Congressional Library

THE LIBRARY OF CONGRESS has already become, by liberal management, the Library of the American people. Every citizen has his share in its vast stores of learning. Opened daily from nine A. M. to ten P. M. in an edifice conceded to be a masterpiece of architecture and of art—a delight to the eye and to the mind.   Ainsworth R. Spofford.

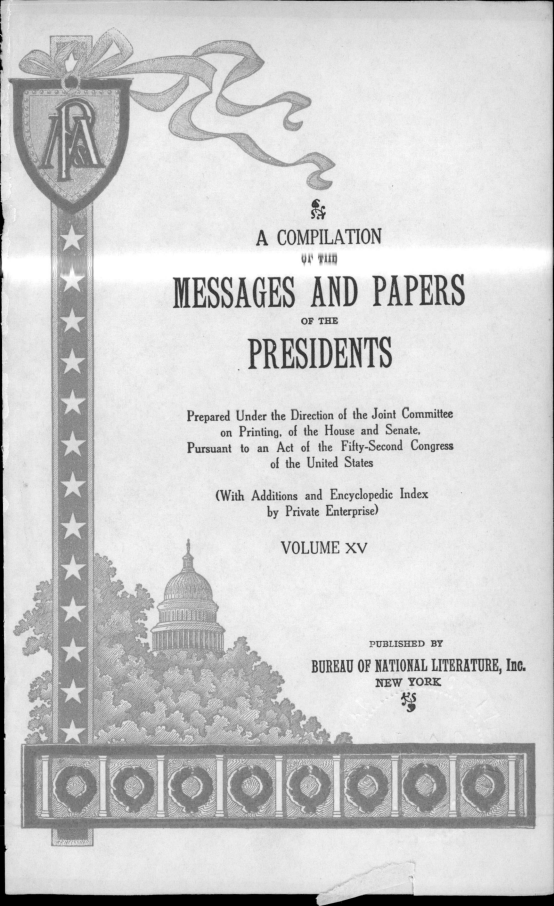

A COMPILATION
OF THE
MESSAGES AND PAPERS
OF THE
PRESIDENTS

Prepared Under the Direction of the Joint Committee
on Printing, of the House and Senate,
Pursuant to an Act of the Fifty-Second Congress
of the United States

(With Additions and Encyclopedic Index
by Private Enterprise)

VOLUME XV

PUBLISHED BY

BUREAU OF NATIONAL LITERATURE, Inc.
NEW YORK

ILLUSTRATIONS IN VOLUME FIFTEEN

of the fifth principal meridian, which are hereby reserved for the Fort Totten school and for the Grey Nuns Department for meadow purposes; and saving and excepting those portions of Lot 2 of Sec. 16 and Lots 2 and 3 of Sec. 17, T. 152 N., R. 65 W., fifth principal meridian not embraced in Allotment No. 585 of Jesse G. Palmer, which are hereby reserved for use for agency purposes; and saving and excepting Lots 4, 5, 6, and 7 of Sec. 10, the NW ¼, the W ½ of the SW ¼ and Lots 5 and 6 of Sec. 15, Lots 1 and 2 of Sec. 9, the E ½ of the NE ¼, the SE ¼ of the SE¼ and Lots 3, 4, and 5 of Sec. 16, T. 152 N., R. 65 W., of the fifth principal meridian, which are hereby reserved for public use as a park to be known as Sully's Hill Park, will, on the sixth day of September, 1904, at 9 o'clock A. M., in the manner herein prescribed, and not otherwise, be opened to entry and settlement and to disposition under the general provisions of the homestead and townsite laws of the United States.

Commencing at 9 o'clock A. M., Monday, August 8th, 1904, and ending at 6 o'clock P. M., Saturday, August 20th, 1904, a registration will be had at Devils Lake and Grand Forks, State of North Dakota, for the purpose of ascertaining what persons desire to enter, settle upon, and acquire title to any of said lands under the homestead law, and of ascertaining their qualifications so to do. To obtain registration each applicant will be required to show himself duly qualified, by written application to be made only on a blank form provided by the Commissioner of the General Land Office, to make homestead entry of these lands under existing laws, and to give the registering officer such appropriate matters of description and identity as will protect the applicant and the Government against any attempted impersonation. Registration cannot be effected through the use of the mails or the employment of an agent, excepting that honorably discharged soldiers and sailors entitled to the benefits of section 2304 of the Revised Statutes of the United States, as amended by the act of Congress approved March 1, 1901 (31 Stat., 847), may present their applications for registration and due proofs of their qualifications through an agent of their own selection, having a duly executed power of attorney, but no person will be permitted to act as agent for more than one such soldier or sailor. No person will be permitted to register more than once or in any other than his true name.

Each applicant who shows himself duly qualified will be registered and given a nontransferable certificate to that effect, which will entitle him to go upon and examine the lands to be opened hereunder; but the only purpose for which he can go upon and examine said lands is that of enabling him later on, as herein provided, to understandingly select the lands for which he will make entry. No one will be permitted to make settlement upon any of said lands in advance of the opening herein provided for, and during the first sixty days following said opening no one but registered applicants will be permitted to make homestead settlement upon any of said lands, and then only in pursuance of a homestead entry duly allowed by the local land officers, or of a soldier's declaratory statement duly accepted by such officers.

The order in which, during the first sixty days following the opening, the registered applicants will be permitted to make homestead entry of the lands opened hereunder, will be determined by a drawing for the district publicly held at Devils Lake, North Dakota, commencing at 9 o'clock A. M., Wednesday, August 24th, 1904, and continuing for such period as may be necessary to complete the same. The drawing will be had under the supervision and immediate observance of a committee of three persons whose integrity is such as to make their control of the drawing a guaranty of its fairness. The members of this committee will be appointed by the Secretary of the Interior, who will prescribe suitable compensation for their services. Preparatory to this drawing the registration officers will, at the time of registering each applicant who shows himself duly qualified, make out a card, which must be signed by the applicant, and giving such a description of the applicant as will enable the local land officers to thereafter identify him. This card will be subsequently sealed in a separate envelope which will bear no other distinguishing label or mark than such as may be necessary to show that it is to go into the drawing. These envelopes will be carefully preserved and remain sealed until opened in the course of the drawing herein provided. When the registration is completed, all of these sealed envelopes will be brought together at the place of drawing and turned over to the committee in charge of the drawing, who, in such manner as in their judgment will be attended with entire fairness and equality of opportunity, shall proceed to draw out and open the separate envelopes and to give to each enclosed card a number in the order in which the envelope containing the same was drawn. The result of the drawing will be certified by the committee to the officers of the district and will determine the order in which the applicants may make homestead entry of said lands and settlement thereon.

Notice of the drawings, stating the name of each applicant and number assigned to him by the drawing, will be posted each day at the place of drawing, and each applicant will be notified of his number, and of the day upon which he must make his entry, by a postal card mailed to him at the address given by him at the time of registration. The result of each day's drawing will also be given to the press to be published as a matter of news. Applications for homestead entry of said lands during the first sixty days following the opening can be made only by registered applicants and in the order established by the drawing. At the land office for the district at Devils Lake, North

Dakota, commencing Tuesday, September 6th, 1904, at 9 o'clock A. M., the applications of those drawing numbers 1 to 50, inclusive, must be presented and will be considered in their numerical order during the first day, and the applications of those drawing numbers 51 to 100, inclusive, must be presented and will be considered in their numerical order 'during the second day, and so on at that rate until all of said lands subject to entry under the homestead law, and desired thereunder, have been entered. If any applicant fails to appear and present his application for entry when the number assigned to him by the drawing is reached, his right to enter will be passed until after the other applications assigned for that day have been disposed of, when he will be given another opportunity to make entry, failing in which he will be deemed to have abandoned his right to make entry under such drawing.

To obtain the allowance of a homestead entry, each applicant must personally present the certificate of registration theretofore issued to him, together with a regular homestead application and the necessary accompanying proofs, and make the first payment of one dollar and fifty cents per acre for the land embraced in his application, together with the regular land office fees, but an honorably discharged soldier or sailor may file his declaratory statement through his agent, who can represent but one soldier or sailor as in the matter of registration. The production of the certificate of registration will be dispensed with only upon satisfactory proof of its loss or destruction. If at the time of considering his regular application for entry it appear that an applicant is disqualified from making homestead entry of these lands, his application will be rejected, notwithstanding his prior registration. If any applicant shall register more than once hereunder, or in any other than his true name, or shall transfer his registration certificate, he will thereby lose all the benefits of the registration and drawing herein provided for, and will be precluded from entering or settling upon any of said lands during the first sixty days following said opening.

Any person, or persons desiring to found, or to suggest establishing, a townsite upon any of said ceded lands, at any point, may, at any time before the opening herein provided for, file in the land office a written application to that effect, describing by legal subdivisions the lands intended to be affected, and stating fully and under oath the necessity or propriety of founding or establishing a town at that place. The local officers will forthwith transmit said petition to the Commissioner of the General Land Office with their recommendation in the premises. Such Commissioner, if he believes the public interests will be subserved thereby, will, if the Secretary of the Interior approve thereof, issue an order withdrawing the lands described in such petition, or any portion thereof, from homestead entry and settlement and directing that the same be held for the time being for townsite settlement, entry, and disposition only. In such event the lands so withheld from homestead entry and settlement will, at the time of said opening, and not before, become subject to settlement, entry, and disposition under the general townsite laws of the United States. None of said ceded lands will be subject to settlement, entry, or disposition under such general townsite laws except in the manner herein prescribed until after the expiration of sixty days from the time of said opening.

All persons are especially admonished that under the said act of Congress approved April 27, 1904, it is provided that no person shall be permitted to settle upon, occupy, or enter any of said ceded lands except in the manner prescribed in this proclamation until after the expiration of sixty days from the time when the same are opened to settlement and entry. After the expiration of the said period of sixty days, but not before, any of said lands remaining undisposed of may be settled upon, occupied, and entered under the general provisions of the homestead and townsite laws of the United States in like manner as if the manner of effecting such settlement, occupancy, and entry had not been prescribed herein in obedience to law, subject, however, to the payment of four dollars and fifty cents per acre for the land entered, in the manner and at the times required by the said act of Congress above mentioned.

The Secretary of the Interior shall prescribe all needful rules and regulations necessary to carry into full effect the opening herein provided for.

In witness whereof, I have hereunto set my hand and caused the seal of the United States to be affixed.

DONE at the City of Washington this 2nd day of June, in [SEAL.] the year of our Lord 1904, and of the Independence of the United States the one hundred and twenty-eighth.

By the President: THEODORE ROOSEVELT.
JOHN HAY, *Secretary of State.*

BY THE PRESIDENT OF THE UNITED STATES OF AMERICA.

A PROCLAMATION.

Whereas, in the opening of the "Cherokee Outlet" in the Territory of Oklahoma, by proclamation dated August 19, 1893, pursuant to section ten of the Act of Congress approved March 3, 1893 (27 Stat., 612, 640), lot one containing four acres, in block forty-eight according to the plat of the official townsite survey of the south half of section twenty-five in township twenty-three north, of range twenty-one west of the Indian principal meridian, known as Woodward Townsite, approved by the Commissioner of the General Land Office, was reserved for the site of a court-house for county "N", now Woodward County, in said Territory;

And Whereas, the county board of commissioners of said county have relinquished all right, title, and interest said county had in said lot one, block forty-eight, known as "Court House Reserve", and have consented and recommended that the same be patented to the "Town of Woodward" for use as a public park, and it appearing that said reserve is no longer used or required for use as a court-house site, and that it is needed and desired by said "Town of Woodward" for public park purposes;

Now, therefore, I, THEODORE ROOSEVELT, President of the United States, by virtue of the power in me vested by section ten of said act of Congress, do hereby declare and make known that said lot one in block forty-eight of said Woodward Townsite is hereby restored to the public domain, to be disposed of to said Town of Woodward for public park purposes under the fourth section of the Act of Congress approved May 14, 1890 (26 Stat., 109).

In witness whereof, I have hereunto set my hand and caused the seal of the United States to be affixed.

[SEAL.]   DONE at the City of Washington this 13th day of October, in the year of our Lord one thousand nine hundred and four, and of the Independence of the United States the one hundred and twenty-ninth.

By the President: THEODORE ROOSEVELT.

JOHN HAY, *Secretary of State.*

THANKSGIVING PROCLAMATION

BY THE PRESIDENT OF THE UNITED STATES OF AMERICA.

A PROCLAMATION.

It has pleased Almighty God to bring the American people in safety and honor through another year, and, in accordance with the long unbroken custom handed down to us by our forefathers, the time has come when a special day shall be set apart in which to thank Him who holds all nations in the hollow of His hand for the mercies thus vouchsafed to us. During the century and a quarter of our national life we as a people have been blessed beyond all others, and for this we owe humble and heartfelt thanks to the Author of all blessings. The year that has closed has been one of peace within our own borders as well as between us and all other nations. The harvests have been abundant, and those who work, whether with hand or brain, are prospering greatly. Reward has waited upon honest effort. We have been enabled to do our duty to ourselves and to others. Never has there been a time when religious and charitable effort has been more evident. Much has been given to us and much will be expected from us. We speak of what has been done by this nation in no spirit of boastfulness or vainglory, but with full and reverent realization that our strength is as nothing unless we are helped from above. Hitherto we have been given the heart and the strength to do the tasks allotted to us as they severally arose. We are thankful for all that has been done for us in the past, and we pray that in the future we may be strengthened in the unending struggle to do our duty fearlessly and honestly, with charity and goodwill, with respect for ourselves and with love toward our fellow-men. In this great republic the effort to combine national strength with personal freedom is being tried on a scale more gigantic than ever before in the world's history. Our success will mean much not only for ourselves, but for the future of all mankind; and every man or woman in our land should feel the grave responsibility resting upon him or her, for in the last analysis this success must depend upon the high average of our individual citizenship, upon the way in which each of us does his duty by himself and his neighbor.

Now, therefore, I, THEODORE ROOSEVELT, President of the United States, do hereby appoint and set apart Thursday, the twenty-fourth of this November, to be observed as a day of festival and thanksgiving by all the people of the United States at home or abroad, and do recommend that on that day they cease from their ordinary occupations and gather in their several places of worship or in their homes, devoutly to give thanks unto Almighty God for the benefits he has conferred upon us as individuals and as a nation, and to beseech Him that in the future His Divine favor may be continued to us.

In witness whereof, I have hereunto set my hand and caused the seal of the United States to be affixed.

DONE at the City of Washington this 1st day of November, [SEAL.] in the year of our Lord one thousand nine hundred and four and of the independence of the United States the one hundred and twenty-ninth.

THEODORE ROOSEVELT.

By the President:

JOHN HAY,
Secretary of State.

INTERNATIONAL PEACE MOVEMENT

[Remarks at the White House, Sept. 24, 1904, on the Occasion of the
Reception of the Interparliamentary Union.]

Gentlemen of the Interparliamentary Union:

I greet you with profound pleasure as representatives in a special
sense of the great international movement for peace and goodwill among
the nations of the earth. It is a matter of gratification to all Americans
that we have had the honor of receiving you here as the Nation's guests.
You are men skilled in the practical work of government in your several
countries; and this fact adds weight to your championship of the cause
of international justice. I thank you for your kind allusions to what the
Government of the United States has accomplished for the policies you
have at heart, and I assure you that this Government's attitude will
continue unchanged in reference thereto. We are even now taking
steps to secure arbitration treaties with all other Governments which
are willing to enter into them with us.

In response to your resolutions I shall at an early date ask the other
nations to join in a second Congress at The Hague. I feel, as I am sure
you do, that our efforts should take the shape of pushing forward toward
completion the work already begun at The Hague, and that whatever is
now done should appear not as something divergent therefrom, but as a
continuance thereof. At the first conference at The Hague several
questions were left unsettled, and it was expressly provided that there
should be a second conference. A reasonable time has elapsed, and I
feel that your body has shown sound judgment in concluding that a
second conference should now be called to carry some steps further
toward completion the work of the first. It would be visionary to expect
too immediate success for the great cause you are championing; but
very substantial progress can be made if we strive with resolution and
good sense toward the goal of securing among the nations of the earth,
as among the individuals of each nation, a just sense of responsibility in
each toward others, and a just recognition in each of the rights of others.
The right and the responsibility must go hand in hand. Our effort must
be unceasing both to secure in each nation full acknowledgment of the
rights of others, and to bring about in each nation an ever growing sense
of its own responsibilities.

At an early date I shall issue the call for the conference you request.

I again greet you and bid you welcome in the name of the American
people, and wish you God-speed in your efforts for the common good of
mankind.

EXECUTIVE ORDERS

WHITE HOUSE, *March 1, 1904.*

All positions in the civil service of the War Department in the Philippines, except those filled by persons employed merely as skilled or unskilled laborers, and by persons appointed by the President, will be treated as classified under the civil-service rules. The present occupants of these positions who have been specially commended for retention by their chiefs, with the approval of the Secretary of War, and whose names appear on the list furnished the United States Civil Service Commission, may be retained, and after three years' service in such positions shall be eligible for transfer to competitive positions in the United States, subject to the civil-service rules and regulations.

THEODORE ROOSEVELT.

WHITE HOUSE, *March 10, 1904.*

All officials of the Government, civil, military, and naval, are hereby directed not only to observe the President's proclamation of neutrality in the pending war between Russia and Japan, but also to abstain from either action or speech which can legitimately cause irritation to either of the combatants. The Government of the United States represents the people of the United States, not only in the sincerity with which it is endeavoring to keep the scales of neutrality exact and even, but in the sincerity with which it deplores the breaking out of the present war, and hopes that it will end at the earliest possible moment and with the smallest possible loss to those engaged. Such a war inevitably increases and inflames the susceptibilities of the combatants to anything in the nature of an injury or slight by outsiders. Too often combatants make conflicting claims as to the duties and obligations of neutrals, so that even when discharging these duties and obligations with scrupulous care it is difficult to avoid giving offense to one or the other party. To such unavoidable causes of offense, due to the performance of national duty, there must not be added any avoidable causes. It is always unfortunate to bring old-world antipathies and jealousies into our life, or by speech or conduct to excite anger and resentment toward our nation in friendly foreign lands; but in a government employee, whose official position makes him in some sense the representative of the people, the mischief of such actions is greatly increased. A strong and self-confident nation should be peculiarly careful not only of the rights but of the susceptibilities of its neighbors; and nowadays all the nations of the world are neighbors one to the other. Courtesy, moderation, and self-restraint should mark international, no less than private, intercourse.

All the officials of the Government, civil, military, and naval, are expected so to carry themselves both in act and in deed as to give no cause of just offense to the people of any foreign and friendly power— and with all mankind we are now in friendship.

THEODORE ROOSEVELT.

WHITE HOUSE, *March 26, 1904.*

Schedule A, Section VI, of the civil-service rules is hereby amended by striking out, in the first line of paragraph 10, the words "at Indian schools" and inserting in their place the words "in the Indian service."

As amended, paragraph 10 will read:

"10. Physicians employed by contract in the Indian service and receiving not more than $720 per annum salary, may lawfully perform their official duties in connection with their private practice, each employment, however, to be subject to the approval of the Commission."

THEODORE ROOSEVELT.

WHITE HOUSE, *November 29, 1904.*

No person shall be appointed or employed in any Executive Department or office for the performance of any service of the character performed by classified employees except in accordance with the provisions of the civil-service rules; and before making any appointment or employment for service with respect to which there may be reasonable doubt as to the requirement of examination the head of the Department or office shall confer with the Civil Service Commission for the purpose of determining whether examination is required, and when such conference does not result in agreement the case shall be presented to the Attorney-General for his opinion.

THEODORE ROOSEVELT.

WHITE HOUSE, *November 15, 1904.*

In the exercise of the power vested in the President by Section 1753 of the Revised Statutes and acts amendatory thereof:

IT IS ORDERED, That the Isthmian Canal Commission be classified and the civil-service act and rules applied thereto, and that no person be hereafter appointed, employed, promoted, or transferred in the service of said Commission until he passes an examination in conformity therewith, unless specifically exempted thereunder. This order shall apply to all officers and employees, except persons employed merely as laborers, persons whose appointments are confirmed by the Senate, and engineers detailed from the army.

The officers and employees included within the provisions of this order are hereby arranged in classes according to annual salary or compensation as follows:

A. Less that $720.
B. $720 or more and less than $840.
C. $840 or more and less than $900.
D. $900 or more and less than $1,000.
E. $1,000 or more and less than $1,200.
1. $1,200 or more and less than $1,400.
2. $1,400 or more and less than $1,600.
3. $1,600 or more and less than $1,800.
4. $1,800 or more and less than $2,000.
5. $2,000 or more and less than $2,500.
6. $2,500 or more.

THEODORE ROOSEVELT.

In connection with this order of classification the President issued an executive order defining the positions which may be filled without competitive examination under the civil-service rules.

FOURTH ANNUAL MESSAGE.

WHITE HOUSE, *December 6, 1904.*

To the Senate and House of Representatives:

The Nation continues to enjoy noteworthy prosperity. Such prosperity is of course primarily due to the high individual average of our citizenship, taken together with our great natural resources; but an important factor therein is the working of our long-continued governmental policies. The people have emphatically expressed their approval of the principles underlying these policies, and their desire that these principles be kept substantially unchanged, although of course applied in a progressive spirit to meet changing conditions.

The enlargement of scope of the functions of the National Government required by our development as a nation involves, of course, increase of expense; and the period of prosperity through which the country is passing justifies expenditures for permanent improvements far greater than would be wise in hard times. Battle ships and forts, public buildings, and improved waterways are investments which should be made when we have the money; but abundant revenues and a large surplus always invite extravagance, and constant care should be taken to guard against unnecessary increase of the ordinary expenses of government. The cost of doing Government business shauld be regulated with the same rigid scrutiny as the cost of doing a private business.

In the vast and complicated mechanism of our modern civilized life the dominant note is the note of industralism; and the relations of capital and labor, and especially of organized capital and organized labor, to each other and to the public at large come second in importance only to the intimate questions of family life. Our peculiar form of government, with its sharp division of authority between the Nation and the several States, has been on the whole far more advantageous to our development than a more strongly centralized government. But it is undoubtedly responsible for much of the difficulty of meeting with adequate legislation the new problems presented by the total change in industrial conditions on this continent during the last half century. In actual practice it has proved exceedingly difficult, and in many cases impossible, to get unanimity of wise action among the various States on these subjects. From the very nature of the case this is especially true of the laws affecting the employment of capital in huge masses.

With regard to labor the problem is no less important, but it is simpler. As long as the States retain the primary control of the police power the circumstances must be altogether extreme which require interference by the Federal authorities, whether in the way of safeguarding the rights of labor or in the way of seeing that wrong is not done by unruly persons who shield themselves behind the name of labor. If there is resistance to the Federal courts, interference with the mails, or interstate commerce, or molestation of Federal property, or if the State authorities in some crisis which they are unable to face call for help, then the Federal Government may interfere; but though such interference may be caused by a condition of things arising out of trouble connected with some question of labor, the interference itself simply takes the form of restoring order without regard to the questions which have caused the breach of order—for to keep order is a primary duty and in a time of disorder and violence all other questions sink into abeyance until order has been restored. In the District of Columbia and in the Territories the Federal law covers the entire field of government; but the labor question is only acute in populous centers of commerce, manufactures, or mining. Nevertheless, both in the enactment and in the enforcement of law the Federal Government within its restricted sphere should set an example to the State governments, especially in a matter so vital as this affecting labor. I believe that under modern industrial conditions it is often necessary, and even where not necessary it is yet often wise, that there should be organization of labor in order better to secure the rights of the individual wage-worker. All encouragement should be given to any such organization, so long as it is conducted with a due and decent regard for the rights of others. There are in this country some labor unions which have habitually, and other labor unions which have often, been among the most effective agents in working for good citizenship and for uplifting the condition of those whose welfare should be closest to our hearts. But when any labor union seeks improper ends, or seeks to achieve proper ends by improper means, all good citizens and more especially all honorable public servants must oppose the wrongdoing as resolutely as they would oppose the wrongdoing of any great corporation. Of course any violence, brutality, or corruption, should not for one moment be tolerated. Wage-workers have an entire right to organize and by all peaceful and honorable means to endeavor to persuade their fellows to join with them in organizations. They have a legal right, which, according to circumstances, may or may not be a moral right, to refuse to work in company with men who decline to join their organizations. They have under no circumstances the right to commit violence upon those, whether capitalists or wage-workers, who refuse to support their organizations, or who side with those with whom they are at odds; for mob rule is intolerable in any form.

The wage-workers are peculiarly entitled to the protection and the encouragement of the law. From the very nature of their occupation railroad men, for instance, are liable to be maimed in doing the legitimate work of their profession, unless the railroad companies are required by law to make ample provision for their safety. The Administration has been zealous in enforcing the existing law for this purpose. That law should be amended and strengthened. Wherever the National Government has power there should be a stringent employer's liability law, which should apply to the Government itself where the Government is an employer of labor.

In my Message to the Fifty-seventh Congress, at its second session, I urged the passage of an employer's liability law for the District of Columbia. I now renew that recommendation, and further recommend that the Congress appoint a commission to make a comprehensive study of employer's liability with the view of extending the provisions of a great and constitutional law to all employments within the scope of Federal power.

The Government has recognized heroism upon the water, and bestows medals of honor upon those persons who by extreme and heroic daring have endangered their lives in saving, or endeavoring to save, lives from the perils of the sea in the waters over which the United States has jurisdiction, or upon an American vessel. This recognition should be extended to cover cases of conspicuous bravery and self-sacrifice in the saving of life in private employments under the jurisdiction of the United States, and particularly in the land commerce of the Nation.

The ever-increasing casualty list upon our railroads is a matter of grave public concern, and urgently calls for action by the Congress. In the matter of speed and comfort of railway travel our railroads give at least as good service as those of any other nation, and there is no reason why this service should not also be as safe as human ingenuity can make it. Many of our leading roads have been foremost in the adoption of the most approved safeguards for the protection of travelers and employees, yet the list of clearly avoidable accidents continues unduly large. The passage of a law requiring the adoption of a block-signal system has been proposed to the Congress. I earnestly concur in that recommendation, and would also point out to the Congress the urgent need of legislation in the interest of the public safety limiting the hours of labor for railroad employees in train service upon railroads engaged in interstate commerce, and providing that only trained and experienced persons be employed in positions of responsibility connected with the operation of trains. Of course nothing can ever prevent accidents caused by human weakness or misconduct; and there should be drastic punishment for any railroad employee, whether officer or man, who by issuance of wrong orders or by disobedience of orders causes disaster. The law of 1901, requiring interstate railroads to make monthly reports of all accidents to passengers and employees on duty, should also be amended so as to empower the Government to make a personal investigation, through proper officers, of all accidents involving loss of life which seem to require investigation, with a requirement that the results of such investigation be made public.

The safety-appliance law, as amended by the act of March 2, 1903, has proved beneficial to railway employees, and in order that its provisions may be properly carried out, the force of inspectors provided for by appropriation should be largely increased. This service is analogous to the Steamboat-Inspection Service, and deals with even more important interests. It has passed the experimental stage and demonstrated its utility, and should receive generous recognition by the Congress.

There is no objection to employees of the Government forming or belonging to unions; but the Government can neither discriminate for nor discriminate against nonunion men who are in its employment, or who seek to be employed under it. Moreover, it is a very grave impropriety for Government employees to band themselves together for the purpose of extorting improperly high salaries from the Government. Especially is this true of those within the classified service. The letter carriers, both municipal and rural, are as a whole an excellent body of public servants. They should be amply paid. But their payment must be obtained by arguing their claims fairly and honorably before the Congress, and not by banding together for the defeat of those Congressmen who refuse to give promises which they can not in conscience give. The Administration has already taken steps to prevent and punish abuses of this nature; but it will be wise for the Congress to supplement this action by legislation.

Much can be done by the Government in labor matters merely by giving publicity to certain conditions. The Bureau of Labor has done excellent work of this kind in many different directions. I shall shortly lay before you in a special message the full report of the investigation of the Bureau of Labor into the Colorado mining strike, as this was a strike in which certain very evil forces, which are more or less at work everywhere under the conditions of modern industrialism, became startlingly prominent. It is greatly to be wished that the Department of Commerce and Labor, through the Labor Bureau, should compile and arrange for the Congress a list of the labor laws of the various States, and should be given the means to investigate and report to the Congress upon the labor conditions in the manufacturing and mining regions throughout the country, both as to wages, as to hours of labor, as to the labor of women and children, and as to the effect in the various labor centers of immigration from abroad. In this investigation especial attention should be paid to the conditions of child labor and child-labor legislation in the several States. Such an investigation must necessarily take into account many of the problems with which this question of child labor is connected. These problems can be actually met, in most cases, only by the States themselves; but the lack of proper legislation in one State in such a matter as child labor often renders it excessively difficult to establish protective restriction upon the work in another State having the same industries, so that the worst tends to drag down the better. For this reason, it would be well for the Nation at least to endeavor to secure comprehensive information as to the conditions of labor of children in the different States. Such investigation and publication by the National Government would tend toward the securing of approximately uniform legislation of the proper character among the several States.

When we come to deal with great corporations the need for the Government to act directly is far greater than in the case of labor, because great corporations can become such only by engaging in interstate commerce, and interstate commerce is peculiarly the field of the General Government. It is an absurdity to expect to eliminate the abuses in great corporations by State action. It is difficult to be patient with an argument that such matters should be left to the States because more than one State pursues the policy of creating on easy terms corporations which are never operated within that

State at all, but in other States whose laws they ignore. The National Government alone can deal adequately with these great corporations. To try to deal with them in an intemperate, destructive, or demagogic spirit would, in all probability, mean that nothing whatever would be accomplished, and, with absolute certainty, that if anything were accomplished it would be of a harmful nature. The American people need to continue to show the very qualities that they have shown—that is, moderation, good sense, the earnest desire to avoid doing any damage, and yet the quiet determination to proceed, step by step, without halt and without hurry, in eliminating or at least in minimizing whatever of mischief or evil there is to interstate commerce in the conduct of great corporations. They are acting in no spirit of hostility to wealth, either individual or corporate. They are not against the rich man any more than against the poor man. On the contrary, they are friendly alike toward rich man and toward poor man, provided only that each acts in a spirit of justice and decency toward his fellows. Great corporations are necessary, and only men of great and singular mental power can manage such corporations successfully, and such men must have great rewards. But these corporations should be managed with due regard to the interest of the public as a whole. Where this can be done under the present laws it must be done. Where these laws come short others should be enacted to supplement them.

Yet we must never forget the determining factor in every kind of work, of head or hand, must be the man's own good sense, courage, and kindliness. More important than any legislation is the gradual growth of a feeling of responsibility and forbearance among capitalists and wage-workers alike; a feeling of respect on the part of each man for the rights of others; a feeling of broad community of interest, not merely of capitalists among themselves, and of wage-workers among themselves, but of capitalists and wage-workers in their relations to each other, and of both in their relations to their fellows who with them make up the body politic. There are many captains of industry, many labor leaders, who realize this. A recent speech by the president of one of our great railroad systems to the employees of that system contains sound common sense. It runs in part as follows:

" It is my belief we can better serve each other, better understand the man as well as his business, when meeting face to face, exchanging views, and realizing from personal contact we serve but one interest, that of our mutual prosperity.

" Serious misunderstandings can not occur where personal good will exists and opportunity for personal explanation is present.

" In my early business life I had experience with men of affairs of a character to make me desire to avoid creating a like feeling of resentment to myself and the interests in my charge, should fortune ever

place me in authority, and I am solicitous of a measure of confidence on the part of the public and our employees that I shall hope may be warranted by the fairness and good fellowship I intend shall prevail in our relationship.

" But do not feel I am disposed to grant unreasonable requests, spend the money of our company unnecessarily or without value received, nor expect the days of mistakes are disappearing, or that cause for complaint will not continually occur; simply to correct such abuses as may be discovered, to better conditions as fast as reasonably may be expected, constantly striving, with varying success, for that improvement we all desire, to convince you there is a force at work in the right direction, all the time making progress—is the disposition with which I have come among you, asking your good will and encouragement.

" The day has gone by when a corporation can be handled successfully in defiance of the public will, even though that will be unreasonable and wrong. A public may be led, but not driven, and I prefer to go with it and shape or modify, in a measure, its opinion, rather than be swept from my bearings, with loss to myself and the interests in my charge.

" Violent prejudice exists towards corporate activity and capital today, much of it founded in reason, more in apprehension, and a large measure is due to the personal traits of arbitrary, unreasonable, incompetent, and offensive men in positions of authority. The accomplishment of results by indirection, the endeavor to thwart the intention, if not the expressed letter of the law (the will of the people), a disregard of the rights of others, a disposition to withhold what is due, to force by main strength or inactivity a result not justified, depending upon the weakness of the claimant and his indisposition to become involved in litigation, has created a sentiment harmful in the extreme and a disposition to consider anything fair that gives gain to the individual at the expense of the company.

" If corporations are to continue to do the world's work, as they are best fitted to, these qualities in their representatives that have resulted in the present prejudice against them must be relegated to the background. The corporations must come out into the open and see and be seen. They must take the public into their confidence and ask for what they want, and no more, and be prepared to explain satisfactorily what advantage will accrue to the public if they are given their desires; for they are permitted to exist not that they may make money solely, but that they may effectively serve those from whom they derive their power.

" Publicity, and not secrecy, will win hereafter, and laws be construed by their intent and not by their letter, otherwise public utilities will be owned and operated by the public which created them, even though

the service be less efficient and the result less satisfactory from a financial standpoint."

The Bureau of Corporations has made careful preliminary investigation of many important corporations. It will make a special report on the beef industry.

The policy of the Bureau is to accomplish the purposes of its creation by co-operation, not antagonism; by making constructive legislation, not destructive prosecution, the immediate object of its inquiries; by conservative investigation of law and fact, and by refusal to issue incomplete and hence necessarily inaccurate reports. Its policy being thus one of open inquiry into, and not attack upon, business, the Bureau has been able to gain not only the confidence, but, better still, the co-operation of men engaged in legitimate business.

The Bureau offers to the Congress the means of getting at the cost of production of our various great staples of commerce.

Of necessity the careful investigation of special corporations will afford the Commissioner knowledge of certain business facts, the publication of which might be an improper infringement of private rights. The method of making public the results of these investigations affords, under the law, a means for the protection of private rights. The Congress will have all facts except such as would give to another corporation information which would injure the legitimate business of a competitor and destroy the incentive for individual superiority and thrift.

The Bureau has also made exhaustive examinations into the legal condition under which corporate business is carried on in the various States; into all judicial decisions on the subject; and into the various systems of corporate taxation in use. I call special attention to the report of the chief of the Bureau; and I earnestly ask that the Congress carefully consider the report and recommendations of the Commissioner on this subject.

The business of insurance vitally affects the great mass of the people of the United States and is national and not local in its application. It involves a multitude of transactions among the people of the different States and between American companies and foreign governments. I urge that the Congress carefully consider whether the power of the Bureau of Corporations can not constitutionally be extended to cover interstate transactions in insurance.

Above all else, we must strive to keep the highways of commerce open to all on equal terms; and to do this it is necessary to put a complete stop to all rebates. Whether the shipper or the railroad is to blame makes no difference; the rebate must be stopped, the abuses of the private car and private terminal-track and side-track systems must be stopped, and the legislation of the Fifty-eighth Congress which

declares it to be unlawful for any person or corporation to offer, grant, give, solicit, accept, or receive any rebate, concession, or discrimination in respect of the transportation of any property in interstate or foreign commerce whereby such property shall by any device whatever be transported at a less rate than that named in the tariffs published by the carrier must be enforced. For some time after the enactment of the Act to Regulate Commerce it remained a mooted question whether that act conferred upon the Interstate Commerce Commission the power, after it had found a challenged rate to be unreasonable, to declare what thereafter should, prima facie, be the reasonable maximum rate for the transportation in dispute. The Supreme Court finally resolved that question in the negative, so that as the law now stands the Commission simply possess the bare power to denounce a particular rate as unreasonable. While I am of the opinion that at present it would be undesirable, if it were not impracticable, finally to clothe the Commission with general authority to fix railroad rates, I do believe that, as a fair security to shippers, the Commission should be vested with the power, where a given rate has been challenged and after full hearing found to be unreasonable, to decide, subject to judicial review, what shall be a reasonable rate to take its place; the ruling of the Commission to take effect immediately, and to obtain unless and until it is reversed by the court of review. The Government must in increasing degree supervise and regulate the workings of the railways engaged in interstate commerce; and such increased supervision is the only alternative to an increase of the present evils on the one hand or a still more radical policy on the other. In my judgment the most important legislative act now needed as regards the regulation of corporations is this act to confer on the Interstate Commerce Commission the power to revise rates and regulations, the revised rate to at once go into effect, and stay in effect unless and until the court of review reverses it.

Steamship companies engaged in interstate commerce and protected in our coastwise trade should be held to a strict observance of the interstate commerce act.

In pursuing the set plan to make the city of Washington an example to other American municipalities several points should be kept in mind by the legislators. In the first place, the people of this country should clearly understand that no amount of industrial prosperity, and above all no leadership in international industrial competition, can in any way atone for the sapping of the vitality of those who are usually spoken of as the working classes. The farmers, the mechanics, the skilled and unskilled laborers, the small shop keepers, make up the bulk of the population of any country; and upon their well-being, generation after generation, the well-being of the country and the race depends.

Rapid development in wealth and industrial leadership is a good thing, but only if it goes hand in hand with improvement, and not deterioration, physical and moral. The over-crowding of cities and the draining of country districts are unhealthy and even dangerous symptoms in our modern life. We should not permit overcrowding in cities. In certain European cities it is provided by law that the population of towns shall not be allowed to exceed a very limited density for a given area, so that the increase in density must be continually pushed back into a broad zone around the center of the town, this zone having great avenues or parks within it. The death-rate statistics show a terrible increase in mortality, and especially in infant mortality, in overcrowded tenements. The poorest families in tenement houses live in one room, and it appears that in these one-room tenements the average death rate for a number of given cities at home and abroad is about twice what it is in a two-room tenement, four times what it is in a three-room tenement, and eight times what it is in a tenement consisting of four rooms or over. These figures vary somewhat for different cities, but they approximate in each city those given above; and in all cases the increase of mortality, and especially of infant mortality, with the decrease in the number of rooms used by the family and with the consequent overcrowding is startling. The slum exacts a heavy total of death from those who dwell therein; and this is the case not merely in the great crowded slums of high buildings in New York and Chicago, but in the alley slums of Washington. In Washington people can not afford to ignore the harm that this causes. No Christian and civilized community can afford to show a happy-go-lucky lack of concern for the youth of to-day; for, if so, the community will have to pay a terrible penalty of financial burden and social degradation in the to-morrow. There should be severe child-labor and factory-inspection laws. It is very desirable that married women should not work in factories. The prime duty of the man is to work, to be the breadwinner; the prime duty of the woman is to be the mother, the housewife. All questions of tariff and finance sink into utter insignificance when compared with the tremendous, the vital importance of trying to shape conditions so that these two duties of the man and of the woman can be fulfilled under reasonably favorable circumstances. If a race does not have plenty of children, or if the children do not grow up, or if when they grow up they are unhealthy in body and stunted or vicious in mind, then that race is decadent, and no heaping up of wealth, no splendor of momentary material prosperity, can avail in any degree as offsets.

The Congress has the same power of legislation for the District of Columbia which the State legislatures have for the various States. The problems incident to our highly complex modern industrial civilization, with its manifold and perplexing tendencies both for good and for evil, are far less sharply eccentuated in the city of Washington than in most other cities. For this very reason it is easier to deal with the various phases of these problems in Washington, and the District of Columbia government should be a model for the other municipal governments of the Nation, in all such matters as supervision of the housing of the poor, the creation of small parks in the districts inhabited by the poor, in laws affecting labor, in laws providing for the taking care of the children, in truant laws, and in providing schools.

In the vital matter of taking care of children, much advantage could be gained by a careful study of what has been accomplished in such States as Illinois and Colorado by the juvenile courts. The work of the juvenile court is really a work of character building. It is now generally recognized that young boys and young girls who go wrong should not be treated as criminals, not even necessarily as needing reformation, but rather as needing to have their characters formed, and for this end to have them tested and developed by a system of probation. Much admirable work has been done in many of our Commonwealths by earnest men and women who have made a special study of the needs of those classes of children which furnish the greatest number of juvenile offenders, and therefore the greatest number of adult offenders ; and by their aid, and by profiting by the experiences of the different States and cities in these matters, it would be easy to provide a good code for the District of Columbia.

Several considerations suggest the need for a systematic investigation into and improvement of housing conditions in Washington. The hidden residential alleys are breeding grounds of vice and disease, and should be opened into minor streets. For a number of years influential citizens have joined with the District Commissioners in the vain endeavor to secure laws permitting the condemnation of insanitary dwellings. The local death rates, especially from preventable diseases, are so unduly high as to suggest that the exceptional wholesomeness of Washington's better sections is offset by bad conditions in her poorer neighborhoods. A special " Commission on Housing and Health Conditions in the National Capital" would not only bring about the reformation of existing evils, but would also formulate an appropriate building code to protect the city from mammoth brick tenements and other evils which threaten to develop here as they have in other cities. That the Nation's Capital should be made a model for other municipalities is an ideal which appeals to all patriotic citizens everywhere, and such a special Commission might map out and organize the city's future development in lines of civic social service, just as Major L'Enfant and the recent Park Commission planned the arrangement of her streets and parks.

It is mortifying to remember that Washington has no compulsory school attendance law and that careful inquiries indicate the habitual absence from school of some twenty per cent of all children between the ages of eight and fourteen. It must be evident to all who consider the problems of neglected child life or the benefits of compulsory education in other cities that one of the most urgent needs of the National Capital is a law requiring the school attendance of all children, this law to be enforced by attendance agents directed by the board of education.

Public play grounds are necessary means for the development of wholesome citizenship in modern cities. It is important that the work inaugurated here through voluntary effort should be taken up and extended through Congressional appropriation of funds sufficient to equip and maintain numerous convenient small play grounds upon land which can be secured without purchase or rental. It is also desirable that small vacant places be purchased and reserved as small-park play grounds in densely settled sections of the city which now have no public open spaces and are destined soon to be built up solidly. All these needs should be met immediately. To meet them would entail expenses; but a corresponding saving could be made by stopping the building of streets and levelling of ground for purposes largely speculative in outlying parts of the city.

There are certain offenders, whose criminality takes the shape of brutality and cruelty towards the weak, who need a special type of punishment. The wife-beater, for example, is inadequately punished by imprisonment; for imprisonment may often mean nothing to him, while it may cause hunger and want to the wife and children who have been the victims of his brutality. Probably some form of corporal punishment would be the most adequate way of meeting this kind of crime.

The Department of Agriculture has grown into an educational institution with a faculty of two thousand specialists making research into all the sciences of production. The Congress appropriates, directly and indirectly, six millions of dollars annually to carry on this work. It reaches every State and Territory in the Union and the islands of the sea lately come under our flag. Co-operation is had with the State experiment stations, and with many other institutions and individuals. The world is carefully searched for new varieties of grains, fruits, grasses, vegetables, trees, and shrubs, suitable to various localities in our country; and marked benefit to our producers has resulted.

The activities of our age in lines of research have reached the tillers of the soil and inspired them with ambition to know more of the principles that govern the forces of nature with which they have to deal. Nearly half of the people of this country devote their energies to growing things from the soil. Until a recent date little has been done to prepare these millions for their life work. In most lines of human activity college-trained men are the leaders. The farmer had no opportunity for special training until the Congress made provision for it forty years ago. During these years progress has been made and teachers have been prepared. Over five thousand students are in attendance at our State agricultural colleges. The Federal Government expends ten millions of dollars annually toward this education and for research in Washington and in the several States and Territories. The Department of Agriculture has given facilities for post-graduate work to five hundred young men during the last seven years, preparing them for advance lines of work in the Department and in the State institutions.

The facts concerning meteorology and its relations to plant and animal life are being systematically inquired into. Temperature and moisture are controlling factors in all agricultural operations. The seasons of the cyclones of the Caribbean Sea and their paths are being forecasted with increasing accuracy. The cold winds that come from the north are anticipated and their times and intensity told to farmers, gardeners, and fruiterers in all southern localities.

We sell two hundred and fifty million dollars' worth of animals and animal products to foreign countries every year, in addition to supplying our own people more cheaply and abundantly than any other nation is able to provide for its people. Successful manufacturing depends primarily on cheap food, which accounts to a considerable extent for our growth in this direction. The Department of Agriculture, by careful inspection of meats, guards the health of our people and gives clean bills of health to deserving exports; it is prepared to deal promptly with imported diseases of animals, and maintain the excellence of our flocks and herds in this respect. There should be an annual census of the live stock of the Nation.

We sell abroad about six hundred million dollars' worth of plants and their products every year. Strenuous efforts are being made to import from foreign countries such grains as are suitable to our varying localities. Seven years ago we bought three-fourths of our rice; by helping the rice growers on the Gulf coast to secure seeds from the Orient suited to their conditions, and by giving them adequate protection, they now supply home demand and export to the islands of the Caribbean Sea and to other rice-growing countries. Wheat and other grains have been imported from light-rainfall countries to our lands in the West and Southwest that have not grown crops because of light precipitation, resulting in an extensive addition to our cropping area and our home-making territory that can not be irrigated. Ten million bushels of first-class macaroni wheat were grown from these experimental importations last year. Fruits suitable to our soils and climates are being imported from all the countries of the Old World—the fig from Turkey, the almond from Spain, the date from Algeria, the mango from India. We are helping our fruit growers to get their crops into European markets by studying methods of preservation through refrigeration, packing, and handling, which have been quite successful. We are helping our hop growers by importing varieties that ripen earlier and later than the kinds they have been raising, thereby lengthening the harvesting season. The cotton crop of the country is threatened with root rot, the bollworm, and the boll weevil. Our pathologists will find immune varieties that will resist the root disease, and the bollworm can be dealt with, but the boll weevil is a serious menace to the cotton crop. It is a Central American insect that has become acclimated in Texas and has done great damage. A scientist of the Department of Agriculture has found the weevil at home in Guatemala being kept in check by an ant, which has been brought to our cotton fields for observation. It is hoped that it may serve a good purpose.

The soils of the country are getting attention from the farmer's standpoint, and interesting results are following. We have duplicates of the soils that grow the wrapper tobacco in Sumatra and the filler tobacco in Cuba. It will be only a question of time when the large amounts paid to these countries will be paid to our own people. The reclamation of alkali lands is progressing, to give object lessons to our people in methods by which worthless lands may be made productive.

The insect friends and enemies of the farmer are getting attention. The enemy of the San Jose scale was found near the Great Wall of China, and is now cleaning up all our orchards. The fig-fertilizing insect imported from Turkey has helped to establish an industry in California that amounts to from fifty to one hundred tons of dried figs annually, and is extending over the Pacific coast. A parasitic fly from South Africa is keeping in subjection the black scale, the worst pest of the orange and lemon industry in California.

Careful preliminary work is being done towards producing our own silk. The mulberry is being distributed in large numbers, eggs are being imported and distributed, improved reels were imported from Europe last year, and two expert reelers were brought to Washington to reel the crop of cocoons and teach the art to our own people.

The crop-reporting system of the Department of Agriculture is being brought closer to accuracy every year. It has two hundred and fifty thousand reporters selected from people in eight vocations in life. It has arrangements with most European countries for interchange of estimates, so that our people may know as nearly as possible with what they must compete.

During the two and a half years that have elapsed since the passage of the reclamation act rapid progress has been made in the surveys and examinations of the opportunities for reclamation in the thirteen States and three Territories of the arid West. Construction has already been begun on the largest and most important of the irrigation works, and plans are being completed for works which will utilize the funds now available. The operations are being carried on by the Reclamation Service, a corps of engineers selected through competitive civil-service examinations. This corps includes experienced consulting and constructing engineers as well as various experts in mechanical and legal matters, and is composed largely of men who have spent most of their lives in practical affairs connected with irrigation. The larger problems have been solved and it now remains to execute with care, economy, and thoroughness the work which has been laid out. All important details are being carefully considered by boards of consulting engineers, selected for their thorough knowledge and practical experience. Each project is taken up on the ground by competent men and viewed from the standpoint of the creation of prosperous homes, and of promptly refunding to the Treasury the cost of construction. The reclamation act has been found to be remarkably complete and effective, and so broad in its provisions that a wide range of undertakings has been possible under it. At the same time, economy is guaranteed by the fact that the funds must ultimately be returned to be used over again.

It is the cardinal principle of the forest-reserve policy of this Administration that the reserves are for use. Whatever interferes with the use of their resources is to be avoided by every possible means. But these resources must be used in such a way as to make them permanent.

The forest policy of the Government is just now a subject of vivid public interest throughout the West and to the people of the United States in general. The forest reserves themselves are of extreme value to the present as well as to the future welfare of all the western public-land States. They powerfully affect the use and disposal of the public lands. They are of special importance because they preserve the water supply and the supply of timber for domestic purposes, and so promote settlement under the reclamation act. Indeed, they are essential to the welfare of every one of the great interests of the West.

Forest reserves are created for two principal purposes. The first is to preserve the water supply. This is their most important use. The principal users of the water thus preserved are irrigation ranchers and settlers, cities and towns to whom their municipal water supplies are of the very first importance, users and furnishers of water power, and the users of water for domestic, manufacturing, mining, and other purposes. All these are directly dependent upon the forest reserves.

The second reason for which forest reserves are created is to preserve the timber supply for various classes of wood users. Among the more important of these are settlers under the reclamation act and other acts, for whom a cheap and accessible supply of timber for domestic uses is absolutely necessary; miners and prospectors, who are in serious danger of losing their timber supply by fire or through export by lumber companies when timber lands adjacent to their mines pass into private ownership; lumbermen, transportation companies, builders, and commercial interests in general.

Although the wisdom of creating forest reserves is nearly everywhere heartily recognized, yet in a few localities there has been misunderstanding and complaint. The following statement is therefore desirable:

The forest reserve policy can be successful only when it has the full support of the people of the West. It can not safely, and should not in any case, be imposed upon them against their will. But neither can we accept the views of those whose only interest in the forest is temporary; who are anxious to reap what they have not sown and then move away, leaving desolation behind them. On the contrary, it is everywhere and always the interest of the permanent settler and the permanent business man, the man with a stake in the country, which must be considered and which must decide.

The making of forest reserves within railroad and wagon-road land-grant limits will hereafter, as for the past three years, be so managed as to prevent the issue, under the act of June 4, 1897, of base for exchange or lieu selection (usually called scrip). In all cases where forest reserves within areas covered by land grants appear to be essential to the prosperity of settlers, miners, or others, the Government lands within such proposed forest reserves will, as in the recent past, be withdrawn from sale or entry pending the completion of such negotiations with the owners of the land grants as will prevent the creation of so-called scrip.

It was formerly the custom to make forest reserves without first getting definite and detailed information as to the character of land and timber within their boundaries. This method of action often resulted in badly chosen boundaries and consequent injustice to settlers and others. Therefore this Administration adopted the present method of first withdrawing the land from disposal, followed by careful examination on the ground and the preparation of detailed maps and descriptions, before any forest reserve is created.

I have repeatedly called attention to the confusion which exists in Government forest matters because the work is scattered among three independent organizations. The United States is the only one of the great nations in which the forest work of the Government is not concentrated under one department, in consonance with the plainest dictates of good administration and common sense. The present arrangement is bad from every point of view. Merely to mention it is to prove that it should be terminated at once. As I have repeatedly recommended, all the forest work of the Government should be concentrated in the Department of Agriculture, where the larger part of that work is already done, where practically all of the trained foresters of the Government are employed, where chiefly in Washington there is comprehensive first-class knowledge of the problems of the reserves acquired on the ground, where all problems relating to growth from the soil are already gathered, and where all the sciences auxiliary to forestry are at hand for prompt and effective co-operation. These reasons are decisive in themselves, but it should be added that the great organizations of citizens whose interests are affected by the forest-reserves, such as the National Live Stock Association, the National Wool Growers' Association, the American Mining Congress, the national Irrigation Congress, and the National Board of Trade, have uniformly, emphatically, and most of them repeatedly, expressed themselves in favor of placing all Government forest work in the Department of Agriculture because of the peculiar adaptation of that Department for it. It is true, also, that the forest services of nearly all the great nations of the world are under the respective departments of agriculture, while in but two of the smaller nations and in one colony are they under the department of the interior. This is the result of long and varied experience and it agrees fully with the requirements of good administration in our own case.

The creation of a forest service in the Department of Agriculture will have for its important results:

First. A better handling of all forest work; because it will be under a single head, and because the vast and indispensable experience of the Department in all matters pertaining to the forest reserves, to forestry in general, and to other forms of production from the soil, will be easily and rapidly accessible.

Second. The reserves themselves, being handled from the point of view of the man in the field, instead of the man in the office, will be more easily and more widely useful to the people of the West than has been the case hitherto.

Third. Within a comparatively short time the reserves will become self-supporting. This is important, because continually and rapidly increasing appropriations will be necessary for the proper care of this exceedingly important interest of the Nation, and they can and should be offset by returns from the National forests. Under similar circumstances the forest possessions of other great nations form an important source of revenue to their governments.

Every administrative officer concerned is convinced of the necessity for the proposed consolidation of forest work in the Department of Agriculture, and I myself have urged it more than once in former messages. Again I commend it to the early and favorable consideration of the Congress. The interests of the Nation at large and of the West in particular have suffered greatly because of the delay.

I call the attention of the Congress again to the report and recommendation of the Commission on the Public Lands forwarded by me to the second session of the present Congress. The Commission has prosecuted its investigations actively during the past season, and a second report is now in an advanced stage of preparation.

In connection with the work of the forest reserves I desire again to urge upon the Congress the importance of authorizing the President to set aside certain portions of these reserves or other public lands as game refuges for the preservation of the bison, the wapiti, and other large beasts once so abundant in our woods and mountains and on our great plains, and now tending toward extinction. Every support should be given to the authorities of the Yellowstone Park in their successful efforts at preserving the large creatures therein; and at very little expense portions of the public domain in other regions which are wholly unsuited to agricultural settlement could be similarly utilized. We owe it to future generations to keep alive the noble and beautiful creatures which by their presence add such distinctive character to the American wilderness. The limits of the Yellowstone Park should be extended southwards. The Canyon of the Colorado should be made a national park; and the national-park system should include the Yosemite and as many as possible of the groves of giant trees in California.

The veterans of the Civil War have a claim upon the Nation such as no other body of our citizens possess. The Pension Bureau has never in its history been managed in a more satisfactory manner than is now the case.

The progress of the Indians toward civilization, though not rapid, is perhaps all that could be hoped for in view of the circumstances. Within the past year many tribes have shown, in a degree greater than ever before, an appreciation of the necessity of work. This changed attitude is in part due to the policy recently pursued of reducing the amount of subsistence to the Indians, and thus forcing them, through sheer necessity, to work for a livelihood. The policy, though severe, is a useful one, but it is to be exercised only with judgment and with a full understanding of the conditions which exist in each community for which it is intended. On or near the Indian reservations there is usually very little demand for labor, and if the Indians are to earn their living and when work can not be furnished from outside (which is always preferable), then it must be furnished by the Government.

Practical instruction of this kind would in a few years result in the forming of habits of regular industry, which would render the Indian a producer and would effect a great reduction in the cost of his maintenance.

It is commonly declared that the slow advance of the Indians is due to the unsatisfactory character of the men appointed to take immediate charge of them, and to some extent this is true. While the standard of the employees in the Indian Service shows great improvement over that of bygone years, and while actual corruption or flagrant dishonesty is now the rare exception, it is nevertheless the fact that the salaries paid Indian agents are not large enough to attract the best men to that field of work. To achieve satisfactory results the official in charge of an Indian tribe should possess the high qualifications which are required in the manager of a large business, but only in exceptional cases is it possible to secure men of such a type for these positions. Much better service, however, might be obtained from those now holding the places were it practicable to get out of them the best that is in them, and this should be done by bringing them constantly into closer touch with their superior officers. An agent who has been content to draw his salary, giving in return the least possible equivalent in effort and service, may, by proper treatment, by suggestion and encouragement, or persistent urging, be stimulated to greater effort and induced to take a more active personal interest in his work.

Under existing conditions an Indian agent in the distant West may be wholly out of touch with the office of the Indian Bureau. He may very well feel that no one takes a personal interest in him or his efforts. Certain routine duties in the way of reports and accounts are required of him, but there is no one with whom he may intelligently consult on matters vital to his work, except after long delay. Such a man would be greatly encouraged and aided by personal contact with some one whose interest in Indian affairs and whose authority in the Indian Bureau were greater than his own, and such contact would be certain to arouse and constantly increase the interest he takes in his work.

The distance which separates the agents—the workers in the field—from the Indian Office in Washington is a chief obstacle to Indian progress. Whatever shall more closely unite these two branches of the Indian Service, and shall enable them to co-operate more heartily and more effectively, will be for the increased efficiency of the work and the betterment of the race for whose improvement the Indian Bureau was established. The appointment of a field assistant to the Commissioner of Indian Affairs would be certain to insure this good end. Such an official, if possessed of the requisite energy and deep interest in the work, would be a most efficient factor in bringing into closer relationship and a more direct union of effort the Bureau in Washington and its agents in the field; and with the co-operation of its branches thus secured the Indian Bureau would, in measure fuller than ever before, lift up the savage toward that self-help and self-reliance which constitute the man.

In 1907 there will be held at Hampton Roads the tricentennial celebration of the settlement at Jamestown, Virginia, with which the history of what has now become the United States really begins. I commend this to your favorable consideration. It is an event of prime historic significance, in which all the people of the United States should feel, and should show, great and general interest.

In the Post-Office Department the service has increased in efficiency, and conditions as to revenue and expenditure continue satisfactory. The increase of revenue during the year was $9,358,181.10, or 6.9 per cent, the total receipts amounting to $143,382,624.34. The expenditures were $152,362,116.70, an increase of about 9 per cent over the previous year, being thus $8,979,492.36 in excess of the current revenue. Included in these expenditures was a total appropriation of $12,956,637.35 for the continuation and extension of the rural free-delivery service, which was an increase of $4,902,237.35 over the amount expended for this purpose in the preceding fiscal year. Large as this expenditure has been the beneficent results attained in extending the free distribution of mails to the residents of rural districts have justified the wisdom of the outlay. Statistics brought down to the 1st of October, 1904, show that on that date there were 27,138 rural routes established, serving approximately 12,000,000 of people in rural districts remote from post-offices, and that there were pending at that time 3,859 petitions for the establishment of new rural routes. Unquestionably some part of the general increase in receipts is due to the increased postal facilities which the rural service has afforded. The revenues have also been aided greatly by amendments in the classification of mail matter, and the curtailment of abuses of the second-class mailing privilege. The average increase in the volume of mail matter for the period beginning with 1902 and ending June, 1905 (that portion for 1905 being estimated), is 40.47 per cent, as compared with 25.46 per cent for the period immediately preceding, and 15.92 for the four-year period immediately preceding that.

Our consular system needs improvement. Salaries should be substituted for fees, and the proper classification, grading, and transfer of consular officers should be provided. I am not prepared to say that a competitive system of examinations for appointment would work well; but by law it should be provided that consuls should be familiar, according to places for which they apply, with the French, German, or

Spanish languages, and should possess acquaintance with the resources of the United States.

The collection of objects of art contemplated in section 5586 of the Revised Statutes should be designated and established as a National Gallery of Art; and the Smithsonian Institution should be authorized to accept any additions to said collection that may be received by gift, bequest, or devise.

It is desirable to enact a proper National quarantine law. It is most undesirable that a State should on its own initiative enforce quarantine regulations which are in effect a restriction upon interstate and international commerce. The question should properly be assumed by the Government alone. The Surgeon-General of the National Public Health and Marine-Hospital Service has repeatedly and convincingly set forth the need for such legislation.

I call your attention to the great extravagance in printing and binding Government publications, and especially to the fact that altogether too many of these publications are printed. There is a constant tendency to increase their number and their volume. It is an understatement to say that no appreciable harm would be caused by, and substantial benefit would accrue from, decreasing the amount of printing now done by at least one-half. Probably the great majority of the Government reports and the like now printed are never read at all, and furthermore the printing of much of the material contained in many of the remaining ones serves no useful purpose whatever.

The attention of the Congress should be especially given to the currency question, and that the standing committees on the matter in the two Houses charged with the duty, take up the matter of our currency and see whether it is not possible to secure an agreement in the business world for bettering the system; the committees should consider the question of the retirement of the greenbacks and the problem of securing in our currency such elasticity as is consistent with safety. Every silver dollar should be made by law redeemable in gold at the option of the holder.

I especially commend to your immediate attention the encouragement of our merchant marine by appropriate legislation.

The growing importance of the Orient as a field for American exports drew from my predecessor, President McKinley, an urgent request for its special consideration by the Congress. In his message of 1898 he stated:

"In this relation, as showing the peculiar volume and value of our trade with China and the peculiarly favorable conditions which exist for their expansion in the normal course of trade, I refer to the communication addressed to the Speaker of the House of Representatives by the Secretary of the Treasury on the 14th of last June, with its as companying letter of the Secretary of State, recommending an appropriation for a commission to study the industrial and commercial conditions in the Chinese Empire and to report as to the opportunities for and the obstacles to the enlargement of markets in China for the raw products and manufactures of the United States. Action was not taken thereon during the last session. I cordially urge that the recommendation receive at your hands the consideration which its importance and timeliness merit."

In his annual message of 1889 he again called attention to this recommendation, quoting it, and stated further:

I now renew this recommendation, as the importance of the subject has steadily grown since it was first submitted to you, and no time should be lost in studying for ourselves the resources of this great field for American trade and enterprise."

The importance of securing proper information and data with a view to the enlargement of our trade with Asia is undiminished. Our consular representatives in China have strongly urged a place for permanent display of American products in some prominent trade center of that Empire, under Government control and management, as an effective means of advancing our export trade therein. I call the attention of the Congress to the desirability of carrying out these suggestions.

In dealing with the questions of immigration and naturalization it is indispensable to keep certain facts ever before the minds of those who share in enacting the laws. First and foremost, let us remember that the question of being a good American has nothing whatever to do with a man's birthplace any more than it has to do with his creed. In every generation from the time this Government was founded men of foreign birth have stood in the very foremost rank of good citizenship, and that not merely in one but in every field of American activity; while to try to draw a distinction between the man whose parents came to this country and the man whose ancestors came to it several generations back is a mere absurdity. Good Americanism is a matter of heart, of conscience, of lofty aspiration, of sound common sense, but not of birthplace or of creed. The medal of honor, the highest prize to be won by those who serve in the Army and the Navy of the United States decorates men born here, and it also decorates men born in Great Britain and Ireland, in Germany, in Scandinavia, in France, and doubtless in other countries also. In the field of statesmanship, in the field of business, in the field of philanthropic endeavor, it is equally true that among the men of whom we are most proud as Americans no distinction whatever can be drawn between those who themselves or whose parents came over in sailing ship or steamer from across the water and those whose ancestors stepped ashore into the wooded wilderness at Plymouth or at the mouth of the Hudson, the Delaware, or the James nearly three centuries ago. No fellow-citizen of ours is entitled to any peculiar regard because of the way in which he worships his Maker, or because of the birthplace of himself or his parents, nor should he be in any way discriminated against therefor. Each must stand on his worth as a man and each is entitled to be judged solely thereby.

There is no danger of having too many immigrants of the right kind. It makes no difference from what country they come. If they are sound in body and in mind, and, above all, if they are of good character, so that we can rest assured that their children and grandchildren will be worthy fellow-citizens of our children and grandchildren, then we should welcome them with cordial hospitality.

But the citizenship of this country should not be debased. It is vital that we should keep high the standard of well-being among our wage-workers, and therefore we should not admit masses of men whose standards of living and whose personal customs and habits are such that they tend to lower the level of the American wage-worker; and above all we should not admit any man of an unworthy type, any man concerning whom we can say that he will himself be a bad citizen, or that his children and grandchildren will detract from instead of adding to the sum of the good citizenship of the country. Similarly we should take the greatest care about naturalization. Fraudulent naturalization, the naturalization of improper persons, is a curse to our Government; and it is the affair of every honest voter, wherever born, to see that no fraudulent voting is allowed, that no fraud in connection with naturalization is permitted.

In the past year the cases of false, fraudulent, and improper naturalization of aliens coming to the attention of the executive branches of the Government have increased to an alarming degree. Extensive sales of forged certificates of naturalization have been discovered, as well as many cases of naturalization secured by perjury and fraud; and in addition, instances have accumulated showing that many courts issue certificates of naturalization carelessly and upon insufficient evidence.

Under the Constitution it is in the power of the Congress "to establish a uniform rule of naturalization," and numerous laws have from time to time been enacted for that purpose, which have been supplemented in a few States by State laws having special application. The Federal statutes permit naturalization by any court of record in the United States having common-law jurisdiction and a seal and clerk, except the police court of the District of Columbia, and nearly all these courts exercise this important function. It results that where so many courts of such varying grades have jurisdiction, there is lack of uniformity in the rules applied in conferring naturalization. Some courts

THE FIRST SPEECH OF A PRESIDENT ON FOREIGN SOIL (ROOSEVELT)

THE FIRST SPEECH OF A PRESIDENT ON FOREIGN SOIL.

Until 1906, it had been unwritten law that a President of the United States must not leave the soil of his country during his incumbency of the Presidency. But as Americans discovered soon after Theodore Roosevelt came to occupy the White House, usefulness and not precedent guided the actions of the hero of San Juan Hill. During the construction of the Panama Canal, so many charges and counter-charges concerning the administration of the task were bandied back and forth that the President determined to pay a visit to the Canal to draw his own conclusions from first-hand information. Naturally, in visiting the Canal Zone, the President was visiting what was virtually a part of the country whose destinies he was guiding. The preceding picture shows Mr. Roosevelt in a characteristic attitude as he delivered a speech on the occasion of his 1906 visit.

are strict and others lax. An alien who may secure naturalization in one place might be denied it in another, and the intent of the constitutional provision is in fact defeated. Furthermore, the certificates of naturalization issued by the courts differ widely in wording and appearance, and when they are brought into use in foreign countries, are frequently subject to suspicion.

There should be a comprehensive revision of the naturalization laws. The courts having power to naturalize should be definitely named by national authority; the testimony upon which naturalization may be conferred should be definitely prescribed; publication of impending naturalization applications should be required in advance of their being in court; the form and wording of all certificates issued should be uniform throughout the country, and the courts should be required to make returns to the Secretary of State at stated periods of all naturalizations conferred.

Not only are the laws relating to naturalization now defective, but those relating to citizenship of the United States ought also to be made the subject of scientific inquiry with a view to probable further legislation. By what acts expatriation may be assumed to have been accomplished, how long an American citizen may reside abroad and receive the protection of our passport, whether any degree of protection should be extended to one who has made the declaration of intention to become a citizen of the United States but has not secured naturalization, are questions of serious import, involving personal rights and often producing friction between this Government and foreign governments. Yet upon these question our laws are silent. I recommend that an examination be made into the subjects of citizenship, expatriation, and protection of Americans abroad, with a view to appropriate legislation.

The power of the Government to protect the integrity of the elections of its own officials is inherent and has been recognized and affirmed by repeated declarations of the Supreme Court. There is no enemy of free government more dangerous and none so insidious as the corruption of the electorate. No one defends or excuses corruption, and it would seem to follow that none would oppose vigorous measures to eradicate it. I recommend the enactment of a law directed against bribery and corruption in Federal elections. The details of such a law may be safely left to the wise discretion of the Congress, but it should go as far as under the Constitution it is possible to go, and should include severe penalties against him who gives or receives a bribe intended to influence his act or opinion as an elector; and provisions for the publication not only of the expenditures for nominations and elections of all candidates but also of all contributions received and expenditures made by political committees.

220

No subject is better worthy the attention of the Congress than that portion of the report of the Attorney-General dealing with the long delays and the great obstruction to justice experienced in the cases of Beavers, Green and Gaynor, and Benson. Were these isolated and special cases, I should not call your attention to them; but the difficulties encountered as regards these men who have been indicted for criminal practices are not exceptional; they are precisely similar in kind to what occurs again and again in the case of criminals who have sufficient means to enable them to take advantage of a system of procedure which has grown up in the Federal courts and which amounts in effect to making the law easy of enforcement against the man who has no money, and difficult of enforcement, even to the point of sometimes securing immunity, as regards the man who has money. In criminal cases the writ of the United States should run throughout its borders. The wheels of justice should not be clogged, as they have been clogged in the cases above mentioned, where it has proved absolutely impossible to bring the accused to the place appointed by the Constitution for his trial. Of recent years there has been grave and increasing complaint of the difficulty of bringing to justice those criminals whose criminality, instead of being against one person in the Republic, is against all persons in the Republic, because it is against the Republic itself. Under any circumstance and from the very nature of the case it is often exceedingly difficult to secure proper punishment of those who have been guilty of wrongdoing against the Government. By the time the offender can be brought into court the popular wrath against him has generally subsided; and there is in most instances very slight danger indeed of any prejudice existing in the minds of the jury against him. At present the interests of the innocent man are amply safeguarded; but the interests of the Government, that is, the interests of honest administration, that is the interests of the people, are not recognized as they should be. No subject better warrants the attention of the Congress. Indeed, no subject better warrants the attention of the bench and the bar throughout the United States.

Alaska, like all our Territorial acquisitions, has proved resourceful beyond the expectations of those who made the purchase. It has become the home of many hardy, industrious, and thrifty American citizens. Towns of a permanent character have been built. The extent of its wealth in minerals, timber, fisheries, and agriculture, while great, is probably not comprehended yet in any just measure by our people. We do know, however, that from a very small beginning its products have grown until they are a steady and material contribution to the wealth of the nation. Owing to the immensity of Alaska and its location in the far north, it is a difficult matter to provide many things essential to its growth and to the happiness and comfort of its people by private enterprise alone. It should, therefore, receive reasonable aid from the Government. The Government has already done excellent work for Alaska in laying cables and building telegraph lines. This work has been done in the most economical and efficient way by the Signal Corps of the Army.

In some respects it has outgrown its present laws, while in others those laws have been found to be inadequate. In order to obtain information upon which I could rely I caused an official of the Department of Justice, in whose judgment I have confidence, to visit Alaska during the past summer for the purpose of ascertaining how government is administered there and what legislation is actually needed at present. A statement of the conditions found to exist, together with some recommendations and the reasons therefor, in which I strongly concur, will be found in the annual report of the Attorney-General. In some instances I feel that the legislation suggested is so imperatively needed that I am moved briefly to emphasize the Attorney-General's proposals.

Under the Code of Alaska as it now stands many purely administrative powers and duties, including by far the most important, devolve upon the district judges or upon the clerks of the district court acting under the direction of the judges, while the governor, upon whom these powers and duties should logically fall, has nothing specific to do except to make annual reports, issue Thanksgiving Day proclamations, and appoint Indian policemen and notaries public. I believe it essential to good government in Alaska, and therefore recommend, that the Congress divest the district judges and the clerks of their courts of the administrative or executive functions that they now exercise and cast them upon the governor. This would not be an innovation; it would simply conform the government of Alaska to fundamental principles, making the governorship a real instead of a merely nominal office, and leaving the judges free to give their entire attention to their judicial duties and at the same time removing them from a great deal of the strife that now embarrasses the judicial office in Alaska.

I also recommend that the salaries of the district judges and district attorneys in Alaska be increased so as to make them equal to those received by corresponding officers in the United States after deducting the difference in the cost of living; that the district attorneys should be prohibited from engaging in private practice; that United States commissioners be appointed by the governor of the Territory instead of by the district judges, and that a fixed salary be provided for them to take the place of the discredited "fee system," which should be abolished in all offices; that a mounted constabulary be created to police the territory outside the limits of incorporated towns—a vast section now wholly without police protection; and that some provision be made to at least lessen the oppressive delays and costs that now attend the prosecution of appeals from the district court of Alaska. There should be a division of the existing judicial districts, and an increase in the number of judges.

Alaska should have a Delegate in the Congress. Where possible, the Congress should aid in the construction of needed wagon roads. Additional light-houses should be provided. In my judgment, it is especially important to aid in such manner as seems just and feasible in the construction of a trunk line of railway to connect the Gulf of Alaska with the Yukon River through American territory. This would be most beneficial to the development of the resources of the Territory, and to the comfort and welfare of its people.

Salmon hatcheries should be established in many different streams, so as to secure the preservation of this valuable food fish. Salmon fisheries and canneries should be prohibited on certain of the rivers where the mass of those Indians dwell who live almost exclusively on fish.

The Alaskan natives are kindly, intelligent, anxious to learn, and willing to work. Those who have come under the influence of civilization, even for a limited period, have proved their capability of becoming self-supporting, self-respecting citizens, and ask only for the just enforcement of law and intelligent instruction and supervision. Others, living in more remote regions, primitive, simple hunters and fisher folk, who know only the life of the woods and the waters, are daily being confronted with twentieth-century civilization with all of its complexities. Their country is being overrun by strangers, the game slaughtered and driven away, the streams depleted of fish, and hitherto unknown and fatal diseases brought to them, all of which combine to produce a state of abject poverty and want which must result in their extinction. Action in their interest is demanded by every consideration of justice and humanity.

The needs of these people are:

The abolition of the present fee system, whereby the native is degraded, imposed upon, and taught the injustice of law.

The establishment of hospitals at central points, so that contagious diseases that are brought to them continually by incoming whites may be localized and not allowed to become epidemic, to spread death and destitution over great areas.

The development of the educational system in the form of practical training in such industries as will assure the Indians self-support under the changed conditions in which they will have to live.

The duties of the office of the governor should be extended to include the supervision of Indian affairs, with necessary assistants in different districts. He should be provided with the means and the power to protect and advise the native people, to furnish medical treatment in time of epidemics, and to extend material relief in periods of famine and extreme destitution.

The Alaskan natives should be given the right to acquire, hold, and dispose of property upon the same conditions as given other inhabitants; and the privilege of citizenship should be given to such as may be able to meet certain definite requirements. In Hawaii Congress should give the governor power to remove all the officials appointed under him. The harbor of Honolulu should be dredged. The Marine Hospital Service should be empowered to study leprosy in the islands. I ask special consideration for the report and recommendation of the governor of Porto Rico.

In treating of our foreign policy and of the attitude that this great Nation should assume in the world at large, it is absolutely necessary to consider the Army and the Navy, and the Congress, through which the thought of the Nation finds its expression, should keep ever vividly in mind the fundamental fact that it is impossible to treat our foreign policy, whether this policy takes shape in the effort to secure justice for others or justice for ourselves, save as conditioned upon the attitude we are willing to take toward our Army, and especially toward our Navy. It is not merely unwise, it is contemptible, for a nation, as for an individual, to use high-sounding language to proclaim its purposes, or to take positions which are ridiculous if unsupported by potential force, and then to refuse to provide this force. If there is no intention of providing and of keeping the force necessary to back up a strong attitude, then it is far better not to assume such an attitude.

The steady aim of this Nation, as of all enlightened nations, should be to strive to bring ever nearer the day when there shall prevail throughout the world the peace of justice. There are kinds of peace which are highly undesirable, which are in the long run as destructive as any war. Tyrants and oppressors have many times made a wilderness and called it peace. Many times peoples who were slothful or timid or shortsighted, who had been enervated by ease or by luxury, or misled by false teachings, have shrunk in unmanly fashion from doing duty that was stern and that needed self-sacrifice, and have sought to hide from their own minds their shortcomings, their ignoble motives, by calling them love of peace. The peace of tyrannous terror, the peace of craven weakness, the peace of injustice, all these should be shunned as we shun unrighteous war. The goal to set before us as a nation, the goal which should be set before all mankind, is the attainment of the peace of justice, of the peace which comes when each nation is not merely safe-guarded in its own rights, but scrupulously recognizes and performs its duty toward others. Generally peace tells for righteousness; but if there is conflict between the two, then our fealty is due first to the cause of righteousness. Unrighteous wars are common, and unrighteous peace is rare; but both should be shunned. The right of freedom and the responsibility for the exercise of that right can not be divorced. One of our great poets has well and finely said that freedom is not a gift that tarries long in the hands of cowards. Neither does it tarry long in the hands of those too slothful, too dishonest, or too unintelligent to exercise it. The eternal vigilance which is the price of liberty must be exercised, sometimes to guard against outside foes; although of course far more often to guard against our own selfish or thoughtless shortcomings.

It these self-evident truths are kept before us, and only if they are so kept before us, we shall have a clear idea of what our foreign policy in its larger aspects should be. It is our duty to remember that a nation has no more right to do injustice to another nation, strong or weak, than an individual has to do injustice to another individual; that the same moral law applies in one case as in the other. But we must also remember that it is as much the duty of the Nation to guard its own rights and its own interests as it is the duty of the individual so to do. Within the Nation the individual has now delegated this right to the State, that is, to the representative of all the individuals, and it is a maxim of the law that for every wrong there is a remedy. But in international law we have not advanced by any means as far as we have advanced in municipal law. There is as yet no judicial way of enforcing a right in international law. When one nation wrongs another or wrongs many others, there is no tribunal before which the wrongdoer can be brought. Either it is necessary supinely to acquiesce in the wrong, and thus put a premium upon brutality and aggression, or else it is necessary for the aggrieved nation valiantly to stand up for its rights. Until some method is devised by which there shall be a degree of international control over offending nations, it would be a wicked thing for the most civilized powers, for those with most sense of international obligations and with keenest and most generous appreciation of the difference between right and wrong, to disarm. If the great civilized nations of the present day should completely disarm, the result would mean an immediate recrudescence of barbarism in one form or another. Under any circumstances a sufficient armament would have to be kept up to serve the purposes of international police; and until international cohesion and the sense of international duties and rights are far more advanced than at present, a nation desirous both of securing respect for itself and of doing good to others must have a force adequate for the work which it feels is allotted to it as its part of the general world duty. Therefore it follows that a self-respecting, just, and far-seeing nation should on the one hand endeavor by every means to aid in the development of the various movements which tend to provide substitutes for war, which tend to render nations in their actions toward one another, and indeed toward their own peoples, more responsive to the general sentiment of humane and civilized mankind; and on the other hand that it should keep prepared, while scrupulously avoiding wrongdoing itself, to repel any wrong, and in exceptional cases to take action which in a more advanced stage of international relations would come under the head of the exercise of the international police. A great free people owes it to itself and to all mankind not to sink into helplessness before the powers of evil.

We are in every way endeavoring to help on, with cordial good will, every movement which will tend to bring us into more friendly relations with the rest of mankind. In pursuance of this policy I shall shortly lay before the Senate treaties of arbitration with all powers which are willing to enter into these treaties with us. It is not possible at this period of the world's development to agree to arbitrate all matters, but there are many matters of possible difference between us and other nations which can be thus arbitrated. Furthermore, at the request of the Interparliamentary Union, an eminent body composed of practical statesmen from all countries, I have asked the Powers to join with this Government in a second Hague conference, at which it is hoped that the work already so happily begun at The Hague may be carried some steps further toward completion. This carries out the desire expressed by the first Hague conference itself.

It is not true that the United States feels any land hunger or entertains any projects as regards the other nations of the Western Hemisphere save such as are for their welfare. All that this country desires is to see the neighboring countries stable, orderly, and prosperous. Any country whose people conduct themselves well can count upon our hearty friendship. If a nation shows that it knows how to act with reasonable efficiency and decency in social and political matters, if it keeps order and pays its obligations, it need fear no interference from the United States. Chronic wrongdoing, or an impotence which results in a general loosening of the ties of civilized society, may in America, as elsewhere, ultimately require intervention by some civilized nation, and in the Western Hemisphere the adherence of the United States to the Monroe Doctrine may force the United States, however reluctantly, in flagrant cases of such wrongdoing or impotence, to the exercise of an international police power. If every country washed by the Caribbean Sea would show the progress in stable and just civilization which with the aid of the Platt amendment Cuba has shown since our troops left the island, and which so many of the republics in both Americas are constantly and brilliantly showing, all question of interference by this Nation with their affairs would be at an end. Our interests and those of our southern neighbors are in reality identical. They have great natural riches, and if within their borders the reign of law and justice obtains, prosperity is sure to come to them. While they thus obey the primary laws of civilized society they may rest assured that they will be treated by us in a spirit of cordial and helpful sympathy. We would interfere with them only in the last resort, and then only if it became evident that their inability or unwillingness to do justice at home and abroad had violated the rights of the United States or had invited foreign aggression to the detriment of the entire body of American nations. It is a mere truism to say that every nation, whether in America or anywhere else, which desires to maintain its freedom, its independence, must ultimately realize that the right of such independence can not be separated from the responsibility of making good use of it.

In asserting the Monroe Doctrine, in taking such steps as we have taken in regard to Cuba, Venezuela, and Panama, and in endeavoring to circumscribe the theater of war in the Far East, and to secure the open door in China, we have acted in our own interest as well as in the interest of humanity at large. There are, however, cases in which, while our own interests are not greatly involved, strong appeal is made to our sympathies. Ordinarily it is very much wiser and more useful for us to concern ourselves with striving for our own moral and material betterment here at home than to concern ourselves with trying to better the condition of things in other nations. We have plenty of sins of our own to war against, and under ordinary circumstances we can do more for the general uplifting of humanity by striving with heart and soul to put a stop to civic corruption, to brutal lawlessness and violent race prejudices here at home than by passing resolutions about wrongdoing elsewhere. Nevertheless there are occasional crimes committed on so vast a scale and of such peculiar horror as to make us doubt whether it is not our manifest duty to endeavor at least to show our disapproval of the deed and our sympathy with those who have suffered by it. The cases must be extreme in which such a course is justifiable. There must be no effort made to remove the mote from our brother's eye if we refuse to remove the beam from our own. But in extreme cases action may be justifiable and proper. What form the action shall take must depend upon the circumstances of the case; that is, upon the degree of the atrocity and upon our power to remedy it. The cases in which we could interfere by force of arms as we interfered to put a stop to intolerable conditions in Cuba are necessarily very few. Yet it is not to be expected that a people like ours, which in spite of certain very obvious shortcomings, nevertheless as a whole shows by its consistent practice its belief in the principles of civil and religious liberty and of orderly freedom, a people among whom even the worst crime, like the crime of lynching, is never more than sporadic, so that individuals and not classes are molested in their fundamental rights—it is inevitable that such a nation should desire eagerly to give expression to its horror on an occasion like that of the massacre of the Jews in Kishenef, or when it witnesses such systematic and long-extended cruelty and oppression as the cruelty and oppression of which the Armenians have been the victims, and which have won for them the indignant pity of the civil-ized world.

Even where it is not possible to secure in other nations the observance of the principles which we accept as axiomatic, it is necessary for us firmly to insist upon the rights of our own citizens without regard to their creed or race; without regard to whether they were born here or born abroad. It has proved very difficult to secure from Russia the right for our Jewish fellow-citizens to receive passports and travel through Russian territory. Such conduct is not only unjust and irritating toward us, but it is difficult to see its wisdom from Russia's standpoint. No conceivable good is accomplished by it. If an American Jew or an American Christian misbehaves himself in Russia he can at once be driven out; but the ordinary American Jew, like the ordinary American Christian, would behave just about as he behaves here, that is, behave as any good citizen ought to behave; and where this is the case it is a wrong against which we are entitled to protest to refuse him his passport without regard to his conduct and character, merely on racial and religious grounds. In Turkey our difficulties arise less from the way in which our citizens are sometimes treated than from the indignation inevitably excited in seeing such fearful misrule as has been witnessed both in Armenia and Macedonia.

The strong arm of the Government in enforcing respect for its just rights in international matters is the Navy of the United States. I most earnestly recommend that there be no halt in the work of up-building the American Navy. There is no more patriotic duty before us a people than to keep the Navy adequate to the needs of this country's position. We have undertaken to build the Isthmian Canal. We have undertaken to secure for ourselves our just share in the trade of the Orient. We have undertaken to protect our citizens from improper treatment in foreign lands. We continue steadily to insist on the application of the Monroe Doctrine to the Western Hemisphere. Unless our attitude in these and all similar matters is to be a mere boastful sham we can not afford to abandon our naval programme. Our voice is now potent for peace, and is so potent because we are not afraid of war. But our protestations upon behalf of peace would neither receive nor deserve the slightest attention if we were impotent to make them good.

The war which now unfortunately rages in the far East has emphasized in striking fashion the new possibilities of naval warfare. The lessons taught are both strategic and tactical, and are political as well as military. The experiences of the war have shown in conclusive fashion that while sea-going and sea-keeping torpedo destroyers are indispensable, and fast lightly armed and armored cruisers very useful, yet that the main reliance, the main standby, in any navy worthy the name must be the great battle ships, heavily armored and heavily gunned. Not a Russian or Japanese battle ship has been sunk by a torpedo boat, or by gunfire, while among the less protected ships, cruiser after cruiser has been destroyed whenever the hostile squadrons have gotten within range of one another's weapons. There will always be a large field of usefulness for cruisers, especially of the more formidable type. We need to increase the number of torpedo-boat destroyers, paying less heed to their having a knot or two extra speed than to their capacity to keep the seas for weeks, and, if necessary, for months at a time. It is wise to build submarine torpedo boats, as under certain circumstances they might be very useful. But most of all we need to continue building our fleet of battle ships, or ships so powerfully armed that they can inflict the maximum of damage upon our opponents, and so well protected that they can suffer a severe hammering in return without fatal impairment of their ability to fight and maneuver. Of course ample means must be provided for enabling the personnel of the Navy to be brought to the highest point of efficiency. Our great fighting ships and torpedo boats must be ceaselessly trained and maneuvered in squadrons. The officers and men can only learn their trade thoroughly by ceaseless practice on the high seas. In the event of war it would be far better to have no ships at all than to have ships of a poor and ineffective type, or ships which, however good, were yet manned by untrained and unskillful crews. The best officers and men in a poor ship could do nothing against fairly good opponents ; and on the other hand a modern war ship is useless unless the officers and men aboard her have become adepts in their duties. The marksmanship in our Navy has improved in an extraordinary degree during the last three years, and on the whole the types of our battleships are improving ; but much remains to be done. Sooner or later we shall have to provide for some method by which there will be promotions for merit as well as for seniority, or else retirement of all those who after a certain age have not advanced beyond a certain grade ; while no effort must be spared to make the service attractive to the enlisted men in order that they may be kept as long as possible in it. Reservation public schools should be provided wherever there are navy-yards.

Within the last three years the United States has set an example in disarmament where disarmament was proper. By law our Army is fixed at a maximum of one hundred thousand and a minimum of sixty thousand men. When there was insurrection in the Philippines we kept the Army at the maximum. Peace came in the Philippines, and now our Army has been reduced to the minimum at which it is possible to keep it with due regard to its efficiency. The guns now mounted require twenty-eight thousand men, if the coast fortifications are to be adequately manned. Relatively to the Nation, it is not now so large as the police force of New York or Chicago relatively to the population of either city. We need more officers; there are not enough to perform the regular army work. It is very important that the officers of the Army should be accustomed to handle their men in masses, as it is also important that the National Guard of the several States should be accustomed to actual field maneuvering, especially in connection with the regulars. For this reason we are to be congratulated upon the success of the field maneuvers at Manassas last fall, maneuvers in which a larger number of Regulars and National Guard took part than was ever before assembled together in time of peace. No other civilized nation has, relatively to its population, such a diminutive Army as ours; and while the Army is so small we are not to be excused if we fail to keep it at a very high grade of proficiency. It must be incessantly practiced; the standard for the enlisted men should be kept very high, while at the same time the service should be made as attractive as possible; and the standard for the officers should be kept even higher—which, as regards the upper ranks, can best be done by introducing some system of selection and rejection into the promotions. We should be able, in the event of some sudden emergency, to put into the field one first-class army corps, which should be, as a whole, at least the equal of any body of troops of like number belonging to any other nation.

Great progress has been made in protecting our coasts by adequate fortifications with sufficient guns. We should, however, pay much more heed than at present to the development of an extensive system of floating mines for use in all our more important harbors. These mines have been proved to be a most formidable safeguard against hostile fleets.

I earnestly call the attention of the Congress to the need of amending the existing law relating to the award of Congressional medals of honor in the Navy so as to provide that they may be awarded to commissioned officers and warrant officers as well as to enlisted men. These justly prized medals are given in the Army alike to the officers and the enlisted men, and it is most unjust that the commissioned officers and warrant officers of the Navy should not in this respect have the same rights as their brethren in the Army and as the enlisted men of the Navy.

In the Philippine Islands there has been during the past year a continuation of the steady progress which has obtained ever since our troops definitely got the upper hand of the insurgents. The Philippine people, or, to speak more accurately, the many tribes, and even races, sundered from one another more or less sharply, who go to make up the people of the Philippine Islands, contain many elements of good, and some elements which we have a right to hope stand for progress. At present they are utterly incapable of existing in independence at all or of building up a civilization of their own. I firmly believe that we can help them to rise higher and higher in the scale of civilization and of capacity for self-government, and I most earnestly hope that in the end they will be able to stand, if not entirely alone, yet in some such relation to the United States as Cuba now stands. This end is not yet in sight, and it may be indefinitely postponed if our people are foolish enough to turn the attention of the Filipinos away from the problems of achieving moral and material prosperity, of working for a stable, orderly, and just government, and toward foolish and dangerous intrigues for a complete independence for which they are as yet totally unfit.

On the other hand our people must keep steadily before their minds the fact that the justification for our stay in the Philippines must ultimately rest chiefly upon the good we are able to do in the islands. I do not overlook the fact that in the development of our interests in the Pacific Ocean and along its coasts, the Philippines have played and will play an important part; and that our interests have been served in more than one way by the possession of the islands. But our chief reason for continuing to hold them must be that we ought in good faith to try to do our share of the world's work, and this particular piece of work has been imposed upon us by the results of the war with Spain. The problem presented to us in the Philippine Islands is akin to, but not exactly like, the problems presented to the other great civilized powers which have possessions in the Orient. There are points of resemblance in our work to the work which is being done by the British in India and Egypt, by the French in Algiers, by the Dutch in Java, by the Russians in Turkestan, by the Japanese in Formosa; but more distinctly than any of these powers we are endeavoring to develop the natives themselves so that they shall take an ever-increasing share in their own government, and as far as is prudent we are already admitting their representatives to a governmental equality with our own. There are commissioners, judges, and governors in the islands who are Filipinos and who have exactly the same share in the government of the islands as have their colleagues who are Americans, while in the lower ranks, of course, the great majority of the public servants are Filipinos. Within two years we shall be trying the experiment of an elective lower house in the Philippine legislature. It may be that the Filipinos will misuse this legislature, and they certainly will misuse it if they are misled by foolish persons here at home into starting an agitation for their own independence or into any factious or improper action. In such case they will do themselves no good and will stop for the time being all further ꜰᴍꜰꜰ ꜰꜰ ꜰꜰꜰꜰꜰꜰꜰ ꜰꜰꜰ ꜰꜰꜰ ꜰꜰꜰ ꜰꜰꜰ ꜰꜰꜰꜰꜰꜰ ꜰꜰꜰꜰ ꜰꜰ ꜰꜰꜰꜰ ꜰꜰꜰ government. But if they act with wisdom and self-restraint, if they show that they are capable of electing a legislature which in its turn is capable of taking a sane and efficient part in the actual work of government, they can rest assured that a full and increasing measure of recognition will be given them. Above all they should remember that their prime needs are moral and industrial, not political. It is a good thing to try the experiment of giving them a legislature; but it is a far better thing to give them schools, good roads, railroads which will enable them to get their products to market, honest courts, an honest and efficient constabulary, and all that tends to produce order, peace, fair dealing as between man and man, and habits of intelligent industry and thrift. If they are safeguarded against oppression, and if their real wants, material and spiritual, are studied intelligently and in a spirit of friendly sympathy, much more good will be done them than by any effort to give them political power, though this effort may in its own proper time and place be proper enough.

Meanwhile our own people should remember that there is need for the highest standard of conduct among the Americans sent to the Philippine Islands, not only among the public servants but among the private individuals who go to them. It is because I feel this so deeply that in the administration of these islands I have positively refused to permit any discrimination whatsoever for political reasons and have insisted that in choosing the public servants consideration should be paid solely to the worth of the men chosen and to the needs of the islands. There is no higher body of men in our public service than we have in the Philippine Islands under Governor Wright and his associates. So far as possible these men should be given a free hand, and their suggestions should receive the hearty backing both of the Executive and of the Congress. There is need of a vigilant and disinterested support of our public servants in the Philippines by good citizens here in the United States. Unfortunately hitherto those of our people here at home who have specially claimed to be the champions of the Filipinos have in reality been their worst enemies. This will continue to be the case as long as they strive to make the Filipinos independent, and stop all industrial development of the islands by crying out against the laws which would bring it on the ground that capitalists must not "exploit" the islands. Such proceedings are not only unwise, but are most harmful to the Filipinos, who do not need independence at all, but who do need good laws, good public servants, and the industrial development that can only come if the investment of American and foreign capital in the islands is favored in all legitimate ways.

Every measure taken concerning the islands should be taken primarily with a view to their advantage. We should certainly give them lower tariff rates on their exports to the United States; if this is not done it will be a wrong to extend our shipping laws to them. I earnestly hope for the immediate enactment into law of the legislation now pending to encourage American capital to seek investment in the islands in railroads, in factories, in plantations, and in lumbering and mining.

THEODORE ROOSEVELT.

INAUGURAL ADDRESS.

My fellow-citizens, no people on earth have more cause to be thankful than ours, and this is said reverently, in no spirit of boastfulness in our own strength, but with gratitude to the Giver of Good who has blessed us with the conditions which have enabled us to achieve so large a measure of well-being and of happiness. To us as a people it has been granted to lay the foundations of our national life in a new continent. We are the heirs of the ages, and yet we have had to pay few of the penalties which in old countries are exacted by the dead hand of a bygone civilization. We have not been obliged to fight for our existence against any alien race; and yet our life has called for the vigor and effort without which the manlier and hardier virtues wither away. Under such conditions it would be our own fault if we failed; and the success which we have had in the past, the success which we confidently believe the future will bring, should cause in us no feeling of vainglory, but rather a deep and abiding realization of all which life has offered us; a full acknowledgment of the responsibility which is ours; and a fixed determination to show that under a free government a mighty people can thrive best, alike as regards the things of the body and the things of the soul.

Much has been given us, and much will rightfully be expected from us. We have duties to others and duties to ourselves; and we can shirk neither. We have become a great nation, forced by the fact of its greatness into relations with the other nations of the earth, and we must behave as beseems a people with such responsibilities. Toward all other nations, large and small, our attitude must be one of cordial and sincere friendship. We must show not only in our words, but in our deeds, that we are earnestly desirous of securing their good will by acting toward them in a spirit of just and generous recognition of all their rights. But justice and generosity in a nation, as in an individual, count most when shown not by the weak but by the strong. While ever careful to refrain from wronging others, we must be no less insistent that we are not wronged ourselves. We wish peace, but we wish the peace of justice, the peace of righteousness. We wish it because we think it is right and not because we are afraid. No weak nation that acts manfully and justly should ever have cause to fear us, and no strong power should ever be able to single us out as a subject for insolent aggression.

Our relations with the other powers of the world are important; but still more important are our relations among ourselves. Such growth in wealth, in population, and in power as this nation has seen during the century and a quarter of its national life is inevitably accompanied by a like growth in the problems which are ever before every nation that rises to greatness. Power invariably means both responsibility and danger. Our forefathers faced certain perils which we have outgrown. We now face other perils, the very existence of which it was impossible that they should foresee. Modern life is both complex and intense, and the tremendous changes wrought by the extraordinary industrial development of the last half century are felt in every fiber of our social and political being. Never before have men tried so vast and formidable an experiment as that of administering the affairs of a continent under the forms of a Democratic republic. The conditions which have told for our marvelous material well-being, which have developed to a very high degree our energy, self-reliance, and individual initiative, have also brought the care and anxiety inseparable from the accumulation of great wealth in industrial centers. Upon the success of our experiment much depends, not only as regards our own welfare, but as regards the welfare of mankind. If we fail, the cause of free self-government throughout the world will rock to its foundations, and therefore our responsibility is heavy, to ourselves, to the world as it is to-day, and to the generations yet unborn. There is no good reason why we should fear the future, but there is every reason why we should face it seriously, neither hiding from ourselves the gravity of the problems before us nor fearing to approach these problems with the unbending, unflinching purpose to solve them aright.

Yet, after all, though the problems are new, though the tasks set before us differ from the tasks set before our fathers who founded and preserved this Republic, the spirit in which these tasks must be undertaken and these problems faced, if our duty is to be well done, remains essentially unchanged. We know that self-government is difficult. We know that no people needs such high traits of character as that people which seeks to govern its affairs aright through the freely expressed will of the freemen who compose it. But we have faith that we shall not prove false to the memories of the men of the mighty past. They did their work, they left us the splendid heritage we now enjoy. We in our turn have an assured confidence that we shall be able to leave this heritage unwasted and enlarged to our children and our children's children. To do so we must show, not merely in great crises, but in the everyday affairs of life, the qualities of practical intelligence, of courage, of hardihood, and endurance, and above all the power of devotion to a lofty ideal, which made great the men who founded this Republic in the days of Washington, which made great the men who preserved this Republic in the days of Abraham Lincoln.

MARCH 4, 1905.

SPECIAL MESSAGES.

WHITE HOUSE, *December 7, 1904.*

To the Senate and House of Representatives:

I transmit herewith a report from the Secretary of State covering statements showing the receipts and disbursements of the Louisiana Purchase Exposition Company for the months of March, April, May, June, July, August, September, and October, 1904, furnished by the Louisiana Purchase Exposition Commission in pursuance of section 11 of the "Act to provide for celebrating the one hundredth anniversary of the purchase of the Louisiana territory," etc., approved March 3, 1901.

THEODORE ROOSEVELT.

WHITE HOUSE, *December 13, 1904.*

To the Senate and House of Representatives:

I transmit herewith, for the information of the Congress, the fourth annual report (with appendices) of the governor of Porto Rico, covering the period from July 1, 1903, to June 30, 1904.

THEODORE ROOSEVELT.

WHITE HOUSE, *December 14, 1904.*

To the Senate and House of Representatives:

Referring to section 32 of the act approved April 12, 1900, entitled "An act temporarily to provide revenues and a civil government for

Porto Rico, and for other purposes," I transmit herewith an ordinance enacted by the executive council of Porto Rico on August 30, 1904, granting to the Ponce Railway and Light Company the right to construct branch tracks or extensions of its present line of railway around the Playa of Ponce, which ordinance was approved by the President of the United States on October 8, 1904, subject to disqualification.

Attention is invited to the accompanying report of the Secretary of State.

THEODORE ROOSEVELT.

WHITE HOUSE, *December 14, 1904.*

To the Senate and House of Representatives:

Referring to section 32 of the act approved April 12, 1900, entitled "An act temporarily to provide revenues and a civil government for Porto Rico, and for other purposes," I transmit herewith an ordinance enacted by the executive council of Porto Rico on August 30, 1904, granting to the Compania de los Ferrocarriles de Puerto Rico and to its assign, the American Railroad Company of Porto Rico, the right to construct a spur or branch railway track connecting its warehouse at the Playa of Ponce with its main line, which ordinance was approved by the President of the United States on October 8, 1904, subject to qualification.

Attention is invited to the accompanying report of the Secretary of State.

THEODORE ROOSEVELT.

WHITE HOUSE, *December 14, 1904.*

To the Senate and House of Representatives:

Referring to section 32 of the act approved April 12, 1900, entitled "An act temporarily to provide revenues and a civil government for Porto Rico, and for other purposes," I transmit herewith an ordinance enacted by the executive council of Porto Rico on July 7, 1904, amending "An ordinance granting to the Vandegrift Construction Company the right to build and operate a line of railway between the municipality of San Juan and the Playa of Ponce, in the island of Porto Rico, and to develop electric energy by water or other power for distribution and sale for railway, lighting, and industrial purposes."

This ordinance was approved by the President of the United States on August 2, 1904, subject to qualification.

Attention is invited to the accompanying report of the Secretary of State.

THEODORE ROOSEVELT.

WHITE HOUSE, *December 14, 1904.*

To the Senate and House of Representatives:

Referring to section 32 of the act approved April 12, 1900, entitled "An act temporarily to provide revenues and a civil government for Porto Rico, and for other purposes," I transmit herewith an ordinance enacted by the executive council of Porto Rico on November 4, 1904, granting to the Campania de los Ferrocarriles de Puerto Rico and to its assign, the American Railroad Company of Porto Rico, the right to construct a spur or branch railway track running from its station of Lajas in the southwest direction toward the district of Boqueron, for a distance of about 7 kilometers, which ordinance was approved by the President of the United States on December 8, 1904, subject to qualification.

Attention is invited to the accompanying report of the Secretary of State.

THEODORE ROOSEVELT.

WHITE HOUSE, *December 14, 1904.*

To the Senate and House of Representatives:

Referring to section 32 of the act approved April 12, 1900, entitled "An act temporarily to provide revenues and a civil government for Porto Rico, and for other purposes," I transmit herewith an ordinance enacted by the executive council of Porto Rico on April 2, 1904, authorizing the transfer to the Ponce and Guayama Railroad Company of the franchise, rights, and exemptions granted to the "Compania de los Ferrocarriles de Puerto Rico" for the construction and maintenance of a railway between Ponce and Guayama, and also the transfer and assignment of such franchise, rights, and exemptions from the American Railroad Company of Porto Rico Central Aguirre Operator to the said Ponce and Guayama Railroad Company.

This ordinance was approved by the President of the United States on May 2, 1904, subject to qualification.

Attention is invited to the accompanying report of the Secretary of State.

THEODORE ROOSEVELT.

WHITE HOUSE, *December 15, 1904*

To the Senate and House of Representatives:

I transmit herewith, for the consideration of Congress, a report by the Secretary of State resubmitting a claim of the owners of the British steamship *Lindisfarne,* amounting to $158.11, for demurrage to that vessel while undergoing repairs necessitated through a collision with the United States army transport *Crook* in New York Harbor on May 23, 1900.

THEODORE ROOSEVELT.

WHITE HOUSE, *December 21, 1904.*

To the Senate and House of Representatives:

I transmit herewith the report of the Commissioner of Corporations, covering the period from the organization of the Bureau to June 30, 1904.

THEODORE ROOSEVELT

WHITE HOUSE, *December 21, 1904.*

To the Senate and House of Representatives:

I transmit herewith, for your consideration, a report and recommendations from the Secretary of State of the United States on the subject of the naturalization of aliens in the United States.

THEODORE ROOSEVELT.

WHITE HOUSE, *January 9, 1905.*

To the Senate and House of Representatives:

I transmit herewith a report, by the Secretary of Agriculture, of the operations of the Bureau of Animal Industry of the Department of Agriculture for the fiscal year ended June 30, 1904, in compliance with the requirements of section 11 of the act approved May 29, 1884, for the establishment of that Bureau.

THEODORE ROOSEVELT.

WHITE HOUSE, *January 9, 1905.*

To the Senate and House of Representatives:

I have, in a former message, stated to the Congress my belief that our Army need not be large, but that it should in every part be brought to the highest point of efficiency. The Secretary of War has called to my attention the fact that the act approved February 2, 1901, which accomplished so much to promote this result, failed to meet the needs of one staff department, in which all of our people are peculiarly interested and of which they have a right to demand a high degree of excellence. I refer to the Medical Department. Not only does a competent medical service by safeguarding the health of the Army contribute greatly to its power, but it gives to the families of the nation a guaranty that their fathers, brothers, and sons who are wounded in battle or sicken in the camp shall have not only skilled medical aid, but also that prompt and well-ordered attention to all their wants which can come only by an adequate and trained personnel.

I am satisfied that the Medical Corps is much too small for the needs of the present Army and therefore very much too small for its successful expansion in time of war to meet the needs of an enlarged Army, and, in addition, to furnish the volunteer service a certain number of officers trained in medical administration. A bill which, in the opinion of the Secretary of War, of the late Secretary of War, and of the General Staff of the Army, supplies these deficiencies was introduced at the last session of Congress and is now before you. I am also advised that it meets the cordial approval of the medical profession of the country. It provides an organization which, when compared with that of other nations, does not seem to err on the side of excessive liberality, but which is believed to be sufficient. I earnestly recommend its passage by the present Congress. If the Medical Department is left as it is, no amount of wisdom or efficiency in its administration would prevent a complete breakdown in the event of a serious war.

I transmit herewith a memorandum which has been prepared for me by the Surgeon-General of the Army, and also the remarks of the former and of the present Secretary of War with reference to this bill.

It is reported to me that the Ordnance Corps is in a position of disadvantage; that its personnel is inadequate to the performance of the duties with which it is charged, and that under existing conditions it is unable to recruit its numbers with officers of the class necessary for the conduct of its very technical work. It is unnecessary for me to lay stress upon the desirability of having the design and manufacture of the material with which we are to fight in competent and sufficient hands, as there is no difference of opinion as to the intention of all concerned to have provided a proper supply of weapons, munitions, engines of war, equal in conception and construction to any in the world, and superior in any respects in which by skill and attention we may be able to compass such superiority.

The greatly increased utilization of the exact sciences in ordnance construction requires a larger personnel for their application, and the process of its selection should be severely and continuously discriminating, under conditions offering stimulus sufficient to cause officers of proper capacity, of whom it appears there are plenty, to wish to subject themselves to it. A bill embodying the necessary provisions and involving no radical departure from existing methods has been prepared by the War Department. I think it should be passed.

THEODORE ROOSEVELT.

WHITE HOUSE, *January 10, 1905.*

To the Senate and House of Representatives:

I transmit herewith, for the consideration of the Congress, a communication from the Secretary of the Interior relative to the re-establishment of the boundary line between the State of Colorado and the Territories of New Mexico and Oklahoma, surveyed under authority of the act of Congress of July 1, 1902. (32 Stat., 552, 574.)

THEODORE ROOSEVELT.

WHITE HOUSE, *January 10, 1905.*

To the Senate and House of Representatives:

I transmit herewith a communication from the Secretary of the Interior relative to the reservation of certain lands in the abandoned Fort Sherman Military Reservation, in view of the contemplated use of such lands in connection with irrigation works to be constructed under the act of June 17, 1902. (32 Stat., 388.)

The matter is presented for the consideration of the Congress.

THEODORE ROOSEVELT.

WHITE HOUSE, *January 11, 1905.*

To the Senate and House of Representatives:

In the fall of 1903, John Henry Lofland, Earl Worden Chaffee, and Joseph Drummond Little, then members of the first or highest class at the Naval Academy, severally committed acts for which they were charged with the offense of hazing, were tried by court-martial, and were dismissed from the academy and from the naval service.

In a letter addressed to the chairman of the Committee on Naval Affairs of the House March 21, 1904, the Secretary of the Navy, after reviewing the facts upon which action in the cases of these midshipmen was based, states that "if discretion in the infliction of punishment had been vested either in the court-martial or the Department a lighter punishment than dismissal from the service might have been inflicted," and concludes that Congress is the proper authority to determine in cases of this character whether exception should be made to the operation of the statute.

The Committee on Naval Affairs (H. R. No. 2554, 58th Cong., 2d sess.), upon consideration of the Department's report, unanimously concludes that "under all the circumstances no detriment will be done the service" by sanctioning the appointment of these midshipmen to the naval service under appropriate conditions and restrictions.

Upon review of the facts in this case I concur generally in the conclusions of the Secretary of the Navy and the Committee on Naval Affairs with respect to the character of the offenses committed by these midshipmen. Their acts were in plain violation of the letter of the statute, but the case presented is not an aggravated one, and I believe that their severance from the academy, their reduction to the foot of the class of which they were members, and their entry into the naval service without formal graduation will be adequate punishment.

The draft of a bill granting authority for the appointment of these midshipmen to the Navy under conditions and restrictions believed to be sufficient to guard the interests of the service is inclosed for the consideration of the Congress.

THEODORE ROOSEVELT.

WHITE HOUSE, *January 13, 1905.*

To the Senate and House of Representatives:

I transmit herewith the report of the Isthmian Canal Commission, accompanied by a letter of the Secretary of War, under whose supervision I have, by Executive order, placed the work of the Commission. I concur with the Secretary of War in the view that the present provision of law, by which the work of building the canal has to be done only through a body of seven members, is inelastic and clumsy, and I earnestly recommend a change so that the President, who is charged with the responsibility of building the canal, may exercise greater discretion in the organization of the personnel through whom he is to discharge this duty. Actual experience has convinced me that it will be impossible to obtain the best and most effective service under the limitations prescribed by law. The general plans for the work must be agreed upon with the aid of the best engineers of the country, who should act as an advisory or consulting body. The consulting engineers should not be put on the Commission, which should be used only as an executive instrument for the executive and administrative work. The actual work of executing the general plans agreed upon by the Commission, after receiving the conclusions of the advising engineers, must be done by an engineer in charge, and we now have an excellent engineer. It is, in my judgment, inadvisable, therefore, to restrict the Executive's choice of commissioners to representatives of the Engineer Corps of the Army or the Navy. The Commission should consist of five, or preferably three, members, whose respective duties, powers, and salaries should be assigned to them by the President, and who should be placed under the member of the Cabinet whom the President desires. Of these men the one appointed as administrator of the Canal Strip should also serve as minister to Panama.

THEODORE ROOSEVELT.

WHITE HOUSE, *January 13, 1905.*

To the Senate and House of Representatives:

I transmit herewith, for the consideration of Congress, a report by the Secretary of State concerning the importance of reform in our extraterritorial judicial system in China and Korea, with accompanying papers, including a draft of an act providing for the establishment of a district court of the United States for China and Korea.

THEODORE ROOSEVELT.

WHITE HOUSE, *January 16, 1905.*

To the Senate and House of Representatives:

I transmit herewith, for the information of the Congress, the annual report of the Philippine Commission, together with the separate reports to the Commission of the civil governor of the islands and of the heads of the four departments.

I also inclose a letter from the Secretary of War, submitting the reports for my consideration.

THEODORE ROOSEVELT.

WHITE HOUSE, *January 18, 1905.*

To the Senate and House of Representatives:

I transmit herewith a communication from the Acting Secretary of State, accompanied by reports from the diplomatic and consular officers, upon the feasibility of regular co-operation between the two branches of our foreign service for the better promotion of American industry and trade. Basing his conclusions upon the views expressed in these reports, the Acting Secretary recommends that provision be made for six special agents, with the diplomatic rank and title of commercial attaché, to be sent abroad to make a practical trial of the proposed plan; to report to the Department of State conditions existing in different countries which might suggest modifications or changes in the general scheme; to prepare, for the Department of Commerce and Labor, reports upon commerce and manufactures, or upon kindred topics, of a more exhaustive and comprehensive character than is ordinarily obtainable at present; and to visit consulates, examine their workings, and suggest such changes, either to the consular officers or to the Department of State, as would tend to the general improvement and strengthening of the service.

It is proposed that these agents shall be chosen primarily for their expert knowledge, but shall be not merely specialists, except for particular investigation that might, from time to time, be required, but practical men of affairs, with the experience best suited to fit them for their executive duties. It is suggested that the consular service might supply the best type of agents desired, and that, for this reason, and also because of the incentive to merit which would thus be provided, appointments should be made preferably from among those consular officers who have demonstrated their special fitness and capacity.

It will, in my opinion, be found upon examination that, while the measure proposed is a modest and more or less tentative one, involving comparatively slight expense, it promises important and far-reaching consequences in the judicious strengthening of our whole foreign service in the interest of trade, and the gradual development of capacities in it but imperfectly available as yet to make it fully adequate to the demands of our productive energy as a nation. Agriculture in the United States has long been dependent for its prosperity upon the demand from abroad for its surplus product; and of late years our manufacturing industries have found that they were outstripping the capacity of even our enormous home market, and are now looking more and more to foreign consumption for relief from accumulating stocks. According to an estimate of the Department of Commerce and Labor, our exports of manufactures in the calendar year 1904 "will not only exceed the highest figures of any earlier year, but may probably pass the $500,000,000 line, as against 434 millions in the high-record year, the fiscal year 1900, 151 millions in 1890, 103 millions in 1880, 68 millions in 1870, and 40 millions in 1860." The magnitude and steady growth of this export movement from our workshops and factories are such as to suggest the grave importance of providing it with all the official apparatus necessary to its full and free development.

It is generally admitted that in recent years the consular service, whatever may be its defects of system, has developed a commercial utility which has been of great practical value. It would be most regrettable, however, if this improvement, which has been brought about by the zeal and energy of individual consuls rather than by the efforts of the service as a whole, and also, to a large extent, by the special direction of the Department of State, should be accepted as fully satisfying even present requirements, not to speak of the prospective demands of a rapidly expanding commerce. For this reason I cordially commend to the consideration of Congress the recommendations of the Acting Secretary of State, looking to the gradual systematizing and equipment of the whole foreign service, by simple and inexpensive means, as an auxiliary, responsive at all points, to what may reasonably be expected of it by the great industrial and commercial interests which are so deeply concerned in enlarging their share of the world's trade.

In view of the interest and importance of the subject to the public, and especially to the business community, I also suggest that authority be given for the printing of a special edition of 5,000 copies of the Acting Secretary's letter, together with the appended reports from diplomatic and consular officers, of which 2,000 copies shall be for distribution by the Department of State.

THEODORE ROOSEVELT.

WHITE HOUSE, *January 19, 1905.*

To the Senate and House of Representatives:

I transmit herewith a report on the condition and needs of the natives of Alaska, made by Lieut. ... Emmons, United States Navy retired.

Lieutenant Emmons had for many years peculiar facilities for ascertaining the facts about the natives of Alaska and has recently concluded an investigation made on the ground by my special direction. I very earnestly ask the attention of the Congress to the facts set forth in this report as to the needs of the native people of Alaska. It seems to me that our honor as a nation is involved in seeing that these needs are met. I earnestly hope that legislation along the general lines advocated by Lieutenant Emmons can be enacted.

THEODORE ROOSEVELT.

WHITE HOUSE, *January 23, 1905.*

To the Senate and House of Representatives:

I transmit herewith a communication from the Secretary of State covering the report of the agent of the United States in the arbitration of the Venezuelan cases before The Hague tribunal, with accompanying appendixes.

The attention of Congress is invited to the request of the Secretary of State that 500 copies of the report and appendixes be printed for the use of the Department of State.

THEODORE ROOSEVELT.

WHITE HOUSE, *January 26, 1905.*

To the Senate and House of Representatives:

. I transmit herewith the final report of the Commission on International Exchange, constituted under the authority of the act of March 3, 1903, in compliance with the requests of the Governments of China and Mexico.

The work of the Commission has assisted greatly in the establishment of the new monetary system of the Philippine Islands, Mexico, and the Republic of Panama. The work done in China has, from the letter of the Prince of Ching, the head of the executive, been very helpful to that Government. Such improvements in the monetary systems of the silver-using countries bring them into closer connection with the gold-standard countries and are of very great benefit to the trade of the United States, and every effort should be made to encourage such reforms.

The attention of Congress is invited to the accompanying report of the Acting Secretary of State, whose request for a suitable appropriation for carrying on this valuable work in the manner which seems to him most practicable I heartily indorse and recommend to your favorable consideration.

THEODORE ROOSEVELT.

WHITE HOUSE, *January 27, 1905.*

To the Senate:

In compliance with a resolution of the Senate of the 25th instant (the House of Representatives concurring), I return herewith Senate bill No. 5501, entitled "An act granting an increase of pension to Sarah A. Rowe."

THEODORE ROOSEVELT

WHITE HOUSE, *January 27, 1905.*

To the Senate and House of Representatives:

I transmit herewith certain reports by the Commissioner of Labor and the Attorney-General on the labor disturbances in Colorado, together with copies of correspondence between the President and the Attorney-General and the Commissioner of Labor upon the matter; and copies of correspondence between the Secretary of War and the governor of Colorado as to the request of the governor of Colorado for aid by the National Executive in dealing with the labor disturbances.

THEODORE ROOSEVELT.

WHITE HOUSE, *January 30, 1905.*

To the Senate and House of Representatives:

I call the attention of the Congress to the fact that no statistics have been collected by the Federal Government upon the subject of marriage and divorce since the year 1886, and that but few of the States have provisions for the collection of such statistics.

The institution of marriage is, of course, at the very foundation of our social organization, and all influences that affect that institution are of vital concern to the people of the whole country. There is a widespread conviction that the divorce laws are dangerously lax and indifferently administered in some of the States, resulting in a diminishing regard for the sanctity of the marriage relation.

The hope is entertained that co-operation amongst the several States can be secured to the end that there may be enacted upon the subject of marriage and divorce uniform laws, containing all possible safeguards for the security of the family. Intelligent and prudent action in that direction will be greatly promoted by securing reliable and trustworthy statistics upon marriage and divorce. I deem the matter of sufficient general importance to recommend that the Director of the Census be authorized by appropriate legislation to collect and publish statistics pertaining to that subject covering the period from 1866 to the present time.

THEODORE ROOSEVELT.

WHITE HOUSE, *January 30, 1905.*

To the Senate and House of Representatives:

I have been informed that the attention of Congress has been drawn to the defects of the law authorizing the formation of corporations in the District of Columbia. The evils growing out of the existing law were brought to my notice by a member of the bar of the District, and I directed the Attorney-General to make me a report upon the subject. From that report it appears that in the past two years there have been incorporated under the law of the District 2,211 companies, with a total authorized capital of nearly $4,000,000,000. Many of the companies thus incorporated represent no actual investment and may be used by unscrupulous persons to perpetrate fraud upon the public and upon those who may be deluded into investing in their stock. The increase of these corporations is going on with alarming rapidity. On one day of last week one person presented for filing articles for the incorporation of fourteen companies; another person presented for filing articles of incorporation for thirty-eight companies. In each of these the same persons were named as trustees. The aggregate authorized capital proposed for these thirty-eight companies amounted to $43,000,000. On one day of this week one person presented for filing articles of incorporation for fifty-four companies, in each of which the same three persons were named as trustees. The authorized capital proposed for these companies was over $200,000,000. The Attorney-General closes his report with the statement that—

"The law governing the formation and control of corporations in the District of Columbia is not, as it should be, a model of its kind, but, on the other hand, is hopelessly vicious."

The evil growing out of these laws is of such magnitude and the necessity for action is so urgent that I recommend to Congress the immediate consideration of the subject. The case calls for the most radical remedy. The right of incorporation ought to be suspended at once until Congress can devise proper legislation for guarding its exercise. Moreover, measures ought to be taken to annul the charters which have already been issued, either by their direct repeal, if that be possible under the Constitution, or by what other legislative action may be deemed necessary. I doubt not that Congress has already seen the necessity of replacing these vicious incorporation laws by those which are governed by sounder principles, which will forbid the issuance of stock or bonds in excess of the actual investment and permit a proper public supervision. When such a law shall have been enacted, all legitimate corporations which have been formed under the existing law may readily be reincorporated.

THEODORE ROOSEVELT.

WHITE HOUSE, *February 7, 1905.*

To the House of Representatives:

In compliance with a resolution of the House of Representatives dated the 4th instant (the Senate concurring), I return herewith House bill No. 3286, entitled "An act granting an increase of pension to Jacob F. French."

THEODORE ROOSEVELT.

WHITE HOUSE, *February 7, 1905.*

To the Senate and House of Representatives:

Circumstances have placed under the control of this Government the Philippine Archipelago. The islands of that group present as many interesting and novel questions with respect to their ethnology, their fauna and flora, and their geology and mineral resources as any region of the world. At my request the National Academy of Sciences appointed a committee to consider and report upon the desirability of instituting scientific explorations of the Philippine Islands. The report of this committee, together with the report of the Board of Scientific Surveys of the Philippine Islands, including draft of a bill providing for surveys of the Philippine Islands, which board was appointed by me, after receiving the report of the committee appointed by the National Academy of Sciences, with instructions to prepare such estimates and make such suggestions as might appear to it pertinent in the circumstances, accompanies this message.

The scientific surveys which should be undertaken go far beyond any surveys or explorations which the government of the Philippine Islands, however completely self-supporting, could be expected to make. The surveys, while of course beneficial to the people of the Philippine

Islands, should be undertaken as a national work for the information not merely of the people of the Philippine Islands, but of the people of this country and of the world. Only preliminary explorations have yet been made in the archipelago, and it should be a matter of pride to the Government of the United States fully to investigate and to describe the entire region. So far as may be convenient and practical, the work of this survey should be conducted in harmony with that of the proper bureaus of the government of the Philippines; but it should not be under the control of the authorities of the Philippine Islands, for it should be undertaken as a national work and subject to a board to be appointed by Congress or the President. The plan transmitted recommends simultaneous surveys in different branches of research, organized on a co-operative system. This would tend to completeness, avoid duplication, and render the work more economical than if the exploration were undertaken piecemeal. No such organized surveys have ever yet been attempted anywhere; but the idea is in harmony with modern, scientific, and industrial methods.

I recommend, therefore, that provision be made for the appointment of a board of surveys to superintend the national surveys and explorations to be made in the Philippine Islands, and that appropriations be made from time to time to meet the necessary expenses of such investigation. It is not probable that the survey would be completed in a less period than that of eight or ten years, but it is well that it should be begun in the near future. The Philippine Commission, and those responsible for the Philippine government, are properly anxious that this survey should not be considered as an expense of that government, but should be carried on and treated as a national duty in the interests of science.

THEODORE ROOSEVELT.

WHITE HOUSE, *February 13, 1905.*

To the Senate and House of Representatives:

For a number of years efforts have been made to confirm the historical statement that the remains of Admiral John Paul Jones were interred in a certain piece of ground in the city of Paris then owned by the Government and used at the time as a burial place for foreign Protestants. These efforts have at last resulted in documentary proof that John Paul Jones was buried, on July 20, 1792, between 8 and 9 o'clock p. m., in the now abandoned cemetery of St. Louis, in the northeastern section of Paris. About 500 bodies were interred there, and the body of the Admiral was probably among the last hundred buried. It was incased in a leaden coffin, calculated to withstand the ravages of time.

The cemetery was about 210 feet long by 120 feet wide. Since its disuse as a burial place the soil has been filled to a level, and covered almost completely by buildings, most of them of an inferior class.

The American ambassador in Paris, being satisfied that it is practical to discover and identify the remains of John Paul Jones, has, after prolonged negotiations with the present holders of the property, and the tenants thereof, secured from them options in writing, which give him the right to dig in all parts of the property during a period of three months for the purpose of making the necessary excavations and searches, upon condition of a stated compensation for the damage and annoyance caused by the work. The actual search is to be conducted by the chief engineer of the municipal department of Paris, having charge of subterranean works, at a cost which has been carefully estimated. The ambassador gives the entire cost of the work, including the options, compensation, cost of excavating, and caring for the remains, as not exceeding 180,000 francs, or $35,000, on the supposition that the body may not be found until the whole area has been searched. If earlier discovered the expense would be proportionately less.

The great interest which our people feel in the story of Paul Jones's life, the national sense of gratitude for the great service done by him toward the achievement of independence, and the sentiment of mingled distress and regret felt because the body of one of our greatest heroes lies, forgotten and unmarked, in foreign soil, lead me to approve the ambassador's suggestion that Congress should take advantage of this unexpected opportunity to do proper honor to the memory of Paul Jones, and appropriate the sum of $35,000, or so much thereof as may be necessary for the purposes above described, to be expended under the direction of the Secretary of State.

The report of Ambassador Porter, with the plans and photograph of the property, is annexed hereto.

In addition to the foregoing recommendation I urge that Congress emphasize the value set by our people upon the achievements of the naval commanders in our war of independence by providing for the erection of appropriate monuments to the memory of two, at least, of those who now lie in undistinguished graves, John Paul Jones and John Barry. These two men hold unique positions in the history of the birth of our Navy. Their services were of the highest moment to the young Republic in the days when it remained to be determined whether or not she should win out in her struggle for independence. It is eminently fitting that these services should now be commemorated in suitable manner.

THEODORE ROOSEVELT.

WHITE HOUSE, *February 13, 1905.*

To the Senate and House of Representatives:

I submit herewith the second partial report of the Public Lands Commission, appointed by me October 22, 1903, to report upon the condition, operation, and effect of the present land laws and to recommend such changes as are needed to effect the largest practical disposition of the public lands to actual settlers who will build homes upon them, and to secure in permanence the fullest and most effective use of the resources of the public lands. The subject is one of such magnitude and importance that I have concluded to submit this second partial report bearing upon some of the larger features which require immediate attention without waiting for the final statement of the Commission, which, from the very nature of the case, it has not been possible to complete at this time. I am in full sympathy with the general conclusions of the Commission in substance and in essence, and I commend its recommendations to your earnest and favorable consideration. The existing conditions, as set forth in this report, seem to require a radical revision of most of the laws affecting the public domain if we are to secure the best possible use of the remaining public lands by actual home makers.

THEODORE ROOSEVELT.

WHITE HOUSE, *February 15, 1905.*

To the Senate and House of Representatives:

I transmit herewith for the information of the Congress a report on the progress of the beet-sugar industry in the United States in 1904. Your attention is respectfully invited to the accompanying letter of the Secretary of Agriculture, recommending that 10,000 copies of the report be printed for the use of the Department of Agriculture in addition to such number as may be desired for the use of the Senate and House of Representatives.

THEODORE ROOSEVELT.

WHITE HOUSE, *February 27, 1905.*

To the Senate and House of Representatives:

In further compliance with the provisions of the act making appropriation for the support of the Army, approved June 30, 1902, relating to "the proper shelter and protection of officers and enlisted men of the Army of the United States lawfully on duty in the Philippine Islands, etc.," I transmit herewith a letter from the Secretary of War together with a supplemental statement from the Quartermaster-General of the Army, showing additional expenditures.

THEODORE ROOSEVELT.

WHITE HOUSE, *March 1, 1905.*

To the Senate and House of Representatives:

Your attention is respectfully called to the necessity of passing some legislation at this session which will supplement existing law intended to prevent the spread of contagious diseases of animals from one State to another or to foreign countries. Two bills, each designed to cure defects in existing law, are now pending before the Congress. The measures are practically identical. One is H. B. 17589, the other S. 7167. These bills have been favorably reported by the Committee on Agriculture of both branches of Congress.

Recent decisions of the Federal courts have held that the statutory powers of the Secretary of Agriculture are inadequate to enforce regulations that prohibit the interstate movement of animals which have been exposed to contagion, but which at the time of shipment have not yet developed visible signs of disease.

The right of the Secretary of Agriculture to regulate interstate movement of animals exposed but not actually diseased must be recognized if the spread of such diseases from State to State and to other countries is to be prevented; and yet this right has recently been attacked in two cases filed in the Supreme Court of the United States, and the Secretary of Agriculture is advised that the trend of recent decisions makes it probable that the Supreme Court may hold that the existing law is not sufficiently clear as to the steps which may be taken to accomplish this object. Each of the bills referred to in this message is accompanied by an able report, which points out the necessity, from a legal standpoint, for the enactment of this legislation.

I fear, if no remedial legislation be granted at this session, that it may not be possible to continue to enforce the necessary measures for controlling this class of diseases, and that serious, widespread, and irreparable injury will be caused to the live-stock interests of the United States. If the Federal quarantine is rendered ineffective, State will quarantine against State, each requiring compliance with differing statutes; the way to market may be blocked or rendered very difficult for shippers of live stock; contagious diseases of live stock may be so disseminated through the stock yards and channels of commerce that foreign countries will restrict the export of animals and possibly meats from the United States, all of which would be disastrous to the live-stock industry.

I therefore put in an earnest plea for early action in this matter, and commend to your favorable consideration the two bills proposed by the Committees on Agriculture and referred to in this message.

THEODORE ROOSEVELT.

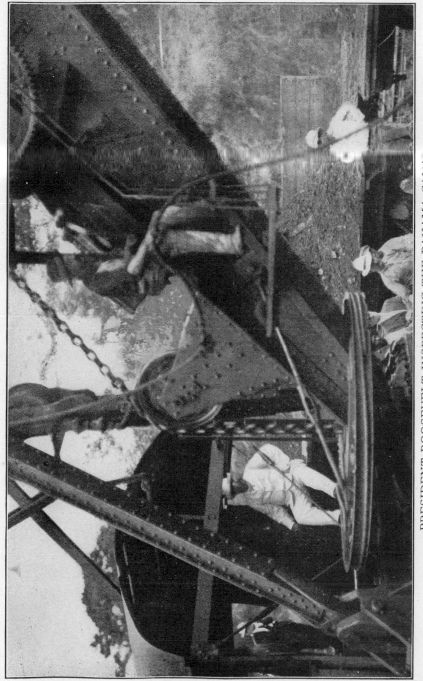

PRESIDENT ROOSEVELT INSPECTING THE PANAMA CANAL

THE PANAMA CANAL

The commencement of the task of constructing the Panama Canal was the most important event of Roosevelt's Administration. The history of the undertaking is written by Roosevelt himself on pages 6664, 6718, 6806, 6827, 7021, 7100, 7231, 7268, 7287, 7305 and 7348. The message commencing on page 7685 describes his visit of inspection to the canal zone. President Taft continued the narrative, pages 7370, 7374, 7423, 7482 and 7518. The reader who desires a brief recital of the facts should refer to the article entitled "Panama Canal" in the Encyclopedic Index. The index references following this article will enable the reader to glean a complete and authentic knowledge of the subject from the messages of the Presidents, from Jackson to Wilson, who have discussed the project.

WHITE HOUSE, *March 2, 1905.*

To the Senate and House of Representatives:

I transmit herewith, for the information of the Congress, a Report on Sugar Cane Experiments, 1903—4. The attention of the Congress is respectfully invited to the accompanying letter of the Secretary of Agriculture, recommending that 10,000 copies of the report be printed for the use of the Department of Agriculture in addition to such number as may be desired for the use of the Senate and House of Representatives.

THEODORE ROOSEVELT.

WHITE HOUSE, *March 2, 1905.*

To the Senate and House of Representatives:

I transmit herewith the appendix to the Report of the Commission on the Public Lands, forwarded by me to the Congress on February 13, 1905.

THEODORE ROOSEVELT.

WHITE HOUSE, *March 2, 1905.*

To the Senate and House of Representatives:

I transmit herewith, for the information of the Congress, a report on the Mexican cotton-boll weevil. Your attention is respectfully invited to the accompanying letter of the Secretary of Agriculture, recommending that at least 10,000 copies of this report be printed for the use of the Department of Agriculture, in addition to such number as may be desired for the use of the Senate and House of Representatives.

THEODORE ROOSEVELT.

WHITE HOUSE, *March 3, 1905.*

To the Senate and House of Representatives:

I transmit herewith a report from the Secretary of Commerce and Labor upon that portion of the resolution of the House of Representatives adopted March 7, 1904, having to do with the prices of cattle and dressed beef, the margins between such prices, and the organization, conduct, and profits of the corporations engaged in the beef-packing industry.

In view of the fact that the Department of Justice is now engaged upon other matters involved in the resolution, the Secretary of Commerce and Labor can not at this time report thereon.

THEODORE ROOSEVELT.

WHITE HOUSE, *March 6, 1905.*

To the Senate:

I wish to call the attention of the Senate at this executive session to the treaty with Santo Domingo. I feel that I ought to state to the Senate that the condition of affairs in Santo Domingo is such that it is very much for the interest of that Republic that action on the treaty should be had at as early a moment as the Senate, after giving the matter full consideration, may find practicable.

I call attention to the following facts:

1. This treaty was entered into at the earnest request of Santo Domingo itself, and is designed to afford Santo Domingo relief and assistance. Its primary benefit will be to Santo Domingo. It offers the method most likely to secure peace and to prevent war in the island.

2. The benefit to the United States will consist chiefly in the tendency under the treaty to secure stability, order, and prosperity in Santo Domingo, and the removal of the apprehension lest foreign powers make aggressions on Santo Domingo in the course of collecting claims due their citizens; for it is greatly to our interest that all the islands in the Caribbean Sea should enjoy peace and prosperity and feel good will toward this country. The benefit to honest creditors will come from the fact that for the first time under this treaty a practicable method of attempting to settle the debts due them will be inaugurated.

3. Many of the debts alleged to be due from Santo Domingo to outside creditors unquestionably on their face represent far more money than ever was actually given Santo Domingo. The proposed treaty provides for a process by which impartial experts will determine what debts are valid and what are in whole or in part invalid, and will apportion accordingly the surplus revenue available for the payment of the debts. This treaty offers the only method for preventing the collection of fraudulent debts, whether owed to Americans or to citizens of other nations.

4. This treaty affords the most practicable means of obtaining payment for the just claims of American citizens.

5. If the treaty is ratified, creditors belonging to other nations will have exactly as good treatment as creditors who are citizens of the United States, and at the same time Santo Domingo will be protected against unjust and exorbitant claims. If it is not ratified, the chances are that American creditors will fare ill as compared with those of other nations; for foreign nations, being denied the opportunity to get what is rightfully due their citizens under the proposed arrangement, will be left to collect the debts due their citizens as they see fit, provided, of course, there is not permanent occupancy of Dominican territory. As in such case the United States will have nothing to say as to what debts

should or should not be collected, and as Santo Domingo will be left without aid, assistance, or protection, it is impossible to state that the sums collected from it will not be improper in amount. In such event, whatever is collected by means of forcible intervention will be applied to the creditors of foreign nations in preference to creditors who are citizens of the United States.

6. The correspondence between the Secretary of State and the Minister of Haiti, submitted to the Senate several days ago, shows that our position is explicitly and unreservedly that under no circumstances do we intend to acquire territory in or possession of either Haiti or Santo Domingo, it being stated in these letters that even if the two republics desired to become a part of the United States the United States would certainly refuse its assent.

7. Santo Domingo grievously needs the aid of a powerful and friendly nation. This aid we are able, and I trust that we are willing, to bestow. She has asked for this aid, and the expressions of friendship, repeatedly sanctioned by the people and the Government of the United States, warrant her in believing that it will not be withheld in the hour of her need.

THEODORE ROOSEVELT.

PROCLAMATION

By the President of the United States of America.

A PROCLAMATION.

Whereas public interests require that the Senate of the United States be convened at 12 o'clock on the 4th day of March next, to receive such communications as may be made by the Executive:

Now, therefore, I, THEODORE ROOSEVELT, President of the United States of America, do hereby proclaim and declare that an extraordinary occasion requires the Senate of the United States to convene at the Capitol in the city of Washington on the 4th day of March next, at 12 o'clock noon, of which all persons who shall at that time be entitled to act as members of that body are hereby required to take notice.

GIVEN under my hand and the seal of the United States at Washington, the 23rd day of February in the year of our [SEAL.] Lord one thousand nine hundred and five, and of the Independence of the United States the one hundred and twenty-ninth.

THEODORE ROOSEVELT.

By the President:
> JOHN HAY,
> > *Secretary of State.*

BY THE PRESIDENT OF THE UNITED STATES OF AMERICA.

A PROCLAMATION.

Whereas the Congress of the United States has passed an Act approved March 3, 1905, and entitled, "An Act To provide for celebrating the birth of the American nation, the first permanent settlement of English-speaking people on the Western Hemisphere, by the holding of an international naval, marine, and military celebration in the vicinity of Jamestown, on the waters of Hampton Roads, in the State of Virginia; to provide for a suitable and permanent commemoration of said event, and to authorize an appropriation in aid thereof. and for other purposes";

And Whereas Section 3 of the said Act reads as follows:

"SEC. 3. The President of the United States is hereby authorized to make proclamation of said celebration, setting forth the event to be commemorated, inviting foreign nations to participate by the sending of their naval vessels and such representation of their military organizations as may be practicable. . . ":

Now, therefore, I THEODORE ROOSEVELT, President of the United States, by virtue of the authority vested in me by the said Act, do hereby declare and proclaim that there shall be inaugurated, in the year nineteen hundred and seven, on and near the waters of Hampton Roads, in the State of Virginia, an international naval, marine and military celebration, beginning May 13, and ending not later than November 1, 1907, for the purpose of commemorating, in a fitting and appropriate manner, the birth of the American nation, the first permanent settlement of English-speaking people on the American Continent, made at Jamestown, Virginia, on the thirteenth day of May, sixteen hundred and seven, and in order that the great events of American history which have resulted therefrom, may be accentuated to the present and future generations of American citizens. And in the name of the Government and of the people of the United States, I do hereby invite all the nations of the earth to take part in the commemoration of an event which has had a far reaching effect upon the course of human history, by sending their naval vessels to the said celebration and by making such representations of their military organizations as may be practicable.

In testimony whereof, I have hereunto set my hand and caused the seal of the United States to be affixed.

DONE at the City of Washington, this 29th day of March, [SEAL.] one thousand nine hundred and five, and of the Independence of the United States, the one hundred and twenty-ninth.

THEODORE ROOSEVELT.

By the President:

ALVEY A. ADEE,
    Acting Secretary of State.

By the President of the United States of America.

A PROCLAMATION.

Whereas, it is provided in the Act of Congress approved March 3, 1893, entitled "An Act Making appropriations for sundry civil expenses of the Government for the fiscal year ending June thirtieth, eighteen hundred and ninety-four, and for other purposes", "That the President is hereby authorized by proclamation to withhold from sale and grant for public use to the municipal corporation in which the same is situated all or any portion of any abandoned military reservation not exceeding twenty acres in one place",

And, Whereas, the Fort Sherman Military reservation at Coeur d'Alene, Idaho, created by Executive orders of August 25, 1879, and April 22, 1880, and enlarged by Executive orders of May 26, 1891, and February 2, 1892, and containing 902.21 acres, more or less, was by Executive order of October 5, 1900, placed under the custody of the Interior Department for disposal under the act of July 5, 1884, being "An Act To provide for the disposal of abandoned and useless military reservations",

And, Whereas, the citizens of the town of Coeur d'Alene, Idaho, have petitioned that a portion of the said reservation be granted to the Municipal Authorities of the town of Coeur d'Alene, Idaho, for the use of a public cemetery,

Now, Therefore, I, Theodore Roosevelt, by virtue of the power in me vested by the Act of Congress aforesaid, do hereby withdraw from sale, entry or other disposition, the land embraced in the legal subdivision, designated on the official plat of survey of the former Fort Sherman Military reservation as Lot 9 in section 14, township 50 north of range 4 west, Boise Meridian, containing 19.45 acres, and do hereby grant, for public use, the said described tract of land to the incorporated town of Coeur d'Alene, in the State of Idaho.

In witness whereof, I have hereunto set my hand and caused the seal of the United States to be affixed.

[SEAL.]   Done at the City of Washington, this 6th day of May, in the year of our Lord one thousand nine hundred and five, and of the Independence of the United States the one hundred and twenty-ninth.

THEODORE ROOSEVELT.

By the President:

Francis B. Loomis,
Acting Secretary of State.

BY THE PRESIDENT OF THE UNITED STATES OF AMERICA.

A PROCLAMATION.

Whereas, satisfactory proof has been given to me by the Government of the Republic of Panama that no discriminating duties of tonnage or imposts are imposed or levied in the ports of that Republic upon vessels wholly belonging to citizens of the United States or upon the produce, manufactures, or merchandise imported in such vessels from the United States, or from any foreign country;

Now, therefore, I, THEODORE ROOSEVELT, President of the United States of America, by virtue of the authority vested in me by section four thousand two hundred and twenty-eight of the Revised Statutes of the United States, do hereby declare and proclaim that, the foreign discriminating duties of tonnage and imposts within the United States are suspended and discontinued so far as respects the vessels of the Republic of Panama, and the produce, manufactures, or merchandise imported into the United States from the Republic of Panama, or from any other foreign country; the suspension to take effect on and after the date of this proclamation and to continue so long as the reciprocal exemption of vessels belonging to citizens of the United States, and their cargoes, shall be continued, and no longer.

In testimony whereof, I have hereunto set my hand and caused the seal of the United States to be affixed.

DONE at the City of Washington, the 15th day of May, in the year of our Lord one thousand nine hundred and five, [SEAL.] and of the Independence of the United States the one hundred and twenty-ninth.   THEODORE ROOSEVELT.

By the President: FRANCIS B. LOOMIS, *Acting Secretary of State.*

BY THE PRESIDENT OF THE UNITED STATES OF AMERICA.

A PROCLAMATION.

Whereas, it is provided by section 13 of the Act of Congress of March 3, 1891, entitled, "An act to amend title sixty, chapter three, of the Revised Statutes of the United States, relating to copyrights", that said act "shall only apply to a citizen or subject of a foreign state or nation when such foreign state or nation permits to citizens of the United States of America the benefit of copyright on substantially the same basis as its own citizens; or when such foreign state or nation is a party to an international agreement which provides for reciprocity in the granting of copyright, by the terms of which agreement the United States of America may, at its pleasure, become a party to such agreement";

And whereas, it is also provided by said section that "the existence of either of the conditions aforesaid shall be determined by the President of the United States by proclamation made from time to time as the purposes of this act may require";

And whereas, satisfactory official assurances have been given that in Norway the law permits to citizens of the United States the benefit of copyright on substantially the same basis as to the citizens of that country;

Now, therefore, I, THEODORE ROOSEVELT, President of the United States of America, do declare and proclaim that the first of the con-
ᴵᴵᴵᴵᴵᴵᴵᴵ ᴵᴵᴵᴵᴵᴵᴵᴵᴵ ᴵᴵ ᴵᴵᴵᴵᴵᴵᴵ ᴵᴵ ᴵᴵ ᴵᴵᴵ ᴵᴵ ᴵᴵ ᴺᴵᴵᴵᴵᴵ ᴵ, ᴵᴵᴵᴵ, ᴵᴵ ᴵᴵᴵᴵ
fulfilled in respect to the subjects of Norway.

In testimony whereof, I have hereunto set my hand and caused the
      seal of the United States to be affixed.

        DONE at the City of Washington this first day of July, in
[SEAL.] the year of our Lord one thousand nine hundred and five,
      and of the Independence of the United States of America,
      the one hundred and twenty-ninth.

              THEODORE ROOSEVELT.
By the President:
    HERBERT H. D. PEIRCE,
      Acting Secretary of State.

BY THE PRESIDENT OF THE UNITED STATES OF AMERICA.

A PROCLAMATION.

John Hay, Secretary of State of the United States, died on July 1st. His death, a crushing sorrow to his friends, is to the people of this country a national bereavement; and it is in addition a serious loss to all mankind, for to him it was given to stand as a leader in the effort to better world-conditions by striving to advance the cause of international peace and justice. He entered the public service as the trusted and intimate companion of Abraham Lincoln, and for well-nigh forty-five years he served his country with loyal devotion and high ability in many positions of honor and trust; and finally he crowned his life work by serving as Secretary of State with such farsighted reading of the future and such loyalty to lofty ideals as to confer lasting benefits not only upon our own country but upon all the nations of the earth.

As a suitable expression of national mourning, I direct that the Diplomatic representatives of the United States in all foreign countries display the flags over their embassies and legations at half-mast for ten days; that for a like period the flag of the United States be displayed at half-mast at all forts and military posts and at all naval stations and on all vessels of the United States.

I further order that on the day of the funeral the Executive Departments in the city of Washington be closed and that on all public buildings throughout the United States the national flag be displayed at half-mast.

DONE at the City of Washington, this third day of July, [SEAL.] A. D., 1905, and of the Independence of the United States of America the one hundred and twenty-ninth.

THEODORE ROOSEVELT.

By the President:

HERBERT H. D. PEIRCE,
Acting Secretary of State.

BY THE PRESIDENT OF THE UNITED STATES OF AMERICA.

A PROCLAMATION.

Whereas, it was provided by the act of Congress, approved May 27, A. D. 1902 (32 Stat., 263), among other things, that on October 1, 1903, the unallotted lands in the Uintah Indian Reservation, in the State of Utah, "shall be restored to the public domain: *Provided*, That persons entering any of said lands under the homestead laws shall pay therefor at the rate of one dollar and twenty-five cents per acre";

And whereas, the time for the opening of said unallotted lands was extended to October 1, 1904, by the act of Congress, approved March 3, 1903 (32 Stat., 998), and was extended to March 10, 1905, by the act of Congress, approved April 21, 1904 (33 Stat., 207) and was again extended to not later than September 1, 1905, by the act of Congress, approved March 3, 1905 (33 Stat., 1069), which last named act provided, among other things:

"That the said unallotted lands, excepting such tracts as may have been set aside as national forest reserve, and such mineral lands as were disposed of by the Act of Congress of May twenty-seventh, nineteen hundred and two, shall be disposed of under the general provisions of the homestead and townsite laws of the United States, and shall be opened to settlement and entry by proclamation of the President, which proclamation shall prescribe the manner in which these lands may be settled upon, occupied, and entered by persons entitled to make entry thereof; and no person shall be permitted to settle upon, occupy, or enter any of said lands, except as prescribed in said proclamation, until after the expiration of sixty days from the time when the same are thereby opened to settlement and entry: *Provided*, That the rights of honorably discharged Union soldiers and sailors of the late civil and the Spanish war or Philippine insurrection, as defined and described in sections twenty-three hundred and four and twenty-three hundred and five of the Revised Statutes, as amended by the Act of March first, nineteen hundred and one, shall not be abridged."

Now, therefore, I, THEODORE ROOSEVELT, President of the United States of America, by virtue of the power in me vested by said acts of Congress, do hereby declare and make known that all the unallotted lands in said reservation, excepting such as have at that time been reserved for military, forestry, and other purposes, and such mineral lands as may have been disposed of under existing laws, will, on and after the 28th day of August, 1905, in the manner hereinafter prescribed, and not otherwise, be opened to entry, settlement, and disposition under the general provisions of the homestead and townsite laws of the United States; and it is further directed and prescribed that:

Commencing at 9 o'clock a. m., Tuesday, August 1, 1905, and ending at 6 o'clock p. m., Saturday, August 12, 1905, a registration will be had at Vernal, Price, and Provo, State of Utah, and at Grand Junction, State of Colorado, for the purpose of ascertaining what persons desire to enter, settle upon, and acquire title to any of said lands under the homestead law, and of ascertaining their qualifications so to do. To obtain registration each applicant will be required to show himself duly qualified, by written application to be made only on a blank form provided by the Commissioner of the General Land Office, to make homestead entry of these lands under existing laws, and to give the registering officer such appropriate matters of description and identity as will protect the applicant and the Government against any attempted impersonation. Registration can not be effected through the use of the mails or the employment of an agent, excepting that honorably discharged soldiers and sailors entitled to the benefits of section 2304 of the Revised Statutes of the United States, as amended by the act of Congress, approved March 1, 1901 (31 Stat., 847), may present their applications for registration and due proofs of their qualifications through an agent of their own selection, having a duly executed power of attorney on a blank form provided by the Commissioner of the General Land Office, but no person will be permitted to act as agent for more than one such soldier or sailor. No person will be permitted to register more than once or in other than his true name.

Each applicant who shows himself duly qualified will be registered and given a nontransferable certificate to that effect, which will entitle him to go upon and examine the lands to be opened hereunder; but the only purpose for which he can go upon and examine said lands is that of enabling him later on, as herein provided, to understandingly select the lands for which he may make entry. No one will be permitted to make settlement upon any of said lands in advance of the opening herein provided for, and during the first sixty days following said opening no one but registered applicants will be permitted to make homestead settlement upon any of said lands, and then only in pursuance of a homestead entry duly allowed by the local land officers, or of a soldier's declaratory statement duly accepted by such officers.

The order in which, during the first sixty days following the opening, the registered applicants will be permitted to make homestead entry of the lands opened hereunder, will be determined by a drawing for the district publicly held at Provo, Utah, commencing at 9 o'clock a. m., Thursday, August 17, 1905, and continuing for such period as may be necessary to complete the same. The drawing will be had under the supervision and immediate observance of a committee of three persons whose integrity is such as to make their control of the drawing a guaranty of its fairness. The members of this committee will be appointed by the Secretary of the Interior, who will prescribe suitable compensation for their services. Preparatory to this drawing the registration officers will, at the time of registering each applicant who shows himself duly qualified, make out a card, which must be signed by the applicant, and giving such a description of the applicant as will enable the local land officers to thereafter identify him. This card will be subsequently sealed in a separate envelope which will bear no other distinguishing label or mark than such as may be necessary to show that it is to go into the drawing. These envelopes will be carefully preserved and remain sealed until opened in the course of the drawing herein provided. When the registration is completed all of these sealed envelopes will be brought together at the place of drawing and turned over to the committee in charge of the drawing, who, in such manner as in their judgment will be attended with entire fairness and equality of opportunity, shall proceed to draw out and open the separate envelopes and to give to each inclosed card a number in the order in which the envelope containing the same is drawn. The result of the drawing will be certified by the committee to the officers of the district and will determine the order in which the applicants may make homestead entry of said lands and settlement thereon.

Notice of the drawings, stating the name of each applicant and number assigned to him by the drawing, will be posted each day at the place of drawing, and each applicant will be notified of his number and of the day upon which he must make his entry by a postal card mailed to him at the address given by him at the time of registration. The result of each day's drawing will also be given to the press to be published as a matter of news. Applications for homestead entry of said lands during the first sixty days following the opening can be made only by registered applicants and in the order established by the drawing.

Commencing on Monday, August 28, 1905, at 9 o'clock a. m., the applications of those drawing numbers 1 to 50, inclusive, must be presented at the land office in the town of Vernal, Utah, in the land district in which said lands are situated, and will be considered in their numerical order during the first day, and the applications of those drawing numbers 51 to 100, inclusive, must be presented and will be considered in their numerical order during the second day, and so on at that rate until all of said lands subject to entry under the homestead law, and desired thereunder, have been entered. If any applicant fails to appear and present his application for entry when the number assigned to him by the drawing is reached, his right to enter will be passed until after the other applications assigned for that day have been disposed of, when he will be given another opportunity to make entry, failing in which he will be deemed to have abandoned his right to make entry under such drawing.

To obtain the allowance of a homestead entry, each applicant must personally present the certificate of registration theretofore issued to him, together with a regular homestead application and the necessary accompanying proofs, together with the regular land office fees, but an honorably discharged soldier or sailor may file his declaratory statement through his agent, who can represent but one soldier or sailor as in the matter of registration.

Persons who make homestead entry for any of these lands will be required to pay therefor at the rate of one dollar and twenty-five cents per acre when they make final proof, but no payment, other than the usual fees and commissions, will be required at the time the entry is made.

Persons who apply to make entry of these lands prior to October 27, 1905, will not be required to file the usual nonmineral affidavit with their applications to enter, but such affidavit must be filed before final proof is accepted under their entries; but all persons who make entry after that date will be required to file that affidavit with their applications to enter.

The production of the certificate of registration will be dispensed with only upon satisfactory proof of its loss or destruction. If at the time of considering his regular application for entry it appears that an applicant is disqualified from making homestead entry of these lands, his application will be rejected, notwithstanding his prior registration. If any applicant shall register more than once hereunder, or in any other than his true name, or shall transfer his registration certificate, he will thereby lose all the benefits of the registration and drawing herein provided for, and will be precluded from entering or settling upon any of said lands during the first sixty days following said opening.

Any person or persons desiring to found, or to suggest establishing, a townsite upon any of the said lands, at any point, may, at any time before the opening herein provided for, file in the land office a written application to that effect, describing by legal subdivisions the lands intended to be affected, and stating fully and under oath the necessity or propriety of founding or establishing a town at that place. The local officers will forthwith transmit said petition to the Commissioner of the General Land Office with their recommendation in the premises. Such Commissioner, if he believes the public interests will be subserved thereby, will, if the Secretary of the Interior approve thereof, issue an order withdrawing the lands described in such petition, or any portion thereof, from homestead entry and settlement and directing that the same be held for the time being for disposal under ithe townsite laws of the United States in such manner as the Secretary !of the Interior may from time to time direct; and, if at any time after !such withdrawal has been made it is determined that the lands so withdrawn are not needed for townsite purposes they may be released from such withdrawal and then disposed of under the general provisions of the homestead laws in the manner prescribed herein.

All persons are especially admonished that under the said act of Congress approved March 3, 1905, it is provided that no person shall be permitted to settle upon, occupy, or enter any of said lands, except in the manner prescribed in this proclamation, until after the expiration of sixty days from the time when the same are opened to settlement and entry. After the expiration of the said period of sixty days, but not before, as hereinbefore prescribed, any of said lands remaining undisposed of may be settled upon, occupied, and entered under the general provisions of the homestead and townsite laws of the United States in like manner as if the manner of effecting such settlement, occupancy, and entry had not been prescribed herein in obedience to law.

The Secretary of the Interior shall prescribe all needful rules and regulations necessary to carry into full effect the opening herein provided for.

In witness whereof, I have hereunto set my hand and caused the seal of the United States to be affixed.

Done at the City of Washington this 14th day of July, in [SEAL.] the year of our Lord one thousand nine hundred and five, and of the Independence of the United States the one hundred and thirtieth.

THEODORE ROOSEVELT.

By the President:

ALVEY A. ADEE,
Acting Secretary of State.

By the President of the United States.

A PROCLAMATION.

ANNOUNCING DEATH OF EX-PRESIDENT GROVER CLEVELAND.

The White House, *June 24, 1908.*

To the People of the United States:

Grover Cleveland, President of the United States from 1885 to 1889 and again from 1893 to 1897, died at 8:40 o'clock this morning at his home in Princeton, New Jersey. In his death, the Nation has been deprived of one of its greatest citizens. By profession a lawyer, his chief services to his country were rendered during his long, varied and honorable career in public life. As Mayor of his city, as Governor of his State, and twice as President, he showed signal power as an administrator, coupled with entire devotion to the country's good and the courage that quailed before no hostility when once he was convinced where his duty lay. Since his retirement from the Presidency he has continued well and faithfully to serve his countrymen by the simplicity, dignity and uprightness of his private life.

In testimony of the respect in which his memory is held by the government and people of the United States, I do hereby direct that the flags on the White House and the several departmental buildings be displayed at half-staff for a period of thirty days; and that suitable military and naval honors, under the orders of the Secretaries of War and of the Navy, be rendered on the day of the funeral.

Done this twenty-fourth day of June in the year of our Lord one thousand nine hundred and eight and of the Independence of the United States of America the one hundred and thirty-second. **THEODORE ROOSEVELT.**

[SEAL.]

By the President:

Alvey A. Adee, *Acting Secretary of State.*

By the President of the United States of America.

A PROCLAMATION.

RECIPROCITY WITH THE NETHERLANDS.

Whereas, the Government of the Netherlands has entered into a Commercial Agreement with the United States in conformity with the provisions of the third section of the Tariff Act of the United States, approved July 24, 1897, by which Agreement in the judgment of the President reciprocal and equivalent concessions are secured in favor of the products of the United States;

Therefore, be it known that I, Theodore Roosevelt, President of the United States of America, acting under the authority conferred by said Act of Congress, do hereby suspend during the continuance in force of said Agreement the imposition and collection of the duties imposed by the first Section of said Act upon the articles hereinafter specified, being the products of the industry of the Netherlands; and do declare in place thereof the rates of duty provided in the third Section of said Act to be in force and effect from and after the date of this, my Proclamation, as follows:

Brandies, or other spirits manufactured or distilled from grain or other materials, one dollar and seventy-five cents per proof gallon.

In testimony whereof, I have hereunto set my hand and caused the seal of the United States to be affixed.

Done at the city of Washington this twelfth day of August, in the year of our Lord one thousand nine hundred and eight, [SEAL.] and of the Independence of the United States of America the one hundred and thirty-third.

THEODORE ROOSEVELT.

By the President:

ALVEY A. ADEE, *Acting Secretary of State.*

The President of the United States and Her Majesty the Queen of the Netherlands, mutually desiring by means of a Commercial Agreement to facilitate the commercial intercourse between the two countries, have appointed for that purpose their respective plenipotentiaries, namely:

The President of the United States of America, Elihu Root, Secretary of State of the United States; and

Her Majesty the Queen of the Netherlands, Jonkheer R. de Marees van Swinderen, Her Majesty's Envoy Extraordinary and Minister Plenipotentiary to the United States;

Who, having exchanged their respective full powers, which were found to be in good and due form, have agreed upon and concluded the following articles:

ARTICLE I.

It is agreed on the part of the United States, pursuant to and in accordance with the provisions of the third section of the Tariff Act of the United States, approved July 24, 1897, and in consideration of the concessions hereinafter made on the part of the Netherlands in favor of the products of the soil and industry of the United States, that brandies, or other spirits manufactured or distilled from grain or other materials, products of the industry of the Netherlands imported into the United States, shall, from and after the date when this Agreement shall be put in force, be subject to the reduced tariff duty provided by said Section 3, namely, one dollar and seventy-five cents per proof gallon.

ARTICLE II.

Reciprocally and in consideration of the preceding concession, the Royal Government of the Netherlands agrees that, during the continuance in force of this Agreement, the duties imposed upon the following named products of the industry of the United States imported into the Netherlands shall not exceed the tariff rates hereinafter specified, viz.:

Upon mutton, salt pork, and salted bacon, 0.75 florin per 100 kilograms.

Upon mutton, salt pork and salted bacon, when smoked or dried, 1 florin per 100 kilograms.

ARTICLE III.

The Royal Government of the Netherlands further guarantees to continue to admit into the Netherlands during the aforesaid period canned meats manufactured in the United States in packages weighing more than four pounds (English) at the rates of duty hitherto levied, namely: one, six, and eight florins per one hundred kilograms, according to quality and the distinctions made in the Tariff of the Netherlands respecting meats, although entitled under strict application of the law to levy upon such canned meats a duty of twenty-five florins per one hundred kilograms.

ARTICLE IV.

It is mutually agreed by the High Contracting Parties that in the event that the Royal Government of the Netherlands shall, at any time during the continuance in force of this Agreement, withdraw from any product of the soil or industry of the United States imported into the Netherlands the benefit of the lowest tariff rates imposed by the Netherlands upon a like product of any other origin, either Party shall thereupon have the right to terminate this Agreement upon giving to the other three months' prior notice of its intention to do so.

ARTICLE V.

It is further agreed on the part of the United States that the instructions to the Customs Officers set forth in the annexed diplomatic note and made a part of the consideration of this Agreement shall go into effect not later than July 1, 1907.

ARTICLE VI.

This Agreement shall be ratified by the Royal Government of the Netherlands as soon as possible, and upon official notice thereof the President of the United States shall issue his proclamation giving full effect to the provisions of Article I of this Agreement. From and after the date of such proclamation this Agreement shall be in full force and effect, and shall continue in force until one year from the date when either Party shall notify the other of its intention to terminate the same.

Done in duplicate in the English and Dutch languages, at Washington this 16th day of May, one thousand nine hundred and seven.

ELIHU ROOT [SEAL.]

R. DE MAREES VAN SWINDEREN [SEAL.]

DEPARTMENT OF STATE,
Washington, May 16, 1907.

SIR: Referring to the Commercial Agreement signed this day between the Government of the Netherlands and the Government of the United States, I have the honor to inform you that instructions will be issued to the Customs Officers of the United States to the following effect:—

> " Market value as defined by section 19 of the Customs Administrative Act shall be construed to mean the export price whenever goods, wares, and merchandise are sold wholly for export, or sold in the home market only in limited quantities, by reason of which facts there can not be established a market value based upon the sale of such goods, wares, and merchandise in usual wholesale quantities, packed ready for shipment to the United States."

These instructions shall take effect not later than July 1, 1907, and shall remain in force thereafter for the term of the aforesaid Agreement. In pursuance thereof the export price of Maastricht pottery imported into the United States from the Netherlands under the conditions described in your Note of March 23, 1907, shall be accepted by the customs officers of the United States as the true market value of the aforesaid articles of merchandise.

Receive, Mr. Minister, the renewed assurance of my highest consideration.

ELIHU ROOT.

JONKHEER R. DE MAREES VAN SWINDEREN,
Minister of the Netherlands.

BY THE PRESIDENT OF THE UNITED STATES OF AMERICA.

THANKSGIVING PROCLAMATION.

Once again the season is at hand when, according to the ancient custom of our people, it becomes the duty of the President to appoint a day of prayer and of thanksgiving to God.

Year by year this Nation grows in strength and worldly power. During the century and a quarter that has elapsed since our entry into the circle of independent peoples we have grown and prospered in material things to a degree never known before, and not now known in any other country. The thirteen colonies which straggled along the seacoast of the Atlantic and were hemmed-in but a few miles west of tidewater by the Indian haunted wilderness, have been transformed into the mightiest republic which the world has ever seen. Its domains stretch across the continent from one to the other of the two greatest oceans, and it exercises dominion alike in the arctic and tropic realms. The growth in wealth and population has surpassed even the growth in territory. Nowhere else in the world is the average of individual comfort and material well-being as high as in our fortunate land.

For tho vory roaoon that in material well being we have thus abounded, we owe it to the Almighty to show equal progress in moral and spiritual things. With a nation, as with the individuals who make up a nation, material well-being is an indispensable foundation. But the foundation avails nothing by itself. That life is wasted, and worse than wasted, which is spent in piling, heap upon heap, those things which minister merely to the pleasure of the body and to the power that rests only on wealth. Upon material well-being as a foundation must be raised the structure of the lofty life of the spirit, if this Nation is properly to fulfil its great mission and to accomplish all that we so ardently hope and desire. The things of the body are good; the things of the intellect better; the best of all are the things of the soul; for, in the nation as in the individual, in the long run it is character that counts. Let us, therefore, as a people set our faces resolutely against evil, and with broad charity, with kindliness and good-will toward all men, but with unflinching determination to smite down wrong, strive with all the strength that is given us for righteousness in public and in private life.

Now, therefore, I, Theodore Roosevelt, President of the United States, do set apart Thursday, the 26th day of November, next, as a day of general thanksgiving and prayer, and on that day I recommend that the people shall cease from their daily work, and, in their homes or in their churches, meet devoutly to thank the Almighty for the many and great blessings they have received in the past, and to pray that they may be given the strength so to order their lives as to deserve a continuation of these blessings in the future.

In witness whereof, I have hereunto set my hand and caused the seal of the United States to be affixed.

Done at the city of Washington this thirty-first day of October in the year of our Lord one thousand nine hundred and eight, [SEAL.] and of the Independence of the United States the one hundred and thirty-third.

THEODORE ROOSEVELT.

By the President:

ALVEY A. ADEE, *Acting Secretary of State.*

BY THE PRESIDENT OF THE UNITED STATES OF AMERICA.

A PROCLAMATION.

CENTENNIAL ANNIVERSARY OF BIRTH OF ABRAHAM LINCOLN.

Whereas, by Joint Resolution of Congress it is provided " That the twelfth day of February, nineteen hundred and nine, the same being the centennial anniversary of the birth of Abraham Lincoln, be and the same is hereby, made a special legal holiday in the District of Columbia and the Territories of the United States ";

And, whereas, by the said Joint Resolution the President is authorized to issue a proclamation in accordance with the foregoing, setting apart the twelfth day of February, nineteen hundred and nine, as a special legal holiday;

Now, therefore, I, Theodore Roosevelt, President of the United States of America, in virtue of the authority conferred upon me by the said Joint Resolution, do hereby set apart the twelfth day of February, nineteen hundred and nine, as a special legal holiday.

In witness whereof, I have hereunto set my hand and caused the seal of the United States to be affixed.

Done at the city of Washington this eleventh day of February in the year of our Lord one thousand nine hundred and nine, [SEAL.]   and of the Independence of the United States the one hundred and thirty-third.

THEODORE ROOSEVELT.

By the President:

ROBERT BACON, *Secretary of State.*

BY THE PRESIDENT OF THE UNITED STATES OF AMERICA.

A PROCLAMATION.

RECIPROCITY WITH SPAIN.

Whereas, the Government of the United States of America and the Government of Spain have, by an exchange of notes at Washington on February 20, 1909, agreed to supplement the Commercial Agreement which they concluded at San Sebastion on August 1, 1906, to the end that sparkling wines produced in and exported from Spain may be admitted on their importation into the United States at the reduced rates authorized by Section 3 of the United States Tariff Act of July 24, 1897, which action, in the judgment of the President, is compensated by reciprocal and equivalent concessions on the part of Spain in favor of the products of the soil or industry of the United States;

Now, therefore, be it known that I, Theodore Roosevelt, President of the United States of America, acting under the authority conferred by the third section of said Tariff Act, do hereby suspend, during the continuance in force of the said Commercial Agreement of August 1, 1906, the imposition and collection of the duties imposed by the first section of said Act upon the articles hereinafter specified, being the products of the soil or industry of Spain; and do declare in place thereof the following rates of duty provided in the third section of said Act to be in force and effect from and after the date of this, my Proclamation, as follows:

On all sparkling wines, in bottles containing not more than one quart and more than one pint, six dollars per dozen; containing not more than one pint each and more than one-half pint, three dollars per dozen; containing one-half pint each or less, one dollar and fifty cents per dozen; in bottles or other vessels containing more than one quart each, in addition to six dollars per dozen bottles on the quantities in excess of one quart, at the rate of one dollar and ninety cents per gallon.

In testimony whereof, I have hereunto set my hand and caused the seal of the United States to be affixed.

Done at the city of Washington this twentieth day of February, in the year of our Lord one thousand nine hundred and nine,

[SEAL.]   and of the Independence of the United States of America the one hundred and thirty-third.

THEODORE ROOSEVELT.

By the President:

ROBERT BACON, *Secretary of State.*

BY THE PRESIDENT OF THE UNITED STATES OF AMERICA.

SPECIAL SESSION PROCLAMATION.

SPECIAL SESSION OF SENATE TO BE CONVENED MARCH 4, 1909.

Whereas, public interests require that the Senate of the United States be convened at 12 o'clock on the 4th day of March next to receive such communications as may be made by the Executive;

Now, therefore, I, Theodore Roosevelt, President of the United States of America, do hereby proclaim and declare that an extraordinary occasion requires the Senate of the United States to convene at the Capitol, in the city of Washington, on the 4th day of March next, at 12 o'clock noon, of which all persons who shall at that time be entitled to act as members of that body are hereby required to take notice.

Given under my hand and the seal of the United States at Wash-

[SEAL.] ington, the 27th day of February in the year of our Lord 1909, and of the Independence of the United States the one hundred and thirty-third.

THEODORE ROOSEVELT.

By the President:

ROBERT BACON, *Secretary of State.*

BY THE PRESIDENT OF THE UNITED STATES OF AMERICA.

A PROCLAMATION.

Whereas by a Joint Resolution, approved April 22, 1898, entitled "Joint Resolution to prohibit the export of coal or other material used in war from any sea-port of the United States", the President is "authorized, in his discretion, and with such limitations and exceptions as shall deem to him expedient, to prohibit the export of coal or other material used in war from any sea-port of the United States until otherwise ordered by the President or by Congress;"

Now, therefore, I, THEODORE ROOSEVELT, President of the United States of America, for good and sufficient reasons unto me appearing, and by virtue of the authority conferred upon me by the said Joint Resolution, do hereby declare and proclaim that the export of arms, ammunition and munitions of war of every kind, from any port in the United States or in Porto Rico to any port in the Dominican Republic, is prohibited, without limitation or exception, from and after the date of this my proclamation until otherwise ordered by the President or by Congress.

And I do hereby enjoin all good citizens of the United States and of Porto Rico and all persons residing or being within the territory or jurisdiction thereof to be governed accordingly.

In witness whereof, I have hereunto set my hand and caused the seal of the United States to be affixed.

[SEAL.] DONE at the City of Washington this 14th day of October in the year of our Lord one thousand nine hundred and five and of the Independence of the United States of America the one hundred and thirtieth.

THEODORE ROOSEVELT.

By the President:

ELIHU ROOT,
Secretary of State.

By the President of the United States of America.

A PROCLAMATION.

When nearly three centuries ago the first settlers came to the country which has now become this great Republic, they fronted not only hardship and privation, but terrible risk to their lives. In those grim years the custom grew of setting apart one day in each year for a special service of thanksgiving to the Almighty for preserving the people through the changing seasons. The custom has now become national and hallowed by immemorial usage. We live in easier and more plentiful times than our forefathers, the men who with rugged strength faced the rugged days; and yet the dangers to national life are quite as great now as at any previous time in our history. It is eminently fitting that once a year our people should set apart a day for praise and thanksgiving to the Giver of Good, and, at the same time that they express their thankfulness for the abundant mercies received, should manfully acknowledge their shortcomings and pledge themselves solemnly and in good faith to strive to overcome them. During the past year we have been blessed with bountiful crops. Our business prosperity has been great. No other people has ever stood on as high a level of material well-being as ours now stands. We are not threatened by foes from without. The foes from whom we should pray to be delivered are our own passions, appetites, and follies; and against these there is always need that we should war.

Therefore, I now set apart Thursday, the thirtieth day of this November, as a day of thanksgiving for the past and of prayer for the future, and on that day I ask that throughout the land the people gather in their homes and places of worship, and in rendering thanks unto the Most High for the manifold blessings of the past year, consecrate themselves to a life of cleanliness, honor and wisdom, so that this nation may do its allotted work on the earth in a manner worthy of those who founded it and of those who preserved it.

In witness whereof, I have hereunto set my hand and caused the seal of the United States to be affixed.

[SEAL.] Done at the City of Washington this 2nd day of November in the year of our Lord one thousand nine hundred and five and of the Independence of the United States the one hundred and thirtieth.

THEODORE ROOSEVELT.

By the President:

Elihu Root,
Secretary of State.

EXECUTIVE ORDERS

WHITE HOUSE, *August 31, 1905.*

It is ordered that each member of the advisory board of engineers upon plans of the Panama Canal shall be allowed $5,000, payable upon the completion of the report of the board. In addition thereto he shall, when on duty with the board, be allowed $15 per day for personal expenses from the date of leaving his home until his return thereto, including Sundays and Holidays. He shall also be allowed the actual cost of transportation incurred by him in travel on duty in connection with the board to include cost of ticket by railway or steamer, sleeper or parlor car accommodations, baggage transportation, cabs and porterage.

It is further ordered that the allowance of $5,000 to Gen. Davis and Gen. Abbott shall be increased by the amount of their retired pay for the time during which they are employed upon the work of the board, it being my intention that these members of the board shall receive the same compensation for this work as the other members, and this increase being made to provide for the usual reduction of retired officers' pay.   THEODORE ROOSEVELT.

WHITE HOUSE, *October 13, 1905.*

No officer or employee of the government shall, directly or indirectly, instruct or be concerned in any manner in the instruction of any person, or classes of persons, with a view to their special preparation for the examination of the United States Civil Service Commission. The fact that any officer or employee is found so engaged shall be considered sufficient cause for his removal from the service.

THEODORE ROOSEVELT.

WHITE HOUSE, *October 17, 1905.*

When the President or head of an executive department is satisfied that an officer or employee in the classified service is inefficient or incapable, and that the public service will be materially improved by his removal, such removal will be made without hearing, but the cause of removal shall be stated in writing and filed. When misconduct is committed in the view and presence of the President or head of an executive department, removal may be made summarily and without notice.

THEODORE ROOSEVELT.

WHITE HOUSE, *November 17, 1905.*

Civil service rule No. 12 is hereby amended to read as follows, concerning removals:

"1.   In making removals or reductions, and in other punishment, penalties like in character shall be imposed for like offenses.

"2.   No person shall be removed from a competitive position except for such cause as will promote the efficiency of the service.   When the President or head of an executive department is satisfied that an officer or employe in the classified service is inefficient or incapable and that the public service will be materially improved by his removal, such removal may be made without notice to such officer or employe, but the cause of removal shall be stated in writing and filed.   When misconduct is committed in the view and presence of the President or head of an executive department, removal may be made summarily, and no statement of reasons need be filed.

"3.   Where a recommendation for removal or reduction in grade or compensation of an officer or employe is made to the head of an executive department by a bureau chief or other subordinate officer, the said head of the department may, in his discretion, require that the person sought to be removed be furnished with a statement in writing of the reason for such action, and be allowed a reasonable time for personally answering the same.

"4.   The civil service commission shall have no jurisdiction to investigate any removal unless it is alleged that the procedure required by section 2 of rule 12 has not been followed or that the removal was made for political or religious reasons."

THEODORE ROOSEVELT.

WHITE HOUSE, *November 17, 1905.*

When the President or head of an executive department is satisfied that an officer or employe in the classified service is inefficient or incapable, and that the public service will be materially improved by his removal, such removal will be made without hearing; but the cause of removal shall be stated in writing and filed.   When misconduct is committed in the view and presence of the President or head of executive department removal may be made summarily and without notice.

THEODORE ROOSEVELT

WHITE HOUSE, *November 18, 1905.*

Schedule A of the civil service rules is hereby amended by adding to Section II, Treasury Department, a new clause to be numbered 12, to read as follows:

12.   One examiner of tobacco and one examiner of tea in the Customs Service at the Port of Chicago.

THEODORE ROOSEVELT.

ADDRESS

[Luther Place Memorial Church, Washington, D. C., Jan. 29, 1905.]

Dr. Butler: It is a great pleasure to meet with you this morning and say a word of greeting on the occasion of the rededication of this church, coming as it does almost simultaneously with the entry of your pastor into his eightieth year.

From the standpoint from which I am obliged so continually to look at matters, there is a peculiar function to be played by the great Lutheran Church in the United States of America. This is a Church which had its rise to power in, and, until it emigrated to this side of the water, had always had its fullest development in the two great races of Northern and Northern Middle Europe—the German and the Scandinavian. The Lutheran Church came to the territory which is now the United States very shortly after the first permanent settlements were made within our limits; for when the earliest settlers came to dwell around the mouth of the Delaware they brought the Lutheran worship with them, and so with the earliest German settlers who came to Pennsylvania and afterward to New York and the mountainous region in the western part of Virginia and the States south of it. From that day to this the history of the growth in population of this Nation has consisted largely, in some respects mainly, of the arrival of successive waves of newcomers to our shores; and the prime duty of those already in the land is to see that their own progress and development are shared by these newcomers. It is a serious and dangerous thing for any man to tear loose from the soil, from the religion in which he and his forbears have taken root, and to be transplanted into a new land. He should receive all possible aid in the new land; and the aid can be tendered him most effectively by those who can appeal to him on the ground of spiritual kinship. Therefore the Lutheran Church can do most in helping upward and onward so many of the newcomers to our shores; and it seems to me that it should be, I am tempted to say, wellnigh the prime duty of this Church to see that the immigrant, especially the immigrant of Lutheran faith from the Old World, whether he comes from Scandinavia or Germany, or whether he belonged to one of the Lutheran countries of Finland, or Hungary, or Austria, may be not suffered to drift off with no friendly hand extended to him out of all the church communion, away from all the influences that tend toward safeguarding and uplifting him, and that he find ready at hand in this country those eager to bring him into fellowship with the existing bodies. The Lutheran Church in this country is of very great power now numerically, and through the intelligence and thrift of its members, but it will grow steadily to even greater power. It is destined to be one of the two or three greatest and most important national churches in the United States; one of the two or three churches most distinctively American, most distinctively among the forces that are to tell for making this great country even greater in the future. Therefore a peculiar load of responsibility rests upon the members of this Church. It is an important thing for the people of this Nation to remember their rights, but it is an even more important thing for them to remember their duties. In the last analysis the work of statesmen and soldiers, the work of the public men, shall go for nothing if it is not based upon the spirit of Christianity working in the millions of homes throughout this country, so that there may be that social, that spiritual, that moral foundation without which no country can ever rise to permanent greatness. For material well-being, material prosperity, success in arts, in letters, great industrial triumphs, all of them and all of the structures raised thereon will be as evanescent as a dream if they do not rest on "the righteousness that exalteth a nation."

Let me congratulate you and congratulate all of us that we live in a land and at a time when we accept it as natural that there should be an interdenominational service of thanksgiving, such a ceremony as is to take place this afternoon, in which the pastors of other churches join to congratulate themselves and you upon the rebuilding of this church. One of the constant problems of life is to try to cultivate breadth without shallowness, just as we want to try to cultivate depth without narrowness. It seems to me that thanksgiving with the combined earnestness, the liberty, of the great body of the pastors who, for our good fortune, are in the various churches of this country can be accepted as in a peculiar measure typifying the American spirit in religious thought; that for our good fortune those men have been able to combine fervor in doing the Lord's work with charity toward their brethren who do it with certain differences in the non-essentials. The forces of evil are strong and mighty in this century and in this country as they are in other countries, as they have been in all the past centuries; and the people who sincerely wish to do the Lord's work will find ample opportunity for all their labor in fighting the common enemy, and in assuming toward their fellows of a different confession an attitude of generous rivalry in the effort to see how the most good can be done to our people as a whole.

FIFTH ANNUAL MESSAGE.

WHITE HOUSE, Dec. 5, 1905.

To the Senate and House of Representatives:

The people of this country continue to enjoy great prosperity. Undoubtedly there will be ebb and flow in such prosperity, and this ebb and flow will be felt more or less by all members of the community, both by the deserving and the undeserving. Against the wrath of the Lord the wisdom of man cannot avail; in time of flood or drought human ingenuity can but partially repair the disaster. A general failure of crops would hurt all of us. Again, if the folly of man mars the general well-being, then those who are innocent of the folly will have to pay part of the penalty incurred by those who are guilty of the folly. A panic brought on by the speculative folly of part of the business community would hurt the whole business community. But such stoppage of welfare, though it might be severe, would not be lasting. In the long run the one vital factor in the permanent prosperity of the country is the high individual character of the average American worker, the average American citizen, no matter whether his work be mental or manual, whether he be farmer or wage-worker, business man or professional man.

In our industrial and social system the interests of all men are so closely intertwined that in the immense majority of cases a straight-dealing man who by his efficiency, by his ingenuity and industry, benefits himself must also benefit others. Normally the man of great productive capacity who becomes rich by guiding the labor of many other men does so by enabling them to produce more than they could produce without his guidance; and both he and they share in the benefit, which comes also to the public at large. The superficial fact that the sharing may be unequal must never blind us to the underlying fact that there is this sharing, and that the benefit comes in some degree to each man concerned. Normally the wage-worker, the man of small means, and the average consumer, as well as the average producer, are all alike helped by making conditions such that the man of exceptional

6974 Messages and Papers of the Presidents

business ability receives an exceptional reward for his ability. Something can be done by legislation to help the general prosperity; but no such help of a permanently beneficial character can be given to the less able and less fortunate, save as the results of a policy which shall inure to the advantage of all industrious and efficient people who act decently; and this is only another way of saying that any benefit which comes to the less able and less fortunate must of necessity come even more to the more able and more fortunate. If, therefore, the less fortunate man is moved by envy of his more fortunate brother to strike at the conditions under which they have both, though unequally, prospered, the result will assuredly be that while danger may come to the one struck at, it will visit with an even heavier load the one who strikes the blow. Taken as a whole we must all go up or down together.

Yet, while not merely admitting, but insisting upon this, it is also true that where there is no governmental restraint or supervision some of the exceptional men use their energies not in ways that are for the common good, but in ways which tell against this common good. The fortunes amassed through corporate organization are now so large, and vest such power in those that wield them, as to make it a matter of necessity to give to the sovereign—that is, to the Government, which represents the people as a whole—some effective power of supervision over their corporate use. In order to insure a healthy social and industrial life, every big corporation should be held responsible by, and be accountable to, some sovereign strong enough to control its conduct I am in no sense hostile to corporations. This is an age of combination, and any effort to prevent all combination will be not only useless, but in the end vicious, because of the contempt for law which the failure to enforce law inevitably produces. We should, moreover, recognize in cordial and ample fashion the immense good effected by corporate agencies in a country such as ours, and the wealth of intellect, energy, and fidelity devoted to their service, and therefore normally to the service of the public, by their officers and directors. The corporation has come to stay, just as the trade union has come to stay. Each can do and has done great good. Each should be favored so long as it does good. But each should be sharply checked where it acts against law and justice.

So long as the finances of the Nation are kept upon an honest basis no other question of internal economy with which the Congress has the power to deal begins to approach in importance the matter of endeavoring to secure proper industrial conditions under which the individuals —and especially the great corporations—doing an interstate business are to act. The makers of our National Constitution provided especially that the regulation of interstate commerce should come within the sphere of the General Government. The arguments in favor of their taking this stand were even then overwhelming. But they are far stronger today, in view of the enormous development of great business agencies, usually corporate in form. Experience has shown conclusively that it is useless to try to get any adequate regulation and supervision of these great corporations by State action. Such regulation and supervision can only be effectively exercised by a sovereign whose jurisdiction is coextensive with the field of work of the corporations—that is, by the National Government. I believe that this regulation and supervision can be obtained by the enactment of law by the Congress. If this proves impossible, it will certainly be necessary ultimately to confer in fullest form such power upon the National Government by a proper amendment of the Constitution. It would obviously be unwise to endeavor to secure such an amendment until it is certain that the result cannot be obtained under the Constitution as it now is. The laws of the Congress and of the several States hitherto, as passed upon by the courts, have resulted more often in showing that the States have no power in the matter than that the National Government has power; so that there at present exists a very unfortunate condition of things, under which these great corporations doing an interstate business occupy the position of subjects without a sovereign, neither any State Government nor the National Government having effective control over them. Our steady aim should be by legislation, cautiously and carefully undertaken, but resolutely persevered in, to assert the sovereignty of the National Government by affirmative action.

This is only in form an innovation. In substance it is merely a restoration; for from the earliest time such regulation of industrial activities has been recognized in the action of the lawmaking bodies; and all that I propose is to meet the changed conditions in such manner as will prevent the Commonwealth abdicating the power it has always possessed not only in this country, but also in England before and since this country became a separate Nation.

It has been a misfortune that the National laws on this subject have hitherto been of a negative or prohibitive rather than an affirmative kind, and still more that they have in part sought to prohibit what could not be effectively prohibited, and have in part in their prohibitions confounded what should be allowed and what should not be allowed. It is generally useless to try to prohibit all restraint on competition, whether this restraint be reasonable or unreasonable; and where it is not useless it is generally hurtful. Events have shown that it is not possible adequately to secure the enforcement of any law of this kind by incessant appeal to the courts. The Department of Justice has for the last four years devoted more attention to the enforcement of the anti-trust legislation than to anything else. Much has been accomplished, particularly marked has been the moral effect of the prosecutions; but it is increasingly evident that there will be a very insufficient beneficial result in the way of economic change. The successful prosecution of one device to evade the law immediately develops another device to accomplish the same purpose. What is needed is not sweeping prohibition of every arrangement, good or bad, which may tend to restrict competition, but such adequate supervision and regulation as will prevent any restriction of competition from being to the detriment of the public—as well as such supervision and regulation as will prevent other abuses in no way connected with restriction of competition. Of these abuses, perhaps the chief, although by no means the only one, is overcapitalization—generally itself the result of dishonest promotion—because of the myriad evils it brings in its train; for such overcapitalization often means an inflation that invites business panic; it always conceals the true relation of the profit earned to the capital actually invested, and it creates a burden of interest payments which is a fertile cause of improper reduction in or limitation of wages; it damages the small investor, discourages thrift, and encourages gambling and speculation; while perhaps worst of all is the trickiness and dishonesty which it implies—for harm to morals is worse than any possible harm to material interests, and the debauchery of politics and business by great dishonest corporations is far worse than any actual material evil they do the public. Until the National Government obtains, in some manner which the wisdom of the Congress may suggest, proper control over the big corporations engaged in interstate commerce—that is, over the great majority of the big corporations—it will be impossible to deal adequately with these evils.

I am well aware of the difficulties of the legislation that I am suggesting, and of the need of temperate and cautious action in securing it. I should emphatically protest against improperly radical or hasty action. The first thing to do is to deal with the great corporations engaged in the business of interstate transportation. As I said in my message of December 6 last, the immediate and most pressing need, so far as legislation is concerned, is the enactment into law of some scheme to secure to the agents of the Government such supervision and regulation of the rates charged by the railroads of the country engaged in interstate traffic as shall summarily and effectively prevent the imposition of unjust or unreasonable rates. It must include putting a complete stop to rebates in every shape and form. This power to regulate rates, like all similar powers over the business world, should be exercised with moderation, caution, and self-restraint; but it should exist, so that it can be effectively exercised when the need arises.

The first consideration to be kept in mind is that the power should be affirmative and should be given to some administrative body created by the Congress. If given to the present Interstate Commerce Commission, or to a reorganized Interstate Commerce Commission, such commission should be made unequivocally administrative. I do not believe in the Government interfering with private business more than is necessary. I do not believe in the Government undertaking any work which can with propriety be left in private hands. But neither do I believe in the Government flinching from overseeing any work when it becomes evident that abuses are sure to obtain therein unless there is governmental supervision. It is not my province to indicate the exact terms of the law which should be enacted; but I call the attention of the Congress to certain existing conditions with which it is desirable to deal. In my judgment the most important provision which such law should contain is that conferring upon some competent administrative body the power to decide, upon the case being brought before it, whether a given rate prescribed by a railroad is reasonable and just, and if it is found to be unreasonable and unjust, then, after full investigation of the complaint, to prescribe the limit of rate beyond which it shall not be lawful to go—the maximum reasonable rate, as it is commonly called—this decision to go into effect within a reasonable time and to obtain from thence onward, subject to review by the courts. It sometimes happens at present not that a rate is too high but that a favored shipper is given too low a rate. In such case the commission would have the right to fix this already established minimum rate as the maximum; and it would need only one or two such decisions by the commission to cure railroad companies of the practice of giving improper minimum rates. I call your attention to the fact that my proposal is not to give the commission power to initiate or originate rates generally, but to regulate a rate already fixed or originated by the roads, upon complaint and after investigation. A heavy penalty should be exacted from any corporation which fails to respect an order of the commission. I regard this power to establish a maximum rate as being essential to any scheme of real reform in the matter of railway regulation. The first necessity is to secure it; and unless it is granted to the commission there is little use in touching the subject at all.

Illegal transactions often occur under the forms of law. It has often occurred that a shipper has been told by a traffic officer to buy a large quantity of some commodity and then after it has been bought an open reduction is made in the rate to take effect immediately, the arrangement resulting to the profit of one shipper and the one railroad and to the damage of all their competitors; for it must not be forgotten that the big shippers are at least as much to blame as any railroad in the matter of rebates. The law should make it clear so that nobody can fail to understand that any kind of commission paid on freight shipments, whether in this form or in the form of fictitious damages, or of a concession, a free pass, reduced passenger rate, or payment of brokerage, is illegal. It is worth while considering whether it would not be wise to confer on the Government the right of civil action against the beneficiary of a rebate for at least twice the value of the rebate; this would help stop what is really blackmail. Elevator allowances should be stopped, for they have now grown to such an extent that they are demoralizing and are used as rebates.

The best possible regulation of rates would, of course, be that regulation secured by an honest agreement among the railroads themselves to carry out the law. Such a general agreement would, for instance, at once put a stop to the efforts of any one big shipper or big railroad to discriminate against or secure advantages over some rival; and such agreement would make the railroads themselves agents for enforcing the law. The power vested in the Government to put a stop to agreements to the detriment of the public should, in my judgment, be accompanied by power to permit, under specified conditions and careful supervision, agreements clearly in the interest of the public. But, in my judgment, the necessity for giving this further power is by no means as great as the necessity for giving the commission or administrative body the other powers I have enumerated above; and it may well be inadvisable to attempt to vest this particular power in the commission or other administrative body until it already possesses and is exercising what I regard as by far the most important of all the powers I recommend—as indeed the vitally important power—that to fix a given maximum rate, which rate, after the lapse of a reasonable time, goes into full effect, subject to review by the courts.

All private-car lines, industrial roads, refrigerator charges, and the like should be expressly put under the supervision of the Interstate Commerce Commission or some similar body so far as rates, and agreements practically affecting rates, are concerned. The private car owners and the owners of industrial railroads are entitled to a fair and reasonable compensation on their investment, but neither private cars nor industrial railroads nor spur tracks should be utilized as devices for securing preferential rates. A rebate in icing charges, or in mileage, or in a division of the rate for refrigerating charges is just as pernicious as a rebate in any other way. No lower rate should apply on goods imported than actually obtains on domestic goods from the American seaboard to destination except in cases where water competition is the controlling influence. There should be publicity of the accounts of common carriers; no common carrier engaged in interstate business should keep any books or memoranda other than those reported pursuant to law or regulation, and these books or memoranda should be open to the inspection of the Government. Only in this way can violations or evasions of the law be surely detected. A system of examination of railroad accounts should be provided similar to that now conducted into the National banks by the bank examiners; a few first-class railroad accountants, if they had proper direction and proper authority to inspect books and papers, could accomplish much in preventing willful violations of the law. It would not be necessary for them to examine into the accounts of any railroad unless for good reasons they were directed to do so by the Interstate Commerce Commission. It is greatly to be desired that some way might be found by which an agreement as to transportation within a State intended to operate as a fraud upon the Federal interstate commerce laws could be brought under the jurisdiction of the Federal authorities. At present it occurs that large shipments of interstate traffic are controlled by concessions on purely State business, which of course amounts to an evasion of the law. The commission should have power to enforce fair treatment by the great trunk lines of lateral and branch lines.

I urge upon the Congress the need of providing for expeditious action by the Interstate Commerce Commission in all these matters, whether in regulating rates for transportation or for storing or for handling property or commodities in transit. The history of the cases litigated under the present commerce act shows that its efficacy has been to a great degree destroyed by the weapon of delay, almost the most formidable weapon in the hands of those whose purpose it is to violate the law.

Let me most earnestly say that these recommendations are not made in any spirit of hostility to the railroads. On ethical grounds, on grounds of right, such hostility would be intolerable; and on grounds of mere National self-interest we must remember that such hostility would tell against the welfare not merely of some few rich men, but of a multitude of small investors, a multitude of railway employes, wage workers, and most severely against the interest of the public as a whole. I believe that on the whole our railroads have done well and not ill; but the railroad men who wish to do well should not be exposed to competition with those who have no such desire, and the only way to secure this end is to give to some Government tribunal the power to see that justice is done by the unwilling exactly as it is gladly done by the willing. Moreover, if some Government body is given increased power the effect will be to furnish authoritative answer on behalf of the railroad whenever irrational clamor against it is raised, or whenever charges made against it are disproved. I ask this legislation not only in the interest of the public but in the interest of the honest railroad man and the honest shipper alike, for it is they who are chiefly jeoparded by the practices of their dishonest competitors. This legislation should be enacted in a spirit as remote as possible from hysteria and rancor. If we of the American body politic are true to the traditions we have inherited we shall always scorn any effort to make us hate any man because he is rich, just as much as we should scorn any effort to make us look down upon or treat contemptuously any man because he is poor. We judge a man by his conduct—that is, by his character—and not by his wealth or intellect. If he makes his fortune honestly, there is no just cause of quarrel with him. Indeed, we have nothing but the kindliest feelings of admiration for the successful business man who behaves decently, whether he has made his success by building or managing a railroad or by shipping goods over that railroad. The big railroad men and big shippers are simply Americans of the ordinary type who have developed to an extraordinary degree certain great business qualities. They are neither better nor worse than their fellow-citizens of smaller means. They are merely more able in certain lines and therefore exposed to certain peculiarly strong temptations. These temptations have not sprung newly into being; the exceptionally successful among mankind have always been exposed to them; but they have grown amazingly in power as a result of the extraordinary development of industrialism along new lines, and under these new conditions, which the law-makers of old could not foresee and therefore could not provide against, they have become so serious and menacing as to demand entirely new remedies. It is in the interest of the best type of railroad man and the best type of shipper no less than of the public that there should be Governmental supervision and regulation of these great business operations, for the same reason that it is in the interest of the corporation which wishes to treat its employes aright that there should be an effective Employers' Liability act, or an effective system of factory laws to prevent the abuse of women and children. All such legislation frees the corporation that wishes to do well from being driven into doing ill, in order to compete with its rival, which prefers to do ill. We desire to set up a moral standard. There can be no delusion more fatal to the Nation than the delusion that the standard of profits, of business prosperity, is sufficient in judging any business or political question—from rate legislation to municipal government. Business success, whether for the individual or for the Nation, is a good thing only so far as it is accompanied by and develops a high standard of conduct—honor, integrity, civic courage. The kind of business prosperity that blunts the standard of honor, that puts an inordinate value on mere wealth, that makes a man ruthless and conscienceless in trade, and weak and cowardly in citizenship, is not a good thing at all, but a very bad thing for the Nation. This Government stands for manhood first and for business only as an adjunct of manhood.

The question of transportation lies at the root of all industrial success, and the revolution in transportation which has taken place during the last half century has been the most important factor in the growth

RUSSO-JAPANESE PEACE ENVOYS AT PORTSMOUTH, N. H.

THE TREATY OF PORTSMOUTH, N. H.

On June 11, 1905, President Roosevelt sent identical notes to the Russian and Japanese Governments, urging the two Governments to open direct peace negotiations. On August 9th, the envoys assembled at Portsmouth N. H., and on September 5th negotiations were concluded.

The articles, "Russo-Japanese War" and "Portsmouth, Treaty of," in the Encyclopedic Index, give all the facts.

of the new industrial conditions. Most emphatically we do not wish to
see the man of great talents refused the reward for his talents. Still
less do we wish to see him penalized; but we do desire to see the system of railroad transportation so handled that the strong man shall be
given no advantage over the weak man. We wish to insure as fair
treatment for the small town as for the big city; for the small shipper
as for the big shipper. In the old days the highway of commerce,
whether by water or by a road on land, was open to all; it belonged to
the public and the traffic along it was free. At present the railway is
this highway, and we must do our best to see that it is kept open to
all on equal terms. Unlike the old highway it is a very difficult and
complex thing to manage, and it is far better that it should be managed
by private individuals than by the Government. But it can only be so
managed on condition that justice is done the public. It is because, in
my judgment, public ownership of railroads is highly undesirable and
would probably in this country entail far-reaching disaster, but I wish
to see such supervision and regulation of them in the interest of the
public as will make it evident that there is no need for public ownership. The opponents of Government regulation dwell upon the difficulties to be encountered and the intricate and involved nature of the
problem. Their contention is true. It is a complicated and delicate
problem, and all kinds of difficulties are sure to arise in connection with
any plan of solution, while no plan will bring all the benefits hoped for
by its more optimistic adherents. Moreover, under any healthy plan,
the benefits will develop gradually and not rapidly. Finally, we must
clearly understand that the public servants who are to do this peculiarly
responsible and delicate work must themselves be of the highest type
both as regards integrity and efficiency. They must be well paid, for
otherwise able men cannot in the long run be secured; and they must
possess a lofty probity which will revolt as quickly at the thought of
pandering to any gust of popular prejudice against rich men as at the
thought of anything even remotely resembling subserviency to rich
men. But while I fully admit the difficulties in the way, I do not for a
moment admit that these difficulties warrant us in stopping in our
effort to secure a wise and just system. They should have no other
effect than to spur us on to the exercise of the resolution, the even-
handed justice, and the fertility of resource, which we like to think of
as typically American, and which will in the end achieve good results
in this as in other fields of activity. The task is a great one and underlies the task of dealing with the whole industrial problem. But the
fact that it is a great problem does not warrant us in shrinking from
the attempt to solve it. At present we face such utter lack of supervision, such freedom from the restraints of law, that excellent men have
often been literally forced into doing what they deplored because other-

wise they were left at the mercy of unscrupulous competitors. To rail at and assail the men who have done as they best could under such conditions accomplishes little. What we need to do is to develop an orderly system, and such a system can only come through the gradually increased exercise of the right of efficient Government control.

In my annual message to the Fifty-eighth Congress, at its third session, I called attention to the necessity for legislation requiring the use of block signals upon railroads engaged in interstate commerce. The number of serious collisions upon unblocked roads that have occurred within the past year adds force to the recommendation then made. The Congress should provide, by appropriate legislation, for the introduction of block signals upon all railroads engaged in interstate commerce at the earliest practicable date, as a measure of increased safety to the traveling public.

Through decisions of the Supreme Court of the United States and the lower Federal courts in cases brought before them for adjudication the safety appliance law has been materially strengthened, and the Government has been enabled to secure its effective enforcement in almost all cases, with the result that the condition of railroad equipment throughout the country is much improved and railroad employes perform their duties under safer conditions than heretofore. The Government's most effective aid in arriving at this result has been its inspection service, and that these improved conditions are not more general is due to the insufficient number of inspectors employed. The inspection service has fully demonstrated its usefulness, and in appropriating for its maintenance the Congress should make provision for an increase in the number of inspectors.

The excessive hours of labor to which railroad employes in train service are in many cases subjected is also a matter which may well engage the serious attention of the Congress. The strain, both mental and physical, upon those who are engaged in the movement and operation of railroad trains under modern conditions is perhaps greater than that which exists in any other industry, and if there are any reasons for limiting by law the hours of labor in any employment, they certainly apply with peculiar force to the employment of those upon whose vigilance and alertness in the performance of their duties the safety of all who travel by rail depends.

In my annual message to the Fifty-seventh Congress, at its second session, I recommended the passage of an employers' liability law for the District of Columbia and in our navy yards. I renewed that recommendation in my message to the Fifty-eighth Congress, at its second session, and further suggested the appointment of a commission to make a comprehensive study of employers' liability, with a view to the enactment of a wise and Constitutional law covering the subject, applicable to all industries within the scope of the Federal power. I hope that such a law will be prepared and enacted as speedily as possible.

The National Government has, as a rule, but little occasion to deal with the formidable group of problems connected more or less directly with what is known as the labor question, for in the great majority of cases these problems must be dealt with by the State and municipal authorities, and not by the National Government. The National Government has control of the District of Columbia, however, and it should see to it that the City of Washington is made a model city in all respects, with its sanitary parks, public playgrounds, proper regulation of the system of housing, so as to do away with the evils of alley tenements, a proper system of education, a proper system of dealing with truancy and juvenile offenders, a proper handling of the charitable work of the District. Moreover, there should be proper factory laws to prevent all abuses in the employment of women and children in the District. These will be useful chiefly as object lessons, but even this limited amount of usefulness would be of real National value.

There has been demand for depriving courts of the power to issue injunctions in labor disputes. Such special limitation of the equity powers of our courts would be most unwise. It is true that some judges have misused this power; but this does not justify a denial of the power any more than an improper exercise of the power to call a strike by a labor leader would justify the denial of the right to strike. The remedy is to regulate the procedure by requiring the judge to give due notice to the adverse parties before granting the writ, the hearing to be ex parte if the adverse party does not appear at the time and place ordered. What is due notice must depend upon the facts of the case; it should not be used as a pretext to permit violation of law or the jeopardizing of life or property. Of course, this would not authorize the issuing of a restraining order or injunction in any case in which it is not already authorized by existing law.

I renew the recommendation I made in my last annual message for an investigation by the Department of Commerce and Labor of general labor conditions, especial attention to be paid to the conditions of child labor and child-labor legislation in the several States. Such an investigation should take into account the various problems with which the question of child labor is connected. It is true that these problems can be actually met in most cases only by the States themselves, but it would be well for the Nation to endeavor to secure and publish comprehensive information as to the conditions of the labor of children in the different States, so as to spur up those that are behindhand and to secure approximately uniform legislation of a high character among the several States. In such a Republic as ours the one thing that we cannot afford to neglect is the problem of turning out decent citizens. The future of the Nation depends upon the citizenship of the generations to come; the children of today are those who tomorrow will shape the destiny of our land, and we cannot afford to neglect them. The Legislature of Colorado has recommended that the National Government provide some general measure for the protection from abuse of children and dumb animals throughout the United States. I lay the matter before you for what I trust will be your favorable consideration.

The Department of Commerce and Labor should also make a thorough investigation of the conditions of women in industry. Over five million American women are now engaged in gainful occupations; yet there is an almost complete dearth of data upon which to base any trustworthy conclusions as regards a subject as important as it is vast and complicated. There is need of full knowledge on which to base action looking toward State and municipal legislation for the protection of working women. The introduction of women into industry is working change and disturbance in the domestic and social life of the Nation. The decrease in marriage, and especially in the birth rate, has been coincident with it. We must face accomplished facts, and the adjustment of factory conditions must be made, but surely it can be made with less friction and less harmful effects on family life than is now the case. This whole matter in reality forms one of the greatest sociological phenomena of our time; it is a social question of the first importance, of far greater importance than any merely political or economic question can be, and to solve it we need ample data, gathered in a sane and scientific spirit in the course of an exhaustive investigation.

In any great labor disturbance not only are employer and employe interested, but a third party—the general public. Every considerable labor difficulty in which interstate commerce is involved should be investigated by the Government and the facts officially reported to the public.

The question of securing a healthy, self-respecting, and mutually sympathetic attitude as between employer and employe, capitalist and wage-worker, is a difficult one. All phases of the labor problem prove difficult when approached. But the underlying principles, the root principles, in accordance with which the problem must be solved are entirely simple. We can get justice and right dealing only if we put as of paramount importance the principle of treating a man on his worth as a man rather than with reference to his social position, his occupation or the class to which he belongs. There are selfish and brutal men in all ranks of life. If they are capitalists their selfishness and brutality may take the form of hard indifference to suffering, greedy disregard of every moral restraint which interferes with the accumulation of wealth, and cold-blooded exploitation of the weak; or, if they are laborers, the form of laziness, of sullen envy of the more fortunate, and of willingness to perform deeds of murderous violence. Such conduct is just as reprehensible in one case as in the other, and all honest and farseeing men should join in warring against it wherever it becomes manifest. Individual capitalist and individual wage-worker, corporation and union, are alike entitled to the protection of the law, and must alike obey the law. Moreover, in addition to mere obedience to the law, each man, if he be really a good citizen, must show broad sympathy for his neighbor and genuine desire to look at any question arising between them from the standpoint of that neighbor no less than from his own, and to this end it is essential that capitalist and wage-worker should consult freely one with the other, should each strive to bring closer the day when both shall realize that they are properly partners and not enemies. To approach the questions which inevitably arise between them solely from the standpoint which treats each side in the mass as the enemy of the other side in the mass is both wicked and foolish. In the past the most direful among the influences which have brought about the downfall of republics has ever been the growth of the class spirit, the growth of the spirit which tends to make a man subordinate the welfare of the public as a whole to the welfare of the particular class to which he belongs, the substitution of loyalty to a class for loyalty to the Nation. This inevitably brings about a tendency to treat each man not on his merits as an individual, but on his position as belonging to a certain class in the community. If such a spirit grows up in this Republic it will ultimately prove fatal to us, as in the past it has proved fatal to every community in which it has become dominant. Unless we continue to keep a quick and lively sense of the great fundamental truth that our concern is with the individual worth of the individual man, this Government cannot permanently hold the place which it has achieved among the nations. The vital lines of cleavage among our people do not correspond, and indeed run at right angles to, the lines of cleavage which divide occupation from occupation, which divide wage-workers from capitalists, farmers from bankers, men of small means from men of large means, men who live in the towns from men who live in the country; for the vital line of cleavage is the line which divides the honest man who tries to do well by his neighbor from the dishonest man who does ill by his neighbor. In other words, the standard we should establish is the standard of conduct, not the standard of occupation, of means, or of social position. It is the man's moral quality, his attitude toward the great questions which concern all humanity, his cleanliness of life, his power to do his duty toward himself and toward others, which really count; and if we substitute for the standard of personal judgment which treats each man according to his merits, another standard in accordance with which all men of one class are favored and all men of another class discriminated against, we shall do irreparable damage to the body politic. I believe that our people are too sane, too self-respecting, too fit for self-government, ever to adopt such an attitude. This Government is not and never shall be government by a plutocracy. This Government is not and never shall be government by a mob. It shall continue to be in the future what it has been in the past, a Government based on the theory that each man, rich or poor, is to be treated simply and solely on his worth as a man, that all his personal and property rights are to be safeguarded, and that he is neither to wrong others nor to suffer wrong from others.

The noblest of all forms of government is self-government; but it is also the most difficult. We who possess this priceless boon, and who desire to hand it on to our children and our children's children, should ever bear in mind the thought so finely expressed by Burke: "Men are qualified for civil liberty in exact proportion to their disposition to put moral chains upon their own appetites; in proportion as they are disposed to listen to the counsels of the wise and good in preference to the flattery of knaves. Society cannot exist unless a controlling power upon will and appetite be placed somewhere, and the less of it there be within the more there must be without. It is ordained in the eternal constitution of things that men of intemperate minds cannot be free. Their passions forge their fetters."

The great insurance companies afford striking examples of corporations whose business has extended so far beyond the jurisdiction of the States which created them as to preclude strict enforcement of supervision and regulation by the parent States. In my last annual message I recommended "that the Congress carefully consider whether the power of the Bureau of Corporations cannot constitutionally be extended to cover interstate transactions in insurance."

Recent events have emphasized the importance of an early and exhaustive consideration of this question, to see whether it is not possible to furnish better safeguards than the several States have been able to furnish against corruption of the flagrant kind which has been exposed. It has been only too clearly shown that certain of the men at the head of these large corporations take but small note of the ethical distinction between honesty and dishonesty; they draw the line only this side of what may be called law-honesty, the kind of honesty necessary in order to avoid falling into the clutches of the law. Of course the only complete remedy for this condition must be found in an aroused public conscience, a higher sense of ethical conduct in the community at large, and especially among business men and in the great profession of the law, and in the growth of a spirit which condemns all dishonesty, whether in rich man or in poor man, whether it takes the shape of bribery or of blackmail. But much can be done by legislation which is not only drastic but practical. There is need of a far stricter and more uniform regulation of the vast insurance interests of this country. The United States should in this respect follow the policy of other nations by providing adequate national supervision of commercial interests which are clearly national in character. My predecessors have repeatedly recognized that the foreign business of these companies is an important part of our foreign commercial relations. During the administrations of President Cleveland, Harrison, and McKinley the State Department exercised its influence, through diplomatic channels, to prevent unjust discrimination by foreign countries against American insurance companies. These negotiations illustrated the propriety of the Congress recognizing the National character of insurance, for in the absence of Federal legislation the State Department could only give expression to the wishes of the authorities of the several States, whose policy was ineffective through want of uniformity.

I repeat my previous recommendation that the Congress should also consider whether the Federal Government has any power or owes any duty with respect to domestic transactions in insurance of an interstate character. That State supervision has proved inadequate is generally conceded. The burden upon insurance companies, and therefore their policy holders, of conflicting regulations of many States, is unquestioned, while but little effective check is imposed upon any able and unscrupulous man who desires to exploit the company in his own interest at the expense of the policy holders and of the public. The inability of a State to regulate effectively insurance corporations created under the laws of other States and transacting the larger part of their business elsewhere is also clear. As a remedy for this evil of conflicting, ineffective, and yet burdensome regulations there has been for many years a widespread demand for Federal supervision. The Congress has already recognized that interstate insurance may be a proper subject for Federal legislation, for in creating the Bureau of Corporations it authorized it to publish and supply useful information concerning interstate corporations, "including corporations engaged in insurance." It is obvious that if the compilation of statistics be the limit of the Federal power it is wholly ineffective to regulate this form of commercial intercourse between the States, and as the insurance business has outgrown in magnitude the possibility of adequate State supervision, the Congress should carefully consider whether further legislation can be had. What is said above applies with equal force to fraternal and benevolent organizations which contract for life insurance.

There is more need of stability than of the attempt to attain an ideal perfection in the methods of raising revenue; and the shock and strain to the business world certain to attend any serious change in these methods render such change inadvisable unless for grave reason. It is not possible to lay down any general rule by which to determine the moment when the reasons for will outweigh the reasons against such a change. Much must depend, not merely on the needs, but on the desires, of the people as a whole; for needs and desires are not necessarily identical. Of course, no change can be made on lines beneficial to, or desired by, one section or one State only. There must be something like a general agreement among the citizens of the several States, as represented in the Congress, that the change is needed and desired in the interest of the people, as a whole; and there should then be a sincere, intelligent, and disinterested effort to make it in such shape as will combine, so far as possible, the maximum of good to the people at large with the minimum of necessary disregard for the special interests of localities or classes. But in time of peace the revenue must on the average, taking a series of years together, equal the expenditures or else the revenues must be increased. Last year there was a deficit. Unless our expenditures can be kept within the revenues then our revenue laws must be readjusted. It is as yet too early to attempt to outline what shape such a readjustment should take, for it is as yet too early to say whether there will be need for it. It should be considered whether it is not desirable that the tariff laws should provide for applying as against or in favor of any other nation maximum and minimum tariff rates established by the Congress, so as to secure a certain reciprocity of treatment between other nations and ourselves. Having in view even larger considerations of policy than those of a purely economic nature, it would, in my judgment, be well to endeavor to bring about closer commercial connections with the other peoples of this continent. I am happy to be able to announce to you that Russia now treats us on the most-favored-nation basis.

I earnestly recommend to Congress the need of economy and to this end of a rigid scrutiny of appropriations. As examples merely, I call your attention to one or two specific matters. All unnecessary offices should be abolished. The Commissioner of the General Land Office recommends the abolishment of the office of Receiver of Public Moneys for the United States Land Office. This will effect a saving of about a quarter of a million dollars a year. As the business of the Nation grows, it is inevitable that there should be from time to time a legitimate increase in the number of officials, and this fact renders it all the more important that when offices become unnecessary they should be abolished. In the public printing also a large saving of public money can be made. There is a constantly growing tendency to publish masses of unimportant information. It is probably not unfair to say that many tens of thousands of volumes are published at which no human being ever looks and for which there is no real demand whatever.

Yet, in speaking of economy, I must in no wise be understood as advocating the false economy which is in the end the worst extravagance. To cut down on the navy, for instance, would be a crime against the Nation. To fail to push forward all work on the Panama Canal would be as great a folly.

In my message of December 2, 1902, to the Congress I said:

"Interest rates are a potent factor in business activity, and in order that these rates may be equalized to meet the varying needs of the seasons and of widely separated communities, and to prevent the recurrence of financial stringencies, which injuriously affect legitimate business, it is necessary that there should be an element of elasticity in our monetary system. Banks are the natural servants of commerce, and, upon them should be placed, as far as practicable, the burden of furnishing and maintaining a circulation adequate to supply the needs of our diversified industries and of our domestic and foreign commerce; and the issue of this should be so regulated that a sufficient supply should be always available for the business interests of the country."

Every consideration of prudence demands the addition of the element of elasticity to our currency system. The evil does not consist in an inadequate volume of money, but in the rigidity of this volume, which does not respond as it should to the varying needs of communities and of seasons. Inflation must be avoided; but some provision should be made that will insure a larger volume of money during the Fall and Winter months than in the less active seasons of the year; so that the currency will contract against speculation, and will expand for the needs of legitimate business. At present the Treasury Department is at irregularly recurring intervals obliged, in the interest of the business world—that is, in the interests of the American public—to try to avert financial crises by providing a remedy which should be provided by Congressional action.

At various times I have instituted investigations into the organization and conduct of the business of the executive departments. While none of these inquiries have yet progressed far enough to warrant final conclusions, they have already confirmed and emphasized the general impression that the organization of the departments is often faulty in principle and wasteful in results, while many of their business methods are antiquated and inefficient. There is every reason why our executive governmental machinery should be at least as well planned, economical, and efficient as the best machinery of the great business organizations, which at present is not the case. To make it so is a task of complex detail and essentially executive in its nature; probably no legislative body, no matter how wise and able, could undertake it with reasonable prospect of success. I recommend that the Congress consider this subject with a view to provide by legislation for the transfer, distribution, consolidation, and assignment of duties and executive organizations or parts of organizations, and for the changes in business methods, within or between the several departments, that will best promote the economy, efficiency, and high character of the Government work.

In my last annual message I said:

"The power of the Government to protect the integrity of the elections of its own officials is inherent and has been recognized and affirmed by repeated declarations of the Supreme Court. There is no enemy of free government more dangerous and none so insidious as the corruption of the electorate. No one defends or excuses corruption, and it would seem to follow that none would oppose vigorous measures to eradicate it. I recommend the enactment of a law directed against bribery and corruption in Federal elections. The details of such a law may be safely left to the wise discretion of the Congress, but it should go as far as under the Constitution it is possible to go, and should include severe penalties against him who gives or receives a bribe intended to influence his act or opinion as an elector; and provisions for the publication not only of the expenditures for nominations and elections of all candidates, but also of all contributions received and expenditures made by political committees."

I desire to repeat this recommendation. In political campaigns in a country as large and populous as ours it is inevitable that there should be much expense of an entirely legitimate kind. This, of course, means that many contributions, and some of them of large size, must be made, and, as a matter of fact, in any big political contest such contributions are always made to both sides. It is entirely proper both to give and receive them, unless there is an improper motive connected with either gift or reception. If they are extorted by any kind of pressure or promise, express or implied, direct or indirect, in the way of favor or immunity, then the giving or receiving becomes not only improper but criminal. It will undoubtedly be difficult, as a matter of practical detail, to shape an act which shall guard with reasonable certainty against such misconduct; but if it is possible to secure by law the full and verified publication in detail of all the sums contributed to and expended by the candidates or committees of any political parties, the result cannot but be wholesome. All contributions by corporations to any political committee or for any political purpose should be forbidden by law; directors should not be permitted to use stockholders' money for such purposes; and, moreover, a prohibition of this kind would be, as far as it went, an effective method of stopping the evils aimed at in corrupt practices acts. Not only should both the National and the several State Legislatures forbid any officer of a corporation from using the money of the corporation in or about any election, but they should also forbid such use of money in connection with any legislation save by the employment of counsel in public manner for distinctly legal services.

The first conference of nations held at The Hague in 1899, being unable to dispose of all the business before it, recommended the consideration and settlement of a number of important questions by another conference to be called subsequently and at an early date. These questions were the following: (1) The rights and duties of neutrals; (2) the limitation of the armed forces on land and sea, and of military budgets; (3) the use of new types and calibres of military and naval guns; (4) the inviolability of private property at sea in times of war; (5) the bombardment of ports, cities, and villages by naval forces. In October, 1904, at the instance of the Interparliamentary Union, which, at a conference held in the United States, and attended by the lawmakers of fifteen different nations, had reiterated the demand for a second conference of nations, I issued invitations to all the powers signatory to The Hague Convention to send delegates to such a conference, and suggested that it be again held at The Hague. In its note of December 16, 1904, the United States Government communicated to the representatives of foreign governments its belief that the conference could be best arranged under the provisions of the present Hague treaty.

From all the powers acceptance was received, coupled in some cases with the condition that we should wait until the end of the war then waging between Russia and Japan. The Emperor of Russia, immediately after the treaty of peace which so happily terminated this war, in a note presented to the President on September 13, through Ambassador Rosen, took the initiative in recommending that the conference be now called. The United States Government in response expressed its cordial acquiescence, and stated that it would, as a matter of course, take part in the new conference and endeavor to further its aims. We assume that all civilized governments will support the movement, and that the conference is now an assured fact. This Government will do everything in its power to secure the success of the conference, to the end that substantial progress may be made in the cause of international peace, justice, and good will.

This renders it proper at this time to say something as to the general attitude of this Government toward peace. More and more war is coming to be looked upon as in itself a lamentable and evil thing. A wanton or useless war, or a war of mere aggression—in short, any war begun or carried on in a conscienceless spirit, is to be condemned as a peculiarly atrocious crime against all humanity. We can, however, do nothing of permanent value for peace unless we keep ever clearly in mind the ethical element which lies at the root of the problem. Our aim is righteousness. Peace is normally the hand-maiden of righteousness; but when peace and righteousness conflict then a great and upright people can never for a moment hesitate to follow the path which leads toward righteousness, even though that path also leads to war. There are persons who advocate peace at any price; there are others who, following a false analogy, think that because it is no longer necessary in civilized countries for individuals to protect their rights with a strong hand, it is therefore unnecessary for nations to be ready to defend their rights. These persons would do irreparable harm to any nation that adopted their principles, and even as it is they seriously hamper the cause which they advocate by tending to render it absurd in the eyes of sensible and patriotic men. There can be no worse foe of mankind in general, and of his own country in particular, than the demagogue of war, the man who in mere folly or to serve his own selfish ends continually rails at and abuses other nations, who seeks to excite his countrymen against foreigners on insufficient pretexts, who excites and inflames a perverse and aggressive national vanity, and who may on occasions wantonly bring on conflict between his nation and some other nation. But there are demagogues of peace just as there are demagogues of war, and in any such movement as this for The Hague conference it is essential not to be misled by one set of extremists any more than by the other. Whenever it is possible for a nation or an individual to work for real peace, assuredly it is failure of duty not so to strive, but if war is necessary and righteous then either the man or the nation shrinking from it forfeits all title to self-respect. We have scant sympathy with the sentimentalist who dreads oppression less than physical suffering, who would prefer a shameful peace to the pain and toil sometimes lamentably necessary in order to secure a righteous peace. As yet there is only a partial and imperfect analogy between international law and internal or municipal law, because there is no sanction of force for executing the former while there is in the case of the latter. The private citizen is protected in his rights by the law, because the law rests in the last resort upon force exercised through the forms of law. A man does not have to defend his rights with his own hand, because he can call upon the police, upon the sheriff's posse, upon the militia, or in certain extreme cases upon the army, to defend him. But there is no such sanction of force for international law. At present there could be no greater calamity than for the free peoples, the enlightened, independent, and peace-loving peoples, to disarm while yet leaving it open to any barbarism or despotism to remain armed. So long as the world is as un-organized as now the armies and navies of those peoples who on the whole stand for justice, offer not only the best, but the only possible, security for a just peace. For instance, if the United States alone, or in company only with the other nations that on the whole tend to act justly, disarmed, we might sometimes avoid bloodshed, but we would cease to be of weight in securing the peace of justice—the real peace for which the most law-abiding and high-minded men must at times be willing to fight. As the world is now, only that nation is equipped for peace that knows how to fight, and that will not shrink from fighting if ever the conditions become such that war is demanded in the name of the highest morality.

So much it is emphatically necessary to say in order both that the position of the United States may not be misunderstood, and that a genuine effort to bring nearer the day of the peace of justice among the nations may not be hampered by a folly which, in striving to achieve the impossible, would render it hopeless to attempt the achievement of the practical. But, while recognizing most clearly all above set forth, it remains our clear duty to strive in every practicable way to bring nearer the time when the sword shall not be the arbiter among nations. At present the practical thing to do is to try to minimize the number of cases in which it must be the arbiter, and to offer, at least to all civilized powers, some substitute for war which will be available in at least a considerable number of instances. Very much can be done through another Hague conference in this direction, and I most earnestly urge that this Nation do all in its power to try to further the movement and to make the result of the decisions of The Hague conference effective. I earnestly hope that the conference may be able to devise some way to make arbitration between nations the customary way of settling international disputes in all save a few classes of cases, which should themselves be as sharply defined and rigidly limited as the present governmental and social development of the world will permit. If possible, there should be a general arbitration treaty negotiated among all the nations represented at the conference. Neutral rights and property should be protected at sea as they are protected on land. There should be an international agreement to this purpose and a similar agreement defining contraband of war.

During the last century there has been a distinct diminution in the number of wars between the most civilized nations. International relations have become closer and the development of The Hague tribunal is not only a symptom of this growing closeness of relationship, but is a means by which the growth can be furthered. Our aim should be from time to time to take such steps as may be possible toward creating something like an organization of the civilized nations, because as the world becomes more highly organized the need for navies and armies will diminish. It is not possible to secure anything like an immediate disarmament, because it would first be necessary to settle what peoples are on the whole a menace to the rest of mankind, and to provide against the disarmament of the rest being turned into a movement which would really chiefly benefit these obnoxious peoples; but it may be possible to exercise some check upon the tendency to swell indefinitely the budgets for military expenditure. Of course such an effort could succeed only if it did not attempt to do too much; and if it were undertaken in a spirit of sanity as far removed as possible from a merely hysterical pseudo-philanthropy. It is worth while pointing out that since the end of the insurrection in the Philippines this Nation has shown its practical faith in the policy of disarmament by reducing its little army one-third. But disarmament can never be of prime importance; there is more need to get rid of the causes of war than of the implements of war.

I have dwelt much on the dangers to be avoided by steering clear of any mere foolish sentimentality because my wish for peace is so genuine and earnest; because I have a real and great desire that this second Hague conference may mark a long stride forward in the direction of securing the peace of justice throughout the world. No object is better worthy the attention of enlightened statesmanship than the establishment of a surer method than now exists of securing justice as between nations, both for the protection of the little nations and for the prevention of war between the big nations. To this aim we should endeavor not only to avert bloodshed, but, above all, effectively to strengthen the forces of right. The Golden Rule should be, and as the world grows in morality it will be, the guiding rule of conduct among nations as among individuals; though the Golden Rule must not be construed, in fantastic manner, as forbidding the exercise of the police power. This mighty and free Republic should ever deal with all other States, great or small, on a basis of high honor, respecting their rights as jealously as it safeguards its own.

One of the most effective instruments for peace is the Monroe Doctrine as it has been and is being gradually developed by this Nation and accepted by other nations. No other policy could have been as efficient in promoting peace in the Western Hemisphere and in giving to each nation thereon the chance to develop along its own lines. If we had refused to apply the doctrine to changing conditions it would now be completely outworn, would not meet any of the needs of the present day, and, indeed, would probably by this time have sunk into complete oblivion. It is useful at home, and is meeting with recognition abroad because we have adapted our application of it to meet the growing and changing needs of the hemisphere. When we announce a policy such as the Monroe Doctrine we thereby commit ourselves to the consequences of the policy, and those consequences from time to time alter. It is out of the question to claim a right and yet shirk the responsibility for its exercise. Not only we, but all American republics who are benefited by the existence of the doctrine, must recognize the obligations each nation is under as regards foreign peoples no less than its duty to insist upon its own rights.

That our rights and interests are deeply concerned in the maintenance of the doctrine is so clear as hardly to need argument. This is especially true in view of the construction of the Panama Canal. As a mere matter of self defense we must exercise a close watch over the approaches to this canal; and this means that we must be thoroughly alive to our interests in the Caribbean Sea.

There are certain essential points which must never be forgotten as regards the Monroe Doctrine. In the first place we must as a Nation make it evident that we do not intend to treat it in any shape or way as an excuse for aggrandizement on our part at the expense of the republics to the south. We must recognize the fact that in some South American countries there has been much suspicion lest we should interpret the Monroe Doctrine as in some way inimical to their interests, and we must try to convince all the other nations of this continent once and for all that no just and orderly Government has anything to fear from us. There are certain republics to the south of us which have already reached such a point of stability, order, and prosperity that they themselves, though as yet hardly consciously, are among the guarantors of this doctrine. These republics we now meet not only on a basis of entire equality, but in a spirit of frank and respectful friendship, which we hope is mutual. If all of the republics to the south of us will only grow as those to which I allude have already grown, all need for us to be the especial champions of the doctrine will disappear, for no stable and growing American Republic wishes to see some great non-American military power acquire territory in its neighborhood. All that this country desires is that the other republics on this continent shall be happy and prosperous; and they cannot be happy and prosperous unless they maintain order within their boundaries and behave with a just regard for their obligations toward outsiders. It must be understood that under no circumstances will the United States use the Monroe Doctrine as a cloak for territorial aggression. We desire peace with all the world, but perhaps most of all with the other peoples of the American Continent. There are, of course, limits to the wrongs which any self-respecting nation can endure. It is always possible that wrong actions toward this Nation, or toward citizens of this Nation, in some State unable to keep order among its own people, unable to secure justice from outsiders, and unwilling to do justice to those outsiders who treat it well, may result in our having to take action to protect our rights; but such action will not be taken with a view to territorial aggression, and it will be taken at all only with extreme reluctance and when it has become evident that every other resource has been exhausted.

Moreover, we must make it evident that we do not intend to permit the Monroe Doctrine to be used by any nation on this Continent as a shield to protect it from the consequences of its own misdeeds against foreign nations. If a republic to the south of us commits a tort against a foreign nation, such as an outrage against a citizen of that nation, then the Monroe Doctrine does not force us to interfere to prevent punishment of the tort, save to see that the punishment does not assume the form of territorial occupation in any shape. The case is more difficult when it refers to a contractual obligation. Our own Government has always refused to enforce such contractual obligations on behalf of its citizens by an appeal to arms. It is much to be wished that all foreign governments would take the same view. But they do not; and in consequence we are liable at any time to be brought face to face with disagreeable alternatives. On the one hand, this country would certainly decline to go to war to prevent a foreign government from collecting a just debt; on the other hand, it is very inadvisable to permit any foreign power to take possession, even temporarily, of the custom houses of an American Republic in order to enforce the payment of its obligations; for such temporary occupation might turn into a permanent occupation. The only escape from these alternatives may at any time be that we must ourselves undertake to bring about some arrangement by which so much as possible of a just obligation shall be paid. It is far better that this country should put through such an arrangement, rather than allow any foreign country to undertake it. To do so insures the defaulting republic from having to pay debt of an improper character under duress, while it also insures honest creditors of the republic from being passed by in the interest of dishonest or grasping creditors. Moreover, for the United States to take such a position offers the only possible way of insuring us against a clash with some foreign power. The position is, therefore, in the interest of peace as well as in the interest of justice. It is of benefit to our people; it is of benefit to foreign peoples; and most of all it is really of benefit to the people of the country concerned.

This brings me to what should be one of the fundamental objects of the Monroe Doctrine. We must ourselves in good faith try to help upward toward peace and order those of our sister republics which need such help. Just as there has been a gradual growth of the ethical element in the relations of one individual to another, so we are, even though slowly, more and more coming to recognize the duty of bear-

STREET AND HARBOR SCENES IN SAN DOMINGO

SAN DOMINGO

" San Domingo is a Republic occupying the eastern portion of the Island of Haiti. The inhabitants are of mixed Spanish, Indian, and negro blood, with some pure Africans. The language is principally Spanish, though French and English are spoken. It claims an area of 18,045 square miles, and the population is estimated at 610,000.

In 1904, in consequence of intimations from Germany and Great Britain that they would be compelled to take action unless the just claims of their subjects received some recognition, the United States was compelled to interfere and it was arranged that the customs should be collected by the United States, one-third of the receipts being returned to carry on the Dominican Government and the other two-thirds being devoted to paying off the various creditors of Santo Domingo. This arrangement has worked very satisfactorily, the share received by the Dominican Government amounting to more than was received when the entire customs were collected by native officials."

Quoted from the article entitled " Santo Domingo " in the Encyclopedic Index, which carries the narrative down to date.

ing one another's burdens, not only as among individuals, but also as among nations.

Santo Domingo, in her turn, has now made an appeal to us to help her, and not only every principle of wisdom but every generous instinct within us bids us respond to the appeal. It is not of the slightest consequence whether we grant the aid needed by Santo Domingo as an incident to the wise development of the Monroe Doctrine or because we regard the case of Santo Domingo as standing wholly by itself, and to be treated as such, and not on general principles or with any reference to the Monroe Doctrine. The important point is to give the incident aid, and the case is certainly wholly peculiar in deserving to be judged purely on its own merits. The conditions in Santo Domingo have for a number of years grown from bad to worse until a year ago all society was on the verge of dissolution. Fortunately, just at this time a ruler sprang up in Santo Domingo, who, with his colleagues, saw the dangers threatening their country and appealed to the friendship of the only great and powerful neighbor who possessed the power, and as they hoped also the will to help them. There was imminent danger of foreign intervention. The previous rulers of Santo Domingo had recklessly incurred debts, and owing to her internal disorders she had ceased to be able to provide means of paying the debts. The patience of her foreign creditors had become exhausted, and at least two foreign nations were on the point of intervention, and were only prevented from intervening by the unofficial assurance of this Government that it would itself strive to help Santo Domingo in her hour of need. In the case of one of these nations, only the actual opening of negotiations to this end by our Government prevented the seizure of territory in Santo Domingo by a European power. Of the debts incurred some were just, while some were not of a character which really renders it obligatory on or proper for Santo Domingo to pay them in full. But she could not pay any of them unless some stability was assured her Government and people.

Accordingly, the Executive Department of our Government negotiated a treaty under which we are to try to help the Dominican people to straighten out their finances. This treaty is pending before the Senate. In the meantime a temporary arrangement has been made which will last until the Senate has had time to take action upon the treaty. Under this arrangement the Dominican Government has appointed Americans to all the important positions in the customs service, and they are seeing to the honest collection of the revenues, turning over 45 per cent. to the Government for running expenses and putting the other 55 per cent. into a safe depository for equitable division in case the treaty shall be ratified, among the various creditors, whether European or American.

The Custom Houses offer well-nigh the only sources of revenue in Santo Domingo, and the different revolutions usually have as their real aim the obtaining of these Custom Houses. The mere fact that the Collectors of Customs are Americans, that they are performing their duties with efficiency and honesty, and that the treaty is pending in the Senate gives a certain moral power to the Government of Santo Domingo which it has not had before. This has completely discouraged all revolutionary movement, while it has already produced such an increase in the revenues that the Government is actually getting more from the 45 per cent. that the American Collectors turn over to it than it got formerly when it took the entire revenue. It is enabling the poor, harassed people of Santo Domingo once more to turn their attention to industry and to be free from the cure of interminable revolutionary disturbance. It offers to all bona-fide creditors, American and European, the only really good chance to obtain that to which they are justly entitled, while it in return gives to Santo Domingo the only opportunity of defense against claims which it ought not to pay, for now if it meets the views of the Senate we shall ourselves thoroughly examine all these claims, whether American or foreign, and see that none that are improper are paid. There is, of course, opposition to the treaty from dishonest creditors, foreign and American, and from the professional revolutionists of the island itself. We have already reason to believe that some of the creditors who do not dare expose their claims to honest scrutiny are endeavoring to stir up sedition in the island and opposition to the treaty. In the meantime, I have exercised the authority vested in me by the joint resolution of the Congress to prevent the introduction of arms into the island for revolutionary purposes.

Under the course taken, stability and order and all the benefits of peace are at last coming to Santo Domingo, danger of foreign intervention has been suspended, and there is at last a prospect that all creditors will get justice, no more and no less. If the arrangement is terminated by the failure of the treaty chaos will follow; and if chaos follows, sooner or later this Government may be involved in serious difficulties with foreign Governments over the island, or else may be forced itself to intervene in the island in some unpleasant fashion. Under the proposed treaty the independence of the island is scrupulously respected, the danger of violation of the Monroe Doctrine by the intervention of foreign powers vanishes, and the interference of our Government is minimized, so that we shall only act in conjunction with the Santo Domingo authorities to secure the proper administration of the customs, and therefore to secure the payment of just debts and to secure the Dominican Government against demands for unjust debts. The proposed method will give the people of Santo Domingo the same chance to move onward and upward which we have already given to the people of Cuba. It will be doubly to our discredit as a Nation if we fail to take advantage of this chance; for it will be of damage to ourselves, and it will be of incalculable damage to Santo Domingo. Every consideration of wise policy, and, above all, every consideration of large generosity, bids us meet the request of Santo Domingo as we are now trying to meet it.

We cannot consider the question of our foreign policy without at the same time treating of the Army and the Navy. We now have a very small army indeed, one well-nigh infinitesimal when compared with the army of any other large nation. Of course the army we do have should be as nearly perfect of its kind and for its size as is possible. I do not believe that any army in the world has a better average of enlisted men or a better type of junior officer; but the army should be trained to act effectively in a mass. Provision should be made by sufficient appropriations for manœuvers of a practical kind, so that the troops may learn how to take care of themselves under actual service conditions; every march, for instance, being made with the soldier loaded exactly as he would be in active campaign. The Generals and Colonels would thereby have opportunity of handling regiments, brigades, and divisions, and the commissary and medical departments would be tested in the field. Provision should be made for the exercise at least of a brigade and by preference of a division in marching and embarking at some point on our coast and disembarking at some other point and continuing its march. The number of posts in which the army is kept in time of peace should be materially diminished and the posts that are left made correspondingly larger. No local interests should be allowed to stand in the way of assembling the greater part of the troops which would at need form our field armies in stations of such size as will permit the best training to be given to the personnel of all grades, including the high officers and staff officers. To accomplish this end we must have not company or regimental garrisons, but brigade and division garrisons. Promotion by mere seniority can never result in a thoroughly efficient corps of officers in the higher ranks unless there accompanies it a vigorous weeding-out process. Such a weeding-out process—that is, such a process of selection—is a chief feature of the four years' course of the young officer at West Point. There is no good reason why it should stop immediately upon his graduation. While at West Point he is dropped unless he comes up to a certain standard of excellence, and when he graduates he takes rank in the army according to his rank of graduation. The results are good at West Point; and there should be in the army itself something that will achieve the same end. After a certain age has been reached the average officer is unfit to do good work below a certain grade. Provision should be made for the promotion of exceptionally meritorious men over the heads of their comrades and for the retirement of all men who have reached a given age without getting beyond a given rank; this age of retirement of course changing from rank to rank. In both the army and the navy there should be some principle of selection, that is, of promotion for merit, and there should be a resolute effort to eliminate the aged officers of reputable character who possess no special efficiency.

There should be an increase in the coast artillery force, so that our coast fortifications can be in some degree adequately manned. There is special need for an increase and reorganization of the Medical Department of the army. In both the army and navy there must be the same thorough training for duty in the staff corps as in the fighting line. Only by such training in advance can we be sure that in actual war field operations and those at sea will be carried on successfully. The importance of this was shown conclusively in the Spanish-American and the Russo-Japanese wars. The work of the medical departments in the Japanese army and navy is especially worthy of study. I renew my recommendation of January 9, 1905, as to the Medical Department of the army and call attention to the equal importance of the needs of the staff corps of the navy. In the Medical Department of the navy the first in importance is the reorganization of the Hospital Corps, on the lines of the Gallinger bill, (S. 3,984, February 1, 1904), and the reapportionment of the different grades of the medical officers to meet service requirements. It seems advisable also that medical officers of the army and navy should have similar rank and pay in their respective grades, so that their duties can be carried on without friction when they are brought together. The base hospitals of the navy should be put in condition to meet modern requirements and hospital ships be provided. Unless we now provide with ample forethought for the medical needs of the army and navy appalling suffering of a preventable kind is sure to occur if ever the country goes to war. It is not reasonable to expect successful administration in time of war of a department which lacks a third of the number of officers necessary to perform the medical service in time of peace. We need men who are not merely doctors; they must be trained in the administration of military medical service.

Our navy must, relatively to the navies of other nations, always be of greater size than our army. We have most wisely continued for a number of years to build up our navy, and it has now reached a fairly high standard of efficiency. This standard of efficiency must not only be maintained, but increased. It does not seem to be necessary, however, that the navy should—at least in the immediate future—be increased beyond the present number of units. What is now clearly necessary is to substitute efficient for inefficient units as the latter become worn out or as it becomes apparent that they are useless. Probably the result would be attained by adding a single battleship to our navy each year, the superseded or outworn vessels being laid up or broken up as they are thus replaced. The four single-turret monitors built immediately after the close of the Spanish war, for instance, are vessels which would be of but little use in the event of war. The money spent upon them could have been more usefully spent in other ways. Thus it would have been far better never to have built a single one of these monitors and to have put the money into an ample supply of reserve guns. Most of the smaller cruisers and gunboats, though they serve a useful purpose so far as they are needed for international police work, would not add to the strength of our navy in a conflict with a serious foe. There is urgent need of providing a large increase in the number of officers, and especially in the number of enlisted men.

Recent naval history has emphasized certain lessons which ought not to, but which do, need emphasis. Seagoing torpedo boats or destroyers are indispensable, not only for making night attacks by surprise upon an enemy, but even in battle for finishing already crippled ships. Under exceptional circumstances submarine boats would doubtless be of use. Fast scouts are needed. The main strength of the navy, however, lies, and can only lie, in the great battleships, the heavily armored, heavily gunned vessels which decide the mastery of the seas. Heavy-armed cruisers also play a most useful part, and unarmed cruisers, if swift enough, are very useful as scouts. Between antagonists of approximately equal prowess the comparative perfection of the instruments of war will ordinarily determine the fight. But it is, of course, true that the man behind the gun, the man in the engine room, and the man in the conning tower, considered not only individually, but especially with regard to the way in which they work together, are even more important than the weapons with which they work. The most formidable battleship is, of course, helpless against even a light cruiser if the men aboard it are unable to hit anything with their guns, and thoroughly well-handled cruisers may count seriously in an engagement with much superior vessels, if the men aboard the latter are ineffective, whether from lack of training or from any other cause. Modern warships are most formidable mechanisms when well handled, but they are utterly useless when not well handled, and they cannot be handled at all without long and careful training. This training can under no circumstance be given when once war has broken out. No fighting ship of the first class should ever be laid up save for necessary repairs, and her crew should be kept constantly exercised on the high seas, so that she may stand at the highest point of perfection. To put a new and untrained crew upon the most powerful battleship and send it out to meet a formidable enemy is not only to invite, but to insure, disaster and disgrace. To improvise crews at the outbreak of a war, so far as the serious fighting craft are concerned, is absolutely hopeless. If the officers and men are not thoroughly skilled in, and have not been thoroughly trained to, their duties, it would be far better to keep the ships in port during hostilities than to send them against a formidable opponent, for the result could only be that they would be either sunk or captured. The marksmanship of our navy is now on the whole in a gratifying condition, and there has been a great improvement in fleet practice. We need additional seamen; we need a large store of reserve guns; we need sufficient money for ample target practice, ample practice of every kind at sea. We should substitute for comparatively inefficient types—the old third-class battleship Texas, the single-turreted monitors above mentioned, and, indeed, all the monitors and some of the old cruisers—efficient, modern seagoing vessels. Seagoing torpedo-boat destroyers should be substituted for some of the smaller torpedo boats. During the present Congress there need be no additions to the aggregate number of units of the navy. Our navy, though very small relatively to the navies of other nations, is for the present sufficient in point of numbers for our needs, and while we must constantly strive to make its efficiency higher, there need be no additions to the total of ships now built and building, save in the way of substitution as above outlined. I recommend the report of the Secretary of the Navy to the careful consideration of the Congress, especially with a view to the legislation therein advocated.

During the past year evidence has accumulated to confirm the expressions contained in my last two annual messages as to the importance of revising by appropriate legislation our system of naturalizing aliens. I appointed last March a commission to make a careful examination of our naturalization laws, and to suggest appropriate measures to avoid the notorious abuses resulting from the improvident or unlawful granting of citizenship. This commission, composed of an officer of the Department of State, of the Department of Justice, and of the Department of Commerce and Labor, has discharged the duty imposed upon it, and has submitted a report, which will be transmitted to the Congress for its consideration, and, I hope, for its favorable action.

The distinguishing recommendations of the commission are:

First—A Federal Bureau of Naturalization, to be established in the Department of Commerce and Labor, to supervise the administration of the naturalization laws and to receive returns of naturalizations pending and accomplished.

Second—Uniformity of naturalization certificates, fees to be charged, and procedure.

Third—More exacting qualifications for citizenship.

Fourth—The preliminary declaration of intention to be abolished and no alien to be naturalized until at least ninety days after the filing of his petition.

Fifth—Jurisdiction to naturalize aliens to be confined to United States district courts and to such State courts as have jurisdiction in civil actions in which the amount in controversy is unlimited; in cities of over 100,000 inhabitants the United States district courts to have exclusive jurisdiction in the naturalization of the alien residents of such cities.

In my last message I asked the attention of the Congress to the urgent need of action to make our criminal law more effective; and I most earnestly request that you pay heed to the report of the Attorney General on this subject. Centuries ago it was especially needful to throw every safeguard round the accused. The danger then was lest he should be wronged by the State. The danger is now exactly the reverse. Our laws and customs tell immensely in favor of the criminal and against the interests of the public he has wronged. Some antiquated and outworn rules which once safeguarded the threatened rights of private citizens, now merely work harm to the general body politic. The criminal law of the United States stands in urgent need of revision. The criminal process of any court of the United States should run throughout the entire territorial extent of our country. The delays of the criminal law, no less than of the civil, now amount to a very great evil.

There seems to be no statute of the United States which provides for the punishment of a United States Attorney or other officer of the Government who corruptly agrees to wrongfully do or wrongfully refrain from doing any act when the consideration for such corrupt agreement is other than one possessing money value. This ought to be remedied by appropriate legislation. Legislation should also be enacted to cover explicitly, unequivocally, and beyond question breach of trust in the shape of prematurely divulging official secrets by an officer or employe of the United States, and to provide a suitable penalty therefor. Such officer or employe owes the duty to the United States to guard carefully and not to divulge or in any manner use, prematurely, information which is accessible to the officer or employe by reason of his official position. Most breaches of public trust are already covered by the law, and this one should be. It is impossible, no matter how much care is used, to prevent the occasional appointment to the public service of a man who when tempted proves unfaithful; but every means should be provided to detect and every effort made to punish the wrongdoer. So far as in my power lies each and every such wrongdoer shall be relentlessly hunted down; in no instance in the past has he been spared; in no instance in the future shall he be spared. His crime is a crime against every honest man in the Nation, for it is a crime against the whole body politic. Yet in dwelling on such misdeeds it is unjust not to add that they are altogether exceptional, and that on the whole the employes of the Government render upright and faithful service to the people. There are exceptions, notably in one or two branches of the service, but at no time in the Nation's history has the public service of the Nation taken as a whole stood on a higher plane than now, alike as regards honesty and as regards efficiency.

Once again I call your attention to the condition of the public land laws. Recent developments have given new urgency to the need for such changes as will fit these laws to actual present conditions. The honest disposal and right use of the remaining public lands is of fundamental importance. The iniquitous methods by which the monopolizing of the public lands is being brought about under the present laws are becoming more generally known, but the existing laws do not furnish effective remedies. The recommendations of the Public Lands Commission upon this subject are wise and should be given effect.

The creation of small irrigated farms under the Reclamation act is a powerful offset to the tendency of certain other laws to foster or permit monopoly of the land. Under that act the construction of great irrigation works has been proceeding rapidly and successfully, the lands reclaimed are eagerly taken up, and the prospect that the policy of National irrigation will accomplish all that was expected of it is bright. The act should be extended to include the State of Texas.

The Reclamation act derives much of its value from the fact that it tends to secure the greatest possible number of homes on the land, and to create communities of freeholders, in part by settlement on public lands, in part by forcing the subdivision of large private holdings before they can get water from Government irrigation works. The law requires that no right to the use of water for land in private ownership shall be sold for a tract exceeding 160 acres to any one land owner. This provision has excited active and powerful hostility, but the success of the law itself depends on the wise and firm enforcement of it. We cannot afford to substitute tenants for freeholders on the public domain.

The greater part of the remaining public lands can not be irrigated. They are at present and will probably always be of greater value for grazing than for any other purpose. This fact has led to the grazing homestead of 640 acres in Nebraska and to the proposed extension of it to other States. It is argued that a family can not be supported on 160 acres of arid grazing land. This is obviously true, but neither can a family be supported on 640 acres of much of the land to which it is proposed to apply the grazing homestead. To establish universally any such arbitrary limit would be unwise at the present time. It would probably result on the one hand in enlarging the holdings of some of the great land owners, and on the other in needless suffering and failure on the part of a very considerable proportion of the bona fide settlers who give faith to the implied assurance of the Government that such an area is sufficient. The best use of the public grazing lands requires the careful examination and classification of these lands in order to give each settler land enough to support his family and no more. While this work is being done, and until the lands are settled, the Government should take control of the open range, under reasonable regulations suited to local needs, following the general policy already in successful operation on the forest reserves. It is probable that the present grazing value of the open public range is scarcely more than half what it once was or what it might easily be again under careful regulation.

The forest policy of the Administration appears to enjoy the unbroken support of the people. The great users of timber are themselves forwarding the movement for forest preservation. All organized opposition to the forest preserves in the West has disappeared. Since the consolidation of all Government forest work in the National Forest Service there has been a rapid and notable gain in the usefulness of the forest reserves to the people and in public appreciation of their value. The National parks within or adjacent to forest reserves should be transferred to the charge of the Forest Service also. The National Government already does something in connection with the construction and maintenance of the great system of levees along the lower course of the Mississippi; in my judgment it should do much more.

To the spread of our trade in peace and the defense of our flag in war a great and prosperous merchant marine is indispensable. We should have ships of our own and seamen of our own to convey our goods to neutral markets, and in case of need to re-inforce our battle line. It cannot but be a source of regret and uneasiness to us that the lines of communication with our sister republics of South America should be chiefly under foreign control. It is not a good thing that American merchants and manufacturers should have to send their goods and letters to South America via Europe if they wish security and dispatch. Even on the Pacific, where our ships have held their own better than on the Atlantic, our merchant flag is now threatened through the liberal aid bestowed by other Governments on their own steam lines. I ask your earnest consideration of the report with which the Merchant Marine Commission has followed its long and careful inquiry.

I again heartily commend to your favorable consideration the tercentennial celebration at Jamestown, Va. Appreciating the desirability of this commemoration, the Congress passed an act, March 3, 1905, authorizing in the year 1907, on and near the waters of Hampton Roads, in the State of Virginia, an international naval, marine, and military celebration in honor of this event. By the authority vested in me by this act, I have made proclamation of said celebration, and have issued, in conformity with its instructions, invitations to all the nations of the earth to participate, by sending their naval vessels and such military organizations as may be practicable. This celebration would fail of its full purpose unless it were enduring in its results and commensurate with the importance of the event to be celebrated, the event from which our Nation dates its birth. I earnestly hope that this celebration, already indorsed by the Congress of the United States, and by the Legislatures of sixteen States since the action of the Congress, will receive such additional aid at your hands as will make it worthy of the great event it is intended to celebrate, and thereby enable the Government of the United States to make provision for the exhibition of its own resources, and likewise enable our people who have undertaken the work of such a celebration to provide suitable and proper entertainment and instruction in the historic events of our country for all who may visit the exposition and to whom we have tendered our hospitality.

It is a matter of unmixed satisfaction once more to call attention to the excellent work of the Pension Bureau; for the veterans of the civil war have a greater claim upon us than any other class of our citizens. To them, first of all among our people, honor is due.

Seven years ago my lamented predecessor, President McKinley, stated that the time had come for the Nation to care for the graves of the Confederate dead. I recommend that the Congress take action toward this end. The first need is to take charge of the graves of the Confederate dead who died in Northern prisons.

The question of immigration is of vital interest to this country. In the year ending June 30, 1905, there came to the United States 1,026,000 alien immigrants. In other words, in the single year that has just elapsed there came to this country a greater number of people than came here during the one hundred and sixty-nine years of our Colonial life which intervened between the first landing at Jamestown and the Declaration of Independence. It is clearly shown in the report of the Commissioner General of Immigration that while much of this enormous immigration is undoubtedly healthy and natural, a considerable proportion is undesirable from one reason or another;

moreover, a considerable proportion of it, probably a very large proportion, including most of the undesirable class, does not come here of its own initiative, but because of the activity of the agents of the great transportation companies. These agents are distributed throughout Europe, and by the offer of all kinds of inducements they wheedle and cajole many immigrants, often against their best interest, to come here. The most serious obstacle we have to encounter in the effort to secure a proper regulation of the immigration to these shores arises from the determined opposition of the foreign steamship lines who have no interest whatever in the matter save to increase the returns on their capital by carrying masses of immigrants hither in the steerage quarters of their ships.

As I said in my last message to the Congress, we cannot have too much immigration of the right sort and we should have none whatever of the wrong sort. Of course, it is desirable that even the right kind of immigration should be properly distributed in this country. We need more of such immigration for the South; and special effort should be made to secure it. Perhaps it would be possible to limit the number of immigrants allowed to come in any one year to New York and other Northern cities, while leaving unlimited the number allowed to come to the South; always provided, however, that a stricter effort is made to see that only immigrants of the right kind come to our country anywhere. In actual practice it has proved so difficult to enforce the immigration laws where long stretches of frontier marked by an imaginary line alone intervene between us and our neighbors that I recommend that no immigrants be allowed to come in from Canada and Mexico save natives of the two countries themselves. As much as possible should be done to distribute the immigrants upon the land and keep them away from the congested tenement-house districts of the great cities. But distribution is a palliative, not a cure. The prime need is to keep out all immigrants who will not make good American citizens. The laws now existing for the exclusion of undesirable immigrants should be strengthened. Adequate means should be adopted, enforced by sufficient penalties, to compel steamship companies engaged in the passenger business to observe in good faith the law which forbids them to encourage or solicit immigration to the United States. Moreover, there should be a sharp limitation imposed upon all vessels coming to our ports as to the number of immigrants in ratio to the tonnage which each vessel can carry. This ratio should be high enough to insure the coming hither of as good a class of aliens as possible. Provision should be made for the surer punishment of those who induce aliens to come to this country under promise or assurance of employment. It should be made possible to inflict a sufficiently heavy penalty on any employer violating this law to deter him from taking the risk. It seems to me wise that there should be an international conference held to deal with this question of immigration, which has more than a merely National significance; such a conference could, among other things, enter at length into the methods for securing a thorough inspection of would-be immigrants at the ports from which they desire to embark before permitting them to embark.

In dealing with this question it is unwise to depart from the old American tradition and to discriminate for or against any man who desires to come here and become a citizen, save on the ground of that man's fitness for citizenship. It is our right and duty to consider his moral and social quality. His standard of living should be such that he will not, by pressure of competition, lower the standard of living of our own wage-workers; for it must ever be a prime object of our legislation to keep high their standard of living. If the man who seeks to come here is from the moral and social standpoint of such a character as to bid fair to add value to the community he should be heartily welcomed. We cannot afford to pay heed to whether he is of one creed or another, of one nation, or another. We cannot afford to consider whether he is Catholic or Protestant, Jew or Gentile; whether he is Englishman or Irishman, Frenchman or German, Japanese, Italian, Scandinavian, Slav, or Magyar. What we should desire to find out is the individual quality of the individual man. In my judgment, with this end in view, we shall have to prepare through our own agents a far more rigid inspection in the countries from which the immigrants come. It will be a great deal better to have fewer immigrants, but all of the right kind, than a great number of immigrants, many of whom are necessarily of the wrong kind. As far as possible we wish to limit the immigration to this country to persons who propose to become citizens of this country, and we can well afford to insist upon adequate scrutiny of the character of those who are thus proposed for future citizenship. There should be an increase in the stringency of the laws to keep out insane, idiotic, epileptic, and pauper immigrants. But this is by no means enough. Not merely the Anarchist, but every man of Anarchistic tendencies, all violent and disorderly people, all people of bad character, the incompetent, the lazy, the vicious, the physically unfit, defective, or degenerate should be kept out. The stocks out of which American citizenship is to be built should be strong and healthy, sound in body, mind, and character. If it be objected that the Government agents would not always select well, the answer is that they would certainly select better than do the agents and brokers of foreign steamship companies, the people who now do whatever selection is done.

The questions arising in connection with Chinese immigration stand by themselves. The conditions in China are such that the entire Chinese coolie class, that is, the class of Chinese laborers, skilled and unskilled, legitimately come under the head of undesirable immigrants to this country, because of their numbers, the low wages for which they work, and their low standard of living. Not only is it to the interest of this country to keep them out, but the Chinese authorities do not desire that they should be admitted. At present their entrance is prohibited by laws amply adequate to accomplish this purpose. These laws have been, are being, and will be, thoroughly enforced. The violations of them are so few in number as to be infinitesimal and can be entirely disregarded. There is no serious proposal to alter the immigration law as regards the Chinese laborer, skilled or unskilled, and there is no excuse for any man feeling or affecting to feel the slightest alarm on the subject.

But in the effort to carry out the policy of excluding Chinese laborers, Chinese coolies, grave injustice and wrong have been done by this Nation to the people of China, and therefore ultimately to this Nation itself. Chinese students, business and professional men of all kinds—not only merchants, but bankers, doctors, manufacturers, professors, travelers, and the like—should be encouraged to come here, and treated on precisely the same footing that we treat students, business men, travelers, and the like of other nations. Our laws and treaties should be framed, not so as to put these people in the excepted classes, but to state that we will admit all Chinese, except Chinese of the coolie class, Chinese skilled or unskilled laborers. There would not be the least danger that any such provision would result in any relaxation of the law about laborers. These will, under all conditions, be kept out absolutely. But it will be more easy to see that both justice and courtesy are shown, as they ought to be shown, to other Chinese, if the law or treaty is framed as above suggested. Examinations should be completed at the port of departure from China. For this purpose there should be provided a more adequate Consular Service in China than we now have. The appropriations both for the offices of the Consuls and for the office forces in the consulates should be increased.

As a people we have talked much of the open door in China, and we expect, and quite rightly intend to insist upon, justice being shown us by the Chinese. But we cannot expect to receive equity unless we do equity. We cannot ask the Chinese to do to us what we are unwilling to do to them. They would have a perfect right to exclude our laboring men if our laboring men threatened to come into their country in such numbers as to jeopardize the well-being of the Chinese population; and as, mutatis mutandis, these were the conditions with which Chinese immigration actually brought this people face to face, we had and have a perfect right, which the Chinese Government in no way contests, to act as we have acted in the matter of restricting coolie immigration. That this right exists for each country was explicitly acknowledged in the last treaty between the two countries. But we must treat the Chinese student, traveler, and business man in a spirit of the broadest justice and courtesy if we expect similar treatment to be accorded to our own people of similar rank who go to China. Much trouble has come during the past Summer from the organized boycott against American goods which has been started in China. The main factor in producing this boycott has been the resentment felt by the students and business people of China, by all the Chinese leaders, against the harshness of our law toward educated Chinamen of the professional and business classes.

This Government has the friendliest feeling for China and desires China's well-being. We cordially sympathize with the announced purpose of Japan to stand for the integrity of China. Such an attitude tends to the peace of the world.

The civil service law has been on the statute books for twenty-two years. Every President and a vast majority of heads of departments who have been in office during that period have favored a gradual extension of the merit system. The more thoroughly its principles have been understood, the greater has been the favor with which the law has been regarded by administration officers. Any attempt to carry on the great executive departments of the Government without this law would inevitably result in chaos. The Civil Service Commissioners are doing excellent work, and their compensation is inadequate considering the service they perform.

The statement that the examinations are not practical in character is based on a misapprehension of the practice of the Commission. The departments are invariably consulted as to the requirements desired and as to the character of questions that shall be asked. General invitations are frequently sent out to all heads of departments asking whether any changes in the scope or character of examinations are required. In other words, the departments prescribe the requirements and qualifications desired, and the Civil Service Commission co-operates with them in securing persons with these qualifications and insuring open and impartial competition. In a large number of examinations (as, for example, those for trades positions), there are no educational requirements whatever, and a person who can neither read nor write may pass with a high average. Vacancies in the service are filled with reasonable expedition, and the machinery of the Commission, which reaches every part of the country, is the best agency that has yet been devised for finding people with the most suitable qualifications for the various offices to be filled. Written competitive examinations do not make an ideal method for filling positions, but they do represent an immeasurable advance upon the "spoils" method, under which outside politicians really make the appointments nominally made by the executive officers, the appointees being chosen by the politicians in question, in the great majority of cases, for reasons totally unconnected with the needs of the service or of the public.

Statistics gathered by the Census Bureau show that the tenure of office in the Government service does not differ materially from that enjoyed by employes of large business corporations. Heads of executive departments and members of the Commission have called my attention to the fact that the rule requiring a filing of charges and three days' notice before an employe could be separated from the service for inefficiency has served no good purpose whatever, because that is not a matter upon which a hearing of the employe found to be inefficient can be of any value, and in practice the rule providing for such notice and hearing has merely resulted in keeping in a certain number of incompetents, because of the reluctance of the heads of departments and bureau chiefs to go through the required procedure. Experience has shown that this rule is wholly ineffective to save any man, if a superior for improper reasons wishes to remove him, and is mischievous because it sometimes serves to keep in the service incompetent men not guilty of specific wrongdoing. Having these facts in view the rule has been amended by providing that where the inefficiency or incapacity comes within the personal knowledge of the head of a department the removal may be made without notice, the reasons therefor being filed and made a record of the department. The absolute right of the removal rests where it always has rested, with the head of a department; any limitation of this absolute right results in grave injury to the public service. The change is merely one of procedure; it was much needed, and it is producing good results.

The civil service law is being energetically and impartially enforced, and in the large majority of cases complaints of violations of either the law or rules are discovered to be unfounded. In this respect this law compares very favorably with any other Federal statute. The question of politics in the appointment and retention of the men engaged in merely ministerial work has been practically eliminated in almost the entire field of Government employment covered by the civil service law. The action of the Congress in providing the commission with its own force instead of requiring it to rely on detailed clerks has been justified by the increased work done at a smaller cost to the Government. I urge upon the Congress a careful consideration of the recommendations contained in the annual report of the commission.

Our copyright laws urgently need revision. They are imperfect in definition, confused and inconsistent in expression; they omit provision for many articles which, under modern reproductive processes are entitled to protection; they impose hardships upon the copyright proprietor which are not essential to the fair protection of the public; they are difficult for the courts to interpret and impossible for the Copyright Office to administer with satisfaction to the public. Attempts to improve them by amendment have been frequent, no less than twelve acts for the purpose having been passed since the Revised Statutes. To perfect them by further amendment seems impracticable. A complete revision of them is essential. Such a revision, to meet modern conditions, has been found necessary in Germany, Austria, Sweden, and other foreign countries, and bills embodying it are pending in England and the Australian colonies. It has been urged here, and proposals for a commission to undertake it have, from time to time, been pressed upon the Congress. The inconveniences of the present conditions being so great, an attempt to frame appropriate legislation has been made by the Copyright Office, which has called conferences of the various interests especially and practically concerned with the operation of the copyright laws. It has secured from them suggestions as to the changes necessary; it has added from its own experience and investigations, and it has drafted a bill which embodies such of these changes and additions as, after full discussion and expert criticism, appeared to be sound and safe. In form this bill would replace the existing insufficient and inconsistent laws by one general copyright statute. It will be presented to the Congress at the coming session. It deserves prompt consideration.

I recommend that a law be enacted to regulate inter-State commerce in misbranded and adulterated foods, drinks, and drugs. Such law would protect legitimate manufacture and commerce, and would tend to secure the health and welfare of the consuming public. Traffic in food-stuffs which have been debased or adulterated so as to injure health or to deceive purchasers should be forbidden.

The law forbidding the emission of dense black or gray smoke in the city of Washington has been sustained by the courts. Something has been accomplished under it, but much remains to be done if we would preserve the capital city from defacement by the smoke nuisance. Repeated prosecutions under the law have not had the desired effect. I recommend that it be made more stringent by increasing both the minimum and maximum fine; by providing for imprisonment in cases of repeated violation, and by affording the remedy of injunction against the continuation of the operation of plants which are persistent offenders. I recommend, also, an increase in the number of inspectors, whose duty it shall be to detect violations of the act.

I call your attention to the generous act of the State of California

THE HAGUE PEACE CONFERENCE—PEACE PALACE

THE HAGUE PEACE CONFERENCE

The article entitled "Hague Peace Conference," in the Encyclopedic Index, so thoroughly covers the case that no further comment here is necessary.

The movement for international peace has been furthered by every President of the United States, from Washington to Taft. Sometimes popular clamor made it extremely difficult to preserve peace. In Washington's time the public heart bled for our former ally, France, when the rest of Europe attacked her, and a strong party stood for the declaration of war against her assailants. But Washington, who had in war won undying fame, stood for peace, and peace was maintained. Again, in Grant's time, the "Alabama" affair was a live coal that had to be quenched. Our people thought of the horrors of the late war, recollected Great Britain's indifference, suspected her even of aiding the Confederates, and knew her officials' hostility to the North had permitted the destructive *Alabama* to sail. But Grant, who had lived through the inferno of war and who knew its lineaments, stood for peace, and the matter was arbitrated.

President Taft, by proposing to Great Britain a treaty that will provide for the arbitration of every question that may arise between us, has taken the longest step yet made toward universal peace.

The arbitration of Grant's time, which set a shining example to the world, is described in the article entitled "Alabama Claims, The," in the Encyclopedic Index.

in conferring upon the United States Government the ownership of the Yosemite Valley and the Mariposa Big Tree Grove. There should be no delay in accepting the gift, and appropriations should be made for the including thereof in the Yosemite National Park, and for the care and policing of the park. California has acted most wisely, as well as with great magnanimity, in the matter. There are certain mighty natural features of our land which should be preserved in perpetuity for our children and our children's children. In my judgment, the Grand Canyon of the Colorado should be made into a National park. It is greatly to be wished that the State of New York should copy as regards Niagara what the State of California has done as regards the Yosemite. Nothing should be allowed to interfere with the preservation of Niagara Falls in all their beauty and majesty. If the State cannot see to this, then it is earnestly to be wished that she should be willing to turn it over to the National Government, which should in such case (if possible, in conjunction with the Canadian Government) assume the burden and responsibility of preserving unharmed Niagara Falls; just as it should gladly assume a similar burden and responsibility for the Yosemite National Park, and as it has already assumed them for the Yellowstone National Park. Adequate provision should be made by the Congress for the proper care and supervision of all these National parks. The boundaries of the Yellowstone National Park should be extended to the south and east, to take in such portions of the abutting forest reservations as will enable the Government to protect the elk on their Winter range.

The most characteristic animal of the Western plains was the great, shaggy-maned wild ox, the bison, commonly known as buffalo. Small fragments of herds exist in a domesticated state here and there, a few of them in the Yellowstone Park. Such a herd as that on the Flathead Reservation should not be allowed to go out of existence. Either on some reservation or on some forest reserve like the Wichita reserve and game refuge provision should be made for the preservation of such a herd. I believe that the scheme would be of economic advantage, for the robe of the buffalo is of high market value, and the same is true of the robe of the crossbred animals.

I call your especial attention to the desirability of giving to the members of the Life Saving Service pensions such as are given to firemen and policemen in all our great cities. The men in the Life Saving Service continually and in the most matter of fact way do deeds such as make Americans proud of their country. They have no political influence, and they live in such remote places that the really heroic services they continually render receive the scantiest recognition from the public. It is unjust for a great nation like this to permit these men to become totally disabled or to meet death in the performance

223

of their hazardous duty and yet to give them no sort of reward. If one of them serves thirty years of his life in such a position he should surely be entitled to retire on half pay, as a fireman or policeman does, and if he becomes totally incapacitated through accident or sickness, or loses his health in the discharge of his duty, he or his family should receive a pension just as any soldier should. I call your attention with especial earnestness to this matter because it appeals not only to our judgment but to our sympathy; for the people on whose behalf I ask it are comparatively few in number, render incalculable service of a particularly dangerous kind, and have no one to speak for them.

During the year just past, the phase of the Indian question which has been most sharply brought to public attention is the larger legal significance of the Indian's induction into citizenship. This has made itself manifest not only in a great access of litigation in which the citizen Indian figures as a party defendant and in a more widespread disposition to levy local taxation upon his personalty, but in a decision of the United States Supreme Court which struck away the main prop on which has hitherto rested the Government's benevolent effort to protect him against the evils of intemperance. The court holds, in effect, that when an Indian becomes, by virtue of an allotment of land to him, a citizen of the State in which his land is situated, he passes from under Federal control in such matters as this, and the acts of the Congress prohibiting the sale or gift to him of intoxicants become substantially inoperative. It is gratifying to note that the States and municipalities of the West which have most at stake in the welfare of the Indians are taking up this subject and are trying to supply, in a measure at least, the abdication of its trusteeship forced upon the Federal Government. Nevertheless, I would urgently press upon the attention of the Congress the question whether some amendment of the internal revenue laws might not be of aid in prosecuting those malefactors, known in the Indian country as "bootleggers," who are engaged at once in defrauding the United States Treasury of taxes and, what is far more important, in debauching the Indians by carrying liquors illicitly into territory still completely under Federal jurisdiction.

Among the crying present needs of the Indians are more day schools situated in the midst of their settlements, more effective instruction in the industries pursued on their own farms, and a more liberal extension of the field-matron service, which means the education of the Indian women in the arts of home making. Until the mothers are well started in the right direction we cannot reasonably expect much from the children who are soon to form an integral part of our American citizenship. Moreover the excuse continually advanced by male adult Indians for refusing offers of remunerative employment at a distance from their homes is that they dare not leave their families too long out of their sight. One effectual remedy for this state of things is to employ the minds and strengthen the moral fibre of the Indian women—the end to which the work of the field matron is especially directed. I trust that the Congress will make its appropriations for Indian day schools and field matrons as generous as may consist with the other pressing demands upon its providence.

During the last year the Philippine Islands have been slowly recovering from the series of disasters which, since American occupation, have greatly reduced the amount of agricultural products below what was produced in Spanish times. The war, the rinderpest, the locusts, the drought, and the cholera have been united as causes to prevent a return of the prosperity much needed in the islands. The most serious is the destruction by the rinderpest of more than 75 per cent. of the draught cattle, because it will take several years of breeding to restore the necessary number of these indispensable aids to agriculture. The commission attempted to supply by purchase from adjoining countries the needed cattle, but the experiments made were unsuccessful. Most of the cattle imported were unable to withstand the change of climate and the rigors of the voyage and died from other diseases than rinderpest.

The income of the Philippine Government has necessarily been reduced by reason of the business and agricultural depression in the islands, and the Government has been obliged to exercise great economy to cut down its expenses, to reduce salaries, and in every way to avoid a deficit. It has adopted an internal revenue law, imposing taxes on cigars, cigarettes, and distilled liquors, and abolishing the old Spanish industrial taxes. The law has not operated as smoothly as was hoped, and although its principle is undoubtedly correct, it may need amendments for the purpose of reconciling the people to its provisions. The income derived from it has partly made up for the reduction in customs revenue.

There has been a marked increase in the number of Filipinos employed in the civil service, and a corresponding decrease in the number of Americans. The Government in every one of its departments has been rendered more efficient by elimination of undesirable material and the promotion of deserving public servants.

Improvements of harbors, roads, and bridges continue, although the cutting down of the revenue forbids the expenditure of any great amount from current income for these purposes. Steps are being taken, by advertisement for competitive bids, to secure the construction and maintenance of 1,000 miles of railway by private corporations under the recent enabling legislation of the Congress. The transfer of the friar lands, in accordance with the contract made some **two** years ago, has been completely effected, and the purchase money paid. Provision has just been made by statute for the speedy settlement in a special proceeding in the Supreme Court of controversies over the possession and title of church buildings and rectories arising between the Roman Catholic Church and schismatics claiming under ancient municipalities. Negotiations and hearings for the settlement of the amount due to the Roman Catholic Church for rent and occupation of churches and rectories by the army of the United States are in progress, and it is hoped a satisfactory conclusion may be submitted to the Congress before the end of the session.

Tranquillity has existed during the past year throughout the Archipelago, except in the Province of Cavite, the Province of Batangas, and the Province of Samar, and in the Island of Jolo among the Moros. The Jolo disturbance was put an end to by several sharp and short engagements, and now peace prevails in the Moro Province. Cavite, the mother of ladrones in the Spanish times, is so permeated with the traditional sympathy of the people for ladronism as to make it difficult to stamp out the disease. Batangas was only disturbed by reason of the fugitive ladrones from Cavite, Samar was thrown into disturbance by the uneducated and partly savage peoples living in the mountains, who, having been given by the municipal code more power than they were able to exercise discreetly, elected municipal officers who abused their trusts, compelled the people raising hemp to sell it at a much less price than it was worth, and by their abuses drove their people into resistance to constituted authority. Cavite and Samar are instances of reposing too much confidence in the self-governing power of a people. The disturbances have all now been suppressed, and it is hoped that with these lessons local governments can be formed which will secure quiet and peace to the deserving inhabitants. The incident is another proof of the fact that if there has been any error as regards giving self-government in the Philippines it has been in the direction of giving it too quickly, not too slowly. A year from next April the first legislative assembly for the islands will be held. On the sanity and self-restraint of this body much will depend so far as the future self-government of the islands is concerned.

The most encouraging feature of the whole situation has been the very great interest taken by the common people in education and the great increase in the number of enrolled students in the public schools. The increase was from 300,000 to half a million pupils. The average attendance is about 70 per cent. The only limit upon the number of pupils seems to be the capacity of the government to furnish teachers and school houses.

The agricultural conditions of the islands enforce more strongly than ever the argument in favor of reducing the tariff on the products of the Philippine Islands entering the United States. I earnestly recommend that the tariff now imposed by the Dingley bill upon the products of the Philippine Islands be entirely removed, except the tariff on sugar and tobacco, and that that tariff be reduced to 25 per cent. of the present rates under the Dingley act; that after July 1, 1909, the tariff upon tobacco and sugar produced in the Philippine Islands be entirely removed, and that free trade between the islands and the United States in the products of each country then be provided for by law.

A statute in force, enacted April 15, 1904, suspends the operation of the coastwise laws of the United States upon the trade between the Philippine Islands and the United States until July 1, 1906. I earnestly recommend that this suspension be postponed until July 1, 1909. I think it of doubtful utility to apply the coastwise laws to the trade between the United States and the Philippines under any circumstances, because I am convinced that it will do no good whatever to American bottoms, and will only interfere and be an obstacle to the trade between the Philippines and the United States, but if the coastwise law must be thus applied, certainly it ought not to have effect until free trade is enjoyed between the people of the United States and the people of the Philippine Islands in their respective products.

I do not anticipate that free trade between the islands and the United States will produce a revolution in the sugar and tobacco production of the Philippine Islands. So primitive are the methods of agriculture in the Philippine Islands, so slow is capital in going to the islands, so many difficulties surround a large agricultural enterprise in the islands, that it will be many, many years before the products of those islands will have any effect whatever upon the markets of the United States. The problem of labor is also a formidable one with the sugar and tobacco producers in the islands. The best friends of the Filipino people and the people themselves are utterly opposed to the admission of Chinese coolie labor. Hence the only solution is the training of Filipino labor, and this will take a long time. The enactment of a law by the Congress of the United States making provision for free trade between the islands and the United States, however, will be of great importance from a political and sentimental standpoint; and, while its actual benefit has doubtless been exaggerated by the people of the islands, they will accept this measure of justice as an indication that the people of the United States are anxious to aid the people of the Philippine Islands in every way, and especially in the agricultural development of their archipelago. It will aid the Filipinos without injuring interests in America.

In my judgment immediate steps should be taken for the fortification of Hawaii. This is the most important point in the Pacific to fortify in order to conserve the interests of this country. It would be hard to overstate the importance of this need. Hawaii is too heavily taxed. Laws should be enacted setting aside for a period of, say, twenty years 75 per cent. of the internal revenue and customs receipts from Hawaii as a special fund to be expended in the islands for educational and public buildings, and for harbor improvements and military and naval defenses. It cannot be too often repeated that our aim must be to develop the territory of Hawaii on traditional American lines. That territory has serious commercial and industrial problems to reckon with; but no measure of relief can be considered which looks to legislation admitting Chinese and restricting them by statute to field labor and domestic service. The status of servility can never again be tolerated on American soil. We cannot concede that the proper solution of its problems is special legislation admitting to Hawaii a class of laborers denied admission to the other States and Territories. There are obstacles, and great obstacles, in the way of building up a representative American community in the Hawaiian Islands; but it is not in the American character to give up in the face of difficulty. Many an American Commonwealth has been built up against odds equal to those that now confront Hawaii.

No merely half-hearted effort to meet its problems as other American communities have met theirs can be accepted as final. Hawaii shall never become a territory in which a governing class of rich planters exists by means of coolie labor. Even if the rate of growth of the Territory is thereby rendered slower, the growth must only take place by the admission of immigrants fit in the end to assume the duties and burdens of full American citizenship. Our aim must be to develop the Territory on the same basis of stable citizenship as exists on this continent.

I earnestly advocate the adoption of legislation which will explicitly confer American citizenship on all citizens of Porto Rico. There is, in my judgment, no excuse for failure to do this. The harbor of San Juan should be dredged and improved. The expenses of the Federal Court of Porto Rico should be met from the Federal Treasury and not from the Porto Rican treasury. The elections in Porto Rico should take place every four years, and the Legislature should meet in session every two years. The present form of government in Porto Rico, which provides for the appointment by the President of the members of the Executive Council or upper house of the Legislature, has proved satisfactory and has inspired confidence in property owners and investors. I do not deem it advisable at the present time to change this form in any material feature. The problems and needs of the island are industrial and commercial rather than political.

I wish to call the attention of the Congress to one question which affects our insular possessions generally; namely, the need of an increased liberality in the treatment of the whole franchise question in these islands. In the proper desire to prevent the islands being exploited by speculators and to have them develop in the interests of their own people an error has been made in refusing to grant sufficiently liberal terms to induce the investment of American capital in the Philippines and in Porto Rico. Elsewhere in this message I have spoken strongly against the jealousy of mere wealth, and especially of corporate wealth as such. But it is particularly regrettable to allow any such jealousy to be developed when we are dealing either with our insular or with foreign affairs. The big corporation has achieved its present position in the business world simply because it is the most effective instrument in business competition. In foreign affairs we cannot afford to put our people at a disadvantage with their competitors by in any way discriminating against the efficiency of our business organizations. In the same way we cannot afford to allow our insular possessions to lag behind in industrial development from any twisted jealousy of business success. It is, of course, a mere truism to say that the business interests of the islands will only be developed if it becomes the financial interest of somebody to develop them. Yet this development is one of the things most earnestly to be wished for in the interest of the islands themselves. We have been paying all possible heed to the political and educational interests of the islands, but, important though these objects are, it is not less important that we should favor their industrial development. The Government can in certain ways help this directly, as by building good roads; but the fundamental and vital help must be given through the development of the industries of the islands, and a most efficient means to this end is to encourage big American corporations to start industries in them, and this means to make it advantageous for them to do so. To limit the ownership of mining claims, as has been done in the Philippines, is absurd. In both the Philippines and Porto Rico the limit of holdings of land should be largely raised.

I earnestly ask that Alaska be given an elective delegate. Some person should be chosen who can speak with authority of the needs of the Territory. The Government should aid in the construction of a railroad from the Gulf of Alaska to the Yukon River, in American territory. In my last two messages I advocated certain additional action on behalf of Alaska. I shall not now repeat those recommendations, but I shall lay all my stress upon the one recommendation of giving to Alaska some one authorized to speak for it. I should prefer that the delegate was made elective, but if this is not deemed wise, then make him appointive. At any rate, give Alaska some person whose business it shall be to speak with authority on her behalf to the Congress. The natural resources of Alaska are great. Some of the chief needs of the peculiarly energetic, self-reliant, and typically American white population of Alaska were set forth in my last message. I also earnestly ask your attention to the needs of the Alaskan Indians. All Indians who are competent should receive the full rights of American citizenship. It is, for instance, a gross and indefensible wrong to deny to such hard-working, decent-living Indians as the Metlakahtlas the right to obtain licenses as captains, pilots, and engineers; the right to enter mining claims, and to profit by the homestead law. These particular Indians are civilized and are competent and entitled to be put on the same basis with the white men round about them.

I recommend that Indian Territory and Oklahoma be admitted as one State and that New Mexico and Arizona be admitted as one State. There is no obligation upon us to treat territorial subdivisions, which are matters of convenience only, as binding us on the question of admission to Statehood. Nothing has taken up more time in the Congress during the past few years than the question as to the Statehood to be granted to the four Territories above mentioned, and after careful consideration of all that has been developed in the discussions of the question, I recommend that they be immediately admitted as two States. There is no justification for further delay; and the advisability of making the four Territories into two States has been clearly established.

In some of the Territories the legislative assemblies issue licenses for gambling. The Congress should by law forbid this practice, the harmful results of which are obvious at a glance.

The treaty between the United States and the Republic of Panama, under which the construction of the Panama Canal was made possible, went into effect with its ratification by the United States Senate on February 23, 1904. The canal properties of the French Canal Company were transferred to the United States on April 23, 1904, on payment of $40,000,000 to that company. On April 1, 1905, the Commission was reorganized, and it now consists of Theodore P. Shonts, Chairman; Charles E. Magoon, Benjamin M. Harrod, Rear Admiral Mordecai T. Endicott, Brig. Gen. Peter C. Hains, and Col. Oswald H. Ernst. John F. Stevens was appointed Chief Engineer on July 1 last. Active work in canal construction, mainly preparatory, has been in progress for less than a year and a half. During that period two points about the canal have ceased to be open to debate: First, the question of route; the canal will be built on the Isthmus of Panama. Second, the question of feasibility; there are no physical obstacles on this route that American engineering skill will not be able to overcome without serious difficulty, or that will prevent the completion of the canal within a reasonable time and at a reasonable cost. This is virtually the unanimous testimony of the engineers who have investigated the matter for the Government.

The point which remains unsettled is the question of type, whether the canal shall be one of several locks above sea level, or at sea level with a single tide lock. On this point I hope to lay before the Congress at an early day the findings of the Advisory Board of American and European Engineers, that at my invitation have been considering the subject, together with the report of the Commission thereon, and such comments thereon or recommendations in reference thereto as may seem necessary.

The American people is pledged to the speediest possible construction of a canal adequate to meet the demands which the commerce of the world will make upon it, and I appeal most earnestly to the Congress to aid in the fulfillment of the pledge. Gratifying progress has been made during the past year, and especially during the past four months. The greater part of the necessary preliminary work has been done. Actual work of excavation could be begun only on a limited scale till the Canal Zone was made a healthful place to live in and to work in. The Isthmus had to be sanitated first. This task has been so thoroughly accomplished that yellow fever has been virtually extirpated from the Isthmus and general health conditions vastly improved. The same methods which converted the island of Cuba from a pest hole, which menaced the health of the world, into a healthful place of abode, have been applied on the Isthmus with satisfactory results. There is no reason to doubt that when the plans for water supply, paving, and sewerage of Panama and Colon and the large labor camps have been fully carried out, the Isthmus will be, for the tropics, an unusually healthy place of abode. The work is so far advanced now that the health of all those employed in canal work is as well guarded as it is on similar work in this country and elsewhere.

In addition to sanitating the Isthmus, satisfactory quarters are being provided for employes and an adequate system of supplying them with wholesome food at reasonable prices has been created. Hospitals have been established and equipped that are without their superiors of their kind anywhere. The country has thus been made fit to work in, and provision has been made for the welfare and comfort of those who are to do the work. During the past year a large portion of the plant with which the work is to be done has been ordered. It is confidently believed that by the middle of the approaching year a sufficient proportion of this plant will have been installed to enable us to resume the work of excavation on a large scale.

What is needed now and without delay is an appropriation by the Congress to meet the current and accruing expenses of the commission. The first appropriation of $10,000,000, out of the $135,000,000 authorized by the Spooner act, was made three years ago. It is nearly exhausted. There is barely enough of it remaining to carry the commission to the end of the year. Unless the Congress shall appropriate before that time all work must cease. To arrest progress for any length of time now, when matters are advancing so satisfactorily, would be deplorable. There will be no money with which to meet pay roll obligations and none with which to meet bills coming due for materials and supplies; and there will be demoralization of the forces, here and on the Isthmus, now working so harmoniously and effectively, if there is delay in granting an emergency appropriation. Estimates of the amount necessary will be found in the accompanying reports of the Secretary of War and the commission.

I recommend more adequate provision than has been made heretofore for the work of the Department of State. Within a few years there has been a very great increase in the amount and importance of the work to be done by that department, both in Washington and abroad. This has been caused by the great increase of our foreign trade, the increase of wealth among our people, which enables them to travel more generally than heretofore, the increase of American capital which is seeking investment in foreign countries, and the growth of our power and weight in the councils of the civilized world. There has been no corresponding increase of facilities for doing the work afforded to the department having charge of our foreign relations.

Neither at home nor abroad is there a sufficient working force to do the business properly. In many respects the system which was adequate to the work of twenty-five years or even ten years ago, is inadequate now, and should be changed. Our Consular force should be classified, and appointments should be made to the several classes, with authority to the Executive to assign the members of each class to duty at such posts as the interests of the service require, instead of the appointments being made as at present to specified posts. There should be an adequate inspection service, so that the department may be able to inform itself how the business of each Consulate is being done, instead of depending upon casual private information or rumor. The fee system should be entirely abolished, and a due equivalent made in salary to the officers who now eke out their subsistence by means of fees. Sufficient provision should be made for a clerical force in every Consulate, composed entirely of Americans, instead of the insufficient provision now made, which compels the employment of great numbers of citizens of foreign countries whose services can be obtained for less money. At a large part of our Consulates the office quarters and the clerical force are inadequate to the performance of the onerous duties imposed by the recent provisions of our immigration laws as well as by our increasing trade. In many parts of the world the lack of suitable quarters for our embassies, legations, and Consulates detracts from the respect in which our officers ought to be held, and seriously impairs their weight and influence.

Suitable provision should be made for the expense of keeping our diplomatic officers more fully informed of what is being done from day to day in the progress of our diplomatic affairs with other countries. The lack of such information, caused by insufficient appropriations available for cable tolls and for clerical and messenger service, frequently puts our officers at a great disadvantage and detracts from their usefulness. The salary list should be readjusted. It does not now correspond either to the importance of the service to be rendered and the degrees of ability and experience required in the different positions, or to the differences in the cost of living. In many cases the salaries are quite inadequate.

THEODORE ROOSEVELT.

SIXTH ANNUAL MESSAGE.

WHITE HOUSE, Dec. 3, 1906.

To the Senate and House of Representatives:

As a nation we still continue to enjoy a literally unprecedented prosperity; and it is probable that only reckless speculation and disregard of legitimate business methods on the part of the business world can materially mar this prosperity.

No Congress in our time has done more good work of importance than the present Congress. There were several matters left unfinished at your last session, however, which I most earnestly hope you will complete before your adjournment.

I again recommend a law prohibiting all corporations from contributing to the campaign expenses of any party. Such a bill has already past one House of Congress. Let individuals contribute as they desire; but let us prohibit in effective fashion all corporations from making contributions for any political purpose, directly or indirectly.

Another bill which has just past one House of the Congress and which it is urgently necessary should be enacted into law is that conferring upon the Government the right of appeal in criminal cases on questions of law. This right exists in many of the States; it exists in the District of Columbia by act of the Congress. It is of course not proposed that in any case a verdict for the defendant on the merits should be set aside. Recently in one district where the Government had indicted certain persons for conspiracy in connection with rebates, the court sustained the defendant's demurrer; while in another jurisdiction an indictment for conspiracy to obtain rebates has been sustained by the court, convictions obtained under it, and two defendants sentenced to imprisonment. The two cases referred to may not be in real conflict with each other, but it is unfortunate that there should even be an apparent conflict. At present there is no way by which the Government can cause such a conflict, when it occurs, to be solved by an appeal to a higher court; and the wheels of justice are blocked without any real decision of the question. I can not too strongly urge the passage of the bill in question. A failure to pass it will result in seriously hampering the Government in its effort to obtain justice, especially against wealthy individuals or corporations who do wrong; and may also prevent the Government from obtaining justice for wage-workers who are not themselves able effectively to contest a case where the judgment of an inferior court has been against them. I have specifically in view a recent decision by a district judge leaving railway employees without remedy for violation of a certain so-called labor statute. It seems an absurdity to permit a single district judge, against what may be the judgment of the immense majority of his colleagues on the bench, to declare a law solemnly enacted by the Congress to be "unconstitutional," and then to deny to the Government the right to have the Supreme Court definitely decide the question.

It is well to recollect that the real efficiency of the law often depends not upon the passage of acts as to which there is great public excitement, but upon the passage of acts of this nature as to which there is not much public excitement, because there is little public understanding of their importance, while the interested parties are keenly alive to the desirability of defeating them. The importance of enacting into law the particular bill in question is further increased by the fact that the Government has now definitely begun a policy of resorting to the criminal law in those trust and interstate commerce cases where such a course offers a reasonable chance of success. At first, as was proper, every effort was made to enforce these laws by civil proceedings; but it has become increasingly evident that the action of the Government in finally deciding, in certain cases, to undertake criminal proceedings was justifiable; and tho there have been some conspicuous failures in these cases, we have had many successes, which have undoubtedly had a deterrent effect upon evil-doers, whether the penalty inflicted was in the shape of fine or imprisonment—and penalties of both kinds have already been inflicted by the courts. Of course, where the judge can see his way to inflict the penalty of imprisonment the deterrent effect of the punishment on other offenders is increased; but sufficiently heavy fines accomplish much. Judge Holt, of the New York district court, in a recent decision admirably stated the need for treating with just severity offenders of this kind. His opinion runs in part as follows:

'The Government's evidence to establish the defendant's guilt was clear, conclusive, and undisputed. The case was a flagrant one. The transactions which took place under this illegal contract were very large; the amounts of rebates returned were considerable; and the amount of the rebate itself was large, amounting to more than one-fifth of the entire tariff charge for the transportation of merchandise from this city to Detroit. It is not too much to say, in my opinion, that if this business was carried on for a considerable time on that basis—that is, if this discrimination in favor of this particular shipper was made with an 18 instead of a 23 cent rate and the tariff rate was maintained as against their competitors—the result might be and not improbably would be that their competitors would be driven out of business. This crime is one which in its nature is deliberate and premeditated. I think over a fortnight elapsed between the date of Palmer's letter requesting the reduced rate and the answer of the railroad company deciding to grant it, and then for months afterwards this business was carried on and these claims for rebates submitted month after month and checks in payment of them drawn month after month. Such a violation of the law, in my opinion, in its essential nature, is a very much more heinous act than the ordinary common, vulgar crimes which come before criminal courts constantly for punishment and which arise from sudden passion or temptation. This crime in this case was committed by men of education and of large business experience, whose standing in the community was such that they might have been expected to set an example of obedience to law, upon the maintenance of which alone in this country the security of their property depends. It was committed on behalf of a great railroad corporation, which, like other railroad corporations, has received gratuitously from the State large and valuable privileges for the public's convenience and its own, which performs quasi public functions and which is charged with the highest obligation in the transaction of its business to treat the citizens of this country alike, and not to carry on its business with unjust discriminations between different citizens or different classes of citizens. This crime in its nature is one usually done with secrecy, and proof of which it is very difficult to obtain. The interstate commerce act was past in 1887, nearly twenty years ago. Ever since that time complaints of the granting of rebates by railroads have been common, urgent, and insistent, and altho the Congress has repeatedly past legislation endeavoring to put a stop to this evil, the difficulty of obtaining proof upon which to bring prosecution in these cases is so great that this is the first case that has ever been brought in this court, and, as I am informed, this case and one recently brought in Philadelphia are the only cases that have ever been brought in the eastern part of this country. In fact, but few cases of this kind have ever been brought in this country, East or West. Now, under these circumstances, I am forced to the conclusion, in a case in which the proof is so clear and the facts are so flagrant, it is the duty of the court to fix a penalty which shall in some degree be commensurate with the gravity of the offense. As between the two defendants, in my opinion, the principal penalty should be imposed on the corporation. The traffic manager in this case, presumably, acted without any advantage to himself and without any interest in the transaction, either by the direct authority or in accordance with what he understood to be the policy or the wishes of his employer.

"The sentence of this court in this case is, that the defendant Pomeroy, for each of the six offenses upon which he has been convicted, be fined the sum of $1,000, making six fines, amounting in all to the sum of $6,000; and the defendant, The New York Central and Hudson River Railroad Company, for each of the six crimes of which it has been convicted, be fined the sum of $18,000, making six fines amounting in the aggregate to the sum of $108,000, and judgment to that effect will be entered in this case."

In connection with this matter, I would like to call attention to the very unsatisfactory state of our criminal law, resulting in large part from the habit of setting aside the judgments of inferior courts on technicalities absolutely unconnected with the merits of the case, and where there is no attempt to show that there has been any failure of substantial justice. It would be well to enact a law providing something to the effect that:

No judgment shall be set aside or new trial granted in any cause, civil or criminal, on the ground of misdirection of the jury or the improper admission or rejection of evidence, or for error as to any matter of pleading or procedure unless, in the opinion of the court to which the application is made, after an examination of the entire cause, it shall affirmatively appear that the error complained of has resulted in a miscarriage of justice.

In my last message I suggested the enactment of a law in connection with the issuance of injunctions, attention having been sharply drawn to the matter by the demand that the right of applying injunctions in labor cases should be wholly abolished. It is at least doubtful whether a law abolishing altogether the use of injunctions in such cases would stand the test of the courts; in which case of course the legislation would be ineffective. Moreover, I believe it would be wrong altogether to prohibit the use of injunctions. It is criminal to permit sympathy for criminals to weaken our hands in upholding the law; and if men seek to destroy life or property by mob violence there should be no impairment of the power of the courts to deal with them in the most summary and effective way possible. But so far as possible the abuse of the power should be provided against by some such law as I advocated last year.

In this matter of injunctions there is lodged in the hands of the judiciary a necessary power which is nevertheless subject to the possibility of grave abuse. It is a power that should be exercised with extreme care and should be subject to the jealous scrutiny of all men, and condemnation should be meted out as much to the judge who fails to use it boldly when necessary as to the judge who uses it wantonly or oppressively. Of course a judge strong enough to be fit for his office will enjoin any resort to violence or intimidation, especially by conspiracy, no matter what his opinion may be of the rights of the original quarrel. There must be no hesitation in dealing with disorder. But there must likewise be no such abuse of the injunctive power as is implied in forbidding laboring men to strive for their own betterment in peaceful and lawful ways; nor must the injunction be used merely to aid some big corporation in carrying out schemes for its own aggrandizement. It must be remembered that a preliminary injunction in a labor case, if granted without adequate proof (even when authority can be found to support the conclusions of law on which it is founded), may often settle the dispute between the parties; and therefore if improperly granted may do irreparable wrong. Yet there are many judges who assume a matter-of-course granting of a preliminary injunction to be the ordinary and proper judicial disposition of such cases; and there have undoubtedly been flagrant wrongs committed by judges in connection with labor disputes even within the last few years, altho I think much less often than in former years. Such judges by their unwise action immensely strengthen the hands of those who are striving entirely to do away with the power of injunction; and therefore such careless use of the injunctive process tends to threaten its very existence, for if the American people ever become convinced that this process is habitually abused, whether in matters affecting labor or in matters affecting corporations, it will be well-nigh impossible to prevent its abolition.

It may be the highest duty of a judge at any given moment to disregard, not merely the wishes of individuals of great political or financial power, but the overwhelming tide of public sentiment; and the judge who does thus disregard public sentiment when it is wrong, who brushes aside the plea of any special interest when the pleading is not founded on righteousness, performs the highest service to the country. Such a judge is deserving of all honor; and all honor can not be paid to this wise and fearless judge if we permit the growth of an absurd convention which would forbid any criticism of the judge of another type, who shows himself timid in the presence of arrogant disorder, or who on insufficient grounds grants an injunction that does grave injustice, or who in his capacity as a construer, and therefore in part a maker, of the law, in flagrant fashion thwarts the cause of decent government. The judge has a power over which no review can be exercised; he himself sits in review upon the acts of both the executive and legislative branches of the Government; save in the most extraordinary cases he is amenable only at the bar of public opinion; and it is unwise to maintain that public opinion in reference to a man with such power shall neither be exprest nor led.

The best judges have ever been foremost to disclaim any immunity from criticism. This has been true since the days of the great English Lord Chancellor Parker, who said: "Let all people be at liberty to know what I found my judgment upon; that, so when I have given it in any cause, others may be at liberty to judge of *me*." The proprieties of the case were set forth with singular clearness and good temper by Judge W. H. Taft, when a United States circuit judge, eleven years ago, in 1895:

"The opportunity freely and publicly to criticize judicial action is of vastly more importance to the body politic than the immunity of courts and judges from unjust aspersions and attack. Nothing tends more to render judges careful in their decisions and anxiously solicitous to do exact justice than the consciousness that every act of theirs is to be subjected to the intelligent scrutiny and candid criticism of their fellow-men. Such criticism is beneficial in proportion as it is fair, dispassionate, discriminating, and based on a knowledge of sound legal principles. The comments made by learned text writers and by the acute editors of the various law reviews upon judicial decisions are therefore highly useful. Such critics constitute more or less impartial tribunals of professional opinion before which each judgment is made to stand or fall on its merits, and thus exert a strong influence to secure uniformity of decision. But non-professional criticism also is by no means without its uses, even if accompanied, as it often is, by a direct attack upon the judicial fairness and motives of the occupants of the bench; for if the law is but the essence of common sense, the protest of many average men may evidence a defect in a judicial conclusion, tho based on the nicest legal reasoning and profoundest learning. The two important elements of moral character in a judge are an earnest desire to reach a just conclusion and courage to enforce it. In so far as fear of public comment does not affect the courage of a judge, but only spurs him on to search his conscience and to reach the result which approves itself to his inmost heart such comment serves a useful purpose. There are few men, whether they are judges for life or for a shorter term, who do not prefer to earn and hold the respect of all, and who can not be reached and made to pause and deliberate by hostile public criticism. In the case of judges having a life tenure, indeed, their very independence makes the right freely to comment on their decisions of greater importance, because it is the only practical and available instrument in the hands of a free people to keep such judges alive to the reasonable demands of those they serve.

"On the other hand, the danger of destroying the proper influence of judicial decisions by creating unfounded prejudice against the courts justifies and requires that unjust attacks shall be met and answered. Courts must ultimately rest their defense upon the inherent strength of the opinions they deliver as the ground for their conclusions and must trust to the calm and deliberate judgment of all the people as their best vindication."

There is one consideration which should be taken into account by the good people who carry a sound proposition to an excess in objecting to any criticism of a judge's decision. The instinct of the American people as a whole is sound in this matter. They will not subscribe to the doctrine that any public servant is to be above all criticism. If the best citizens, those most competent to express their judgment in such matters, and above all those belonging to the great and honorable profession of the bar, so profoundly influential in American life, take the position that there shall be no criticism of a judge under any circumstances, their view will not be accepted by the American people as a whole. In such event the people will turn to, and tend to accept as justifiable, the intemperate and improper criticism uttered by unworthy agitators. Surely it is a misfortune to leave to such critics a function, right, in itself, which they are certain to abuse. Just and temperate criticism, when necessary, is a safeguard against the acceptance by the people as a whole of that intemperate antagonism towards the judiciary which must be combated by every right-thinking man, and which, if it became widespread among the people at large, would constitute a dire menace to the Republic.

In connection with the delays of the law, I call your attention and the attention of the Nation to the prevalence of crime among us, and above all to the epidemic of lynching and mob violence that springs up, now in one part of our country, now in another. Each section, North, South, East, or West, has its own faults; no section can with wisdom spend its time jeering at the faults of another section; it should be busy trying to amend its own shortcomings. To deal with the crime of corruption it is necessary to have an awakened public conscience, and to supplement this by whatever legislation will add speed and certainty in the execution of the law. When we deal with lynching even more is necessary. A great many white men are lynched, but the crime is peculiarly frequent in respect to black men. The greatest existing cause of lynching is the perpetration, especially by black men, of the hideous crime of rape—the most abominable in all the category of crimes, even worse than murder. Mobs frequently avenge the commission of this crime by themselves torturing to death the man committing it; thus avenging in bestial fashion a bestial deed, and reducing themselves to a level with the criminal.

Lawlessness grows by what it feeds upon; and when mobs begin to lynch for rape they speedily extend the sphere of their operations and lynch for many other kinds of crimes, so that two-thirds of the lynchings are not for rape at all; while a considerable proportion of the individuals lynched are innocent of all crime. Governor Candler, of Georgia, stated on one occasion some years ago: "I can say of a verity that I have, within the last month, saved the lives of half a dozen innocent negroes who were pursued by the mob, and brought them to trial in a court of law in which they were acquitted." As Bishop Galloway, of Mississippi, has finely said: "When the rule of a mob obtains, that which distinguishes a high civilization is surrendered. The mob which lynches a negro charged with rape will in a little while lynch a white man suspected of crime. Every Christian patriot in America needs to lift up his voice in loud and eternal protest against the mob spirit that is threatening the integrity of this Republic." Governor Jelks, of Alabama, has recently spoken as follows: "The lynching of any person for whatever crime is inexcusable anywhere—it is a defiance of orderly government; but the killing of innocent people under any provocation is infinitely more horrible; and yet innocent people are likely to die when a mob's terrible lust is once aroused. The lesson is this: No good citizen can afford to countenance a defiance of the statutes, no matter what the provocation. The innocent frequently suffer, and, it is my observation, more usually suffer than the guilty. The white people of the South indict the whole colored race on the ground that even the better elements lend no assistance whatever in ferreting out criminals of their own color. The respectable colored people must learn not to harbor their criminals, but to assist the officers in bringing them to justice. This is the larger crime, and it provokes such atrocious offenses as the one at Atlanta. The two races can never get on until there is an understanding on the part of both to make common cause with the law-abiding against criminals of any color."

Moreover, where any crime committed by a member of one race against a member of another race is avenged in such fashion that it seems as if not the individual criminal, but the whole race, is attacked, the result is to exasperate to the highest degree race feeling. There is but one safe rule in dealing with black men as with white men; it is the same rule that must be applied in dealing with rich men and poor men; that is, to treat each man, whatever his color, his creed, or his social position, with even-handed justice on his real worth as a man. White people owe it quite as much to themselves as to the colored race to treat well the colored man who shows by his life that he deserves such treatment; for it is surely the highest wisdom to encourage in the colored race all those individuals who are honest, industrious, law-abiding, and who therefore make good and safe neighbors and citizens. Reward or punish the individual on his merits as an individual. Evil will surely come in the end to both races if we substitute for this just rule the habit of treating all the members of the race, good and bad, alike. There is no question of "social equality" or "negro domination" involved; only the question of relentlessly punishing bad men, and of securing to the good man the right to his life, his liberty, and the pursuit of his happiness as his own qualities of heart, head, and hand enable him to achieve it.

Every colored man should realize that the worst enemy of his race is the negro criminal, and above all the negro criminal who commits the dreadful crime of rape; and it should be felt as in the highest degree an offense against the whole country, and against the colored race in particular, for a colored man to fail to help the officers of the law in hunting down with all possible earnestness and zeal every such infamous offender. Moreover, in my judgment, the crime of rape should always be punished with death, as is the case with murder; assault with intent to commit rape should be made a capital crime, at least in the discretion of the court; and provision should be made by which the punishment may follow immediately upon the heels of the offense; while the trial should be so conducted that the victim need not be wantonly shamed while giving testimony, and that the least possible publicity shall be given to the details.

The members of the white race on the other hand should understand that every lynching represents by just so much a loosening of the bands of civilization; that the spirit of lynching inevitably throws into prominence in the community all the foul and evil creatures who dwell therein. No man can take part in the torture of a human being without having his own moral nature permanently lowered. Every lynching means just so much moral deterioration in all the children who have any knowledge of it, and therefore just so much additional trouble for the next generation of Americans.

Let justice be both sure and swift; but let it be justice under the law, and not the wild and crooked savagery of a mob.

There is another matter which has a direct bearing upon this matter of lynching and of the brutal crime which sometimes calls it forth and at other times merely furnishes the excuse for its existence. It is out of the question for our people as a whole permanently to rise by treading down any of their own number. Even those who themselves for the moment profit by such maltreatment of their fellows will in the long run also suffer. No more shortsighted policy can be imagined than, in the fancied interest of one class, to prevent the education of another class. The free public school, the chance for each boy or girl to get a good elementary education, lies at the foundation of our whole political situation. In every community the poorest citizens, those who need the schools most, would be deprived of them if they only received school facilities proportioned to the taxes they paid. This is as true of one portion of our country as of another. It is as true for the negro as for the white man. The white man, if he is wise, will decline to allow the negroes in a mass to grow to manhood and womanhood without education. Unquestionably education such as is obtained in our public schools does not do everything towards making a man a good citizen; but it does much. The lowest and most brutal criminals, those for instance who commit the crime of rape, are in the great majority men who have had either no education or very little; just as they are almost invariably men who own no property; for the man who puts money by out of his earnings, like the man who acquires education, is usually lifted above mere brutal criminality. Of course the best type of education for the colored man, taken as a whole, is such education as is conferred in schools like Hampton and Tuskegee; where the boys and girls, the young men and young women, are trained industrially as well as in the ordinary public school branches. The graduates of these schools turn out well in the great majority of cases, and hardly any of them become criminals, while what little criminality there is never takes the form of that brutal violence which invites lynch law. Every graduate of these schools—and for the matter of that every other colored man or woman—who leads a life so useful and honorable as to win the good will and respect of those whites whose neighbor he or she is, thereby helps the whole colored race as it can be helped in no other way; for next to the negro himself, the man who can do most to help the negro is his white neighbor who lives near him; and our steady effort should be to better the relations between the two. Great tho the benefit of these schools has been to their colored pupils and to the colored people, it may well be questioned whether the benefit has not been at least as great to the white people among whom these colored pupils live after they graduate.

Be it remembered, furthermore, that the individuals who, whether from folly, from evil temper, from greed for office, or in a spirit of mere base demagogy, indulge in the inflammatory and incendiary speeches and writings which tend to arouse mobs and to bring about lynching, not only thus excite the mob, but also tend by what criminologists call "suggestion," greatly to increase the likelihood of a repetition of the very crime against which they are inveighing. When the mob is composed of the people of one race and the man lynched is of another race, the men who in their speeches and writings either excite or justify the action tend, of course, to excite a bitter race feeling and to cause the people of the opposite race to lose sight of the abominable act of the criminal himself; and in addition, by the prominence they give to the hideous deed they undoubtedly tend to excite in other brutal and depraved natures thoughts of committing it. Swift, relentless, and orderly punishment under the law is the only way by which criminality of this type can permanently be supprest.

In dealing with both labor and capital, with the questions affecting both corporations and trades unions, there is one matter more important to remember than aught else, and that is the infinite harm done by preachers of mere discontent. These are the men who seek to excite a violent class hatred against all men of wealth. They seek to turn wise and proper movements for the better control of corporations and for doing away with the abuses connected with wealth, into a campaign of hysterical excitement and falsehood in which the aim is to inflame to madness the brutal passions of mankind. The sinister demagogs and foolish visionaries who are always eager to undertake such a campaign of destruction sometimes seek to associate themselves with those working for a genuine reform in governmental and social methods, and sometimes masquerade as such reformers. In reality they are the worst enemies of the cause they profess to advocate, just as the purveyors of sensational slander in newspaper or magazine are the worst enemies of all men who are engaged in an honest effort to better what is bad in our social and governmental conditions. To preach hatred of the rich man as such, to carry on a campaign of slander and invective against him, to seek to mislead and inflame to madness honest men whose lives are hard and who have not the kind of mental training which will permit them to appreciate the danger in the doctrines preached—all this is to commit a crime against the body politic and to be false to every worthy principle and tradition of American national life. Moreover, while such preaching and such agitation may give a livelihood and a certain notoriety to some of those who take part in it, and may result in the temporary political success of others, in the long run every such movement will either fail or else will provoke a violent reaction, which will itself result not merely in undoing the mischief wrought by the demagog and the agitator, but also in undoing the good that the honest reformer, the true upholder of popular rights, has painfully and laboriously achieved. Corruption is never so rife as in communities where the demagog and the agitator bear full sway, because in such communities all moral bands become loosened, and hysteria and sensationalism replace the spirit of sound judgment and fair dealing as between man and man.. In sheer revolt against the squalid anarchy thus produced men are sure in the end to turn toward any leader who can restore order, and then their relief at being free from the intolerable burdens of class hatred, violence, and demagogy is such that they can not for some time be aroused to indignation against misdeeds by men of wealth; so that they permit a new growth of the very abuses which were in part responsible for the original outbreak. The one hope for success for our people lies in a resolute and fearless, but sane and cool-headed, advance along the path marked out last year by this very Congress. There must be a stern refusal to be misled into following either that base creature who appeals and panders to the lowest instincts and passions in order to arouse one set of Americans against their fellows, or that other creature, equally base but no baser, who in a spirit of greed, or to accumulate or add to an already huge fortune, seeks to exploit his fellow-Americans with callous disregard to their welfare of soul and body. The man who debauches others in order to obtain a high office stands on an evil equality of corruption with the man who debauches others for financial profit; and when hatred is sown the crop which springs up can only be evil.

The plain people who think—the mechanics, farmers, merchants, workers with head or hand, the men to whom American traditions are dear, who love their country and try to act decently by their neighbors, owe it to themselves to remember that the most damaging blow that can be given popular government is to elect an unworthy and sinister agitator on a platform of violence and hypocrisy. Whenever such an issue is raised in this country nothing can be gained by flinching from it, for in such case democracy is itself on trial, popular self-government under republican forms is itself on trial. The triumph of the mob is just as evil a thing as the triumph of the plutocracy, and to have escaped one danger avails nothing whatever if we succumb to the other. In the end the honest man, whether rich or poor, who earns his own living and tries to deal justly by his fellows, has as much to fear from the insincere and unworthy demagog, promising much and performing nothing, or else performing nothing but evil, who would set on the mob to plunder the rich, as from the crafty corruptionist, who, for his own ends, would permit the common people to be exploited by the very wealthy. If we ever let this Government fall into the hands of men of either of these two classes, we shall show ourselves false to America's past. Moreover, the demagog and the corruptionist often work hand in hand. There are at this moment wealthy reactionaries of such obtuse morality that they regard the public servant who prosecutes them when they violate the law, or who seeks to make them bear their proper share of the public burdens, as being even more objectionable than the violent agitator who hounds on the mob to plunder the rich. There is nothing to choose between such a reactionary and such an agitator; fundamentally they are alike in their selfish disregard of the rights of others; and it is natural that they should join in opposition to any movement of which the aim is fearlessly to do exact and even justice to all.

I call your attention to the need of passing the bill limiting the number of hours of employment of railroad employees. The measure is a very moderate one and I can conceive of no serious objection to it. Indeed, so far as it is in our power, it should be our aim steadily to reduce the number of hours of labor, with as a goal the general introduction of an eight-hour day. There are industries in which it is not possible that the hours of labor should be reduced; just as there are communities not far enough advanced for such a movement to be for their good, or, if in the Tropics, so situated that there is no analogy between their needs and ours in this matter. On the Isthmus of Panama, for instance, the conditions are in every way so different from what they are here that an eight-hour day would be absurd; just as it is absurd, so far as the Isthmus is concerned, where white labor can not be employed, to bother as to whether the necessary work is done by alien black men or by alien yellow men. But the wageworkers of the United States are of so high a grade that alike from the merely industrial standpoint and from the civic standpoint it should be our object to do what we can in the direction of securing the general observance of an eight-hour day. Until recently the eight-hour law on our Federal statute books has been very scantily observed. Now, however, largely thru the instrumentality of the Bureau of Labor, it is being rigidly enforced, and I shall speedily be able to say whether or not there is need of further legislation in reference thereto; for our purpose is to see it obeyed in spirit no less than in letter. Half holidays during summer should be established for Government employees; it is as desirable for wageworkers who toil with their hands as for salaried officials whose labor is mental that there should be a reasonable amount of holiday.

The Congress at its last session wisely provided for a truant court for the District of Columbia; a marked step in advance on the path of properly caring for the children. Let me again urge that the Congress provide for a thoro investigation of the conditions of child labor and of the labor of women in the United States. More and more our people are growing to recognize the fact that the questions which are not merely of industrial but of social importance outweigh all others; and these two questions most emphatically come in the category of those which affect in the most far-reaching way the home life of the Nation. The horrors incident to the employment of young children in factories or at work anywhere are a blot on our civilization. It is true that each State must ultimately settle the question in its own way; but a thoro official investigation of the matter, with the results published broadcast, would greatly help toward arousing the public conscience and securing unity of State action in the matter. There is, however, one law on the subject which should be enacted immediately, because there is no need for an investigation in reference thereto, and the failure to enact it is discreditable to the National Government. A drastic and thorogoing child-labor law should be enacted for the District of Columbia and the Territories.

Among the excellent laws which the Congress past at the last session was an employers' liability law. It was a marked step in advance to get the recognition of employers' liability on the statute books; but the law did not go far enough. In spite of all precautions exercised by employers there are unavoidable accidents and even deaths involved in nearly every line of business connected with the mechanic arts. This inevitable sacrifice of life may be reduced to a minimum, but it can not be completely eliminated. It is a great social injustice to compel the employee, or rather the family of the killed or disabled victim, to bear the entire burden of such an inevitable sacrifice. In other words, society shirks its duty by laying the whole cost on the victim, whereas the injury comes from what may be called the legitimate risks of the trade. Compensation for accidents or deaths due in any line of industry to the actual conditions under which that industry is carried on, should be paid by that portion of the community for the benefit of which the industry is carried on—that is, by those who profit by the industry. If the entire trade risk is placed upon the employer he will promptly and properly add it to the legitimate cost of production and assess it proportionately upon the consumers of his commodity. It is therefore clear to my mind that the law should place this entire "risk of a trade" upon the employer. Neither the Federal law, nor, as far as I am informed, the State laws dealing with the question of employers' liability are sufficiently thorogoing. The Federal law should of course include employees in navy-yards, arsenals, and the like.

The commission appointed by the President October 16, 1902, at the request of both the anthracite coal operators and miners, to inquire into, consider, and pass upon the questions in controversy in connection with the strike in the anthracite regions of Pennsylvania and the causes out of which the controversy arose, in their report, findings, and award exprest the belief "that the State and Federal governments should provide the machinery for what may be called the compulsory investigation of controversies between employers and employees when they arise." This expression of belief is deserving of the favorable consideration of the Congress and the enactment of its provisions into law. A bill has already been introduced to this end.

Records show that during the twenty years from January 1, 1881, to December 31, 1900, there were strikes affecting 117,509 establishments, and 6,105,694 employees were thrown out of employment. During the same period there were 1,005 lockouts, involving nearly 10,000 establishments, throwing over one million people out of employment. These strikes and lockouts involved an estimated loss to employees of $307,000,000 and to employers of $143,000,000, a total of $450,000,000. The public suffered directly and indirectly probably as great additional loss. But the money loss, great as it was, did not measure the anguish and suffering endured by the wives and children of employees whose pay stopt when their work stopt, or the disastrous effect of the strike or lockout upon the business of employers, or the increase in the cost of products and the inconvenience and loss to the public.

Many of these strikes and lockouts would not have occurred had the parties to the dispute been required to appear before an unprejudiced body representing the nation and, face to face, state the reasons for their contention. In most instances the dispute would doubtless be found to be due to a misunderstanding by each of the other's rights, aggravated by an unwillingness of either party to accept as true the statements of the other as to the justice or injustice of the matters in dispute. The exercise of a judicial spirit by a disinterested body representing the Federal Government, such as would be provided by a commission on conciliation and arbitration, would tend to create an atmosphere of friendliness and conciliation between contending parties; and the giving each side an equal opportunity to present fully its case in the presence of the other would prevent many disputes from developing into serious strikes or lockouts, and, in other cases, would enable the commission to persuade the opposing parties to come to terms.

In this age of great corporate and labor combinations, neither employers nor employees should be left completely at the mercy of the stronger party to a dispute, regardless of the righteousness of their respective claims. The proposed measure would be in the line of securing recognition of the fact that in many strikes the public has itself an interest which can not wisely be disregarded; an interest not merely of general convenience, for the question of a just and proper public policy must also be considered. In all legislation of this kind it is well to advance cautiously, testing each step by the actual results; the step proposed can surely be safely taken, for the decisions of the commission would not bind the parties in legal fashion, and yet would give a chance for public opinion to crystallize and thus to exert its full force for the right.

It is not wise that the Nation should alienate its remaining coal lands. I have temporarily withdrawn from settlement all the lands which the Geological Survey has indicated as containing, or in all probability containing, coal. The question, however, can be properly settled only by legislation, which in my judgment should provide for the withdrawal of these lands from sale or from entry, save in certain especial circumstances. The ownership would then remain in the United States, which should not, however, attempt to work them, but permit them to be worked by private individuals under a royalty system, the Government keeping such control as to permit it to see that no excessive price was charged consumers. It would, of course, be as necessary to supervise the rates charged by the common carriers to transport the product as the rates charged by those who mine it; and the supervision must extend to the conduct of the common carriers, so that they shall in no way favor one competitor at the expense of another. The withdrawal of these coal lands would constitute a policy analogous to that which has been followed in withdrawing the forest lands from ordinary settlement. The coal, like the forests, should be treated as the property of the public and its disposal should be under conditions which would inure to the benefit of the public as a whole.

The present Congress has taken long strides in the direction of securing proper supervision and control by the National Government over corporations engaged in interstate business—and the enormous majority of corporations of any size are engaged in interstate business. The passage of the railway rate bill, and only to a less degree the passage of the pure food bill, and the provision for increasing and rendering more effective national control over the beef-packing industry, mark an important advance in the proper direction. In the short session it will perhaps be difficult to do much further along this line; and it may be best to wait until the laws have been in operation for a number of months before endeavoring to increase their scope, because only operation will show with exactness their merits and their shortcomings and thus give opportunity to define what further remedial legislation is needed. Yet in my judgment it will in the end be advisable in connection with the packing house inspection law to provide for putting a date on the label and for charging the cost of inspection to the packers. All these laws have already justified their enactment. The interstate commerce law, for instance, has rather amusingly falsified the predictions, both of those who asserted that it would ruin the railroads and of those who asserted that it did not go far enough and would accomplish nothing. During the last five months the railroads have shown increased earnings and some of them unusual dividends; while during the same period the mere taking effect of the law has produced an unprecedented, a hitherto unheard of, number of voluntary reductions in freights and fares by the railroads. Since the founding of the Commission there has never been a time of equal length in which anything like so many reduced tariffs have been put into effect. On August 27, for instance, two days before the new law went into effect, the Commission received notices of over five thousand separate tariffs which represented reductions from previous rates.

It must not be supposed, however, that with the passage of these laws it will be possible to stop progress along the line of increasing the power of the National Government over the use of capital in interstate commerce. For example, there will ultimately be need of enlarging the powers of the Interstate Commerce Commission along several different lines, so as to give it a larger and more efficient control over the railroads.

It can not too often be repeated that experience has conclusively shown the impossibility of securing by the actions of nearly half a hundred different State legislatures anything but ineffective chaos in the way of dealing with the great corporations which do not operate exclusively within the limits of any one State. In some method, whether by a national license law or in other fashion, we must exercise, and that at an early date, a far more complete control than at present over these great corporations—a control that will among other things prevent the evils of excessive overcapitalization, and that will compel the disclosure by each big corporation of its stockholders and of its properties and business, whether owned directly or thru subsidiary or affiliated corporations. This will tend to put a stop to the securing of inordinate profits by favored individuals at the expense whether of the general public, the stockholders, or the wageworkers. Our effort should be not so much to prevent consolidation as such, but so to supervise and control it as to see that it results in no harm to the people. The reactionary or ultraconservative apologists for the misuse of wealth assail the effort to secure such control as a step toward socialism. As a matter of fact it is these reactionaries and ultraconservatives who are themselves most potent in increasing socialistic feeling. One of the most efficient methods of averting the consequences of a dangerous agitation, which is 80 per cent wrong, is to remedy the 20 per cent of evil as to which the agitation is well founded. The best way to avert the very undesirable move for the government ownership of railways is to secure by the Government on behalf of the people as a whole such adequate control and regulation of the great interstate common carriers as will do away with the evils which give rise to the agitation against them. So the proper antidote to the dangerous and wicked agitation against the men of wealth as such is to secure by proper legislation and executive action the abolition of the grave abuses which actually do obtain in connection with the business use of wealth under our present system—or rather no system—of failure to exercise any adequate control at all. Some persons speak as if the exercise of such governmental control would do away with the freedom of individual initiative and dwarf individual effort. This is not a fact. It would be a veritable calamity to fail to put a premium upon individual initiative, individual capacity and effort; upon the energy, character, and foresight which it is so important to encourage in the individual. But as a matter of fact the deadening and degrading effect of pure socialism, and especially of its extreme form communism, and the destruction of individual character which they would bring about, are in part achieved by the wholly unregulated competition which results in a single individual or corporation rising at the expense of all others until his or its rise effectually checks all competition and reduces former competitors to a position of utter inferiority and subordination.

In enacting and enforcing such legislation as this Congress already has to its credit, we are working on a coherent plan, with the steady endeavor to secure the needed reform by the joint action of the moderate men, the plain men who do not wish anything hysterical or dangerous, but who do intend to deal in resolute common-sense fashion with the real and great evils of the present system. The reactionaries and the violent extremists show symptoms of joining hands against us. Both assert, for instance, that, if logical, we should go to government ownership of railroads and the like; the reactionaries, because on such an issue they think the people would stand with them, while the extremists care rather to preach discontent and agitation than to achieve solid results. As a matter of fact, our position is as remote from that of the Bourbon reactionary as from that of the impracticable or sinister visionary. We hold that the Government should not conduct the business of the nation, but that it should exercise such supervision as will insure its being conducted in the interest of the nation. Our aim is, so far as may be, to secure, for all decent, hard working men, equality of opportunity and equality of burden.

The actual working of our laws has shown that the effort to prohibit all combination, good or bad, is noxious where it is not ineffective. Combination of capital like combination of labor is a necessary element of our present industrial system. It is not possible completely to prevent it; and if it were possible, such complete prevention would do damage to the body politic. What we need is not vainly to try to prevent all combination, but to secure such rigorous and adequate control and supervision of the combinations as to prevent their injuring the public, or existing in such form as inevitably to threaten injury—for the mere fact that a combination has secured practically complete control of a necessary of life would under any circumstances show that such combination was to be presumed to be adverse to the public interest. It is unfortunate that our present laws should forbid all combinations, instead of sharply discriminating between those combinations which do good and those combinations which do evil. Rebates, for instance, are as often due to the pressure of big shippers (as was shown in the investigation of the Standard Oil Company and as has been shown since by the investigation of the tobacco and sugar trusts) as to the initiative of big railroads. Often railroads would like to combine for the purpose of preventing a big shipper from maintaining improper advantages at the expense of small shippers and of the general public. Such a combination, instead of being forbidden by law, should be favored. In other words, it should be permitted to railroads to make agreements, provided these agreements were sanctioned by the Interstate Commerce Commission and were published. With these two conditions complied with it is impossible to see what harm such a combination could do to the public at large. It is a public evil to have on the statute books a law incapable of full enforcement because both judges and juries realize that its full enforcement would destroy the business of the country; for the result is to make decent railroad men violators of the law against their will, and to put a premium on the behavior of the wilful wrongdoers. Such a result in turn tends to throw the decent man and the wilful wrongdoer into close association, and in the end to drag down the former to the latter's level; for the man who becomes a lawbreaker in one way unhappily tends to lose all respect for law and to be willing to break it in many ways. No more scathing condemnation could be visited upon a law than is contained in the words of the Interstate Commerce Commission when, in commenting upon the fact that the numerous joint traffic associations do technically violate the law, they say: "The decision of the United States Supreme Court in the Trans-Missouri case and the Joint Traffic Association case has produced no practical effect upon the railway operations of the country. Such associations, in fact, exist now as they did before these decisions, and with the same general effect. In justice to all parties, we ought probably to add that it is difficult to see how our interstate railways could be operated with due regard to the interest of the shipper and the railway without concerted action of the kind afforded thru these associations."

This means that the law as construed by the Supreme Court is such that the business of the country can not be conducted without breaking it. I recommend that you give careful and early consideration to this subject, and if you find the opinion of the Interstate Commerce

Commission justified, that you amend the law so as to obviate the evil disclosed.

The question of taxation is difficult in any country, but it is especially difficult in ours with its Federal system of government. Some taxes should on every ground be levied in a small district for use in that district. Thus the taxation of real estate is peculiarly one for the immediate locality in which the real estate is found. Again, there is no more legitimate tax for any State than a tax on the franchises conferred by that State upon street railroads and similar corporations which operate wholly within the State boundaries, sometimes in one and sometimes in several municipalities or other minor divisions of the State. But there are many kinds of taxes which can only be levied by the General Government so as to produce the best results, because, among other reasons, the attempt to impose them in one particular State too often results merely in driving the corporation or individual affected to some other locality or other State. The National Government has long derived its chief revenue from a tariff on imports and from an internal or excise tax. In addition to these there is every reason why, when next our system of taxation is revised, the National Government should impose a graduated inheritance tax, and, if possible, a graduated income tax. The man of great wealth owes a peculiar obligation to the State, because he derives special advantages from the mere existence of government. Not only should he recognize this obligation in the way he leads his daily life and in the way he earns and spends his money, but it should also be recognized by the way in which he pays for the protection the State gives him. On the one hand, it is desirable that he should assume his full and proper share of the burden of taxation; on the other hand, it is quite as necessary that in this kind of taxation, where the men who vote the tax pay but little of it, there should be clear recognition of the danger of inaugurating any such system save in a spirit of entire justice and moderation. Whenever we, as a people, undertake to remodel our taxation system along the lines suggested, we must make it clear beyond peradventure that our aim is to distribute the burden of supporting the Government more equitably than at present; that we intend to treat rich man and poor man on a basis of absolute equality. and that we regard it as equally fatal to true democracy to do or permit injustice to the one as to do or permit injustice to the other.

I am well aware that such a subject as this needs long and careful study in order that the people may become familiar with what is proposed to be done, may clearly see the necessity of proceeding with wisdom and self-restraint, and may make up their minds just how far they are willing to go in the matter; while only trained legislators can work out the project in necessary detail. But I feel that in the near future our national legislators should enact a law providing for a graduated inheritance tax by which a steadily increasing rate of duty should be put upon all moneys or other valuables coming by gift, bequest, or devise to any individual or corporation. It may be well to make the tax heavy in proportion as the individual benefited is remote of kin. In any event, in my judgment the pro rata of the tax should increase very heavily with the increase of the amount left to any one individual after a certain point has been reached. It is most desirable to encourage thrift and ambition, and a potent source of thrift and ambition is the desire on the part of the breadwinner to leave his children well off. This object can be attained by making the tax very small on moderate amounts of property left; because the prime object should be to put a constantly increasing burden on the inheritance of those swollen fortunes which it is certainly of no benefit to this country to perpetuate.

There can be no question of the ethical propriety of the Government thus determining the conditions upon which any gift or inheritance should be received. Exactly how far the inheritance tax would, as an incident, have the effect of limiting the transmission by devise or gift of the enormous fortunes in question it is not necessary at present to discuss. It is wise that progress in this direction should be gradual. At first a permanent national inheritance tax, while it might be more substantial than any such tax has hitherto been, need not approximate, either in amount or in the extent of the increase by graduation, to what such a tax should ultimately be.

This species of tax has again and again been imposed, altho only temporarily, by the National Government. It was first imposed by the act of July 6, 1797, when the makers of the Constitution were alive and at the head of affairs. It was a graduated tax; tho small in amount, the rate was increased with the amount left to any individual, exceptions being made in the case of certain close kin. A similar tax was again imposed by the act of July 1, 1862; a minimum sum of one thousand dollars in personal property being excepted from taxation, the tax then becoming progressive according to the remoteness of kin. The war-revenue act of June 13, 1898, provided for an inheritance tax on any sum exceeding the value of ten thousand dollars, the rate of the tax increasing both in accordance with the amounts left and in accordance with the legatee's remoteness of kin. The Supreme Court has held that the succession tax imposed at the time of the Civil War was not a direct tax but an impost or excise which was both constitutional and valid. More recently the Court, in an opinion delivered by Mr. Justice White, which contained an exceedingly able and elaborate discussion of the powers of the Congress to impose death duties, sustained the constitutionality of the inheritance-tax feature of the war-revenue act of 1898.

In its incidents, and apart from the main purpose of raising revenue, an income tax stands on an entirely different footing from an inheritance tax; because it involves no question of the perpetuation of fortunes swollen to an unhealthy size. The question is in its essence a question of the proper adjustment of burdens to benefits. As the law now stands it is undoubtedly difficult to devise a national income tax which shall be constitutional. But whether it is absolutely impossible is another question; and if possible it is most certainly desirable. The first purely income-tax law was past by the Congress in 1861, but the most important law dealing with the subject was that of 1894. This the court held to be unconstitutional.

The question is undoubtedly very intricate, delicate, and troublesome. The decision of the court was only reached by one majority. It is the law of the land, and of course is accepted as such and loyally obeyed by all good citizens. Nevertheless, the hesitation evidently felt by the court as a whole in coming to a conclusion, when considered together with the previous decisions on the subject, may perhaps indicate the possibility of devising a constitutional income-tax law which shall substantially accomplish the results aimed at. The difficulty of amending the Constitution is so great that only real necessity can justify a resort thereto. Every effort should be made in dealing with this subject, as with the subject of the proper control by the National Government over the use of corporate wealth in interstate business, to devise legislation which without such action shall attain the desired end; but if this fails, there will ultimately be no alternative to a constitutional amendment.

It would be impossible to overstate (tho it is of course difficult quantitatively to measure) the effect upon a nation's growth to greatness of what may be called organized patriotism, which necessarily includes the substitution of a national feeling for mere local pride; with as a resultant a high ambition for the whole country. No country can develop its full strength so long as the parts which make up the whole each put a feeling of loyalty to the part above the feeling of loyalty to the whole. This is true of sections and it is just as true of classes. The industrial and agricultural classes must work together, capitalists and wageworkers must work together, if the best work of which the country is capable is to be done. It is probable that a thoroly efficient system of education comes next to the influence of patriotism in bringing about national success of this kind. Our federal form of government, so fruitful of advantage to our people in certain ways, in other ways undoubtedly limits our national effectiveness. It is not possible, for instance, for the National Government

By the President of the United States of America.

A PROCLAMATION

WHEREAS by a Joint Resolution approved the 30th day of May, 1908, it is provided

"That the twelfth day of February, nineteen hundred and nine,

the same being the centennial anniversary of the birth of

Abraham Lincoln, be and the same is hereby, made a special

legal holiday in the District of Columbia and the Territo-

ries of the United States";

AND WHEREAS by the said Joint Resolution the President

is authorized to issue a proclamation in accordance with the

foregoing setting apart the twelfth day of February, nineteen

hundred and nine, as a special legal holiday;

NOW, THEREFORE, I, THEODORE ROOSEVELT, President of the

United States of America, in virtue of the authority conferred

upon me by the said Joint Resolution, do hereby set apart the

twelfth day of February, nineteen hundred and nine, as a

special legal holiday.

ROOSEVELT'S PROCLAMATION OF SPECIAL HOLIDAY FOR
CELEBRATION OF CENTENNIAL OF LINCOLN'S BIRTH.

IN WITNESS WHEREOF, I have hereunto set my

hand and caused the seal of the United States to be affixed.

DONE at the City of Washington this eleventh day

of February in the year of our Lord one thou-

sand nine hundred and nine, and of the

Independence of the United States

the one hundred and thirty-

third.

Theodore Roosevelt

By the President:

Robert Bacon

Secretary of State.

LAST PAGE AND SIGNATURE OF ROOSEVELT'S ANNOUNCEMENT
OF CENTENNIAL OF LINCOLN'S BIRTH.

to take the lead in technical industrial education, to see that the public school system of this country develops on all its technical, industrial, scientific, and commercial sides. This must be left primarily to the several States. Nevertheless, the National Government has control of the schools of the District of Columbia, and it should see that these schools promote and encourage the fullest development of the scholars in both commercial and industrial training. The commercial training should in one of its branches deal with foreign trade. The industrial training is even more important. It should be one of our prime objects as a Nation, so far as feasible, constantly to work toward putting the mechanic, the wageworker who works with his hands, on a higher plane of efficiency and reward, so as to increase his effectiveness in the economic world, and the dignity, the remuneration, and the power of his position in the social world. Unfortunately, at present the effect of some of the work in the public schools is in the exactly opposite direction. If boys and girls are trained merely in literary accomplishments, to the total exclusion of industrial, manual, and technical training, the tendency is to unfit them for industrial work and to make them reluctant to go into it, or unfitted to do well if they do go into it. This is a tendency which should be strenuously combated. Our industrial development depends largely upon technical education, including in this term all industrial education, from that which fits a man to be a good mechanic, a good carpenter, or blacksmith, to that which fits a man to do the greatest engineering feat. The skilled mechanic, the skilled workman, can best become such by technical industrial education. The far-reaching usefulness of institutes of technology and schools of mines or of engineering is now universally acknowledged, and no less far-reaching is the effect of a good building or mechanical trades school, a textile, or watchmaking, or engraving school. All such training must develop not only manual dexterity but industrial intelligence. In international rivalry this country does not have to fear the competition of pauper labor as much as it has to fear the educated labor of specially trained competitors; and we should have the education of the hand, eye, and brain which will fit us to meet such competition.

In every possible way we should help the wageworker who toils with his hands and who must (we hope in a constantly increasing measure) also toil with his brain. Under the Constitution the National Legislature can do but little of direct importance for his welfare save where he is engaged in work which permits it to act under the interstate commerce clause of the Constitution; and this is one reason why I so earnestly hope that both the legislative and judicial branches of the Government will construe this clause of the Constitution in the broadest possible manner. We can, however, in

224

such a matter as industrial training, in such a matter as child labor and factory laws, set an example to the States by enacting the most advanced legislation that can wisely be enacted for the District of Columbia.

The only other persons whose welfare is as vital to the welfare of the whole country as is the welfare of the wageworkers are the tillers of the soil, the farmers. It is a mere truism to say that no growth of cities, no growth of wealth, no industrial development can atone for any falling off in the character and standing of the farming population. During the last few decades this fact has been recognized with ever-increasing clearness. There is no longer any failure to realize that farming, at least in certain branches, must become a technical and scientific profession. This means that there must be open to farmers the chance for technical and scientific training, not theoretical merely but of the most severely practical type. The farmer represents a peculiarly high type of American citizenship, and he must have the same chance to rise and develop as other American citizens have. Moreover, it is exactly as true of the farmer, as it is of the business man and the wageworker, that the ultimate success of the Nation of which he forms a part must be founded not alone on material prosperity but upon high moral, mental, and physical development. This education of the farmer—self-education by preference, but also education from the outside, as with all other men—is peculiarly necessary here in the United States, where the frontier conditions even in the newest States have now nearly vanished, where there must be a substitution of a more intensive system of cultivation for the old wasteful farm management, and where there must be a better business organization among the farmers themselves.

Several factors must cooperate in the improvement of the farmer's condition. He must have the chance to be educated in the widest possible sense—in the sense which keeps ever in view the intimate relationship between the theory of education and the facts of life. In all education we should widen our aims. It is a good thing to produce a certain number of trained scholars and students; but the education superintended by the State must seek rather to produce a hundred good citizens than merely one scholar, and it must be turned now and then from the class book to the study of the great book of nature itself. This is especially true of the farmer, as has been pointed out again and again by all observers most competent to pass practical judgment on the problems of our country life. All students now realize that education must seek to train the executive powers of young people and to confer more real significance upon the phrase "dignity of labor," and to prepare the pupils so that, in addition to each developing in the highest degree his individual capacity for work, they may together help create a right public opinion, and show in many ways social and cooperative spirit. Organization has become necessary in the business world; and it has accomplished much for good in the world of labor. It is no less necessary for farmers. Such a movement as the grange movement is good in itself and is capable of a well-nigh infinite further extension for good so long as it is kept to its own legitimate business. The benefits to be derived by the association of farmers for mutual advantage are partly economic and partly sociological.

Moreover, while in the long run voluntary effort will prove more efficacious than government assistance, while the farmers must primarily do most for themselves, yet the Government can also do much. The Department of Agriculture has broken new ground in many directions, and year by year it finds how it can improve its methods and develop fresh usefulness. Its constant effort is to give the governmental assistance in the most effective way; that is, thru associations of farmers rather than to or thru individual farmers. It is also striving to coordinate its work with the agricultural departments of the several States, and so far as its own work is educational to coordinate it with the work of other educational authorities. Agricultural education is necessarily based upon general education, but our agricultural educational institutions are wisely specializing themselves, making their courses relate to the actual teaching of the agricultural and kindred sciences to young country people or young city people who wish to live in the country.

Great progress has already been made among farmers by the creation of farmers' institutes, of dairy associations, of breeders' associations, horticultural associations, and the like. A striking example of how the Government and the farmers can cooperate is shown in connection with the menace offered to the cotton growers of the Southern States by the advance of the boll weevil. The Department is doing all it can to organize the farmers in the threatened districts, just as it has been doing all it can to organize them in aid of its work to eradicate the cattle fever tick in the South. The Department can and will cooperate with all such associations, and it must have their help if its own work is to be done in the most efficient style.

Much is now being done for the States of the Rocky Mountains and Great Plains thru the development of the national policy of irrigation and forest preservation; no Government policy for the betterment of our internal conditions has been more fruitful of good than this. The forests of the White Mountains and Southern Appalachian regions should also be preserved; and they can not be unless the people of the States in which they lie, thru their representatives in the Congress, secure vigorous action by the National Government.

I invite the attention of the Congress to the estimate of the Secretary of War for an appropriation to enable him to begin the preliminary work for the construction of a memorial amphitheater at Arlington. The Grand Army of the Republic in its national encampment has urged the erection of such an amphitheater as necessary for the proper observance of Memorial Day and as a fitting monument to the soldier and sailor dead buried there. In this I heartily concur and commend the matter to the favorable consideration of the Congress.

I am well aware of how difficult it is to pass a constitutional amendment, Nevertheless in my judgment the whole question of marriage and divorce should be relegated to the authority of the National Congress. At present the wide differences in the laws of the different States on this subject result in scandals and abuses; and surely there is nothing so vitally essential to the welfare of the nation, nothing around which the nation should so bend itself to throw every safeguard, as the home life of the average citizen. The change would be good from every standpoint. In particular it would be good because it would confer on the Congress the power at once to deal radically and efficiently with polygamy; and this should be done whether or not marriage and divorce are dealt with. It is neither safe nor proper to leave the question of polygamy to be dealt with by the several States. Power to deal with it should be conferred on the National Government.

When home ties are loosened; when men and women cease to regard a worthy family life, with all its duties fully performed, and all its responsibilities lived up to, as the life best worth living; then evil days for the commonwealth are at hand. There are regions in our land, and classes of our population, where the birth rate has sunk below the death rate. Surely it should need no demonstration to show that wilful sterility is, from the standpoint of the nation, from the standpoint of the human race, the one sin for which the penalty is national death, race death; a sin for which there is no atonement; a sin which is the more dreadful exactly in proportion as the men and women guilty thereof are in other respects, in character, and bodily and mental powers, those whom for the sake of the state it would be well to see the fathers and mothers of many healthy children, well brought up in homes made happy by their presence. No man, no woman, can shirk the primary duties of life, whether for love of ease and pleasure, or for any other cause, and retain his or her self-respect.

Let me once again call the attention of the Congress to two subjects concerning which I have frequently before communicated with them. One is the question of developing American shipping. I trust that a law embodying in substance the views, or a major part of the views, exprest in the report on this subject laid before the House at its last session will be past. I am well aware that in former years objectionable measures have been proposed in reference to the encouragement of American shipping; but it seems to me that the proposed measure is as nearly unobjectionable as any can be. It will of course benefit primarily our seaboard States, such as Maine, Louisiana, and Washington; but what benefits part of our people in the end benefits all; just as Government aid to irrigation and forestry in the West is really of benefit, not only to the Rocky Mountain States, but to all our country. If it prove impracticable to enact a law for the encouragement of shipping generally, then at least provision should be made for better communication with South America, notably for fast mail lines to the chief South American ports. It is discreditable to us that our business people, for lack of direct communication in the shape of lines of steamers with South America, should in that great sister continent be at a disadvantage compared to the business people of Europe.

I especially call your attention to the second subject, the condition of our currency laws. The national bank act has ably served a great purpose in aiding the enormous business development of the country; and within ten years there has been an increase in circulation per capita from $21.41 to $33.08. For several years evidence has been accumulating that additional legislation is needed. The recurrence of each crop season emphasizes the defects of the present laws. There must soon be a revision of them, because to leave them as they are means to incur liability of business disaster. Since your body adjourned there has been a fluctuation in the interest on call money from 2 per cent to 30 per cent; and the fluctuation was even greater during the preceding six months. The Secretary of the Treasury had to step in and by wise action put a stop to the most violent period of oscillation. Even worse than such fluctuation is the advance in commercial rates and the uncertainty felt in the sufficiency of credit even at high rates. All commercial interests suffer during each crop period. Excessive rates for call money in New York attract money from the interior banks into the speculative field; this depletes the fund that would otherwise be available for commercial uses, and commercial borrowers are forced to pay abnormal rates; so that each fall a tax, in the shape of increased interest charges, is placed on the whole commerce of the country.

The mere statement of these facts shows that our present system is seriously defective. There is need of a change. Unfortunately, however, many of the proposed changes must be ruled from consideration because they are complicated, are not easy of comprehension, and tend to disturb existing rights and interests. We must also rule out any plan which would materially impair the value of the United States

2 per cent bonds now pledged to secure circulation, the issue of which was made under conditions peculiarly creditable to the Treasury. I do not press any especial plan. Various plans have recently been proposed by expert committees of bankers. Among the plans which are possibly feasible and which certainly should receive your consideration is that repeatedly brought to your attention by the present Secretary of the Treasury, the essential features of which have been approved by many prominent bankers and business men. According to this plan national banks should be permitted to issue a specified proportion of their capital in notes of a given kind, the issue to be taxed at so high a rate as to drive the notes back when not wanted in legitimate trade. This plan would not permit the issue of currency to give banks additional profits, but to meet the emergency presented by times of stringency.

I do not say that this is the right system. I only advance it to emphasize my belief that there is need for the adoption of some system which shall be automatic and open to all sound banks, so as to avoid all possibility of discrimination and favoritism. Such a plan would tend to prevent the spasms of high money and speculation which now obtain in the New York market; for at present there is too much currency at certain seasons of the year, and its accumulation at New York tempts bankers to lend it at low rates for speculative purposes; whereas at other times when the crops are being moved there is urgent need for a large but temporary increase in the currency supply. It must never be forgotten that this question concerns business men generally quite as much as bankers; especially is this true of stockmen, farmers, and business men in the West; for at present at certain seasons of the year the difference in interest rates between the East and the West is from 6 to 10 per cent, whereas in Canada the corresponding difference is but 2 per cent. Any plan must, of course, guard the interests of western and southern bankers as carefully as it guards the interests of New York or Chicago bankers; and must be drawn from the standpoints of the farmer and the merchant no less than from the standpoints of the city banker and the country banker.

The law should be amended so as specifically to provide that the funds derived from customs duties may be treated by the Secretary of the Treasury as he treats funds obtained under the internal-revenue laws. There should be a considerable increase in bills of small denominations. Permission should be given banks, if necessary under settled restrictions, to retire their circulation to a larger amount than three millions a month.

I most earnestly hope that the bill to provide a lower tariff for or else absolute free trade in Philippine products will become a law. No harm will come to any American industry; and while there will be some small but real material benefit to the Filipinos, the main benefit will come by the showing made as to our purpose to do all in our power for their welfare. So far our action in the Philippines has been abundantly justified, not mainly and indeed not primarily because of the added dignity it has given us as a nation by proving that we are capable honorably and efficiently to bear the international burdens which a mighty people should bear, but even more because of the immense benefit that has come to the people of the Philippine Islands. In these islands we are steadily introducing both liberty and order, to a greater degree than their people have ever before known. We have secured justice. We have provided an efficient police force, and have put down ladronism. Only in the islands of Leyte and Samar is the authority of our Government resisted and this by wild mountain tribes under the superstitious inspiration of fakirs and pseudo-religious leaders. We are constantly increasing the measure of liberty accorded the islanders, and next spring, if conditions warrant, we shall take a great stride forward in testing their capacity for self-government by summoning the first Filipino legislative assembly; and the way in which they stand this test will largely determine whether the self-government thus granted will be increased or decreased; for if we have erred at all in the Philippines it has been in proceeding too rapidly in the direction of granting a large measure of self-government. We are building roads. We have, for the immeasurable good of the people, arranged for the building of railroads. Let us also see to it that they are given free access to our markets. This nation owes no more imperative duty to itself and mankind than the duty of managing the affairs of all the islands under the American flag—the Philippines, Porto Rico, and Hawaii—so as to make it evident that it is in every way to their advantage that the flag should fly over them.

American citizenship should be conferred on the citizens of Porto Rico. The harbor of San Juan in Porto Rico should be dredged and improved. The expenses of the federal court of Porto Rico should be met from the Federal Treasury. The administration of the affairs of Porto Rico, together with those of the Philippines, Hawaii, and our other insular possessions, should all be directed under one executive department; by preference the Department of State or the Department of War.

The needs of Hawaii are peculiar; every aid should be given the islands; and our efforts should be unceasing to develop them along the lines of a community of small freeholders, not of great planters with coolie-tilled estates. Situated as this Territory is, in the middle of the Pacific, there are duties imposed upon this small community which do not fall in like degree or manner upon any other American community. This warrants our treating it differently from the way in which we treat Territories contiguous to or surrounded by sister Territories or other States, and justifies the setting aside of a portion of our revenues to be expended for educational and internal improvements therein. Hawaii is now making an effort to secure immigration fit in the end to assume the duties and burdens of full American citizenship, and whenever the leaders in the various industries of those islands finally adopt our ideals and heartily join our administration in endeavoring to develop a middle class of substantial citizens, a way will then be found to deal with the commercial and industrial problems which now appear to them so serious. The best Americanism is that which aims for stability and permanency of prosperous citizenship, rather than immediate returns on large masses of capital.

Alaska's needs have been partially met, but there must be a complete reorganization of the governmental system, as I have before indicated to you. I ask your especial attention to this. Our fellow-citizens who dwell on the shores of Puget Sound with characteristic energy are arranging to hold in Seattle the Alaska Yukon Pacific Exposition. Its special aims include the upbuilding of Alaska and the development of American commerce on the Pacific Ocean. This exposition, in its purposes and scope, should appeal not only to the people of the Pacific slope, but to the people of the United States at large. Alaska since it was bought has yielded to the Government eleven millions of dollars of revenue, and has produced nearly three hundred millions of dollars in gold, furs, and fish. When properly developed it will become in large degree a land of homes. The countries bordering the Pacific Ocean have a population more numerous than that of all the countries of Europe; their annual foreign commerce amounts to over three billions of dollars, of which the share of the United States is some seven hundred millions of dollars. If this trade were thoroly understood and pushed by our manufacturers and producers, the industries not only of the Pacific slope, but of all our country, and particularly of our cotton-growing States, would be greatly benefited. Of course, in order to get these benefits, we must treat fairly the countries with which we trade.

It is a mistake, and it betrays a spirit of foolish cynicism, to maintain that all international governmental action is, and must ever be, based upon mere selfishness, and that to advance ethical reasons for such action is always a sign of hypocrisy. This is no more necessarily true of the action of governments than of the action of individuals. It is a sure sign of a base nature always to ascribe base motives for the actions of others. Unquestionably no nation can afford to disregard proper considerations of self-interest, any more than a private individual can so do. But it is equally true that the average private individual in any really decent community does many actions with reference to other men

In which he is guided, not by self-interest, but by public spirit, by regard for the rights of others, by a disinterested purpose to do good to others, and to raise the tone of the community as a whole. Similarly, a really great nation must often act, and as a matter of fact often does act, toward other nations in a spirit not in the least of mere self-interest, but paying heed chiefly to ethical reasons; and as the centuries go by this disinterestedness in international action, this tendency of the individuals comprizing a nation to require that nation to act with justice toward its neighbors, steadily grows and strengthens. It is neither wise nor right for a nation to disregard its own needs, and it is foolish --and may be wicked--to think that other nations will disregard theirs. But it is wicked for a nation only to regard its own interest, and foolish to believe that such is the sole motive that actuates any other nation. It should be our steady aim to raise the ethical standard of national action just as we strive to raise the ethical standard of individual action.

Not only must we treat all nations fairly, but we must treat with justice and good will all immigrants who come here under the law. Whether they are Catholic or Protestant, Jew or Gentile; whether they come from England or Germany, Russia, Japan, or Italy, matters nothing. All we have a right to question is the man's conduct. If he is honest and upright in his dealings with his neighbor and with the State, then he is entitled to respect and good treatment. Especially do we need to remember our duty to the stranger within our gates. It is the sure mark of a low civilization, a low morality, to abuse or discriminate against or in any way humiliate such stranger who has come here lawfully and who is conducting himself properly. To remember this is incumbent on every American citizen, and it is of course peculiarly incumbent on every Government official, whether of the nation or of the several States.

I am prompted to say this by the attitude of hostility here and there assumed toward the Japanese in this country. This hostility is sporadic and is limited to a very few places. Nevertheless, it is most discreditable to us as a people, and it may be fraught with the gravest consequences to the nation. The friendship between the United States and Japan has been continuous since the time, over half a century ago, when Commodore Perry, by his expedition to Japan, first opened the islands to western civilization. Since then the growth of Japan has been literally astounding. There is not only nothing to parallel it, but nothing to approach it in the history of civilized mankind. Japan has a glorious and ancient past. Her civilization is older than that of the nations of northern Europe—the nations from whom the people of the United States have chiefly sprung. But fifty years ago Japan's development was still that of the Middle Ages. During that fifty years the

progress of the country in every walk in life has been a marvel to mankind, and she now stands as one of the greatest of civilized nations;
great in the arts of war and in the arts of peace; great in military, in
industrial, in artistic development and achievement.   Japanese soldiers
and sailors have shown themselves equal in combat to any of whom
history makes note.   She has produced great generals and mighty
admirals; her fighting men, afloat and ashore, show all the heroic courage, the unquestioning, unfaltering loyalty, the splendid indifference
to hardship and death, which marked the Loyal Ronins; and they show
also that they possess the highest ideal of patriotism.   Japanese artists
of every kind see their products eagerly sought for in all lands.   The
industrial and commercial development of Japan has been phenomenal;
greater than that of any other country during the same period.   At the
same time the advance in science and philosophy is no less marked.
The admirable management of the Japanese Red Cross during the late
war, the efficiency and humanity of the Japanese officials, nurses, and
doctors, won the respectful admiration of all acquainted with the facts.
Thru the Red Cross the Japanese people sent over $100,000 to the
sufferers of San Francisco, and the gift was accepted with gratitude
by our people.   The courtesy of the Japanese, nationally and individually, has become proverbial.   To no other country has there been such
an increasing number of visitors from this land as to Japan.   In return,
Japanese have come here in great numbers.   They are welcome, socially
and intellectually, in all our colleges and institutions of higher learning,
in all our professional and social bodies.   The Japanese have won in a
single generation the right to stand abreast of the foremost and most
enlightened peoples of Europe and America; they have won on their
own merits and by their own exertions the right to treatment on a basis
of full and frank equality.   The overwhelming mass of our people
cherish a lively regard and respect for the people of Japan, and in
almost every quarter of the Union the stranger from Japan is treated
as he deserves; that is, he is treated as the stranger from any part of
civilized Europe is and deserves to be treated.   But here and there a
most unworthy feeling has manifested itself toward the Japanese—the
feeling that has been shown in shutting them out from the common
schools in San Francisco, and in mutterings against them in one or
two other places, because of their efficiency as workers.   To shut them
out from the public schools is a wicked absurdity, when there are no
first-class colleges in the land, including the universities and colleges of
California, which do not gladly welcome Japanese students and on
which Japanese students do not reflect credit.   We have as much to
learn from Japan as Japan has to learn from us; and no nation is fit
to teach unless it is also willing to learn.   Thruout Japan Americans are
well treated, and any failure on the part of Americans at home to treat

the Japanese with a like courtesy and consideration is by just so much a confession of inferiority in our civilization.

Our nation fronts on the Pacific, just as it fronts on the Atlantic. We hope to play a constantly growing part in the great ocean of the Orient. We wish, as we ought to wish, for a great commercial development in our dealings with Asia; and it is out of the question that we should permanently have such development unless we freely and gladly extend to other nations the same measure of justice and good treatment which we expect to receive in return. It is only a very small body of our citizens that act badly. Where the National Government has power it will deal summarily with any such. Where the several States have power I earnestly ask that they also deal wisely and promptly with such conduct, or else this small body of wrongdoers may bring shame upon the great mass of their innocent and right-thinking fellows—that is, upon our nation as a whole. Good manners should be an international no less than an individual attribute. I ask fair treatment for the Japanese as I would ask fair treatment for Germans or Englishmen, Frenchmen, Russians, or Italians. I ask it as due to humanity and civilization. I ask it as due to ourselves because we must act uprightly toward all men.

I recommend to the Congress that an act be past specifically providing for the naturalization of Japanese who come here intending to become American citizens. One of the great embarrassments attending the performance of our international obligations is the fact that the Statutes of the United States are entirely inadequate. They fail to give to the National Government sufficiently ample power, thru United States courts and by the use of the Army and Navy, to protect aliens in the rights secured to them under solemn treaties which are the law of the land. I therefore earnestly recommend that the criminal and civil statutes of the United States be so amended and added to as to enable the President, acting for the United States Government, which is responsible in our international relations, to enforce the rights of aliens under treaties. Even as the law now is something can be done by the Federal Government toward this end, and in the matter now before me affecting the Japanese everything that it is in my power to do will be done, and all of the forces, military and civil, of the United States which I may lawfully employ will be so employed. There should, however, be no particle of doubt as to the power of the National Government completely to perform and enforce its own obligations to other nations. The mob of a single city may at any time perform acts of lawless violence against some class of foreigners which would plunge us into war. That city by itself would be powerless to make defense against the foreign power thus assaulted, and if independent of this Government it would never venture to perform or permit the performance of the acts complained of. The entire power and the whole duty to protect the offending city or the offending community lies in the hands of the United States Government. It is unthinkable that we should continue a policy under which a given locality may be allowed to commit a crime against a friendly nation, and the United States Government limited, not to preventing the commission of the crime, but, in the last resort, to defending the people who have committed it against the consequences of their own wrongdoing.

Last August an insurrection broke out in Cuba which it speedily grew evident that the existing Cuban Government was powerless to quell. This Government was repeatedly asked by the then Cuban Government to intervene, and finally was notified by the President of Cuba that he intended to resign; that his decision was irrevocable; that none of the other constitutional officers would consent to carry on the Government, and that he was powerless to maintain order. It was evident that chaos was impending, and there was every probability that if steps were not immediately taken by this Government to try to restore order the representatives of various European nations in the island would apply to their respective governments for armed intervention in order to protect the lives and property of their citizens. Thanks to the preparedness of our Navy, I was able immediately to send enough ships to Cuba to prevent the situation from becoming hopeless; and I furthermore dispatched to Cuba the Secretary of War and the Assistant Secretary of State, in order that they might grapple with the situation on the ground. All efforts to secure an agreement between the contending factions, by which they should themselves come to an amicable understanding and settle upon some modus vivendi—some provisional government of their own—failed. Finally the President of the Republic resigned. The quorum of Congress assembled failed by deliberate purpose of its members, so that there was no power to act on his resignation, and the Government came to a halt. In accordance with the so-called Platt amendment, which was embodied in the constitution of Cuba, I thereupon proclaimed a provisional government for the island, the Secretary of War acting as provisional governor until he could be replaced by Mr. Magoon, the late minister to Panama and governor of the Canal Zone on the Isthmus; troops were sent to support them and to relieve the Navy, the expedition being handled with most satisfactory speed and efficiency. The insurgent chiefs immediately agreed that their troops should lay down their arms and disband; and the agreement was carried out. The provisional government has left the personnel of the old government and the old laws, so far as might be, unchanged, and will thus administer the island for a few months until tranquillity can be restored, a new election properly held, and a new government inaugurated. Peace has come in the island; and the harvesting of the sugar-cane crop, the great crop of the island, is about to proceed.

When the election has been held and the new government inaugu-rated in peaceful and orderly fashion the provisional government will come to an end. I take this opportunity of expressing upon behalf of the American people, with all possible solemnity, our most earnest hope that the people of Cuba will realize the imperative need of preserving justice and keeping order in the Island. The United States wishes nothing of Cuba except that it shall prosper morally and materially, and wishes nothing of the Cubans save that they shall be able to preserve order among themselves and therefore to preserve their independence. If the elections become a farce, and if the insurrectionary habit be-comes confirmed in the Island, it is absolutely out of the question that the Island should continue independent; and the United States, which has assumed the sponsorship before the civilized world for Cuba's career as a nation, would again have to intervene and to see that the government was managed in such orderly fashion as to secure the safety of life and property. The path to be trodden by those who exercise self-government is always hard, and we should have every charity and patience with the Cubans as they tread this difficult path. I have the utmost sympathy with, and regard for, them; but I most earnestly adjure them solemnly to weigh their responsibilities and to see that when their new government is started it shall run smoothly, and with freedom from flagrant denial of right on the one hand, and from insur-rectionary disturbances on the other.

The Second International Conference of American Republics, held in Mexico in the years 1901-2, provided for the holding of the third conference within five years, and committed the fixing of the time and place and the arrangements for the conference to the governing board of the Bureau of American Republics, composed of the representatives of all the American nations in Washington. That board discharged the duty imposed upon it with marked fidelity and painstaking care, and upon the courteous invitation of the United States of Brazil the conference was held at Rio de Janeiro, continuing from the 23d of July to the 29th of August last. Many subjects of common interest to all the American nations were discust by the conference, and the con-clusions reached, embodied in a series of resolutions and proposed con-ventions, will be laid before you upon the coming in of the final report of the American delegates. They contain many matters of importance relating to the extension of trade, the increase of communication, the smoothing away of barriers to free intercourse, and the promotion of a better knowlege and good understanding between the different countries represented. The meetings of the conference were harmonious and the conclusions were reached with substantial unanimity. It is interesting to observe that in the successive conferences which have been held the representatives of the different American nations have been learning to work together effectively, for, while the First Conference in Washington in 1889, and the Second Conference in Mexico in 1901-2, occupied many months, with much time wasted in an unregulated and fruitless discussion, the Third Conference at Rio exhibited much of the facility in the practical dispatch of business which characterizes permanent deliberative bodies, and completed its labors within the period of six weeks originally allotted for its sessions.

Quite apart from the specific value of the conclusions reached by the conference, the example of the representatives of all the American nations engaging in harmonious and kindly consideration and discussion of subjects of common interest is itself of great and substantial value for the promotion of reasonable and considerate treatment of all international questions. The thanks of this country are due to the Government of Brazil and to the people of Rio de Janeiro for the generous hospitality with which our delegates, in common with the others, were received, entertained, and facilitated in their work.

Incidentally to the meeting of the conference, the Secretary of State visited the city of Rio de Janeiro and was cordially received by the conference, of which he was made an honorary president. The announcement of his intention to make this visit was followed by most courteous and urgent invitations from nearly all the countries of South America to visit them as the guest of their Governments. It was deemed that by the acceptance of these invitations we might appropriately express the real respect and friendship in which we hold our sister Republics of the southern continent, and the Secretary, accordingly, visited Brazil, Uruguay, Argentina, Chile, Peru, Panama, and Colombia. He refrained from visiting Paraguay, Bolivia, and Ecuador only because the distance of their capitals from the seaboard made it impracticable with the time at his disposal. He carried with him a message of peace and friendship, and of strong desire for good understanding and mutual helpfulness; and he was everywhere received in the spirit of his message. The members of government, the press, the learned professions, the men of business, and the great masses of the people united everywhere in emphatic response to his friendly expressions and in doing honor to the country and cause which he represented.

In many parts of South America there has been much misunderstanding of the attitude and purposes of the United States towards the other American Republics. An idea had become prevalent that our assertion of the Monroe Doctrine implied, or carried with it, an assumption of superiority, and of a right to exercise some kind of protectorate over the countries to whose territory that doctrine applies.

Nothing could be farther from the truth. Yet that impression continued to be a serious barrier to good understanding, to friendly intercourse, to the introduction of American capital and the extension of American trade. The impression was so widespread that apparently it could not be reached by any ordinary means.

It was part of Secretary Root's mission to dispel this unfounded impression, and there is just cause to believe that he has succeeded. In an address to the Third Conference at Rio on the 31st of July—an address of such note that I send it in, together with this message—he said:

"We wish for no victories but those of peace, for no territory except our own; for no sovereignty except the sovereignty over ourselves. We deem the independence and equal rights of the smallest and weakest member of the family of nations entitled to as much respect as those of the greatest empire, and we deem the observance of that respect the chief guaranty of the weak against the oppression of the strong. We neither claim nor desire any rights or privileges or powers that we do not freely concede to every American Republic. We wish to increase our prosperity, to extend our trade, to grow in wealth, in wisdom, and in spirit, but our conception of the true way to accomplish this is not to pull down others and profit by their ruin, but to help all friends to a common prosperity and a common growth, that we may all become greater and stronger together. Within a few months for the first time the recognized possessors of every foot of soil upon the American continents can be and I hope will be represented with the acknowledged rights of equal sovereign states in the great World Congress at The Hague. This will be the world's formal and final acceptance of the declaration that no part of the American continents is to be deemed subject to colonization. Let us pledge ourselves to aid each other in the full performance of the duty to humanity which that accepted declaration implies, so that in time the weakest and most unfortunate of our Republics may come to march with equal step by the side of the stronger and more fortunate. Let us help each other to show that for all the races of men the liberty for which we have fought and labored is the twin sister of justice and peace. Let us unite in creating and maintaining and making effective an all-American public opinion, whose power shall influence international conduct and prevent international wrong, and narrow the causes of war, and forever preserve our free lands from the burden of such armaments as are massed behind the frontiers of Europe, and bring us ever nearer to the perfection of ordered liberty. So shall come security and prosperity, production and trade, wealth, learning, the arts, and happiness for us all."

These words appear to have been received with acclaim in every part of South America. They have my hearty approval, as I am sure they will have yours, and I can not be wrong in the conviction that they correctly represent the sentiments of the whole American people. I can not better characterize the true attitude of the United States in its assertion of the Monroe Doctrine than in the words of the distinguished former minister of foreign affairs of Argentina, Doctor Drago, in his speech welcoming Mr. Root at Buenos Ayres. He spoke of—

"The traditional policy of the United States (which) without accentuating superiority or seeking preponderance, condemned the oppression of the nations of this part of the world and the control of their destinies by the great Powers of Europe."

It is gratifying to know that in the great city of Buenos Ayres, upon the arches which spanned the streets, entwined with Argentine and American flags for the reception of our representative, there were emblazoned not only the names of Washington and Jefferson and Marshall, but also, in appreciative recognition of their services to the cause of South American independence, the names of James Monroe, John Quincy Adams, Henry Clay, and Richard Rush. We take especial pleasure in the graceful courtesy of the Government of Brazil, which has given to the beautiful and stately building first used for the meeting of the conference the name of "Palacio Monroe." Our grateful acknowledgments are due to the Governments and the people of all the countries visited by the Secretary of State for the courtesy, the friendship, and the honor shown to our country in their generous hospitality to him.

In my message to you on the 5th of December, 1905, I called your attention to the embarrassment that might be caused to this Government by the assertion by foreign nations of the right to collect by force of arms contract debts due by American republics to citizens of the collecting nation, and to the danger that the process of compulsory collection might result in the occupation of territory tending to become permanent. I then said:

"Our own Government has always refused to enforce such contractual obligations on behalf of its citizens by an appeal to arms. It is much to be wisht that all foreign governments would take the same view."

This subject was one of the topics of consideration at the conference at Rio and a resolution was adopted by that conference recommending to the respective governments represented "to consider the advisability of asking the Second Peace Conference at The Hague to examine the question of the compulsory collection of public debts, and, in general, means tending to diminish among nations conflicts of purely pecuniary origin."

This resolution was supported by the representatives of the United States in accordance with the following instructions:

"It has long been the established policy of the United States not to use its armed forces for the collection of ordinary contract debts due to its citizens by other governments. We have not considered the use of force for such a purpose consistent with that respect for the independent sovereignty of other members of the family of nations which is the most important principle of international law and the chief protection of weak nations against the oppression of the strong. It seems to us that the practise is injurious in its general effect upon the relations of nations and upon the welfare of weak and disordered states, whose development ought to be encouraged in the interests of civilization; that it offers frequent temptation to bullying and oppression and to unnecessary and unjustifiable warfare. We regret that other powers, whose opinions and sense of justice we esteem highly, have at times taken a different view and have permitted themselves, tho we believe with reluctance, to collect such debts by force. It is doubtless true that the non-payment of public debts may be accompanied by such circumstances of fraud and wrongdoing or violation of treaties as to justify the use of force. This Government would be glad to see an international consideration of the subject which shall discriminate between such cases and the simple nonperformance of a contract with a private person, and a resolution in favor of reliance upon peaceful means in cases of the latter class.

"It is not felt, however, that the conference at Rio should undertake to make such a discrimination or to resolve upon such a rule. Most of the American countries are still debtor nations, while the countries of Europe are the creditors. If the Rio conference, therefore, were to take such action it would have the appearance of a meeting of debtors resolving how their creditors should act, and this would not inspire respect. The true course is indicated by the terms of the program, which proposes to request the Second Hague Conference, where both creditors and debtors will be assembled, to consider the subject."

Last June trouble which had existed for some time between the Republics of Salvador, Guatemala, and Honduras culminated in war— a war which threatened to be ruinous to the countries involved and very destructive to the commercial interests of Americans, Mexicans, and other foreigners who are taking an important part in the development of these countries. The thoroly good understanding which exists between the United States and Mexico enabled this Government and that of Mexico to unite in effective mediation between the warring Republics; which mediation resulted, not without long-continued and patient effort, in bringing about a meeting of the representatives of the hostile powers on board a United States warship as neutral territory, and peace was there concluded; a peace which resulted in the saving of thousands of lives and in the prevention of an incalculable amount of misery and the destruction of property and of the means of livelihood. The Rio Conference past the following resolution in reference to this action:

"That the Third International American Conference shall address to the Presidents of the United States of America and of the United States of Mexico a note in which the conference which is being held at Rio expresses its satisfaction at the happy results of their mediation for the celebration of peace between the Republics of Guatemala, Honduras, and Salvador."

This affords an excellent example of one way in which the influence of the United States can properly be exercised for the benefit of the peoples of the Western Hemisphere; that is, by action taken in concert with other American republics and therefore free from those suspicions and prejudices which might attach if the action were taken by one alone. In this way it is possible to exercise a powerful influence toward the substitution of considerate action in the spirit of justice for the insurrectionary or international violence which has hitherto been so great a hindrance to the development of many of our neighbors. Repeated examples of united action by several or many American republics in favor of peace, by urging cool and reasonable, instead of excited and belligerent, treatment of international controversies, can not fail to promote the growth of a general public opinion among the American nations which will elevate the standards of international action, strengthen the sense of international duty among governments, and tell in favor of the peace of mankind.

I have just returned from a trip to Panama and shall report to you at length later on the whole subject of the Panama Canal.

The Algeciras Convention, which was signed by the United States as well as by most of the powers of Europe, supersedes the previous convention of 1880, which was also signed both by the United States and a majority of the European powers. This treaty confers upon us equal commercial rights with all European countries and does not entail a single obligation of any kind upon us, and I earnestly hope it may be speedily ratified. To refuse to ratify it would merely mean that we forfeited our commercial rights in Morocco and would not achieve another object of any kind. In the event of such refusal we would be left for the first time in a hundred and twenty years without any commercial treaty with Morocco; and this at a time when we are everywhere seeking new markets and outlets for trade.

The destruction of the Pribilof Islands fur seals by pelagic sealing still continues. The herd which, according to the surveys made in 1874 by direction of the Congress, numbered 4,700,000, and which, according to the survey of both American and Canadian commissioners in 1891, amounted to 1,000,000, has now been reduced to about 180,000. This result has been brought about by Canadian and some other sealing vessels killing the female seals while in the water during their annual pilgrimage to and from the south, or in search of food. As a rule the female seal when killed is pregnant, and also has an unweaned pup on land, so that, for each skin taken by pelagic sealing, as a rule, three lives are destroyed—the mother, the unborn offspring, and the nursing pup, which is left to starve to death. No damage whatever is done to the herd by the carefully regulated killing on land; the custom of pelagic sealing is solely responsible for all of the present evil, and is alike indefensible from the economic standpoint and from the standpoint of humanity.

In 1896 over 16,000 young seals were found dead from starvation on the Pribilof Islands. In 1897 it was estimated that since pelagic sealing began upward of 400,000 adult female seals had been killed at sea, and over 300,000 young seals had died of starvation as the result. The revolting barbarity of such a practise, as well as the wasteful destruction which it involves, needs no demonstration and is its own condemnation. The Bering Sea Tribunal, which sat in Paris in 1893, and which decided against the claims of the United States to exclusive jurisdiction in the waters of Bering Sea and to a property right in the fur seals when outside of the three-mile limit, determined also upon certain regulations which the Tribunal considered sufficient for the proper protection and preservation of the fur seal in, or habitually resorting to, the Bering Sea. The Tribunal by its regulations established a close season, from the 1st of May to the 31st of July, and excluded all killing in the waters within 60 miles around the Pribilof Islands. They also provided that the regulations which they had determined upon, with a view to the protection and preservation of the seals, should be submitted every five years to new examination, so as to enable both interested Governments to consider whether, in the light of past experience, there was occasion for any modification thereof.

The regulations have proved plainly inadequate to accomplish the object of protection and preservation of the fur seals, and for a long time this Government has been trying in vain to secure from Great Britain such revision and modification of the regulations as were contemplated and provided for by the award of the Tribunal of Paris.

The process of destruction has been accelerated during recent years by the appearance of a number of Japanese vessels engaged in pelagic sealing. As these vessels have not been bound even by the inadequate limitations prescribed by the Tribunal of Paris, they have paid no attention either to the close season or to the sixty-mile limit imposed upon the Canadians, and have prosecuted their work up to the very islands themselves. On July 16 and 17 the crews from several Japanese vessels made raids upon the island of St. Paul, and before they were beaten off by the very meager and insufficiently armed guard, they succeeded in killing several hundred seals and carrying off the skins of most of them. Nearly all the seals killed were females and the work was done with frightful barbarity. Many of the seals appear to have been skinned alive and many were found half skinned and still alive. The raids were repelled only by the use of firearms, and five of the raiders were killed, two were wounded, and twelve captured, including the two wounded. Those captured have since been tried and sentenced to imprisonment. An attack of this kind had been wholly unlookt for, but such provision of vessels, arms, and ammunition will now be made that its repetition will not be found profitable.

Suitable representations regarding the incident have been made to the Government of Japan, and we are assured that all practicable measures will be taken by that country to prevent any recurrence of the outrage. On our part, the guard on the island will be increased and better equipped and organized, and a better revenue-cutter patrol service about the islands will be established; next season a United States war vessel will also be sent there.

We have not relaxed our efforts to secure an agreement with Great Britain for adequate protection of the seal herd, and negotiations with Japan for the same purpose are in progress.

The laws for the protection of the seals within the jurisdiction of the United States need revision and amendment. Only the islands of St. Paul and St. George are now, in terms, included in the Government reservation, and the other islands are also to be included. The landing of aliens as well as citizens upon the islands, without a permit from the Department of Commerce and Labor, for any purpose except in case of stress of weather or for water, should be prohibited under adequate penalties. The approach of vessels for the excepted purposes should be regulated. The authority of the Government agents on the islands should be enlarged, and the chief agent should have the powers of a committing magistrate. The entrance of a vessel into the territorial waters surrounding the islands with intent to take seals should be made a criminal offense and cause of forfeiture. Authority for seizures in such cases should be given and the presence on any such vessel of seals or sealskins, or the paraphernalia for taking them, should be made *prima facie* evidence of such intent. I recommend what legislation is needed to accomplish these ends; and I commend to your attention the report of Mr. Sims, of the Department of Commerce and Labor, on this subject.

In case we are compelled to abandon the hope of making arrangements with other governments to put an end to the hideous cruelty now incident to pelagic sealing, it will be a question for your serious consideration how far we should continue to protect and maintain the seal herd on land with the result of continuing such a practise, and whether it is not better to end the practise by exterminating the herd ourselves in the most humane way possible.

In my last message I advised you that the Emperor of Russia had taken the initiative in bringing about a second peace conference at The Hague. Under the guidance of Russia the arrangement of the preliminaries for such a conference has been progressing during the past year. Progress has necessarily been slow, owing to the great number of countries to be consulted upon every question that has arisen. It is a matter of satisfaction that all of the American Republics have now, for the first time, been invited to join in the proposed conference.

The close connection between the subjects to be taken up by the Red Cross Conference held at Geneva last summer and the subjects which naturally would come before The Hague Conference made it apparent that it was desirable to have the work of the Red Cross Conference completed and considered by the different powers before the meeting at The Hague. The Red Cross Conference ended its labors on the 6th day of July, and the revised and amended convention, which was signed by the American delegates, will be promptly laid before the Senate.

By the special and highly appreciated courtesy of the Governments of Russia and the Netherlands, a proposal to call The Hague Conference together at a time which would conflict with the Conference of the American Republics at Rio de Janeiro in August was laid aside. No other date has yet been suggested. A tentative program for the conference has been proposed by the Government of Russia, and the subjects which it enumerates are undergoing careful examination and consideration in preparation for the conference.

It must ever be kept in mind that war is not merely justifiable, but imperative, upon honorable men, upon an honorable nation. where peace can only be obtained by the sacrifice of conscientious conviction or of national welfare. Peace is normally a great good, and normally it coincides with righteousness; but it is righteousness and not peace which should bind the conscience of a nation as it should bind the conscience of an individual; and neither a nation nor an individual can surrender conscience to another's keeping. Neither can a nation, which is an entity, and which does not die as individuals die, refrain from taking thought for the interest of the generations that are to come, no less than for the interest of the generation of to-day; and no public men have a right, whether from shortsightedness, from selfish indifference, or from sentimentality, to sacrifice national interests which are vital in character. A just war is in the long run far better for a nation's soul than the most prosperous peace obtained by acquiescence in wrong or injustice. Moreover, tho it is criminal for a nation not to prepare for war, so that it may escape the dreadful consequences of being defeated in war, yet it must always be remembered that even to be defeated in war may be far better than not to have fought at all. As has been well and finely said, a beaten nation is not necessarily a disgraced nation; but the nation or man is disgraced if the obligation to defend right is shirked.

We should as a nation do everything in our power for the cause of honorable peace. It is morally as indefensible for a nation to commit a wrong upon another nation, strong or weak, as for an individual thus to wrong his fellows. We should do all in our power to hasten the day when there shall be peace among the nations—a peace based upon justice and not upon cowardly submission to wrong. We can accomplish a good deal in this direction, but we can not accomplish everything, and the penalty of attempting to do too much would almost inevitably be to do worse than nothing; for it must be remembered that fantastic extremists are not in reality leaders of the causes which they espouse, but are ordinarily those who do most to hamper the real leaders of the cause and to damage the cause itself. As yet there is no likelihood of establishing any kind of international power, of whatever sort, which can effectively check wrongdoing, and in these circumstances it would be both a foolish and an evil thing for a great and free nation to deprive itself of the power to protect its own rights and even in exceptional cases to stand up for the rights of others. Nothing would more promote iniquity, nothing would further defer the reign upon earth of peace and righteousness, than for the free and enlightened peoples which, tho with much stumbling and many shortcomings, nevertheless strive toward justice, deliberately to render themselves powerless while leaving every despotism and barbarism armed and able to work their wicked will. The chance for the settlement of disputes peacefully, by arbitration, now depends mainly upon the possession by the nations that mean to do right of sufficient armed strength to make their purpose effective.

The United States Navy is the surest guarantor of peace which this country possesses. It is earnestly to be wisht that we would profit by the teachings of history in this matter. A strong and wise people will study its own failures no less than its triumphs, for there is wisdom to be learned from the study of both, of the mistake as well as of the success. For this purpose nothing could be more instructive than a rational study of the war of 1812, as it is told, for instance, by Captain-Mahan. There was only one way in which that war could have been avoided. If during the preceding twelve years a navy relatively as strong as that which this country now has had been built up, and an army provided relatively as good as that which the country now has, there never would have been the slightest necessity of fighting the war; and if the necessity had arisen the war would under such circumstances have ended with our speedy and overwhelming triumph. But our people during those twelve years refused to make any preparations whatever, regarding either the Army or the Navy. They saved a million or two of dollars by so doing; and in mere money paid a hundredfold for each million they thus saved during the three years of war which followed—a war which brought untold suffering upon our people, which at one time threatened the gravest national disaster, and which, in spite of the necessity of waging it, resulted merely in what was in effect a drawn battle, while the balance of defeat and triumph was almost even.

I do not ask that we continue to increase our Navy. I ask merely that it be maintained at its present strength; and this can be done only if we replace the obsolete and outworn ships by new and good ones, the equals of any afloat in any navy. To stop building ships for one year means that for that year the Navy goes back instead of forward. The old battle ship Texas, for instance, would now be of little service in a stand-up fight with a powerful adversary. The old double-turret monitors have outworn their usefulness, while it was a waste of money to build the modern single-turret monitors. All these ships should be replaced by others; and this can be done by a well-settled program of providing for the building each year of at least one first-class battle ship equal in size and speed to any that any nation is at the same time building; the armament presumably to consist of as large a number as possible of very heavy guns of one caliber, together with smaller guns to repel torpedo attack; while there should be heavy armor, turbine engines, and in short, every modern device. Of course, from time to time, cruisers, colliers, torpedo-boat destroyers or torpedo boats, will have to be built also. All this, be it remembered, would not increase our Navy, but would merely keep it at its present strength. Equally of course, the ships will be absolutely useless if the men aboard them are not so trained that they can get the best possible service out of the formidable but delicate and complicated mechanisms intrusted to their care. The marksmanship of our men has so improved during the last five years that I deem it within bounds to say that the Navy is more than twice as efficient, ship for ship, as half a decade ago. The Navy can only attain proper efficiency if enough officers and men are pro·vided, and if these officers and men are given the chance (and required to take advantage of it) to stay continually at sea and to exercise the fleets singly and above all in squadron, the exercise to be of every kind and to include unceasing practise at the guns, conducted under conditions that will test marksmanship in time of war.

In both the Army and the Navy there is urgent need that every-thing possible should be done to maintain the highest standard for the personnel, alike as regards the officers and the enlisted men. I do not believe that in any service there is a finer body of enlisted men and of junior officers than we have in both the Army and the Navy, including the Marine Corps. All possible encouragement to the enlisted men should be given, in pay and otherwise, and everything practicable done to render the service attractive to men of the right type. They should be held to the strictest discharge of their duty, and in them a spirit should be encouraged which demands not the mere performance of duty, but the performance of far more than duty, if it conduces to the honor and the interest of the American nation; and in return the amplest consideration should be theirs.

West Point and Annapolis already turn out excellent officers. We do not need to have these schools made more scholastic. On the con-trary we should never lose sight of the fact that the aim of each school is to turn out a man who shall be above everything else a fighting man. In the Army in particular it is not necessary that either the cavalry or infantry officer should have special mathematical ability. Probably in both schools the best part of the education is the high standard of character and of professional morale which it confers.

But in both services there is urgent need for the establishment of a principle of selection which will eliminate men after a certain age if they can not be promoted from the subordinate ranks, and which will bring into the higher ranks fewer men, and these at an earlier age. This principle of selection will be objected to by good men of mediocre capacity, who are fitted to do well while young in the lower posi-tions, but who are not fitted to do well when at an advanced age they come into positions of command and of great responsibility. But the desire of these men to be promoted to positions which they are not competent to fill should not weigh against the interest of the Navy and the country. At present our men, especially in the Navy, are kept far too long in the junior grades, and then, at much too advanced an age, are put quickly thru the senior grades, often not attaining to these senior grades until they are too old to be of real use in them; and if they are of real use, being put thru them so quickly that little benefit to the Navy comes from their having been in them at all.

The Navy has one great advantage over the Army in the fact that

the officers of high rank are actually trained in the continual performance of their duties; that is, in the management of the battle ships and
armored cruisers gathered into fleets. This is not true of the army
officers, who rarely have corresponding chances to exercise command
over troops under service conditions. The conduct of the Spanish
war showed the lamentable loss of life, the useless extravagance, and
the inefficiency certain to result, if during peace the high officials of
the War and Navy Departments are praised and rewarded only if
they save money at no matter what cost to the efficiency of the service,
and if the higher officers are given no chance whatever to exercise and
practise command. For years prior to the Spanish war the Secretaries of War were praised chiefly if they practised economy; which
economy, especially in connection with the quartermaster, commissary,
and medical departments, was directly responsible for most of the
mismanagement that occurred in the war itself—and parenthetically
be it observed that the very people who clamored for the misdirected
economy in the first place were foremost to denounce the mismanagement, loss, and suffering which were primarily due to this same misdirected economy and to the lack of preparation it involved. There
should soon be an increase in the number of men for our coast defenses; these men should be of the right type and properly trained;
and there should therefore be an increase of pay for certain skilled
grades, especially in the coast artillery. Money should be appropriated
to permit troops to be massed in body and exercised in maneuvers, particularly in marching. Such exercise during the summer just past has
been of incalculable benefit to the Army and should under no circumstances be discontinued. If on these practise marches and in these
maneuvers elderly officers prove unable to bear the strain, they should
be retired at once, for the fact is conclusive as to their unfitness for
war; that is, for the only purpose because of which they should be
allowed to stay in the service. It is a real misfortune to have scores
of small company or regimental posts scattered thruout the country;
the Army should be gathered in a few brigade or division posts; and
the generals should be practised in handling the men in masses. Neglect to provide for all of this means to incur the risk of future disaster
and disgrace.

The readiness and efficiency of both the Army and Navy in dealing
with the recent sudden crisis in Cuba illustrate afresh their value to
the Nation. This readiness and efficiency would have been very much
less had it not been for the existence of the General Staff in the Army
and the General Board in the Navy; both are essential to the proper
development and use of our military forces afloat and ashore. The
troops that were sent to Cuba were handled flawlessly. It was the
swiftest mobilization and dispatch of troops over sea ever accom-

plished by our Government. The expedition landed completely equipped and ready for immediate service, several of its organizations hardly remaining in Havana over night before splitting up into detachments and going to their several posts. It was a fine demonstration of the value and efficiency of the General Staff. Similarly, it was owing in large part to the General Board that the Navy was able at the outset to meet the Cuban crisis with such instant efficiency; ship after ship appearing on the shortest notice at any threatened point, while the Marine Corps in particular performed indispensable service. The Army and Navy War Colleges are of incalculable value to the two services, and they cooperate with constantly increasing efficiency and importance.

The Congress has most wisely provided for a National Board for the promotion of rifle practise. Excellent results have already come from this law, but it does not go fa enough. Our Regular Army is so small that in any great war we lould have to trust mainly to volunteers; and in such event these volunteers should already know how to shoot; for if a soldier has the fighting edge, and ability to take care of himself in the open, his efficiency on the line of battle is almost directly proportionate to excellence in marksmanship. We should establish shooting galleries in all the large public and military schools, should maintain national target ranges in different parts of the country, and should in every way encourage the formation of rifle clubs thruout all parts of the land. The little Republic of Switzerland offers us an excellent example in all matters connected with building up an efficient citizen soldiery.

THEODORE ROOSEVELT.

SEVENTH ANNUAL MESSAGE.

WHITE HOUSE, Dec. 3, 1907.

To the Senate and House of Representatives:

No nation has greater resources than ours, and I think it can be truthfully said that the citizens of no nation possess greater energy and industrial ability. In no nation are the fundamental business conditions sounder than in ours at this very moment; and it is foolish, when such is the case, for people to hoard money instead of keeping it in sound banks; for it is such hoarding that is the immediate occasion of money stringency. Moreover, as a rule, the business of our people is conducted with honesty and probity, and this applies alike to farms and factories, to railroads and banks, to all our legitimate commercial enterprises.

In any large body of men, however, there are certain to be some who are dishonest, and if the conditions are such that these men prosper or commit their misdeeds with impunity, their example is a very evil thing for the community. Where these men are business men of great sagacity and of temperament both unscrupulous and reckless, and where the conditions are such that they act without supervision or control and at first without effective check from public opinion, they delude many innocent people into making investments or embarking in kinds of business that are really unsound. When the misdeeds of these successfully dishonest men are discovered, suffering comes not only upon them, but upon the innocent men whom they have misled. It is a painful awakening, whenever it occurs; and, naturally, when it does occur those who suffer are apt to forget that the longer it was deferred the more painful it would be. In the effort to punish the guilty it is both wise and proper to endeavor so far as possible to minimize the distress of those who have been misled by the guilty. Yet it is not possible to refrain because of such distress from striving to put an end to the misdeeds that are the ultimate causes of the suffering, and, as a means to this end, where possible to punish those responsible for them. There may be honest differences of opinion as to many governmental policies; but surely there can be no such differences as to the need of unflinching perseverance in the war against successful dishonesty.

In my Message to the Congress on December 5, 1905, I said:

"If the folly of man mars the general well-being, then those who are innocent of the folly will have to pay part of the penalty incurred by those who are guilty of the folly. A panic brought on by the speculative folly of part of the business community would hurt the whole business community; but such stoppage of welfare, though it might be severe, would not be lasting. In the long run, the one vital factor in the permanent prosperity of the country is the high individual character of the average American worker, the average American citizen, no matter whether his work be mental or manual, whether he be farmer or wage-worker, business man or professional man.

"In our industrial and social system the interests of all men are so closely intertwined that in the immense majority of cases a straight-dealing man, who by his efficiency, by his ingenuity and industry, benefits himself, must also benefit others. Normally, the man of great productive capacity who becomes rich by guiding the labor of many other men does so by enabling them to produce more than they could produce without his guidance; and both he and they share in the benefit, which comes also to the public at large. The superficial fact that the sharing may be unequal must never blind us to the underlying fact that there is this sharing, and that the benefit comes in some degree to each man concerned. Normally, the wageworker, the man of small means, and the average consumer, as well as the average producer, are all alike helped by making conditions such that the man of exceptional business ability receives an exceptional reward for his ability. Something can be done by legislation to help the general prosperity; but no such help of a permanently beneficial character can be given to the less able and less fortunate save as the results of a policy which shall inure to the advantage of all industrious and efficient people who act decently; and this is only another way of saying that any benefit which comes to the less able and less fortunate must of necessity come even more to the more able and more fortunate. If, therefore, the less fortunate man is moved by envy of his more fortunate brother to strike at the conditions under which they have both, though unequally, prospered, the result will assuredly be that while damage may come to the one struck at, it will visit with an even heavier load the one who strikes the blow. Taken as a whole, we must all go up or go down together.

"Yet, while not merely admitting, but insisting upon this, it is also true that where there is no governmental restraint or supervision some of the exceptional men use their energies, not in ways that are for the common good, but in ways which tell against this common good. The fortunes amassed through corporate organization are now so large, and vest such power in those that wield them, as to make it a matter of necessity to give to the sovereign—that is, to the Government, which represents the people as a whole—some effective power of supervision over their corporate use. In order to insure a healthy social and industrial life, every big corporation should be held responsible by, and be accountable to, some sovereign strong enough to control its conduct. I am in no sense hostile to corporations. This is an age of combination, and any effort to prevent all combination will be not only useless, but in the end vicious, because of the contempt for law which the failuure to enforce law inevitably produces. We should, moreover, recognize in cordial and ample fashion the immense good effected by corporate agencies in a country such as ours, and the wealth of intellect, energy, and fidelity devoted to their service, and therefore normally to the service of the public, by their officers and directors. The corporation has come to stay, just as the trade union has come to stay. Each can do and has done great good. Each should be favored so long as it does good. But each should be sharply checked where it acts against law and justice.

" * * * The makers of our National Constitution provided especially that the regulation of interstate commerce should come within the sphere of the General Government. The arguments in favor of their taking this stand were even then overwhelming. But they are far stronger to-day, in view of the enormous development of great business agencies, usually corporate in form. Experience has shown conclusively that it is useless to try to get any adequate regulation and supervision of these great corporations by State action. Such regulation and supervision can only be effectively exercised by a sovereign whose jurisdiction is coextensive with the field of work of the corporations —that is, by the National Government. I believe that this regulation and supervision can be obtained by the enactment of law by the Congress. * * * Our steady aim should be by legislation, cautiously and carefully undertaken, but resolutely persevered in, to assert the sovereignty of the National Government by affirmative action.

"This is only in form an innovation. In substance it is merely a restoration; for from the earliest time such regulation of industrial activities has been recognized in the action of the lawmaking bodies; and all that I propose is to meet the changed conditions in such manner as will prevent the Commonwealth abdicating the power it has always possessed, not only in this country, but also in England before and since this country became a separate nation.

"It has been a misfortune that the National laws on this subject have hitherto been of a negative or prohibitive rather than an affirmative kind, and still more that they have in part sought to prohibit what could not be effectively prohibited, and have in part in their prohibitions confounded what should be allowed and what should not be allowed. It is generally useless to try to prohibit all restraint on competition, whether this restraint be reasonable or unreasonable; and where it is not useless it is generally hurtful. * * * The successful prosecution of one device to evade the law immediately develops another device to accomplish the same purpose. What is needed is not sweeping prohibition of every arrangement, good or bad, which may tend to restrict competition, but such adequate supervision and regulation as will prevent any restriction of competition from being to the detriment of the public, as well as such supervision and regulation as will prevent other abuses in no way connected with restriction of competition."

I have called your attention in these quotations to what I have already said because I am satisfied that it is the duty of the National Government to embody in action the principles thus expressed.

No small part of the trouble that we have comes from carrying to an extreme the national virtue of self-reliance, of independence in initiative and action. It is wise to conserve this virtue and to provide for its fullest exercise, compatible with seeing that liberty does not become a liberty to wrong others. Unfortunately, this is the kind of liberty that the lack of all effective regulation inevitably breeds. The founders of the Constitution provided that the National Government should have complete and sole control of interstate commerce. There was then practically no interstate business save such as was conducted by water, and this the National Government at once proceeded to regulate in thoroughgoing and effective fashion. Conditions have now so wholly changed that the interstate commerce by water is insignificant compared with the amount that goes by land, and almost all big business concerns are now engaged in interstate commerce. As a result, it can be but partially and imperfectly controlled or regulated by the action of any one of the several States; such action inevitably tending to be either too drastic or else too lax, and in either case ineffective for purposes of justice. Only the National Government can in thoroughgoing fashion exercise the needed control. This does not mean that there should be any extension of Federal authority, for such authority already exists under the Constitution in amplest and most far-reaching form; but it does mean that there should be an extension of Federal activity. This is not advocating centralization. It is merely looking facts in the face, and realizing that centralization in business has already come and can not be avoided or undone, and that the public at large can only protect itself from certain evil effects of this business centralization by providing better methods for the exercise of control through the authority already centralized in the National Government by the Constitution itself. There must be no halt in the healthy constructive course of action which this Nation has elected to pursue, and has steadily pursued, during the last six years, as shown both in the legislation of the Congress and the administration of the law by the Department of Justice. The most vital need is in connection with the railroads. As to these, in my judgment there should now be either a national incorporation act or a law licensing railway companies to engage in interstate commerce upon certain conditions. The law should be so framed as to give to the Interstate Commerce Commission power to pass upon the future issue of securities, while ample means should be provided to enable the Commission, whenever in its judgment it is necessary, to make a physical valuation of any railroad. As I stated in my Message to the Congress a year ago, railroads should be given power to enter into agreements, subject to these argreements being made public in minute detail and to the consent of the Interstate Commerce Commission being first obtained. Until the National Government assumes proper control of interstate commerce, in the exercise of the authority it already possesses, it will be impossible either to give to or to get from the railroads full justice. The railroads and all other great corporations will do well to recognize that this control must come; the only question is as to what governmental body can most wisely exercise it. The courts will determine the limits within which the Federal authority can exercise it, and there will still remain ample work within each State for the railway commission of that State; and the National Interstate Commerce Commission will work in harmony with the several State commissions, each within its own province, to achieve the desired end.

Moreover, in my judgment there should be additional legislation looking to the proper control of the great business concerns engaged in interstate business, this control to be exercised for their own benefit and prosperity no less than for the protection of investors and of the general public. As I have repeatedly said in Messages to the Congress and elsewhere experience has definitely shown not merely the unwisdom but the futility of endeavoring to put a stop to all business combinations. Modern industrial conditions are such that combination is not only necessary but inevitable. It is so in the world of business just as it is so in the world of labor, and it is as idle to desire to put an end to all corporations, to all big combinations of capital, as to desire to put an end to combinations of labor. Corporation and labor union alike have come to stay. Each if properly managed is a source of good and not evil. Whenever in either there is evil, it should be promptly held to account; but it should receive hearty encouragement so long as it is properly managed. It is profoundly immoral to put or keep on the statute books a law, nominally in the interest of public morality. that really puts a premium upon public immorality, by undertaking to forbid honest men from doing what must be done under modern business conditions, so that the law itself provides that its own infraction must be the condition precedent upon business success. To aim at the accomplishment of too much usually means the accomplishment of too little, and often the doing of positive damage. In my Message to the Congress a year ago, in speaking of the antitrust laws, I said:

"The actual working of our laws has shown that the effort to prohibit all combination, good or bad, is noxious where it is not ineffective. Combination of capital, like combination of labor, is a necessary element in our present industrial system. It is not possible completely to prevent it; and if it were possible, such complete prevention would do damage to the body politic. What we need is not vainly to try to prevent all combination, but to secure such rigorous and adequate control and supervision of the combinations as to prevent their injuring the public, or existing in such forms as inevitably to threaten injury. * * * It is unfortunate that our present laws should forbid all combinations instead of sharply discriminating between those combinations which do evil. * * * Often railroads would like to combine for the purpose of preventing a big shipper from maintaining improper advantages at the expense of small shippers and of the general public. Such a combination, instead of being forbidden by law, should be favored. * * * It is a public evil to have on the statute books a law incapable of full enforcement, because both judges and juries realize that its full enforcement would destroy the business of the country; for the result is to make decent men violators of the law against their will, and to put a premium on the behavior of the willful wrongdoers. Such a result in turn tends to throw the decent man and the willful wrongdoer into close association, and in the end to drag down the former to the latter's level; for the man who becomes a lawbreaker in one way unhappily tends to lose all respect for law and to be willing to break it in many ways. No more scathing condemnation could be visited upon a law than is contained in the words of the Interstate Commerce Commission when, in commenting upon the fact that the numerous joint traffic associations do technically violate the law, they say: 'The decision of the United States Supreme Court in the Trans-Missouri case and the Joint Traffic Association case has produced no practical effect upon the railway operations of the country. Such associations, in fact, exist now as they did before these decisions, and with the same general effect. In justice to all parties, we ought probably to add that it is difficult to see how our interstate railways could be operated with due regard to the interest of the shipper and the railway without concerted action of the kind afforded through these asociations.'

"This means that the law as construed by the Supreme Court is such that the business of the country can not be conducted without breaking it."

As I have elsewhere said:

'All this is substantially what I have said over and over again. Surely it ought not to be necessary to say that it in no shape or way represents any hostility to corporations as such. On the contrary, it means a frank recognition of the fact that combinations of capital, like combinations of labor, are a natural result of modern conditions and of our National development. As far as in my ability lies my endeavor is and will be to prevent abuse of power by either and to favor both so long as they do well. The aim of the National Government is quite as much to favor and protect honest corporations, honest business men of wealth, as to bring to justice those individuals and corporations representing dishonest methods. Most certainly there will be no relaxation by the Government authorities in the effort to get at any great railroad wrecker—any man who by clever swindling devices robs investors, oppresses wage-workers, and does injustice to the general public. But any such move as this is in the interest of nonest railway operators, of honest corporations, and of those who, when they invest their small savings in stocks and bonds, wish to be assured that these will represent money honestly expended for legiti-

JAPANESE BATTERY BOMBARDING PORT ARTHUR

THE ATTACK ON PORT ARTHUR

Port Arthur, as the eastern end of the Siberian railway, became naturally the centre of Russian influence in the Far East, and as such was the logical point for attack by the Japanese so soon as hostilities against Russia were declared. On February 8, 1904, three days after the breaking of diplomatic negotiations, Admiral Togo attacked Port Arthur from the sea, and then blockaded it, while transports had already landed troops for an attack upon the fortress by land. The Japanese land forces finally drove the Russian defenders into the city late in July, and began their assault upon the city on July 30. It was not until January 2, 1905, however, that the fortress surrendered, after a siege which produced much fierce fighting on both sides, and which taught many new lessons in the art of modern warfare. (See article Russo-Japanese War in Encyclopedic Index.)

mate business purposes. To confer upon the National Government the power for which I ask would be a check upon overcapitalization and upon the clever gamblers who benefit by overcapitalization. But it alone would mean an increase in the value, an increase in the safety of the stocks and bonds of law-abiding, honestly managed railroads, and would render it far easier to market their securities. I believe in proper publicity. There has been complaint of some of the investigations recently carried on, but those who complain should put the blame where it belongs—upon the misdeeds which are done in darkness and not upon the investigations which brought them to light The Administration is responsible for turning on the light, but it is not responsible for what the light showed. I ask for full power to be given the Federal Government, because no single State can by legislation effectually cope with these powerful corporations engaged in interstate commerce, and, while doing them full justice, exact from them in return full justice to others. The conditions of railroad activity, the conditions of our immense interstate commerce, are such as to make the Central Government alone competent to exercise full supervision and control

"The grave abuses in individual cases of railroad management in the past represent wrongs not merely to the general public, but, above all, wrongs to fair-dealing and honest corporations and men of wealth, because they excite a popular anger and distrust which from the very nature of the case tends to include in the sweep of its resentment good and bad alike. From the standpoint of the public I can not too earnestly say that as soon as the natural and proper resentment aroused by these abuses becomes indiscriminate and unthinking, it also becomes not merely unwise and unfair, but calculated to defeat the very ends which those feeling it have in view. There has been plenty of dishonest work by corporations in the past. There will not be the slightest let-up in the effort to hunt down and punish every dishonest man. But the bulk of our business is honestly done. In the natural indignation the people feel over the dishonesty, it is essential that they should not lose their heads and get drawn into an indiscriminate raid upon all corporations, all people of wealth, whether they do well or ill. Out of any such wild movement good will not come, can not come, and never has come. On the contrary, the surest way to invite reaction is to follow the lead of either demagogue or visionary in a sweeping assault upon property values and upon public confidence, which would work incalculable damage in the business world and would produce such distrust of the agitators that in the revulsion the distrust would extend to honest men who, in sincere and same fashion, are trying to remedy the evils."

The antitrust law should **not be repealed**; but it should be made both

225

more efficient and more in harmony with actual conditions. It should be so amended as to forbid only the kind of combination which does harm to the general public, such amendment to be accompanied by, or to be an incident of, a grant of supervisory power to the Government over these big concerns engaged in interstate business. This should be accompanied by provision for the compulsory publication of accounts and the subjection of books and papers to the inspection of the Government officials. A beginning has already been made for such supervision by the establishment of the Bureau of Corporations.

The antitrust law should not prohibit combinations that do no injustice to the public, still less those the existence of which is on the whole of benefit to the public. But even if this feature of the law were abolished, there would remain as an equally objectionable feature the difficulty and delay now incident to its enforcement. The Government must now submit to irksome and repeated delay before obtaining a final decision of the courts upon proceedings instituted, and even a favorable decree may mean an empty victory. Moreover, to attempt to control these corporations by lawsuits means to impose upon both the Department of Justice and the courts an impossible burden; it is not feasible to carry on more than a limited number of such suits. Such a law to be really effective must of course be administered by an executive body, and not merely by means of lawsuits. The design should be to prevent the abuses incident to the creation of unhealthy and improper combinations, instead of waiting until they are in existence and then attempting to destroy them by civil or criminal proceedings.

A combination should not be tolerated if it abuse the power acquired by combination to the public detriment. No corporation or association of any kind should be permitted to engage in foreign or interstate commerce that is formed for the purpose of, or whose operations create, a monopoly or general control of the production, sale, or distribution of any one or more of the prime necessities of life or articles of general use and necessity. Such combinations are against public policy; they violate the common law; the doors of the courts are closed to those who are parties to them, and I believe the Congress can close the channels of interstate commerce against them for its protection. The law should make its prohibitions and permissions as clear and definite as possible, leaving the least possible room for arbitrary action, or allegation of such action, on the part of the Executive, or of divergent interpretations by the courts. Among the points to be aimed at should be the prohibition of unhealthy competition, such as by rendering service at an actual loss for the purpose of crushing out competition, the prevention of inflation of capital, and the prohibition of a corporation's making exclusive trade with itself a condition of having any trade with itself. Reasonable agreements between, or combinations of, corporations should be permitted, provided they are submitted to and approved by some appropriate Government body.

The Congress has the power to charter corporations to engage in interstate and foreign commerce, and a general law can be enacted under the provisions of which existing corporations could take out Federal charters and new Federal corporations could be created. An essential provision of such a law should be a method of predetermining by some Federal board or commission whether the applicant for a Federal charter was an association or combination within the restrictions of the Federal law. Provision should also be made for complete publicity in all matters affecting the public and complete protection to the investing public and the shareholders in the matter of issuing corporate securities. If an incorporation law is not deemed advisable, a license act for big interstate corporations might be enacted; or a combination of the two might be tried. The supervision established might be analogous to that now exercised over national banks. At least, the antitrust act should be supplemented by specific prohibitions of the methods which experience has shown have been of most service in enabling monopolistic combinations to crush out competition. The real owners of a corporation should be compelled to do business in their own name. The right to hold stock in other corporations should hereafter be denied to interstate corporations, unless on approval by the Government officials, and a prerequisite to such approval should be the listing with the Government of all owners and stockholders, both by the corporation owning such stock and by the corporation in which such stock is owned.

To confer upon the National Government, in connection with the amendment I advocate in the antitrust law, power of supervision over big business concerns engaged in interstate commerce, would benefit them as it has benefited the national banks. In the recent business crisis it is noteworthy that the institutions which failed were institutions which were not under the supervision and control of the National Government. Those which were under National control stood the test.

National control of the kind above advocated would be to the benefit of every well-managed railway. From the standpoint of the public there is need for additional tracks, additional terminals, and improvements in the actual handling of the railroads, and all this as rapidly as possible. Ample, safe, and speedy transportation facilities are even more necessary than cheap transportation. Therefore, there is need for the investment of money which will provide for all these things while at the same time securing as far as is possible better wages and shorter hours for their employees. Therefore, while there must be just and reasonable regulation of rates, we should be the first to protest against any arbitrary and unthinking movement to cut them down without the fullest and most careful consideration of all interests concerned and of the actual needs of the situation. Only a special body of men acting for the National Government under authority conferred upon it by the Congress ic competent to pass judgment on such a matter.

Those who fear, from any reason, the extension of Federal activity will do well to study the history not only of the national banking act but of the pure-food law, and notably the meat inspection law recently enacted. The pure-food law was opposed so violently that its passage was delayed for a decade; yet it has worked unmixed and immediate good. The meat inspection law was even more violently assailed; and the same men who now denounce the attitude of the National Government in seeking to oversee and control the workings of interstate common carriers and business concerns, then asserted that we were "discrediting and ruining a great American industry." Two years have not elapsed, and already it has become evident that the great benefit the law confers upon the public is accompanied by an equal benefit to the reputable packing establishments. The latter are better off under the law than they were without it. The benefit to interstate common carriers and business concerns from the legislation I advocate would be equally marked.

Incidentally, in the passage of the pure-food law the action of the various State food and dairy commissioners showed in striking fashion how much good for the whole people results from the hearty cooperation of the Federal and State officials in securing a given reform. It is primarily to the action of these State commissioners that we owe the enactment of this law; for they aroused the people, first to demand the enactment and enforcement of State laws on the subject, and then the enactment of the Federal law, without which the State laws were largely ineffective. There must be the closest cooperation between the National and State governments in administering these laws.

In my Message to the Congress a year ago I spoke as follows of the currency:

"I especially call your attention to the condition of our currency laws. The national-bank act has ably served a great purpose in aiding the enormous business development of the country, and within ten years there has been an increase in circulation per capita from $21.41 to $33.08. For several years evidence has been accumulating that additional legislation is needed. The recurrence of each crop season emphasizes the defects of the present laws. There must soon be a revision of them, because to leave them as they are means to incur liability of business disaster. Since your body adjourned there has been a fluctuation in the interest on call money from 2 per cent to 30 per cent, and the fluctuation was even greater during the preceding six months. The Secretary of the Treasury had to step in and by wise action put a stop to the most violent period of oscillation. Even worse than such fluctuation is the advance in commercial rates and the uncertainty felt in the sufficiency of credit even at high rates. All commercial interests suffer during each crop period. Excessive rates for call money in New York attract money from the interior banks into the speculative field. This depletes the fund that would otherwise be available for commercial uses, and commercial borrowers are forced to pay abnormal rates, so that each fall a tax, in the shape of increased interest charges, is placed on the whole commerce of the country.

"The mere statement of these facts shows that our present system is seriously defective. There is need of a change. Unfortunately, however, many of the proposed changes must be ruled from consideration because they are complicated, are not easy of comprehension, and tend to disturb existing rights and interests. We must also rule out any plan which would materially impair the value of the United States 2 per cent bonds now pledged to secure circulation, the issue of which was made under conditions peculiarly creditable to the Treasury. I do not press any especial plan. Various plans have recently been proposed by expert committees of bankers. Among the plans which are possibly feasible and which certainly should receive your consideration is that repeatedly brought to your attention by the present Secretary of the Treasury, the essential features of which have been approved by many prominent bankers and business men. According to this plan national banks should be permitted to issue a specified proportion of their capital in notes of a given kind, the issue to be taxed at so high a rate as to drive the notes back when not wanted in legitimate trade. This plan would not permit the issue of currency to give banks additional profits, but to meet the emergency presented by times of stringency.

"I do not say that this is the right system. I only advance it to emphasize my belief that there is need for the adoption of some system which shall be automatic and open to all sound banks, so as to avoid all possibility of discrimination and favoritism. Such a plan would tend to prevent the spasms of high money and speculation which now obtain in the New York market; for at present there is too much currency at certain seasons of the year, and its accumulation at New York tempts bankers to lend it at low rates for speculative purposes; whereas at other times when the crops are being moved there is urgent need for a large but temporary increase in the currency supply. It must never be forgotten that this question concerns business men generally quite as much as bankers; especially is this true of stockmen, farmers, and business men in the West; for at present at certain seasons of the year the difference in interest rates between the East and the West is from 6 to 10 per cent, whereas in Canada the corresponding difference is but 2 per cent. Any plan must, of course, guard the interests of western and southern bankers as carefully as it guards the interests of New York or Chicago bankers, and must be drawn from the standpoints of the farmer and the merchant no less than from the standpoints of the city banker and the country banker."

I again urge on the Congress the need of immediate attention to this matter. We need a greater elasticity in our currency; provided, of course, that we recognize the even greater need of a safe and secure currency. There must always be the most rigid examination by the National authorities. Provision should be made for an emergency currency. The emergency issue should, of course, be made with an effective guaranty, and upon conditions carefully prescribed by the Government. Such emergency issue must be based on adequate securities approved by the Government, and must be issued under a heavy tax. This would permit currency being issued when the demand for it was urgent, while securing its requirement as the demand fell off. It is worth investigating to determine whether officers and directors of national banks should ever be allowed to loan to themselves. Trust companies should be subject to the same supervision as banks; legislation to this effect should be enacted for the District of Columbia and the Territories.

Yet we must also remember that even the wisest legislation on the subject can only accomplish a certain amount. No legislation can by any possibility guarantee the business community against the results of speculative folly any more than it can guarantee an individual against the results of his extravagance. When an individual mortgages his house to buy an automobile he invites disaster; and when wealthy men, or men who pose as such, or are unscrupulously or foolishly eager to become such, indulge in reckless speculation—especially if it is accompanied by dishonesty—they jeopardize not only their own future but the future of all their innocent fellow-citizens, for they expose the whole business community to panic and distress.

The income account of the Nation is in a most satisfactory condition. For the six fiscal years ending with the 1st of July last, the total expenditures and revenues of the National Government, exclusive of the postal revenues and expenditures, were, in round numbers, revenues, $3,465,000,0000, and expenditures, $3,275,000,000. The net excess of income over expenditures, including in the latter the fifty millions expended for the Panama Canal, was one hundred and ninety million dollars for the six years, an average of about thirty-one millions a year. This represents an approximation between income and outgo which it would be hard to improve. The satisfactory working of the

present tariff law has been chiefly responsible for this excellent showing. Nevertheless, there is an evident and constantly growing feeling
among our people that the time is rapidly approaching when our system of revenue legislation must be revised.

This country is definitely committed to the protective system and
any effort to uproot it could not but cause widespread industrial disaster. In other words, the principle of the present tariff law could not
with wisdom be changed. But in a country of such phenomenal growth
as ours it is probably well that every dozen years or so the tariff laws
should be carefully scrutinized so as to see that no industry or any
proper benefit is interfered thereby, that proper revenue is provided,
and that our foreign trade is encouraged. There must always be as a
minimum a tariff which will not only allow for the collection of an
ample revenue but which will at least make good the difference in cost
of production here and abroad; that is, the difference in the labor cost
here and abroad, for the well-being of the wage-worker must ever be a
cardinal point of American policy. The question should be approached
purely from a business standpoint; both the time and the manner of
the change being such as to arouse the minimum of agitation and disturbance in the business world, and to give the least play for selfish
and factional motives. The sole consideration should be to see that
the sum total of changes represents the public good. This means that
the subject can not with wisdom be dealt with in the year preceding a
Presidential election, because as a matter of fact experience has conclusively shown that at such a time it is impossible to get men to treat
it from the standpoint of the public good. In my judgment the wise
time to deal with the matter is immediately after such election.

When our tax laws are revised the question of an income tax and
an inheritance tax should receive the careful attention of our legislators. In my judgment both of these taxes should be part of our system of Federal taxation. I speak diffidently about the income tax because one scheme for an income tax was declared unconstitutional by
the Supreme Court; while in addition it is a difficult tax to administer
in its practical working, and great care would have to be exercised to
see that it was not evaded by the very men whom it was most desirable
to have taxed, for if so evaded it would, of course, be worse than no
tax at all; as the least desirable of all taxes is the tax which bears
heavily upon the honest as compared with the dishonest man. Nevertheless, a graduated income tax of the proper type would be a desirable
feature of Federal taxation, and it is to be hoped that one may be devised which the Supreme Court will declare constitutional. The inheritance tax, however, is both a far better method of taxation, and
far more important for the purpose of having the fortunes of the country bear in proportion to their increase in size a corresponding increase

and burden of taxation. The Government has the absolute right to decide as to the terms upon which a man shall receive a bequest or devise from another, and this point in the devolution of property is especially appropriate for the imposition of a tax. Laws imposing such taxes have repeatedly been placed upon the National statute books and as repeatedly declared constitutional by the courts; and these laws contained the progressive principle, that is, after a certain amount is reached the bequest or gift, in life or death, is increasingly burdened and the rate of taxation is increased in proportion to the remoteness of blood of the man receiving the bequest. These principles are recognized already in the leading civilized nations of the world. In Great Britain all the estates worth $5,000 or less are practically exempt from death duties, while the increase is such that when an estate exceeds five millions of dollars in value and passes to a distant kinsman or stranger in blood the Government receives all told an amount equivalent to nearly a fifth of the whole estate. In France so much of an inheritance as exceeds $10,000,000 pays over a fifth to the State if it passes to a distant relative. The German law is especially interesting to us because it makes the inheritance tax an imperial measure while allotting to the individual States of the Empire a portion of the proceeds and permitting them to impose taxes in addition to those imposed by the Imperial Government. Small inheritances are exempt, but the tax is so sharply progressive that when the inheritance is still not very large, provided it is not an agricultural or a forest land, it is taxed at the rate of 25 per cent if it goes to distant relatives. There is no reason why in the United States the National Government should not impose inheritance taxes in addition to those imposed by the States, and when we last had an inheritance tax about one-half of the States levied such taxes concurrently with the National Government, making a combined maximum rate, in some cases as high as 25 per cent. The French law has one feature which is to be heartily commended. The progressive principle is so applied that each higher rate is imposed only on the excess above the amount subject to the next lower rate; so that each increase of rate will apply only to a certain amount above a certain maximum. The tax should if possible be made to bear more heavily upon those residing without the country than within it. A heavy progressive tax upon a very large fortune is in no way such a tax upon thrift or industry as a like would be on a small fortune. No advantage comes either to the country as a whole or to the individuals inheriting the money by permitting the transmission in their entirety of the enormous fortunes which would be affected by such a tax; and as an incident to its function of revenue raising, such a tax would help to preserve a measurable equality of opportunity for the people of the generations growing to manhood. We have not the slightest sympathy with that socialistic idea which would try to put laziness, thrift-lessness and inefficiency on a par with industry, thrift and efficiency; which would strive to break up not merely private property, but what is far more important, the home, the chief prop upon which our whole civilization stands. Such a theory, if ever adopted, would mean the ruin of the entire country—a ruin which would bear heaviest upon the weakest, upon those least able to shift for themselves. But proposals for legislation such as this herein advocated are directly opposed to this class of socialistic theories. Our aim is to recognize what Lincoln pointed out: The fact that there are some respects in which men are obviously not equal, but also to insist that there should be an equality of self-respect and of mutual respect, an equality of rights before the law, and at least an approximate equality in the conditions under which each man obtains the chance to show the stuff that is in him when com-pared to his fellows.

A few years ago there was loud complaint that the law could not be invoked against wealthy offenders. There is no such complaint now. The course of the Department of Justice during the last few years has been such as to make it evident that no man stands above the law, that no corporation is so wealthy that it can not be held to account. The Department of Justice has been as prompt to proceed against the wealthiest malefactor whose crime was one of greed and cunning as to proceed against the agitator who incites to brutal violence. Every-thing that can be done under the existing law, and with the existing state of public opinion, which so profoundly influences both the courts and juries, has been done. But the laws themselves need strengthen-ing in more than one important point; they should be made more definite, so that no honest man can be led unwittingly to break them, and so that the real wrongdoer can be readily punished.

Moreover, there must be the public opinion back of the laws or the laws themselves will be of no avail. At present, while the average juryman undoubtedly wishes to see trusts broken up, and is quite ready to fine the corporation itself, he is very reluctant to find the facts proven beyond a reasonable doubt when it comes to sending to jail a member of the business community for indulging in practices which are profoundly unhealthy, but which, unfortunately, the business com-munity has grown to recognize as well-nigh normal. Both the present condition of the law and the present temper of juries render it a task of extreme difficulty to get at the real wrongdoer in any such case, especially by imprisonment. Yet it is from every standpoint far preferable to punish the prime offender by imprisonment rather than to fine the corporation, with the attendant damage to stockholders.

The two great evils in the execution of our criminal laws to-day are sentimentality and technicality. For the latter the remedy must come from the hands of the legislatures, the courts, and the lawyers. The other must depend for its cure upon the gradual growth of a sound public opinion which shall insist that regard for the law and the demands of reason shall control all other influences and emotions in the jury box. Both of these evils must be removed or public discontent with the criminal law will continue.

Instances of abuse in the granting of injunctions in labor disputes continue to occur, and the resentment in the minds of those who feel that their rights are being invaded and their liberty of action and of speech unwarrantably restrained continues likewise to grow. Much of the attack on the use of the process of injunction is wholly without warrant; but I am constrained to express the belief that for some of it there is warrant. This question is becoming more and more one of prime importance, and unless the courts will themselves deal with it in effective manner, it is certain ultimately to demand some form of legislative action. It would be most unfortunate for our social welfare if we should permit many honest and law-abiding citizens to feel that they had just cause for regarding our courts with hostility. I earnestly commend to the attention of the Congress this matter, so that some way may be devised which will limit the abuse of injunctions and protect those rights which from time to time it unwarrantably invades. Moreover, discontent is often expressed with the use of the process of injunction by the courts, not only in labor disputes, but where State laws are concerned. I refrain from discussion of this question as I am informed that it will soon receive the consideration of the Supreme Court.

The Federal courts must of course decide ultimately what are the respective spheres of State and Nation in connection with any law, State or National, and they must decide definitely and finally in matters affecting individual citizens, not only as to the rights and wrongs of labor but as to the rights and wrongs of capital; and the National Government must always see that the decision of the court is put into effect. The process of injunction is an essential adjunct of the court's doing its work well; and as preventive measures are always better than remedial, the wise use of this process is from every standpoint commendable. But where it is recklessly or unnecessarily used, the abuse should be censured, above all by the very men who are properly anxious to prevent any effort to shear the courts of this necessary power. The court's decision must be final; the protest is only against the conduct of individual juudges in needlessly anticipating such final decision, or in the tyrannical use of what is nominally a temporary injunction to accomplish what is in fact a permanent decision.

The loss of life and limb from railroad accidents in this country has become appalling. It is a subject of which the National Government should take supervision. It might be well to begin by providing for a Federal inspection of interstate railroads somewhat along the lines of Federal inspection of steamboats, although not going so far; perhaps at first all that it would be necessary to have would be some officer whose duty would be to investigate all accidents on interstate railroads and report in detail the causes thereof. Such an officer should make it his business to get into close touch with railroad operating men so as to become thoroughly familiar with every side of the question, the idea being to work along the lines of the present steamboat inspection law.

The National Government should be a model employer. It should demand the highest quality of service from each of its employees and it should care for all of them properly in return. Congress should adopt legislation providing limited but definite compensation for accidents to all workmen within the scope of the Federal power, including employees of navy yards and arsenals. In other words, a model employers' liability act, far-reaching and thoroughgoing, should be enacted which should apply to all positions, public and private, over which the National Government has jurisdiction. The number of accidents to wage-workers, including those that are preventable and those that are not, has become appalling in the mechanical, manufacturing, and transportation operations of the day. It works grim hardship to the ordinary wage-worker and his family to have the effect of such an accident fall solely upon him; and, on the other hand, there are whole classes of attorneys who exist only by inciting men who may or may not have been wronged to undertake suits for negligence. As a matter of fact a suit for negligence is generally an inadequate remedy for the person injured, while it often causes altogether disproportionate annoyance to the employer. The law should be made such that the payment for accidents by the employer would be automatic instead of being a matter for lawsuits. Workmen should receive certain and definite compensation for all accidents in industry irrespective of negligence. The employer is the agent of the public and on his own responsibility and for his own profit he serves the public. When he starts in motion agencies which create risks for others, he should take all the ordinary and extraordinary risks involved; and the risk he thus at the moment assumes will ultimately be assumed, as it ought to be, by the general public. Only in this way can the shock of the accident be diffused, instead of falling upon the man or woman least able to bear it, as is now the case. The community at large should share the burdens as well as the benefits of industry. By the proposed law, employers would gain a desirable certainty of obligation and get rid of litigation to determine it, while the workman and his family would be relieved from a crushing load. With such a policy would come increased care, and accidents would be reduced in number. The National laws pro-viding for employers' liability on railroads engaged in interstate commerce and for safety appliances, as well as for diminishing the hours any employee of a railroad should be permitted to work, should all be strengthened wherever in actual practice they have shown weakness; they should be kept on the statute books in thoroughgoing form.

The constitutionality of the employers' liability act passed by the preceding Congress has been carried before the courts. In two jurisdictions the law has been declared unconstitutional, and in three jurisdictions its constitutionality has been affirmed. The question has been carried to the Supreme Court, the case has been heard by that tribunal, and a decision is expected at an early date. In the event that the court should affirm the constitutionality of the act, I urge further legislation along the lines advocated in my Message to the preceding Congress. The practice of putting the entire burden of loss to life or limb upon the victim or the victim's family is a form of social injustice in which the United States stands in unenviable prominence. In both our Federal and State legislation we have, with few exceptions, scarcely gone farther than the repeal of the fellow-servant principle of the old law of liability, and in some of our States even this slight modification of a completely outgrown principle has not yet been secured. The legislation of the rest of the industrial world stands out in striking contrast to our backwardness in this respect. Since 1895 practically every country of Europe, together with Great Britain, New Zealand, Australia, British Columbia, and the Cape of Good Hope has enacted legislation embodying in one form or another the complete recognition of the principle which places upon the employer the entire trade risk in the various lines of industry. I urge upon the Congress the enactment of a law which will at the same time bring Federal legislation up to the standard already established by all the European countries, and which will serve as a stimulus to the various States to perfect their legislation in this regard.

The Congress should consider the extension of the eight-hour law. The constitutionality of the present law has recently been called into question, and the Supreme Court has decided that the existing legislation is unquestionably within the powers of the Congress. The principle of the eight-hour day should as rapidly and as far as practicable be extended to the entire work carried on by the Government; and the present law should be amended to embrace contracts on those public works which the present wording of the act has been construed to exclude. The general introduction of the eight-hour day should be the goal toward which we should steadily tend, and the Government should set the example in this respect.

Strikes and lockouts, with their attendant loss and suffering, continue to increase. For the five years ending December 31, 1905, the number of strikes was greater than those in any previous ten years and was double the number in the preceding five years. These figures indicate the increasing need of providing some machinery to deal with this class of disturbance in the interest alike of the employer, the employee, and the general public. I renew my previous recommendation that the Congress favorably consider the matter of creating the machinery for compulsory investigation of such industrial controversies as are of sufficient magnitude and of sufficient concern to the people of the country as a whole to warrant the Federal Government in taking action.

The need for some provision for such investigation was forcibly illustrated during the past summer. A strike of telegraph operators seriously interfered with telegraphic communication, causing great damage to business interests and serious inconvenience to the general public. Appeals were made to me from many parts of the country, from city councils, from boards of trade, from chambers of commerce, and from labor organizations, urging that steps be taken to terminate the strike. Everything that could with any propriety be done by a representative of the Government was done, without avail, and for weeks the public stood by and suffered without recourse of any kind. Had the machinery existed and had there been authority for compulsory investigation of the dispute, the public would have been placed in possession of the merits of the controversy, and public opinion would probably have brought about a prompt adjustment.

Each successive step creating machinery for the adjustment of labor difficulties must be taken with caution, but we should endeavor to make progress in this direction.

The provisions of the act of 1898 creating the chairman of the Interstate Commerce Commission and the Commissioner of Labor a board of mediation in controversies between interstate railroads and their employees has, for the first time, been subjected to serious tests within the past year, and the wisdom of the experiment has been fully demonstrated. The creation of a board for compulsory investigation in cases where mediation fails and arbitration is rejected is the next logical step in a progressive program.

It is certain that for some time to come there will be a constant increase absolutely, and perhaps relatively, of those among our citizens who dwell in cities or towns of some size and who work for wages. This means that there will be an ever-increasing need to consider the problems inseparable from a great industrial civilization. Where an immense and complex business, especially in those branches relating to manufacture and transportation, is transacted by a large number of capitalists who employ a very much larger number of wage-earners, the former tend more and more to combine into corporations and the latter into unions. The relations of the capitalist and wage-worker to one another, and of each to the general public, are not always easy to adjust; and to put them and keep them on a satisfactory basis is one of the most important and one of the most delicate tasks before our whole civilization. Much of the work for the accomplishment of this end must be done by the individuals concerned themselves, whether singly or in combination; and the one fundamental fact that must never be lost track of is that the character of the average man, whether he be a man of means or a man who works with his hands, is the most important factor in solving the problem aright. But it is almost equally important to remember that without good laws it is also impossible to reach the proper solution. It is idle to hold that without good laws evils such as child labor, as the over-working of women, as the failure to protect employees from loss of life or limb, can be effectively reached, any more than the evils of rebates and stock-watering can be reached without good laws. To fail to stop these practices by legislation means to force honest men into them, because otherwise the dishonest who surely will take advantage of them will have everything their own way. If the States will correct these evils, well and good; but the Nation must stand ready to aid them.

No question growing out of our rapid and complex industrial development is more important than that of the employment of women and children. The presence of women in industry reacts with extreme directness upon the character of the home and upon family life, and the conditions surrounding the employment of children bear a vital relation to our future citizenship. Our legislation in those areas under the control of the Congress is very much behind the legislation of our more progressive States. A thorough and comprehensive measure should be adopted at this session of the Congress relating to the employment of women and children in the District of Columbia and the Territories. The investigation into the condition of women and children wage-earners recently authorized and directed by the Congress is now being carried on in the various States, and I recommend that the appropriation made last year for beginning this work be renewed, in order that we may have the thorough and comprehensive investigation which the subject demands. The National Government has as an ultimate resort for control of child labor the use of the interstate commerce clause to prevent the products of child labor from entering into interstate commerce. But before using this it ought certainly to enact model laws on the subject for the Territories under its own immediate control.

There is one fundamental proposition which can be laid down as regards all these matters, namely: While honesty by itself will not

solve the problem, yet the insistence upon honesty—not merely technical honesty, but honesty in purpose and spirit—is an essential element
in arriving at a right conclusion. Vice in its cruder and more archaic
forms shocks everybody; but there is very urgent need that public
opinion should be just as severe in condemnation of the vice which
hides itself behind class or professional loyalty, or which denies that it
is vice if it can escape conviction in the courts. The public and the
representatives of the public, the high officials, whether on the bench
or in executive or legislative positions, need to remember that often the
most dangerous criminals, so far as the life of the Nation is concerned,
are not those who commit the crimes known to and condemned by the
popular conscience for centuries, but those who commit crimes only
rendered possible by the complex conditions of our modern industrial
life. It makes not a particle of difference whether these crimes are
committed by a capitalist or by a laborer, by a leading banker or manu-
facturer or railroad man, or by a leading representative of a labor
union. Swindling in stocks, corrupting legislatures, making fortunes
by the inflation of securities, by wrecking railroads, by destroying competitors through rebates—these forms of wrongdoing in the capitalist,
are far more infamous than any ordinary form of embezzlement or
forgery; yet it is a matter of extreme difficulty to secure the punishment of the man most guilty of them, most responsible for them. The
business man who condones such conduct stands on a level with the
labor man who deliberately supports a corrupt demagogue and agitator,
whether head of a union or head of some municipality, because he is
said to have "stood by the union." The members of the business community, the educators, or clergymen, who condone and encourage the
first kind of wrongdoing, are no more dangerous to the community,
but are morally even worse, than the labor men who are guilty of the
second type of wrongdoing, because less is to be pardoned those who
have no such excuse as is furnished either by ignorance or by dire
need.

When the Department of Agriculture was founded there was much
sneering as to its usefulness. No Department of the Government,
however, has more emphatically vindicated its usefulness, and none
save the Post-Office Department comes so continually and intimately
into touch with the people. The two citizens whose welfare is in the
aggregate most vital to the welfare of the Nation, and therefore to
the welfare of all other citizens, are the wage-worker who does manual
labor and the tiller of the soil, the farmer. There are, of course, kinds
of labor where the work must be purely mental, and there are other
kinds of labor where, under existing conditions, very little demand indeed is made upon the mind, though I am glad to say that the proportion of men engaged in this kind of work is diminishing. But in

any community with the solid, healthy qualities which make up a really great nation the bulk of the people should do work which calls for the exercise of both body and mind.   Progress can not permanently exist in the abandonment of physical labor, but in the development of physical labor, so that it shall represent more and more the work of the trained mind in the trained body.   Our school system is gravely defective in so far as it puts a premium upon mere literary training and tends therefore to train the boy away from the farm and the work-shop.   Nothing is more needed than the best type of industrial school, the school for mechanical industries in the city, the school for prac-tically teaching agriculture in the country.   The calling of the skilled tiller of the soil, the calling of the skilled mechanic, should alike be recognized as professions, just as emphatically as the callings of law-yer, doctor, merchant, or clerk.   The schools recognize this fact and it should equally be recognized in popular opinion.   The young man who has the farsightedness and courage to recognize it and to get over the idea that it makes a difference whether what he earns is called salary or wages, and who refuses to enter the crowded field of the so-called professions, and takes to constructive industry instead, is reason-ably sure of an ample reward in earnings, in health, in opportunity to marry early, and to establish a home with a fair amount of freedom from worry.   It should be one of our prime objects to put both the farmer and the mechanic on a higher plane of efficiency and reward, so as to increase their effectiveness in the economic world, and there-fore the dignity, the remuneration, and the power of their positions in the social world.

No growth of cities, no growth of wealth, can make up for any loss in either the number or the character of the farming population.   We of the United States should realize this above almost all other peoples. We began our existence as a nation of farmers, and in every great crisis of the past a peculiar dependence has had to be placed upon the farming population; and this dependence has hitherto been justified. But it can not be justified in the future if agriculture is permitted to sink in the scale as compared with other employments.   We can not afford to lose that preeminently typical American, the farmer who owns his own medium-sized farm.   To have his place taken by either a class of small peasant proprietors, or by a class of great landlords with tenant-farmed estates would be a veritable calamity.   The growth of our cities is a good thing but only in so far as it does not mean a growth at the expense of the country farmer.   We must welcome the rise of physical sciences in their application to agricultural practices, and we must do all we can to render country conditions more easy and pleasant.   There are forces which now tend to bring about both these results, but they are, as yet, in their infancy.   The National Government through the Department of Agriculture should do all it can by joining with the State governments and with independent associations of farmers to encourage the growth in the open farming country of such institutional and social movements as will meet the demand of the best type of farmers, both for the improvement of their farms and for the betterment of the life itself. The Department of Agriculture has in many places, perhaps especially in certain districts of the South, accomplished an extraordinary amount by cooperating with and teaching the farmers through their associations, on their own soil, how to increase their income by managing their farms better than they were hitherto managed. The farmer must not lose his independence, his initiative, his rugged self-reliance, yet he must learn to work in the heartiest cooperation with his fellows, exactly as the business man has learned to work; and he must prepare to use to constantly better advantage the knowledge that can be obtained from agricultural colleges, while he must insist upon a practical curriculum in the schools in which his children are taught. The Department of Agriculture and the Department of Commerce and Labor both deal with the fundamental needs of our people in the production of raw material and its manufacture and distribution, and, therefore, with the welfare of those who produce it in the raw state, and of those who manufacture and distribute it. The Department of Commerce and Labor has but recently been founded but has already justified its existence; while the Department of Agriculture yields to no other in the Government in the practical benefits which it produces in proportion to the public money expended. It must continue in the future to deal with growing crops as it has dealt in the past, but it must still further extend its field of usefulness hereafter by dealing with live men, through a farreaching study and treatment of the problems of farm life alike from the industrial and economic and social standpoint. Farmers must cooperate with one another and with the Government, and the Government can best give its aid through associations of farmers, so as to deliver to the farmer the large body of agricultural knowledge which has been accumulated by the National and State governments and by the agricultural colleges and schools.

The grain producing industry of the country, one of the most important in the United States, deserves special consideration at the hands of the Congress. Our grain is sold almost exclusively by grades. To secure satisfactory results in our home markets and to facilitate our trade abroad, these grades should approximate the highest degree of uniformity and certainty. The present diverse methods of inspection and grading throughout the country under different laws and boards, result in confusion and lack of uniformity, destroying that confidence which is necessary for healthful trade. Complaints against the present methods have continued for years and they are growing in volume and intensity, not only in this country but abroad. I therefore suggest to the Congress the advisability of a National system of inspection and grading of grain entering into interstate and foreign commerce as a remedy for the present evils.

The conservation of our natural resources and their proper use constitute the fundamental problem which underlies almost every other problem of our National life. We must maintain for our civilization the adequate material basis without which that civilization can not exist. We must show foresight, we must look ahead. As a nation we not only enjoy a wonderful measure of present prosperity but if this prosperity is used aright it is an earnest of future success such as no other nation will have. The reward of foresight for this Nation is great and easily foretold. But there must be the look ahead, there must be a realization of the fact that to waste, to destroy, our natural resources, to skin and exhaust the land instead of using it so as to increase its usefulness, will result in undermining in the days of our children the very prosperity which we ought by right to hand down to them amplified and developed. For the last few years, through several agencies, the Government has been endeavoring to get our people to look ahead and to substitute a planned and orderly development of our resources in place of a haphazard striving for immediate profit. Our great river systems should be developed as National water highways, the Mississippi, with its tributaries, standing first in importance, and the Columbia second, although there are many others of importance on the Pacific, the Atlantic and the Gulf slopes. The National Government should undertake this work, and I hope a beginning will be made in the present Congress; and the greatest of all our rivers, the Mississippi, should receive especial attention. From the Great Lakes to the mouth of the Mississippi there should be a deep waterway, with deep waterways leading from it to the East and the West. Such a waterway would practically mean the extension of our coast line into the very heart of our country. It would be of incalculable benefit to our people. If begun at once it can be carried through in time appreciably to relieve the congestion of our great freight-carrying lines of railroads. The work should be systematically and continuously carried forward in accordance with some well-conceived plan. The main streams should be improved to the highest point of efficiency before the improvement of the branches is attempted; and the work should be kept free from every taint of recklessness or jobbery. The inland waterways which lie just back of the whole eastern and southern coasts should likewise be developed. Moreover, the development of our waterways involves many other important water problems, all of which should be considered as part of the same general scheme. The

Government dams should be used to produce hundreds of thousands of horsepower as an incident to improving navigation; for the annual value of the unused water-power of the United States perhaps exceeds the annual value of the products of all our mines. As an incident to creating the deep waterways down the Mississippi, the Government should build along its whole lower length levees which taken together with the control of the headwaters, will at once and forever put a complete stop to all threat of floods in the immensely fertile Delta region. The territory lying adjacent to the Mississippi along its lower course will thereby become one of the most prosperous and populous, as it already is one of the most fertile, farming regions in all the world. I have appointed an Inland Waterways Commission to study and outline a comprehensive scheme of development along all the lines indicated. Later I shall lay its report before the Congress.

Irrigation should be far more extensively developed than at present, not only in the States of the Great Plains and the Rocky Mountains, but in many others, as, for instance, in large portions of the South Atlantic and Gulf States, where it should go hand in hand with the reclamation of swamp land. The Federal Government should seriously devote itself to this task, realizing that utilization of waterways and water-power, forestry, irrigation, and the reclamation of lands threatened with overflow, are all interdependent parts of the same problem. The work of the Reclamation Service in developing the larger opportunities of the western half of our country for irrigation is more important than almost any other movement. The constant purpose of the Government in connection with the Reclamation Service has been to use the water resources of the public lands for the ultimate greatest good of the greatest number; in other words, to put upon the land permanent home-makers, to use and develop it for themselves and for their children and children's children. There has been, of course, opposition to this work; opposition from some interested men who desire to exhaust the land for their own immediate profit without regard to the welfare of the next generation, and opposition from honest and well-meaning men who did not fully understand the subject or who did not look far enough ahead. This opposition is, I think, dying away, and our people are understanding that it would be utterly wrong to allow a few individuals to exhaust for their own temporary personal profit the resources which ought to be developed through use so as to be conserved for the permanent common advantage of the people as a whole.

The effort of the Government to deal with the public land has been based upon the same principle as that of the Reclamation Service. The land law system which was designed to meet the needs of the fertile and well-watered regions of the Middle West has largely broken down when applied to the dryer regions of the Great Plains, the mountains, and much of the Pacific slope, where a farm of 160 acres is inadequate for self-support. In these regions the system lent itself to fraud, and much land passed out of the hands of the Government without passing into the hands of the home-maker. The Department of the Interior and the Department of Justice joined in prosecuting the offenders against the law; and they have accomplished much, while where the administration of the law has been defective it has been changed. But the laws themselves are defective. Three years ago a public lands commission was appointed to scrutinize the law, and defects, and recommend a remedy. Their examination specifically showed the existence of great fraud upon the public domain, and their recommendations for changes in the law were made with the design of conserving the natural resources of every part of the public lands by putting it to its best use. Especial attention was called to the prevention of settlement by the passage of great areas of public land into the hands of a few men, and to the enormous waste caused by unrestricted grazing upon the open range. The recommendations of the Public Lands Commission are sound, for they are especially in the interest of the actual home-maker; and where the small home-maker can not at present utilize the land they provide that the Government shall keep control of it so that it may not be monopolized by a few men. The Congress has not yet acted upon these recommendations; but they are so just and proper, so essential to our National welfare, that I feel confident, if the Congress will take time to consider them, that they will ultimately be adopted.

Some such legislation as that proposed is essential in order to preserve the great stretches of public grazing land which are unfit for cultivation under present methods and are valuable only for the forage which they supply. These stretches amount in all to some 300,000,000 acres, and are open to the free grazing of cattle, sheep, horses and goats, without restriction. Such a system, or lack of system, means that the range is not so much used as wasted by abuse. As the West settles the range becomes more and more over-grazed. Much of it can not be used to advantage unless it is fenced, for fencing is the only way by which to keep in check the owners of nomad flocks which roam hither and thither, utterly destroying the pastures and leaving a waste behind so that their presence is incompatible with the presence of home-makers. The existing fences are all illegal. Some of them represent the improper exclusion of actual settlers, actual home-makers, from territory which is usurped by great cattle companies. Some of them represent what is in itself a proper effort to use the range for those upon the land, and to prevent its use by nomadic outsiders. All these fences, those that are hurtful and those that are beneficial, are alike illegal and must come down. But it is an outrage that the law should necessitate such action on the part of the Administration. The unlawful fencing of public lands for private grazing must be stopped, but the necessity which occasioned it must be provided for. The Federal Government should have control of the range, whether by permit or lease, as local necessities may determine. Such control could secure the great benefit of legitimate fencing, while at the same time securing and promoting the settlement of the country. In some places it may be that the tracts of range adjacent to the homesteads of actual settlers should be allotted to them severally or in common for the summer grazing of their stock. Elsewhere it may be that a lease system would serve the purpose; the leases to be temporary and subject to the rights of settlement, and the amount charged being large enough merely to permit of the efficient and beneficial control of the range by the Government, and of the payment to the county of the equivalent of what it would otherwise receive in taxes. The destruction of the public range will continue until some such laws as these are enacted. Fully to prevent the fraud in the public lands which, through the joint action of the Interior Department and the Department of Justice, we have been endeavoring to prevent, there must be further legislation, and especially a sufficient appropriation to permit the Department of the Interior to examine certain classes of entries on the ground before they pass into private ownership. The Government should part with its title only to the actual home-maker, not to the profit-maker who does not care to make a home.. Our prime object is to secure the rights and guard the interests of the small ranchman, the man who plows and pitches hay for himself. It is this small ranchman, this actual settler and home-maker, who in the long run is most hurt by permitting thefts of the public land in whatever form.

Optimism is a good characteristic, but if carried to an excess it becomes foolishness. We are prone to speak of the resources of this country as inexhaustible; this is not so. The mineral wealth of the country, the coal, iron, oil, gas, and the like, does not reproduce itself, and therefore is certain to be exhausted ultimately; and wastefulness in dealing with it to-day means that our descendants will feel the exhaustion a generation or two before they otherwise would. But there are certain other forms of waste which could be entirely stopped—the waste of soil by washing, for instance, which is among the most dangerous of all wastes now in progress in the United States, is easily preventable, so that this present enormous loss of fertility is entirely unnecessary. The preservation or replacement of the forests is one of the most important means of preventing this loss. We have made a beginning in forest preservation, but it is only a beginning. At present lumbering is the fourth greatest industry in the United States; and yet, so rapid has been the rate of exhaustion of timber in the United States in the past, and so rapidly is the remainder being exhausted, that the country is unquestionably on the verge of a timber famine which will be felt in every household in the land. There has already been a rise in the price of lumber, but there is certain to be a more rapid and heavier rise in the future. The present annual consumption of lumber is certainly three times as great as the annual growth; and if the consumption and growth continue unchanged, practically all our lumber will be exhausted in another generation, while long before the limit to complete exhaustion is reached the growing scarcity will make itself felt in many blighting ways upon our National welfare. About 20 per cent of our forested territory is now reserved in National forests; but these do not include the most valuable timber lands, and in any event the proportion is too small to expect that the reserves can accomplish more than a mitigation of the trouble which is ahead for the nation. Far more drastic action is needed. Forests can be lumbered so as to give to the public the full use of their mercantile timber without the slightest detriment to the forest, any more than it is a detriment to a farm to furnish a harvest; so that there is no parallel between forests and mines, which can only be completely used by exhaustion. But forests, if used as all our forests have been used in the past and as most of them are still used, will be either wholly destroyed, or so damaged that many decades have to pass before effective use can be made of them again. All these facts are so obvious that it is extraordinary that it should be necessary to repeat them. Every business man in the land, every writer in the newspapers, every man or woman of an ordinary school education, ought to be able to see that immense quantities of timber are used in the country, that the forests which supply this timber are rapidly being exhausted, and that, if no change takes place, exhaustion will come comparatively soon, and that the effects of it will be felt severely in the every-day life of our people. Surely, when these facts are so obvious, there should be no delay in taking preventive measures. Yet we seem as a nation to be willing to proceed in this matter with happy-go-lucky indifference even to the immediate future. It is this attitude which permits the self-interest of a very few persons to weigh for more than the ultimate interest of all our people. There are persons who find it to their immense pecuniary benefit to destroy the forests by lumbering. They are to be blamed for thus sacrificing the future of the Nation as a whole to their own self-interest of the moment; but heavier blame attaches to the people at large for permitting such action, whether in the White Mountains, in the southern Alleghenies, or in the Rockies and Sierras. A big lumbering company, impatient for immediate returns and not caring to look far enough ahead, will often deliberately destroy all the good timber in a region, hoping afterwards to move on to some new country. The shiftless man of small means, who does not care to become an actual home-maker but would like immediate profit, will find it to his advantage to take up timber land simply to turn it over to such a big company, and leave it valueless for future settlers. A big mine owner, anxious only to develop his mine at the moment, will care only to cut all the timber that he wishes without regard to the future—probably not looking ahead to the condition of the country when the forests are exhausted, any more than he does to the condition when the mine is worked out. I do not blame these men nearly as much as I blame the ignorant public opinion, the indifferent public opinion, which permits their action to go unchecked. Of course to check the waste of timber means that there must be on the part of the public the acceptance of a temporary restriction in the lavish use of the timber, in order to prevent the total loss of this use in the future. There are plenty of men in public and private life who actually advocate the continuance of the present system of unchecked and wasteful extravagance, using as an argument the fact that to check it will of course mean interference with the ease and comfort of certain people who now get lumber at less cost than they ought to pay, at the expense of the future generations. Some of these persons actually demand that the present forest reserves be thrown open to destruction, because, forsooth, they think that thereby the price of lumber could be put down again for two or three or more years. Their attitude is precisely like that of an agitator protesting against the outlay of money by farmers on manure and in taking care of their farms generally. Undoubtedly, if the average farmer were content absolutely to ruin his farm, he could for two or three years avoid spending any money on it, and yet make a good deal of money out of it. But only a savage would, in his private affairs, show such reckless disregard of the future; yet it is precisely this reckless disregard of the future which the opponents of the forestry system are now endeavoring to get the people of the United States to show. The only trouble with the movement for the preservation of our forests is that it has not gone nearly far enough, and was not begun soon enough. It is a most fortunate thing, however, that we began it when we did. We should acquire in the Appalachian and White Mountain regions all the forest lands that it is possible to acquire for the use of the Nation. These lands, because they form a National asset, are as emphatically national as the rivers which they feed, and which flow through so many States before they reach the ocean.

There should be no tariff on any forest product grown in this country; and, in especial, there should be no tariff on wood pulp; due notice of the change being of course given to those engaged in the business so as to enable them to adjust themselves to the new conditions.

The repeal of the duty on wood pulp should if possible be accompanied by an agreement with Canada that there shall be no export duty on Canadian pulp wood.

In the eastern United States the mineral fuels have already passed into the hands of large private owners, and those of the West are rapidly following. It is obvious that these fuels should be conserved and not wasted, and it would be well to protect the people against unjust and extortionate prices, so far as that can still be done. What has been accomplished in the great oil fields of the Indian Territory by the action of the Administration, offers a striking example of the good results of such a policy. In my judgment the Government should have the right to keep the fee of the coal, oil, and gas fields in its own possession and to lease the rights to develop them under proper regulations; or else, if the Congress will not adopt this method, the coal deposits should be sold under limitations, to conserve them as public utilities, the right to mine coal being separated from the title to the soil. The regulations should permit coal lands to be worked in sufficient quantity by the several corporations. The present limitations have been absurd, excessive, and serve no useful purpose, and often render it necessary that there should be either fraud or close abandonment of the work of getting out the coal.

Work on the Panama Canal is proceeding in a highly satisfactory manner. In March last, John F. Stevens, chairman of the Commission and chief engineer, resigned, and the Commission was reorganized and constituted as follows: Lieut. Col. George W. Goethals, Corps. of Engineers, U. S. Army, chairman and chief engineer; Maj. D. D. Gaillard, Corps of Engineers, U. S. Army; Maj. William L. Sibert, Corps of Engineers, U. S. Army; Civil Engineer H. H. Rousseau, U. S. Navy; Mr. J. C. S. Blackburn; Col. W. C. Gorgas, U. S. Army, and Mr. Jackson Smith, Commissioners. This change of authority and direction went into effect on April 1, without causing a perceptible check to the progress of the work. In March the total excavation in the Culebra Cut, where effort was chiefly concentrated, was 815,270 cubic yards. In April this was increased to 879,527 cubic yards. There was a considerable decrease in the output for May and June owing partly to the advent of the rainy season and partly to temporary trouble with the steam shovel men over the question of wages. This trouble was settled satisfactorily to all parties and in July the total excavation advanced materially and in August the grand total from all points in the canal prism by steam shovels and dredges exceeded all previous United States records, reaching 1,274,404 cubic yards. In September this record was eclipsed and a total of 1,517,412 cubic yards was removed. Of this amount 1,481,307 cubic yards were from the canal prism and 36,105 cubic yards were from accessory works.. These results were achieved in the rainy season with a rainfall in August of 11.89 inches and in September of 11.65 inches. Finally, in October, the record was again eclipsed, the total excavation being 1,868,729 cubic yards; a truly extraordinary record, especially in view of the heavy rainfall, which was 17.1 inches. In fact, experience during the last two rainy seasons demonstrates that the rains are a less serious obstacle to progress than has hitherto been supposed.

Work on the locks and dams at Gatun, which began actively in March last, has advanced so far that it is thought that masonry work on the locks can be begun within fifteen months. In order to remove all doubt as to the satisfactory character of the foundations for the locks of the Canal, the Secretary of War requested three eminent civil engineers, of special experience in such construction, Alfred Noble, Frederic P. Stearns and John R. Freeman, to visit the Isthmus and make thorough personal investigations of the sites. These gentlemen went to the Isthmus in April and by means of test pits which had been dug for the purpose, they inspected the proposed foundations, and also examined the borings that had been made. In their report to the Secretary of War, under date of May 2, 1907, they said: "We found that all of the locks, of the dimensions now propesed, will rest upon rock of such character that it will furnish a safe and stable foundation." Subsequent new borings, conducted by the present Commission, have fully confirmed this verdict. They show that the locks will rest on rock for their entire length. The cross section of the dam and method of construction will be such as to insure against any slip or sloughing off. Similar examination of the foundations of the locks and dams on the Pacific side are in progress. I believe that the locks should be made of a width of 120 feet.

Last winter bids were requested and received for doing the work of canal construction by contract. None of them was found to be satisfactory and all were rejected. It is the unanimous opinion of the present Commission that the work can be done better, more cheaply, and more quickly by the Government than by private contractors. Fully 80 per cent of the entire plant needed for construction has been purchased or contracted for; machine shops have been erected and equipped for making all needed repairs to the plant; many thousands of employees have been secured; an effective organization has been perfected; a recruiting system is in operation which is capable of furnishing more labor than can be used advantageously; employees are well sheltered and well fed; salaries paid are satisfactory, and the work is not only going forward smoothly, but it is producing results far in advance of the most sanguine anticipations. Under these favorable conditions, a change in the method of prosecuting the work would be unwise and unjustifiable, for it would inevitably disorganize existing conditions, check progress, and increase the cost and lengthen the time of completing the Canal.

The chief engineer and all his professional associates are firmly convinced that the 85 feet level lock canal which they are constructing is the best that could be desired. Some of them had doubts on this point when they went to the Isthmus. As the plans have developed under their direction their doubts have been dispelled. While they may decide upon changes in detail as construction advances they are in hearty accord in approving the general plan. They believe that it provides a canal not only adequate to all demands that will be made upon it but superior in every way to a sea level canal. I concur in this belief.

I commend to the favorable consideration of the Congress a postal savings bank system, as recommended by the Postmaster-General. The primary object is to encourage among our people economy and thrift and by the use of postal savings banks to give them an opportunity to husband their resources, particularly those who have not the facilities at hand for depositing their money in savings banks. Viewed, however, from the experience of the past few weeks, it is evident that the advantages of such an institution are still more far-reaching. Timid depositors have withdrawn their savings for the time being from national banks, trust companies, and savings banks; individuals have hoarded their cash and the workingmen their earnings; all of which money has been withheld and kept in hiding or in safe deposit box to the detriment of prosperity. Through the agency of the postal savings banks such money would be restored to the channels of trade, to the mutual benefit of capital and labor.

I further commend to the Congress the consideration of the Postmaster-General's recommendation for an extension of the parcel post, especially on the rural routes. There are now 38,215 rural routes, serving nearly 15,000,000 people who do not have the advantages of the inhabitants of cities in obtaining their supplies. These recommendations have been drawn up to benefit the farmer and the country storekeeper; otherwise, I should not favor them, for I believe that it is good policy for our Government to do everything possible to aid the small town and the country district. It is desirable that the country merchant should not be crushed out.

The fourth-class postmasters' convention has passed a very strong resolution in favor of placing the fourth-class postmasters under the civil-service law. The Administration has already put into effect the policy of refusing to remove any fourth-class postmasters save for reasons connected with the good of the service; and it is endeavoring so far as possible to remove them from the domain of partisan politics. It would be a most desirable thing to put the fourth-class postmasters in the classified service. It is possible that this might be done without

Congressional action, but, as the matter is debatable, I earnestly recommend that the Congress enact a law providing that they be included under the civil-service law and put in the classified service.

Oklahoma has become a State, standing on a full equality with her elder sisters, and her future is assured by her great natural resources. The duty of the National Government to guard the personal and property rights of the Indians within her borders remains of course unchanged.

I reiterate my recommendations of last year as regards Alaska. Some form of local self-government should be provided, as simple and inexpensive as possible; it is impossible for the Congress to devote the necessary time to all the little details of necessary Alaskan legislation. Road building and railway building should be encouraged. The Governor of Alaska should begiven an ample appropriation wherewith to organize a force to preserve the public peace. Whisky selling to the natives should be made a felony. The coal land laws should be changed so as to meet the peculiar needs of the Territory. This should be attended to at once; for the present laws permit individuals to locate large areas of the public domain for speculative purposes; and cause an immense amount of trouble, fraud, and litigation. There should be another judicial division established. As early as possible lighthouses and buoys should be established as aids to navigation, especially in and about Prince William Sound, and the survey of the coast completed. There is need of liberal appropriations for lighting and buoying the southern coast and improving the aids to navigation in southeastern Alaska. One of the great industries of Alaska, as of Puget Sound and the Columbia, is salmon fishing. Gradually, by reason of lack of proper laws, this industry is being ruined; it should now be taken in charge, and effectively protected, by the United States Government.

The courage and enterprise of the citizens of the far Northwest in their projected Alaskan-Yukon-Pacific Exposition, to be held in 1909, should receive liberal encouragement. This exposition is not sentimental in its conception, but seeks to exploit the natural resources of Alaska and to promote the commerce, trade, and industry of the Pacific States with their neighboring States and with our insular possessions and the neighboring countries of the Pacific. The exposition asks no loan from the Congress but seeks appropriations for National exhibits and exhibits of the western dependencies of the General Government. The State of Washington and the city of Seattle have shown the characteristic western enterprise in large donations for the conduct of this exposition in which other States are lending generous assistance.

The unfortunate failure of the shipping bill at the last session or the last Congress was followed by the taking off of certain Pacific steamships, which has greatly hampered the movement of passengers between Hawaii and the mainland. Unless the Congress is prepared by positive encouragement to secure proper facilities in the way of shipping between Hawaii and the mainland, then the coastwise shipping laws should be so far relaxed as to prevent Hawaii suffering as it is now suffering. I again call your attention to the capital importance from every standpoint of making Pearl Harbor available for the largest deep water vessels, and of suitably fortifying the island.

The Secretary of War has gone to the Philippines. On his return I shall submit to you his report on the islands.

I again recommend that the rights of citizenship be conferred upon the people of Porto Rico.

A bureau of mines should be created under the control and direction of the Secretary of the Interior; the bureau to have power to collect statistics and make investigations in all matters pertaining to mining and particularly to the accidents and dangers of the industry. If this can not now be done, at least additional appropriations should be given the Interior Department to be used for the study of mining conditions, for the prevention of fraudulent mining schemes, for carrying on the work of mapping the mining districts, for studying methods for minimizing the accidents and dangers in the industry; in short, to aid in all proper ways the development of the mining industry.

I strongly recommend to the Congress to provide funds for keeping up the Hermitage, the home of Andrew Jackson; these funds to be used through the existing Hermitage Association for the preservation of a historic building which should ever be dear to Americans.

I further recommend that a naval monument be established in the Vicksburg National Park. This national park gives a unique opportunity for commemorating the deeds of those gallant men who fought on water, no less than of those who fought on land, in the great civil war.

Legislation should be enacted at the present session of the Congress for the Thirteenth Census. The establishment of the permanent Census Bureau affords the opportunity for a better census than we have ever had, but in order to realize the full advantage of the permanent organization, ample time must be given for preparation.

There is a constantly growing interest in this country in the question of the public health. At last the public mind is awake to the fact that many diseases, notably tuberculosis, are National scourges. The work of the State and city boards of health should be supplemented by a constantly increasing interest on the part of the National Government. The Congress has already provided a bureau of public health and has provided for a hygienic laboratory. There are other valuable laws relating to the public health connected with the various departments. This whole branch of the Government should be strengthened and aided in every way.

I call attention to two Government commissions which I have appointed and which have already done excellent work. The first of these has to do with the organization of the scientific work of the Government, which has grown up wholly without plan and is in consequence so unwisely distributed among the Executive Departments that much of its effect is lost for the lack of proper coordination. This commission's chief object is to introduce a planned and orderly development and operation in the place of the ill assorted and often ineffective grouping and methods of work which have prevailed. This can not be done without legislation, nor would it be feasible to deal in detail with so complex an administrative problem by specific provisions of law. I recommend that the President be given authority to concentrate related lines of work and reduce duplication by Executive order through transfer and consolidation of lines of work.

The second committee, that on Department methods, was instructed to investigate and report upon the changes needed to place the conduct of the executive force of the Government on the most economical and effective basis in the light of the best modern business practice. The committee has made very satisfactory progress. Antiquated practices and bureaucratic ways have been abolished, and a general renovation of departmental methods has been inaugurated. All that can be done by Executive order has already been accomplished or will be put into effect in the near future. The work of the main committee and its several assistant committees has produced a wholesome awakening on the part of the great body of officers and employees engaged in Government work. In nearly every Department and office there has been a careful self-inspection for the purpose of remedying any defects before they could be made the subject of adverse criticism. This has led individuals to a wider study of the work on which they were engaged, and this study has resulted in increasing their efficiency in their respective lines of work. There are recommendations of special importance from the committee on the subject of personnel and the classification of salaries which will require legislative action before they can be put into effect. It is my intention to submit to the Congress in the near future a special message on those subjects.

Under our form of government voting is not merely a right but a duty, and, moreover, a fundamental and necessary duty if a man is to be a good citizen. It is well to provide that corporations shall not contribute to Presidential or National campaigns, and furthermore to provide for the publication of both contributions and expenditures. There is, however, always danger in laws of this kind, which from their very nature are difficult of enforcement; the danger being lest they be obeyed only by the honest, and disobeyed by the unscrupulous, so as to act only as a penalty upon honest men. Moreover, no such law would hamper an unscrupulous man of unlimited means from buying his own way into office. There is a very radical measure which would, I believe, work a substantial improvement in our system of conducting a campaign, although I am well aware that it will take some time for people so to familiarize themselves with such a proposal as to be willing to consider its adoption. The need for collecting large campaign funds would vanish if Congress provided an appropriation for the proper and legitimate expenses of each of the great national parties, an appropriation ample enough to meet the necessity for thorough organization and machinery, which requires a large expenditure of money. Then the stipulation should be made that no party receiving campaign funds from the Treasury should accept more than a fixed amount from any individual subscriber or donor; and the necessary publicity for receipts and expenditures could without difficulty be provided.

There should be a National gallery of art established in the capita' city of this country. This is important not merely to the artistic but to the material welfare of the country; and the people are to be congratulated on the fact that the movement to establish such a gallery is taking definite form under the guidance of the Smithsonian Institution. So far from there being a tariff on works of art brought into the country, their importation should be encouraged in every way. There have been no sufficient collections of objects of art by the Government, and what collections have been acquired are scattered and are generally placed in unsuitable and imperfectly lighted galleries.

The Biological Survey is quietly working for the good of our agricultural interests, and is an excellent example of a Government bureau which conducts original scientific research the findings of which are of much practical utility. For more than twenty years it has studied the food habits of birds and mammals that are injurious or beneficial to agriculture, horticulture, and forestry; has distributed illustrated bulletins on the subject, and has labored to secure legislative protection for the beneficial species. The cotton boll-weevil, which has recently overspread the cotton belt of Texas and is steadily extending its range, is said to cause an annual loss of about $3,000,000. The Biological Survey has ascertained and gives wide publicity to the fact that at least 43 kinds of birds prey upon this destructive insect. It has discovered that 57 species of birds feed upon scale-insects—dreaded enemies of the fruit grower. It has shown that woodpeckers as a class, by destroying the larvæ of wood-boring insects, are so essential to tree life that it is doubtful if our forests could exist without them. It has shown that cuckoos and orioles are the natural enemies of the leaf-eating caterpillars that destroy our shade and fruit trees; that our quails and sparrows consume annually hundreds of tons of seeds of noxious weeds; that hawks and owls as a class (excepting the few that kill poultry and game birds) are markedly beneficial, spending their lives in catching grasshoppers, mice, and other pests that prey upon the products of husbandry. It has conducted field experiments for the purpose of devising and perfecting simple methods for holding in check the hordes of destructive rodents—rats, mice, rabbits, gophers, prairie dogs, and ground squirrels—which annually destroy crops worth many millions of dollars, and it has published practical directions for the destruction of wolves and coyotes on the stock ranges of the West, resulting during the past year in an estimated saving of cattle and sheep valued at upwards of a million dollars.

It has inaugurated a system of inspection at the principal ports of entry on both Atlantic and Pacific coasts by means of which the introduction of noxious mammals and birds is prevented, thus keeping out the mongoose and certain birds which are as much to be dreaded as the previously introduced English sparrow and the house rats and mice.

In the interest of game protection it has cooperated with local officials in every State in the Union, has striven to promote uniform legislation in the several States, has rendered important service in enforcing the Federal law regulating interstate traffic in game, and has shown how game protection may be made to yield a large revenue to the State—a revenue amounting in the case of Illinois to $128,000 in a single year.

The Biological Survey has explored the faunas and floras of America with reference to the distribution of animals and plants; it has defined and mapped the natural life areas—areas in which, by reason of prevailing climatic conditions, certain kinds of animals and plants occur—and has pointed out the adaptability of these areas to the cultivation of particular crops. The results of these investigations are not only of high educational value but are worth each year to the progressive farmers of the country many times the cost of maintaining the Survey, which, it may be added, is exceedingly small. I recommend to Congress that this bureau, whose usefulness is seriously handicapped by lack of funds, be granted an appropriation in some degree commensurate with the importance of the work it is doing.

I call your especial attention to the unsatisfactory condition of our foreign mail service, which, because of the lack of American steamship lines is now largely done through foreign lines, and which, particularly so far as South and Central America are concerned, is done in a manner which constitutes a serious barrier to the extension of our commerce.

The time has come, in my judgment, to set to work seriously to make our ocean mail service correspond more closely with our recent commercial and political development. A beginning was made by the ocean mail act of March 3, 1891, but even at that time the act was known to be inadequate in various particulars. Since that time events have moved rapidly in our history. We have acquired Hawaii, the Philippines, and lesser islands in the Pacific. We are steadily prosecuting the great work of uniting at the Isthmus the waters of the Atlantic and the Pacific. To a greater extent than seemed probable even a dozen years ago, we may look to an American future on the sea worthy of the traditions of our past. As the first step in that direction, and the step most feasible at the present time, I recommend the extension of the ocean mail act of 1891. This act has stood for some years free from successful criticism of its principle and purpose. It was based on theories of the obligations of a great maritime nation, undisputed in our own land and followed by other nations since the beginning of steam navigation. Briefly those theories are, that it is the duty of a first-class Power so far as practicable to carry its ocean mails under its own flag; that the fast ocean steamships and their crews, required for such mail service, are valuable auxiliaries to the sea power of a nation. Furthermore, the construction of such steamships insures the maintenance in an efficient condition of the shipyards in which our battleships must be built.

The expenditure of public money for the performance of such necessary functions of government is certainly warranted, nor is it necessary to dwell upon the incidental benefits to our foreign commerce, to the shipbuilding industry, and to ship owning and navigation which will accompany the discharge of these urgent public duties, though they, too, should have weight.

The only serious question is whether at this time we can afford to improve our ocean mail service as it should be improved. All doubt on this subject is removed by the reports of the Post-Office Department. For the fiscal year ended June 30, 1907, that Department estimates that the postage collected on the articles exchanged with foreign countries other than Canada and Mexico amounted to $6,579,043.48, or $3,637,226.81 more than the net cost of the service exclusive of the cost of transporting the articles between the United States exchange postoffices and the United States postoffices at which they were mailed or delivered. In other words, the Government of the United States, having assumed a monopoly of carrying the mails for the people, is making a profit of over $3,600,000 by rendering a cheap and inefficient service. That profit I believe should be devoted to strengthening our maritime power in those directions where it will best promote our prestige. The country is familiar with the facts of our maritime im-

PANAMA CANAL: OPERATION OF GATUN LOCKS

THE CHANNEL OF THE CANAL

The Panama Canal has a summit elevation of eighty-five feet above the sea and is reached by a flight of three locks at the Atlantic or northern end, one in the interior at Pedro Miguel and two at the Pacific or southern end. It is about fifty miles in length from deep water in the Caribbean Sea to deep water in the Pacific Ocean.

The channel from mile o in the Caribbean to mile 6.70 is 500 feet wide; from the south end of Gatun locks to mile 23.50, not less than 1,000 feet wide; from mile 23.50 to mile 26.50, 800 feet wide; from mile 26.50 to mile 27.00, 700 feet wide; from mile 27.00 to mile 31.25, 500 feet wide; from mile 31.25 to Pedro Miguel lock (mile 39.36) 300 feet wide, and from Pedro Miguel lock to Miraflores locks and from Miraflores locks to deep water in Panama Bay, 500 feet wide. The average bottom width of the channel in this project is 649 feet, and the minimum width is 300 feet. The Canal has a minimum depth of 41 feet. A full description of the Panama Canal will be found in the Encyclopedic Index.

potence in the harbors of the great and friendly Republics of South America. Following the failure of the shipbuilding bill we lost our only American line of steamers to Australasia, and that loss on the Pacific has become a serious embarrassment to the people of Hawaii, and has wholly cut off the Samoan islands from regular communication with the Pacific coast. Puget Sound, in the year, has lost over half (four out of seven) of its American steamers trading with the Orient.

We now pay under the act of 1891 $4 a statute mile outward to 20-knot American mail steamships, built according to naval plans, available as cruisers, and manned by Americans. The warships of that speed are confined exclusively to trans-Atlantic trade with New York. To steamships of 16 knots or over only $2 a mile can be paid, and it is steamships of this speed and type which are needed to meet the requirements of mail service to South America, Asia (including the Philippines), and Australia. I strongly recommend, therefore, a simple amendment to the ocean mail act of 1891 which shall authorize the Postmaster-General in his discretion to enter into contracts for the transportation of mails to the Republics of South America, to Asia, the Philippines, and Australia at a rate not to exceed $4 a mile for steamships of 16 knots speed or upwards, subject to the restrictions and obligations of the act of 1891. The profit of $3,600,000 which has been mentioned will fully cover the maximum annual expenditure involved in this recommendation, and it is believed will in time establish the lines so urgently needed. The proposition involves no new principle, but permits the efficient discharge of public functions now inadequately performed or not performed at all.

Not only there is not now, but there never has been, any other nation in the world so wholly free from the evils of militarism as is ours. There never has been any other large nation, not even China, which for so long a period has had relatively to its numbers so small a regular army as has ours. Never at any time in our history has this Nation suffered from militarism or been in the remotest danger of suffering from militarism. Never at any time of our history has the Regular Army been of a size which caused the slightest appreciable tax upon the tax-paying citizens of the Nation. Almost always it has been too small in size and underpaid. Never in our entire history has the Nation suffered in the least particular because too much care has been given to the Army, too much prominence given it, too much money spent upon it, or because it has been too large. But again and again we have suffered because enough care has not been given to it, because it has been too small, because there has not been sufficient preparation in advance for possible war. Every foreign war in which we have engaged has cost us many times the amount which, if wisely expended during the preceding years of peace on the Regular Army, would have insured the war ending in but a fraction of the time and but for a fraction of the cost that was actually the case. As a Nation we have always been shortsighted in providing for the efficiency of the Army in time of peace. It is nobody's especial interest to make such provision and no one looks ahead to war at any period, no matter how remote, as being a serious possibility; while an improper economy, or rather niggardliness, can be practiced at the expense of the Army with the certainty that those practicing it will not be called to account therefor, but that the price will be paid by the unfortunate persons who happen to be in office when a war does actually come.

I think it is only lack of foresight that troubles us, not any hostility to the Army. There are, of course, foolish people who denounce any care of the Army or Navy as "militarism," but I do not think that these people are numerous. This country has to contend now, and has had to contend in the past, with many evils, and there is ample scope for all who would work for reform. But there is not one evil that now exists, or that ever has existed in this country, which is, or ever has been, owing in the smallest part to militarism. Declamation against militarism has no more serious place in an earnest and intelligent movement for righteousness in this country than declamation against the worship of Baal or Astaroth. It is declamation against a non-existent evil, one which never has existed in this country, and which has not the slightest chance of appearing here. We are glad to help in any movement for international peace, but this is because we sincerely believe that it is our duty to help all such movements provided they are sane and rational, and not because there is any tendency toward militarism on our part which needs to be cured. The evils we have to fight are those in connection with industrialism, not militarism. Industry is always necessary, just as war is sometimes necessary. Each has its price, and industry in the United States now exacts, and has always exacted, a far heavier toll of death than all our wars put together. The statistics of the railroads of this country for the year ended June 30, 1906, the last contained in the annual statistical report of the Interstate Commerce Commission, show in that one year a total of 108,324 casualties to persons, of which 10,618 represent the number of persons killed. In that wonderful hive of human activity, Pittsburg, the deaths due to industrial accidents in 1906 were 919, all the result of accidents in mills, mines or on railroads. For the entire country, therefore, it is safe to say that the deaths due to industrial accidents aggregate in the neighborhood of twenty thousand a year. Such a record makes the death rate in all our foreign wars utterly trivial by comparison. The number of deaths in battle in all the foreign wars put together, for the last century and a quarter, aggregate considerably less than one year's death record for our industries. A mere glance at these figures is sufficient to show the absurdity of the outcry against militarism.

But again and again in the past our little Regular Army has rendered service literally vital to the country, and it may at any time have to do so in the future. Its standard of efficiency and instruction is higher now than ever in the past. But it is too small. There are not enough officers; and it is impossible to secure enough enlisted men. We should maintain in peace a fairly complete skeleton of a large army. A great and long-continued war would have to be fought by volunteers. But months would pass before any large body of efficient volunteers could be put in the field, and our Regular Army should be large enough to meet any immediate need. In particular it is essential that we should possess a number of extra officers trained in peace to perform efficiently the duties urgently required upon the breaking out of war.

The Medical Corps should be much larger than the needs of our Regular Army in war. Yet at present it is smaller than the needs of the service demand even in peace. The Spanish war occurred less than ten years ago. The chief loss we suffered in it was by disease among the regiments which never left the country. At the moment the Nation seemed deeply impressed by this fact; yet seemingly it has already been forgotten, for not the slightest effort has been made to prepare a medical corps of sufficient size to prevent the repetition of the same disaster on a much larger scale if we should ever be engaged in a serious conflict. The trouble in the Spanish war was not with the then existing officials of the War Department; it was with the representatives of the people as a whole who, for the preceding thirty years, had declined to make the necessary provision for the Army. Unless ample provision is now made by Congress to put the Medical Corps where it should be put disaster in the next war is inevitable, and the responsibility will not lie with those then in charge of the War Department, but with those who now decline to make the necessary provision. A well organized medical corps, thoroughly trained before the advent of war in all the important administrative duties of a military sanitary corps, is essential to the efficiency of any large army, and especially of a large volunteer army. Such knowledge of medicine and surgery as is possessed by the medical profession generally will not alone suffice to make an efficient military surgeon. He must have, in addition, knowledge of the administration and sanitation of large field hospitals and camps, in order to safeguard the health and lives of men intrusted in great numbers to his care. A bill has long been pending before the Congress for the reorganization of the Medical Corps; its passage is urgently needed.

But the Medical Department is not the only department for which increased provision should be made. The rate of pay for the officers should be greatly increased; there is no higher type of citizen than the American regular officer, and he should have a fair reward for his admirable work. There should be a relatively even greater increase in the pay for the enlisted men. In especial provision should be made for establishing grades equivalent to those of warrant officers in the Navy which should be open to the enlisted men who serve sufficiently long and who do their work well. Inducements should be offered sufficient to encourage really good men to make the Army a life occupation. The prime needs of our present Army is to secure and retain competent noncommissioned officers. This difficulty rests fundamentally on the question of pay. The noncommissioned officer does not correspond with an unskilled laborer; he corresponds to the best type of skilled workman or to the subordinate official in civil institutions. Wages have greatly increased in outside occupations in the last forty years and the pay of the soldier, like the pay of the officers, should be proportionately increased. The first sergeant of a company, if a good man, must be one of such executive and administrative ability, and such knowledge of his trade, as to be worth far more than we at present pay him. The same is true of the regimental sergeant major. These men should be men who had fully resolved to make the Army a life occupation and they should be able to look forward to ample reward; while only men properly qualified should be given a chance to secure these final rewards. The increase over the present pay need not be great in the lower grades for the first one or two enlistments, but the increase should be marked for the noncommissioned officers of the upper grades who serve long enough to make it evident that they intend to stay permanently in the Army, while additional pay should be given for high qualifications in target practice. The position of warrant officer should be established and there should be not only an increase of pay, but an increase of privileges and allowances and dignity, so as to make the grade open to noncommissioned officers capable of filling them desirably from every standpoint. The rate of desertion in our Army now in time of peace is alarming. The deserter should be treated by public opinion as a man guilty of the greatest crime; while on the other hand the man who serves steadily in the Army should be treated as what he is, that is, as preeminently one of the best citizens of this Republic. After twelve years' service in the Army my own belief is that the man should be given a preference according to his ability for certain types of office over all civilian applicants without examination. This should also apply, of course, to the men who have served twelve years in the Navy. A special corps should be provided to do the manual labor now necessarily demanded of the privates themselves.

Among the officers there should be severe examinations to weed out the unfit up to the grade of major. From that position on appointments should be solely by selection and it should be understood that a man of merely average capacity could never get beyond the position of major, while every man who serves in any grade a certain length of time prior to promotion to the next grade without getting the promotion to the next grade should be forthwith retired. The practice marches and field maneuvers of the last two or three years have been invaluable to the Army. They should be continued and extended. A rigid and not a perfunctory examination of physical capacity has been provided for the higher grade officers. This will work well. Unless an officer has a good physique, unless he can stand hardship, ride well, and walk fairly, he is not fit for any position, even after he has become a colonel. Before he has become a colonel the need for physical fitness in the officers is almost as great as in the enlisted man. I hope speedily to see introduced into the Army a far more rigid and thoroughgoing test of horsemanship for all field officers than at present. There should be a Chief of Cavalry just as there is a Chief of Artillery.

Perhaps the most important of all legislation needed for the benefit of the Army is a law to equalize and increase the pay of officers and enlisted men of the Army, Navy, Marine Corps, and Revenue-Cutter Service. Such a bill has been prepared, which it is hoped will meet with your favorable consideration. The next most essential measure is to authorize a number of extra officers as mentioned above. To make the Army more attractive to enlisted men, it is absolutely essential to create a service corps, such as exists in nearly every modern army in the world, to do the skilled and unskilled labor, inseparably connected with military administration, which is now exacted, without just compensation, of enlisted men who voluntarily entered the Army to do service of an altogether different kind. There are a number of other laws necessary to so organize the Army as to promote its efficiency and facilitate its rapid expansion in time of war; but the above are the most important.

It was hoped The Hague Conference might deal with the question of the limitation of armaments. But even before it had assembled informal inquiries had developed that as regards naval armaments, the only ones in which this country had any interest, it was hopeless to try to devise any plan for which there was the slightest possibility of securing the assent of the nations gathered at The Hague. No plan was even proposed which would have had the assent of more than one first class Power outside of the United States. The only plan that seemed at all feasible, that of limiting the size of battleships, met with no favor at all. It is evident, therefore, that it is folly for this Nation to base any hope of securing peace on any international agreement as to the limitations of armaments. Such being the fact it would be most unwise for us to stop the upbuilding of our Navy. To build one battleship of the best and most advanced type a year would barely keep our fleet up to its present force. This is not enough. In my judgment, we should this year provide for four battleships. But it is idle to build battleships unless in addition to providing the men, and the means for thorough training, we provide the auxiliaries for them, unless we provide docks, the coaling stations, the colliers and supply ships that they need. We are extremely deficient in coaling stations and docks on the Pacific, and this deficiency should not longer be permitted to exist. Plenty of torpedo boats and destroyers should be built. Both on the Atlantic and Pacific coasts, fortifications of the best type should be provided for all our greatest harbors.

We need always to remember that in time of war the Navy is not to be used to defend harbors and sea-coast cities; we should perfect our system of coast fortifications. The only efficient use for the Navy is for offense. The only way in which it can efficiently protect our own coast against the possible action of a foreign navy is by destroying that foreign navy. For defense against a hostile fleet which actually attacks them, the coast cities must depend upon their forts, mines, torpedoes, submarines, and torpedo boats and destroyers. All of these together are efficient for defensive purposes, but they in no way supply the place of a thoroughly efficient navy capable of acting on the offensive; for parrying never yet won a fight. It can only be won by hard hitting, and an aggressive sea-going navy alone can do this hard hitting of the offensive type. But the forts and the like are necessary so that the Navy may be footloose. In time of war there is sure to be demand, under pressure, of fright, for the ships to be scattered so as to defend all kind of ports. Under penalty of terrible disaster, this demand must be refused. The ships must be kept together, and their objective made the enemies' fleet. If fortifications are sufficiently strong, no modern navy will venture to attack them, so long as the foe has in existence a hostile navy of anything like the same size or efficiency. But unless there exists such a navy then the fortifications are powerless by themselves to secure the victory. For of course the mere deficiency means that any resolute enemy can at his leisure combine all his forces upon one point with the certainty that he can take it.

Until our battle fleet is much larger than at present it should never be split into detachments so far apart that they could not in event of emergency be speedily united. Our coast line is on the Pacific just as much as on the Atlantic. The interests of California, Oregon, and Washington are as emphatically the interests of the whole Union as those of Maine and New York, of Louisiana and Texas. The battle fleet should now and then be moved to the Pacific, just as at other times it should be kept in the Atlantic. When the Isthmian Canal is built the transit of the battle fleet from one ocean to the other will be comparatively easy. Until it is built I earnestly hope that the battle fleet will be thus shifted between the two oceans every year or two. The marksmanship on all our ships has improved phenomenally during the last five years. Until within the last two or three years it was not possible to train a battle fleet in squadron maneuvers under service conditions, and it is only during these last two or three years that the training under these conditions has become really effective. Another and most necessary stride in advance is now being taken. The battle fleet is about starting by the Straits of Magellan to visit the Pacific coast.. Sixteen battleships are going under the command of Rear-Admiral Evans, while eight armored cruisers and two other battleships will meet him at San Francisco, whither certain torpedo destroyers are also going. No fleet of such size has ever made such a voyage, and it will be of very great educational use to all engaged in it.. The only way by which to teach officers and men how to handle the fleet so as to meet every possible strain and emergency in time of war is to have them practice under similar conditions in time of peace. Moreover, the only way to find out our actual needs is to perform in time of peace whatever maneuvers might be necessary in time of war. After war is declared it is too late to find out the needs; that means to invite disaster. This trip to the Pacific will show what some of our needs are and will enable us to provide for them. The proper place for an officer to learn his duty is at sea, and the only way in which a navy can ever be made efficient is by practice at sea, under all the conditions which would have to be met if war existed.

I bespeak the most liberal treatment for the officers and enlisted men of the Navy. It is true of them, as likewise of the officers and enlisted men of the Army, that they form a body whose interests should be close to the heart of every good American. In return the most rigid performance of duty should be exacted from them. The reward should be ample when they do their best; and nothing less than their best should be tolerated. It is idle to hope for the best results when the men in the senior grades come to those grades late in life and serve too short a time in them. Up to the rank of lieutenant-commander promotion in the Navy should be as now, by seniority, subject, however, to such rigid tests as would eliminate the unfit. After the grade of lieutenant-commander, that is, when we come to the grade of command rank, the unfit should be eliminated in such manner that only the conspicuously fit would remain, and sea service should be a principal test of fitness. Those who are passed by should, after a certain length of service in their respective grades, be retired. Of a given number of men it may well be that almost all would make good lieutenants and most of them good lieutenant-commanders, while only a minority be fit to be captains, and but three or four to be admirals. Those who object to promotion otherwise than by mere seniority should reflect upon the elementary fact that no business in private life could be successfully managed if those who enter at the lowest rungs of the ladder should each in turn, if he lived, become the head of the firm, its active director, and retire after he had held the position a few months. On its face such a scheme is an absurdity. Chances for improper favoritism can be minimized by a properly formed board; such as the board of last June, which did such conscientious and excellent work in elimination.

If all that ought to be done can not now be done, at least let a beginning be made. In my last three annual Messages, and in a special Message to the last Congress, the necessity for legislation that will cause officers of the line of the Navy to reach the grades of captain and rear-admiral at less advanced ages and which will cause them to have more sea training and experience in the highly responsible duties of those grades, so that they may become thoroughly skillful in handling battleships, divisions, squadrons, and fleets in action, has been fully explained and urgently recommended. Upon this subject the Secretary of the Navy has submitted detailed and definite recommendations which have received my approval, and which, if enacted into law, will accomplish what is immediately necessary, and will, as compared with existing law, make a saving of more than five millions of dollars during the next seven years. The navy personnel act of 1899 has accomplished all that was expected of it in providing satisfactory periods of service in the several subordinate grades, from the grade of ensign to the grade of lieutenant-commander, but the law is inadequate in the upper grades and will continue to be inadequate on account of the expansion of the personnel since its enactment. Your attention is invited to the following quotations from the report of the personnel board of 1906, of which the Assistant Secretary of the Navy was president:

"Congress has authorized a considerable increase in the number of midshipmen at the Naval Academy, and these midshipmen upon graduation are promoted to ensign and lieutenant (junior-grade). But no provision has been made for a corresponding increase in the upper grades, the result being that the lower grades will become so congested that a midshipman now in one of the lowest classes at Annapolis may possibly not be promoted to lieutenant until he is between 45 and 50 years of age. So it will continue under the present law, congesting at the top and congesting at the bottom. The country fails to get from the officers of the service the best that is in them by not providing opportunity for their normal development and training. The board believes that this works a serious detriment to the efficiency of the Navy and is a real menace to the public safety."

As stated in my special Message to the last Congress: "I am firmly of the opinion that unless the present conditions of the higher commissioned personnel is rectified by judicious legislation the future of our Navy will be gravely compromised." It is also urgently necessary to increase the efficiency of the Medical Corps of the Navy. Special legislation to this end has already been proposed; and I trust it may be enacted without delay.

It must be remembered that everything done in the Navy to fit it to do well in time of war must be done in time of peace. Modern wars are short; they do not last the length of time requisite to build a battleship; and it takes longer to train the officers and men to do well on a battleship than it takes to build it. Nothing effective can be done for the Navy once war has begun, and the result of the war, if the combatants are otherwise equally matched, will depend upon which power has prepared best in time of peace. The United States Navy is the best guaranty the Nation has that its honor and interest will not be neglected; and in addition it offers by far the best insurance for peace that can by human ingenuity be devised.

I call attention to the report of the official Board of Visitors to the Naval Academy at Annapolis which has been forwarded to the Congress. The report contains this paragraph:

"Such revision should be made of the courses of study and methods of conducting and marking examinations as will develop and bring out the average all-round ability of the midshipman rather than to give him prominence in any one particular study. The fact should be kept in mind that the Naval Academy is not a university but a school, the primary object of which is to educate boys to be efficient naval officers. Changes in curriculum, therefore, should be in the direction of making the course of instruction less theoretical and more practical. No portion of any future class should be graduated in advance of the full four years' course, and under no circumstances should the standard of instruction be lowered. The Academy in almost all of its departments is now magnificently equipped, and it would be very unwise to make the course of instruction less exacting than it is to-day."

Acting upon this suggestion I designated three seagoing officers, Capt. Richard Wainwright, Commander Robert S. Griffin, and Lieut. Commander Albert L. Key, all graduates of the Academy, to investigate conditions and to recommend to me the best method of carrying into effect this general recommendation. These officers performed the duty promptly and intelligently, and, under the personal direction of

Capt. Charles J. Badger, Superintendent of the Academy, such of the proposed changes as were deemed to be at present advisable were put into effect at the beginning of the academic year, October 1, last. The results, I am confident, will be most beneficial to the Academy, to the midshipmen, and to the Navy.

In foreign affairs this country's steady policy is to behave toward other nations as a strong and self-respecting man should behave toward the other men with whom he is brought into contact.. In other words, our aim is disinterestedly to help other nations where such help can be wisely given without the appearance of meddling with what does not concern us; to be careful to act as a good neighbor; and at the same time, in good-natured fashion, to make it evident that we do not intend to be imposed upon.

The Second International Peace Conference was convened at The Hague on the 15th of June last and remained in session until the 18th of October. For the first time the representatives of practically all the civilized countries of the world united in a temperate and kindly discussion of the methods by which the causes of war might be narrowed and its injurious effects reduced.

Although the agreements reached in the Conference did not in any direction go to the length hoped for by the more sanguine, yet in many directions important steps were taken, and upon every subject on the programme there was such full and considerate discussion as to justify the belief that substantial progress has been made toward further agreements in the future. Thirteen conventions were agreed upon embodying the definite conclusions which had been reached, and resolutions were adopted marking the progress made in matters upon which agreement was not yet sufficiently complete to make conventions practicable.

The delegates of the United States were instructed to favor an agreement for obligatory arbitration, the establishment of a permanent court of arbitration to proceed judicially in the hearing and decision of international causes, the prohibition of force for the collection of contract debts alleged to be due from governments to citizens of other countries until after arbitration as to the justice and amount of the debt and the time and manner of payment, the immunity of private property at sea, the better definition of the rights of neutrals, and, in case any measure to that end should be introduced, the limitation of armaments.

In the field of peaceful disposal of international differences several important advances were made. First, as to obligatory arbitration. Although the Conference failed to secure a unanimous agreement upon the details of a convention for obligatory arbitration, it did resolve as follows:

"It is unanimous: (1) In accepting the principle for obligatory arbitration; (2) In declaring that certain differences, and notably those relating to the interpretation and application of international conventional stipulations are susceptible of being submitted to obligatory arbitration without any restriction."

In view of the fact that as a result of the discussion the vote upon the definite treaty of obligatory arbitration, which was proposed, stood 32 in favor to 9 against the adoption of the treaty, there can be little doubt that the great majority of the countries of the world have reached a point where they are now ready to apply practically the principles thus unanimously agreed upon by the Conference.

The second advance, and a very great one, is the agreement which relates to the use of force for the collection of contract debts. Your attention is invited to the paragraphs upon this subject in my Message of December, 1906, and to the resolution of the Third American Conference at Rio in the summer of 1906. The convention upon this subject adopted by the Conference substantially as proposed by the American delegates is as follows: :

"In order to avoid between nations armed conflicts of a purely pecuniary origin arising from contractual debts claimed of the government of one country by the government of another country to be due to its nationals, the signatory Powers agree not to have recourse to armed force for the collection of such contractual debts.

"However, this stipulation shall not be applicable when the debtor State refuses or leaves unanswered an offer to arbitrate, or, in case of acceptance, makes it impossible to formulate the terms of submission, or, after arbitration, fails to comply with the award rendered.

"It is further agreed that arbitration here contemplated shall be in conformity, as to procedure, with Chapter III of the Convention for the Pacific Settlement of International Disputes adopted at The Hague, and that it shall determine, in so far as there shall be no agreement between the parties, the justice and the amount of the debt, the time and mode of payment thereof."

Such a provision would have prevented much injustice and extortion in the past, and I cannot doubt that its effect in the future will be most salutary.

A third advance has been made in amending and perfecting the convention of 1899 for the voluntary settlement of international disputes, and particularly the extension of those parts of that convention which relate to commissions of inquiry. The existence of those provisions enabled the Governments of Great Britain and Russia to avoid war, notwithstanding great public excitement, at the time of the Dogger Bank incident, and the new convention agreed upon by the Conference gives practical effect to the experience gained in that inquiry.

Substantial progress was also made towards the creation of a permanent judicial tribunal for the determination of international causes. There was very full discussion of the proposal for such a court and a general agreement was finally reached in favor of its creation. The Conference recommended to the signatory Powers the adoption of a draft upon which it agreed for the organization of the court, leaving to be determined only the method by which the judges should be selected. This remaining unsettled question is plainly one which time and good temper will solve.

A further agreement of the first importance was that for the creation of an international prize court. The constitution, organization and procedure of such a tribunal were provided for in detail. Anyone who recalls the injustices under which this country suffered as a neutral power during the early part of the last century can not fail to see in this provision for an international prize court the great advance which the world is making towards the substitution of the rule of reason and justice in place of simple force. Not only will the international prize court be the means of protecting the interests of neutrals, but it is in itself a step towards the creation of the more general court for the hearing of international controversies to which reference has just been made. The organization and action of such a prize court can not fail to accustom the different countries to the submission of international questions to the decision of an international tribunal, and we may confidently expect the results of such submission to bring about a general agreement upon the enlargement of the practice.

Numerous provisions were adopted for reducing the evil effects of war and for defining the rights and duties of neutrals.

The Conference also provided for the holding of a third Conference within a period similar to that which elapsed between the First and Second Conferences.

The delegates of the United States worthily represented the spirit of the American people and maintained with fidelity and ability the policy of our Government upon all the great questions discussed in the Conference.

The report of the delegation, together with authenticated copies of the conventions signed, when received, will be laid before the Senate for its consideration.

When we remember how difficult it is for one of our own legislative bodies, composed of citizens of the same country, speaking the same language, living under the same laws, and having the same customs, to reach an agreement, or even to secure a majority upon any difficult and important subject which is proposed for legislation, it becomes plain that the representatives of forty-five different countries, speaking many different languages, accustomed to different methods of procedure, with widely diverse interests, who discussed so many different subjects and reached agreements upon so many, are entitled to grateful appreciation for the wisdom, patience, and moderation with which they have discharged their duty. The example of this temperate discussion, and the agreements and the efforts to agree, among representatives of all the nations of the earth, acting with universal recognition of the supreme obligation to promote peace, can not fail to be a powerful influence for good in future international relations.

A year ago in consequence of a revolutionary movement in Cuba which threatened the immediate return to chaos of the island, the United States intervened, sending down an army and establishing a provisional government under Governor Magoon. Absolute quiet and prosperity have returned to the island because of this action. We are now taking steps to provide for elections in the island and our expectation is within the coming year to be able to turn the island over again to a government chosen by the people thereof. Cuba is at our doors. It is not possible that this Nation should permit Cuba again to sink into the condition from which we rescued it. All that we ask of the Cuban people is that they be prosperous, that they govern themselves so as to bring content, order and progress to their island, the Queen of the Antilles; and our only interference has been and will be to help them achieve these results.

An invitation has been extended by Japan to the Government and people of the United States to participate in a great national exposition to be held at Tokyo from April 1 to October 31, 1912, and in which the principal countries of the world are to be invited to take part. This is an occasion of special interest to all the nations of the world, and peculiarly so to us; for it is the first instance in which such a great national exposition has been held by a great power dwelling on the Pacific; and all the nations of Europe and America will, I trust, join in helping to success this first great exposition ever held by a great nation of Asia. The geographical relations of Japan and the United States as the possessors of such large portions of the coasts of the Pacific, the intimate trade relations already existing between the two countries, the warm friendship which has been maintained between them without break since the opening of Japan to intercourse with the western nations, and her increasing wealth and production, which we regard with hearty goodwill and wish to make the occasion of mutually beneficial commerce, all unite in making it eminently desirable that this invitation should be accepted. I heartily recommend such legislation as will provide in generous fashion for the representation of this Government and its people in the proposed exposition. Action should be taken now. We are apt to underestimate the time necessary for preparation in such cases. The invitation to the French Exposition of 1900 was brought to the attention of the Congress by President Cleveland in December, 1895; and so many are the delays necessary to such proceedings that the period of four years and a half which then intervened before the exposition proved none too long for the proper preparation of the exhibits.

The adoption of a new tariff by Germany, accompanied by conventions for reciprocal tariff concessions between that country and most of the other countries of continental Europe, led the German Government to give the notice necessary to terminate the reciprocal commercial agreement with this country proclaimed July 13, 1900. The notice was to take effect on the 1st of March, 1906, and in default of some other arrangements this would have left the exports from the United States to Germany subject to the general German tariff duties, from 25 to 50 per cent higher than the conventional duties imposed upon the goods of most of our competitors for German trade.

Under a special agreement made between the two Governments in February, 1906, the German Government postponed the operation of their notice until the 30th of June, 1907. In the meantime, deeming it to be my duty to make every possible effort to prevent a tariff war between the United States and Germany arising from misunderstanding by either country of the conditions existing in the other, and acting upon the invitation of the German Government, I sent to Berlin a commission composed of competent experts in the operation and administration of the customs tariff, from the Departments of the Treasury and Commerce and Labor. This commission was engaged for several months in conference with a similar commission appointed by the German Government, under instructions, so far as practicable, to reach a common understanding as to all the facts regarding the tariffs of the United States and Germany material and relevant to the trade relations between the two countries. The commission reported, and upon the basis of the report, a further temporary commercial agreement was entered into by the two countries, pursuant to which, in the exercise of the authority conferred upon the President by the third section of the tariff act of July 24, 1897, I extended the reduced tariff rates provided for in that section to champagne and all other sparkling wines, and pursuant to which the German conventional or minimum tariff rates were extended to about 96½ per cent of all the exports from the United States to Germany. This agreement is to remain in force until the 30th of June, 1908, and until six months after notice by either party to terminate it.

The agreement and the report of the commission on which it is based will be laid before the Congress for its information.

This careful examination into the tariff relations between the United States and Germany involved an inquiry into certain of our methods of administration which had been the cause of much complaint on the part of German exporters. In this inquiry I became satisfied that certain vicious and unjustifiable practices had grown up in our customs administration, notably the practice of determining values of imports upon detective reports never disclosed to the persons whose interests were affected. The use of detectives, though often necessary, tends towards abuse, and should be carefully guarded. Under our practice as I found it to exist in this case, the abuse had become gross and discreditable. Under it, instead of seeking information as to the market value of merchandise from the well-known and respected members of the commercial community in the country of its production, secret statements were obtained from informers and discharged employees and business rivals, and upon this kind of secret evidence the values of imported goods were frequently raised and heavy penalties were frequently imposed upon importers who were never permitted to know what the evidence was and who never had an opportunity to meet it. It is quite probable that this system tended towards an increase of the duties collected upon imported goods, but I conceive it to be a violation of law to exact more duties than the law provides, just as it is a violation to admit goods upon the payment of less than the legal rate of duty. This practice was repugnant to the spirit of American law and to American sense of justice. In the judgment of the most competent experts of the Treasury Department and the Department of Commerce and Labor it was wholly unnecessary for the due collection of the customs revenues, and the attempt to defend it merely illustrates the demoralization which naturally follows from a long continued course of reliance upon such methods. I accordingly caused the regulations governing this branch of the customs service to be modified so that values are determined upon a hearing in which all the parties interested have an opportunity to be heard and to know the evidence against them. Moreover our Treasury agents are accredited to the government of the country in which they seek information, and in Germany receive the assistance of the quasi-official chambers of commerce in determining the actual market value of goods, in accordance with what I am advised to be the true construction of the law.

These changes of regulations were adapted to the removal of such manifest abuses that I have not felt that they ought to be confined to our relations with Germany; and I have extended their operation to all other countries which have expressed a desire to enter into similar administrative relations.

I ask for authority to re-form the agreement with China under which the indemnity of 1900 was fixed, by remitting and cancelling the obligation of China for the payment of all that part of the stipulated indemnity which is in excess of the sum of eleven million, six hundred and fifty-five thousand, four hundred and ninety-two dollars and sixty-nine cents, and interest at four per cent. After the rescue of the foreign legations in Peking during the Boxer troubles in 1900 the Powers required from China the payment of equitable indemnities to the several nations, and the final protocol under which the troops were withdrawn, signed at Peking, September 7, 1901, fixed the amount of this indemnity allotted to the United States at over $20,000,000, and China paid, up to and including the 1st day of June last, a little over $6,-000,000. It was the first intention of this Government at the proper time, when all claims had been presented and all expenses ascertained as fully as possible, to revise the estimates and account, and as a proof of sincere friendship for China voluntarily to release that country from its legal liability for all payments in excess of the sum which should prove to be necessary for actual indemnity to the United States and its citizens.

This Nation should help in every practicable way in the education of the Chinese people, so that the vast and populous Empire of China may gradually adapt itself to modern conditions. One way of doing this is by promoting the coming of Chinese students to this country and making it attractive to them to take courses at our universities and higher educational institutions. Our educators should, so far as possible, take concerted action toward this end.

On the courteous invitation of the President of Mexico, the Secretary of State visited that country in September and October and was received everywhere with the greatest kindness and hospitality.

He carried from the Government of the United States to our southern neighbor a message of respect and good will and of desire for better acquaintance and increasing friendship. The response from the Government and the people of Mexico was hearty and sincere. No pains were spared to manifest the most friendly attitude and feeling toward the United States.

In view of the close neighborhood of the two countries the relations which exist between Mexico and the United States are just cause for gratification. We have a common boundary of over 1,500 miles from the Gulf of Mexico to the Pacific. Much of it is marked only by the shifting waters of the Rio Grande. Many thousands of Mexicans are residing upon our side of the line and it is estimated that over 40,000 Americans are resident in Mexican territory and that American investments in Mexico amount to over seven hundred million dollars. The extraordinary industrial and commercial prosperity of Mexico has been greatly promoted by American enterprise, and Americans are sharing largely in its results. The foreign trade of the Republic already exceeds $240,000,000 per annum, and of this two-thirds both of exports and imports are exchanged with the United States. Under these circumstances numerous questions necessarily arise between the two countries. These questions are always approached and disposed of in a spirit of mutual courtesy and fair dealing. Americans carrying on business in Mexico testify uniformly to the kindness and consideration with which they are treated and their sense of the security of their property and enterprises under the wise administration of the great statesman who has so long held the office of Chief Magistrate of that Republic.

The two Governments have been uniting their efforts for a considerable time past to aid Central America in attaining the degree of peace and order which have made possible the prosperity of the northern ports of the Continent. After the peace between Guatemala, Honduras, and Salvador, celebrated under the circumstances described in my last Message, a new war broke out between the Republics of Nicaragua, Honduras, and Salvador. The effort to compose this new difficulty has resulted in the acceptance of the joint suggestion of the Presidents of Mexico and of the United States for a general peace conference between all the countries of Central America. On the 17th day of September last a protocol was signed between the representatives of the five Central American countries accredited to this Government agreeing upon a conference to be held in the City of Washington "in order to devise the means of preserving the good relations among said Republics and bringing about permanent peace in those countries." The protocol includes the expression of a wish that the Presidents of the United States and Mexico should appoint "representatives to lend their good and impartial offices in a purely friendly way toward the realization of the objects of the conference." The conference is now in session and will have our best wishes and, where it is practicable, our friendly assistance.

One of the results of the Pan American Conference at Rio Janeiro in the summer of 1906 has been a great increase in the activity and usefulness of the International Bureau of American Republics. That institution, which includes all the American Republics in its membership and brings all their representatives together, is doing a really valuable work in informing the people of the United States about the other Republics and in making the United States known to them. Its action is now limited by appropriations determined when it was doing a work on a much smaller scale and rendering much less valuable service. I recommend that the contribution of this Government to the expenses of the Bureau be made commensurate with its increased work.

THEODORE ROOSEVELT.

THE WHITE HOUSE.
December 3, 1907.

SPECIAL MESSAGE.

WHITE HOUSE, Jan. 31, 1908.

To the Senate and House of Representatives:

The recent decision of the Supreme Court in regard to the employers' liability act, the experience of the Interstate Commerce Commission and of the Department of Justice in enforcing the interstate commerce and antitrust laws, and the gravely significant attitude toward the law and its administration recently adopted by certain heads of great corporations, render it desirable that there should be additional legislation as regards certain of the relations between labor and capital, and between the great corporations and the public.

The Supreme Court has decided the employers' liability law to be unconstitutional because its terms apply to employees engaged wholly in intrastate commerce as well as to employees engaged in interstate commerce. By a substantial majority the Court holds that the Congress has power to deal with the question in so far as interstate commerce is concerned.

As regards the employers' liability law, I advocate its immediate reenactment, limiting its scope so that it shall apply only to the class of cases as to which the Court says it can constitutionally apply, but strengthening its provisions within this scope. Interstate employment being thus covered by an adequate national law, the field of intrastate employment will be left to the action of the several States. With this clear definition of responsibility the States will undoubtedly give to the performance of their duty within their field the consideration the importance of the subject demands.

I also very urgently advise that a comprehensive act be passed providing for compensation by the Government to all employees injured in the Government service. Under the present law an injured workman in the employment of the Government has no remedy, and the entire burden of the accident falls on the helpless man, his wife, and his young children. This is an outrage. It is a matter of humiliation to the Nation that there should not be on our statute books provision to meet and partially to atone for cruel misfortune when it comes upon a man through no fault of his own while faithfully serving the public. In no other prominent industrial country in the world could such gross injustice occur; for almost all civilized nations have enacted legislation embodying the complete recognition of the principle which places the entire trade risk for industrial accidents (excluding, of course, accidents due to willful misconduct by the employee) on the industry as represented by the employer, which in this case is the Government. In all these countries the principle applies to the Government just as much as to the private employer. Under no circumstances should the injured employee or his surviving dependents be required to bring suit against the Government, nor should there be the requirement that in order to insure recovery negligence in some form on the part of the Government should be shown. Our proposition is not to confer a right of action upon the Government employee, but to secure him suitable provision against injuries received in the course of his employment. The burden of the trade risk should be placed upon the Government. Exactly as the workingman is entitled to his wages, so he should be entitled to indemnity for the injuries sustained in the natural course of his labor. The rates of compensation and the regulations for its payment should be specified in the law, and the machinery for determining the amount to be paid should in each case be provided in such manner that the employee is properly represented without expense to him. In other words, the compensation should be paid automatically, while the application of the law in the first instance should be vested in the Department of Commerce and Labor. The law should apply to all laborers, mechanics, and other civilian employees of the Government of the United States, including those in the service of the Panama Canal Commission and of the insular governments.

The same broad principle which should apply to the Government should ultimately be made applicable to all private employers. Where the Nation has the power it should enact laws to this effect. Where the States alone have the power they should enact the laws. It is to be observed that an employers' liability law does not really mean mulcting employers in damages. It merely throws upon the employer the burden of accident insurance against injuries which are sure to occur. It requires him either to bear or to distribute through insurance the loss which can readily be borne when distributed, but which, if undistributed, bears with frightful hardship upon the unfortunate victim of accident. In theory, if wages were always freely and fairly adjusted, they would always include an allowance as against the risk of injury, just as certainly as the rate of interest for money includes an allowance for insurance against the risk of loss. In theory, if employees were all experienced business men, they would employ that part of their wages which is received because of the risk of injury to secure accident insurance. But as a matter of fact it is not practical to expect that this will be done by the great body of employees. An employers' liability law makes it certain that it will be done, in effect, by the employer, and it will ultimately impose no real additional burden upon him.

There is a special bill to which I call your attention. Secretary Taft has urgently recommended the immediate passage of a law providing for compensation to employees of the Government injured in the work of the Isthmian Canal, and that $100,000 be appropriated for this purpose each year. I earnestly hope this will be done; and that a special bill be passed covering the case of Yardmaster Banton, who was injured nearly two years ago while doing his duty. He is now helpless to support his wife and his three little boys.

I again call your attention to the need of some action in connection with the abuse of injunctions in labor cases. As regards the rights and wrongs of labor and capital, from blacklisting to boycotting, the whole subject is covered in admirable fashion by the report of the Anthracite Coal Strike Commission, which report should serve as a chart for the guidance of both legislative and executive officers. As regards injunctions, I can do little but repeat what I have said in my last message to the Congress. Even though it were possible, I should consider it most unwise to abolish the use of the process of injunction. It is necessary in order that the courts may maintain their own dignity and in order that they may in effective manner check disorder and violence. The judge who uses it cautiously and conservatively, but who, when the need arises, uses it fearlessly, confers the greatest service upon our people, and his preeminent usefulness as a public servant should be heartily recognized. But there is no question in my mind that it has sometimes been used heedlessly and unjustly, and that some of the injunctions issued inflict grave and occasionally irreparable wrong upon those enjoined.

It is all wrong to use the injunction to prevent the entirely proper and legitimate actions of labor organizations in their struggle for industrial betterment, or under the guise of protecting property rights unwarrantably to invade the fundamental rights of the individual. It is futile to concede, as we all do, the right and the necessity of organized effort on the part of wage-earners and yet by injunctive process to forbid peaceable action to accomplish the lawful objects for which they are organized and upon which their success depends. The fact that the punishment for the violation of an injunction must, to make the order effective, necessarily be summary and without the intervention of a jury makes its issuance in doubtful cases a dangerous practice, and in itself furnishes a reason why the process should be surrounded with safeguards to protect individuals against being enjoined from exercising their proper rights. Reasonable notice should be given the adverse party.

This matter is daily becoming of graver importance and I can not too urgently recommend that the Congress give careful consideration to the subject. If some way of remedying the abuses is not found the feeling of indignation against them among large numbers of our citizens will tend to grow so extreme as to produce a revolt against the whole use of the process of injunction. The ultra-conservatives who object to cutting out the abuses will do well to remember that if the popular feeling does become strong many of those upon whom they rely to defend them will be the first to turn against them. Men of property can not afford to trust to anything save the spirit of justice and fair play; for those very public men who, while it is to their interest, defend all the abuses committed by capital and pose as the champions of conservatism, will, the moment they think their interest changes, take the lead in just such a matter as this and pander to what they esteem popular feeling by endeavoring, for instance, effectively to destroy the power of the courts in matters of injunction; and will even seek to render nugatory the power to punish for contempt, upon which power the very existence of the orderly administration of justice depends.

It is my purpose as soon as may be to submit some further recommendations in reference to our laws regulating labor conditions within the sphere of Federal authority. A very recent decision of the Supreme Court of the United States rendered since this message was written, in the case of Adair *v.* United States, seemingly of far-reaching import and of very serious probable consequences, has modified the previously entertained views on the powers of the Congress in the premises to such a degree as to make necessary careful consideration of the opinions therein filed before it is possible definitely to decide in what way to call the matter to your attention.

Not only should there be action on certain laws affecting wage-earners; there should also be such action on laws better to secure control over the great business concerns engaged in interstate commerce, and especially over the great common carriers. The Interstate Commerce Commission should be empowered to pass upon any rate or practice on its own initiative. Moreover, it should be provided that whenever the Commission has reason to believe that a proposed advance in a rate ought not to be made without investigation, it should have authority to issue an order prohibiting the advance pending examination by the Commission.

I would not be understood as expressing an opinion that any or even a majority of these advances are improper. Many of the rates in this country have been abnormally low. The operating expenses of our railroads, notably the wages paid railroad employees, have greatly increased. These and other causes may in any given case justify an advance in rates, and if so the advance should be permitted and approved. But there may be, and doubtless are, cases where this is not true; and our law should be so framed that the Government, as the representative of the whole people, can protect the individual against unlawful exaction for the use of these public highways. The Interstate Commerce Commission should be provided with the means to make a physical valuation of any road as to which it deems this valuation necessary. In some form the Federal Government should exercise supervision over the financial operations of our interstate railroads. In no other way can justice be done between the private owners of those properties and the public which pay their charges. When once an inflated capitalization has gone upon the market and has become fixed in value, its existence must be recognized. As a practical matter it is then often absolutely necessary to take account of the thousands of innocent stockholders who have purchased their stock in good faith. The usual result of such inflation is therefore to impose upon the public an unnecessary but everlasting tax, while the innocent purchasers of the stock are also harmed and only a few speculators are benefited. Such wrongs when once accomplished can with difficulty be undone; but they can be prevented with safety and with justice. When combinations of interstate railways must obtain Government sanction; when it is no longer possible for an interstate railway to issue stock or bonds, save in the manner approved by the Federal Government; when that Government makes sure that the proceeds of every stock and bond issue go into the improvement of the property and not the enrichment of some individual or syndicate; when, whenever it becomes material for guidance in the regulative action of the Government, the physical value of one of these properties is determined and made known—there will be eliminated from railroad securities that element of uncertainty which lends to them their speculative quality and which has contributed much to the financial stress of the recent past.

I think that the Federal Government must also assume a certain measure of control over the physical operation of railways in the handling of interstate traffic. The Commission now has authority to establish through routes and joint rates. In order to make this provision effective and in order to promote in times of necessity the proper movement of traffic, I think it must also have authority to determine the conditions upon which cars shall be interchanged between different interstate railways. It is also probable that the Commission should have authority, in particular instances, to determine the schedule upon which perishable commodities shall be moved.

In this connection I desire to repeat my recommendation that railways be permitted to form traffic associations for the purpose of conferring about and agreeing upon rates, regulations, and practices affecting interstate business in which the members of the association are mutually interested. This does not mean that they should be given the right to pool their earnings or their traffic. The law requires that rates shall be so adjusted as not to discriminate between individuals, localities, or different species of traffic. Ordinarily, rates by all competing lines must be the same. As applied to practical conditions, the railway operations of this country can not be conducted according to law without what is equivalent to conference and agreement. The articles under which such associations operate should be approved by the Commission; all their operations should be open to public inspection; and the rates, regulations, and practices upon which they agree should be subject to disapproval by the Commission.

I urge this last provision with the same earnestness that I do the others. This country provides its railway facilities by private capital. Those facilities will not be adequate unless the capital employed is assured of just treatment and an adequate return. In fixing the charges of our railroads, I believe that, considering the interests of the public alone, it is better to allow too liberal rather than too scanty earnings, for, otherwise, there is grave danger that our railway development may not keep pace with the demand for transportation. But the fundamental idea that these railways are public highways must be recognized, and they must be open to the whole public upon equal terms and upon reasonable terms.

In reference to the Sherman antitrust law, I repeat the recommendations made in my message at the opening of the present Congress, as well as in my message to the previous Congress. The attempt in this law to provide in sweeping terms against all combinations of whatever character, if technically in restraint of trade as such restraint has been defined by the courts, must necessarily be either futile or mischievous, and sometimes both. The present law makes some combinations illegal, although they may be useful to the country. On the other hand, as to some huge combinations which are both noxious and illegal, even if the action undertaken against them under the law by the Government is successful, the result may be to work but a minimum benefit to the public. Even though the combination be broken up and a small measure of reform thereby produced, the real good aimed at can not be obtained, for such real good can come only by a thorough and continuing supervision over the acts of the combination in all its parts, so as to prevent stock watering, improper forms of competition, and, in short, wrongdoing generally. The law should correct that portion of the Sherman Act which prohibits all combinations of the character above described, whether they be reasonable or unreasonable; but this should be done only as a part of a general scheme to provide for this effective and thoroughgoing supervision by the National Government of all the operations of the big interstate business concerns. Judge Hough, of New York, in his recent decision in the Harriman case, states that the Congress possesses the power to limit the interstate operations of corporations not complying with Federal safeguards against the recurrence of obnoxious practices, and to license those which afford the public adequate security against methods calculated to diminish solvency, and therefore efficiency and economy in interstate transportation. The judge adds that in these matters "the power of Congress is ample, though as yet not fruitful in results." It is very earnestly to be desired that either along the lines the judge indicates, or in some other way equally efficacious, the Congress may exercise the power which he holds it possesses.

Superficially it may seem that the laws, the passage of which I herein again advocate—for I have repeatedly advocated them before—are not connected. But in reality they are connected. Each and every one of these laws, if enacted, would represent part of the campaign against privilege, part of the campaign to make the class of great property holders realize that property has its duties no less than its rights. When the courts guarantee to the employer, as they should, the rights of the employer, and to property the rights of property, they should no less emphatically make it evident that they will exact from property and from the employer the duties which should necessarily accompany these rights; and hitherto our laws have failed in precisely this point of enforcing the performance of duty by the man of property toward the man who works for him, by the man of great wealth, especially if he uses that wealth in corporate form, toward the investor, the wage-worker, and the general public. The permanent failure of the man of property to fulfill his obligations would ultimately assure the wresting from him of the privileges which he is entitled to enjoy only if he recognizes the obligations accompanying them. Those who assume or share the responsibility for this failure are rendering but a poor service to the cause which they believe they champion.

I do not know whether it is possible, but if possible, it is certainly desirable, that in connection with measures to restrain stock watering and overcapitalization there should be measures taken to prevent at least the grosser forms of gambling in securities and commodities, such as making large sales of what men do not possess and "cornering" the market. Legitimate purchases of commodities and of stocks and securities for investment have no connection whatever with purchases of stocks or other securities or commodities on a margin for speculative and gambling purposes. There is no moral differenece between gambling at cards or in lotteries or on the race track and gambling in the stock market. One method is just as pernicious to the body politic as the other in kind, and in degree the evil worked is far greater. But it is a far more difficult subject with which to deal. The great bulk of the business transacted on the exchanges is not only legitimate, but is necessary to the working of our modern industrial system, and extreme care would have to be taken not to interfere with this business in doing away with the "bucket shop" type of operation. We should study both the successes and the failures of foreign legislators who, notably in Germany, have worked along this line, so as not to do anything harmful. Moreover, there is a special difficulty in dealing with this matter by the Federal Government in a Federal Republic like ours. But if it is possible to devise a way to deal with it the effort should be made, even if only in a cautious and tentative way. It would seem that the Federal Government could at least act by forbidding the use of the mails, telegraph and telephone wires for mere gambling in stocks and futures, just as it does in lottery transactions.

I inclose herewith a statement issued by the Chief of the Bureau of Corporations (Appendix 1) in answer to certain statements (which I also inclose) 'made by and on behalf of the agents of the Standard Oil Corporation (Appendix 2) and a letter of the Attorney-General (Appendix 3) containing an answer to certain statements, also inclosed, made by the president of the Santa Fe Railway Company (Appendix 4). The Standard Oil Corporation and the railway company have both been found guilty by the courts of criminal misconduct; both have been sentenced to pay heavy fines; and each has issued and published broadcast these statements, asserting their innocence and denouncing as improper the action of the courts and juries in convicting them of guilt. These statements are very elaborate, are very ingenious, and are untruthful in important particulars. The following letter and inclosure from Mr. Heney sufficiently illustrate the methods of the high officials of the Santa Fe and show the utter falsity of their plea of ignorance, the similar plea of the Standard Oil being equally without foundation:

DEPARTMENT OF JUSTICE,
OFFICE OF THE UNITED STATES ATTORNEY,
DISTRICT OF OREGON,
PORTLAND, Jan. 11, 1908.

The PRESIDENT,

Washington, D. C.

DEAR MR. PRESIDENT: I understand that Mr. Ripley, of the Atchison, Topeka and Santa Fe Railway system, has commented with some severity upon your attitude toward the payment of rebates by certain transcontinental railroads and that he has declared that he personally never knew anything about any rebates being granted by his road. * * * I inclose you herewith copy of a letter from Edward Chambers, general freight traffic manager of the Atchison, Topeka and Santa Fe Railway system, to Mr. G. A. Davidson, auditor of the same company, dated February 27, 1907. * * *

This letter does not deal with interstate shipments, but the constitution of the State of California makes the payment of rebates by railroads a felony, and Mr. Ripley has apparently not been above the commission of crime to secure business. You are at liberty to use this inclosure in any way that you think it can be of service to yourself or the public. * * *

Sincerely, yours,   FRANCIS J. HENEY.

SAN FRANCISCO, Feb. 27, 1907.

DEAR SIR: I hand you herewith a file of papers covering the movement of fuel oil shipped by the Associated Oil Company over our line from January 1, 1906, up to and including November 15, 1906.

We agreed with the Associated Oil Co.'s negotiations with Mr. Ripley, Mr. Wells, and myself, that in consideration of their making us a special price on oil for company use, which is covered by a contract, and the further consideration that we would take a certain quantity, they would in turn ship from Bakersfield over our line to San Francisco Bay points a certain minimum number of barrels of fuel oil at rate of 25 cents per barrel from Bakersfield, exclusive of the switching charge.

These statements cover the movement, except that they have included Stockton, which is not correct, as it is not a bay point and could not be reached as conveniently by water. We have paid them on account of this movement $7,239 which should be deducted from the total of movement shown in the attached papers.

I wish you would arrange to make up a statement, check the same, and refund to the Associated Oil Company down to the basis of 25 cents per barrel from Bakersfield where they are the shippers, regardless of who is consignee, as all their fuel oil is sold delivered. The reason for making this deal in addition to what I have stated, is that the Associated Oil Company have their own boats and carry oil from fields controlled by themselves along the coast near San Luis Obispo to San Francisco at a much lower cost than the special rate we have made them and in competition with the Union Oil Company and the Standard Oil Company, it was necessary for them to sell at the San Francisco Bay points on the basis of the cost of water transportation from the coast fields. They figured they could only afford to pay us the 25 cents per barrel if by doing this they sold our company a certain amount of fuel oil, otherwise the business covered by the attached papers would have come in by boat from the coast fields.

I am writing this up completely so that there may be in the papers a history of the reasons why this arrangement was made. I wish you would go ahead and make the adjustment as soon as possible, as the Associated Oil Company are very anxious to have the matter closed up.

The arrangement was canceled on November 15th at a conference between Mr. Ripley, Mr. Wells, Mr. Porter, and myself.

Yours, truly, EDWARD CHAMBERS.

SHIPMENTS-ASSOCIATED OIL COMPANY,
  Mr. G. A. DAVIDSON,
    Auditor, Los Angeles.

The attacks by these great corporations on the Administration's actions have been given a wide circulation throughout the country, in the newspapers and otherwise, by those writers and speakers who, consciously or unconsciously, act as the representatives of predatory wealth—of the wealth accumulated on a giant scale by all forms of iniquity, ranging from the oppression of wageworkers to unfair and unwholesome methods of crushing out competition, and to defrauding the public by stock jobbing and the manipulation of securities. Certain wealthy men of this stamp, whose conduct should be abhorrent to every man of ordinarily decent conscience, and who commit the hideous wrong of teaching our young men that phenomenal business success must ordinarily be based on dishonesty, have during the last few months made it apparent that they have banded together to work for a reaction. Their endeavor is to overthrow and discredit all who honestly administer the law, to prevent any additional legislation which would check and restrain them, and to secure if possible a freedom from all restraint which will permit every unscrupulous wrongdoer to do what he wishes unchecked provided he has enough money. The only way to counteract the movement in which these men are engaged is to make clear to the public just what they have done in the past and just what they are seeking to accomplish in the present.

The Administration and those who support its views are not only not engaged in an assault on property, but are strenuous upholders of the rights of property. The wise attitude to take is admirably stated by Governor Fort, of New Jersey, in his recent inaugural address; the principles which he upholds as regards the State being of course identical with those which should obtain as regards the Nation.

"Just and fair regulation can only be objected to by those misconceiving the rights of the State. The State grants all corporate powers to its railways and other public utility corporations, and may not only modify, but repeal all charters and charter privileges it confers. It may, therefore, impose conditions upon their operation at its pleasure. Of course in the doing of these things, it should act wisely and with conservatism, protecting all vested rights of property and the interests of the innocent holders of the securities of existing *quasi*-public corporations. Regulation, therefore, upon a wise basis, of the operation of these public utilities companies, including the fixing of rates and public charges, upon complaint and subject to court review, should be intrusted to a proper board, as well as the right to regulate the output of stock and the bonded issues of such corporations. If this were done, it would inure to the benefit of the people and the companies, for it would fix the value of such securities, and act as a guaranty against their depreciation. Under such a law, the holders of existing securities would find them protected, and new securities offered would have the confidence of the people, because of the guaranty of the State that they were only issued for extensions or betterments and upon some basis of the cost of such extensions and betterments. It is difficult to suggest any legislation that would give greater confidence to the public and investors than a wise public utilities bill; and the mere suggestion of its enactment should cause this class of security holders to feel that their holdings were strengthened, and that the State was about to aid the managers of its public utility corporations to conserve their corporate property for the public benefit and for the protection of invested capital. * * *

"The time has come for the strict supervision of these great corporations and the limitation of their stock and bond issues under some proper public official. It will make for conservatism, and strengthen the companies doing a legitimate business, and eliminate, let us hope, those which are merely speculative in character and organized simply to catch the unsuspecting or credulous investor. Corporations have come in our business world to remain for all time. Corporate methods are the most satisfactory for business purposes in many cases. Every business or enterprise honestly incorporated should be protected, and the public made to feel confidence in its corporate organization. Capital invested in corporations must be as free from wrongful attack as that invested by individuals, and the State should do everything to foster and protect invested corporate capital and encourage the public in giving to it support and confidence. Nothing will do so much to achieve this desirable result as proper supervision and reasonable control over stock and bond issues, so that overcapitalization will be prevented and the people may know when they buy a share of stock or a bond * * * that the name of the State upon it stands as a guaranty that there is value behind it and reasonable safety in its purchase. The act must make it clear that the intent of the supervision by the Commissioner is not for the purpose of striking at corporate organizations or invested corporate capital, but rather to recognize and protect existing conditions and insure greater safeguards for the future. * * *

"Capital does not go into a State where reprisals are taken or vested interests are injured; it comes only where wise, conservative, safe treatment is assured, and it should be our policy to encourage and secure corporate rights and the best interests of stock and bond holders committed to our legal care."

Under no circumstances would we countenance attacks upon law-abiding property, or do aught but condemn those who hold up rich men as being evil men because of their riches. On the contrary, our whole effort is to insist upon conduct, and neither wealth nor property nor any other class distinction, as being the proper standard by which to judge the actions of men. For the honest man of great wealth we have a hearty regard, just as we have a hearty regard for the honest politician and honest newspaper. But part of the movement to up hold honesty must be a movement to frown on dishonesty. We attack only the corrupt men of wealth, who find in the purchased politician the most efficient instrument of corruption and in the purchased news-paper the most efficient defender of corruption. Our main quarrel is not with these agents and representatives of the interests. They derive their chief power from the great sinister offenders who stand behind them. They are but puppets who move as the strings are pulled. It is not the puppets, but the strong cunning men and the mighty forces working for evil behind and through the puppets, with whom we have to deal. We seek to control law-defying wealth; in the first place to prevent its doing dire evil to the Republic, and in the next place to avoid the vindictive and dreadful radicalism which, if left uncontrolled, it is certain in the end to arouse. Sweeping attacks upon all property, upon all men of means, without regard to whether they do well or ill, would sound the death-knell of the Republic; and such attacks become inevitable if decent citizens permit those rich men whose lives are corrupt and evil to domineer in swollen pride, unchecked and unhindered, over the destinies of this country. We act in no vindictive spirit, and we are no respecters of persons. If a labor union does wrong, we oppose it as firmly as we oppose a corporation which does wrong; and we stand equally stoutly for the rights of the man of wealth and for the rights of the wageworker. We seek to protect the property of every man who acts honestly, of every corporation that represents wealth honestly accumulated and honestly used. We seek to stop wrongdoing, and we desire to punish the wrongdoers only so far as is necessary to achieve this end.

There are ample material rewards for those who serve with fidelity the mammon of unrighteousness; but they are dearly paid for by the people who permit their representatives, whether in public life, in the press, or in the colleges where their young men are taught, to preach and to practice that there is one law for the rich and another for the poor. The amount of money the representatives of certain great moneyed interests are willing to spend can be gauged by their recent publication broadcast throughout the papers of this country, from the Atlantic to the Pacific, of huge advertisements attacking with envenomed bitterness the Administration's policy of warring against successful dishonesty, and by their circulation of pamphlets and books prepared with the same object; while they likewise push the circulation of the writings and speeches of men who, whether because they are misled, or because, seeing the light, they are willing to sin against the light, serve these their masters of great wealth to the cost of the plain people. The books and pamphlets, the controlled newspapers, the speeches by public or private men to which I refer, are usually and especially in the interest of the Standard Oil Trust and of certain notorious railroad combinations, but they also defend other individuals and corporations of great wealth that have been guilty of wrongdoing. It is only rarely that the men responsible for the wrongdoing themselves speak or write. Normally they hire others to do their bidding, or find others who will do it without hire. From the railroad-rate law to the pure-food law, every measure for honesty in business that has been passed during the last six years has been opposed by these men on its passage and in its administration with every resource that bitter and unscrupulous craft could suggest and the command of almost unlimited money secure. But for the last year the attack has been made with most bitterness upon the actual administration of the law, especially through the Department of Justice, but also through the Interstate Commerce Commission and the Bureau of Corporations. The extraordinary violence of the assaults upon our policy contained in these speeches, editorials, articles, advertisements, and pamphlets, and the enormous sums of money spent in these various ways, give a fairly accurate measure of the anger and terror which our public actions have caused the corrupt men of vast wealth to feel in the very marrow of their being. The attack is sometimes made openly against us for enforcing the law, and sometimes with a certain cunning, for not trying to enforce it in some other way than that which experience shows to be practical. One of the favorite methods of the latter class of assailant is to attack the Administration for not procuring the imprisonment instead of the fine of offenders under these antitrust laws. The man making this assault is usually either a prominent lawyer or an editor who takes his policy from the financiers and his arguments from their attorneys. If the former, he has defended and advised many wealthy malefactors, and he knows well that, thanks to the advice of lawyers like himself, a certain kind of modern corporation has been turned into an admirable instrument by which to render it well-nigh impossible to get at the head of the corporation, at the man who is really most guilty. When we are able to put the real wrongdoer in prison, this is what we strive to do; this is what we have actually done with some very wealthy criminals, who, moreover, represented that most baneful of all alliances, the alliance between the corruption of organized politics and the corruption of high finance. This is what we have done in the Gaynor and Greene case, in the case of the misapplication of funds in connection with certain great banks in Chicago, in the land-fraud cases, where, as in other cases likewise, neither the highest political position nor the possession of great wealth, has availed to save the offenders from prison. The Federal Government does scourge sin; it does bid sinners fear; for it has put behind the bars with impartial severity, the powerful financier, the powerful politician, the rich land thief, the rich contractor—all, no matter how high their station, against whom criminal misdeeds can be proved. All their wealth and power can not protect them. But it often happens that the effort to imprison a given defendant is certain to be futile, while it is possible to fine him or to fine the corporation of which he is head; so that, in other words, the only way of punishing the wrong is by fining the corporation, unless we are content to proceed personally against the minor agents. The corporation lawyers to whom I refer and their employers are the men mainly responsible for this state of things, and their responsibility is shared with all who ingeniously oppose the passing of just and effective laws, or who fail to execute them when they have been put on the statute books.

Much is said, in these attacks upon the policy of the present Administration, about the rights of "innocent stockholders." That stockholder is not innocent who voluntarily purchases stock in a corporation whose methods and management he knows to be corrupt; and "innocent stockholders" when a great law-defying corporation is punished, are the first estopped from complaining about the proceedings the Government finds necessary in order to compel the corporation to obey the law. There has been in the past grave wrong done innocent stockholders by overcapitalization, stock-watering, stock jobbing, stock-manipulation. This we have sought to prevent, first, by exposing the thing done and punishing the offender when any existing law had been violated; second, by recommending the passage of laws which would make unlawful similar practices for the future. The public men, lawyers, and editors who loudly proclaim their sympathy for the "innocent stockholders" when a great lawdefying corporation is punished, are the first to protest with frantic vehemence against all efforts by law to put a stop to the practices which are the real and ultimate sources of the damage alike to the stockholders and the public. The apologists of successful dishonesty always declaim against any effort to punish or prevent it, on the ground that any such effort will "unsettle business." It is they who by their acts have unsettled business; and the very men raising this cry spend hundreds of thousands of dollars in securing, by speech, editorial, book, or pamphlet, the defense by misstatements of what they have done; and yet when public servants correct their misstatements by telling the truth they declaim against them for breaking silence, lest "values be depreciated." They have hurt honest business men, honest workingmen, honest farmers; and now they clamor against the truth being told.

The keynote of all these attacks upon the effort to secure honesty in business and in politics is well expressed in brazen protests against any effort for the moral regeneration of the business world, on the ground that it is unnatural, unwarranted, and injurious, and that business panic is the necessary penalty for such effort to secure business honesty. The morality of such a plea is precisely as great as if made on behalf of the men caught in a gambling establishment when that gambling establishment is raided by the police. If such words mean anything they mean that those whose sentiments they represent stand against the effort to bring about a moral regeneration of business which will prevent a repetition of the insurance, banking, and street railroad scandals in New York; a repetition of the Chicago and Alton deal; a repetition of the combination between certain professional politicians, certain professional labor leaders, and certain big financiers, from the disgrace of which San Francisco has just been rescued; a repetition of the successful effort by the Standard Oil people to crush out every competitor, to overawe the common carriers, and to establish a monopoly which treats the public with a contempt which the public deserves so long as it permits men of such principles and such sentiments to avow and act on them with impunity. The outcry against stopping dishonest practices among wrongdoers who happen to be wealthy is precisely similar to the outcry raised against every effort for cleanliness and decency in city government, because, forsooth, it will "hurt business." The same outcry is made aginst the Department of Justice for prosecuting the heads of colossal corporations that has been made against the men who in San Francisco have prosecuted with impartial severity the wrongdoers among business men, public officials, and labor leaders alike. The principle is the same in the two cases. Just as the blackmailer and bribe giver stand on the same evil eminence of infamy, so the man who makes an enormous fortune by corrupting legislatures and municipalities and fleecing his stockholders and the public, stands on the same moral level with the creature who fattens on the blood money of the gambling house and the saloon. Moreover, in the last analysis, both kinds of corruption are far more intimately connected than would at first sight appear; the wrongdoing is at bottom the same. Corrupt business and corrupt politics act and react with ever increasing debasement, one on the other; the corrupt head of a corporation and the corrupt labor leader are both in the same degree the enemies of honest corporations and honest labor unions; the rebate taker, the franchise trafficker, the manipulator of

PANAMA CANAL: THE CUT AT BAS OBISPO, LOOKING SOUTH

THE PANAMA CANAL.

The commencement of the task of constructing the Panama Canal was the most important event of Roosevelt's Administration. The history of the undertaking is written by Roosevelt himself on pages 6662, 6758, 6881, 6901, 7401, 7480, 7611, 7648, 7667, 7685 and 7728. The message commencing on page 7685 describes his visit of inspection to the canal zone. President Taft continued the narrative, pages 7750, 7754, 7803, 7863 and 7898. The reader who desires a brief recital of the facts should refer to the article entitled "Panama Canal" in the encyclopedic index. The index references following this article will enable the reader to glean a complete and authentic knowledge of the subject from the messages of the Presidents, from Jackson to Taft, who have discussed the project.

Bas Obispo is at the beginning of the Culebra Cut as one enters the Canal from the Atlantic side. Bas Obispo really represents the beginning of the Continental Divide on the Isthmus.

securities, the purveyor and protector of vice, the blackmailing ward boss, the ballot-box stuffer, the demagogue, the mob leader, the hired bully, and mankiller—all alike work at the same web of corruption, and all alike should be abhorred by honest men.

The "business" which is hurt by the movement for honesty is the kind of business which, in the long run, it pays the country to have hurt. It is the kind of business which has tended to make the very name "high finance" a term of scandal to which all honest American men of business should join in putting an end. The special pleaders for business dishonesty, in denouncing the present Administration for enforcing the law against the huge and corrupt corporations which have defied the law, also denounce it for endeavoring to secure sadly needed labor legislation, such as a far-reaching law making employer liable for injuries to their employees. It is meet and fit that the apologists for corrupt wealth should oppose every effort to relieve weak and helpless people from crushing misfortune brought upon them by injury in the business from which they gain a bare livelihood. The burden should be distributed.. It is hypocritical baseness to speak of a girl who works in a factory where the dangerous machinery is unprotected as having the "right" freely to contract to expose herself to dangers to life and limb. She has no alternative but to suffer want or else to expose herself to such dangers, and when she loses a hand or is otherwise maimed or disfigured for life, it is a moral wrong that the whole burden of the risk necessarily incidental to the business should be placed with crushing weight upon her weak shoulders, and all who profit by her work escape scot-free. This is what opponents of a just employers' liability law advocate; and it is consistent that they should usually also advocate immunity for those most dangerous members of the criminal class—the criminals of great wealth.

Our opponents have recently been bitterly criticising the two judges referred to in the accompanying communications from the Standard Oil Company and the Santa Fe Railroad for having imposed heavy fines on these two corporations; and yet these same critics of these two judges exhaust themselves in denouncing the most respectful and cautious discussion of the official action of a judge which results in immunity to wealthy and powerful wrongdoers or which renders nugatory a temperate effort to better the conditions of life and work among those of our fellow countrymen whose need is greatest. Most certainly it behooves us all to treat with the utmost respect the high office of judge; and our judges, as a whole, are brave and upright men. Respect for the law must go hand in hand with respect for the judges; and, as a whole, it is true now as in the past that the judges stand in character and service above all other men among their fellow-servants of the public. There is all the greater need that the few who fail in

227

this great office, who fall below this high standard of integrity, of wisdom, of sympathetic understanding and of courage, should have their eyes opened to the needs of their countrymen. A judge who on the bench either truckles to the mob and shrinks from sternly repressing violence and disorder, or bows down before a corporation; who fails to stand up valiantly for the rights of property on the one hand, or on the other by misuse of the process of injunction or by his attitude toward all measures for the betterment of the conditions of labor, makes the wageworker feel with bitterness that the courts are hostile to him; or who fails to realize that all public servants in their several stations must strive to stop the abuses of the criminal rich—such a man performs an even worse service to the body politic than the legislator or executive who goes wrong. The judge who does his full duty well stands higher, and renders a better service to the people, than any other public servant; he is entitled to greater respect; and if he is a true servant of the people, if he is upright, wise and fearless, he will unhesitatingly disregard even the wishes of the people if they conflict with the eternal principles of right as against wrong. He must serve the people; but he must serve his own conscience first. All honor to such a judge; and all honor can not be rendered him if it is rendered equally to his brethren who fall immeasurably below the high ideals for which he stands. Untruthful criticism is wicked at all times, and whoever may be the object; but it is a peculiarly flagrant iniquity when a judge is the object. No man should lightly criticize a judge; no man shall, even in his own mind, condemn a judge unless he is sure of the facts. If a judge is assailed for standing against popular folly, and above all for standing against mob violence, all honorable men should rally instantly to his support. Nevertheless if he clearly fails to do his duty by the public in dealing with lawbreaking corporations lawbreaking men of wealth, he must expect to feel the weight of public opinion; and this is but right, for except in extreme cases this is the only way in which he can be reached at all. No servant of the people has a right to expect to be free from just and honest criticism.

The opponents of the measures we champion single out now one and now another measure for especial attack, and speak as if the movement in which we are engaged was purely economic. It has a large economic side, but it is fundamentally an ethical movement. It is not a movement to be completed in one year, or two or three years; it is a movement which must be persevered in until the spirit which lies behind it sinks deep into the heart and the conscience of the whole people. It is always important to choose the right means to achieve our purpose, but it is even more important to keep this purpose clearly before us; and this purpose is to secure national honesty in business and in politics. We do not subscribe to the cynical belief that dishonesty

and unfair dealing are essential to business success, and are to be con-
doned when the success is moderate and applauded when the success
is great. The methods by which the Standard Oil people and those
engaged in the other combinations of which I have spoken above have
achieved great fortunes can only be justified by the advocacy of a system of morality which would also justify every form of criminality on
the part of a labor union, and every form of violence, corruption, and
fraud, from murder to bribery and ballot-box stuffing in politics. We
are trying to secure equality of opportunity for all; and the struggle
for honesty is the same whether it is made on behalf of one set of men
or of another. In the interest of the small settlers and landowners,
and against the embittered opposition of wealthy owners of huge
wandering flocks of sheep, or of corporations desiring to rob the
people of coal and timber, we strive to put an end to the theft of public
land in the West. When we do this, and protest against the action of
all men, whether in public life or in private life, who either take part in
or refuse to try to stop such theft, we are really engaged in the same
policy as when we endeavor to put a stop to rebates or to prevent the
upgrowth of uncontrolled monopolies. Our effort is simply to enforce
the principles of common honesty and common sense. It would indeed be ill for the country should there be any halt in our work.

The laws must in the future be administered as they are now being
administered, so that the Department of Justice may continue to be,
what it now is, in very fact the Department of Justice, where so far as
our ability permits justice is meted out with an even hand to great and
small, rich and poor, weak and strong. Moreover, there should be no
delay in supplementing the laws now on the statute books by the enactment of further legislation as outlined in the message I sent to the
Congress on its assembling. Under the existing laws much, very much,
has been actually accomplished during the past six years, and it has
been shown by actual experience that they can be enforced against the
wealthiest corporation and the richest and most powerful manager or
manipulator of that corporation, as rigorously and fearlessly as against
the humblest offender. Above all, they have been enforced against the
very wrongdoers and agents of wrongdoers who have for so many
years gone scot-free and flouted the laws with impunity, against great
law-defying corporations of immense wealth, which, until within the
last half dozen years, have treated themselves and have expected others
to treat them as being beyond and above all possible check from law.

It is especially necessary to secure to the representatives of the National Government full power to deal with the great corporations
engaged in interstate commerce, and above all, with the great interstate common carriers. Our people should clearly recognize that while

there are difficulties in any course of conduct to be followed in dealing with these great corporations, these difficulties must be faced, and one of three courses followed.

The first course is to abandon all effort to oversee and control their actions in the interest of the general public and to permit a return to the utter lack of control which would obtain if they were left to the common law. I do not for one moment believe that our people would tolerate this position. The extraordinary growth of modern industrialism has rendered the common law, which grew up under and was adapted to deal with totally different conditions, in many respects inadequate to deal with the new conditions. These new conditions make it necessary to shackle cunning as in the past we have shackled force. The vast individual and corporate fortunes, the vast combinations of capital, which have marked the development of our industrial system, create new conditions, and necessitate a change from the old attitude of the State and the Nation toward the rules regulating the acquisition and untrammeled business use of property, in order both that property may be adequately protected, and that at the same time those who hold it may be prevented from wrongdoing.

The second and third courses are to have the regulation undertaken either by the Nation or by the States. Of course in any event both the National Government and the several State governments must do each its part, and each can do a certain amount that the other can not do, while the only really satisfactory results must be obtained by the representatives of the National and State governments working heartily together within their respective spheres. But in my judgment thoroughgoing and satisfactory control can in the end only be obtained by the action of the National Government, for almost all the corporations of enormous wealth—that is, the corporations which it is especially desirable to control—are engaged in interstate commerce, and derive their power and their importance not from that portion of their business which is intrastate, but from the interstate business. It is not easy always to decide just where the line of demarcation between the two kinds of business falls. This line must ultimately be drawn by the Federal courts. Much of the effort to secure adequate control of the great corporations by State action has been wise and effective, but much of it has been neither; for when the effort is made to accomplish by the action of the State what can only be accomplished by the action of the Nation, the result can only be disappointment, and in the end the law will probably be declared unconstitutional. So likewise in the national arena, we who believe in the measures herein advocated are hampered and not aided by the extremists who advocate action so violent that it would either be useless or else would cause more mischief than it would remedy.

In a recent letter from a learned judge of the supreme court of one of the Gulf States, the writer speaks as follows:

"In all matters pertaining to interstate commerce the authority of the National Government already exists and does not have to be acquired, and the exercise of this existing authority can be in no sense a usurpation of, or infringement upon, the rights of the States. On the contrary, had the Federal Government given this question more attention in the past and applied a vigorous check to corporate abuses, conditions would now be better, because the States would have had fewer real or imaginary grievances and have had less cause not only to attempt and overpass at the authority reserved to the National Government, but to act without proper moderation in matters peculiarly within their own provinces. The National Government has been remiss in the past, but even at this late day it can solve this problem, and the sooner the National authority is exercised the less apt are the States to take action which will represent encroachment upon the National domain. There is a field of operations for both powers, and plenty alike for National and State governments to do in order to protect both the people and the public utilities. The line of demarcation between Federal and State authority ean and should be speedily settled by the Federal courts. The fact that the National Government has omitted to exercise the authority conferred upon it by the interstate commerce clause of the Constitution has made the States restive under what they deem corporate abuses, and in some cases has probably stimulated them to go too far in the attempt to correct these abuses, with the result that all measures which they passed, good or bad, have been held up by the Federal courts. The necessary equitable and uniform regulation can not be obtained by the separate action of the States, but only by the affirmative action of the National Government."

This is an appeal by a high State judge, alarmed, as good citizens should be alarmed, by conflicts over the matter of jurisdiction, and by the radical action advocated by honest people smarting from a sense of injury received from corporations; which injury the Federal courts forbid the States to try to remedy, while the Federal Government nevertheless refrains from itself taking adequate measures to provide a remedy. It can not too strongly be insisted that the defenders and apologists of the great corporations, who have sought in the past and still seek to prevent adequate action by the Federal Government to control these great corporations, are not only proving false to the people, but are laying up a day of wrath for the great corporations themselves. The Nation will not tolerate an utter lack of control over very wealthy men of enormous power in the industrial, and therefore in the social, lives of all our people, some of whom have shown themselves cynically and brutally indifferent to the interests of the people; and if the Congress does not act, with good tempered and sensible but resolute thoroughness, in cutting out the evils and in providing an effective supervision, the result is certain to be action on the part of the separate States, sometimes wise, sometimes ill-judged and extreme, sometimes unjust and damaging to the railroads or other corporations, more often ineffective from every standpoint, because the Federal courts declare it unconstitutional.

We have just passed through two months of acute financial stress. At any such time it is a sad fact that entirely innocent people suffer from no fault of their own; and everyone must feel the keenest sympathy for the large body of honest business men, of honest investors, of honest wageworkers, who suffer because involved in a crash for which they are in no way responsible. At such a time there is a natural tendency on the part of many men to feel gloomy and frightened at the outlook; but there is no justification for this feeling. There is no nation so absolutely sure of ultimate success as ours. Of course we shall succeed. Ours is a nation of masterful energy, with a continent for its domain, and it feels within its veins the thrill which comes to those who know that they possess the future. We are not cast down by the fear of failure. We are upheld by the confident hope of ultimate triumph. The wrongs that exist are to be corrected; but they in no way justify doubt as to the final outcome, doubt as to the great material prosperity of the future, or of the lofty spiritual life which is to be built upon that prosperity as a foundation. No misdeeds in the present must be permitted to shroud from our eyes the glorious future of the Nation; but because of this very fact it behooves us never to swerve from our resolute purpose to cut out wrongdoing and uphold what is right.

I do not for a moment believe that the actions of this Administration have brought on business distress; so far as this is due to local and not world-wide causes, and to the actions of any particular individuals, it is due to the speculative folly and flagrant dishonesty of a few men of great wealth, who seek to shield themselves from the effects of their own wrongdoing by ascribing its results to the actions of those who have sought to put a stop to the wrongdoing. But if it were true that to cut out rottenness from the body politic meant a momentary check to an unhealthy seeming prosperity, I should not for one moment hesitate to put the knife to the corruption. On behalf of all our people, on behalf no less of the honest man of means than of the honest man who earns each day's livelihood by that day's sweat of his brow, it is necessary to insist upon honesty in business and politics alike, in all walks of life, in big things and in little things; upon just and fair dealing as between man and man. Those who demand this are striving for the right in the spirit of Abraham Lincoln when he said:

"Fondly do we hope, fervently do we pray, that this mighty scourge may speedily pass away. Yet, if God wills that it continue until all the wealth piled by the bondsmen's two hundred and fifty years of unrequited toil shall be sunk, and until every drop of blood drawn with the lash shall be paid by another drawn with the sword, as was said three thousand years ago so still it must be said, 'The judgments of the Lord are true and righteous altogether.'

"With malice toward none, with charity for all, with firmness in the right, as God gives us to see the right, let us strive on to finish the work we are in."

In the work we of this generation are in, there is, thanks be to the Almighty, no danger of bloodshed and no use for the sword; but there is grave need of those stern qualities shown alike by the men of the North and the men of the South in the dark days when each valiantly battled for the light as it was given each to see the light. Their spirit should be our spirit, as we strive to bring nearer the day when greed and trickery and cunning shall be trampled under foot by those who fight for the righteousness that exalteth a nation.

THEODORE ROOSEVELT.

THE WHITE HOUSE,
   January 31, 1908.

SPECIAL MESSAGE.

To the Senate and House of Representatives:

Let me again urge upon the Congress the need of providing for four battle ships of the best and most advanced type at this session. Prior to the recent Hague Conference it had been my hope that an agreement could be reached between the different nations to limit the increase of naval armaments, and especially to limit the size of warships. Under these circumstances I felt that the construction of one battle ship a year would keep our Navy up to its then positive and relative strength. But actual experience showed not merely that it was impossible to obtain such an agreement for the limitation of armaments among the various leading powers, but that there was no likelihood whatever of obtaining it in the future within any reasonable time. Coincidentally with this discovery occurred a radical change in the building of battle ships among the great military nations—a change in accordance with which the most modern battle ships have been or are being constructed, of a size and armament which doubles, or more probably trebles, their effectiveness. Every other great naval nation has or is building a number of ships of this kind; we have provided for but two, and therefore the balance of power is now inclining against us. Under these conditions, to provide for but one or two battle ships a year is to provide that this Nation, instead of advancing, shall go backward in naval rank and relative power among the great nations. Such a course would be unwise for us if we fronted merely on one ocean, and it is doubly unwise when we front on two oceans. As Chief Executive of the Nation, and as Commander in Chief of the Navy, there is imposed upon me the solemn responsibility of advising the Congress of the measures vitally necessary to secure the peace and welfare of the Republic in the event of international complications which are even remotely possible. Having in view this solemn responsibility, I earnestly advise that the Congress now provide four battle ships of the most advanced type. I can not too emphatically say that this is a measure of peace and not of war. I can conceive of no circumstances under which this Republic would enter into an aggressive war; most certainly, under no circumstances would it enter into an aggressive war to extend its territory or in any other manner seek material aggrandizement. I advocate that the United States build a navy commensurate with its powers and its needs, because I feel that such a navy will be the surest guaranty and safeguard of peace. We are not a military nation. Our army is so small as to present an almost absurd contrast to our size, and is properly treated as little more than a nucleus for organization in case of serious war. Yet we are a rich Nation, and undefended wealth invites aggression. The very liberty of individual speech and action, which we so prize and guard, renders it possible that at times unexpected causes of friction with foreign powers may suddenly develop. At this moment we are negotiating arbitration treaties with all the other great powers that are willing to enter into them. These arbitration treaties have a special usefulness because in the event of some sudden disagreement they render it morally incumbent upon both nations to seek first to reach an agreement through arbitration, and at least secure a breathing space during which the cool judgment of the two nations involved may get the upper hand over any momentary burst of anger. These arbitration treaties are entered into not only with the hope of preventing wrongdoing by others against us, but also as a proof that we have no intention of doing wrong ourselves.

Yet it is idle to assume, and from the standpoint of national interest and honor it is mischievous folly for any statesman to assume, that this world has yet reached the stage, or has come within measurable distance of the stage, when a proud nation, jealous of its honor and conscious of its great mission in the world, can be content to rely for peace upon the forbearance of other powers. It would be equally foolish to rely upon each of them possessing at all times and under all circumstances and provocations an altruistic regard for the rights of others. Those who hold this view are blind indeed to all that has gone on before their eyes in the world at large. They are blind to what has happened in China, in Turkey, in the Spanish possessions, in Central and South Africa, during the last dozen years. For centuries China has cultivated the very spirit which our own peace-at-any-price men wish this country to adopt. For centuries China has refused to provide military forces and has treated the career of the soldier as inferior in honor and regard to the career of the merchant or of the man of letters. There never has been so large an empire which for so long a time has so persistently proceeded on the theory of doing away with what is called "militarism." Whether the result has been happy in internal affairs I need not discuss; all the advanced reformers and farsighted patriots in the Chinese Empire are at present seeking (I may add, with our hearty good will) for a radical and far-reaching reform in internal affairs. In external affairs the policy has resulted in various other nations now holding large portions of Chinese territory, while there is a very acute fear in China lest the Empire, because of its defenselessness, be exposed to absolute dismemberment, and its well-wishers are able to help it only in a small measure, because no nation can help any other unless that other can help itself.

The State Department is continually appealed to to interfere on behalf of peoples and nationalities who insist that they are suffering from oppression; now Jews in one country, now Christians in another; now black men said to be oppressed by white men in Africa. Armenians, Koreans, Finns, Poles, representatives of all appeal at times to this Government. All of this oppression is alleged to exist in time of profound peace, and frequently, although by no means always, it is alleged to occur at the hands of people who are not very formidable in a military sense. In some cases the accusations of oppression and wrongdoing are doubtless ill-founded. In others they are well founded, and in certain cases the most appalling loss of life is shown to have occurred, accompanied with frightful cruelty. It is not our province to decide which side has been right and which has been wrong in all or any of these controversies. I am merely referring to the loss of life. It is probably a conservative statement to say that within the last twelve years, at periods of profound peace, and not as the result of war, massacres and butcheries have occurred in which more lives of men, women, and children have been lost than in any single great war since the close of the Napoleonic struggles. To any public man who knows of the complaints continually made to the State Department there is an element of grim tragedy in the claim that the time has gone by when weak nations or peoples can be oppressed by those that are stronger, without arousing effective protest from other strong interests. Events still fresh in the mind of every thinking man show that neither arbitration nor any other device can as yet be invoked to prevent the gravest and most terrible wrongdoing to peoples who are either few in numbers, or who, if numerous, have lost the first and most important of national virtues—the capacity for self-defense.

When a nation is so happily situated as is ours—that is, when it has no reason to fear or to be feared by its land neighbors—the fleet is all the more necessary for the preservation of peace. Great Britain has been saved by its fleet from the necessity of facing one of the two alternatives—of submission to conquest by a foreign power or of itself becoming a great military power. The United States can hope for a permanent career of peace on only one condition, and that is, on condition of building and maintaining a first-class navy; and the step to be taken toward this end at this time is to provide for the building of four additional battle ships. I earnestly wish that the Congress would pass the measures for which I have asked for strengthening and rendering more efficient the Army as well as the Navy; all of these measures as affecting every branch and detail of both services are sorely needed, and it would be the part of farsighted wisdom to enact them all into laws, but the most vital and immediate need is that of the four battle ships.

To carry out this policy is but to act in the spirit of George Washington; is but to continue the policies which he outlined when he said, "Observe good faith and justice toward all nations. Cultivate peace and harmony with all. * * * Nothing is more essential than that permanent, inveterate antipathies against particular nations and passionate attachments for others should be excluded and that in place of them just and amicable feelings toward all should be cultivated. * * *

"I can not recommend to your notice measures for the fulfillment of our duties to the rest of the world without again pressing upon you the necessity of placing ourselves in a condition of complete defense and of exacting from them the fulfillment of their duties toward us. The United States ought not to indulge a persuasion that, contrary to the order of human events, they will forever keep at a distance those painful appeals to arms with which the history of every other nation abounds. There is a rank due to the United States among nations which will be withheld, if not absolutely lost, by the reputation of weakness. If we desire to avoid insult, we must be able to repel it; if we desire to secure peace, one of the most powerful instruments of our rising prosperity, it must be known that we are at all times ready for war."

THEODORE ROOSEVELT.

THE WHITE HOUSE, *April 14, 1908.*

VETO MESSAGES

To the House of Representatives:

I return herewith without my approval House bill 17707 to authorize William H. Standish to construct a dam across James River, in
Stone County, Mo., and divert a portion of its waters through a
tunnel into the said river again to create electric power. My reasons
for not signing the bill are:

The bill gives to the grantee a valuable privilege, which by its very
nature is monopolistic, and does not contain the conditions essential
to protect the public interest.

In pursuance of a policy declared in my message of February 26,
1908 (S. Doc. No. 325), transmitting the report of the Inland Waterways Commission to Congress, I wrote on March 13, 1908, the following letter to the Senate Committee on Commerce:

Numerous bills granting water rights in conformity with the general
act of June 21, 1906, have been introduced during the present session
of Congress, and some of these have already passed. While the general act authorizes the limitation and restriction of water rights in the
public interest and would seem to warrant making a reasonable charge
for the benefits conferred, those bills which have come to my attention
do not seem to guard the public interests adequately in these respects.
The effect of granting privileges such as are conferred by these bills,
as I said in a recent message, "taken together with rights already
acquired under state laws, would be to give away properties of enormous value. Through lack of foresight we have formed the habit of
granting without compensation extremely valuable rights, amounting
to monopolies, on navigable streams and on the public domain. The
repurchase at great expense of water rights thus carelessly given away
without return has already begun in the East, and before long will be
necessary in the West also. No rights involving water power should
be granted to any corporation in perpetuity, but only for a length of
time sufficient to allow them to conduct their business profitably. A
reasonable charge should, of course, be made for valuable rights and
privileges which they obtain from the National Government. The
values for which this charge is made will ultimately, through the
natural growth and orderly development of our population and industries, reach enormous amounts. A fair share of the increase should
be safeguarded for the benefit of the people, from whose labor it
springs. The proceeds thus secured, after the cost of administration
and improvement has been met, should naturally be devoted to the
development of our inland waterways." Accordingly I have decided
to sign no bills hereafter which do not provide specifically for the right
to fix and make a charge and for a definite limitation in time of the
rights conferred.

In my veto message of April 13, 1908, returning House bill 15444,
to extend the time for the construction of a dam across Rainy River,
I said:

We are now at the beginning of great development in **water power.** Its use through electrical transmission is entering more and more largely into every element of the daily life of the people. Already the evils of monopoly are becoming manifest; already the experience of the past shows the necessity of caution in making unrestricted grants of this great power.

The present policy pursued in making these grants is unwise in giving away the property of the people in the flowing waters to individuals or organizations practically unknown, and granting in perpetuity these valuable privileges in advance of the formulation of definite plans as to their use. In some cases the grantees apparently have little or no financial or other ability to utilize the gift, and have sought it merely because it could be had for the asking.

The Rainy River Company, by an agreement in writing, approved by the War Department, subsequently promised to submit to and abide by such conditions as may be imposed by the Secretary of War, including a time limit and a reasonable charge. Only because of its compliance in this way with these conditions did the bill extending the time limit for that project finally become a law.

An amendment to the present bill expressly authorizing the Government to fix a limitation of time and impose a charge was proposed by the War Department. The letter, veto message, and amendment above referred to were considered by the Senate Committee on Commerce, as appears by the committee's report on the present bill, and the proposed amendment was characterized by the committee as a "new departure from the policy heretofore pursued in respect to legislation authorizing the construction of such dams." Their report set forth an elaborate legal argument intended to show that the Federal Government has no power to impose any charge whatever for such a privilege.

The fact that the proposed policy is new is in itself no sufficient argument against its adoption. As we are met with new conditions of industry seriously affecting the public welfare, we should not hesitate to adopt measures for the protection of the public merely because those measures are new. When the public welfare is involved, Congress should resolve any reasonable doubt as to its legislative power in favor of the people and against the seekers for a special privilege.

My reason for believing that the Federal Government, in granting a license to dam a navigable river, has the power to impose any conditions it finds necessary to protect the public, including a charge and a limitation of the time, is that its consent is legally essential to an enterprise of this character. It follows that Congress can impose conditions upon its consent. This principle was clearly stated in the House of Representatives on March 28, 1908, by Mr. Williams, of Mississippi, when he said:

* * * There can be no doubt in the mind of any man seeking merely the public good and public right, independently of any desire for local legislation, of this general proposition: that whenever any sovereignty, state or federal, is required to issue a charter or a license or a consent, in order to confer powers upon individuals or corpora- tions, it is the duty of that sovereignty in the interests of the people so to condition the grant of that power as that it shall redound to the interest of all the people, and that utilities of vast value should not be gratuitously granted to individuals or corporations and perpetually alienated from the people or the state or the government.

* * * It is admitted that this power to erect dams in navigable streams can not be exercised by anybody except by an act of Congress. Now, then, if it require an act of Congress to permit any man to put a dam in a navigable stream, then two things follow: Congress should so exercise the power in making that grant as, first, to prevent any harm to the navigability of the stream itself, and, secondly, so as to prevent any individual or any private corporation from securing through the act of Congress any uncompensated advantage of private profit.

The authority of Congress in this matter was asserted by Secretary Taft on April 17, 1908, in his report on Senator Newlands's Inland Waterways Commission bill (S. 500), where he said:

In the execution of any project and as incidental to and inseparably connected with the improvement of navigation, the power of Congress extends to the regulation of the use and development of the waters for purposes subsidiary to navigation.

And by the Solicitor-General in a memorandum prepared after a careful investigation of the subject.

Believing that the National Government has this power, I am convinced that its power ought to be exercised. The people of the country are threatened by a monopoly far more powerful, because in far closer touch with their domestic and industrial life, than any- thing known to our experience. A single generation will see the exhaustion of our natural resources of oil and gas and such a rise in the price of coal as will make the price of electrically transmitted water power a controlling factor in transportation, in manufactur- ing, and in household lighting and heating. Our water power alone, if fully developed and wisely used, is probably sufficient for our present transportation, industrial, municipal, and domestic needs. Most of it is undeveloped and is still in national or state control.

To give away, without conditions, this, one of the greatest of our resources, would be an act of folly. If we are guilty of it, our children will be forced to pay an annual return upon a capitalization based upon the highest prices which "the traffic will bear." They will find themselves face to face with powerful interests intrenched behind the doctrine of "vested rights" and strengthened by every defense which money can buy and the ingenuity of able corporation lawyers can devise. Long before that time they may and very probably will have become a consolidated interest, controlled from the great financial centers, dictating the terms upon which the citizen can conduct his business or earn his livelihood, and not amenable to the wholesome check of local opinion.

The total water power now in use by power plants in the United States is estimated by the Bureau of the Census and the Geological Survey as 5,300,000 horsepower. Information collected by the Bureau of Corporations shows that thirteen large concerns, of which the General Electric Company and the Westinghouse Electric and Manufacturing Company are most important, now hold water-power installations and advantageous power sites aggregating about 1,046,000 horsepower, where the control by these concerns is practically admitted. This is a quantity equal to over 19 per cent of the total now in use. Further evidence of a very strong nature as to additional intercorporate relations, furnished by the bureau, leads me to the conclusion that this total should be increased to 24 per cent; and still other evidence, though less conclusive, nevertheless affords reasonable ground for enlarging this estimate by 9 per cent additional. In other words, it is probable that these thirteen concerns directly or indirectly control developed water power and advantageous power sites equal to more than 33 per cent of the total water power now in use. This astonishing consolidation has taken place practically within the last five years. The movement is still in its infancy, and unless it is controlled the history of the oil industry will be repeated in the hydroelectric power industry, with results far more oppressive and disastrous for people. It is true that the great bulk of our potential water power is as yet undeveloped, but the sites which are now controlled by combinations are those which offer the greatest advantages and therefore hold a strategic position. This is certain to be strengthened by the increasing demand for power and the extension of long-distance electrical transmission.

It is, in my opinion, relatively unimportant for us to know whether or not the promoters of this particular project are affiliated with any of these great corporations. If we make an unconditional grant to this grantee, our control over it ceases. He, or any purchaser from him, will be free to sell his rights to any one of them at pleasure. The time to attach conditions and prevent monopoly is when a grant is made.

The great corporations are acting with foresight, singleness of purpose, and vigor to control the water powers of the country. They pay no attention to state boundaries and are not interested in the constitutional law affecting navigable streams except as it affords what has been aptly called a "twilight zone," where they may find a convenient refuge from any regulation whatever by the public, whether through the national or the state governments. It is significant that they are opposing the control of water power on the Desplaines River by the State of Illinois with equal vigor and with like arguments to those with which they oppose the National Government pursuing the policy I advocate. Their attitude is the same with reference to their projects upon the mountain streams of the West, where the jurisdiction of the Federal Government as the owner of the public lands and national forests is not open to question. They are demanding legislation for unconditional grants in perpetuity of land for reservoirs, conduits, power houses, and transmission lines to replace the existing statute which authorizes the administrative officers of the Government to impose conditions to protect the public when any permit is issued. Several bills for that purpose are now pending in both Houses, among them the bill, S. 6626, to subject lands owned or held by the United States to condemnation in the state courts, and the bills, H. R. 11356 and S. 2661, respectively, to grant locations and rights of way for electric and other power purposes through the public lands and reservations of the United States. These bills were either drafted by representatives of the power companies, or are similar in effect to those thus drafted. On the other hand, the administration proposes that authority be given to issue power permits for a term not to exceed fifty years, irrevocable except for breach of condition. This provision to prevent revocation would remove the only valid ground of objection to the act of 1901, which expressly makes all permits revocable at discretion. The following amendment to authorize this in national forests was inserted in last year's agricultural appropriation bill:

And hereafter permits for power plants within national forests may be made irrevocable, except for breach of condition, for such term, not exceeding fifty years, as the Secretary of Agriculture may by regulation prescribe, and land covered by such permits issued in pursuance of an application filed before entry, location or application, subsequently approved under the act of June 11, 1906, shall in perpetuity remain subject to such permit and renewals thereof.

The representatives of the power companies present in Washington during the last session agreed upon the bill above mentioned as the most favorable to their interests. At their request frequent conferences were held between them and the representatives of the administration for the purpose of reaching an agreement if possible. The companies refused to accept anything less than a grant in perpetuity and insisted that the slight charge now imposed by the Forest Service was oppressive. But they made no response to the specific proposal that the reasonableness of the charge be determined through an investigation of their business by the Bureau of Corporations.

The amendment of the agricultural bill providing for irrevocable permits being new legislation was stricken out under the House rules upon a point of order made by friends of the House bill—that is, by friends of the power companies. Yet, in the face of this record, the power companies complain that they are forced to accept revocable permits by the policy of the administration.

The new legislation sought in their own interest by some companies in the West, and the opposition of other companies in the East to proposed legislation in the public interest, have a common source and a common purpose. Their source is the rapidly growing water-power combination. Their purpose is a centralized monopoly of hydro-electric power development free of all public control. It is obvious that a monopoly of power in any community calls for strict public supervision and regulation.

The suggestion of the Senate Committee on Commerce in their report on the present bill that many of the streams for the damming of which a federal license is sought are, in fact, unnavigable is sufficiently answered in this case by the action of the House Committee on Interstate and Foreign Commerce upon this very measure. As stated in the House on March 18, 1908, by Mr. Russell, of Missouri, a bill to declare this river unnavigable was rejected by that committee.

I repeat the words with which I concluded my message vetoing the Rainy River bill:

In place of the present haphazard policy of permanently alienating valuable public property we should substitute a definite policy along the following lines:

First. There should be a limited or carefully guarded grant in the nature of an option or opportunity afforded within reasonable time for development of plans and for execution of the project.

Second. Such a grant or concession should be accompanied in the act making the grant by a provision expressly making it the duty of a designated official to annul the grant if the work is not begun or plans are not carried out in accordance with the authority granted.

Third. It should also be the duty of some designated official to see to it that in approving the plans the maximum development of the navigation and power is assured, or at least that in making the plans these may not be so developed as ultimately to interfere with the better utilization of the water or complete development of the power.

Fourth. There should be a license fee or charge which, though small or nominal at the outset, can in the future be adjusted so as to secure a control in the interest of the public.

Fifth. Provision should be made for the termination of the grant or privilege at a definite time, leaving to future generations the power or authority to renew or extend the concessions in accordance with the conditions which may prevail at that time.

Further reflection suggests a sixth condition, viz:

The license should be forfeited upon proof that the licensee has joined in any conspiracy or unlawful combination in restraint ot trade, as is provided for grants of coal lands in Alaska by the act of May 28, 1908.

I will sign no bill granting a privilege of this character which does not contain the substance of these conditions. I consider myself bound, as far as exercise of my executive power will allow, to do for the people, in prevention of monopoly of their resources, what I believe they would do for themselves if they were in a position to act. Accordingly I shall insist upon the conditions mentioned above not only in acts which I sign, but also in passing upon plans for use of water power presented to the executive departments for action. The imposition of conditions has received the sanction of Congress in the general act of 1906, regulating the construction of dams in navigable waters, which authorizes the imposing of "such conditions and stipulations as the Chief of Engineers and the Secretary of War may deem necessary to protect the present and future interests of the United States."

I inclose a letter from the Commissioner of Corporations, setting forth the results of his investigations and the evidence of the far-reaching plans and operations of the General Electric Company, the Westinghouse Electric and Manufacturing Company, and other large concerns, for consolidation of the water powers of the country under their control. I also inclose the memorandum of the Solicitor-General above referred to.

I esteem it my duty to use every endeavor to prevent this growing monopoly, the most threatening which has ever appeared, from being fastened upon the people of this nation.

THEODORE ROOSEVELT.

THE WHITE HOUSE, *January 15, 1909.*

DEPARTMENT OF COMMERCE AND LABOR,
BUREAU OF CORPORATIONS,
Washington, January 14, 1909.

SIR: I have the honor to submit herewith a report on certain features of the concentration of water powers.

The water-power situation has been greatly changed by recent improvements in electric-power transmission. Two-hundred-mile transmission is now regarded as commercially possible even in the cheaper coal areas. A two-hundred-mile radius opens an area of 120,000 square miles for the marketing of power from a given power plant.

A strong movement toward concentrating the control of water powers has accompanied this change. A very significant fact is that this concentration has taken place practically in the last five years. The chief existing concentrations are as follows:

(1) *General Electric*—being those power companies controlled by or affiliated with the General Electric Company or its subsidiary corporations.

(2) *Westinghouse*—being those similarly connected with the Westinghouse Electric and Manufacturing Company.

(3) *Other concentrations* of water power which can not at present be identified with either of the first two.

Inter-company relations are easily concealed. Strictly judicial proof of such community of interests is rarely obtainable, nor is it necessary for practical purposes. It is sufficient to give, as herein, the significant evidential facts, leaving the obvious deductions to be made therefrom.

Therefore the General Electric and the Westinghouse concentrations are classified in the following groups:

(*a*) Those where a control by one or the other of these parent companies, directly or through subsidiary corporations, is admitted.

(*b*) Those where such control is inferred from substantial evidence (herinafter summarized) with reasonable conclusiveness.

(*c*) Those where such control is at least partially indicated, though not proven, by the available evidence.

This report does not by any means assume to be a complete survey even of the present conditions of concentration. There may be many further affiliations as yet undiscovered.

The exact relations, if any, between these two groups (General Electric and Westinghouse) can not now be stated. General Electric and Westinghouse patents have been pooled since 1896, and certain individuals are interested in both General Electric and Westinghouse power companies.

(1) GENERAL ELECTRIC.

The control of the General Electric Company is shown directly or through subsidiary corporations, or indicated by the appearance of the names of certain individuals unquestionably connected with the General Electric Company.

Such subsidiary corporations are:

United Electric Securities Company (Maine, 1890).

Electrical Securities Corporation (New York, 1904).

Electric Bond and Share Company (New York, 1905).

Such individuals most closely connected with General Electric Company water-power control are—

Sydney Z. Mitchell, vice-president and treasurer Electric Bond and Share Company (General Electric; see above), formerly with Stone & Webster, of Boston, to be mentioned later.

J. D. Mortimer, assistant secretary Electric Bond and Share Company (General Electric; see above) and director of American Gas and Electric Company.

C. N. Mason, vice-president Electrical Securities Corporation and of United Electric Securities Company (General Electric; see above).

H. L. Doherty, president American Gas and Electric Company, which in 1908 controlled at least 19 lighting and gas companies in various parts of the United States, and is, in turn, controlled by the Electric Bond and Share Company (General Electric; see above).

Other names which may be mentioned are—

C. A. Coffin, president General Electric Company.

A. W. Burchard, assistant to the president, General Electric Company, and director of American Gas and Electric Company (General Electric).

C. W. Wetmore, director of Electric Bond and Share Company.

Hinsdill Parsons, vice-president General Electric Company and director of Electric Bond and Share Company.

(a) Those water-power companies which are admittedly controlled by the General Electric Company or its subsidiary companies are—

Schenectady Power Company, New York developments on the Hoosick River at Schaghticoke and Johnsonville, with a total development of 26,000 horsepower. This company is owned outright by the General Electric Company.

Carolina Power and Light Company, at Raleigh, N. C., with 4,000 horsepower installed on the Cape Fear River, and leasing power, in addition, on the Neuse River. The stock of this company is held by the Electric Bond and Share Company (General Electric) and voted by Mr. J. D. Mortimer. C. Elmer Smith, of Smith interests in Westinghouse group, is also interested.

Rockingham Power Company, in North Carolina, on the Yadkin River, in process of construction, with an installation to be of 32,000 horsepower. This company is financed by the Electrical Securities Corporation (General Electric), C. N. Mason of the latter being president. C. Elmer Smith (see above) is also interested.

Animas Power and Water Company, Colorado, on the Animas River, with 8,000 horsepower installed, is controlled through the Electric Bond and Share Company (General Electric).

Central Colorado Power Company, in Colorado, on the Grand River, with an installation to be of 18,000 horsepower, is also controlled through the Electric Bond and Share Company (General Electric).

(b) Those water-power companies, the control of which by the General Electric Company or its subsidiary companies is reasonably inferred, are—

Montgomery Light and Water Power Company, near Montgomery, Ala., on the Tallapoosa River, with an installation of 6,000 horsepower. H. L. Doherty, president American Gas and Electric Company (General Electric), is first vice-president of this company.

The Summit County Power Company, at Dillon, Colo., with an

installation of 1,600 horsepower, has Mr. H. L. Doherty, of American Gas and Electric Company (General Electric), on its directorate.

Butte Electric and Power Company (Montana), a holding company for various subsidiary power companies, to wit: Montana Power Transmission Company, Madison River Power Company, Billings and Eastern Montana Power Company. These companies comprise six water-power developments in operation, with a total installation of 43,000 horsepower. The holding company (Butte Electric) is apparently controlled jointly by C. W. Wetmore, of Electric Bond and Share Company (General Electric), and C. A. Coffin, president of General Electric Company. P. E. Bisland, secretary, was formerly with Electrical Securities Corporation (General Electric).

Washington Water Power Company has three developments in Washington and Idaho, on the Spokane River, with a total installation of 61,000 horsepower. Mr. Hinsdill Parsons, vice-president of General Electric Company and Electric Bond and Share Company (General Electric), is on the directorate.

Great Western Power Company, in California, on the north fork of the Feather River in Butte County, with an installed capacity of 53,000 horsepower. On its directorate are Mr. A. W. Burchard, of the General Electric Company, and Mr. A. C. Bedford, of the Standard Oil Company.

(*c*) Control partially indicated.

There are also a number of other water-power companies, with a total of about 420,000 horsepower (including installations and power sites), whose connection with the General Electric Company is at least partially indicated, though the evidence thereto is by no means conclusive.

(2) WESTINGHOUSE.

The Westinghouse group contains the following companies:

The Security Investment Company;

Electric Properties Company (New York, 1906), successor to Westinghouse, Church, Kerr & Co.; and the

Smith interests, represented by C. Elmer Smith and S. Fahs Smith. of S. Morgan Smith Company, important manufacturers of water turbines. While C. Elmer Smith is interested in at least two General Electric power companies (Carolina and Rockingham; see above), the Smith interests seem especially harmonious with the Westinghouse group, and are so classified.

The individual names most prominently identified are:

John F. Wallace, of New York, president Electric Properties Company.

George C. Smith, of Pittsburg and New York, vice-president and director of the Electric Properties Company.

C. Elmer Smith, of Smith interests.

(*a*) Those power companies which are admittedly Westinghouse are:

Atlanta Water and Electric Power Company, on the Chattahoochee River above Atlanta, Ga., with an installation of 17,000 horsepower. C. Elmer Smith is president and George C. Smith and S. Fahs Smith directors.

Ontario Power Company of Niagara Falls, a Canadian corporation on the Canadian side, with an installation of 66,000 horsepower. Together with its distributing company in the United States, the Niagara, Lockport, and Ontario Power Company, it is known as a Westinghouse concern, H. H. Westinghouse being president of the latter, and the majority of its stock being voted by the Electric Power Securities Company of New York, a construction company owned by Westinghouse interests.

(*b*) Those power companies whose connection with Westinghouse interests is inferred from substantial evidence (hereinafter summarized) are:

Albany Power and Manufacturing Company, near Albany, Ga., with 3,500 horsepower installed, on the Kinchafoonee, and owning besides a site on the Flint River, estimated at 10,000 horsepower, has for its vice-president C. Elmer Smith (Smith interests).

Electric Manufacturing and Power Company, on the Broad River, near Spartanburg, S. C., with 11,500 horsepower installed, has on its directorate E. H. Jennings, of Pittsburg, a director of the Electric Properties Company (Westinghouse).

Savannah River Power Company, on the Savannah River, near Anderson, S. C., has an installed development of 3,000 horsepower, and owns besides a site of 6,000 horsepower. This company has on its directorate C. Elmer Smith (Smith interests).

Gainesville Electric Railway Company, with 1,500 horsepower installed, on the Chestagee River, a tributary of the Chattahoochee, near Gainesville, Ga. Eighty-five per cent of its stock is owned by the North Georgia Electric Company (Smith interests).

North Georgia Electric Company; one development of 3,000 horsepower and at least seven other power sites on the upper waters of the Chattahoochee, and through the Etowah Power Company, personally identified with itself, it owns four other sites on the headwaters of the Coosa River. C. Elmer Smith is vice-president.

Chattanooga and Tennessee River Power Company, in process of construction at Hale Bar on the Tennessee River, below Chattanooga, in cooperation with the War Department, by which the Government obtains slack-water navigation. The company in return receives ownership of the power of 58,000 horsepower to be installed. This company is being personally financed by A. N. Brady, of New York, a director of the Westinghouse Electric and Manufacturing Company.

Mr. Brady is also a director of the American Tobacco Company, whose interests control the Southern Power Company (see below).

Northern Colorado Power Company, which has a steam development at Lafayette, Colo., and is projecting power plants on the Platte, has John F. Wallace and George C. Smith on its directorate (Westinghouse).

(*c*) Control partially indicated.

There are also a number of other water-power companies, with a total of about 102,000 horsepower (including installations and sites), whose connection with the Westinghouse Company is at least partially indicated, though the evidence thereto is by no means conclusive.

(3) OTHER CONCENTRATIONS.

The General Electric and Westinghouse companies present the most important examples of water-power concentration, as above set forth. There are, however, a number of other companies and interests further showing the facts and tendencies of concentration.

The more important instances are as follows:

The Gould interests, located in Virginia, with undeveloped powers and power sites on the James and Appomattox amounting to 20,000 horsepower, and owning besides other sites on the Appomattox and Rappahannock rivers.

Southern Power Company, the largest operating power company in the South, has 90,000 horsepower installed in three developments, 31,000 horsepower in process of construction, and at least seven other power sites in North Carolina and South Carolina, with a total potential capacity of 75,000 horsepower. This company supplies 110 cotton mills and other factories in at least 28 towns, including a population of about 200,000. Messrs. B. N. Duke, J. B. Duke, and Junius Parker, of the American Tobacco Company, are officers and directors.

Stone & Webster, of Boston. This concern owns and controls powers and sites in Florida, Georgia, Minnesota, and Wisconsin, and in the Puget Sound region, with a total capacity of about 150,000 horsepower. Mr. Sydney Z. Mitchell, now of the Electric Bond and Share Company (General Electric), was formerly connected with Stone & Webster, and in 1908, according to Moody's Manual, 1908, was still a director in three of Stone & Webster's subsidiary corporations, to wit, Puget Sound Electric Railway, Tacoma Railway and Power Company, and Puget Sound Power Company.

Charles H. Baker interests; having proposed developments in Alabama estimated at 130,000 horsepower.

Commonwealth Power Company, together with the Grand Rapids-Muskegon Power Company (both under same interests), controlling

13 developed water powers in Michigan, with a total installation of 43,000 horsepower. A harmonious connection apparently exists with the Eastern Michigan Power Company, which controls all the power sites on the Au Sable River, Michigan.

United Missouri River Power Company, a holding company controlling at least three subsidiaries, which, with a closely related company, have five developed powers and one in construction, making a total of 57,500 horsepower.

Portland General Electric Company, with developments on the Clackamas and Willamette rivers amounting to 22,500 horsepower, near Portland, Ore. A. C. Bedford, a director of the Standard Oil Company, is president, and F. D. Pratt, also of the Standard Oil Company, is a director.

Pacific Gas and Electric Company. This is a very important holding company of the California Gas and Electric Corporation and the San Francisco Gas and Electric Company. These two latter companies in turn represent the consolidation or acquisition of the stock or property of over thisty power or power-distributing companies in California. They control 11 water-power developments, with a total installed plant of 118,000 horsepower.

Pacific Light and Power Company, with another company controlled by the same interests, known as the Huntington interests, represent eight developments in California, with a total of 30,000 horsepower. Henry E. Huntington is vice-president and Howard E. Huntington a director.

Edison Electric Company, with six developments in California and a total of 33,000 horsepower.

Hudson River Electric Power Company, a holding company for the Hudson River Water Power Company, Hudson River Power Transmission Company, Empire State Power Company, with developments at Spiers Falls and Mechanicsville on the upper Hudson, and Schoharie Creek near Amsterdam, N. Y., amounting to 45,000 horsepower installed, and sites owned in the Mohawk, Sacandaga, and Upper Hudson valleys, amounting to 30,000 horsepower, or a total of 75,000 horsepower. C. Elmer Smith was director of the holding company to within a year.

SUMMARY

An estimate of the water power, developed and potential, now controlled by the General Electric interests, admitted or sufficiently proven, is about 252,000 horsepower; by the Westinghouse interests, similarly known, about 180,000 horsepower, and by other large power companies, 875,000 horsepower. This makes a total of 1,307,000 horsepower. Adding the horsepowers of the third class (*c*), those whose connection with these two great interests is at least probable.

to wit, 520,000 horsepower, we have a small group of 13 selected companies or interests controlling a total of 1,827,000 horsepower.

Assuming that the water power at present in use by water-power plants in the United States is 5,300,000 horsepower, as estimated by the United States Census and Geological Survey from figures of installation, it is seen that approximately a quantity of horsepower equal to more than 33 per cent of that amount is now probably controlled by this small group of interests. Furthermore, this percentage by no means tells the whole truth. The foregoing powers naturally represent a majority of the best power sites. These sites are strategic points for large power and market control. Poorer sites will not generally be developed until these strategic sites are developed to their full capacity. And should these strategic sites be "coupled up" they become still more strategic. There are powerful economic reasons for such coupling. The great problem of water-power companies is that of the "uneven load," and not only of an uneven load but of an uneven source of power, because of the fluctuating flow of the stream. A coupling-up utilizes not only the different storages in the same drainage basin, but, of still greater import, the different drainage flows of different basins. Also, by coupling-up, powers which have largely "day loads" can at night help out other powers which have largely "night loads," and vice versa. Coupling-up is rapidly in progress in the United States. The Niagara Falls Power Company and the Canadian Niagara Power Company are coupled. The Southern Power Company, in North Carolina and South Carolina; the Commonwealth Power Company, in Michigan; the Pacific Gas and Electric Company, the Pacific Light and Power Company, and the Edison Electric Company, in California—each concern has its various developments coupled-up into one unit.

The economic reasons urging water-power concentration are thus obvious. The facts set forth above show the very rapid and very recent concentration that has already occurred, practically all in the last five years. These economic reasons and business facts indicate clearly the further progress toward concentration that is likely to occur in the near future. It is obvious that the effect on the public of such present and future conditions is a matter for serious public consideration.

Very respectfully yours,

HERBERT KNOX SMITH,

Commissioner of Corporations.

THE PRESIDENT.

[Memorandum by the Solicitor-General on the power of Congress, in granting licenses for dams and other structures in navigable streams, to impose certain conditions.]

MAY 11, 1908.

The general principle that a grant of property or of any right or
privilege may be upon conditions needs no citation of authority. If
a grantor may give or withhold, he may give upon terms. The
authority to make a grant generally carries with it the authority to
withhold, to impose conditions, to modify, and to terminate.

The Pacific Railroad charters contained the condition that the
government in service in transporting mails, troops, supplies, etc.,
should have the preference, and in some cases in consideration of the
land grants the transportation was to be free from all toll or other
charge upon any property or troops of the United States. (Sec. 6, act
of July 1, 1862, 12 Stat., 489, 493, Union Pacific; sec. 3, act of
March 3, 1863, id., 772, 773, Missouri Pacific; see also act of July 1,
1864, 13 Stat., 339; sec. 11, act of July 2, 1864, id., 365, 370, Northern
Pacific, in which Congress reserved the right to restrict charges for
government transportation; sec. 11, act of July 27, 1866, 14 Stat.,
292, 297.) In the acts to aid in the construction of telegraph lines
"to secure to the Government the use of the same for postal, military,
and other purposes," it was provided that the government business
shall have priority over all other business, and shall be sent at rates
to be annually fixed by the Postmaster-General (e. g., sec. 2, act of
July 24, 1866, 14 Stat., 221).

These charters, licenses, and grants were made under the federal
authority over interstate commerce and over post-roads, and manifestly the reservations or conditions were germane to the grants and
for the benefit of the whole people, being for the benefit of their government. In reference to the proposal in connection with the control of the Government over navigation and the improvement of inland waterways to limit permissive licenses for dams and other structures to a definite time, and to impose a charge for the power developed or for any use of the surplus water, it is objected that this is to
usurp power or to pervert and misapply federal power to an end or
object to which it has no relation.

There is no doubt of the national power over navigation, and the
inquiry presupposes governmental control as proposed and the grant
of licenses only in navigable streams. The question is wholly one of
power. No one questions the power of Congress over navigation
and navigable waters as a branch of its power to regulate interstate
and foreign commerce, and the power fails here, it is said, because of
the lack of connection between navigation and the purpose for which
the power is to be used, because to impose terms for the use of water
made possible by structures in aid of navigation or structures permitted and licensed as not seriously interfering with navigation, by

limiting the time during which that privilege or right shall be enjoyed and by imposing a charge for it, is not germane to the only branch of power which Congress may constitutionally exercise here; that is, the power over navigation. It is said that the State and not the United States controls and administers the rights which riparian owners may possess in the water or the use of the water; that riparian owners do possess rights of property which may not be taken from them under the guise of a power to regulate navigation; and that the States and not the United States are clothed as matter of sovereignty and dominion with the power over and the property in the waters themselves and the beds of the streams.

But first and in general, whatever the rights of the individual riparian or the particular State, which we will examine later, there is no doubt whatever that the federal authority over navigation is paramount to everything within its sphere, and the only question here would be the truth as a fact of the federal exercise of power, whether it was actually the authority over navigation which is being exercised, and whether the proposed law or laws which carry that authority into effect are a legitimate means of exercising the power, and whether there is a genuine and legitimate relation between the power and the objects and purposes to which it is applied.

The question is, then, as to the reality and degree of connection between the power and the method and effect of its exercise. In the recent measures proposed for acquiring lands in the Southern Appalachian and White mountains for national forest purposes the test is that the land shall be situated on the watersheds of navigable streams and shall be more valuable for the regulation of stream flow than for other purposes. The House committee reports show, amid divergent views as to whether the particular thing proposed was in fact a legitimate exercise of the power, that all agreed Congress, having an unquestioned right to improve navigable streams, may take land for that purpose whenever in the judgment of Congress it is necessary to the proper exercise of the power. Thus the committee resolved that the Federal Government has no power to acquire lands within a State solely for forest reserves, but under its constitutional power over navigation may appropriate for the purchase of lands for forest reserves in a State, provided it clearly appears that such reserves have a direct and substantial connection with the conservation and improvement of the navigability of a river actually navigable in whole or in part; and that any appropriation made therefor is limited to that purpose (Mr. Jenkins). Mr. Parker did not concur, thinking the question at least doubtful, and that the United States has no interest in rivers except for purposes of navigation, and "it may fairly be said that the rivers of the Atlantic slope are not navigable above tidal flow."

Messrs. Littlefield, Diekema, and Bannon have no doubt of the power, and think that if reforesting the watershed at its source is an appropriate means plainly adapted to that end of preventing the depositing in the river of accumulations that would obstruct its navigable portion, Congress has the right to acquire and control for that purpose. But the improvement of navigability in this way by increasing the flow of the water must not be theoretical, but physical, tangible, actual, and substantial, demonstrable by satisfactory, competent testimony in order to justify an appropriation. And the protection and improvement of navigability must also be the real objective, and not the incidental, purpose of the appropriation.

Mr. Brantley holds that Congress has the constitutional power to acquire lands and forest reserves in a State by purchase, condemnation, or otherwise, as an aid to navigation, if it be made to appear to Congress that such reserves would materially or substantially aid navigation.

It is thus evident from all these views that there is no doubt of the power, and that the only real question is whether navigability is substantially aided, or whether the proposed exercise of the power is too remote and fanciful to commend itself to the judgment of Congress as an appropriate means.

It is to be said respecting structures in navigable streams that the legislation of Congress has passed through an evolution up to the point now reached and the proposals now made. The Government has built many public works in aid of navigation where the improvement and protection were obvious by dams, locks, and canals, an example of which is the canalization of the St. Marys River on the connecting waters of the Great Lakes just as they issue from Lake Superior and on the international boundary between this country and Canada. Another feature of this evolution may be noted here in that region. The United States granted an easement for a right of way through public reserved lands of the United States to the State of Michigan for purposes of this canal, and then the state administration was surrendered and all rights reconveyed to the United States so that locks and other works in aid of navigation there might be undertaken commensurate with the power and interests of the nation and adequate for the enormous traffic passing that point and still increasing by leaps and bounds.

Sometimes Congress commits to municipalities or corporations or private individuals the construction and operation of works in aid of navigation where actual and practical navigation already exists and is being improved, as by the act of April 26, 1904 (33 Stat., 309) ; and at points along such reaches of the stream where, except for the government canals and other works in aid of navigation, the river itself is not actually navigable (e. g., act of May 9, 1906, 34 Stat., 183; id.,

211, 1288; act of March 6, 1906, 34 Stat., 52; extract from river
and harbor act of March 2, 1907, 34 Stat., 1073, 1094); or permits
structures for power development at points in rivers where government plans of navigation improvement by locks, dams, and canals
have already been adopted and the work begun, as at Muscle Shoals
on the Tennessee River, or on the Coosa River in Alabama; or gives
the right to build a dam, maintain and operate power stations in connection with it in consideration of the construction of locks, and a dry
dock in place of existing ones owned and operated by the United
States, namely, Des Moines Rapids Canal, act of February 9, 1905
(33 Stat., 712); or the particular structure is also subjected to the
provisions of the general dam act of June 21, 1906, hereafter to be
referred to (act of February 25, 1907, 34 Stat., 929; act of April 23,
1906, id., 130; act of March 3, 1905, 33 Stat., 1004).

It is difficult to see any difference in principle between such a case,
granting the right to develop and use power in consideration of improving navigation facilities and the imposition of any other reasonable amount or kind of charge. Of course, an illegal power can not
be justified because it has already been illegally exercised; but the
actual exercise of the power and the development of the matter under
the acts of Congress are instructive and significant.

In the numerous cases where permissive licenses have been given
to build dams or other structures in navigable streams at points where
they are not at present actually navigable or practically used for purposes of navigation there is no question, first, that the stream being
navigable as an integral thing or unit, the control over it as such
belongs to Congress and not to the State. The action of Congress is an
exclusion of any state authority which might otherwise exist, and the
theory appears to be that although the structure may be an interference with the existing navigability, such as it is, it is, in the opinion of
Congress, a reasonable interference. Congress by the very fact of its
interposition and grant of license is looking to navigable character
alone and to the future improvement or protection of navigation,
and accordingly invariably Congress either imposes the necessity of
making a proper lock or dam in all such cases, and sluices, or reserves
the right to compel the construction in the future of a suitable lock
for navigation purposes in connection therewith, subjects all plans to
the approval of the Secretary of War, reserves the right at any time
to take possession of the dam without compensation and control the
same for purposes of navigation, and imposes the duty of building in
connection with the dam or canal or other works a wagon and foot
bridge if desired in connection therewith for the purpose of travel; and
the right to alter, amend, and repeal the grant or to require the alter-
ation or removal of the structure is also reserved (act of June 4, 1906,
34 Stat., 265; act of June 16, 1906, id., 296).

Not all these conditions appear in every such grant or license, but they all do appear from time to time in different acts, and it is clear that whether Congress is itself actually improving and protecting navigation or authorizing some other agency or instrumentality to do so in its behalf, or permitting a reasonable obstruction in the particular stream and place when the interests of navigation do not forbid, Congress is proceeding altogether under that power, expressly reserves full control in that behalf, and either provides for locks and canals in the particular construction authorized as part of the authority to build, or else reserves the right to do so whenever the interests of navigation demand. There are many instances of such acts. I cite a few: Act of July 3, 1886 (24 Stat., 123); act of February 27, 1899 (30 Stat., 904); act of June 14, 1906 (34 Stat., 266).

These other points are to be observed in this development of the law: The present and future interests of the United States are provided for (sec. 1, act of June 21, 1906, 34 Stat., 386); uniformly there is a stipulation that the United States shall be entitled to free use of the water power developed (id., and many other acts); a general limit of time for construction is imposed (id.); it is a standing provision and reservation that the construction authorized shall not interfere with navigation; the licensee shall be liable to riparians for damages caused by overflow, etc.; the dam and works authorized shall be limited to the use of the surplus water not required for navigation (act of May 9, 1906, 34 Stat., 183); Congress may revoke, and there are provisions for forfeiture for breach of conditions. Such provisions and conditions, as I have said, appear throughout all these statutes.

Note also the special provisions in the river and harbor act of June 13, 1902 (32 Stat., 358), and in the act of June 28, 1902 (id., 408), by which leases or licenses for the use of water power in the Cumberland River, Tennessee, may be granted by the Secretary of War to the highest responsible bidders, after advertisement, limited to the use of the surplus water not required for navigation and under the condition that no structures shall be built and no operations conducted which shall injure navigation in any manner or interfere with the operations of the Government or impair the usefulness of any government improvement for the benefit of navigation.

In some cases these acts provide not only for sluiceways for logs, etc., but for sluiceways and ladders for fish. It might be as reasonably objected that the United States could make no such condition in connection with its licenses for the preservation of fish in the interest of all the people, because that was solely a matter of state control and largely a matter of riparian right, as to say that it could not impose conditions and charges respecting the power developed by the surplus water.

Occasionally the title of the act recognizes the joint purpose or the collateral and subsidiary incident of power. Thus, an act of May 1, 1906 (34 Stat., 155), relative to the Rock River license, is entitled "An act permitting the building of dams, etc., in aid of navigation and for the development of water power."

In an act of June 29, 1906 (34 Stat., 628), permitting the erection of a lock and dam in aid of navigation in the White River, Arkansas, it is provided that the licensee shall purchase and pay for certain lands necessary for the successful construction and operation of the lock and dam and leave them to the United States, and that, in consideration of the construction of these structures free of cost to the United States, the United States grants to the licensee the rights possessed by it to use the water power produced by the dam and to convert the same into electric power or otherwise utilize it for a period of ninety-nine years, but to furnish to the United States, free of cost, sufficient power to operate the locks and to light the United States buildings and grounds.

Another instance of authority granted to the Secretary of War to make leases or issue licenses for the use of water power is shown by the river and harbor act of September 19, 1890, respecting the Green and Barren rivers.

Without dwelling further on this subject, it is plain that considering this whole body of laws, the United States is legitimately exercising the power over interstate commerce under the heading of the improvement and protection of navigation, and is imposing proper- -that is, not only just, but legal—terms, conditions, and reservations, and as a question of power this is as clearly true when the United States licenses a structure which is a temporary and partial obstruction to navigation at some point where the Government is not yet ready to complete and unify the navigable use of the stream, as where the Government is itself developing an actual plant for the improvement of navigation by constructing the appropriate works. And the connection between the power and its application is as evident and germane even when water power is developed and a charge made for it, because, while that or some other use of the water outside navigation use is the primary or the sole object of the licensee and the navigation use is only incidental to that use, so far as the licensee is concerned, that other use from the standpoint of the Government and the people at large is always and only incidental to the improvement and protection of navigation and that use. This is true as a real fact and principle controlling the subject, even if the ultimate improvement of navigation—the actual navigation use, that is—is remote in time and as a practical undertaking, and is contemplated, so to speak, far ahead.

State law, it is true, in general determines the title of riparian owners in the beds of both navigable and nonnavigable streams, and their rights of user in the flowing water. This riparian property and right, which, respecting title to the beds of nonnavigable streams as extending ad filum aquae, is pretty uniform throughout the States, varies as to navigable streams according as States have followed the common-law rule of stopping the private title at the shore, or having followed the rule on unnavigable waters and extended it to the middle thread of the stream. Regarding the rights of the riparian in the water, the rules vary from the common-law doctrine in the humid States that the upland owner is entitled to the flow of the water as it was accustomed to flow to the doctrine of prior appropriation for beneficial use in the arid States, including the combination of the two doctrines known as the California rule. But always and everywhere the use must be reasonable, and there is an order of preference in the uses beginning with domestic use. Even on public navigable rivers the riparian owner has many rights of user subject to the limitation that his use must be reasonable, so as not to injure the rights of others above or below him on the stream, and subject to the public easement of navigation, and generally to the public right of fishing. The riparian owner has, for instance, the right of access, but when the paramount control over navigation interferes this is a barren right and he is not entitled to compensation; and it seems that even in States where he has the title to the submerged lands out to the middle of the stream the title is a bare, technical title not available for access or any other purpose, or at least not entitling him to compensation if the United States, for any lawful purpose, should appropriate and occupy the subaqueous lands. (Scranton *v.* Wheeler, 179 U. S., 141.)

So much for the private and individual interest of the riparian owner; and it is to be observed respecting the pending proposals that such rights are always capable of being asserted in a court of law; that presumably the Government or the government licensee will have acquired the necessary riparian ownership, and that provision is expressly made in all statutes of this character for compensation by the licensee to the riparian or others for all damages caused.

Now, as to the state interest, there is no doubt that a State may undertake the improvement of a navigable stream within her borders, or license structures over it or in it, until the United States under legislation by Congress assumes jurisdiction. In this matter and in similar instances the Supreme Court has held that there is a concurrent function and power, and that nonaction by Congress amounts to permission to the State to occupy the field. (Willson et al. *v.* The Black Bird Creek Marsh Co., 2 Pet., 245, 252-253; The Passaic Bridges, 3 Wall., 793; Pound *v.* Turck, 95 U. S., 463; Escanaba Co. *v.* Chicago, 107 U. S., 683; Morgan *v.* Louisiana, 118 U. S., 465; New York, etc., R. R. Co. *v.* New York, 165 U. S., 631; United States *v.* Rio Grande Irrigation Co., 174 U. S., 690, 703.) But of course it can not be admitted that a State has any jurisdiction or control whatsoever after Congress has determined that the stream is navigable (whether it is explicitly so denominated or not) and pro- ceeds to improve or protect the navigation or navigable capacity. Then the federal jurisdiction becomes plenary, paramount, and exclusive. The very fact that Congress has legislated as it has done respecting the various streams and waters embraced in the legislation above reviewed is conclusive proof that the national jurisdiction has completely ousted state jurisdiction over those waters and at those points. This seems to be the view of the States themselves and on all hands, and I do not understand that this position is disputed even by those who claim that for purposes of power and all other incidental uses of the water other than for navigation the state authority is supreme and exclusive.

It is a mistake to suppose that the federal jurisdiction and the navigability are doubtful because the stream may not be navigable now at the particular point. It is to make it navigable at some time, even if a remote future is contemplated, and slow progress toward a comprehensive and unifying plan—it is to improve navi- gation, to increase navigable capacity, and in the meantime to pro- tect navigation that the national power interposes. In many senses a navigable stream is a unit. It is none the less a navigable stream because there is an obstruction at a particular point (The Montello, 20 Wall., 430), being navigable above or below or both. And while the test of navigability at any particular point is whether the stream is navigable in fact, the upper reaches of a stream and the preservation and maintenance of flow at the sources, although the stream is not navigable there, are clearly within the scope of the power as directed to the continuing protection as well as the immediate improvement of navigation. The case of United States *v.* Rio Grande Irrigation Co. (174 U. S., 690), by the necessary effect of the final order at page 710, sustains the contention that the United States may interpose to control or prevent the irrigation or other use of water above the limit of navigability, if it shall appear as a fact that such use impairs the navigable capacity over that portion of the stream where navigation does exist.

The preliminary report of the Inland Waterways Commission with the President's message transmitting it to Congress, and the bill introduced in the Senate by Mr. Newlands (S. 500), with the report and recommendations of the Secretary of War upon the same, are very instructive and significant in this matter. The bill reflects and embodies the main ideas and recommendations of the report and will

CRUISE OF THE BATTLE-SHIP FLEET.

"The most notable achievement of the Navy in time of peace was the voyage of the battle-ship fleet. This proved an epoch-making cruise, the longest ever undertaken by such a number of battle-ships, and enlisted the interested attention of the naval world.

The fleet sailed from Hampton Roads December 16, 1907, after a review by the President, and made the passage to various ports for coaling and incidental stops at points in South America; engaged in target practice upon arrival at Magdalena Bay, Mexico, arranged by permission of the Mexican Government; and reached San Francisco, May 1, 1908, without a single mishap to mar the voyage."

Quoted from the article entitled "Cruise of the Battle-Ship Fleet" in the encyclopedic index.

One of the panels shows Roosevelt bidding God-speed to the fleet; another panel, sailors from the fleet parading on land in the course of their trip; and the third, the fleet in battle-line. Roosevelt's genius was a hard-headed, practical, open-air sort of genius. He looked upon the Army and Navy, the sailor and soldier, as machines intended for fighting; and military efficiency in his mind meant, not snappy dress parades, but readiness and ability to sustain and deliver hard knocks. Under his Administration both branches of the service prospered. The principle underlying his military doctrines are set forth fully in his messages. It will be worth while to turn to "Roosevelt, Theodore," in the encyclopedic index, run the eye over the range of subjects he has discussed, and refer to the pages there mentioned for his utterances on topics that interest you. See also "Army" and "Navy."

alone serve the purposes of our consideration after one or two references to the report. The report and the President's message point out that a river system from the forest headwaters to the mouth is a unit and that navigation of the lower reaches can not be fully developed without the control of floods and low waters by storage and drainage; that navigable channels are directly concerned with the protection of source waters and with soil erosion which forms bars and shoals from the richest portions of farms; and that the uses of a stream for domestic and municipal supply, for power and often for irrigation, must be taken into account. The development of waterways and the conservation of forests are promising needs and are indissoluble .... The systematic development of interstate commerce by improvement of inland waterways should proceed in coordination with all other uses of the waters and benefit to be derived from them, which constitute a public asset of incalculable value. The report notes that irrigation projects involving the storage of flood waters (in which, of course, reclamation of arid lands is the chief and primary object) create canals as well as tend to purify and clarify waters and to conserve supply by seepage during droughts; that on the other hand works designed to improve navigation commonly produce headwater and develop power; that western projects are "chiefly thus far for irrigation, but prospectively for navigation and power."

Accordingly the great central idea of Mr. Newlands's measure is the conservation and correlation of the natural resources of the country in navigable waters which are national resources, because essentially dependent upon and developed from the preservation and regulation of stream flow and the improvement of navigation. For example, section 2 of the bill provides for examinations, surveys, and investigations—

with a view to the promotion of transportation; and to consider and coordinate the questions of irrigation, swamp-land reclamation, clarification of streams, utilization of water power, prevention of soil waste, protection of forests, regulation of flow, control of floods, transfer facilities and sites, and the regulation and control thereof, and such other questions regarding waterways as are related to the development of rivers, lakes, and canals for the purposes of commerce.

And again, by section 6, the projects authorized and begun under section 5—

may include such collateral works for the irrigation of arid lands (for reclamation and conservation as specified) and for the utilization of water power as may be deemed advisable in connection with the development of a channel for navigation, or as aiding in a compensatory way in the diminution of the cost of such project.

Section 7 authorizes the commission to be appointed "to enter into cooperation with States, municipalities, communities, corporations, and individuals in such collateral works."

The report of the Secretary of War on this bill, dated April 17, substantially and by inference approves its purpose and general provisions, while making certain specific suggestions. That report notes the provision for coordination between navigation and other uses of the waters in connection with their improvement for the promotion of commerce among the States, and the provision for cooperation with States, municipalities, etc., so as to promote "union of interests through mutual beneficial cooperation," which "feature is recognized by the War Department as highly desirable." The report also notes the provision for correlating the existing agencies in the departments of War, Interior, Agriculture, and Commerce and Labor, and "the utilization and control of water power available in navigable and source streams developed by works for improving navigation." To meet constitutional and legal objections, certain changes are suggested in order to make it clear that the bill contemplates no extension of federal authority beyond its recognized limits, by language which expressly restricts the plan to the development of navigable inland waterways for the purpose of regulating, improving, and protecting interstate and foreign commerce, and also by language which makes the dependence and connection of irrigation and other uses upon the navigation use more clear and certain.

If the power exists, it is for Congress to say whether the occasion for its exercise is real, and whether the connection between the occasion and the method and results of exercise of the power is substantial, and whether the means employed to carry the power into effect are legitimate. The wisdom, expediency, and justice of the means employed are all for Congress to determine. Certainly it is no objection to a power that its exercise is manifestly of vital importance and advantage to the general welfare. As I have suggested already, the interests of navigation may be a secondary or even negligible consideration with the licensees of the Government, but that does not make the government jurisdiction any the less a constitutional control over navigation, and the real object of the licensee, whether it be the development of power or irrigation, is none the less merely subsidiary and incidental from the government point of view. If the Government by its own works in actual aid of navigation, or by such works undertaken by its licensees and agents, or by private licensed and permitted structures in navigable streams where navigation is not yet in actual course of improvement, develops power. which is the natural, and indeed necessary, result of such works, it is preposterous to say that the Government can not deal with the subject on the basis of or with any reference to the power thus incidentally or intentionally developed, but must let it go to waste or give it away or turn it over to the State.

I repeat that the development of power or of irrigation from surplus waters is subsidiary and collateral to, but nevertheless germane to, an actual development of navigation or to an exercise of the navigation jurisdiction where development is in abeyance.

Of course the terms to licensees should be fair, and this is a matter for the justice as well as the wisdom of Congress to settle. The period of license should be long enough to permit the enterprise to be financed. In some cases it may very likely be that all charges should be nominal for a reasonable period, and the rate per horsepower unit might ultimately be varied in accordance with different conditions of time, place, population, and other tributary factors.

Take a case in illustration: The proposal for the Long Saut on the St. Lawrence River contemplates a 20-foot channel in the river where now there is no navigable channel at all, and, under our conventional arrangements with Great Britain, vessels of the United States must use the canal on the Canadian side. This is navigation and an improvement to navigation of tremendous consequence and value. The power developed is enormous and correspondingly valuable. Of course the private enterprise which undertakes this public work is entitled to protection and reward. It may be that the contractors, in consideration of the creation of that most valuable channel, should be relieved from any government charges for the power developed for a term of years; but on the other hand the power developed, which belongs ultimately to and is held in trust for all the people of the United States, should not be granted forever and for nothing.

I understand that the government engineers and experts estimate that the proper use of the water powers of the country as an asset of the people would in time pay for all contemplated and possible improvement of the navigable inland waterways.

The proposed use of the funds to be produced is further evidence of the essential connection between the improvement of navigation and other uses of water thereby stored and made available, because the charges made are to constitute a permanent and general fund in aid of the development of all navigable waterways. The various States manifest concurrence and willingness toward the government plans, and while that fact would not authorize a scheme otherwise unconstitutional, it is of vast practical importance that local jealousies will not be aroused and that the proposals contemplate and would receive cooperation from States, municipalities, and all others locally interested in plans which in the end are for the benefit of the whole people.

Keeping in mind the general principles established and the considerations of proper methods and particular equities which are committed to Congress, the strict constitutionality of the programme proposed can not well be doubted.

VETO MESSAGE

To the House of Representatives:

I herewith return, without approval, H. R. 16954, entitled "An act to provide for the Thirteenth and subsequent decennial censuses." I do this with extreme reluctance, because I fully realize the importance of supplying the Director of the Census at as early a date as possible with the force necessary to the carrying on of his work. But it is of high consequence to the country that the statistical work of the census shall be conducted with entire accuracy. This is as important from the standpoint of business and industry as from the scientific standpoint. It is, therefore, in my judgment, essential that the result should not be open to the suspicion of bias on political and personal grounds; that it should not be open to the reasonable suspicion of being a waste of the people's money and a fraud.

Section 7 of the act provides in effect that appointments to the census shall be under the spoils system, for this is the real meaning of the provision that they shall be subject only to noncompetitive examination. The proviso is added that they shall be selected without regard to political party affiliations. But there is only one way to guarantee that they shall be selected without regard to politics and on merit, and that is by choosing them after competitive examination from the lists of eligibles provided by the Civil Service Commission. The present Director of the Census in his last report states the exact fact about these noncompetitive examinations when he says:

"A noncompetitive examination means that every one of the many thousands who will pass the examinations will have an equal right to appointment, and that personal and political pressure must in the end, as always before, become the determining factor with regard to the great body of these temporary employments. I can not too earnestly urge that the Director of the Census be relieved from this unfortunate situation."

To provide that the clerks and other employees shall be appointed after noncompetitive examination, and yet to provide that they shall be selected without regard to political party affiliations, means merely that the appointments shall be treated as the perquisites of the politicians of both parties, instead of as the perquisites of the politicians of one party. I do not believe in the doctrine that to the victor belong the spoils; but I think even less of the doctrine that the spoils shall be divided without a fight by the professional politicians on both sides; and this would be the result of permitting the bill in its present shape to become a law. Both of the last censuses, the Eleventh and the Twelfth, were taken under a provision of law excluding competition; that is, necessitating the appointments being made under the spoils system. Every man competent to speak with authority because of his knowledge of and familiarity with the work of those censuses has stated that the result was to produce extravagance and demoralization. Mr. Robert P. Porter, who took the census of 1890, states that—

"The efficiency of the decennial census would be greatly improved and its cost materially lessened if it were provided that the employees should be selected in accordance with the terms of the civil service law."

Mr. Frederick H. Wines, the Assistant Director of the Census of 1900, states as follows:

"A mathematical scale was worked out by which the number of 'assignments' to each Senator and Representative was determined in advance, so many appointments to a Senator, a smaller number to a Representative, half as many to a Democrat as a Republican, and in Democratic States and congressional districts the assignments were made to the Republican state and district committees. The assignees named in the first instance the persons to be examined. They were afterwards furnished each with a list of those names who had 'passed' and requested to name those whom they desired to have appointed. Vacancies were filled in the same manner. This system was thoroughly satisfactory to the majority of the politicians interested, though there were a few who refused to have anything to do with it. The effect upon the bureau was, as may readily be imagined, thoroughly demoralizing."

Mr. Carroll D. Wright, who had charge of the Census Bureau after the census of 1890, estimates that $2,000,000, and more than a year's time, would have been saved if the census force had been brought into the classified service, and adds:

"I do not hesitate to say one-third of the amount expended under my own administration was absolutely wasted, and wasted principally on account of the fact that the office was not under civil service rules. * * * In October, 1893, when I took charge of the Census Office, there was an office force of 1,092. There had been a constant reduction for many months and this was kept up without cessation till the close of the census. There was never a month after October, 1893, that the clerical force reached the number then in office; nevertheless, while these general reductions were being made and in the absence of any necessity for the increase of the force, 389 new appointments were made."

This of course meant the destruction of economy and efficiency for purely political considerations.

In view of the temporary character of the work, it would be well to waive the requirements of the civil service law as regards geographical apportionment, but the appointees should be chosen by competitive examination from the lists provided by the Civil Service Commission. The noncompetitive examination in a case like this is not only vicious, but is in effect a fraud upon the public. No essential change is effected by providing that it be conducted by the Civil Service Commission; and to provide that the employees shall be selected without regard to political party affiliations is empty and misleading, unless, at the same time, it is made effective in the only way in which it is possible to make it effective—that is, by providing that the examination shall be made competitive.

I also recommend that if provision is made that the census printing work may be done outside the Government Printing Office, it shall be explicitly provided that the Government authorities shall see that the eight-hour law is applied in effective fashion to these outside offices.

Outside of these matters, I believe that the bill is, on the whole, satisfactory and represents an improvement upon previous legislation on the subject. But it is of vital consequence that we should not once again permit the usefulness of this great decennial undertaking on behalf of the whole people to be marred by permitting it to be turned into an engine to further the self-interest of that small section of the people which makes a profession of politics. The evil effects of the spoils system and of the custom of treating appointments to the public service as personal perquisites of professional politicians are peculiarly evident in the case of a great public work like the taking of the census, a work which should emphatically be done for the whole people and with an eye single to their interest.

THEODORE ROOSEVELT.

The White House, *February 5, 1909.*

[H. R. 16954. Sixtieth Congress of the United States of America; at the second session. Begun and held at the city of Washington on Monday, the seventh day of December, one thousand nine hundred and eight.]

An act to provide for the Thirteenth and subsequent decennial censuses.

Be it enacted by the Senate and House of Representatives of the United States of America in Congress Assembled, That a census of the population, agriculture, manufactures, and mines and quarries of the

United States shall be taken by the Director of the Census m the year nineteen hundred and ten and every ten years thereafter. The census herein provided for shall include each State and Territory on the mainland of the United States, the District of Columbia, and Alaska, Hawaii, and Porto Rico.

SEC. 2. That the period of three years beginning the first day of July next preceding the census provided for in section one of this Act shall be known as the decennial census period, and the reports upon the inquiries provided for in said section shall be completed and published within such period.

SEC. 3. That after June thirtieth, nineteen hundred and nine, and during the decennial census period only, there may be employed in the Census Office, in addition to the force provided for by the Act of March sixth, nineteen hundred and two, entitled "An Act to provide for a permanent Census Office," an Assistant Director, who shall be an experienced practical statistician; a geographer, a chief statistician, who shall be a person of known and tried experience in statistical work, an appointment clerk, a private secretary to the Director, two stenographers, and eight expert chiefs of division. These officers, with the exception of the Assistant Director, shall be appointed without examination by the Secretary of Commerce and Labor upon the recommendation of the Director of the Census. The Assistant Director shall be appointed by the President, by and with the advice and consent of the Senate.

SEC. 4. That the Assistant Director shall perform such duties as may be prescribed by the Director of the Census. In the absence of the Director the Assistant Director shall serve as Director, and in the absence of the Director and Assistant Director the chief clerk shall serve as Director.

The appointment clerk shall perform the appointment duties assigned to the disbursing clerk in section four of the Act entitled "An Act to provide for a permanent Census Office," approved March sixth, nineteen hundred and two. The disbursing clerk of the Census Office shall, at the beginning of the decennial census period, give additional bond to the Secretary of the Treasury in the sum of one hundred thousand dollars, surety to be approved by the Solicitor of the Treasury, which bond shall be conditioned that the said officer shall render, quarter yearly, a true and faithful account to the proper accounting officers of the Treasury of all moneys and properties which shall be received by him by virtue of his office during the said decennial census period. Such bond shall be filed in the office of the Secretary of the Treasury, to be by him put in suit upon any breach of the conditions thereof.

SEC. 5. That during the decennial census period the annual compensation of the officials of the Census Office shall be as follows: The Director of the Census, seven thousand five hundred dollars; the private secretary to the Director, two thousand five hundred dollars; the Assistant Director, five thousand dollars; the chief statisticians, three thousand five hundred dollars each; the chief clerk, three thousand dollars; the disbursing clerk, three thousand dollars; the appointment clerk, three thousand dollars; the geographer, three thousand dollars; the chiefs of division, two thousand two hundred and fifty dollars each; and the stenographers provided for in section three of this Act, two thousand dollars each.

SEC. 6. That in addition to the force hereinbefore provided for and to that already authorized by law there may be employed in the Census Office during the decennial census period, and no longer, as many clerks of classes four, three, two, and one; as many clerks, copyists, computers, and skilled laborers, with salaries at the rate of not less than six hundred dollars nor more than one thousand dollars per annum, and as many messengers, assistant messengers, messenger boys, watchmen, unskilled laborers, and charwomen, as may be found necessary for the proper and prompt performance of the duties herein required, these additional clerks and employees to be appointed by the Director of the Census: *Provided,* That the total number of such additional clerks of classes two, three, and four shall at no time exceed one hundred: *And provided further,* That employees engaged in the compilation or tabulation of statistics by the use of mechanical devices may be compensated on a piece-price basis to be fixed by the Director.

SEC. 7. That the additional clerks and other employees provided for in section six shall be subject to such noncompetitive examination as the Director of the Census may prescribe, the said examination to be conducted by the United States Civil Service Commission: *Provided,* That they shall be selected without regard to the law of apportionment or to the political party affiliations of the applicants, and that preference may be given to persons having previous experience in census work whose efficiency records are satisfactory to the said Director, who may, in his discretion, accept such records in lieu of said examination: *And provided further,* That employees in other branches of the departmental classified service who have had previous experience in census work may be transferred without examination to the Census Office to serve during the whole or a part of the decennial census period, and at the end of such service the employees so transferred shall be eligible to appointment to poistions of similar grade in any Department without examination: *And provided further,* That during the decennial census period and no longer the Director of the Census may fill vacancies in the permanent force of the Census Office by the promotion or transfer of clerks or other employees employed on the temporary force authorized by section six of this Act: *And provided further,* That at the expiration of the decennial census period the term of service of all employees so transferred and of all other temporary officers and employees appointed under the provisions of this Act shall terminate, and such officers and employees shall not thereafter be eligible to appointment or transfer into the classified service of the Government by virtue of their examination or appointment under this Act.

SEC. 8. That the Thirteenth Census shall be restricted to inquiries relating to population, to agriculture, to manufactures, and to mines and quarries. The schedules relating to population shall include for each inhabitant the name, relationship to head of family, color, sex, age, conjugal condition, place of birth, place of birth of parents, number of years in the United States, citizenship, occupation, whether or not employer or employee, school attendance, literacy, and tenure of home and whether or not a survivor of the Union or Confederate Army or Navy; and for the enumeration of institutions, shall include paupers, prisoners, juvenile delinquents, insane, feeble-minded, blind, deaf and dumb, and inmates of benevolent institutions.

The schedules relating to agriculture shall include name and color of occupant of each farm, tenure, acreage of farm, value of farm and improvements, value of farm implements, number and value of live stock on farms and ranges, number and value of domestic animals not on farms and ranges, and the acreage of crops as of the date of enumeration, and the acreage of crops and the quantity and value of crops and other farm products for the year ending December thirty-first next preceding the enumeration.

The schedules of inquiries relating to manufactures and to mines and quarries shall include the name and location of each establishment; character of organization, whether individual, cooperative, or other form; character of business or kind of goods manufactured; amount of capital actually invested; number of proprietors, firm members, copartners, stockholders, and officers and the amount of their salaries; number of employees and the amount of their wages; quantity and cost of materials used in manufactures; amount of miscellaneous expenses; quantity and value of products; time in operation during the census year; character and quantity of power used, and character and number of machines employed.

The census of manufactures and of mines and quarries shall relate to the year ending December thirty-first next preceding the enumeration of population and shall be confined to mines and quarries and manufacturing establishments which were in active operation during all or a portion of that year. The census of manufactures shall furthermore be confined to manufacturing establishments conducted under what is known as the factory system, exclusive of the so-called neighborhood household and hand industries.

The inquiry concerning manufactures shall cover the production of turpentine and rosin and the report concerning this industry shall show, in addition to the other facts covered by the regular schedule of manufactures, the quantity of crude turpentine gathered, the quantity of turpentine and rosin manufactured, the sources, methods, and extent of the industry.

Whenever he shall deem it expedient, the Director of the Census may charge the collection of these statistics upon special agents or upon detailed employees, to be employed without respect to locality.

The form and subdivision of inquiries necessary to secure the information under the foregoing topics shall be determined by the Director of the Census.

SEC. 9. That the Director of the Census shall, at least six months prior to the date fixed for commencing the enumeration at the Thirteenth and each succeeding decennial census, designate the number, whether one or more, of supervisors of census for each State and Territory, the District of Columbia, Alaska, the Hawaiian Islands, and Porto Rico, and shall define the districts within which they are to act; except that the Director of the Census, in his discretion, need not designate supervisors for Alaska and the Hawaiian Islands, but in lieu thereof may employ special agents as hereinafter provided. The supervisors shall be appointed by the President, by and with the advice and consent of the Senate; *Provided,* That the whole number of supervisors shall not exceed three hundred and thirty: *And provided further,* That so far as practicable and desirable the boundaries of the supervisors' distrcts shall conform to the boundaries of the Congressional districts: *And provided further,* That if in any supervisor's distrct the supervisor has not been appointed and qualified ninety days preceding the date fixed for the commencement of the enumeration, or if any vacancy shall occur thereafter, either through death, removal, or resignation of the supervisor, or from any other cause, the Director of the Census may appoint a temporary supervisor or detail an employee of the Census Office to act as supervisor for that district.

SEC. 10. That each supervisor of census shall be charged with the performance, within his own district, of the following duties: To consult with the Director of the Census in regard to the division of his district into subdivisions most convenient for the purpose of the enumeration, which subdivisions or enumeration districts shall be defined and the boundaries thereof fixed by the Director of the Census; to designate to the Director suitable persons, and, with his consent, to employ such persons as enumerators, one or more for each subdivision; to communicate to enumerators the necessary instructions and directions relating to their duties; to examine and scrutinize the returns of the enumerators, and in the event of discrepancies or deficiencies appearing in any of the said returns to use all diligence in causing the same to be corrected or supplied; to forward the completed returns of the enumerators to the Director at such time and in such manner as shall be prescribed, and to make up and forward to the Director the accounts of each enumerator in his district for service rendered, which accounts shall be duly certified to by the enumerator, and the same shall be certified as true and correct, if so found, by the supervisor, and said accounts so certified shall be accepted and paid by the Director. The duties imposed upon the supervisor by this Act shall be performed in any and all particulars in accordance with the orders and instructions of the Director of the Census.

SEC. 11. That each supervisor of the census shall, upon the completion of his duties to the satisfaction of the Director of the Census, receive the sum of one thousand five hundred dollars and, in addition thereto, one dollar for each thousand or majority fraction of a thousand of population enumerated in his district, such sums to be in full compensation for all services rendered and expenses incurred by him: *Provided,* That of the above-named compensation a sum not to exceed six hundred dollars, in the discretion of the Director of the Census, may be paid to any supervisor prior to the completion of his duties in one or more payments, as the Director of the Census may determine: *Provided further,* That in emergencies arising in connection with the work of preparation for, or during the progress of, the enumeration in his district, or in connection with the reenumeration of any subdivision, a supervisor may, in the discretion of the Director of the Census, be allowed actual and necessary traveling expenses and an allowance in lieu of subsistence not exceeding four dollars per day during his necessary absence from his usual place of residence: *And provided further,* That an appropriate allowance to supervisors for clerk hire may be made when deemed necessary by the Director of the Census.

SEC. 12. That each enumerator shall be charged with the collection in his subdivision of the facts and statistics required by the population and agricultural schedules and such other schedules as the Director of the Census may determine shall be used by him in connection with the census, as provided in section eight of this Act. It shall be the duty of each enumerator to visit personally each dwelling house in his subdivision, and each family therein, and each individual living out of a family in any place of abode, and by inquiry made of the head of each family, or of the member thereof deemed most competent and trustworthy, or of such individual living out of a family, to obtain each and every item of information and all particulars required by this Act as of date April fifteenth of the year in which the enumeration shall be made; and in case no person shall be found at the usual place of abode of such family, or individual living out of a family, competent to answer the inquiries made in compliance with the requirements of this Act, then it shall be lawful for the enumerator to obtain the required information as nearly as may be practicable from families or persons living in the neighborhood of such place of abode. It shall be the duty also of each enumerator to forward the original schedules, properly filled out and duly certified, to the supervisor of his district as his returns under the provisions of this Act; and in the event of discrepancies or deficiencies being discovered in these schedules he shall use all diligence in correcting or supplying the same. In case an enumeration district embraces all or any part of any incorporated borough, village, town, or city, and also other territory not included within the limits of such incorporated borough, village, town or city, it shall be the duty of the enumerator to clearly and plainly distinguish and separate, upon the population schedules, the inhabitants of such borough, village, town or city from the inhabitants of the territory not included therein. No enumerator shall be deemed qualified to enter upon his duties until he has received from the supervisor of the district to which he belongs a commission, signed by the supervisor, authorizing him to perform the duties of an enumerator, and setting forth the boundaries of the subdivision within which such duties are to be performed.

SEC. 13. That the territory assigned to each supervisor shall be divided into as many enumeration districts as may be necessary to carry out the purposes of this Act, and, in the discretion of the Director of the Census, two or more enumeration districts may be given to one enumerator, and the boundaries of all the enumeration districts shall be clearly described by civil divisions, rivers, roads, public surveys, or other easily distinguishable lines: *Provided,* That enumerators may be assigned for the special enumeration of institutions, when desirable, without reference to the number of inmates.

SEC. 14. That any supervisor of census may, with the approval of the Director of the Census, remove any enumerator in his district and fill the vacancy thus caused or otherwise occurring. Whenever it shall appear that any portion of the census provided for in this Act has been negligently or improperly taken, and is by reason thereof incomplete or erroneous, the Director of the Census may cause such incomplete and unsatisfactory enumeration and census to be amended or made anew.

SEC. 15. That the Director of the Census may authorize and direct supervisors of census to employ interpreters to assist the enumerators of their respective districts in the enumeration of persons not speaking the English language, but no authorization shall be given for such employment in any district until due and proper effort has been made to secure an enumerator who can speak the language or languages for which the services of an interpreter would otherwise be required. The compensation of such interpreters shall be fixed by the Director of the Census in advance, and shall not exceed five dollars per day for each day actually and necessarily employed.

SEC. 16. That the compensation of enumerators shall be determined by the Director of the Census as follows: In subdivisions where he shall deem such remuneration sufficient, an allowance of not less than two nor more than four cents for each inhabitant; not less than twenty nor more than thirty cents for each farm reported; ten cents for each barn and enclosure containing live stock not on farms, and not less than twenty nor more than thirty cents for each establishment of productive industry reported. In other subdivisions the Director of the Census may fix a mixed rate of not less than one nor more than two dollars per day and, in addition, an allowance of not less than one nor more than three cents for each inhabitant enumerated, and not less than fifteen nor more than twenty cents for each farm and each establishment of productive industry reported. In other subdivisions per diem rates shall be fixed by the Director according to the difficulty of enumeration, having special reference to the regions to be canvassed and the sparsity of settlement or other considerations pertinent thereto. The compensation allowed to an enumerator in any such district shall be not less than three nor more than six dollars per day of eight hours actual field work, and no payment shall be made for time in excess of eight hours for any one day. The subdivisions or enumeration districts to which the several rates of compensation shall apply shall be designated by the Director of the Census at least two weeks in advance of the enumeration. No claim for mileage or traveling expenses shall be allowed any enumerator in either class of subdivisions, except in extreme cases, and then only when authority has been previously granted by the Director of the Census; and the decision of the Director as to the amount due any enumerator shall be final.

SEC. 17. That in the event of the death of any supervisor or enumerator after his appointment and entrance on his duties, the Director of the Census is authorized to pay to his widow or his legal representative such sum as he may deem just and fair for the services rendered by such supervisor or enumerator.

SEC. 18. That special agents may be appointed by the Director of the Census to carry out the provisions of this Act and of the Act to provide for a permanent Census Office approved March sixth, nineteen hundred and two, and Acts amendatory thereof or supplemental thereto. The special agents thus appointed shall have like authority with the enumerators in respect to the subjects committed to them under this Act, and shall receive compensation at rates to be fixed by the Director of the Census: *Provided,* That the same shall in no case exceed six dollars per day and actual necessary traveling expenses, and an allowance in lieu of subsistence not exceeding four dollars per day during necessary absence from their usual place of residence: *Provided further,* That no pay or allowance in lieu of subsistence shall be allowed special agents when employed in the Census Office on other than the special work committed to them, and no appointments of special agents shall be made for clerical work: *And provided further,* That the Director of the Census shall have power, and is hereby authorized, to appoint special agents to assist the supervisors whenever he may deem it proper, in connection with the work of preparation for, or during the progress of, the enumeration or in connection with the reenumeration of any district or a part thereof; or he may, in his discretion, employ for this purpose any of the permanent or temporary employees of the Census Office: *And provided further,*

That the Director of the Census may, in his discretion, fix the compensation of special agents on a piece-price basis.

SEC. 19. That every supervisor, supervisor's clerk, enumerator,
interpreter, special agent, or other employee shall take and subscribe
to an oath or affirmation, to be prescribed by the Director of the
Census. All appointees and employees provided for in this Act shall
be appointed or employed, and examined, if examination is required
by this Act, solely with reference to their fitness to perform the duties
required of them by the provisions of this Act, and without reference
to their political party affiliations.

SEC. 20. That the enumeration of the population required by section one of this Act shall be taken as of the fifteenth day of April;
and it shall be the duty of each enumerator to enumerate the enumeration of his district on that day, unless the Director of the Census
in his discretion shall defer the enumeration in said district by reason
of climatic or other conditions which would materially interfere with
the proper conduct of the work; but in any event it shall be the duty
of each enumerator to prepare the returns hereinbefore required to be
made except those relating to paupers, prisoners, juvenile delinquents,
insane, feeble-minded, blind, deaf and dumb, and inmates of benevolent institutions, and to forward the same to the supervisor of his
district, within thirty days from the commencement of the enumeration of his district: *Provided*, That in any city having five thousand
inhabitants or more under the preceding census the enumeration of
the population shall be commenced on the fifteenth day of April aforesaid and shall be completed within two weeks thereafter.

SEC. 21. That if any person shall receive or secure to himself any
fee, reward, or compensation as a consideration for the appointment
or employment of any person as enumerator or clerk or other employee, or shall in any way receive or secure to himself any part of
the compensation paid to any enumerator or clerk or other employee,
he shall be deemed guilty of a misdemeanor, and upon conviction
thereof shall be fined not more than three thousand dollars and be
imprisoned not more than five years.

SEC. 22. That any supervisor, supervisor's clerk, enumerator, interpreter, special agent, or other employee, who, having taken and sub-
scribed the oath of office required by this Act, shall, without justifiable cause, neglect or refuse to perform the duties enjoined on him by
this Act, shall be deemed guilty of a misdemeanor, and upon conviction thereof, shall be fined not exceeding five hundred dollars; or if
he shall, without the authority of the Director of the Census, publish
or communicate any information coming into his possession by reason
of his employment under the provisions of this Act, or the Act to
provide for a permanent Census Office, or Acts amendatory thereof
or supplemental thereto, he shall be guilty of a misdemeanor and shall
upon conviction thereof be fined not to exceed one thousand dollars,
or be imprisoned not to exceed two years, or both so fined and imprisoned, in the discretion of the court; or if he shall willfully and
knowingly swear to or affirm falsely, he shall be deemed guilty of
perjury, and upon conviction thereof shall be imprisoned not exceeding five years and be fined not exceeding two thousand dollars; or if
he shall willfully and knowingly make a false certificate or a fictitious
return, he shall be guilty of a misdemeanor, and upon conviction
of either of the last-named offenses he shall be fined not exceeding

two thousand dollars and be imprisoned not exceeding five years; or if any person who is or has been an enumerator shall knowingly or willfully furnish, or cause to be furnished, directly or indirectly, to the Director of the Census, or to any supervisor of the census, any false statement or false information with reference to any inquiry for which he was authorized and required to collect information, he shall be guilty of a misdemeanor, and upon conviction thereof shall be fined not exceeding two thousand dollars and be imprisoned not exceeding five years.

Sec. 23. That it shall be the duty of all persons over twenty-one years of age when requested by the Director of the Census, or by any supervisor, enumerator, or special agent, or other employee of the Census Office, acting under the instructions of the said Director, to answer correctly, to the best of their knowledge, all questions on the census schedules applying to themselves and to the family to which they belong or are related, and to the farm or farms of which they or their families are the occupants; and any person over twenty-one years of age who, under the conditions hereinbefore stated, shall refuse or willfully neglect to answer any of these questions, or shall willfully give answers that are false, shall be guilty of a misdemeanor, and upon conviction thereof shall be fined not exceeding one hundred dollars.

And it shall be the duty of every owner, proprietor, manager, superintendent, or agent of a hotel, apartment house, boarding or lodging house, tenement, or other building, when requested by the Director of the Census, or by any supervisor, enumerator, special agent, or other employee of the Census Office, acting under the instructions of the said Director, to furnish the names of the occupants of said hotel, apartment house, boarding or lodging house, tenement, or other building, and to give thereto free ingress and egress to any duly accredited representative of the Census Office, so as to permit of the collection of statistics for census purposes, including the proper and correct enumeration of all persons having their usual place of abode in said hotel, apartment house, boarding or lodging house, tenement, or other building; and any owner, proprietor, manager, superintendent, or agent of a hotel, apartment house, boarding or lodging house, tenement, or other building who shall refuse or willfully neglect to give such information or assistance under the conditions hereinbefore stated shall be guilty of a misdemeanor, and upon conviction thereof shall be fined not exceeding five hundred dollars.

Sec. 24. And it shall be the duty of every owner, president, treasurer, secretary, director, or other officer or agent of any manufacturing establishment, mine, quarry, or other establishment of productive industry, whether conducted as a corporation, firm, limited liability company, or by private individuals, when requested by the Director of the Census or by any supervisor, enumerator, special agent, or other employee of the Census Office acting under the instructions of the said Director, to answer completely and correctly to the best of his knowledge all questions of any census schedule applying to such establishment; and any owner, president, secretary, director, or other officer or agent of any manufacturing establishment, mine, quarry, or other establishment of productive industry, who under the conditions hereinbefore stated shall refuse or willfully neglect to answer any of these questions or shall willfully give answers that are false, shall be guilty of a misdemeanor, and upon conviction thereof shall be fined not exceeding ten thousand dollars, or imprisonment for a period not exceeding one year, or both so fined and imprisoned, at the discretion of the court. The provisions of this section shall also apply to the collection of the information required and authorized by the Act entitled "An Act to provide for a permanent Census Office," and by Acts amendatory thereof or supplemental thereto.

SEC. 25. That the information furnished under the provisions of the next preceding section shall be used only for the statistical purposes for which it is supplied. No publication shall be made by the Census Office whereby the data furnished by any particular establishment can be identified, nor shall the Director of the Census permit anyone other than the sworn employees of the Census Office to examine the individual reports.

SEC. 26. That all fines and penalties imposed by this Act may be enforced by indictment or information in any court of competent jurisdiction.

SEC. 27. That the Director of the Census may authorize the expenditure of necessary sums for the actual and necessary traveling expenses of the officers and employees of the Census Office, including an allowance in lieu of subsistence not exceeding four dollars per day during their necessary absence from the Census Office, or, instead of such an allowance, their actual subsistence expenses, not exceeding five dollars per day; and he may authorize the incidental, miscellaneous, and contingent expenses necessary for the carrying out of this Act, as herein provided, and not otherwise, including advertising in newspapers, the purchase of manuscripts, books of reference and periodicals, the rental of sufficient quarters in the District of Columbia or elsewhere and the furnishing thereof, and expenditures necessary for the compiling, printing, publishing, and distributing the results of the census, and purchase of necessary paper and other supplies, the purchase, rental, construction, and repair of mechanical appliances, the compensation of such permanent and temporary clerks as may be employed under the provisions of this Act and the Act establishing the permanent Census Office and Acts amendatory thereof or supplemental thereto, and all other expenses incurred under authority conveyed in this Act.

SEC. 28. That the Director of the Census is hereby authorized to make requisition upon the Public Printer for such printing as may be necessary to carry out the provisions of this Act, to wit: Blanks, schedules, circulars, pamphlets, envelopes, work sheets, and other items of miscellaneous printing; that he is further authorized to have printed by the Public Printer, in such editions as the Director may deem necessary, preliminary and other Census bulletins, and final reports of the results of the several investigations authorized by this Act, or by the Act to establish a permanent Census Office and Acts amendatory thereof or supplemental thereto, and to publish and distribute said bulletins and reports: *Provided,* That whenever in the opinion of the Director of the Census the Public Printer does not produce the printing and binding required under the provisions of this Act with sufficient promptness, or whenever said printing and binding are not produced by the Public Printer in a manner satisfactory to the Director of the Census in quality or price, said Director is hereby authorized, with the approval of the Secretary of Commerce and Labor, to contract with private parties for printing and binding after due competition.

Sec. 29. That all mail matter, of whatever class, relating to the census and addressed to the Census Office, or to any official thereof, and indorsed "Official business, Census Office," shall be transmitted free of postage, and by registered mail if necessary, and so marked: *Provided,* That if any person shall make use of such indorsement to avoid the payment of postage or registry fee on his or her private letter, package, or other matter in the mail, the person so offending shall be guilty of a misdemeanor and subject to a fine of three hundred dollars, to be prosecuted in any court of competent jurisdiction.

Sec. 30. That the Secretary of Commerce and Labor, whenever he may deem it advisable, or on request of the Director of the Census, is hereby authorized to call upon any other department or office of the Government for information pertinent to the work herein provided for.

Sec. 31. That there shall be in the year nineteen hundred and fifteen, and once every ten years thereafter, a census of agriculture and live stock, which shall show the acreage of farm land, the acreage of the principal crops, and the number and value of domestic animals on the farms and ranges of the country. The schedule employed in this census shall be prepared by the Director of the Census. Such census shall be taken as of October first, and shall relate to the current year. The Director of the Census may appoint enumerators or special agents for the purpose of this census, in accordance with the provisions of the permanent Census Act.

Sec. 32. That the Director of the Census is hereby authorized, at his discretion, upon the written request of the governor of any State or Territory, or of a court of record, to furnish such governor or court of record with certified copies of so much of the population or agricultural returns as may be requested, upon the payment of the actual cost of making such copies, and one dollar additional for certification; and that the Director of the Census is further authorized, in his discretion, to furnish to individuals such data from the population schedules as may be desired for genealogical or other proper purposes, upon payment of the actual cost of searching the records and one dollar for supplying a certificate; and the amounts so received shall be covered into the Treasury of the United States, to be placed to the credit of, and in addition to, the appropriations made for taking the census.

Sec. 33. That the Director of the Census, under the supervision of the Secretary of Commerce and Labor, be, and he is hereby, authorized and directed to acquire by purchase, condemnation, or otherwise, for the use of the Census Office, and for other governmental purposes, the site and buildings thereon, containing about one hundred and eighteen thousand square feet of ground, and constituting the southern three hundred and fifty feet, more or less, of square numbered five hundred and seventy-four, in Washington, District of Columbia, bounded on the north by a public alley, on the south by B street, on the east by First street, and on the west by Second street northwest: *Provided,* That not more than four hundred and thirty thousand dollars shall be paid for the property herein referred to.

That the said Director of the Census, under the supervision of the Secretary of Commerce and Labor, is instructed to cause to be erected on such portion of the site as is not now occupied by buildings a commodious and substantial building with fire-proof vaults, heating and ventilating apparatus, elevators, and approaches, for the use of the Census Office, and for other governmental purposes, the cost of such building not to exceed two hundred and fifty thousand dollars. A sum of money sufficient to pay for the property and the erection of the said building is hereby appropriated out of any money in the Treasury not otherwise appropriated: *Provided,* That no part of the said appropriation shall be expended until a valid title to the property referred to shall be vested in the United States.

SEC. 34. That the Act establishing the permanent Census Office, approved March sixth, nineteen hundred and two, and Acts amenda tory thereof and supplemental thereto, except as herein provided, shall remain in full force. That the Act entitled "An Act to provide for taking the Twelfth and subsequent censuses," approved March third, eighteen hundred and ninety-nine, and all other laws and parts of laws inconsistent with the provisions of this Act are hereby repealed.

J. G. CANNON,
Speaker of the House of Representatives.
CHARLES W. FAIRBANKS,
Vice-President of the United States and
President of the Senate.

I certify that this Act originated in the House of Representatives.
A. McDOWELL, *Clerk.*

SPECIAL MESSAGE.

To the Senate and House of Representatives:

In my message to the Congress of March 25, 1908, I outlined certain measures which I believe the majority of our countrymen desire to have enacted into law at this time. These measures do not represent by any means all that I would like to see done if I thought it possible, but they do represent what I believe can now be done if an earnest effort toward this end is made.

Since I wrote this message an employers' liability law has been enacted which, it is true, comes short of what ought to have been done, but which does represent a real advance. Apparently there is good ground to hope that there will be further legislation providing for recompensing all employees who suffer injury while engaged in the public service; that there will be a child-labor law enacted for the District of Columbia; that the Waterways Commission will be continued with sufficient financial support to increase the effectiveness of its preparatory work; that steps will be taken to provide for such investigation into tariff conditions, by the appropriate committee of the House of Representatives and by Government experts in the Executive service, as will secure the full information necessary for immediate action in revising the tariff at the hands of the Congress elected next fall; and finally, that financial legislation will be enacted providing for temporary measures for meeting any trouble that may arise in the next year or two, and for a commission of experts who shall thoroughly investigate the whole matter, both here and in the great commercial countries abroad, so as to be able to recommend legislation which will put our financial system on an efficient and permanent basis. It is much to be wished that one feature of the financial legislation of this session should be the establishment of postal savings banks. Ample appropriations should be made to enable the Interstate Commerce Commission to carry out the very important feature of the Hepburn law which gives to the Commission supervision and control over the accounting system of the railways. Failure to provide means which will enable the Commission to examine the books of the railways would amount to an attack on the law at its most vital point, and would benefit, as nothing else could benefit, those railways which are corruptly or incompetently managed. Forest reserves should be established throughout the Appalachian Mountain region wherever it can be shown that they will have a direct and real connection with the conservation and improvement of navigable rivers.

There seems, however, much doubt about two of the measures I have recommended: the measure to do away with abuse of the power of injunction and the measure or group of measures to strengthen and render both more efficient and more wise the control by the National Government over the great corporations doing an interstate business.

First, as to the power of injunction and of punishment for contempt. In contempt cases, save where immediate action is imperative, the trial should be before another judge. As regards injunctions, some such legislation as that I have previously recommended should be enacted. They are blind who fail to realize the extreme bitterness caused among large bodies of worthy citizens by the use that has been repeatedly made of the power of injunction in labor disputes. Those in whose judgment we have most right to trust are of the opinion that while much of the complaint against the use of the injunction is unwarranted, yet that it is unquestionably true that in a number of cases this power has been used to the grave injury of the rights of laboring men. I ask that it be limited in some such way as that I have already pointed out in my previous messages, for the very reason that I do not wish to see an embittered effort made to destroy it. It is unwise stubbornly to refuse to provide against a repetition of the abuses which have caused the present unrest. In a democracy like ours it is idle to expect permanently to thwart the determination of the great body of our citizens. It may be and often is the highest duty of a court, a legislature, or an executive, to resist and defy a gust of popular passion; and most certainly no public servant, whatever may be the consequences to himself, should yield to what he thinks wrong. But in a question which is emphatically one of public policy, the policy which the public demands is sure in the end to be adopted; and a persistent refusal to grant to a large portion of our people what is right is only too apt in the end to result in causing such irritation that when the right is obtained it is obtained in the course of a movement so ill considered and violent as to be accompanied by much that is wrong. The process of injunction in labor disputes, as well as where State laws are involved, should be used sparingly, and only when there is the clearest necessity for it; but it is one so necessary to the efficient performance of duty by the court on behalf of the Nation that it is in the highest degree to be regretted that it should be liable to reckless use; for this reckless use tends to make honest men desire so to hamper its operation as to destroy its usefulness.

Every farsighted patriot should protest first of all against the growth in this country of that evil thing which is called "class consciousness." The demagogue, the sinister or foolish socialist visionary who strives to arouse this feeling of class consciousness in our working people, does a foul and evil thing; for he is no true American, he is no self-respecting citizen of this Republic, he forfeits his right to stand with manly self-reliance on a footing of entire equality with all other citizens, who bows to envy and greed, who erects the doctrine of class hatred into a shibboleth, who substitutes loyalty to men of a particular status, whether rich or poor, for loyalty to those eternal and immutable principles of righteousness which bid us treat each man on his worth as a man without regard to his wealth or his poverty. But evil though the influence of these demagogues and visionaries is, it is no worse in its consequences than the influence exercised by the man of great wealth or the man of power and position in the industrial world, who by his lack of sympathy with, and lack of understanding of, still more by any exhibition of uncompromising hostility to, the millions of our working people, tends to unite them against their fellow-Americans who are better off in this world's goods. It is a bad thing to teach our working people that men of means, that men who have the largest proportion of the substantial comforts of life, are necessarily greedy, grasping, and cold-hearted, and that they unjustly demand and appropriate more than their share of the substance of the many. Stern condemnation should be visited upon demagogue and visionary who teach this untruth, and even sterner upon those capitalists who are in truth grasping and greedy and brutally disregardful of the rights of others, and who by their actions teach the dreadful lesson far more effectively than any mere preacher of unrest. A "class grievance" left too long without remedy breeds "class consciousness" and therefore class resentment.

The strengthening of the antitrust law is demanded upon both moral and economic grounds. Our purpose in strengthening it is to secure more effective control by the National Government over the business use of the vast masses of individual, and especially of corporate wealth, which at the present time monopolize most of the interstate business of the country; and we believe the control can best be exercised by preventing the growth of abuses, rather than merely by trying to destroy them when they have already grown. In the highest sense of the word this movement for thorough control of the business use of this great wealth is conservative. We are trying to steer a safe middle course, which alone can save us from a plutocratic class government on the one hand, or a socialistic class government on the other, either of which would be fraught with disaster to our free institutions, State and National. We are trying to avoid alike the evils which would flow from Government ownership of the public utilities by which interstate commerce is chiefly carried on, and the evils which flow from the riot and chaos of unrestricted individualism. There is grave danger to our free institutions in the corrupting influence exercised by great wealth suddenly concentrated in the hands of the few. We sh uld in sane manner try to remedy this danger, in spite of the sullen opposition of these few very powerful men, and with the full purpose to protect them in all their rights at the very time that we require them to deal rightfully with others.

When with steam and electricity modern business conditions went through the astounding revolution which in this country began over half a century ago, there was at first much hesitation as to what particular governmental agency should be used to grapple with the new conditions. At almost the same time, about twenty years since, the effort was made to control combinations by regulating them through the Interstate Commerce Commission, and to abolish them by means of the antitrust act; the two remedies therefore being in part mutually incompatible. The interstate commerce law has produced admirable results, especially since it was strengthened by the Hepburn law two years ago. The antitrust law, though it worked some good, because anything is better than anarchy and complete absence of regulation, nevertheless has proved in many respects not merely inadequate but mischievous. Twenty years ago the misuse of corporate power had produced almost every conceivable form of abuse, and had worked the gravest injury to business morality and the public conscience. For a long time Federal regulation of interstate commerce had been purely negative, the National judiciary merely acting in isolated cases to restrain the State from exercising a power which it was clearly unconstitutional as well as unwise for them to exercise, but which nevertheless the National Government itself failed to exercise. Thus the corporations monopolizing commerce made the law for themselves, State power and common law being inadequate to accomplish any effective regulation, and the National power not yet having been put forth. The result was mischievous in the extreme, and only shortsighted and utter failure to appreciate the grossness of the evils to which the lack of regulation gave rise can excuse the well-meaning persons who now desire to abolish the antitrust law outright, or to amend it by simply condemning "unreasonable" combinations.

Power should unquestionably be lodged somewhere in the Executive branch of the Government to permit combinations which will further the public interest; but it must always be remembered that, as regards the great and wealthy combinations through which most of the interstate business of today is done, the burden of proof should be on them to show that they have a right to exist. No judicial tribunal has the knowledge or the experience to determine in the first place whether a given combination is advisable or necessary in the interest of the public. Some body, whether a commission, or a bureau under the Department of Commerce and Labor, should be given this power. My personal belief is that ultimately we shall have to adopt a National incorporation law, though I am well aware that this may be impossible at present. Over the actions of the Executive body in which the power is placed the courts should possess merely a power of review analogous to that obtaining in connection with the work of the Interstate Commerce Commission at present. To confer this power would not be a leap in the dark; it would merely be to carry still further the theory of effective Governmental control of corporations which was responsible for the creation of the Interstate Commerce Commission and for the enlargement of its powers, and for the creation of the Bureau of Corporations. The interstate commerce legislation has worked admirably. It has benefitted the public; it has benefitted honestly managed and wisely conducted railroads; and in spite of the fact that the business of the country has enormously increased, the value of this Federal legislation has been shown by the way in which it has enabled the Federal Government to correct the most pronounced of the great and varied abuses which existed in the business world twenty years ago— while the many abuses that still remain emphasize the need of further and more thoroughgoing legislation. Similarly, the Bureau of Corporations has amply justified its creation. In other words, it is clear that the principles employed to remedy the great evils in the business world have worked well, and they can now be employed to correct the evils that further commercial growth has brought more prominently to the surface. The powers and scope of the Interstate Commerce Commission, and of any similar body, such as the Bureau of Corporations, which has to deal with the matter in hand, should be greatly enlarged so as to meet the requirements of the present day.

The decisions of the Supreme Court in the Minnesota and North Carolina cases illustrate how impossible is a dual control of National commerce. The States can not control it. All they can do is to control intrastate commerce, and this now forms but a small fraction of the commerce carried by the railroads through each State. Actual experience has shown that the effort at State control is sure to be nullified in one way or another sooner or later. The Nation alone can act with effectiveness and wisdom; it should have the control both of the business and of the agent by which the business is done, for any attempt to separate this control must result in grotesque absurdity. This means that we must rely upon National legislation to prevent the commercial abuses that now exist and the others that are sure to arise unless some efficient Governmental body has adequate power of control over them. At present the failure of the Congress to utilize and exercise the great powers conferred upon it as regards interstate commerce leaves this commerce to be regulated, not by the State nor yet by the Congress, but by the ocasional and necessarily inadequate and one-sided action of the Federal judiciary. However upright and able a court is, it can not act constructively; it can only act negatively or destructively, as an agency of government; and this means that the courts are and must always be unable to deal effectively with a problem like the present, which requires constructive action. A court can decide what is faulty, but it has no power to make better what it thus finds to be faulty. There should be an efficient Executive body created with power enough to correct abuses and scope enough to work out the complex problems that this great country has developed. It is not sufficient objection to say that such a body may be guilty of unwisdom or of abuses. Any Governmental body, whether a court or a commission, whether executive, legislative or judicial, if given power enough to enable it to do effective work for good, must also inevitably receive enough power to make it possibly effective for evil.

Therefore, it is clear that (unless a National incorporation law can be forthwith enacted) some body or bodies in the Executive service should be given power to pass upon any combination or agreement in relation to interstate commerce, and every such combination or agreement not thus approved should be treated as in violation of law and prosecuted accordingly. The issuance of the securities of any combination doing interstate business should be under the supervision of the National Government.

A strong effort has been made to have labor organizations completely exempted from any of the operations of this law, whether or not their acts are in restraint of trade. Such exception would in all probability make the bill unconstitutional, and the Legislature has no more right to pass a bill without regard to whether it is constitutional than the courts have lightly to declare unconstitutional a law which the Legislature has solemnly enacted. The responsibility is as great on the one side as on the other, and an abuse of power by the Legislature in one direction is equally to be condemned with an abuse of power by the courts in the other direction. It is not possible wholly to except labor organizations from the workings of this law, and they who insist upon totally excepting them are merely providing that their status shall be kept wholly unchanged, and that they shall continue to be exposed to the action which they now dread. Obviously, an organization not formed for profit should not be required to furnish statistics in any way as complete as those furnished by organizations for profit. Moreover, so far as labor is engaged in pproduction only, its claims to be exempted from the antitrust law are sound. This would substantially cover the right of laborers to combine, to strike peaceably, and to enter into trade agreements with the employers. But when labor undertakes in a wrongful manner to prevent the distribution and sale of the products of labor, as by certain forms of the boycott, it has left the field of production, and its action may plainly be in restraint of interstate trade, and must necessarily be subject to inquiry, exactly as in the case of any other combination for the same purpose, so as to determine whether such action is contrary to sound public policy. The heartiest encouragement should be given to the wageworkers to form labor unions and to enter into agreements with their employers; and their right to strike, so long as they act peaceably, must be preserved. But we should sanction neither a boycott nor a blacklist which would be illegal at common law.

The measures I advocate are in the interest both of decent corporations and of law-abiding labor unions. They are, moreover, preeminently in the interest of the public, for in my judgment the American people have definitely made up their minds that the days of the reign of the great law-defying and law-evading corporations are over, and that from this time on the mighty organizations of capital necessary for the transaction of business under modern conditions, while encouraged so long as they act honestly and in the interest of the general public, are to be subjected to careful supervision and regulation of a kind so effective as to insure their acting in the interest of the people as a whole.

Allegations are often made to the effect that there is no real need for these laws looking to the more effective control of the great corporations, upon the ground that they will do their work well without such control. I call your attention to the accompanying copy of a report just submitted by Mr. Nathan Matthews, Chairman of the Finance Commission, to the Mayor and City Council of Boston, relating to certain evil practices of various corporations which have been bidders for furnishing to the city iron and steel. This report shows that there have been extensive combinations formed among the various corporations which have business with the city of Boston, including, for instance, a carefully planned combination embracing practically all the firms and corporations engaged in structural steel work in New England. This combination included substantially all the local concerns, and many of the largest corporations in the United States, engaged in manufacturing or furnishing structural steel for use in any part of New England; it affected the States, the cities and towns, the railroads and street railways, and generally all persons having occasion to use iron or steel for any purpose in that section of the country. As regards the city of Boston, the combination resulted in parceling cut the work by collusive bids, plainly dishonest, and supported by false affirmations. In its conclusion, the Commission recommends as follows:

"Comment on the moral meaning of these methods and transactions would seem superfluous; but as they were defended at the public hearings of the Commission and asserted to be common and entirely proper incidents of business life, and as these practices have been freely resorted to by some of the largest industrial corporations that the world has ever known, the Commission deems it proper to record its own opinion.

"The Commission dislikes to believe that these practices are, as alleged, established by the general custom of the business community; and this defense itself, if unchallenged, amounts to a grave accusation against the honesty of present business methods.

"To answer an invitation for public or private work by sending in what purport to be genuine bids, but what in reality are collusive figures purposely made higher than the bid which is known will be submitted by one of the supposed competitors, is an act of plain dishonesty.

"To support these misrepresentations by false affirmations in writing that the bids are submitted in good faith, and without fraud, collusion, or connection with any other bidder, is a positive and deliberate fraud; the successful bidder in the competition is guilty of obtaining money by false pretenses; and the others have made themselves parties to a conspiracy clearly unlawful at the common law.

"Where, as in the case of the 'Boston Agreement,' a number of the most important manufacturers and dealers in structural steel in this country, including the American Bridge Company, one of the constituent members of the United States Steel Corporation, have combined together for the purpose of raising prices by means of collusive bids and false representations, their conduct is not only repugnant to common honesty, but is plainly obnoxious to the Federal statute known as the Sherman or antitrust law.

"The Commission believes that an example should be made of these men, and that the members of the 'Boston Agreement,' or at least all those who, in October and November, 1905, entered in the fraud-ulent competitions for the Cove Street draw span and the Brookline

Street Bridge, should be brought before a Federal grand jury for violation of the act of Congress of July 2, 1890. The three years' limitation for participation in these transactions has not yet elapsed, and the evidence obtained by the Commission is so complete that there should be no difficulty in the Government's securing a conviction in this case."

I have submitted this report to the Department of Justice for thorough investigation and for action, if action shall prove practicable.

Surely such a state of affairs as that above set forth emphasizes the need of further Federal legislation, not merely because of the material benefits such legislation will secure, but above all because this Federal action should be part, and a large part, of the campaign to waken our people as a whole to a lively and effective condemnation of the low standard of morality implied in such conduct on the part of great business concerns. The first duty of every man is to provide a livelihood for himself and for those dependent upon him; it is from every standpoint desirable that each of our citizens should endeavor by hard work and honorable methods to secure for him and his such a competence as will carry with it the opportunity to enjoy in reasonable fashion the comforts and refinements of life; and, furthermore, the man of great business ability who obtains a fortune in upright fashion inevitably in so doing confers a benefit upon the community as a whole and is entitled to reward, to respect, and to admiration. But among the many kinds of evil, social, industrial, and political, which it is our duty as a nation sternly to combat, there is none at the same time more base and more dangerous than the greed which treats the plain and simple rules of honesty with cynical contempt if they interfere with making a profit; and as a nation we can not be held guiltless if we condone such action. The man who preaches hatred of wealth honestly acquired, who inculcates envy and jealousy and slanderous ill will toward those of his fellows who by thrift, energy, and industry have become men of means, is a menace to the community. But his counterpart in evil is to be found in that particular kind of multimillionaire who is almost the least enviable, and is certainly one of the least admirable, of all our citizens; a man of whom it has been well said that his face has grown hard and cruel while his body has grown soft; whose son is a fool and his daughter a foreign princess; whose nominal pleasures are at best those of a tasteless and extravagant luxury, and whose real delight, whose real life work, is the accumulation and use of power in its most sordid and least elevating form. In the chaos of an absolutely unrestricted commercial individualism under modern conditions, this is a type that becomes prominent as inevitably as the marauder baron becomes prominent in the physical chaos of the dark ages. We are striving for legislation to minimize the abuses which give this type its flourishing prominence, partly for the sake of what can be accomplished by the legislation itself, and partly because the legislation marks our participation in a great and stern moral movement to bring our ideals and our conduct into measurable accord.

THEODORE ROOSEVELT.

THE WHITE HOUSE, *April 27*, 1908.

EIGHTH ANNUAL MESSAGE

WHITE HOUSE, Dec. 8, 1908.

To the Senate and House of Representatives:

FINANCES.

The financial standing of the Nation at the present time is excellent, and the financial management of the Nation's interests by the Government during the last seven years has shown the most satisfactory results. But our currency system is imperfect, and it is earnestly to be hoped that the Currency Commission will be able to propose a thoroughly good system which will do away with the existing defects.

During the period from July 1, 1901, to September 30, 1908, there was an increase in the amount of money in circulation of $902,991,399. The increase in the per capita during this period was $7.06. Within this time there were several occasions when it was necessary for the Treasury Department to come to the relief of the money market by purchases or redemptions of United States bonds; by increasing deposits in national banks; by stimulating additional issues of national bank notes, and by facilitating importations from abroad of gold. Our imperfect currency system has made these proceedings necessary, and they were effective until the monetary disturbance in the fall of 1907 immensely increased the difficulty of ordinary methods of relief. By the middle of November the available working balance in the Treasury had been reduced to approximately $5,000,000. Clearing house associations throughout the country had been obliged to resort to the expedient of issuing clearing house certificates, to be used as money. In this emergency it was determined to invite subscriptions for $50,000,000 Panama Canal bonds, and $100,000,000 three per cent certificates of indebtedness authorized by the act of June 13, 1898. It was proposed to re-deposit in the national banks the proceeds of these issues, and to permit their use as a basis for additional circulating notes of national banks. The moral effect of this procedure was so great that it was necessary to issue only $24,631,980 of the Panama Canal bonds and $15,436,500 of the certificates of indebtedness.

During the period from July 1, 1901, to September 30, 1908, the balance between the net ordinary receipts and the net ordinary expenses of the Government showed a surplus in the four years

1902, 1903, 1906 and 1907, and a deficit in the years 1904, 1905, 1908 and a fractional part of the fiscal year 1909. The net result was a surplus of $99,283,413.54. **The** financial operations of the Government during this period, based upon these differences between receipts and expenditures, resulted in a net reduction of the interest-bearing debt of the United States from $987,141,040 to $897,253,990, notwithstanding that there had been two sales of Panama Canal bonds amounting in the aggregate to $54,631,980, and an issue of three per cent certificates of indebtedness under the act of June 13, 1898, amounting to $15,436,500. Refunding operations of the Treasury Department under the act of March 14, 1900, resulted in the conversion into two per cent consols of 1930 of $200,309,400 bonds bearing higher rates of interest. A decrease of $8,687,956 in the annual interest charge resulted from these operations.

In short, during the seven years and three months there has been a net surplus of nearly one hundred millions of receipts over expenditures, a reduction of the interest-bearing debt by ninety millions, in spite of the extraordinary expense of the Panama Canal, and a saving of nearly nine millions on the annual interest charge. This is an exceedingly satisfactory showing, especially in view of the fact that during this period the Nation has never hesitated to undertake any expenditure that it regarded as necessary. There have been no new taxes and no increase of taxes; on the contrary, some taxes have been taken off; there has been a reduction of taxation.

CORPORATIONS.

As regards the great corporations engaged in interstate business, and especially the railroad, I can only repeat what I have already again and again said in my messages to the Congress. I believe that under the interstate clause of the Constitution the United States has complete and paramount right to control all agencies of interstate commerce, and I believe that the National Government alone can exercise this right with wisdom and effectiveness so as both to secure justice from, and to do justice to, the great corporations which are the most important factors in modern business. I believe that it is worse than folly to attempt to prohibit all combinations as is done by the Sherman anti-trust law, because such a law can be enforced only imperfectly and unequally, and its enforcement works almost as much hardship as good. I strongly advocate that instead of an unwise effort to prohibit all combinations there shall be substituted a law which shall expressly permit combinations which are in the interest of the public, but shall at the same time give to some agency of the National Government full power of control and supervision over them. One of the chief features of this control should be securing entire publicity in all matters which the public has a right to know, and furthermore, the power, not by judicial but by executive action, to prevent or put a stop to every form of improper favoritism or other wrongdoing.

The railways of the country should be put completely under the Interstate Commerce Commission and removed from the domain of the anti-trust law. The power of the Commission should be made thoroughgoing, so that it could exercise complete supervision and control over the issue of securities as well as over the raising and lowering of rates. As regards rates, at least, this power should be summary. The power to investigate the financial operations and accounts of the railways has been one of the most valuable features in recent legislation. Power to make combinations and traffic agreements should be explicitly conferred upon the railroads, the permission of the Commission being first gained and the combination or agreement being published in all its details. In the interest of the public the representatives of the public should have complete power to see that the railroads do their duty by the public, and as a matter of course this power should also be exercised so as to see that no injustice is done to the railroads. The shareholders, the employees and the shippers all have interests that must be guarded. It is to the interest of all of them that no swindling stock speculation should be allowed, and that there should be no improper issuance of securities. The guiding intelligences necessary for the successful building and successful management of railroads should receive ample remuneration; but no man should be allowed to make money in connection with railroads out of fraudulent over-capitalization and kindred stock-gambling performances; there must be no defrauding of investors, oppression of the farmers and business men who ship freight, or callous disregard of the rights and needs of the employees. In addition to this the interests of the shareholders, of the employees, and of the shippers should all be guarded as against one another. To give any one of them undue and improper consideration is to do injustice to the others. Rates must be made as low as is compatible with giving proper returns to all the employees of the railroad, from the highest to the lowest, and proper returns to the shareholders; but they must not, for instance, be reduced in such fashion as to necessitate a cut in the wages of the employees or the abolition of the proper and legitimate profits of honest shareholders.

Telegraph and telephone companies engaged in interstate business should be put under the jurisdiction of the Interstate Commerce Commission.

It is very earnestly to be wished that our people, through their representatives, should act in this matter. It is hard to say whether most damage to the country at large would come from entire failure on the part of the public to supervise and control the actions of the great corporations, or from the exercise of the necessary governmental power in a way which would do injustice and wrong to the corporations. Both the preachers of an unrestricted individualism, and the preachers of an oppression which would deny to able men of business the just reward of their initiative and business sagacity, are advocating policies that would be fraught with the gravest harm to the whole country. To permit every lawless capitalist, every law-defying corporation, to take any action, no matter how iniquitous, in the effort to secure an improper profit and to build up privilege, would be ruinous to the Republic and would mark the abandonment of the effort to secure in the industrial world the spirit of democratic fair dealing. On the other hand, to attack these wrongs in that spirit of demagogy which can see wrong only when committed by the man of wealth, and is dumb and blind in the presence of wrong committed against men of property or by men of no property, is exactly as evil as corruptly to defend the wrongdoing of men of wealth. The war we wage must be waged against misconduct, against wrongdoing wherever it is found; and we must stand heartily for the rights of every decent man, whether he be a man of great wealth or a man who earns his livelihood as a wage-worker or a tiller of the soil.

It is to the interest of all of us that there should be a premium put upon individual initiative and individual capacity, and an ample reward for the great directing intelligences alone competent to manage the great business operations of to-day. It is well to keep in mind that exactly as the anarchist is the worst enemy of liberty and the reactionary the worst enemy of order, so the men who defend the rights of property have most to fear from the wrongdoers of great wealth, and the men who are championing popular rights have most to fear from the demagogues who in the name of popular rights would do wrong to and oppress honest business men, honest men of wealth; for the success of either type of wrongdoer necessarily invites a violent reaction against the cause the wrongdoer nominally upholds. In point of danger to the Nation there is nothing to choose between on the one hand the corruptionist, the bribe-giver, the bribe-taker, the man who employs his great talent to swindle his fellow-citizens on a large scale, and, on the other hand, the preacher of class hatred, the man who, whether from ignorance or from willingness to sacrifice his country to his ambition, persuades well-meaning but wrong-headed men to try to destroy the instruments upon which our prosperity mainly rests. Let each group of men beware of and guard against the shortcomings to which that group is itself most liable. Too often we see the business community in a spirit of unhealthy class consciousness deplore the effort to hold to account under the law the wealthy men who in their management of great corporations, whether railroads, street railways, or other industrial enterprises, have behaved in a way that revolts the conscience of the plain, decent people.

Such an attitude can not be condemned too severely, for men of property should recognize that they jeopardize the rights of property when they fail heartily to join in the effort to do away with the abuses of wealth.　On the other hand, those who advocate proper control on behalf of the public, through the State, of these great corporations, and of the wealth engaged on a giant scale in business operations, must ever keep in mind that unless they do scrupulous justice to the corporation, unless they permit ample profit, and cordially encourage capable men of business so long as they act with honesty, they are striking at the root of our national wellbeing; for in the long run, under the mere pressure of material distress, the people as a whole would probably go back to the reign of an unrestricted individualism rather than submit to a control by the State so drastic and so foolish, conceived in a spirit of such unreasonable and narrow hostility to wealth, as to prevent business operations from being profitable, and therefore to bring ruin upon the entire business community, and ultimately upon the entire body of citizens.

The opposition to Government control of these great corporations makes its most effective effort in the shape of an appeal to the old doctrine of State's rights.　Of course there are many sincere men who now believe in unrestricted individualism in business, just as there were formerly many sincere men who believed in slavery—that is, in the unrestricted right of an individual to own another individual.　These men do not by themselves have great weight, however. The effective fight against adequate Government control and supervision of individual, and especially of corporate, wealth engaged in interstate business is chiefly done under cover; and especially under cover of an appeal to State's rights.　It is not at all infrequent to read in the same speech a denunciation of predatory wealth fostered by special privilege and defiant of both the public welfare and law of the land, and a denunciation of centralization in the Central Government of the power to deal with this centralized and organized wealth.　Of course the policy set forth in such twin denunciations amounts to absolutely nothing, for the first half is nullified by the second half.　The chief reason, among the many sound and compelling reasons, that led to the formation of the National Government was the absolute need that the Union, and not the several States, should deal with interstate and foreign commerce; and the power to deal with interstate commerce was granted absolutely and plenarily to the Central Government and was exercised completely as regards the only instruments of interstate commerce known in those days—the waterways, the highroads, as well as the partnerships of individuals who then conducted all of what business there was.　Interstate commerce is now chiefly conducted by railroads; and the great corporation has supplanted the mass of small partnerships or individuals.　The proposal to make the National Government supreme over, and therefore to give it complete control over, the railroads and other instruments of interstate commerce is merely a proposal to carry out to the letter one of the prime purposes, if not the prime purpose, for which the Constitution was founded.   It does not represent centralization.   It represents merely the acknowledgment of the patent fact that centralization has already come in business.   If this irresponsible outside business power is to be controlled in the interest of the general public it can only be controlled in one way—by giving adequate power of control to the one sovereignty capable of exercising such power—the National Government. Forty or fifty separate state governments can not exercise that power over corporations doing business in most or all of them; first, because they absolutely lack the authority to deal with interstate business in any form; and second, because of the inevitable conflict of authority sure to arise in the effort to enforce different kinds of state regulation, often inconsistent with one another and sometimes oppressive in themselves. Such divided authority can not regulate commerce with wisdom and effect. The Central Government is the only power which, without oppression, can nevertheless thoroughly and adequately control and supervise the large corporations. To abandon the effort for National control means to abandon the effort for all adequate control and yet to render likely continual bursts of action by State legislatures, which can not achieve the purpose sought for, but which can do a great deal of damage to the corporation without conferring any real benefit on the public.

I believe that the more farsighted corporations are themselves coming to recognize the unwisdom of the violent hostility they have displayed during the last few years to regulation and control by the National Government of combinations engaged in interstate business.   The truth is that we who believe in this movement of asserting and exercising a genuine control, in the public interest, over these great corporations have to contend against two sets of enemies, who, though nominally opposed to one another, are really allies in preventing a proper solution of the problem.   There are, first, the big corporation men, and the extreme individualists among business men, who genuinely believe in utterly unregulated business—that is, in the reign of plutocracy; and, second, the men who, being blind to the economic movements of the day, believe in a movement of repression rather than of regulation of corporations, and who denounce both the power of the railroads and the exercise of the Federal power which alone can really control the railroads. Those who believe in efficient national control, on the other hand, do not in the least object to combinations; do not in the least object to concentration in business administration. On the contrary, they favor both, with the all important proviso that there shall be such publicity about their workings, and such thoroughgoing control over them, as to insure their being in the interest, and not against the interest, of the general public. We do not object to the concentration of wealth and administration; but we do believe in the distribution of the wealth in profits to the real owners, and in securing to the public the full benefit of the concentrated administration. We believe that with concentration in administration there can come both the advantage of a larger ownership and of a more equitable distribution of profits, and at the same time a better service to the commonwealth. We believe that the administration should be for the benefit of the many; and that greed and rascality, practiced on a large scale, should be punished as relentlessly as if practiced on a small scale.

We do not for a moment believe that the problem will be solved by any short and easy method. The solution will come only by pressing various concurrent remedies. Some of these remedies must lie outside the domain of all government. Some must lie outside the domain of the Federal Government. But there is legislation which the Federal Government alone can enact and which is absolutely vital in order to secure the attainment of our purpose. Many laws are needed. There should be regulation by the National Government of the great interstate corporations, including a simple method of account keeping, publicity, supervision of the issue of securities, abolition of rebates, and of special privileges. There should be short time franchises for all corporations engaged in public business; including the corporations which get power from water rights. There should be National as well as State guardianship of mines and forests. The labor legislation hereinafter referred to should concurrently be enacted into law.

To accomplish this, means of course a certain increase in the use of—not the creation of—power, by the Central Government. The power already exists; it does not have to be created; the only question is whether it shall be used or left idle—and meanwhile the corporations over which the power ought to be exercised will not remain idle. Let those who object to this increase in the use of the only power available, the national power, be frank, and admit openly that they propose to abandon any effort to control the great business corporations and to exercise supervision over the accumulation and distribution of wealth; for such supervision and control can only come through this particular kind of increase of power. We no more believe in that empiricism which demands absolutely unrestrained individualism than we do in that empiricism which clamors for a deadening socialism which would destroy all individual initiative and would ruin the country with a completeness that not even an unrestrained individualism itself could achieve

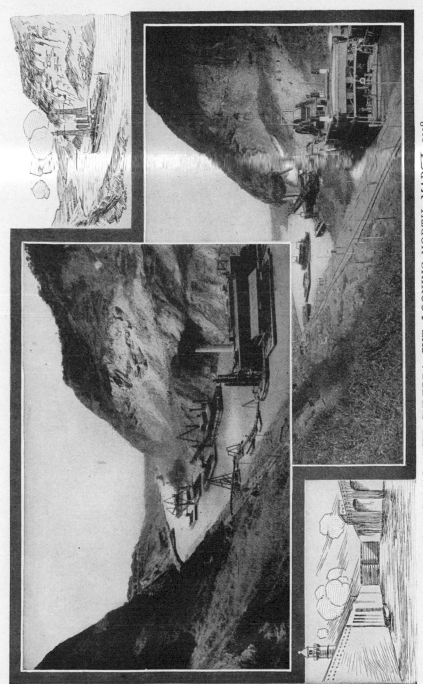

PANAMA CANAL: THE CULEBRA CUT, LOOKING NORTH, MARCH, 1908

PANAMA CANAL NEUTRAL

It is provided by treaties that the Panama Canal shall remain absolutely neutral. It "shall be free and open to the vessels of commerce and war of all nations and shall never be blockaded, nor shall any right of war be exercised nor any act of hostility be committed within it."

Strict rules of neutrality have been devised for the passage of war vessels of the nations engaged in conflict. The warships will be compelled to pass through with the least possible delay and with only such intermissions as may result from the necessities of the service.

No belligerent may "embark or disembark troops, munitions of war or warlike materials in the Canal, except in the case of accidental hindrance of the transit, and in such case the transit shall be resumed with all possible despatch."

The treaty provides that no warship will have the right to exercise the law of search on a commercial ship in transit through the Canal and the provision likewise protects all ships within three marine miles of either terminal.

Ships carrying contraband either in the Atlantic or Pacific do so at their own risk, but warships may not remain in the three-mile zone longer than twenty-four hours, and the treaty stipulates that "a vessel of one belligerent shall not depart within twenty-four hours from the departure of a vessel of war of the other belligerent."

The danger to American democracy lies not in the least in the concentration of administrative power in responsible and accountable hands. It lies in having the power insufficiently concentrated, so that no one can be held responsible to the people for its use. Concentrated power is palpable, visible, responsible, easily reached, quickly held to account. Power scattered through many administrators, many legislators, many men who work behind and through legislators and administrators, is impalpable, is unseen, is irresponsible, can not be reached, can not be held to account. Democracy is in peril wherever the administration of political power is scattered among a variety of men who work in secret, whose very names are unknown to the common people. It is not in peril from any man who derives authority from the people, who exercises it in sight of the people, and who is from time to time compelled to give an account of its exercise to the people.

LABOR.

There are many matters affecting labor and the status of the wage-worker to which I should like to draw your attention, but an exhaustive discussion of the problem in all its aspects is not now necessary. This administration is nearing its end; and, moreover, under our form of government the solution of the problem depends upon the action of the States as much as upon the action of the Nation. Nevertheless, there are certain considerations which I wish to set before you, because I hope that our people will more and more keep them in mind. A blind and ignorant resistance to every effort for the reform of abuses and for the readjustment of society to modern industrial conditions represents not true conservatism, but an incitement to the wildest radicalism; for wise radicalism and wise conservatism go hand in hand, one bent on progress, the other bent on seeing that no change is made unless in the right direction. I believe in a steady effort, or perhaps it would be more accurate to say in steady efforts in many different directions, to bring about a condition of affairs under which the men who work with hand or with brain, the laborers, the superintendents, the men who produce for the market and the men who find a market for the articles produced, shall own a far greater share than at present of the wealth they produce, and be enabled to invest it in the tools and instruments by which all work is carried on. As far as possible I hope to see a frank recognition of the advantages conferred by machinery, organization, and division of labor, accompanied by an effort to bring about a larger share in the ownership by wage-worker of railway, mill and factory. In farming, this simply means that we wish to see the farmer own his own land; we do not wish to see the farms so large that they become the property of absentee landlords who farm them by tenants, nor yet so small that the farmer becomes like a European peasant. Again, the depositors in our savings banks now number over one-tenth of our entire population. These are all capitalists, who through the savings banks loan their money to the workers—that is, in many cases to themselves—to carry on their various industries. The more we increase their number, the more we introduce the principles of cooperation into our industry. Every increase in the number of small stockholders in corporations is a good thing, for the same reasons; and where the employees are the stockholders the result is particularly good. Very much of this movement must be outside of anything that can be accomplished by legislation; but legislation can do a good deal. Postal savings banks will make it easy for the poorest to keep their savings in absolute safety. The regulation of the national highways must be such that they shall serve all people with equal justice. Corporate finances must be supervised so as to make it far safer than at present for the man of small means to invest his money in stocks. There must be prohibition of child labor, diminution of woman labor, shortening of hours of all mechanical labor; stock watering should be prohibited, and stock gambling so far as is possible discouraged. There should be a progressive inheritance tax on large fortunes. Industrial education should be encouraged. As far as possible we should lighten the burden of taxation on the small man. We should put a premium upon thrift, hard work, and business energy; but these qualities cease to be the main factors in accumulating a fortune long before that fortune reaches a point where it would be seriously affected by any inheritance tax such as I propose. It is eminently right that the Nation should fix the terms upon which the great fortunes are inherited. They rarely do good and they often do harm to those who inherit them in their entirety.

PROTECTION FOR WAGEWORKERS.

The above is the merest sketch, hardly even a sketch in outline, of the reforms for which we should work. But there is one matter with which the Congress should deal at this session. There should no longer be any paltering with the question of taking care of the wageworkers who, under our present industrial system, become killed, crippled, or worn out as part of the regular incidents of a given business. The majority of wageworkers must have their rights secured for them by State action; but the National Government should legislate in thoroughgoing and far-reaching fashion not only for all employees of the National Government, but for all persons engaged in interstate commerce. The object sought for could be achieved to a measurable degree, as far as those killed or crippled are concerned, by proper employers' liability laws. As far as concerns those who have been worn out, I call your attention to the fact that definite steps toward providing old-age pensions have been taken in many of our private industries. These may be indefinitely extended through voluntary association and contributory schemes, or through the agency of savings banks, as under the recent Massachusetts plan. To strengthen these practical measures should be our immediate duty; it is not at present necessary to consider the larger and more general governmental schemes that most European governments have found themselves obliged to adopt.

Our present system, or rather no system, works dreadful wrong, and is of benefit to only one class of people—the lawyers. When a workman is injured what he needs is not an expensive and doubtful lawsuit, but the certainty of relief through immediate administrative action. The number of accidents which result in the death or crippling of wageworkers, in the Union at large, is simply appalling; in a very few years it runs up a total far in excess of the aggregate of the dead and wounded in any modern war. No academic theory about "freedom of contract" or "constitutional liberty to contract" should be permitted to interfere with this and similar movements. Progress in civilization has everywhere meant a limitation and regulation of contract. I call your especial attention to the bulletin of the Bureau of Labor which gives a statement of the methods of treating the unemployed in European countries, as this is a subject which in Germany, for instance, is treated in connection with making provision for worn-out and crippled workmen.

Pending a thoroughgoing investigation and action there is certain legislation which should be enacted at once. The law, passed at the last session of the Congress, granting compensation to certain classes of employees of the Government, should be extended to include all employees of the Government and should be made more liberal in its terms. There is no good ground for the distinction made in the law between those engaged in hazardous occupations and those not so engaged. If a man is injured or killed in any line of work, it was hazardous in his case. Whether 1 per cent or 10 per cent of those following a given occupation actually suffer injury or death ought not to have any bearing on the question of their receiving compensation. It is a grim logic which says to an injured employee or to the dependents of one killed that he or they are entitled to no compensation because very few people other than he have been injured or killed in that occupation. Perhaps one of the most striking omissions in the law is that it does not embrace peace officers and others whose lives may be sacrificed in enforcing the laws of the United States. The terms of the act providing compensation should be made more liberal than in the present act. A year's compensation is not adequate for a wage-earner's family in the event of his death by accident in the course of his employment. And in the event of death occurring, say, ten or eleven months after the accident, the family would only receive as compensation the equivalent of one or two months' earnings. In this respect the generosity of the United States towards its employees compares most unfavorably with that of every country in Europe—even the poorest.

The terms of the act are also a hardship in prohibiting payment in cases where the accident is in any way due to the negligence of the employee. It is inevitable that daily familiarity with danger will lead men to take chances that can be construed into negligence. So well is this recognized that in practically all countries in the civilized world, except the United States, only a great degree of negligence acts as a bar to securing compensation. Probably in no other respect is our legislation, both State and National, so far behind practically the entire civilized world as in the matter of liability and compensation for accidents in industry. It is humiliating that at European international congresses on accidents the United States should be singled out as the most belated among the nations in respect to employers' liability legislation. This Government is itself a large employer of labor, and in its dealings with its employees it should set a standard in this country which would place it on a par with the most progressive countries in Europe. The laws of the United States in this respect and the laws of European countries have been summarized in a recent Bulletin of the Bureau of Labor, and no American who reads this summary can fail to be struck by the great contrast between our practices and theirs—a contrast not in any sense to our credit.

The Congress should without further delay pass a model employers' liability law for the District of Columbia. The employers' liability act recently declared unconstitutional, on account of apparently including in its provisions employees engaged in intrastate commerce as well as those engaged in interstate commerce, has been held by the local courts to be still in effect so far as its provisions apply to the District of Columbia. There should be no ambiguity on this point. If there is any doubt on the subject, the law should be reenacted with special reference to the District of Columbia. This act, however, applies only to employees of common carriers. In all other occupations the liability law of the District is the old common law. The severity and injustice o fthe common law in this matter has been in some degree or another modified in the majority of our States, and the only jurisdiction under the exclusive control of the Congress should be ahead and not behind the States of the Union in this respect. A comprehensive employers' liability law should be passed for the District of Columbia.

I renew my recommendation made in a previous message that half-holidays be granted during summer to all wageworkers in Government employ.

I also renew my recommendation that the principle of the eight-hour day should as rapidly and as far as practicable be extended to the entire work being carried on by the Government; the present law should be amended to embrace contracts on those public works which the present wording of the act seems to exclude.

THE COURTS.

I most earnestly urge upon the Congress the duty of increasing the totally inadequate salaries now given to our Judges. On the whole there is no body of public servants who do as valuable work, nor whose moneyed reward is so inadequate compared to their work. Beginning with the Supreme Court, the Judges should have their salaries doubled. It is not befitting the dignity of the Nation that its most honored public servants should be paid sums so small compared to what they would earn in private life that the performance of public service by them implies an exceedingly heavy pecuniary sacrifice.

It is earnestly to be desired that some method should be devised for doing away with the long delays which now obtain in the administration of justice, and which operate with peculiar severity against persons of small means, and favor only the very criminals whom it is most desirable to punish. These long delays in the final decisions of cases make in the aggregate a crying evil; and a remedy should be devised. Much of this intolerable delay is due to improper regard paid to technicalities which are a mere hindrance to justice. In some noted recent cases this over-regard for technicalities has resulted in a striking denial of justice, and flagrant wrong to the body politic.

At the last election certain leaders of organized labor made a violent and sweeping attack upon the entire judiciary of the country, an attack couched in such terms as to include the most upright, honest and broad-minded judges, no less than those of narrower mind and more restricted outlook. It was the kind of attack admirably fitted to prevent any successful attempt to reform abuses of the judiciary, because it gave the champions of the unjust judge their eagerly desired opportunity to shift their ground into a championship of just judges who were unjustly assailed. Last year, before the House Committee on the Judiciary, these same labor leaders formulated their demands, specifying the bill that contained them, refusing all compromise, stating they wished the principle of that bill or nothing. They insisted on a provision that in a labor dispute no injunction should issue except to protect a property right, and specifically provided that the right to carry on business should not be construed as a property right; and in a second provision their bill made legal in a labor dispute any act or agreement by or between two or more persons that would not have been unlawful if done by a single person. In other words, this bill legalized blacklisting and boycotting in every form, legalizing, for instance, those forms of the secondary boycott which the anthracite coal strike commission so unreserv-edly condemned; while the right to carry on a business was explicitly taken out from under that protection which the law throws over property. The demand was made that there should be trial by jury in contempt cases, thereby most seriously impairing the authority of the courts. All this represented a course of policy which, if car-ried out, would mean the enthronement of class privilege in its crudest and most brutal form, and the destruction of one of the most essential functions of the judiciary in all civilized lands.

The violence of the crusade for this legislation, and its complete failure, illustrate two truths which it is essential our people should learn. In the first place, they ought to teach the workingman, the laborer, the wageworker, that by demanding what is improper and impossible he plays into the hands of his foes. Such a crude and vicious attack upon the courts, even if it were temporarily success-ful, would inevitably in the end cause a violent reaction and would band the great mass of citizens together, forcing them to stand by all the judges, competent and incompetent alike, rather than to see the wheels of justice stopped. A movement of this kind can ultimately result in nothing but damage to those in whose behalf it is nominally undertaken. This is a most healthy truth, which it is wise for all our people to learn. Any movement based on that class hatred which at times assumes the name of "class consciousness" is cer-tain ultimately to fail, and if it temporarily succeeds, to do far-reaching damage. "Class consciousness," where it is merely another name for the odious vice of class selfishness, is equally noxious whether in an employer's association or in a workingman's associa-tion. The movement in question was one in which the appeal was made to all workingmen to vote primarily, not as American citi-zens, but as individuals of a certain class in society. Such an appeal in the first place revolts the more high-minded and far-sighted among the persons to whom it is addressed, and in the second place tends to arouse a strong antagonism among all other classes of citizens, whom it therefore tends to unite against the very organization on whose behalf it is issued. The result is therefore unfortunate from every standpoint. This healthy truth, by the way, will be learned by the socialists if they ever succeed in establishing in this country an impor tant national party based on such class consciousness and selfish class interest.

The wageworkers, the workingmen, the laboring men of the coun-try, by the way in which they repudiated the effort to get them to cast their votes in response to an appeal to class hatred, have empha-sized their sound patriotism and Americanism. The whole country has cause to feel pride in this attitude of sturdy independence, in this uncompromising insistence upon acting simply as good citizens, as good Americans, without regard to fancied—and improper—class interests. Such an attitude is an object-lesson in good citizenship to the entire nation.

But the extreme reactionaries, the persons who blind themselves to the wrongs now and then committed by the courts on laboring men, should also think seriously as to what such a movement as this portends. The judges who have shown themselves able and willing effectively to check the dishonest activity of the very rich man who works iniquity by the mismanagement of corporations, who have shown themselves alert to do justice to the wageworker, and sympathetic with the needs of the mass of our people, so that the dweller in the tenement houses, the man who practices a dangerous trade, the man who is crushed by excessive hours of labor, feel that their needs are understood by the courts—these judges are the real bulwark of the courts; these judges, the judges of the stamp of the President-elect, who have been fearless in opposing labor when it has gone wrong, but fearless also in holding to strict account corporations that work iniquity, and far-sighted in seeing that the working-man gets his rights, are the men of all others to whom we owe it that the appeal for such violent and mistaken legislation has fallen on deaf ears, that the agitation for its passage proved to be without substantial basis. The courts are jeopardized primarily by the action of those Federal and State judges who show inability or unwillingness to put a stop to the wrongdoing of very rich men under modern industrial conditions, and inability or unwillingness to give relief to men of small means or wageworkers who are crushed down by these modern industrial conditions; who, in other words, fail to understand and apply the needed remedies for the new wrongs produced by the new and highly complex social and industrial civilization which has grown up in the last half century.

The rapid changes in our social and industrial life which have attended this rapid growth have made it necessary that, in applying to concrete cases the great rule of right laid down in our Constitution, there should be a full understanding and appreciation of the new conditions to which the rules are to be applied. What would have been an infringement upon liberty half a century ago may be the necessary safeguard of liberty to-day. What would have been an injury to property then may be necessary to the enjoyment of property now. Every judicial decision involves two terms—one, as interpretation of the law; the other, the understanding of the facts to which it is to be applied. The great mass of our judicial officers are, I believe, alive to those changes of conditions which so materially affect the performance of their judicial duties. Our judicial system is sound and effective at core, and it remains, and must ever be maintained, as the safeguard of those principles of liberty and justice which stand at the foundation of American institutions; for, as Burke finely said, when liberty and justice are separated, neither is safe. There are, however, some members of the judicial body who have lagged behind in their understanding of these great and vital changes in the body politic, whose minds have never been opened to the new applications of the old principles made necessary by the new conditions. Judges of this stamp do lasting harm by their decisions, because they convince poor men in need of protection that the courts of the land are profoundly ignorant of and out of sympathy with their needs, and profoundly indifferent or hostile to any proposed remedy. To such men it seems a cruel mockery to have any court decide against them on the ground that it desires to preserve "liberty" in a purely technical form, by withholding liberty in any real and constructive sense. It is desirable that the legislative body should possess, and wherever necessary exercise, the power to determine whether in a given case employers and employees are not on an equal footing, so that the necessities of the latter compel them to submit to such exactions as to hours and conditions of labor as unduly to tax their strength; and only mischief can result when such determination is upset on the ground that there must be no "interference with the liberty to contract"—often a merely academic "liberty," the exercise of which is the negation of real liberty.

There are certain decisions by various courts which have been exceedingly detrimental to the rights of wageworkers. This is true of all the decisions that decide that men and women are, by the Constitution, "guaranteed their liberty" to contract to enter a dangerous occupation, or to work an undesirable or improper number of hours, or to work in unhealthy surroundings; and therefore can not recover damages when maimed in that occupation and can not be forbidden to work what the legislature decides is an excessive number of hours, or to carry on the work under conditions which the legislature decides to be unhealthy. The most dangerous occupations are often the poorest paid and those where the hours of work are longest; and in many cases those who go into them are driven by necessity so great that they have practically no alternative. Decisions such as those alluded to above nullify the legislative effort to protect the wageworkers who most need protection from those employers who take advantage of their grinding need. They halt or hamper the movement for securing better and more equitable conditions of labor. The talk about preserving to the misery-hunted beings who make contracts for such service their "liberty" to make them, is either to speak in a spirit of heartless irony or else to show an utter lack of knowledge of the conditions of life among the great masses of our fellow-countrymen, a lack which unfits a judge to do good service just as it would unfit any executive or legislative officer.

There is also, I think, ground for the belief that substantial injustice is often suffered by employees in consequence of the custom of courts issuing temporary injunctions without notice to them, and punishing them for contempt of court in instances where, as a matter of fact, they have no knowledge of any proceedings. Outside of organized labor there is a widespread feeling that this system often works great injustice to wageworkers when their efforts to better their working condition result in industrial disputes. A temporary injunction procured ex parte may as a matter of fact have all the effect of a permanent injunction in causing disaster to the wageworkers' side in such a dispute. Organized labor is chafing under the unjust restraint which comes from repeated resort to this plan of procedure. Its discontent has been unwisely expressed, and often improperly expressed, but there is a sound basis for it, and the orderly and law-abiding people of a community would be in a far stronger position for upholding the courts if the undoubtedly existing abuses could be provided against.

Such proposals as those mentioned above as advocated by the extreme labor leaders contain the vital error of being class legislation of the most offensive kind, and even if enacted into law I believe that the law would rightly be held unconstitutional. Moreover, the labor people are themselves now beginning to invoke the use of the power of injunction. During the last ten years, and within my own knowledge, at least fifty injunctions have been obtained by labor unions in New York City alone, most of them being to protect the union label (a "property right"), but some being obtained for other reasons against employers. The power of injunction is a great equitable remedy, which should on no account be destroyed. But safeguards should be erected against its abuse. I believe that some such provisions as those I advocated a year ago for checking the abuse of the issuance of temporary injunctions should be adopted. In substance, provision should be made that no injunction or temporary restraining order issue otherwise than on notice, except where irreparable injury would otherwise result; and in such case a hearing on the merits of the order should be had within a short fixed period, and, if not then continued after hearing, it should forthwith lapse. Decisions should be rendered immediately, and the chance of delay minimized in every way. Moreover, I believe that the procedure should be sharply defined, and the judge required minutely to state the particulars both of his action and of his reasons therefor, so that the Congress can, if it desires, examine and investigate the same.

The chief lawmakers in our country may be, and often are, the judges, because they are the final seat of authority. Every time they interpret contract, property, vested rights, due process of law, liberty, they necessarily enact into law parts of a system of social philosophy; and as such interpretation is fundamental, they give direction to all law-making. The decisions of the courts on economic and social questions depend upon their economic and social philosophy; and for the peaceful progress of our people during the twentieth century we shall owe most to those judges who hold to a twentieth century economic and social philosophy and not to a long outgrown philosophy, which was itself the product of primitive economic conditions. Of course a judge's views on progressive social philosophy are entirely second in importance to his possession of a high and fine character; which means the possession of such elementary virtues as honesty, courage, and fairmindedness. The judge who owes his election to pandering to demagogic sentiments or class hatreds and prejudices, and the judge who owes either his election or his appointment to the money or the favor of a great corporation, are alike unworthy to sit on the bench, are alike traitors to the people; and no profundity of legal learning, or correctness of abstract conviction on questions of public policy, can serve as an offset to such shortcomings. But it is also true that judges, like executives and legislators, should hold sound views on the questions of public policy which are of vital interest to the people.

The legislators and executives are chosen to represent the people in enacting and administering the laws. The judges are not chosen to represent the people in this sense. Their function is to interpret the laws. The legislators are responsible for the laws; the judges for the spirit in which they interpret and enforce the laws. We stand aloof from the reckless agitators who would make the judges mere pliant tools of popular prejudice and passion; and we stand aloof from those equally unwise partisans of reaction and privilege who deny the proposition that, inasmuch as judges are chosen to serve the interests of the whole people, they should strive to find out what those interests are, and, so far as they conscientiously can, should strive to give effect to popular conviction when deliberately and duly expressed by the lawmaking body. The courts are to be highly commended and staunchly upheld when they set their faces against wrongdoing or tyranny by a majority; but they are to be blamed when they fail to recognize under a government like ours the deliberate judgment of the majority as to a matter of legitimate policy, when duly expressed by the legislature. Such lawfully expressed and deliberate judgment should be given effect by the courts, save in the extreme and exceptional cases where there has been a clear violation of a constitutional provision. Anything like frivolity or wantonness in upsetting such clearly taken governmental action is a grave offense against the Republic. To protest against tyranny, to protect minorities from oppression, to nullify an act committed in a spasm of popular fury, is to render a service to the Republic. But for the courts to arrogate to themselves functions which properly belong to the legislative bodies is all wrong, and in the end works mischief. The people should not be permitted to pardon evil and slipshod legislation on the theory that the court will set it right; they should be taught that the right way to get rid of a bad law is to have the legislature repeal it, and not to have the courts by ingenious hairsplitting nullify it. A law may be unwise and improper; but it should not for these reasons be declared unconstitutional by a strained interpretation, for the result of such action is to take away from the people at large their sense of responsibility and ultimately to destroy their capacity for orderly self restraint and self government. Under such a popular government as ours, founded on the theory that in the long run the will of the people is supreme, the ultimate safety of the Nation can only rest in training and guiding the people so that what they will shall be right, and not in devising means to defeat their will by the technicalities of strained construction.

For many of the shortcomings of justice in our country our people as a whole are themselves to blame, and the judges and juries merely bear their share together with the public as a whole. It is discreditable to us as a people that there should be difficulty in convicting murderers, or in bringing to justice men who as public servants have been guilty of corruption, or who have profited by the corruption of public servants. The result is equally unfortunate, whether due to hairsplitting technicalities in the interpretation of law by judges, to sentimentality and class consciousness on the part of juries, or to hysteria and sensationalism in the daily press. For much of this failure of justice no responsibility whatever lies on rich men as such. We who make up the mass of the people can not shift the responsibility from our own shoulders. But there is an important part of the failure which has specially to do with inability to hold to proper account men of wealth who behave badly.

The chief breakdown is in dealing with the new relations that arise from the mutualism, the interdependence of our time. Every new social relation begets a new type of wrongdoing—of sin, to use an old-fashioned word—and many years always elapse before society is able to turn this sin into crime which can be effectively punished at law. During the lifetime of the older men now alive the social relations have changed far more rapidly than in the preceding two centuries. The immense growth of corporations, of business done by associations, and the extreme strain and pressure of modern life, have produced conditions which render the public confused as to who its really dangerous foes are; and among the public servants who have not only shared this confusion, but by some of their acts have increased it, are certain judges. Marked inefficiency has been shown in dealing with corporations and in re-settling the proper attitude to be taken by the public not only towards corporations, but towards labor and towards the social questions arising out of the factory system and the enormous growth of our great cities.

The huge wealth that has been accumulated by a few individuals of recent years, in what has amounted to a social and industrial revolution, has been as regards some of these individuals made possible only by the improper use of the modern corporation. A certain type of modern corporation, with its officers and agents, its many issues of securities, and its constant consolidation with allied undertakings, finally becomes an instrument so complex as to contain a greater number of elements that, under various judicial decisions, lend themselves to fraud and oppression than any device yet evolved in the human brain. Corporations are necessary instruments of modern business. They have been permitted to become a menace largely because the governmental representatives of the people have worked slowly in providing for adequate control over them.

The chief offender in any given case may be an executive, a legislature, or a judge. Every executive head who advises violent, instead of gradual, action, or who advocates ill-considered and sweeping measures of reform (especially if they are tainted with vindictiveness and disregard for the rights of the minority) is particularly blameworthy. The several legislatures are responsible for the fact that our laws are often prepared with slovenly haste and lack of consideration. Moreover, they are often prepared, and still more frequently amended during passage, at the suggestion of the very parties against whom they are afterwards enforced. Our great clusters of corporations, huge trusts and fabulously wealthy multimillionaires, employ the very best lawyers they can obtain to pick flaws in these statutes after their passage; but they also employ a class of secret agents who seek, under the advice of experts, to render hostile legislation innocuous by making it unconstitutional, often through the insertion of what appear on their face to be drastic and sweeping provisions against the interests of the parties inspiring them; while the demagogues, the corrupt creatures who introduce blackmailing schemes to "strike" corporations, and all who demand extreme, and undesirably radical, measures, show themselves to be the worst enemies of the very public whose loud-mouthed champions they profess to be. A very striking illustration of the consequences of carelessness in the preparation of a statute was the employers' liability law of 1906. In the cases arising under that law, four out of six courts of first instance held it unconstitutional; six out of nine justices of the Supreme Court held that its subject-matter was within the province of congressional action; and four of the nine justices held it valid. It was, however, adjudged unconstitutional by a bare majority of the court—five to four. It was surely a very slovenly piece of work to frame the legislation in such shape as to leave the question open at all.

Real damage has been done by the manifold and conflicting interpretations of the interstate commerce law. Control over the great corporations doing interstate business can be effective only if it is vested with full power in an administrative department, a branch of the Federal executive, carrying out a Federal law; it can never be effective if a divided responsibility is left in both the States and the Nation; it can never be effective if left in the hands of the courts to be decided by lawsuits

The courts hold a place of peculiar and deserved sanctity under our form of government. Respect for the law is essential to the permanence of our institutions; and respect for the law is largely conditioned upon respect for the courts. It is an offense against the Republic to say anything which can weaken this respect, save for the gravest reason and in the most carefully guarded manner. Our judges should be held in peculiar honor; and the duty of respectful and truthful comment and criticism, which should be binding when we speak of anybody, should be especially binding when we speak of them. On an average they stand above any other servants of the community, and the greatest judges have reached the high level held by those few greatest patriots whom the whole country delights to honor. But we must face the fact that there are wise and unwise judges, just as there are wise and unwise executives and legislators. When a president or a governor behaves improperly or unwisely, the remedy is easy, for his term is short; the same is true with the legislator, although not to the same degree, for he is one of many who belong to some given legislative body, and it is therefore less easy to fix his personal responsibility and hold him accountable therefor. With a judge, who, being human, is also likely to err, but whose tenure is for life, there is no similar way of holding him to responsibility. Under ordinary conditions the only forms of pressure to which he is in any way amenable are public opinion and the action of his fellow judges. It is the last which is most immediately effective, and to which we should look for the reform of abuses. Any remedy applied from without is fraught with risk. It is far better, from every standpoint, that the remedy should come from within. In no other nation in the world do the courts wield such vast and far-reaching power as in the United States. All that is necessary is that the courts as a whole should exercise this power with the farsighted wisdom already shown by those judges who scan the future while they act in the present. Let them exercise this great power not only honestly and bravely, but with wise insight into the needs and fixed purposes of the people, so that they may do justice and work equity, so that they may protect all persons in their rights, and yet break down the barriers of privilege, which is the foe of right.

FORESTS

If there is any one duty which more than another we owe it to our children and our children's children to perform at once, it is to save the forests of this country, for they constitute the first and most important element in the conservation of the natural resources of the country. There are of course two kinds of natural resources. One is the kind which can only be used as part of a process of exhaustion; this is true of mines, natural oil and gas wells, and the like. The other, and of course ultimately by far the most important, includes the resources which can be improved in the process of wise use; the soil, the rivers, and the forests come under this head. Any really civilized nation will so use all of these three great national assets that the nation will have their benefit in the future. Just as a farmer, after all his life making his living from his farm, will, if he is an expert farmer, leave it as an asset of increased value to his son, so we should leave our national domain to our children, increased in value and not worn out. There are small sections of our own country, in the East and the West, in the Adriondacks, the White Mountains, and the Appalachians, and in the Rocky Mountains, where we can already see for ourselves the damage in the shape of permanent injury to the soil and the river systems which comes from reckless deforestation. It matters not whether this deforestation is due to the actual reckless cutting of timber, to the fires that inevitably follow such reckless cutting of timber, or to reckless and uncontrolled grazing, especially by the great migratory bands of sheep, the unchecked wandering of which over the country means destruction to forests and disaster to the small home makers, the settlers of limited means.

Shortsighted persons, or persons blinded to the future by desire to make money in every way out of the present, sometimes speak as if no great damage would be done by the reckless destruction of our forests. It is difficult to have patience with the arguments of these persons. Thanks to our own recklessness in the use of our splendid forests, we have already crossed the verge of a timber famine in this country, and no measures that we now take can, at least for many years, undo the mischief that has already been done. But we can prevent further mischief being done; and it would be in the highest degree reprehensible to let any consideration of temporary convenience or temporary cost interfere with such action, especially as regards the National Forests which the nation can *now*, at this very moment, control.

All serious students of the question are aware of the great damage that has been done in the Mediterranean countries of Europe, Asia, and Africa by deforestation. The similar damage that has been done in Eastern Asia is less well known. A recent investigation into conditions in North China by Mr. Frank N. Meyer, of the Bureau of Plant Industry of the United States Department of Agriculture, has incidentally furnished in very striking fashion proof of the ruin that comes from reckless deforestation of mountains, and ,of the further fact that the damage once done may prove practically irreparable. So important are these investigations that I herewith attach as an appendix to my message certain photographs showing present conditions in China. They show in vivid fashion the appalling desolation, taking the shape of barren mountains and gravel- and sand-covered plains, which immediately follows and depends upon the deforestation of the mountains. Not many centuries ago the country of northern China was one of the most fertile and beautiful spots in the entire world, and was heavily forested. We know this not only from the old Chinese records, but from the accounts given by the traveler, Marco Polo. He, for instance, mentions that in visiting the provinces of Shansi and Shensi he observed many plantations of mulberry trees. Now there is hardly a single mulberry tree in either of these provinces, and the culture of the silkworm has moved farther south, to regions of atmospheric moisture. As an illustration of the complete change in the rivers, we may take Polo's statement that a certain river, the Hun Ho, was so large and deep that merchants ascended it from the sea with heavily laden boats; today this river is simply a broad sandy bed, with shallow, rapid currents wandering hither and thither across it, absolutely unnavigable. But we do not have to depend upon written records. The dry wells, and the wells with water far below the former watermark, bear testimony to the good days of the past and the evil days of the present. Wherever the native vegetation has been allowed to remain, as, for instance, here and there around a sacred temple or imperial burying ground, there are still huge trees and tangled jungle, fragments of the glorious ancient forests. The thick, matted forest growth formerly covered the mountains to their summits. All natural factors favored this dense forest growth, and as long as it was permitted to exist the plains at the foot of the mountains were among the most fertile on the globe, and the whole country was a garden. Not the slightest effort was made, however, to prevent the unchecked cutting of the trees, or to secure reforestation. Doubtless for many centuries the tree-cutting by the inhabitants of the mountains worked but slowly in bringing about the changes that have now come to pass; doubtless for generations the inroads were scarcely noticeable. But there came a time when the forest had shrunk sufficiently to make each year's cutting a serious matter, and from that time on the destruction proceeded with appalling rapidity; for of course each year of destruction rendered the forest less able to recuperate, less able to resist next year's inroad. Mr. Meyer describes the ceaseless progress of the destruction even now, when there is so little left to destroy. Every morning men and boys go out armed with mattox or axe, scale the steepest mountain sides, and cut down and grub out, root and branch, the small trees and shrubs still to be found. The big trees disappeared centuries ago, so that now one of these is never seen save in the neighborhood of temples, where they are artificially protected; and even here it takes all the watch and care of the tree-loving priests to prevent their destruction. Each family, each community, where there is no common care exercised in the interest of all of them to prevent deforestation, finds its profit in the immediate use of the fuel which would otherwise be used by some other family or some other community. In the total absence of regulation of the matter in the interest of the whole people, each small group is inevitably pushed into a policy of destruction which can not afford to take thought for the morrow. This is just one of those matters which it is fatal to leave to unsupervised individual control. The forest can only be protected by the State, by the Nation; and the liberty of action of individuals must be conditioned upon what the State or Nation determines to be necessary for the common safety.

The lesson of deforestation in China is a lesson which mankind should have learned many times already from what has occurred in other places. Denudation leaves naked soil; then gullying cuts down to the bare rock; and meanwhile the rock-waste buries the bottom-lands. When the soil is gone, men must go; and the process does not take long.

This ruthless destruction of the forests in northern China has brought about, or has aided in bringing about, desolation, just as the destruction of the forests in central Asia aid in bringing ruin to the once rich central Asian cities; just as the destruction of the forest in northern Africa helped towards the ruin of a region that was a fertile granary in Roman days. Shortsighted man, whether barbaric, semi-civilized, or what he mistakenly regards as fully civilized, when he has destroyed the forests, has rendered certain the ultimate destruction of the land itself. In northern China the mountains are now such as are shown by the accompanying photographs, absolutely barren peaks. Not only have the forests been destroyed, but because of their destruction the soil has been washed off the naked rock. The terrible consequence is that it is impossible now to undo the damage that has been done. Many centuries would have to pass before soil would again collect, or could be made to collect, in sufficient quantity once more to support the old-time forest growth. In consequence the Mongol Desert is practically extending eastward over northern China. The climate has changed and is still changing. It has changed even within the last half century, as the work of tree destruction has been consummated. The great masses of arboreal vegetation on the mountains formerly absorbed the heat of the sun and sent up currents of cool air which brought the moisture-laden clouds lower and forced them to precipitate in rain a part of their burden of water. Now that there is no vegetation, the barren mountains, scorched by the sun, send up currents of heated air which drive away instead of attracting the rain clouds, and cause their moisture to be disseminated. In consequence, instead of the regular and plentiful rains which existed in these regions of China when the forests were still in evidence, the unfortunate inhabitants of the deforested lands now see their crops wither for lack of rainfall, while the seasons grow more and more irregular; and as the air becomes dryer certain crops refuse longer to grow at all. That everything dries out faster than formerly is shown by the fact that the level of the wells all over the land has sunk perceptibly, many of them having become totally dry. In addition to the resulting agricultural distress, the watercourses have changed. Formerly they were narrow and deep, with an abundance of clear water the year around; for the roots and humus of the forests caught the rainwater and let it escape by slow, regular seepage. They have now become broad, shallow stream beds, in which muddy water trickles in slender currents during the dry seasons, while when it rains there are freshets, and roaring muddy torrents come tearing down, bringing disaster and destruction everywhere. Moreover, these floods and freshets, which diversify the general dryness, wash away from the mountain sides, and either wash away or cover in the valleys, the rich fertile soil which it took tens of thousands of years for Nature to form; and it is lost forever, and until the forests grow again it can not be replaced. The sand and stones from the mountain sides are washed loose and come rolling down to cover the arable lands, and in consequence, throughout this part of China, many formerly rich districts are now sandy wastes, useless for human cultivation and even for pasture. The cities have been of course seriously affected, for the streams have gradually ceased to be navigable. There is testimony that even within the memory of men now living there has been a serious diminution of the rainfall of northeastern China. The level of the Sungari River in northern Manchuria has been sensibly lowered during the last fifty years, at least partly as the result of the indiscriminate cutting of the forests forming its watershed. Almost all the rivers of northern China have become uncontrollable, and very dangerous to the dwellers along their banks, as a direct result of the destruction of the forests. The journey from Pekin to Jehol shows in melancholy fashion how the soil has been washed away from whole valleys. so that they have been converted into deserts.

In northern China this disastrous process has gone on so long and has proceeded so far that no complete remedy could be applied. There are certain mountains in China from which the soil is gone so utterly that only the slow action of the ages could again restore it; although of course much could be done to prevent the still further eastward extension of the Mongolian Desert if the Chinese Government would act at once. The accompanying cuts from photographs show the inconceivable desolation of the barren mountains in which certain of these rivers rise—mountains, be it remembered, which formerly supported dense forests of larches and firs, now unable to produce any wood, and because of their condition a source of danger to the whole country. The photographs also show the same rivers after they have passed through the mountains, the beds having become broad and sandy because of the deforestation of the mountains. One of the photographs shows a caravan passing through a valley. Formerly, when the mountains were forested, it was thickly peopled by prosperous peasants. Now the floods have carried destruction all over the land and the valley is a stony desert. Another photograph shows a mountain road covered with the stones and rocks that are brought down in the rainy season from the mountains which have already been deforested by human hands. Another shows a pebbly river-bed in southern Manchuria where what was once a great stream has dried up owing to the deforestation in the mountains. Only some scrub wood is left, which will disappear within a half century. Yet another shows the effect of one of the washouts, destroying an arable mountain side, these washouts being due to the removal of all vegetation; yet in this photograph the foreground shows that reforestation is still a possibility in places.

What has thus happened in northern China, what has happened in Central Asia, in Palestine, in North Africa, in parts of the Mediterranean countries of Europe, will surely happen in our country if we do not exercise that wise forethought which should be one of the chief marks of any people calling itself civilized. Nothing should be permitted to stand in the way of the preservation of the forests, and it is criminal to permit individuals to purchase a little gain for themselves through the destruction of forests when this destruction is fatal to the wellbeing of the whole country in the future.

INLAND WATERWAYS.

Action should be begun forthwith, during the present session of the Congress, for the improvement of our inland waterways—action which will result in giving us not only navigable but navigated rivers. We have spent hundreds of millions of dollars upon these waterways, yet the traffic on nearly all of them is steadily declining. This condition is the direct result of the absence of any comprehensive and far-seeing plan of waterway improvement. Obviously we can not continue thus to expend the revenues of the Government without return. It is poor business to spend money for inland navigation unless we get it.

Inquiry into the condition of the Mississippi and its principal tributaries reveals very many instances of the utter waste caused by the methods which have hitherto obtained for the so-called "improvement" of navigation. A striking instance is supplied by the "improvement" of the Ohio, which, begun in 1824, was continued under a single plan for half a century. In 1875 a new plan was adopted and followed for a quarter of a century. In 1902 still a different plan was adopted and has since been pursued at a rate which only promises a navigable river in from twenty to one hundred years longer.

Such shortsighted, vacillating, and futile methods are accompanied by decreasing water-borne commerce and increasing traffic congestion on land, by increasing floods, and by the waste of public money. The remedy lies in abandoning the methods which have so signally failed and adopting new ones in keeping with the needs and demands of our people.

In a report on a measure introduced at the first session of the present Congress, the Secretary of War said: "The chief defect in the methods hitherto pursued lies in the absence of executive authority for originating comprehensive plans covering the country or natural divisions thereof." In this opinion I heartily concur. The present methods not only fail to give us inland navigation, but they are injurious to the army as well. What is virtually a permanent detail of the corps of engineers to civilian duty necessarily impairs the efficiency of our military establishment. The military engineers have undoubtedly done efficient work in actual construction, but they are necessarily unsuited by their training and traditions to take the broad view, and to gather and transmit to the Congress the commercial and industrial information and forecasts, upon which waterway improvement must always so largely rest. Furthermore, they have failed to grasp the great underlying fact that every stream is a unit from its source to its mouth, and that all its uses are interdependent. Prominent officers of the Engineer Corps have recently even gone so far as to assert in print that waterways are not dependent upon the conservation of the forests about their headwaters. This position is opposed to all the recent work of the scientific bureaus of the Government and to the general experience of mankind. A physician who disbelieved in vaccination would not be the right man to handle an epidemic of smallpox, nor should we leave a doctor skeptical about the transmission of yellow fever by the Stegomyia mosquito in charge of sanitation at Havana or Panama. So with the improvement of our rivers; it is no longer wise or safe to leave this great work in the hands of men who fail to grasp the essential relations between navigation and general development and to assimilate and use the central facts about our streams.

Until the work of river improvement is undertaken in a modern way it can not have results that will meet the needs of this modern nation. These needs should be met without further dilly-dallying or delay. The plan which promises the best and quickest results is that of a permanent commission authorized to coordinate the work of all the Government departments relating to waterways, and to frame and supervise the execution of a comprehensive plan. Under such a commission the actual work of construction might be entrusted to the reclamation service; or to the military engineers acting with a sufficient number of civilians to continue the work in time of war; or it might be divided between the reclamation service and the corps of engineers. Funds should be provided from current revenues if it is deemed wise—otherwise from the sale of bonds. The essential thing is that the work should go forward under the best possible plan, and with the least possible delay. We should have a new type of work and a new organization for planning and directing it. The time for playing with our waterways is past. The country demands results.

NATIONAL PARKS.

I urge that all our National parks adjacent to National forests be placed completely under the control of the forest service of the Agricultural Department, instead of leaving them as they now are, under the Interior Department and policed by the army. The Congress should provide for superintendents with adequate corps of first-class civilian scouts, or rangers, and, further, place the road construction under the superintendent instead of leaving it with the War Department. Such a change in park management would result in economy and avoid the difficulties of administration which now arise from having the responsibility of care and protection divided between different departments. The need for this course is peculiarly great in the Yellowstone Park. This, like the Yosemite, is a great wonderland, and should be kept as a national playground. In both, all wild things should be protected and the scenery kept wholly unmarred.

I am happy to say that I have been able to set aside in various parts of the country small, well-chosen tracts of ground to serve as sanctuaries and nurseries for wild creatures.

DENATURED ALCOHOL.

I had occasion in my message of May 4, 1906, to urge the passage of some law putting alcohol, used in the arts, industries, and manufactures, upon the free list—that is, to provide for the withdrawal free of tax of alcohol which is to be denatured for those purposes. The law of June 7, 1906, and its amendment of March 2, 1907, accomplished what was desired in that respect, and the use of denatured alcohol, as intended, is making a fair degree of progress and is entitled to further encouragement and support from the Congress.

PURE FOOD.

The pure food legislation has already worked a benefit difficult to overestimate.

INDIAN SERVICE.

It has been my purpose from the beginning of my administration to take the Indian Service completely out of the atmosphere of political activity, and there has been steady progress toward that end. The last remaining stronghold of politics in that service was the agency system, which had seen its best days and was gradually falling to pieces from natural or purely evolutionary causes, but, like all such survivals, was decaying slowly in its later stages. It seems clear that its extinction had better be made final now, so that the ground can be cleared for larger constructive work on behalf of the Indians, preparatory to their induction into the full measure of responsible citizenship. On November 1 only eighteen agencies were left on the roster; with two exceptions, where some legal questions seemed to stand temporarily in the way, these have been changed to superintendencies, and their heads brought into the classified civil service.

SECRET SERVICE.

Last year an amendment was incorporated in the measure providing for the Secret Service, which provided that there should be no detail from the Secret Service and no transfer therefrom. It is not too much to say that this amendment has been of benefit only, and could be of benefit only, to the criminal classes. If deliberately introduced for the purpose of diminishing the effectiveness of war against crime it could not have been better devised to this end. It forbade the practices that had been followed to a greater or less extent by the executive heads of various departments for twenty years. To these practices we owe the securing of the evidence which enabled us to drive great lotteries out of business and secure a quarter of a million of dollars in fines from their promoters. These practices have enabled us to get some of the evidence indispensable in order in connection with the theft of government land and government timber by great corporations and by individuals. These practices have enabled us to get some of the evidence indispensable in order to secure the conviction of the wealthiest and most formidable criminals with whom the Government has to deal, both those operating in violation of the anti-trust law and others. The amendment in question was of benefit to no one excepting to these criminals, and it seriously hampers the Government in the detection of crime and the securing of justice. Moreover, it not only affects departments outside of the Treasury, but it tends to hamper the Secretary of the Treasury himself in the effort to utilize the employees of his department so as to best meet the requirements of the public service. It forbids him from preventing frauds upon the customs service, from investigating irregularities in branch mints and assay offices, and has seriously crippled him. It prevents' the promotion of employees in the Secret Service, and this further discourages good effort. In its present form the restriction operates only to the advantage of the criminal, of the wrongdoer. The chief argument in favor of the provision was that the Congressmen did not themselves wish to be investigated by Secret Service men. Very little of such investigation has been done in the past; but it is true that the work of the Secret Service agents was partly responsible for the indictment and conviction of a Senator and a Congressman for land frauds in Oregon. I do not believe that it is in the public interest to protect criminally in any branch of the public service, and exactly as we have again and again during the past seven years prosecuted and convicted such criminals who were in the executive branch of the Government, so in my belief we should be given ample means to prosecute them if found in the legislative branch. But if this is not considered desirable a special exception could be made in the law prohibiting the use of the Secret Service force in investigating members of the Congress. It would be far better to do this than to do what actually was done, and strive to prevent or at least to hamper effective action against criminals by the executive branch of the Government.

POSTAL SAVINGS BANKS.

I again renew my recommendation for postal savings banks, for depositing savings with the security of the Government behind them. The object is to encourage thrift and economy in the wage-earner and person of moderate means. In 14 States the deposits in savings banks as reported to the Comptroller of the Currency amount to $3,590,245,402, or 98.4 per cent of the entire deposits, while in the remaining 32 States there are only $70,308,543, or 1.6 per cent, showing conclusively that there are many localities in the United States where sufficient opportunity is not given to the people to deposit their savings. The result is that money is kept in hiding and unemployed. It is believed that in the aggregate vast sums of money would be brought into circulation through the instrumentality of the postal savings banks. While there are only 1,453 savings banks reporting to the Comptroller there are more than

61,000 post-offices, 40,000 of which are money order offices. Postal savings banks are now in operation in practically all of the great civilized countries with the exception of the United States.

PARCEL POST.

In my last annual message I commended the Postmaster-General's recommendation for an extension of the parcel post on the rural routes. The establishment of a local parcel post on rural routes would be to the mutual benefit of the farmer and the country storekeeper, and it is desirable that the routes, serving more than 15,000,000 people, should be utilized to the fullest practicable extent An amendment was proposed in the Senate at the last session, at the suggestion of the Postmaster-General, providing that, for the purpose of ascertaining the practicability of establishing a special local parcel post system on the rural routes throughout the United States, the Postmaster-General be authorized and directed to experiment and report to the Congress the result of such experiment by establishing a special local parcel post system on rural delivery routes in not to exceed four counties in the United States for packages of fourth-class matter originating on a rural route or at the distributing post office for delivery by rural carriers. It would seem only proper that such an experiment should be tried in order to demonstrate the practicability of the proposition, especially as the Postmaster-General estimates that the revenue derived from the operation of such a system on all the rural routes would amount to many million dollars.

EDUCATION.

The share that the National Government should take in the broad work of education has not received the attention and the care it rightly deserves. The immediate responsibility for the support and improvement of our educational systems and institutions rests and should always rest with the people of the several States acting through their state and local governments, but the Nation has an opportunity in educational work which must not be lost and a duty which should no longer be neglected.

The National Bureau of Education was established more than forty years ago. Its purpose is to collect and diffuse such information "as shall aid the people of the United States in the establishment and maintenance of efficient school systems and otherwise promote the cause of education throughout the country." This purpose in no way conflicts with the educational work of the States, but may be made of great advantage to the States by giving them the fullest, most accurate, and hence the most helpful information and suggestion regarding the best educational systems. The Nation, through its broader field of activities, its wider opportunity for obtaining information from all the States and from foreign countries, is able to do that which not even the richest States can do, and with the distinct additional advantage that the information thus obtained is used for the immediate benefit of all our people.

With the limited means hitherto provided, the Bureau of Education has rendered efficient service, but the Congress has neglected to adequately supply the bureau with means to meet the educational growth of the country. The appropriations for the general work of the bureau, outside education in Alaska, for the year 1909 are but $87,500—an amount less than they were ten years ago, and some of the important items in these appropriations are less than they were thirty years ago. It is an inexcusable waste of public money to appropriate an amount which is so inadequate as to make it impossible properly to do the work authorized, and it is unfair to the great educational interests of the country to deprive them of the value of the results which can be obtained by proper appropriations.

I earnestly recommend that this unfortunate state of affairs as regards the national educational office be remedied by adequate appropriations. This recommendation is urged by the representatives of our common schools and great state universities and the leading educators, who all unite in requesting favorable consideration and action by the Congress upon this subject.

CENSUS.

I strongly urge that the request of the Director of the Census in connection with the decennial work so soon to be begun be complied with and that the appointments to the census force be placed under the civil service law, waiving the geographical requirements as requested by the Director of the Census. The supervisors and enumerators should not be appointed under the civil service law, for the reasons given by the Director. I commend to the Congress the careful consideration of the admirable report of the Director of the Census, and I trust that his recommendations will be adopted and immediate action thereon taken.

PUBLIC HEALTH

It is highly advisable that there should be intelligent action on the part of the Nation on the question of preserving the health of the country. Through the practical extermination in San Francisco of disease-bearing rodents our country has thus far escaped the bubonic plague. This is but one of the many achievements of American health officers; and it shows what can be accomplished with a better organization than at present exists. The dangers to public health from food adulteration and from many other sources, such as the menace to the physical, mental and moral development of children from child labor, should be met and overcome. There are numerous diseases, which are now known to be preventable, which are, nevertheless, not prevented. The recent International Congress on Tuberculosis has made us painfully aware of the inadequacy of American public health legislation. This Nation can not afford to lag behind in the world-wide battle now being waged by all civilized people with the microscopic foes of mankind, nor ought we longer to ignore the reproach that this Government takes more pains to protect the lives of hogs and of cattle than of human beings.

REDISTRIBUTION OF BUREAUS.

The first legislative step to be taken is that for the concentration of the proper bureaus into one of the existing departments. I therefore urgently recommend the passage of a bill which shall authorize a redistribution of the bureaus which shall best accomplish this end.

GOVERNMENT PRINTING OFFICE.

I recommend that legislation be enacted placing under the jurisdiction of the Department of Commerce and Labor the Government Printing Office. At present this office is under the combined control, supervision, and administrative direction of the President and of the Joint Committee on Printing of the two Houses of the Congress. The advantage of having the 4,069 employees in this office and the expenditure of the $5,761,377.57 appropriated therefor supervised by an executive department is obvious, instead of the present combined supervision.

SOLDIERS' HOMES.

All Soldiers' Homes should be placed under the complete jurisdiction and control of the War Department.

INDEPENDENT BUREAUS AND COMMISSIONS.

Economy and sound business policy require that all existing independent bureaus and commissions should be placed under the jurisdiction of appropriate executive departments. It is unwise from every standpoint, and results only in mischief, to have any executive work done save by the purely executive bodies, under the control of the President; and each such executive body should be under the immediate supervision of a Cabinet Minister.

STATEHOOD.

I advocate the immediate admission of New Mexico and Arizona as States. This should be done at the present session of the Congress. The people of the two Territories have made it evident by their votes that they will not come in as one State. The only alternative is to admit them as two, and I trust that this will be done without delay.

INTERSTATE FISHERIES.

I call the attention of the Congress to the importance of the problem of the fisheries in the interstate waters. On the Great Lakes we are now, under the very wise treaty of April 11th of this year, endeavoring to come to an international agreement for the preservation and satisfactory use of the fisheries of these waters which can not otherwise be achieved. Lake Erie, for example, has the richest fresh water fisheries in the world; but it is now controlled by the statutes of two Nations, four States, and one Province, and in this Province by different ordinances in different counties. All these political divisions work at cross purposes, and in no case can they achieve protection to the fisheries, on the one hand, and justice to the localities and individuals on the other. The case is similar in Puget Sound.

But the problem is quite as pressing in the interstate waters of the United States. The salmon fisheries of the Columbia River are now but a fraction of what they were twenty-five years ago, and what they would be now if the United States Government had taken complete charge of them by intervening between Oregon and Washington. During these twenty-five years the fishermen of each State have naturally tried to take all they could get, and the two legislatures have never been able to agree on joint action of any kind adequate in degree for the protection of the fisheries. At the moment the fishing on the Oregon side is practically close 1, while there is no limit on the Washington side of any kind, and no one can tell what the courts will decide as to the very statutes under which this action and non-action result. Meanwhile very few salmon reach the spawning grounds, and probably four years hence the fisheries will amount to nothing; and this comes from a struggle between the associated, or gill-net, fishermen on the one hand, and the owners of the fishing wheels up the river. The fisheries of the Mississippi, the Ohio, and the Potomac are also in a bad way. For this there is no remedy except for the United States to control and legislate for the interstate fisheries as part of the business of interstate commerce. In this case the machinery for scientific investigation and for control already exists in the United States Bureau of Fisheries. In this as in similar problems the obvious and simple rule should be followed of having those matters which no particular State can manage taken in hand by the United States; problems which in the seesaw of conflicting State legislatures are absolutely unsolvable are easy enough for Congress to control.

FISHERIES AND FUR SEALS.

The federal statute regulating interstate traffic in game should be extended to include fish. New federal fish hatcheries should be established. The administration of the Alaskan fur-seal service should be vested in the Bureau of Fisheries.

FOREIGN AFFAIRS.

This Nation's foreign policy is based on the theory that right must be done between nations precisely as between individuals, and in our actions for the last ten years we have in this matter proven our faith by our deeds. We have behaved, and are behaving, towards other nations as in private life an honorable man would behave towards his fellows.

LATIN-AMERICAN REPUBLICS.

The commercial and material progress of the twenty Latin-American Republics is worthy of the careful attention of the Congress. No other section of the world has shown a greater proportionate development of its foreign trade during the last ten years and none other has more special claims on the interest of the United States. It offers to-day probably larger opportunities for the legitimate expansion of our commerce than any other group of countries. These countries will want our products in greatly increased quantities, and we shall correspondingly need theirs. The International Bureau of the American Republics is doing a useful work in making these nations and their resources better known to us, and in acquainting them not only with us as a people and with our purposes towards them, but with what we have to exchange for their goods. It is an international institution supported by all the governments of the two Americas.

PANAMA CANAL.

The work on the Panama Canal is being done with a speed, efficiency and entire devotion to duty which make it a model for all work of the kind. No task of such magnitude has ever before been undertaken by any nation; and no task of the kind has ever been better performed. The men on the isthmus, from Colonel Goethals and his fellow commissioners through the entire list of employees who are faithfully doing their duty, have won their right to the ungrudging respect and gratitude of the American people.

OCEAN MAIL LINERS.

I again recommend the extension of the ocean mail act of 1891 so that satisfactory American ocean mail lines to South America, Asia, the Philippines, and Australiasia may be established. The creation of such steamship lines should be the natural corollary of the voyage of the battle fleet. It should precede the opening of the Panamal Canal. Even under favorable conditions several years must elapse before such lines can be put into operation. Accordingly I urge that the Congress act promptly where foresight already shows that action sooner or later will be inevitable.

HAWAII.

I call particular attention to the Territory of Hawaii. The importance of those islands is apparent, and the need of improving their condition and developing their resources is urgent. In recent years industrial conditions upon the islands have radically changed. The importation of coolie labor has practically ceased, and there is now developing such a diversity in agricultural products as to make possible a change in the land conditions of the Territory, so that an opportunity may be given to the small land owner similar to that on the mainland. To aid these changes, the National Government must provide the necessary harbor improvements on each island, so that the agricultural products can be carried to the markets of the world. The coastwise shipping laws should be amended to meet the special needs of the islands, and the alien contract labor law should be so modified in its application to Hawaii as to enable American and European labor to be brought thither.

We have begun to impr ve Pearl Harbor for a naval base and to provide the necessary military fortifications for the protection of the islands, but I can not too strongly emphasize the need of appropriations for these purposes of such an amount as will within the shortest possible time make those islands practically impregnable. It is useless to develop the industrial conditions of the islands and establish there bases of supply for our naval and merchant fleets unless we insure, as far as human ingenuity can, their safety from foreign seizure.

One thing to be remembered with all our fortifications is that it is almost useless to make them impregnable from the sea if they are left open to land attack. This is true even of our own coast, but it is doubly true of our insular possessions. In Hawaii, for instance, it is worse than useless to establish a naval station unless we establish it behind fortifications so strong that no landing force can take them save by regular and long-continued siege operations.

THE PHILIPPINES.

Real progress toward self-government is being made in the Philippine Islands. The gathering of a Philippine legislative body and Philippine assembly marks a process absolutely new in Asia, not only as regards Asiatic colonies of European powers but as regards Asiatic possessions of other Asiatic powers; and, indeed, always excepting the striking and wonderful example afforded by the great Empire of Japan, it opens an entirely new departure when compared with anything which has happened among Asiatic powers which are their own masters. Hitherto this Philippine legislature has acted with moderation and self-restraint, and has seemed in practical fashion to realize the eternal truth that there must always be government, and that the only way in which any body of individuals can escape the necessity of being governed by outsiders is to show that they are able to restrain themselves, to keep down wrongdoing and disorder. The Filipino people, through their officials, are therefore making real steps in the direction of self-government. I hope and believe that these steps mark the beginning of a course which will continue till the Filipinos become fit to decide for themselves whether they desire to be an independent nation. But it is well for them (and well also for those Americans who during the past decade have done so much damage to the Filipinos by agitation for an immediate independence for which they were totally unfit) to remember that self-government depends, and must depend, upon the Filipinos themselve... All we can do is to give them the opportunity to develop the capacity for self-government. If we had followed the advice of the foolish doctrinaires who wished us at any time during the last ten years to turn the Filipino people adrift, we should have shirked the plainest possible duty and have inflicted a lasting wrong upon the Filipino people. We have acted in exactly the opposite spirit. We have given the Filipinos constitutional government—a government based upon justice—and we have shown that we have governed them for their good and not for our aggrandizement. At the present time, as during the past ten years, the inexorable logic of facts shows that this government must be supplied by us and not by them. We must be wise and generous; we must help the Filipinos to master the difficult art of self-control, which is simply another name for self-government. But we can not give them self-government save in the sense of gov· erning them so that gradually they may, if they are able, learn to govern themselves. Under the present system of just laws and sympathetic administration, we have every reason to believe that they are gradually acquiring the character which lies at the basis of self-government, and for which, if it be lacking, no system of laws, no paper constitution, will in any wise serve as a substitute. Our people in the Philippines have achieved what may legitimately be called a marvelous success in giving to them a government which marks on the part of those in authority both the necessary understanding of the people and the necessary purpose to serve them disinterestedly and in good faith. I trust that within a generation the time will arrive when the Philippines can decide for themselves whether it is well for them to become independent, or to continue under the protection of a strong and disinterested power, able to guarantee to the islands order at home and protection from foreign invasion. But no one can prophesy the exact date when it will be wise to consider independence as a fixed and definite policy. It would be worse than folly to try to set down such a date in advance, for it must depend upon the way in which the Philippine people themselves develop the power of self-mastery.

PORTO RICO.

I again recommend that American citizenship be conferred upon the people of Porto Rico.

CUBA.

In Cuba our occupancy will cease in about two months' time; the Cubans have in orderly manner elected their own governmental authorities, and the island will be turned over to them. Our occupation on this occasion has lasted a little over two years, and Cuba has thriven and prospered under it. Our earnest hope and one desire is that the people of the island shall now govern themselves with justice, so that peace and order may be secure. We will gladly help them to this end; but I would solemnly warn them to remember the great truth that the only way a people can permanently avoid being governed from without is to show that they both can and will govern themselves from within.

JAPANESE EXPOSITION.

The Japanese Government has postponed until 1917 the date of the great international exposition, the action being taken so as to insure ample time in which to prepare to make the exposition all that it should be made. The American commissioners have visited Japan and the postponement will merely give ampler opportunity for America to be represented at the exposition. Not since the first international exposition has there been one of greater importance than this will be, marking as it does the fiftieth anniversary of the ascension to the throne of the Emperor of Japan. The extraordinary leap to a foremost place among the nations of the world made by Japan during this half century is something unparalleled in all previous history. This exposition will fitly commemorate and signalize the giant progress that has been achieved. It is the first exposition of its kind that has ever been held in Asia. The United States, because of the ancient friendship between the two peoples, because each of us fronts on the Pacific, and because of the growing commercial relations between this country and Asia, takes a peculiar interest in seeing the exposition made a success in every way.

I take this opportunity publicly to state my appreciation of the way in which in Japan, in Australia, in New Zealand, and in all the States of South America, the battle fleet has been received on its practice voyage around the world. The American Government can not too strongly express its appreciation of the abounding and generous hospitality shown our ships in every port they visited.

THE ARMY.

As regards the Army I call attention to the fact that while our junior officers and enlisted men stand very high, the present system of promotion by seniority results in bringing into the higher grades many men of mediocre capacity who have but a short time to serve. No man should regard it as his vested right to rise to the highest rank in the Army any more than in any other profession. It is a curious and by no means creditable fact that there should be so often a failure on the part of the public and its representatives to understand the great need, from the standpoint of the service and the Nation, of refusing to promote respectable, elderly incompetents. The higher places should be given to the most deserving men without regard to seniority; at least seniority should be treated as only one consideration. In the stress of modern industrial competition no business firm could succeed if those responsible for its management were chosen simply on the ground that they were the oldest people in its employment; yet this is the course advocated as regards the Army, and required by law for all grades except those of general officer. As a matter of fact, all of the best officers in the highest ranks of the Army are those who have attained their present position wholly or in part by a process of selection.

The scope of retiring boards should be extended so that they could consider general unfitness to command for any cause, in order to secure a far more rigid enforcement than at present in the elimination of officers for mental, physical or temperamental disabilities. But this plan is recommended only if the Congress does not see fit to provide what in my judgment is far better; that is, for selection in promotion, and for elimination for age. Officers who fail to attain a certain rank by a certain age should be retired—for instance, if a man should not attain field rank by the time he is 45 he should of course be placed on the retired list. General officers should be selected as at present, and one-third of the other promotions should be made by selection, the selection to be made by the President or the Secretary of War from a list of at least two candidates proposed for each vacancy by a board of officers from the arm of the service from which the promotion is to be made. A bill is now before the Congress having for its object to secure the promotion of officers to various grades at reasonable ages through a process of selection, by boards of officers, of the least efficient for retirement with a percentage of their pay depending upon length of service. The bill, although not accomplishing all that should be done, is a long step in the right direction; and I earnestly recommend its passage, or that of a more completely effective measure.

The cavalry arm should be reorganized upon modern lines. This is an arm in which it is peculiarly necessary that the field officers should not be old. The cavalry is much more difficult to form than infantry, and it should be kept up to the maximum both in efficiency and in strength, for it can not be made in a hurry. At present both infantry and artillery are too few in number for our needs. Especial attention should be paid to development of the machine gun. A general service corps should be established. As things are now the average soldier has far too much labor of a nonmilitary character to perform.

NATIONAL GUARD.

Now that the organized militia, the National Guard, has been incorporated with the Army as a part of the national forces, it behooves the Government to do every reasonable thing in its power to perfect its efficiency. It should be assisted in its instruction and otherwise aided more liberally than heretofore. The continuous services of many well-trained regular officers will be essential in this connection. Such officers must be specially trained at service schools best to qualify them as instructors of the National Guard. But the detailing of officers for training at the service schools and for duty with the National Guard entails detaching them from their regiments which are already greatly depleted by detachment of officers for assignment to duties prescribed by acts of the Congress.

A bill is now pending before the Congress creating a number of extra officers in the Army, which if passed, as it ought to be, will enable more officers to be trained as instructors of the National Guard and assigned to that duty. In case of war it will be of the utmost importance to have a large number of trained officers to use for turning raw levies into good troops.

There should be legislation to provide a complete plan for organizing the great body of volunteers behind the Regular Army and National Guard when war has come. Congressional assistance should be given those who are endeavoring to promote rifle practice so that our men, in the services or out of them, may know how to use the rifle. While teams representing the United States won the rifle and revolver championships of the world against all comers in England this year, it is unfortunately true that the great body of our citizens shoot less and less as time goes on. To meet this we should encourage rifle practice among schoolboys, and indeed among all classes, as well as in the military services, by every means in our power. Thus, and not otherwise, may we be able to assist in preserving the peace of the world. Fit to hold our own against the strong nations of the earth, our voice for peace will carry to the ends of the earth. Unprepared, and therefore unfit, we must sit dumb and helpless to defend ourselves, protect others, or preserve peace. The first step— in the direction of preparation to avert war if possible, and to be fit for war if it should come—is to teach our men to shoot.

THE NAVY.

I approve the recommendations of the General Board for the increase of the Navy, calling especial attention to the need of additional destroyers and colliers, and, above all, of the four battleships. It is desirable to complete as soon as possible a squadron

JAPANESE FIELD ARTILLERY

THE RUSSO-JAPANESE WAR.

At the outbreak of the Russo-Japanese War, few laymen believed that the little nation of the Pacific would be able to defeat the largest nation on the face of the earth. The war itself arose from Russia's commercial expansion in the East, to which Japan had yielded temporarily, while she was preparing her fighting strength to a point where it would be able to support a more assertive diplomatic policy toward Russia. In the years preceding the war, Japan had been preparing for it by utilizing every new development of military science, while Russia had continued to plod along beaten paths in military preparation. Moreover, the Japanese nation had become strongly unified, and Russia was a poorly-integrated combination of many peoples and many opinions. The Japanese fought with all the intensity inspired by a great patriotic zeal, and not without cause did they emerge from the conflict with the name of the "little brown devils." (See articles Japan, Russia, and Russo-Japanese War in the Encyclopedic Index.)

of eight battleships of the best existing type. The *North Dakota, Delaware, Florida,* and *Utah* will form the first division of this squadron. The four vessels proposed will form the second division. It will be an improvement on the first, the ships being of the heavy, single caliber, all big gun type. All the vessels should have the same tactical qualities—that is, speed and turning circle—and as near as possible these tactical qualities should be the same as in the four vessels before named now being built.

I most earnestly recommend that the General Board be by law turned into a General Staff. There is literally no excuse whatever for continuing the present bureau organization of the Navy. The Navy should be treated as a purely military organization, and everything should be subordinated to the one object of securing military efficiency. Such military efficiency can only be guaranteed in time of war if there is the most thorough previous preparation in time of peace—a preparation, I may add, which will in all probability prevent any need of war. The Secretary must be supreme, and he should have as his official advisers a body of line officers who should themselves have the power to pass upon and coordinate all the work and all the proposals of the several bureaus. A system of promotion by merit, either by selection or by exclusion, or by both processes, should be introduced. It is out of the question, if the present principle of promotion by mere seniority is kept, to expect to get the best results from the higher officers. Our men come too old, and stay for too short a time, in the high command positions.

Two hospital ships should be provided. The actual experience of the hospital ship with the fleet in the Pacific has shown the invaluable work which such a ship does, and has also proved that it is well to have it kept under the command of a medical officer. As was to be expected, all of the anticipations of trouble from such a command have proved completely baseless. It is as absurd to put a hospital ship under a line officer as it would be to put a hospital on shore under such a command. This ought to have been realized before, and there is no excuse for failure to realize it now.

Nothing better for the Navy from every standpoint has ever occurred than the cruise of the battle fleet around the world. The improvement of the ships in every way has been extraordinary, and they have gained far more experience in battle tactics than they would have gained if they had stayed in the Atlantic waters. The American people have cause for profound gratification, both in view of the excellent condition of the fleet as shown by this cruise, and in view of the improvement the cruise has worked in this already high condition. I do not believe that there is any other service in the world in which the average of character and efficiency in the enlisted men is as high as is now the case in our own. I believe that the same statement can be made as to our officers, taken as a whole; but there must be a reservation made in regard to those in the highest ranks—as to which I have already spoken—and in regard to those who have just entered the service; because we do not now get full benefit from our excellent naval school at Annapolis. It is absurd not to graduate the midshipmen as ensigns; to keep them for two years in such an anomalous position as at present the law requires is detrimental to them and to the service. In the academy itself, every first classman should be required in turn to serve as petty officer and officer; his ability to discharge his duties as such should be a prerequisite to his going into the line, and his success in commanding should largely determine his standing at graduation. The Board of Visitors should be appointed in January, and each member should be required to give at least six days' service, only from one to three days' to be performed during June week, which is the least desirable time for the board to be at Annapolis so far as benefiting the Navy by their observations is concerned.

THEODORE ROOSEVELT.

THE WHITE HOUSE,
    Tuesday, December 8, 1908.

REPORT OF SPECIAL COMMITTEE ON PRESIDENT'S MESSAGE RELATING TO THE SECRET SERVICE.

Mr. PERKINS, from the special committee to consider a portion of the annual message of the President, submitted the following

REPORT.

The special committee to consider a portion of the President's annual message submitted a privileged report on the following resolution, recommending its passage:

Whereas the annual message of the President contained the following paragraphs:

"Last year an amendment was incorporated in the measure providing for the Secret Service which provided that there should be no detail from the Secret Service and no transfer therefrom. It is not too much to say that this amendment has been of benefit only, and could be of benefit only, to the criminal classes. If deliberately introduced for the purpose of diminishing the effectiveness of war against crime, it could not have been better devised to this end. It forbade the practices that had been followed to a greater or less extent by the executive heads of various departments for twenty years. To these practices we owe the securing of the evidence which enabled us to drive great lotteries out of business and secure a quarter of a million of dollars in fines from their promoters.

"These practices have enabled us to discover some of the most outrageous frauds in connection with the theft of government land and government timber by great corporations and by individuals. These practices have enabled us to get some of the evidence indispensable in order to secure the conviction of the wealthiest and most formidable criminals with whom the Government has to deal, both those operating in violation of the antitrust law and others. The amendment in question was of benefit to no one excepting to these criminals, and it seriously hampers the Government in the detection of crime and the securing of justice. Moreover, it not only affects departments outside of the Treasury, but it tends to hamper the Secretary of the Treasury himself in the effort to utilize the employees of his department so as to best meet the requirements of the public service. It forbids him from preventing frauds upon the customs service, from investigating irregularities in branch mints and assay offices, and has seriously crippled him. It prevents the promotion of employees in the Secret Service, and this further discourages good effort. In its present form the restriction operates only to the advantage of the criminal, of the wrongdoer.

"The chief argument in favor of the provision was that the Congressmen did not themselves wish to be investigated by Secret Service men. Very little of such investigation has been done in the past; but it is true that the work of the Secret Service agents was partly responsible for the indictment and conviction of a Senator and a Congressman for land frauds in Oregon. I do not believe that it is in the public interest to protect criminals in any branch of the public service, and exactly as we have again and again during the past seven years prosecuted and convicted such criminals who were in the executive branch of the Government, so in my belief we should be given ample means to prosecute them if found in the legislative branch. But if this is not considered desirable a special exception could be made in the law prohibiting the use of the Secret Service force in investigating Members of the Congress. It would be far better to do this than to do what actually was done, and strive to prevent or at least to hamper effective action against criminals by the executive branch of the Government."

Understanding this language to be a reflection on the integrity of its membership, and aware of its own constitutional duty as to its membership, the House in respectful terms called on the President for any information that would justify the language of the message or assist it in its constitutional duty to purge itself of corruption.

The President in his message of January 4 denies that the paragraph of the annual message casts reflections on the integrity of the

House; attributes to the House "an entire failure to understand my message;" declares that he has made no charge of corruption against any Member of this House, and by implication states that he has no proof of corruption on the part of any Member of this House.

Whether the House in its resolution of December 17, 1908, correctly interpreted the meaning of the words used by the President in his annual message, or whether it misunderstood that language as the President implies, will be judged now and in the future according to the accepted interpretations of the English language. This House, charged only with its responsibility to the people of the United States and its obligation to transmit unimpaired to the future the representative institutions inherited from the past, and to preserve its own dignity, must insist on its own capacity to understand the import of the President's language. We consider the language of the President in his message of December 8, 1908, unjustified and without basis of fact, and that it constitutes a breach of the privileges of the House; therefore, be it

Resolved, That the House in the exercise of its constitutional prerogatives declines to consider any communication from any source which is not in its own judgment respectful; and be it further

Resolved, That the special committee and the Committee of the Whole House on the state of the Union be discharged from any consideration of so much of the President's annual message as relates to the Secret Service, and is above set forth, and that the said portion of the message be laid on the table; and be it further

Resolved, That the message of the President sent to the House on January 4, 1909, being unresponsive to the inquiry of the House and constituting an invasion of the privileges of this House by questioning the motives and intelligence of members in the exercise of their constitutional rights and functions, be laid on the table.

SPECIAL MESSAGE.

To the House of Representatives:

I have received the resolution of the House of Representatives of December 17, 1908, running as follows:

"Whereas there was contained in the sundry civil appropriation bill which passed Congress at its last session and became a law a provision in reference to the employment of the Secret Service in the Treasury Department; and

"Whereas in the last annual message of the President of the United States to the two Houses of Congress it was stated in refer-

ence to that provision: 'It is not too much to say that this amendment has been of benefit only, and could be of benefit only, to the
criminal classes,' and it was further stated, 'The chief argument in
favor of the provision was that the Congressmen did not themselves
wish to be investigated by Secret Service men,' and it was further
stated: 'But if this is not considered desirable a special exception
could be made in the law, prohibiting the use of the Secret Service
force in investigating Members of Congress. It would be far better
to do this than to do what actually was done, and strive to prevent
or at least to hamper effective action against criminals by the executive branch of the Government;' and

"Whereas the plain meaning of the above words is that the majority
of the Congressmen were in fear of being investigated by Secret
Service men and that Congress as a whole was actuated by that motive
in enacting the provision in question; and

"Whereas your committee appointed to consider these statements
of the President and to report to the House can not find in the hearings before committees nor in the records of the House or Senate
any justification of this impeachment of the honor and integrity of
the Congress; and

"Whereas your committee would prefer, in order to make an intelligent and comprehensive report, just to the President as well as to
the Congress, to have all the information which the President may
have to communicate: Now, therefore,

"*Be it resolved,* That the President be requested to transmit to the
House any evidence upon which he based his statements that the
'chief argument in favor of the provision was that the Congressmen did not themselves wish to be investigated by Secret Service
men,' and also to transmit to the House any evidence connecting
any Member of the House of Representatives of the Sixtieth Congress with corrupt action in his official capacity, and to inform the
House whether he has instituted proceedings for the punishment of
any such individual by the courts or has reported any such alleged
delinquencies to the House of Representatives."

I am wholly at a loss to understand the concluding portion of the
resolution. I have made no charges of corruption against Congress
nor against any Member of the present House. If I had proof of
such corruption affecting any Member of the House in any matter
as to which the Federal Government has jurisdiction, action would
at once be brought, as was done in the cases of Senators Mitchell
and Burton and Representatives Williamson, Herrmann, and Driggs
at different times since I have been President. This would simply
be doing my duty in the execution and enforcement of the laws
without respect to persons. But I do not regard it as within the
province or the duties of the President to report to the House

"alleged delinquencies" of members or the supposed "corrupt action" of a member "in his official capacity." The membership of the House is by the Constitution placed within the power of the House alone. In the prosecution of criminals and the enforcement of the laws the President must resort to the courts of the United States.

In the third and fourth clauses of the preamble it is stated that the meaning of my words is that "the majority of the Congressmen are in fear of being investigated by Secret Service men" and that "Congress as a whole was actuated by that motive in enacting the provision in question," and that this is an impeachment of the honor and integrity of the Congress. These statements are not, I think, in accordance with the facts. The portion of my message referred to runs as follows:

"Last year an amendment was incorporated in the measure providing for the Secret Service which provided that there should be no detail from the Secret Service and no transfer therefrom. It is not too much to say that this amendment has been of benefit only, and could be of benefit only, to the criminal classes. If deliberately introduced for the purpose of diminishing the effectiveness of war against crime it could not have been better devised to this end. It forbade the practices that had been followed to a greater or less extent by the executive heads of various departments for twenty years. To these practices we owe the securing of the evidence which enabled us to drive great lotteries out of business and secure a quarter of a million of dollars in fines from their promoters. These practices have enabled us to discover some of the most outrageous frauds in connection with the theft of government land and government timber by great corporations and by individuals. These practices have enabled us to get some of the evidence indispensable in order to secure the conviction of the wealthiest and most formidable criminals with whom the Government has to deal, both those operating in violation of the anti-trust law and others. The amendment in question was of benefit to no one excepting to these criminals, and it seriously hampers the Government in the detection of crime and the securing of justice. Moreover, it not only affects departments outside of the Treasury, but it tends to hamper the Secretary of the Treasury himself in the effort to utilize the employees of his department so as to best meet the requirements of the public service. It forbids him from preventing frauds upon the customs service, from investigating irregularities in branch mints and assay offices, and has seriously crippled him. It prevents the promotion of employees in the Secret Service, and this further discourages good effort. In its present form the restriction operates only to the advantage of the criminal, of the wrongdoer.

"The chief argument in favor of the provision was that the Congressmen did not themselves wish to be investigated by Secret Service men. Very little of such investigation has been done in the past; but it is true that the work of the Secret Service agents was partly responsible for the indictment and conviction of a Senator and a Congressman for land frauds in Oregon. I do not believe that it is in the public interest to protect criminals in any branch of the public service, and exactly as we have again and again during the past seven years prosecuted and convicted such criminals who were in the executive branch of the Government, so in my belief we should be given ample means to prosecute them if found in the legislation branch. But if this is not considered desirable a special exception could be made in the law prohibiting the use of the Secret Service force in investigating Members of the Congress. It would be far better to do this than to do what actually was done, and strive to prevent or at least to hamper effective action against criminals by the executive branch of the Government."

A careful reading of this message will show that I said nothing to warrant the statement that "the majority of the Congressmen were in fear of being investigated by the Secret Service men," or "that Congress as a whole was actuated by that motive." I did not make any such statement in this message. Moreover, I have never made any such statement about Congress as a whole, nor, with a few inevitable exceptions, about the Members of Congress, in any message or article or speech. On the contrary, I have always not only deprecated but vigorously resented the practice of indiscriminate attack upon Congress, and indiscriminate condemnation of all Congressmen, wise and unwise, fit and unfit, good and bad alike. No one realizes more than I the importance of cooperation between the Executive and Congress, and no one holds the authority and dignity of the Congress of the United States in higher respect than I do. I have not the slightest sympathy with the practice of judging men, for good or for ill, not on their several merits, but in a mass, as members of one particular body or one caste. To put together all men holding or who have held a particular office, whether it be the office of President, or Judge, or Senator, or Member of the House of Representatives, and to class them all, without regard to their individual differences, as good or bad, seems to me utterly indefensible; and it is equally indefensible whether the good are confounded with the bad in a heated and unwarranted championship of all, or in a heated and unwarranted assault upon all. I would neither attack nor defend all executive officers in a mass, whether Presidents, Governors, Cabinet officers, or officials of lower rank; nor would I attack or defend all legislative officers in a mass. The safety of free government rests very largely in the ability of the plain, everyday citizen to discriminate between those public servants who serve him well and those public servants who serve him ill. He can not thus discriminate if he is persuaded to pass judgment upon a man, not with reference to whether he is a fit or unfit public servant, but with reference to whether he is an executive or legislative officer, whether he belongs to one branch or the other of the Government.

This allegation in the resolution, therefore, must certainly be due to an entire failure to understand my message.

The resolution continues: "That the President be requested to transmit to the House any evidence upon which he based his statements that the 'chief argument in favor of the provision was that the Congressmen did not themselves wish to be investigated by Secret Service men.'" This statement, which was an attack upon no one, still less upon the Congress, is sustained by the facts.

If you will turn to the Congressional Record for May 1 last, pages 5553 to 5560, inclusive, you will find the debate on this subject. Mr. Tawney of Minnesota, Mr. Smith of Iowa, Mr. Sherley of Kentucky, and Mr. Fitzgerald of New York appear in this debate as the special champions of the provision referred to. Messrs. Parsons, Bennet, and Driscoll were the leaders of those who opposed the adoption of the amendment and upheld the right of the Government to use the most efficient means possible in order to detect criminals and to prevent and punish crime. The amendment was carried in the Committee of the Whole, where no votes of the individual members are recorded, so I am unable to discriminate by mentioning the members who voted for and the members who voted against the provision, but its passage, the Journal records, was greeted with applause. I am well aware, however, that in any case of this kind many members who have no particular knowledge of the point at issue are content simply to follow the lead of the committee which had considered the matter, and I have no doubt that many Members of the House simply followed the lead of Messrs. Tawney and Smith, without having had the opportunity to know very much as to the rights and wrongs of the question.

I would not ordinarily attempt in this way to discriminate between Members of the House, but as objection has been taken to my language, in which I simply spoke of the action of the House as a whole, and as apparently there is a desire that I should thus discriminate, I will state that I think the responsibility rested on the Committee on Appropriations, under the lead of the members whom I have mentioned.

Now as to the request of the Congress that I give the evidence for my statement that the chief argument in favor of the provision was that the Congressmen did not themselves wish to be investigated by Secret Service men.

The part of the Congressional Record to which I have referred above entirely supports this statement. Two distinct lines of argument were followed in the debate. One concerned the question whether the law warranted the employment of the Secret Service in departments other than the Treasury, and this did not touch the merits of the service in the least. The other line of argument went to the merits of the service, whether lawfully or unlawfully employed, and here the chief if not the only argument used was that the service should be cut down and restricted because its members had "shadowed" or investigated Members of Congress and other officers of the Government. If we examine the debate in detail it appears that most of what was urged in favor of the amendment took the form of the simple statement that the committee held that there had been a "violation of law" by the use of the Secret Service for other purposes than suppressing counterfeiting (and one or two other matters which can be disregarded), and that such language was now to be used as would effectually prevent all such "violation of law" hereafter. Mr. Tawney, for instance, says: "It was for the purpose of stopping the use of this service in every possible way by the departments of the Government that this provision was inserted;" and Mr. Smith says: "Now, that was the only way in which any limitation could be put upon the activities of the Secret Service." Mr. Fitzgerald followed in the same vein, and by far the largest part of the argument against the employment of the Secret Service was confined to the statement that it was in "violation of law." Of course such a statement is not in any way an argument in favor of the justice of the provision. It is not an argument for the provision at all. It is simply a statement of what the gentlemen making it conceive to have been the law. There was both by implication and direct statement the assertion that it was the law, and ought to be the law, that the Secret Service should only be used to suppress counterfeiting; and that the law should be made more rigid than ever in this respect.

Incidentally I may say that in my judgment there is ample legal authority for the statement that this appropriation law to which reference was made imposes no restrictions whatever upon the use of the Secret Service men, but relates solely to the expenditure of the money appropriated. Mr. Tawney in the debate stated that he had in his possession "a letter from the Secretary of the Treasury, received a few days ago," in which the Secretary of the Treasury "himself admits that the provisions under which the appropriation has been made have been violated year after year for a number of years in his own Department." I append herewith as Appendix A the letter referred to. It makes no such admission as that which Mr. Tawney alleges. It contains, on the contrary, as you will see by reading it, an "emphatic protest against any such abridgment of the rights delegated to the Secretary of the Treasury by existing law," and concludes by asserting that he "is quite within his rights in thus employing the service of these agents" and that the proposed modification which Mr. Tawney succeeded in carrying through would be "distinctly to the advantage of violators of criminal stat-utes of the United States." I call attention to the fact that in this letter of Secretary Cortelyou to Mr. Tawney, as in my letter to the Speaker quoted below, the explicit statement is made that the pro-posed change will be for the benefit of the criminals—a statement which I simply reiterated in public form in my message to the Congress this year, and which is also contained in effect in the report of the Secretary of the Treasury to the Congress.

A careful reading of the Congressional Record will also show that practically the only arguments advanced in favor of the limitation proposed by Mr. Tawney's committee, beyond what may be sup-posed to be contained by implication in certain sentences as to "abuses" which were not specified, were those contained in the repeated statements of Mr. Sherley. Mr. Sherley stated that there had been "pronounced abuses growing out of the use of the Secret Service for purposes other than those intended," putting his state-ment in the form of a question, and in the same form further stated that the "private conduct" of "Members of Congress, Senators," and others ought not to be investigated by the Secret Service, and that they should not investigate a "Member of Congress" who had been accused of "conduct unbecoming a gentleman and a Member of Congress." In addition to these assertions couched as questions, he made one positive declaration, that "This Secret Service at one time was used for the purpose of looking into the personal conduct of a Member of Congress." This argument of Mr. Sherley, the only real argument as to the merits of the question made on behalf of the Committee on Appropriations, will be found in columns 1 and 2 of page 5556 and column 1 of page 5557 of the Congressional Record. In column 1 of page 5556 Mr. Sherley refers to the impropriety of permitting the Secret Service men to investigate men in the depart-ments, officers of the army and navy, and Senators and Congress-men; in column 2 he refers to officers of the navy and Members of Congress; in column 1, page 5557, he refers only to Members of Congress. His speech puts most weight on the investigation of Mem-bers of Congress.

What appears in the record is filled out and explained by an article which appeared in the Chicago Inter-Ocean of January 3, 1904, under a Washington headline, and which marked the beginning of this agitation against the Secret Service. It was a special article of about 3,000 words, written, as I was then informed and now understand, by Mr. L. W. Busbey, at that time private secretary to the Speaker of the House. I inclose a copy of certain extracts from the article, marked Appendix B. It contained an utterly unwarranted attack on the Secret Service Division of the Treasury Department and its chief. The opening paragraph includes, for instance, statements like the following:

"He (the chief of the division) and his men are desirous of doing the secret detective work for the whole Government and are not particular about drawing the line between the lawmakers and the lawbreakers. They are ready to shadow the former as well as the latter."

Then, after saying that Congress will insist that the men shall only be used to stop counterfeiting, the article goes on:

"Congress does not intend to have a Fouche or any other kind of minister of police to be used by the executive departments against the legislative branch of the Government. It has been so used, and it is suspected that it has been so used recently. * * * The legislative branch of the Government will not tolerate the meddling of detectives, whether they represent the President, Cabinet officers, or only themselves. * * * Congressmen resented the secret interference of the Secret Service men, who for weeks shadowed some of the most respected Members of the House and Senate. * * * When it was discovered that the Secret Service men were shadowing Congressmen there was a storm of indignation at the Capitol, and the bureau came near being abolished and the appropriation for the suppression of counterfeiting cut off. * * * At another time the chief of the Secret Service had his men shadow Congressmen with a view to involving them in scandals that would enable the bureau to dictate to them as to the price of silence. * * * The Secret Service men have shown an inclination again to shadow Members of Congress, knowing them to be lawmakers, and this is no joke. Several of the departments have asked Congress for secret funds for investigation, and the Treasury Department wants the limitation removed from the appropriation for suppressing counterfeiting. This shows a tendency toward Foucheism and a secret watch on other officials than themselves."

At the time of this publication the work of the Secret Service which was thus assailed included especially the investigation of great land frauds in the West and the securing of evidence to help the Department of Justice in the beef-trust investigations at Chicago, which resulted in successful prosecutions.

In view of Mr. Busbey's position, I have accepted the above quoted statements as fairly expressing the real meaning and animus of the attacks made in general terms on the use of the Secret Service for the punishment of criminals. Furthermore, in the performance of my duty, to endeavor to find the feelings of Congressmen on public questions of note, I have frequently discussed this particular matter with Members of Congress, and on such occasions the reasons alleged to me for the hostility of Congress to the Secret Service, both by those who did and by those who did not share this hostility, were almost invariably the same as those set forth in Mr. Busbey's article. I may add, by the way, that these allegations as to the Secret Service are wholly without foundation in fact.

But all of this is of insignificant importance compared with the main, the real, issue. This issue is simply, Does Congress desire that the Government shall have at its disposal the most efficient instrument for the detection of criminals and the prevention and punishment of crime, or does it not? The action of the House last May was emphatically an action against the interest of justice and against the interest of law-abiding people, and in its effect of benefit only to lawbreakers. I am not now dealing with motives; whatever may have been the motive that induced the action of which I speak, this was beyond all question the effect of that action. Is the House now willing to remedy the wrong?

For a long time I contented myself with endeavoring to persuade the House not to permit the wrong, speaking informally on the subject with those members who, I believed, knew anything of the matter, and communicating officially only in the ordinary channels, as through the Secretary of the Treasury. In a letter to the Speaker on April 30, protesting against the cutting down of the appropriation vitally necessary if the Interstate Commerce Commission was to carry into effect the twentieth section of the Hepburn law, I added: "The provision about the employment of the Secret Service men will work very great damage to the Government in its endeavor to prevent and punish crime. There is no more foolish outcry than this against 'spies;' only criminals *need fear our detectives.*" (I inclose copy of the whole letter, marked "Appendix C." The postscript is blurred in my copybook, and two or three of the words can not be deciphered.) These methods proved unavailing to prevent the wrong. Messrs. Tawney and Smith and their fellow members on the Appropriations Committee paid no heed to the protests; and as the obnoxious provision was incorporated in the sundry civil bill, it was impossible for me to consider or discuss it on its merits, as I should have done had it been in a separate bill. Therefore I have now taken the only method available, that of discussing it in my message to Congress; and as all efforts to secure what I regard as proper treatment of the subject without recourse to plain speaking had failed, I have spoken plainly and directly, and have set forth the facts in explicit terms.

Since 1901 the investigations covered by the Secret Service Division—under the practice which had been for many years recognized as proper and legitimate, and which had received the sanction of the highest law officers of the Government—have covered a wide range of offenses against the federal law. By far the most important of these related to the public domain, as to which there was uncovered a far-reaching and widespread system of fraudulent transactions involving both the illegal acquisition and the illegal fencing of Government land, and, in connection with both these offenses, the crimes of perjury and subornation of perjury. Some of the persons involved in these violations were of great wealth and of wide political and social influence. Both their corporate associations and their political affiliations and the lawless character of some of their employees made the investigations not only difficult but dangerous. In Colorado one of the Secret Service men was assassinated. In Nebraska it was necessary to remove a United States attorney and a United States marshal before satisfactory progress could be made in the prosecution of the offenders.

The evidence in all these cases was chiefly secured by men trained in the Secret Service and detailed to the Department of Justice at the request of that Department and of the Department of the Interior. In the State of Nebraska alone sixty defendants were indicted, and of the thirty-two cases thus far brought to trial twenty-eight have resulted in conviction, two of the principals, Messrs. Comstock and Richards, men of wealth and wide influence, being sentenced to twelve months in jail and fined $1,500 each. The following Secret Service memorandum made in the course of a pending case illustrates the ramifications of interest with which the Government has to deal:

"Charles T. Stewart, of Council Bluffs, was indicted at Omaha for conspiracy to defraud the Government of the title to public lands in McPherson County, Nebr.; also indicted for maintaining an unlawful inclosure of the public lands, and also under indictment for perjury in connection with final proof submitted by him on lands filed on by him as a homestead. In his final proof he swore that he and his family had resided on the lands in McPherson County (which are within his unlawful inclosure), when as a matter of fact his family has at all times resided in Council Bluffs, Iowa. He is engaged in the wholesale grocery business, his store being located in Omaha, in the wholesale district there. He is reputed to be quite wealthy. Stewart's attorneys are Harl & Tinley, of Council Bluffs, Iowa, who are also the attorneys at that place for the Omaha and Council Bluffs Street Railway Company, in which company Harl holds considerable stock, Stewart being also a stockholder and possibly a director of the company. He is also represented in Omaha by W. J. Connell, one of the attorneys there for the same company. Stewart is also represented in his perjury case by 'Bill' Gurley, of

Omaha, Nebr., who at one time was quite closely connected in a political way with the U. P. R. R. Company; Stewart is also closely associated with C. B. Hazleton, postmaster at Council Bluffs. Harl & Tinley and Hazleton are all members of the same lodge. Another close personal friend of Stewart's is Ed. Hart, alias 'Waterworks' Hart, president of the Council Bluffs Water Company, and interested in the street railway. Stewart's father was interested in, and practically owned and controlled, during his lifetime, a large ranch along the U. P. R. R. in Nebraska, and did a great deal of business with that road."

Concerning this case the United States attorney at Omaha states: "There are three cases against Stewart, one for fencing, one conspiracy, one perjury—all good cases and chances of conviction good."

In connection with the Nebraska prosecution the Government has by decree secured the return to the Government of over a million acres of grazing land, in Colorado of more than 2,000 acres of mineral land, and suits are now pending involving 150,000 acres more.

All these investigations in the land cases were undertaken in consequence of Mr. Hitchcock, the then Secretary of the Interior, becoming convinced that there were extensive frauds committed in his Department; and the ramifications of the frauds were so far-reaching that he was afraid to trust his own officials to deal in thoroughgoing fashion with them. One of the Secret Service men accordingly resigned and was appointed in the Interior Department to carry on this work. The first thing he discovered was that the special agents' division or corps of detectives of the Land Office of the Interior Department was largely under the control of the land thieves, and in consequence the investigations above referred to had to be made by Secret Service men.

If the present law, for which Messrs. Tawney, Smith, and the other gentlemen I have above mentioned are responsible, had then been in effect, this action would have been impossible, and most of the criminals would unquestionably have escaped. No more striking instance can be imagined of the desirability of having a central corps of skilled investigating agents who can at any time be assigned, if necessary in large numbers, to investigate some violation of the Federal statutes, in no matter what branch of the public service. In this particular case most of the men investigated who were public servants were in the executive branch of the Government. But in Oregon, where an enormous acreage of fraudulently alienated public land was recovered for the Government, a United States Senator, Mr. Mitchell, and a Member of the lower House, Mr. Williamson, were convicted on evidence obtained by men transferred from the Secret Service, and another Member of Congress was indicted.

From 1901 to 1904 a successful investigation of naturalization affairs was made by the Secret Service, with the result of obtaining hundreds of convictions of conspirators who were convicted of selling fraudulent papers of naturalization. (Subsequently, Congress passed a very wise law providing a special service and appropriation for the prevention of naturalization frauds; but unfortunately, at the same time that the action against the Secret Service was taken, Congress also cut down the appropriation for this special service, with the result of crippling the effort to stop frauds in naturalization.) The fugitives Greene and Gaynor, implicated in a peculiarly big Government contract fraud, were located and arrested in Canada by the Secret Service, and thanks to this they have since gone to prison for their crimes.

The Secret Service was used to assist in the investigation of crimes under the peonage laws, and owing partly thereto numerous convictions were secured and the objectionable practice was practically stamped out, at least in many districts. The most extensive smuggling of silk and opium in the history of the Treasury Department was investigated by agents of the Secret Service in New York and Seattle and a successful prosecution of the offenders undertaken. Assistance of the utmost value was rendered to the Department of Justice in the beef-trust investigation at Chicago, prosecutions were followed up and fines inflicted. The cotton-leak scandal in the Agricultural Department was investigated and the responsible parties located. What was done in connection with lottery investigations is disclosed in a letter just sent to me by the United States attorney for Delaware, running as follows:

"The destruction of the Honduras National Lottery Company, successor to the Louisiana Lottery Company, was entirely the work of the Secret Service. * * * This excellent work was accomplished by Mr. Wilkie and his subordinates. I thought it might be timely to recall this prosecution."

Three hundred thousand dollars in fines were collected by the Government in the lottery cases. Again, the ink contract fraud in the Bureau of Engraving and Printing (a bureau of the Treasury Department) was investigated by the Secret Service and the guilty parties brought to justice. Mr. Tawney stated in the debate that this was not investigated by the Secret Service, but by a clerk "down there," conveying the impression that the clerk was not in the Secret Service. As a matter of fact, he was in the Secret Service; his name was Moran, and he was promoted to assistant chief for the excellence of his work in this case. The total expense for the office and field force of the Secret Service last year was $135,000, and by this one investigation they saved to the Government over $100,-000 a year. Thanks to the restriction imposed by Congress, it is now very difficult for the Secretary of the Treasury to use the

Secret Service freely even in his own department; for instance, to use them to repeat what they did so admirably in the case of this ink contract. The Government is further crippled by the law forbidding it to employ detective agencies. Of course the Government can detect the most dangerous crimes, and punish the worst criminals, only by the use, either of the Secret Service or of private detectives; to hamper it in using the one, and forbid it to resort to the other, can inure to the benefit of none save the criminals.

The facts above given show beyond possibility of doubt that what the Secretary of the Treasury and I had both written prior to the enactment of the obnoxious provision, and what I have since written in my message to the Congress, state the facts exactly as they are. The obnoxious provision is of benefit only to the criminal class and can be of benefit only to the criminal class. If it had been embodied in the law at the time when I became President all the prosecutions above mentioned, and many others of the same general type, would either not have been undertaken or would have been undertaken with the Government at a great disadvantage; and many, and probably most, of the chief offenders would have gone scot-free instead of being punished for their crimes.

Such a body as the Secret Service, such a body of trained investigating agents, occupying a permanent position in the Government service, and separate from local investigating forces in different Departments, is an absolute necessity if the best work is to be done against criminals. It is by f · the most efficient instrument possible to use against crime. Of course the more efficient an instrument is, the more dangerous 't is 'f misused. To the argument that a force like this can be misused '+ is only necessary to answer that the condition of its usefulness if handled properly is that it shall be so efficient as to be dangerous 'f handled improperly. Any instance of abuse by the Secret Service or other investigating force in the Departments should be unsparingly punished; and Congress should hold itself ready at any and all times to investigate the executive departments whenever there is reason to believe that any such instance of abuse has occurred. I wish to emphasize my more than cordial acquiescence in the view that this is not only the right of Congress, but emphatically its duty. To use the Secret Service in the investigation of purely private or political matters would be a gross abuse. But there has been no single instance of such abuse during my term as President.

In conclusion, I most earnestly ask, in the name of good government and decent administration, in the name of honesty and for the purpose of bringing to justice violators of the federal laws wherever they may be found, whether in public or private life, that the action taken by the House last year be reversed. When this action was taken, the Senate committee, under the lead of the late Senator Allison, having before it a strongly-worded protest (Appendix D) from Secretary Cortelyou like that he had sent to Mr. Tawney, accepted the Secretary's views; and the Senate passed the bill in the shape presented by Senator Allison. In the conference, however, the House conferees insisted on the retention of the provision they had inserted, and the Senate yielded.

The Chief of the Secret Service is paid a salary utterly inadequate to the importance of his functions and to the admirable way in which he has performed them. I earnestly urge that it be increased to $6,000 per annum. I also urge that the Secret Service be placed where it properly belongs, and made a bureau in the Department of Justice, as the Chief of the Secret Service has repeatedly requested; but whether this is done or not, it should be explicitly provided that the Secret Service can be used to detect and punish crime wherever it is found.

THEODORE ROOSEVELT.

THE WHITE HOUSE, *January 4, 1909.*

SPECIAL MESSAGE.

To the Senate and House of Representatives:

I transmit herewith the report of the Commission on Country Life. At the outset I desire to point out that not a dollar of the public money has been paid to any commissioner for his work on the commission.

The report shows the general condition of farming life in the open country, and points out its larger problems; it indicates ways in which the Government, National and State, may show the people how to solve some of these problems; and it suggests a continuance of the work which the commission began.

Judging by thirty public hearings, to which farmers and farmers' wives from forty States and Territories came, and from 120,000 answers to printed questions sent out by the Department of Agriculture, the commission finds that the general level of country life is high compared with any preceding time or with any other land. If it has in recent years slipped down in some places, it has risen in more places. Its progress has been general, if not uniform.

Yet farming does not yield either the profit or the satisfaction that it ought to yield and may be made to yield. There is discontent in the country, and in places discouragement. Farmers as a class do not magnify their calling, and the movement to the towns, though, I am happy to say, less than formerly, is still strong.

Under our system, it is helpful to promote discussion of ways in

which the people can help themselves. There are three main directions in which the farmers can help themselves; namely, better farming, better business, and better living on the farm. The National Department of Agriculture, which has rendered services equaled by no
other similar department in any other time or place; the state departments of agriculture; the state colleges of agriculture and the
mechanic arts, especially through their extension work; the state agricultural experiment stations; the Farmers' Union; the Grange; the
agricultural press; and other similar agencies; have all combined to
place within the reach of the American farmer an amount and quality
of agricultural information which, if applied, would enable him, over
large areas, to double the production of the farm.

The object of the Commission on Country Life therefore is not
to help the farmer raise better crops, but to call his attention to the
opportunities for better business and better living on the farm. If
country life is to become what it should be, and what I believe it ultimately will be—one of the most dignified, desirable, and sought-after
ways of earning a living—the farmer must take advantage not only
of the agricultural knowledge which is at his disposal, but of the
methods which have raised and continue to raise the standards of
living and of intelligence in other callings.

Those engaged in all other industrial and commercial callings have
found it necessary, under modern economic conditions, to organize
themselves for mutual advantage and for the protection of their own
particular interests in relation to other interests. The farmers of every
progressive European country have realized this essential fact and
have found in the co-operative system exactly the form of business
combination they need.

Now whatever the State may do toward improving the practice of
agriculture, it is not within the sphere of any government to reor-
ganize the farmers' business or reconstruct the social life of farming communities. It is, however, quite within its power to use its
influence and the machinery of publicity which it can control for
calling public attention to the needs and the facts. For example, it is
the obvious duty of the Government to call the attention of farmers
to the growing monopolization of water power. The farmers above
all should have that power, on reasonable terms, for cheap transportation, for lighting their homes, and for innumerable uses in the daily
tasks on the farm.

It would be idle to assert that life on the farm occupies as good a
position in dignity, desirability, and business results as the farmers
might easily give it if they chose. One of the chief difficulties is the
failure of country life, as it exists at present, to satisfy the higher
social and intellectual aspirations of country people. Whether the con-

stant draining away of so much of the best elements in the rural population into the towns is due chiefly to this cause or to the superior business opportunities of city life may be open to question. But no one at all familiar with farm life throughout the United States can fail to recognize the necessity for building up the life of the farm upon its social as well as upon its productive side.

It is true that country life has improved greatly in attractiveness, health and comfort, and that the farmer's earnings are higher than they were. But city life is advancing even more rapidly, because of the greater attention which is being given by the citizens of the towns to their own betterment. For just this reason the introduction of effective agricultural co-operation throughout the United States is of the first importance. Where farmers are organized co-operatively they not only avail themselves much more readily of business opportunities and improved methods, but it is found that the organizations which bring them together in the work of their lives are used also for social and intellectual advancement.

The co-operative plan is the best plan of organization wherever men have the right spirit to carry it out. Under this plan any business undertaking is managed by a committee; every man has one vote and only one vote; and everyone gets profits according to what he sells or buys or supplies. It develops individual responsibility and has a moral as well as a financial value over any other plan.

I desire only to take counsel with the farmers as fellow-citizens. It is not the problem of the farmers alone that I am discussing with them, but a problem which affects every city as well as every farm in the country. It is a problem which the working farmers will have to solve for themselves; but it is a problem which also affects in only less degree all the rest of us, and therefore if we can render any help toward its solution it is not only our duty but our interest to do so.

The foregoing will, I hope, make it clear why I appointed a commission to consider problems of farm life which have hitherto had far too little attention, and the neglect of which has not only held back life in the country, but also lowered the efficiency of the whole nation. The welfare of the farmer is of vital consequence to the welfare of the whole community. The strengthening of country life, therefore, is the strengthening of the whole nation.

The commission has tried to help the farmers to see clearly their own problem and to see it as a whole; to distinguish clearly between what the Government can do and what the farmers must do for themselves; and it wishes to bring not only the farmers but the Nation as a whole to realize that the growing of crops, though an essential part, is only a part of country life. Crop growing is the essential foundation; but it is no less essential that the farmer shall get an adequate return for what he grows; and it is no less essential—indeed it is literally vital—that he and his wife and his children shall lead the right kind of life.

For this reason, it is of the first importance that the United States Department of Agriculture, through which as prime agent the ideas the commission stands for must reach the people, should become without delay in fact a Department of Country Life, fitted to deal not only with crops, but also with all the larger aspects of life in the open country.

From all that has been done and learned three great general and immediate needs of country life stand out:

First, effective co-operation among farmers, to put them on a level with the organized interests with which they do business.

Second, a new kind of schools in the country, which shall teach the children as much outdoors as indoors and perhaps more, so that they will prepare for country life, and not, as at present, mainly for life in town.

Third, better means of communication, including good roads and a parcels post, which the country people are everywhere, and rightly, unanimous in demanding.

To these may well be added better sanitation; for easily preventable diseases hold several million country people in the slavery of continuous ill health.

The commission points out, and I concur in the conclusion, that the most important help that the Government, whether National or State, can give is to show the people how to go about these tasks of organization, education and communication with the best and quickest results. This can be done by the collection and spread of information. One community can thus be informed of what other communities have done, and one country of what other countries have done. Such help by the people's government would lead to a comprehensive plan of organization, education and communication, and make the farming country better to live in, for intellectual and social reasons as well as for purely agricultural reasons.

The Government through the Department of Agriculture does not cultivate any man's farm for him. But it does put at his service useful knowledge that he would not otherwise get. In the same way the National and State Governments might put into the people's hands the new and right knowledge of school work. The task of maintaining and developing the schools would remain, as now, with the people themselves.

The only recommendation I submit is that an appropriation of $25,000 be provided, to enable the commission to digest the material it has collected, and to collect and to digest much more that is within its reach, and thus complete its work. This would enable the commission to gather in the harvest of suggestion which is resulting from the discussion it has stirred up. The commissioners have served without compensation, and I do not recommend any appropriation for their services, but only for the expenses that will be required to finish the task that they have begun.

To improve our system of agriculture seems to me the most urgent of the tasks which lie before us. But it can not, in my judgment, be obtained by measures which touch only the material and technical side of the subject; the whole business and life of the farmer must also be taken into account. Such considerations led me to appoint the Commission on Country Life. Our object should be to help develop in the country community the great ideals of community life as well as of personal character. One of the most important adjuncts to this end must be the country church, and I invite your attention to what the commission says of the country church and of the need of an extension of such work as that of the Young Men's Christian Association in country communities. Let me lay special emphasis upon what the Commission says at the very end of its report on personal ideals and local leadership. Everything resolves itself in the end into the question of personality. Neither society nor government can do much for country life unless there is voluntary response in the personal ideals of the men and women who live in the country. In the development of character, the home should be more important than the school, or than society at large. When once the basic material needs have been met, high ideals may be quite independent of income; but they can not be realized without sufficient income to provide adequate foundation; and where the community at large is not financially prosperous it is impossible to develop a high average personal and community ideal. In short, the fundamental facts of human nature apply to men and women who live in the country just as they apply to men and women who live in the towns. Given a sufficient foundation of material well being, the influence of the farmers and farmers' wives on their children becomes the factor of first importance in determining the attitude of the next generation toward farm life. The farmer should realize that the person who most needs consideration on the farm is his wife. I do not in the least mean that she should purchase ease at the expense of duty. Neither man nor woman is really happy or really useful save on condition of doing his or her duty. If the woman shirks her duty as housewife, as home keeper, as the mother whose prime function it is to bear and rear a sufficient number of healthy children, then she is not entitled to our regard. But if she does her duty she is more entitled to our regard even than the man who does his duty; and the man should show special consideration for her needs.

I warn my countrymen that the great recent progress made in city life is not a full measure of our civilization; for our civilization rests at bottom on the wholesomeness, the attractiveness and the completeness, as well as the prosperity, of life in the country. The men and women on the farms stand for what is fundamentally best and most needed in our American life. Upon the development of country life rests ultimately our ability, by methods of farming requiring the highest intelligence, to continue to feed and clothe the hungry nations; to supply the city with fresh blood, clean bodies and clear brains that can endure the terrific strain of modern life; we need the development of men in the open country, who will be in the future, as in the past, the stay and strength of the nation in time of war, and its guiding and controlling spirit in time of peace.

THEODORE ROOSEVELT.

THE WHITE HOUSE, *February* 9, 1909.

SPECIAL MESSAGE.

To the Senate and House of Representatives:

I transmit herewith a report of the National Conservation Commission, together with the accompanying papers. This report, which is the outgrowth of the conference of governors last May, was unanimously approved by the recent joint conference held in this city between the National Conservation Commission and governors of States, state conservation commissions, and conservation committees of great organizations of citizens. It is therefore in a peculiar sense representative of the whole nation and all its parts.

With the statements and conclusions of this report I heartily concur, and I commend it to the thoughtful consideration both of the Congress and of our people generally. It is one of the most fundamentally important documents ever laid before the American people. It contains the first inventory of its natural resources ever made by any nation. In condensed form it presents a statement of our available capital in material resources, which are the means of progress, and calls attention to the essential conditions upon which the perpetuity, safety and welfare of this nation now rest and must always continue to rest. It deserves, and should have, the widest possible distribution among the people.

The facts set forth in this report constitute an imperative call to action. The situation they disclose demands that we, neglecting for a time, if need be, smaller and less vital questions, shall concentrate an effective part of our attention upon the great material foundations of national existence, progress and prosperity.

This first inventory of natural resources prepared by the National Conservation Commission is undoubtedly but the beginning of a series which will be indispensable for dealing intelligently with what we have. It supplies as close an approximation to the actual facts as it was possible to prepare with the knowledge and time available. The progress of our knowledge of this country will continually lead to more accurate information and better use of the sources of national strength. But we can not defer action until complete accuracy in the estimates can be reached, because before that time many of our resources will be practically gone. It is not necessary that this inventory should be exact in every minute detail. It is essential that it should correctly describe the general situation; and that the present inventory does. As it stands it is an irrefutable proof that the conservation of our resources is the fundamental question before this nation, and that our first and greatest task is to set our house in order and begin to live within our means.

The first of all considerations is the permanent welfare of our people; and true moral welfare, the highest form of welfare, can not permanently exist save on a firm and lasting foundation of material well-being. In this respect our situation is far from satisfactory. After every possible allowance has been made, and when every hopeful indication has been given its full weight, the facts still give reason for grave concern. It would be unworthy of our history and our intelligence, and disastrous to our future, to shut our eyes to these facts or attempt to laugh them out of court. The people should and will rightly demand that the great fundamental questions shall be given attention by their representatives. I do not advise hasty or ill-considered action on disputed points, but I do urge, where the facts are known, where the public interest is clear, that neither indifference and inertia, nor adverse private interests, shall be allowed to stand in the way of the public good.

The great basic facts are already well known. We know that our population is now adding about one-fifth to its numbers in ten years, and that by the middle of the present century perhaps one hundred and fifty million Americans, and by its end very many millions more, must be fed and clothed from the products of our soil. With the steady growth in population and the still more rapid increase in consumption our people will hereafter make greater and not less demands per capita upon all the natural resources for their livelihood, comfort and convenience. It is high time to realize that our responsibility to the coming millions is like that of parents to their children, and that in wasting our resources we are wronging our descendants.

We know now that our rivers can and should be made to serve our people effectively in transportation, but that the vast expenditures for our waterways have not resulted in maintaining, much less in promoting, inland navigation. Therefore, let us take immediate steps to ascertain the reasons and to prepare and adopt a comprehensive plan for inland-waterway navigation that will result in giving the people the benefits for which they have paid, but which they have not yet received. We know now that our forests are fast disappearing, that less than one-fifth of them are being conserved, and that no good purpose can be met by failing to provide the relatively small sums needed for the protection, use and improvement of all forests still owned by the Government, and to enact laws to check the wasteful destruction of the forests in private hands. There are differences of opinion as to many public questions; but the American people stand nearly as a unit for waterway development and for forest protection.

We know now that our mineral resources once exhausted are gone forever, and that the needless waste of them costs us hundreds of human lives and nearly $300,000,000 a year. Therefore, let us undertake without delay the investigations necessary before our people will be in position, through state action or otherwise, to put an end to this huge loss and waste, and conserve both our mineral resources and the lives of the men who take them from the earth.

I desire to make grateful acknowledgment to the men, both in and out of the government service, who have prepared the first inventory of our natural resources. They have made it possible for this nation to take a great step forward. Their work is helping us to see that the greatest questions before us are not partisan questions, but questions upon which men of all parties and all shades of opinion may be united for the common good. Among such questions, on the material side, the conservation of natural resources stands first. It is the bottom round of the ladder on our upward progress toward a condition in which the nation as a whole, and its citizens as individuals, will set national efficiency and the public welfare before personal profit.

The policy of conservation is perhaps the most typical example of the general policies which this Government has made peculiarly its own during the opening years of the present century. The function of our Government is to insure to all its citizens, now and hereafter, their rights to life, liberty and the pursuit of happiness. If we of this generation destroy the resources from which our children would otherwise derive their livelihood, we reduce the capacity of our land to support a population, and so either degrade the standard of living or deprive the coming generations of their right to life on this continent. If we allow great industrial organizations to exercise unregulated control of the means of production and the necessaries of life, we deprive the Americans of today and of the future of industrial liberty, a right no less precious and vital than political freedom. Industrial liberty was a fruit of political liberty, and in turn has become one of its chief supports, and exactly as we stand for political democracy so we must stand for industrial democracy.

The rights to life and liberty are fundamental, and like other fundamental necessities, when once acquired, they are little dwelt upon. The right to the pursuit of happiness is the right whose presence or absence is most likely to be felt in daily life. In whatever it has accomplished, or failed to accomplish, the administration which is just drawing to a close has at least seen clearly the fundamental need of freedom of opportunity for every citizen. We have realized that the right of every man to live his own life, provide for his family, and endeavor, according to his abilities, to secure for himself and for them a fair share of the good things of existence, should be subject to one limitation and to no other. The freedom of the individual should be limited only by the present and future rights, interests and needs of the other individuals who make up the community. We should do all in our power to develop and protect individual liberty, individual initiative, but subject always to the need of preserving and promoting the general good. When necessary, the private right must yield, under due process of law and with proper compensation, to the welfare of the commonwealth. The man who serves the community greatly should be greatly rewarded by the community; as there is great inequality of service, so there must be great inequality of reward; but no man and no set of men should be allowed to play the game of competition with loaded dice.

All this is simply good common sense. The underlying principle of conservation has been described as the application of common sense to common problems for the common good. If the description is correct, then conservation is the great fundamental basis for national efficiency. In this stage of the world's history to be fearless, to be just, and to be efficient are the three great requirements of national life. National efficiency is the result of natural resources well handled, of freedom of opportunity for every man, and of the inherent capacity, trained ability, knowledge and will, collectively and individually to use that opportunity.

This administration has achieved some things; it has sought, but has not been able, to achieve others; it has doubtless made mistakes; but all it has done or attempted has been in the single, consistent effort to secure and enlarge the rights and opportunities of the men and women of the United States. We are trying to conserve what is good in our social system, and we are striving toward this end when we endeavor to do away with what is bad. Success may be made too hard for some if it is made too easy for others. The rewards of common industry and thrift may be too small if the rewards for other, and on the whole less valuable, qualities, are made too large, and especially if the rewards for qualities which are really, from the public standpoint, undesirable, are permitted to become too large. Our aim is so far as possible to provide such conditions that there shall be equality of opportunity where there is equality of energy, fidelity and intelligence; when there is a reasonable equality of opportunity the distribution of rewards will take care of itself.

The unchecked existence of monopoly is incompatible with equality of opportunity. The reason for the exercise of government control over great monopolies is to equalize opportunity. We are fighting against privilege. It was made unlawful for corporations to contribute money for election expenses in order to abridge the power of special privilege at the polls. Railroad-rate control is an attempt to secure an equality of opportunity for all men affected by rail transportation; and that means all of us. The great anthracite coal strike was settled, and the pressing danger of a coal famine averted, because we recognized that the control of a public necessity involves a duty to the people, and that public intervention in the affairs of a public-service corporation is neither to be resented as usurpation nor permitted as a privilege by the corporations, but on the contrary to be accepted as a duty and exercised as a right by the Government in the interest of all the people. The efficiency of the army and the navy has been increased so that our people may follow in peace the great work of making this country a better place for Americans to live in, and our navy was sent round the world for the same ultimate purpose. All the acts taken by the Government during the last seven years, and all the policies now being pursued by the Government, fit in as parts of a consistent whole.

Our public-land policy has for its aim the use of the public land so that it will promote local development by the settlement of home makers; the policy we champion is to serve all the people legitimately and openly, instead of permitting the lands to be converted, illegitimately and under cover, to the private benefit of a few. Our forest policy was established so that we might use the public forests for the permanent public good, instead of merely for temporary private gain. The reclamation act, under which the desert parts of the public domain are converted to higher uses for the general benefit, was passed so that more Americans might have homes on the land.

These policies were enacted into law and have justified their enactment. Others have failed, so far, to reach the point of action. Among such is the attempt to secure public control of the open range and thus to convert its benefits to the use of the small man, who is the home maker, instead of allowing it to be controlled by a few great cattle and sheep owners.

The enactment of a pure food law was a recognition of the fact that the public welfare outweighs the right to private gain, and that no man may poison the people for his private profit. The employers' liability bill recognized the controlling fact that while the employer usually has at stake no more than his profit, the stake of the employee is a living for himself and his family.

We are building the Panama Canal; and this means that we are engaged in the giant engineering feat of all time. We are striving to add in all ways to the habitability and beauty of our country. We are striving to hold in the public hands the remaining supply of unappropriated coal, for the protection and benefit of all the people. We have taken the first steps toward the conservation of our natural resources, and the betterment of country life, and the improvement of our waterways. We stand for the right of every child to a childhood free from grinding toil, and to an education; for the civic responsibility and decency of every citizen; for prudent foresight in public matters, and for fair play in every relation of our national and economic life. In international matters we apply a system of diplomacy which puts the obligations of international morality on a level with those that govern the actions of an honest gentleman in dealing with his fellow-men. Within our own border we stand for truth and honesty in public and in private life; and we war sternly against wrongdoers of every grade. All these efforts are integral parts of the same attempt, the attempt to enthrone justice and righteousness, to secure freedom of opportunity to all of our citizens, now and hereafter, and to set the ultimate interest of all of us above the temporary interest of any individual, class, or group.

The nation, its government, and its resources exist, first of all, for the American citizen, whatever his creed, race, or birthplace, whether he be rich or poor, educated or ignorant, provided only that he is a good citizen, recognizing his obligations to the nation for the rights and opportunities which he owes to the nation.

The obligations, and not the rights, of citizenship increase in proportion to the increase of a man's wealth or power. The time is coming when a man will be judged, not by what he has succeeded in getting for himself from the common store, but by how well he has done his duty as a citizen, and by what the ordinary citizen has gained in freedom of opportunity because of his service for the common good. The highest value we know is that of the individual citizen, and the highest justice is to give him fair play in the effort to realize the best there is in him.

The tasks this nation has to do are great tasks. They can only be done at all by our citizens acting together, and they can be done best of all by the direct and simple application of homely common sense. The application of common sense to common problems for the common good, under the guidance of the principles upon which this republic was based, and by virtue of which it exists, spells perpetuity for the nation, civil and industrial liberty for its citizens, and freedom of opportunity in the pursuit of happiness for the plain American, for whom this nation was founded, by whom it was preserved, and through whom alone it can be perpetuated. Upon this platform— larger than party differences, higher than class prejudice, broader than any question of profit and loss—there is room for every American who realizes that the common good stands first.

The National Conservation Commission wisely confined its report to the statement of facts and principles, leaving the Executive to recommend the specific steps to which these facts and principles inevitably lead. Accordingly, I call your attention to some of the larger features of the situation disclosed by the report, and to the action thereby clearly demanded for the general good.

WATERS.

The report says:

"Within recent months it has been recognized and demanded by the people, through many thousand delegates from all States assembled in convention in different sections of the country, that the waterways should and must be improved promptly and effectively as a means of maintaining national prosperity.

"The first requisite for waterway improvement is the control of the waters in such manner as to reduce floods and regulate the regimen of the navigable rivers. The second requisite is development of terminals and connection in such manner as to regulate commerce."

Accordingly, I urge that the broad plan for the development of our waterways, recommended by the Inland Waterways Commission, be put in effect without delay. It provides for a comprehensive system of waterway improvement extending to all the uses of the waters and benefits to be derived from their control, including navigation, the development of power, the extension of irrigation, the drainage of swamp and overflow lands, the prevention of soil wash, and the purification of streams for water supply. It proposes to carry out the work by co-ordinating agencies in the federal departments through the medium of an administrative commission or board, acting in cooperation with the States and other organizations and individual citizens.

The work of waterway development should be undertaken without delay. Meritorious projects in known conformity with the general outlines of any comprehensive plan should proceed at once. The cost of the whole work should be met by direct appropriation if possible, but if necessary by the issue of bonds in small denominations.

It is especially important that the development of water power should be guarded with the utmost care both by the National Government and by the States in order to protect the people against the up-growth of monopoly and to insure to them a fair share in the benefits which will follow the development of this great asset which belongs to the people and should be controlled by them.

FORESTS.

I urge that provision be made for both protection and more rapid development of the national forests. Otherwise, either the increasing use of these forests by the people must be checked or their protection against fire must be dangerously weakened. If we compare the actual fire damage on similar areas on private and national forest lands during the past year, the government fire patrol saved commercial timber worth as much as the total cost of caring for all national forests at the present rate for about ten years.

I especially commend to the Congress the facts presented by the commission as to the relation between forests and stream flow in its bearing upon the importance of the forest lands in national ownership. Without an understanding of this intimate relation the conservation of both these natural resources must largely fail.

The time has fully arrived for recognizing in the law the responsibility to the community, the State, and the nation which rests upon the private owners of private lands. The ownership of forest land is a public trust. The man who would so handle his forest as to cause erosion and to injure stream flow must be not only educated, but he must be controlled.

The report of the National Conservation Commission says:

"Forests in private ownership can not be conserved unless they are protected from fire. We need good fire laws, well enforced. Fire control is impossible without an adequate force of men whose sole duty is fire patrol during the dangerous season."

I hold as first among the tasks before the States and the nation in their respective shares in forest conservation the organization of efficient fire patrols and the enactment of good fire laws on the part of the States.

The report says further:

"Present tax laws prevent reforestation of cut-over land and the perpetuation of existing forests by use. An annual tax upon the land itself, exclusive of the timber, and a tax upon the timber when cut is well adapted to actual conditions of forest investment and is practicable and certain. It is far better that forest land should pay a moderate tax permanently than that it should pay an excessive revenue temporarily and then cease to yield at all."

Second only in importance to good fire laws well enforced is the enactment of tax laws which will permit the perpetuation of existing forests by use.

LANDS.

With our increasing population the time is not far distant when the problem of supplying our people with food will become pressing. The possible additions to our arable area are not great, and it will become necessary to obtain much larger crops from the land, as is now done in more densely settled countries. To do this, we need better farm practice and better strains of wheat, corn and other crop plants, with a reduction in losses from soil erosion and from insects, animals and other enemies of agriculture. The United States Department of Agriculture is doing excellent work in these directions and it should be liberally supported.

The remaining public lands should be classified and the arable lands disposed of to home makers. In their interest the timber and stone act and the commutation clause of the homestead act should be repealed, and the desert-land law should be modified in accordance with the recommendations of the Public Lands Commission.

The use of the public grazing lands should be regulated in such ways as to improve and conserve their value.

Rights to the surface of the public land should be separated from rights to forests upon it and to minerals beneath it, and these should be subject to separate disposal.

The coal, oil, gas and phosphate rights still remaining with the Government should be withdrawn from entry and leased under conditions favorable for economic development.

MINERALS.

The accompanying reports show that the consumption of nearly all of our mineral products is increasing more rapidly than our population. Our mineral waste is about one-sixth of our product, or nearly $1,000,000 for each working day in the year. The loss of structural materials through fire is about another million a day. The loss of life in the mines is appalling. The larger part of these losses of life and property can be avoided.

Our mineral resources are limited in quantity and can not be increased or reproduced. With the rapidly increasing rate of consumption the supply will be exhausted while yet the nation is in its infancy, unless better methods are devised or substitutes are found. Further investigation is urgently needed in order to improve methods and to develop and apply substitutes.

It is of the utmost importance that a Bureau of Mines be established in accordance with the pending bill to reduce the loss of life in mines and the waste of mineral resources and to investigate the methods and substitutes for prolonging the duration of our mineral supplies. Both the need and the public demand for such a bureau are rapidly becoming more urgent. It should co-operate with the States in supplying data to serve as a basis for state mine regulations. The establishment of this bureau will mean merely the transfer from other bureaus of work which it is agreed should be transferred and slightly enlarged and reorganized for these purposes.

CONCLUSIONS.

The joint conference already mentioned adopted two resolutions to which I call your special attention. The first was intended to promote co-operation between the States and the nation upon all of the great questions here discussed. It is as follows:

"*Resolved*, That a joint committee be appointed by the chairman, to consist of six members of state conservation commissions and three members of the National Conservation Commission, whose duty it shall be to prepare and present to the state and national commissions, and through them to the governors and the President, a plan for united action by all organizations concerned with the conservation of natural resources. (On motion of Governor Noel, of Mississippi, the chairman and secretary of the conference were added to and constituted a part of this committee.)"

The second resolution of the joint conference to which I refer calls upon the Congress to provide the means for such co-operation. The principle of the community of interest among all our people in the great natural resources runs through the report of the National Conservation Commission and the proceedings of the joint conference. These resources, which form the common basis of our welfare, can be wisely developed, rightly used, and prudently conserved only by the common action of all the people, acting through their representatives in State and nation. Hence the fundamental necessity for co-operation. Without it we shall accomplish but little, and that little badly. The resolution follows:

"We also especially urge on the Congress of the United States the high desirability of maintaining a national commission on the conservation of the resources of the country, empowered to co-operate with state commissions to the end that every sovereign commonwealth and every section of the country may attain the high degree of prosperity and the sureness of perpetuity naturally arising in the abundant resources and the vigor, intelligence and patriotism of our people."

In this recommendation I most heartily concur, and I urge that an appropriation of at least $50,000 be made to cover the expenses of the National Conservation Commission for necessary rent, assistance and traveling expenses. This is a very small sum. I know of no other way in which the appropriation of so small a sum would result in so large a benefit to the whole nation.

THEODORE ROOSEVELT.

THE WHITE HOUSE, *January 22,* 1909.

SPECIAL MESSAGE.

To the Senate and House of Representatives:

I submit herewith the report of the engineers appointed by me to accompany the ex-Secretary of War, the Hon. William H. Taft, to the isthmian canal to look into the condition of the canal work, and especially to report upon the feasibility and safety of the Gatun dam project, with a view to deciding whether or not there should be any change in the plans in accordance with which the canal is being constructed, these plans having been adopted by the Congress. I am happy to report to you that the accompanying document shows in clearest fashion that the Congress was wise in the position it took, and that it would be an inexcusable folly to change from the proposed lock canal to a sea-level canal. In fact this report not only determines definitely the type of canal, but makes it evident that hereafter attack on this type—the lock type—is in reality merely attack upon the policy of building any canal at all. The board of engineers who signed this report are of all the men in their profession, within or without the United States, the men who are on the whole best qualified to pass upon these very questions which they examined. I commend to you the most careful consideration of their report. They show that the only criticism that can be made of the work on the Isthmus is that there has sometimes been almost an excess of caution in providing against possible trouble. As to the Gatun dam itself, they show that not only is the dam safe, but that on the whole the plan already adopted would make it needlessly high and strong, and accordingly they recommend that the height be reduced by 20 feet, which change in the plans I have accordingly directed. Every American citizen should feel not merely gratification, but a very keen sense of pride in the statement made by this distinguished body of engineers as to the way in which present Treaty.

Article V.

The present Treaty shall be ratified by the President of the United States, by and with the advice and consent of the Senate thereof, and by His Britannic Majesty; and the ratifications shall be exchanged at Washington or at London at the earliest possible time within six months from the date hereof.

In faith whereof the respective Plenipotentiaries have signed this Treaty and thereunto affixed their seals.

Done in duplicate at Washington, the 18th day of November, in the year of Our Lord one thousand nine hundred and one.

John Hay
Pauncefote.

FACSIMILE: THE HAY-PAUNCEFOTE TREATY

THE HAY-PAUNCEFOTE TREATY.

This treaty was signed on November 18, 1901, the United States being represented by John Hay, Secretary of State, and Great Britain by Sir Julian Pauncefote, Ambassador to the United States from Great Britain. The treaty provided regulations covering any future construction of a canal connecting the Atlantic and the Pacific oceans, and displaced the Clayton-Bulwer treaty, signed in 1856, which had long caused great and widespread dissatisfaction in the United States. The Clayton-Bulwer treaty had provided that a canal across the Isthmus, either at Panama or Nicaragua, might not be under exclusive control of either Great Britain or the United States, and in other ways had restricted the control of the United States over such an undertaking. The treaty signed in 1901 is rather indefinite in its provisions, but definitely dissipates the restrictions of the Clayton-Bulwer treaty, and provides that the canal is to be free and open to vessels of all nations, on equitable conditions and charges. The Hay-Pauncefote treaty also permits the United States to fortify the Canal, and to close it in time of war. (See article Great Britain, Treaties with, in the Encyclopedic Index.)

the work has been done, and in which it is now proceeding. The American people are to be heartily congratulated on everything of importance that has been done in connection with the building of the Panama Canal.

THEODORE ROOSEVELT.

THE WHITE HOUSE, *February* 17, 1909.

WASHINGTON, D. C., *February* 16, 1909.

SIR: In accordance with your instructions, we have visited the Isthmian canal, in company with Hon. William H. Taft, and have examined the work in progress and the plans for the structures as far as now developed.

We have given especial consideration, under the instructions of Mr. Taft, to the foundations for the Gatun dam, and the feasibility of constructing and maintaining thereon a safe dam for retaining water at 85 feet above sea level.

We have examined the slides in the banks of the canal and the surveys, plottings and sections that have been made of them. The subsidence in the fills in the toes of the dams and in the railway embankments has also been examined, and we have considered the effect of the qualities of materials thus disclosed upon the construction of the various works and upon their ultimate stability.

We have also considered the evidence that has been accumulated as to the permeability of the different materials and the possible loss of water by percolation through the bed and banks of the future Gatun lake; and the question whether such loss of water by seepage would result in materially reducing the water supply or in undermining and ultimately crippling the structure.

GATUN DAM.

The Gatun earth dam is the central point of discussion, and we were instructed by Mr. Taft to give it first consideration in the light of all new evidence.

We are satisfied, both from the records of the experiments that have been made and from our own personal examination of the materials, as seen in cuts now open and as disclosed by samples from test borings, that there will be no dangerous or objectionable seepage through the materials under the base of the dam, nor are they so soft as to be liable to be pushed aside by the weight of the proposed dam so as to cause dangerous settlement.

We are also satisfied that the materials available and which it is proposed to use are suitable and can be readily placed to form a tight, stable and permanent dam.

The type of dam now under construction is one which meets with our unanimous approval. It is a combination of rock fill and hydraulic fill, in which the exterior faces are to be composed largely of rock of all sizes obtained from the canal excavation, dumped and laid on slopes much flatter than are ordinarily found in earth dams, while the interior of the great mass will consist of clayey material obtained by hydraulic dredging from large deposits at a little distance from the dam and carried by water through pipes to the places where it is to be used. The material as delivered is a mixture of earth and water. The material held in suspension slowly deposits, finally forming a solid, water-tight embankment. The pond necessarily maintained on the top of the dam during construction tests the embankment at all stages of its growth, searches out any weak points, and leads to the closure of any voids or cracks.

The most practical question in the construction of the Gatun dam is the possible slipping and sliding of the materials underneath and in the body of the dam. The materials, speaking broadly, are of a clayey nature, generally impervious to water, but sometimes slipping when subjected to heavy unbalanced pressure or on high steep slopes when saturated with water. In this respect the materials differ radically from the sandy and gravelly materials which have been frequently used in the construction of other earth dams.

In order to build a dam of these clayey materials that will be stable and permanent, it is necessary that the slopes should be flatter than would be needed to secure the stability of a dam of siliceous, sandy, or gravelly materials.

The evidence that has been accumulated as to the degrees of slope that are stable with these materials seems to us conclusive. The fact that the materials are slippery does not mean that a dam built from them is necessarily less stable than a dam built of materials that do not slip so easily. It does mean that, in order to secure stability and permanency, the dam must be built with a greater thickness at the bottom.

The dam as proposed is more than a third of a mile in horizontal thickness at its base, including the rock-fill portions.

The design upon which the work is now being prosecuted abundantly fulfills the required degree of stability and goes far beyond the limits of what would be regarded as sufficient and safe in any less important structure.

As a matter of convenience and economy during construction, materials have been piled up on slopes much steeper than those contemplated in the finished work. Generally, the materials so placed have remained in position, but in some cases slips have occurred. The occurrence of these slips is of no serious consequence either in the practical execution of the work or in the ultimate stability of the structures. We can readily understand how incorrect deductions may have been drawn from these occurrences, especially by those not fully informed as to the character of the materials and the ample dimensions and much less steep slopes of the proposed structures in their final form.

We were requested to consider the proper height for the crest of the Gatun dam, and after consideration concluded that it could be safely reduced 20 feet from that originally proposed, namely, to an elevation of 115 feet above sea level, or 30 feet above the normal level of the water against the dam. We are also of the opinion that the sheet piling recently proposed under the base of the dam may be safely omitted. The narrow cut-off trench now in progress through the upper earth stratum on Gatun Island and elsewhere and designed to be refilled with sluiced material should be continued.

Changes in these respects will facilitate the work of construction and will reduce somewhat the cost of the proposed work.

A full study of all the data at hand, and of the materials, and of the plans that are proposed with the above modifications leaves no doubt in our minds as to the safe, tight and durable character of the Gatun dam.

CHANGES IN PLAN OF CANAL.

It was suggested to us by Mr. Taft that we give special consideration to those changes which have been made in the plans of the minority of the Board of Consulting Engineers of 1905 since the adoption of the project.

Change in position of lower Pacific locks.

One of the most important of these changes is the moving of the lower locks on the Pacific end of the canal from La Boca, on the shore of Panama Bay, to Miraflores, about 4 miles inland.

This change involved abandoning the construction of two earth dams at and near La Boca and the substitution of about 4 miles of deep-sea level channel 500 feet wide from La Boca to Miraflores in place of a wider channel through the lake that would have been created by the dams.

Before this change was made work had been commenced upon the toes of one of the dams. The material had been piled up to a considerable height on slopes steeper than were capable of being supported by the underlying material. Under these conditions settlements occurred with lateral displacement of some of the underlying material. Your board, after carefully inspecting the ground and the partially completed work, is of the opinion that these settlements cause no reason to doubt the stability of the proposed dams. We are unanimously of the opinion that stable and water-tight dams of substantially the proposed dimensions could have been constructed on the proposed sites without recourse to dredging out the underlying soft material.

The report of the minority of the Board of Consulting Engineers of 1905 recognized that an objection might be made from a military point of view to placing locks on the shore of the bay, exposed to guns of hostile ships. We now understand that the controlling reason for the change was a military one. This change in the plans will result in an increase in cost of the canal by an amount judged from evidence at our disposal to be not less than $10,000,000. We are informed, however, that this change would greatly lessen the cost of fortification.

Increased width of canal.

Another change is the increase of the minimum bottom width of the canal from 200 feet to 300 feet. This applies to a length of about 4.7 miles in the Culebra cut. We understand that this change will increase the cost of the work by about $13,000,000. The work upon the excavation of the Culebra cut under the revised plan has now so far advanced that this widening will not delay the completion of the canal.

The widening will permit ships to pass one another in this portion of the canal, as they may under the original plan in all other portions, and will otherwise facilitate navigation through it.

If slides occur after the completion of the canal, the wider canal is not as likely to be blocked as a narrow one.

We understand that this change was authorized directly by you on the presentation of its advantages by the chief engineer, and we merely call attention to it as one reason for the increased cost of the canal.

Increased size of locks.

Another change is the increase of the dimensions of the locks from 95 by 900 feet to 110 by 1,000 feet. The increase in width we understand has been made in compliance with a request from the General Board of the Navy Department, in order to allow the passage of the largest war vessels contemplated.

A large increase in cost is involved in these enlarged dimensions.

Changes in breakwaters

An important change is proposed in the location of the breakwater at the Atlantic end of the canal. The plan provisionally adopted by the Board of Consulting Engineers of 1905, and adopted for the purpose of estimate by the minority of that board, was for a breakwater generally parallel with the channel, which included less than one-third of Limon Bay; whereas the breakwater in the location now proposed will protect the entire bay and furnish a more commodious harbor not only for ships using the canal, but for all other shipping which makes use of the port. A considerable increase in cost is involved in this change.

We had an opportunity to view the present harbor during what is said to have been the only severe norther of the past two years, and have no doubt that a good breakwater is a desirable adjunct to the canal. We are not prepared to pass on the precise location, form, or cost of this.

A change of less importance has been made at the Pacific end by relocating the dredged channel leading to deep water and increasing its width from 300 feet to 500 feet and by constructing a breakwater from the shore at La Boca to Naos Island with material excavated from the Culebra cut. This breakwater, now under construction, serves to prevent currents across the canal cut and tends to prevent deposits in the dredged channel and to increase the safety of navigation. The breakwater may also serve to carry a roadway to Naos Island. These changes involve some additional expense.

Relocation of Panama Railroad

The alignment of the Panama Railroad has been materially changed south of Gatun. This change was made because it was found that the swamp near the Gatuncillo River would not support the very high railroad embankment required, if made with ordinary slopes, and a line crossing at a point higher up the river was selected, which does not, however, materially increase the length of the railroad. The construction of the railroad will cost much more than was estimated by the minority of the Board of Consulting Engineers, who were unable to procure surveys of the proposed location. The recent change in location affords more ample and convenient anchorage immediately above the locks.

Other changes

Some further changes or additions which have not yet been fully worked out have been mentioned to us as likely to be made as the work progresses, namely, the dredging out of a broad anchorage basin immediately downstream from the Gatun locks, another for anchorage and room for turning of long ships near La Boca, and possibly another just below the Miraflores locks. These can all be delayed until the completion of the main work of canal excavation and lock building, and then executed by the dredges that have done the main work. The work can thus be done without additional equipment, and at a low price per cubic yard.

PRESENT CONDITION OF WORK

It has been suggested that we report upon the condition of the work and the progress being made, and, if found possible in the time at our disposal, upon the probable time of completion.

Organization.

We have seen the work under way on all parts of the canal. We have become acquainted with the engineers in responsible positions and have noted the organization and equipment.

It is our impression that the work is well organized and is being conducted energetically and well.

The work is done by day labor and not by the contract system.

The men are well paid, well housed, well fed and well cared for in case of sickness or accident. Houses, furniture, fuel, water, drainage and lights are furnished to employees without cost. Roads are built, schools supported and Young Men's Christian Association buildings provided, which are practically club buildings. Parts of the running expenses are also paid. The premises are cleared and drained and the grass kept cut. The climate is especially adapted to outdoor life, and the ample porches, entirely inclosed by bronze-wire screens, give the greatest facility for this. We are especially pleased with the architectural arrangements of the houses. They are admirably adapted to the climatic conditions.

Bachelor quarters and hotels furnishing meals at moderate prices are also provided by the Government.

Hospitals are provided, free medical attendance is furnished to employees and medical attendance at low rates is supplied to families of employees.

A limited amount of free transportation, namely, one excursion trip each month to any station, is furnished on the Panama Railroad to employees, and half rates are given in all other cases, and also half rates to families of employees. Free transportation in some cases, and in all other cases transportation at reduced rates to and from the Isthmus, is provided to employees and their families.

Six weeks' leave of absence each year, with full pay, is given to all monthly employees, and this includes not only office and engineering forces but also the mechanical forces on the monthly basis.

The medical and sanitary department is especially to be commended for its success in exterminating yellow fever and controlling malaria, and for other measures which have made the Isthmus a thoroughly healthful place in which to live.

The cost of the sanitary department, which represents the cost of keeping the Isthmus healthful, amounts to about $2,000,000 per year. This is a large sum, but the work is well done, and any decrease in the efficiency of the sanitary service might readily prove disastrous to the prosecution of the main work.

We believe that in no other great construction work has so much been done for employees in the way of furnishing necessities, comforts, and luxuries of life at the cost of the work as has been done in this case. This is one reason for the high cost of the canal.

Progress and time of completion

We have examined diagrams and statistics showing the amount of work accomplished by years and by months since the work was taken over by the United States, and showing the amounts of the various classes of work remaining to be done and the estimated rates of progress and times required for completion. It has been impossible for us to check these in detail, but we have compared them with other estimates, and with the work obviously done, and they seem reasonable to us. In the light of this showing, we see no reason why the canal should not be completed, as estimated by the chief engineer, by January 1, 1915; in fact, it seems that a somewhat earlier completion is probable if all goes well, but in view of possible contingencies it is not prudent at this time to count on an earlier date.

Cost of work.

In examining the expenditures thus far made it must be borne in mind that large sums have been paid for steamships, dredges, steam shovels, locomotives, cars, tracks, shops and all the equipment that is necessary to prosecute a work of this magnitude, and also that large sums have been spent for dwellings, offices, buildings of various kinds, for waterworks, sewers, paving and other equipment, and that these expenditures have been made, in large measure, for the whole work, and that corresponding disbursements hereafter will be very much less in proportion than they have been to date.

Colonel Goethals has presented to us an estimate of the quantities of materials and the cost involved in the construction of the canal as now planned, including all disbursements thus far made and the estimated amounts required for completion. These cover the greater width of excavation, the increased size of locks, the extra canal channel required by moving the Pacific locks from La Boca to Miraflores, the improved harbor arrangements at Colon, and all other changes which have been adopted or which are now seriously contemplated. The payments to the New Panama Canal Company are included, and also the payments to the Republic of Panama and the cost of sanitation and zone government, for which items the Board of Consulting Engineers of 1905 stated that it presented no estimates.

The estimates and allowances so made seem ample to us. In some items it would seem that considerable reductions could be made, but, on the other hand, the work is large and novel and unforeseen contingencies must be expected, so that it may be that the aggregate estimate as presented is not too large.

After deducting $15,000,000, representing the estimated receipts from the return of money loaned the Panama Railroad, and from the collection of water rates to cover the cost of municipal improvements made in Panama and Colon, and from miscellaneous sources, this present estimate of the complete cost of the lock canal amounts to $360,000,000.

In making this estimate no reduction has been made for whatever salvage may be realized from the construction plant at the termination of the work, which plant has cost to date about $30,000,000.

The cost of the canal, as estimated in 1905, is frequently stated to be $140,000,000, but this is incorrect, as the minority report expressly excluded sanitation and zone government, and the payments to Panama and the French company had already been made. Adding these amounts, using the present estimates of sanitation and zone government, we have in round numbers the following:

Estimate of the minority of the Board of Consulting Engineers for the cost of construction, exclusive of sanitation and zone government	$140,000,000
Payments made to the Republic of Panama and to the New Panama Canal Company	50,000,000
Sanitation and zone government, as now estimated	27,000,000
Total	**$217,000,000**

The difference between this cost and the total cost as now estimated is therefore $143,000,000. Of this amount nearly one-half can be accounted for by the changes in the canal and appurtenant works to which we have already referred, and the remainder is to be attributed mainly to the higher unit cost of the different items of the work, caused in part by the higher prices for plant, supplies and labor which have prevailed in the United States since the estimate of 1905 was made, and which made it necessary to offer very high wages and special inducements in order to obtain the requisite force in a locality where the reputation for health was not good in the earlier years, in part to the adoption of an eight-hour day for most of the work instead of a ten-hour day, in part to the much greater expenditure for housing and care of employees and for auxiliary works than was anticipated, and in part, in our opinion, to the evident purpose to make the estimates ample and to provide liberally for contingencies.

When the work at Panama is completed, in addition to having the canal, the United States will own the Panama Railroad and the steamship line operated in connection therewith.

TYPE OF CANAL.

In view of the fact that the cost of the lock canal, as now proposed, will largely overrun the estimate of the minority of the Board of Consulting Engineers of 1905, and that the excavation in the Culebra cut is being made somewhat more rapidly than was anticipated, we have considered in a very general way the relative cost and time of construction of a sea-level canal.

Most of the factors which have operated to increase the cost of the lock canal would operate with similar effect to increase the cost of the sea-level canal, and at the present time there are additional factors of even greater importance to be considered as affecting the time of completion and cost of a sea-level canal. One of these is to be found in the Gamboa dam, proposed to be nearly 200 feet in height above its foundations, which would be about 60 feet below the normal river level. Prior to the construction of this dam a long and deep diversion channel must be provided of far greater magnitude than that for the Gatun dam, which has been about two years in progress, and is not yet completed.

Judging by the time required for the construction of dams of similar magnitude in the United States, it is probable that were work on the Gamboa dam to be started as soon as possible this one feature of the sea-level project of the Board of Consulting Engineers of 1905 could not be completed until after the time required for the completion of the lock canal. The construction of this dam at Gamboa for the control of the Chagres is an essential preliminary to the excavation of the sea-level canal for the 13 miles from Bohio to Bas Obispo.

Furthermore, in addition to the Gamboa dam, the sea-level project provides for building for the control of tributary streams three large dams, the sites of which have not been examined.

Work is already far advanced on nearly all parts of the lock canal, and a change in the type would result in abandoning work done which represents large expenditure.

Under the plan now being carried out, the River Chagres and each of the other rivers on the Isthmus tributary thereto is made an ally of the project. The waters of these rivers are handled economically and in such a way as to facilitate the operation of the canal. With the sea-level project, these rivers instead of being allies would be enemies of the canal, and floods in them would greatly interfere with the work.

The excavation of the canal would be carried to 40 feet or more below sea level and to a much greater depth below the bottoms of the valleys in which the upper streams now flow.

It would further be necessary to cut long and large diversion channels on each side of the canal for streams entering the Chagres Valley. The cost of such lateral channels to protect the Culebra cut alone from the comparatively small streams formerly entering it, including work done by the French, has probably been not less than $2,000,000. The channels required for the lower valley of the Chagres would be necessarily much longer, larger and far more expensive.

ROCK EXCAVATION UNDER WATER.

Much has been said about the economy of excavating rock under water by modern appliances as compared with the cost of such excavation in the dry with steam shovels after blasting.

We concur in the opinion of those in charge of work at the Isthmus that it is more economical, where the conditions are favorable, to excavate rock in the dry than by any under-water process now in use. Experience is not yet available to us which will justify the belief that, with the depth of cut and the quality of rock found on the Isthmus, the general adoption of subaqueous methods would prove more expeditious or cheaper.

It is probable that more economical subaqueous methods will be sometime developed, but it would not be wise to base a change in plan of important work upon prospective results to be obtained by any method not yet thoroughly tried.

EARTHQUAKES.

It has been suggested that the canal region is liable to earthquake shocks and that a sea-level canal would be less subject to injury by earthquakes than a lock canal.

We have seen, in the city of Panama, the ruins of an old church, said to have been destroyed by fire, containing a long and extremely flat arch of great age, which convinces us that there has been no earthquake shock on the Isthmus during the one hundred and fifty years, more or less, that this structure has been in existence, that would have injured the work proposed.

Dams and locks are structures of great stability and little subject to damage by earthquake shocks. The successful resistance of the dams and reservoirs supplying San Francisco with water, even when those structures were located near the line of fault of the earthquake, gives confidence in the ability of well-designed masonry structures and earth embankments to resist earthquake shocks.

We do not regard such shocks as a source of serious damage to any type of canal at the Isthmus, but if they were so their effect upon the dams, locks and regulating works proposed for the sea-level canal would be much the same as upon similar structures of the lock canal. The Gamboa dam for controlling the floods of the Chagres in connection with the sea-level canal provides for a lake having an area of 29 square miles when full, and if this water were suddenly let loose into the sea-level canal it would seriously injure large portions thereof and wreck ships therein. A similar result would be reached if the other three dams of the sea-level canal retaining lakes, having an aggregate area of 10 square miles, were to be suddenly destroyed.

WATER SUPPLY.

We believe that the sufficiency of the water supply for a lock canal has never been seriously questioned. It is true that during the dry season the natural flow of the streams would not be sufficient to furnish the water required for numerous lockages. There would even be times when the natural flow would not suffice to make good the loss by evaporation from the surface of the water in Gatun Lake. During the rainy season there is a great excess of water which can be readily stored in Gatun Lake with its area of 163 square miles. It is proposed to fill this lake during the rainy season 2 feet above its normal level, and to draw it as needed during the dry season. It is computed that by drawing it 5 feet below normal level, which draft would leave 40 feet of water through Culebra cut, the supply in a dry year would be sufficient to serve from 30 to 40 lockages up and an equal number of lockages down daily. Each lockage might consist of a single large vessel, or a fleet of smaller vessels capable of being in the lock at one time, as is common at Sault Ste. Marie. For comparison the published record shows that an average of only 12 ships per day passed through the Suez Canal in 1907.

Ultimately, if needed for increased traffic, additional water may be held from wet seasons and made available in dry ones. This may be accomplished either by raising further the high-water level in Gatun Lake or by lowering the low-water level in the lake, this lowering being accompanied, if necessary, by the deepening of the canal, or storage may be provided by an entirely independent reservoir, for which there are excellent sites.

From our examinations in the neighborhood of Gatun dam, we can find no reason to apprehend important loss of water by seepage through the ridges surrounding the lake, while in our judgment the bed of the lake will be practically impervious to water.

The water supply in sight is so much greater than any need that can be reasonably anticipated that the best method of securing more water when the time of need arrives does not require to be considered now

CONCLUSIONS.

Your board is satisfied that the dams and locks, the lock gates, and all other engineering structures involved in the lock-canal project are feasible and safe, and that they can be depended upon to perform with certainty their respective functions.

We do not find any occasion for changing the type of canal that has been adopted.

A change to a sea-level plan at the present time would add greatly to the cost and time of construction, without compensating advantages, either in capacity of canal or safety of navigation, and hence would be a public misfortune.

We do find in the detailed designs that have been adopted, or that are under consideration, some matters where other arrangements than those now considered seem worthy of study. As these proposed changes are of a tentative nature and do not in any case affect the main questions herein discussed, they are not taken up in this report.

Very respectfully,

FREDERICK P. STEARNS.
ARTHUR P. DAVIS.
HENRY A. ALLEN.
JAMES D. SCHUYLER.
ISHAM RANDOLPH.
JOHN R. FREEMAN.
ALLEN HAZEN.

THE PRESIDENT.

SPECIAL MESSAGE.

WHITE HOUSE, January 8, 1906.

To the Senate and House of Representatives:

I inclose herewith the annual report of the Isthmian Canal Commission, the annual report of the Panama Railroad Company and the Secretary of War's letter transmitting the same, together with certain papers.

The work on the isthmus is being admirably done, and great progress has been made, especially during the last nine months. The plant is being made ready and the organization perfected. The first work to be done was the work of sanitation, the necessary preliminary to the work of actual construction; and this has been pushed forward with the utmost energy and means. In a short while I shall lay before you the recommendations of the commission and of the board of consulting engineers as to the proper plan to be adopted for the canal itself, together with my own recommendations thereon. All the work so far has been done, not only with the utmost expedition, but in the most careful and thorough manner, and what has been accomplished gives us good reason to believe that the canal will be dug in a shorter time than has been anticipated and at an expenditure within the estimated amount. All our citizens have a right to congratulate themselves upon the high standard of efficiency and integrity which has been hitherto maintained by the representatives of the government in doing this great work. If this high standard of efficiency and integrity can be maintained in the future at the same level which it has now reached, the construction of the Panama canal will be one of the feats to which the people of this republic will look back with the highest pride.

From time to time various publications have been made, and from time to time in the future various similar publications doubtless will be made, purporting to give an account of jobbery, or immorality, or inefficiency, or misery, as obtaining on the isthmus. I have carefully examined into each of these accusations which seemed worthy of attention. In every instance the accusations have proved to be without foundation in any shape or form. They spring from several sources. Sometimes they take the shape of statements by irresponsible investigators of a sensational habit of mind, incapable of observing or repeating with accuracy what they see, and desirous of obtaining notoriety by widespread slander. More often they originate with, or are given currency by, individuals with a personal grievance. The sensation-mongers, both those who stay at home and those who visit the isthmus, may ground their accusations on false statements by some engineer, who having applied for service on the commission and been refused such service, now endeavors to discredit his successful competitors; or by some lessee or owner of real estate who has sought action, or inaction by the commission to increase the value of his lots, and is bitter because the commission cannot be used for such purposes; or on the tales of disappointed bidders for contracts; or of office holders who have proved incompetent or who have been suspected of corruption and dismissed, or who have been overcome by panic and have fled from the isthmus. Every specific charge relating to jobbery, to immorality or to inefficiency, from whatever source it has come, has been immediately investigated, and in no single instance have the statements of these sensation-mongers and the interested complainants behind them proved true. The only discredit inhering in these false accusations is to those who originate and give them currency, and who, to the extent of their abilities, thereby hamper and obstruct the completion of the great work in which both the honor and the interest of America are so deeply involved. It matters not whether those guilty of these false accusations utter them in mere wanton recklessness and folly or in spirit of sinister malice to gratify some personal or political grudge.

Any attempt to cut down the salaries of the officials of the Isthmian Commission or of their subordinates who are doing important work would be ruinous from the standpoint of accomplishing the work effectively. To quote the words of one of the best observers on the isthmus: "Demoralization of the service is certain if the reward for successful endeavor is a reduction of pay." We are undertaking in Panama a gigantic task—the largest piece of engineering ever done. The employment of the men engaged thereon is only temporary, and yet it will require the highest order of ability if it is to be done economically, honestly and efficiently. To attempt to secure men to do this work on insufficient salaries would amount to putting a premium upon inefficiency and corruption. Men fit for the work will not undertake it unless they are well paid. In the end the men who do undertake it will be left to seek other employment with, as their chief reward, the reputations they achieve. Their work is infinitely more difficult than any private work, both because of the peculiar conditions of the tropical land in which it is laid and because it is impossible to free them from the peculiar limitations inseparably connected with government employment; while it is unfortunately true that men engaged in public work, no matter how devoted and disinterested their services, must expect to be made the objects of misrepresentation and attack. At best, therefore, the positions are not attractive in proportion to their importance, and among the men fit to do the task only those with a genuine sense of public spirit and eager to do the great work for the work's sake can be obtained, and such men cannot be kept if they are to be treated with niggardliness and parsimony, in addition to the certainty that false accusations will continually be brought against them.

I repeat that the work on the isthmus has been done and is being done admirably. The organization is good. The mistakes are extraordinarily few, and these few have been of practically no consequence. The zeal, intelligence and efficient public service of the Isthmian Commission and its subordinates have been noteworthy. I court the fullest, most exhaustive and most searching investigation of any act of theirs, and if any one of them is ever shown to have done wrong his punishment shall be exemplary. But I ask that they be decently paid and that their hands be upheld as long as they act decently. On any other conditions we shall not be able to get men of the right type to do the work, and this means that on any other condition we shall insure, if not failure, at least delay, scandal and inefficiency in the task of digging the giant canal.

THEODORE ROOSEVELT.

By the President of the United States.

A PROCLAMATION.

Whereas, the government of Germany has taken action, extending, on and after March 1, 1906, and until June 30, 1907, or until further notice, the benefit of the German conventional customs tariff to the products of the soil or industry of the United States, by which action, in the judgment of the President, reciprocal concessions are established in favor of the said products of the United States;

Now, therefore, be it known that I, Theodore Roosevelt, President of the United States of America, acting under the authority conferred by the third section of the tariff act of the United States, approved July 24, 1897, do hereby suspend, during the continuance in force of the said concessions by the government of Germany, the imposition and collection of the duties imposed by the first section of said act upon the articles hereinafter specified, being the products of the soil or industry of Germany; and do declare in place thereof the following rates of duty provided in the third section of said act to be in force and effect on and after March 1, 1906, of which the officers and citizens of the United States will take notice, namely:

Upon argols, or crude tartar, or wine lees, crude, 5 per centum ad valorem.

Upon brandies or other spirits manufactured or distilled from grain or other materials, $1.75 per proof gallon.

Upon still wines and vermuth, in casks, 35 cents per gallon; in bottles or jugs, per case of one dozen bottles or jugs containing each not more than one quart and more than one pint, or twenty-four bottles or jugs containing each not more than one pint, $1.25 per case, and any excess beyond these quantities found in such bottles or jugs shall be subject to a duty of 4 cents per pint or fractional part thereof, but no separate or additional duty shall be assessed upon the bottles or jugs.

Upon paintings in oil or water colors, pastels, pen-and-ink drawings, and statuary, 15 per centum ad valorem.

In testimony whereof, I have hereunto set my hand and caused the seal of the United States to be affixed.

Done at the city of Washington this twenty-seventh day of February, 1906, and of the independence of the United States of
[SEAL.] America the one hundred and thirtieth.

THEODORE ROOSEVELT.

By the President:
ELIHU ROOT,
Secretary of State.

SPECIAL MESSAGE.

THE WHITE HOUSE, March 5, 1906.

To the Senate and House of Representatives:

Our coast defenses, as they existed in 1860, were not surpassed in efficiency by those of any country, but within a few years the introduction of rifled cannon and armor in the navies of the world, against which the smooth-bore guns were practically useless, rendered them obsolete. For many years no attempt was made to remedy the deficiencies of these seacoast fortifications. There was no establishment in the country equipped for the manufacture of high-power rifled guns, there was no definite adopted policy of coast defense, and Congress was reluctant to undertake a work the cost of which could not be stated, even approximately, and the details of which had not advanced—so far as could be ascertained—beyond the experimental stages.

The act of March 3, 1883, was the first decisive step taken to secure suitable and adequate ordnance for military purposes. Under the provisions of this act a joint board of officers of the army and navy was appointed " for the purpose of examining and reporting to Congress which of the navy yards or arsenals owned by the government has the best location and is best adapted for the establishment of a government foundry or what other method, if any, should be adopted for the manufacture of heavy ordnance adapted to modern warfare for the use of the army and navy of the United States."

This board, known as the " gun foundry board," made its report in 1884, and directed public attention not only to the defenseless condition of our coasts, but to the importance and necessity of formulating a comprehensive scheme for the protection of our harbors and coast cities.

As a result, the act of Congress, approved March 3, 1885, provided that " the President of the United States shall appoint a board, * * which board shall examine and report at what ports fortifications or other defenses are most urgently required, the character and kind of defenses best adapted to each, with reference to armament, the utilization of torpedoes, mines, and other defensive appliances."

The board organized under the foregoing provision of law, popularly known as the " Endicott board," in its report of January 23, 1886, cited the principles on which any system of coast defense should be based, and clearly stated the necessity of having our important strategic and commercial centers made secure against naval attack. In determining the ports that were in urgent need of defense, since a fleet did not exist for the protection of the merchant marine, fortifications were

provided at every harbor of importance along the coast and at several
of the Lake ports.

For any particular harbor or locality the report specifies the armament considered necessary for proper protection, the character of
emplacements to be used, the number of submarine mines and torpedo
boats, with detailed estimates of cost for these various items. The
proposed guns, mounts, and emplacements were of types that seemed
at that time best suited to accomplish the desired results, based on the
only data available, namely, experiments and information of similar
work from abroad.

Since this report was made part of the public records, the development and adoption of a suitable disappearing gun carriage caused the
substitution of open emplacements for the expensive turrets and
armored casemates, materially reducing the cost of installing the
armament; the great advances in ordnance, increasing the power and
range of the later guns, caused a diminution in the number and caliber
of the pieces to be mounted, and this fact, combined with advances
in the science of engineering, rendered unnecessary the construction
of the expensive "floating batteries" designed by the Endicott board
for mounting guns to give sufficient fire for the defense of wide channels, or for harbors where suitable foundations could not be secured
on land.

Furthermore, keeping pace with the gradual development and improvement in the engines and implements of war, fortified harbors are
equipped with rapid-fire guns, and, to a certain extent, with power
plants, searchlights, and a system of fire control and direction now
essential adjuncts of a complete system of defense, though not so considered by that board.

While the details of the scheme of defense recommended by the
Endicott board have been departed from in making provision for later
developments of war material, the great value of its report lies in the
fact that it sets forth a definite and intelligible plan or policy, upon
which the very important work of coast defense should proceed, and
which is as applicable to-day as when formulated.

The greater effective ranges possible with the later rifled cannon, the
necessity of thoroughly covering with gun-fire all available waters of
approach and the growth of seacoast towns beyond the limits of some
of the military reservations have combined to move defensive works
more to the front, and many of the gun positions now occupied have
been obtained from private ownership. The cost of such sites has
been a large item in the present cost of fortifications, and this purchase
of land was not included in its estimates by the Endicott board.

An examination of the report also discloses the fact that no estimates were submitted covering a supply of ammunition to be kept
in reserve for the service of the guns that were recommended, due

perhaps to the fact that a satisfactory powder to give the energy desired and a suitable projectile to accomplish the desired destruction of armor were still in experimental stages. These questions, however, are no longer in doubt, and Congress already has made provision for some of the ammunition needed.

The omissions in the estimates of the Endicott board and the changes in the details of its plans have caused doubts in the minds of many as to the money that will be needed to defend completely our coasts by guns, mines, and their adjuncts. New localities are pressing their claims for defense. The insular possessions cannot be held unless the principal ports, naval bases, and coaling stations are fortified before the outbreak of war.

These considerations have led me to appoint a joint board of officers of the army and navy " to recommend the armament, fixed and floating, mobile torpedoes, submarine mines, and all other defensive appliances that may be necessary to complete the harbor defense with the most economical and advantageous expenditures of money." The board was further instructed " to extend its examinations so as to include estimates and recommendations relative to defenses of the insular possessions," and to " recommend the order in which the proposed defense shall be completed, so that all the elements of harbor defense may be properly and effectively co-ordinated."

The board has completed its labors and its report, together with a letter of transmittal by the Secretary of War, is herewith transmitted for the information of the Congress. It is to be noted that the entrance to Chesapeake Bay, not heretofore recommended or authorized by Congress, is added to the list of ports in the United States to be defended, with the important reasons therefor clearly stated: that the gun defense proper is well advanced toward completion, and that the greater part of the estimate is for new work of gun defense, for the accessories now so necessary for efficiency, and for an allowance of ammunition, which, added to that already on hand, will give the minimum supply that should be kept in reserve to successfully meet any sudden attack.

The letter of the Secretary of War contains a comparison of the estimates of the Endicott board, with the amounts already appropriated for the present defense and the estimates of the new board, from which it appears that a completed defense of our coasts, omitting cost of ammunition and sites, can be accomplished for less that the amount estimated by the Endicott board, even including the additional localities not recommended by it.

In the insular possessions the great naval bases at Guantanamo, Subig Bay, and Pearl Harbor, the coaling stations at Guam and San Juan require protection, and, in addition, defenses are recommended for Manila Bay and Honolulu, because of the strategic importance of these localities. In the letter of the Secretary of War will be found the sums already appropriated for defenses at some of these ports or harbors, and the estimates are for the completion of an adequate defense at each locality.

Defenses are recommended for the entrances to the Panama Canal, as contemplated by the act of June 28, 1902 (Spooner act), and under the terms of this act the cost of such fortifications would probably be paid from appropriations for the construction and defense of the canal.

The necessity for a complete and adequate system of coast defense is greater to-day than twenty years ago, for the increased wealth of the country offers more tempting inducements to attack, and a hostile fleet can reach our coast in a much shorter period of time.

The fact that we now have a navy does not in any wise diminish the importance of coast defenses; on the contrary, that fact emphasizes their value and the necessity for their construction. It is an accepted naval maxim that a navy can be used to strategic advantage only when acting on the offensive, and it can be free to so operate only after our coast defense is reasonably secure and so recognized by the country.

It was due to the securely defended condition of the Japanese ports that the Japanese fleet was free to seek out and watch its proper objective—the Russian fleet—without fear of interruption or recall to guard its home ports against raids by the Vladivostok squadron. This, one of the most valuable lessons of the late war in the East, is worthy of serious consideration by our country, with its extensive coast line, its many important harbors, and its many wealthy manufacturing coast cities.

The security and protection of our interests require the completion of the defenses of our coast, and the accompanying plan merits and should receive the generous support of the Congress.

THEODORE ROOSEVELT.

SPECIAL MESSAGE.

THE WHITE HOUSE, March 7, 1906.

To the Senate and House of Representatives:

I have signed the Joint Resolution " Instructing the Interstate Commerce Commission to make examinations into the subject of railroad discriminations and monopolies in coal and oil, and report on the same from time to time." I have signed it with hesitation because in the form in which is was passed it achieves very little and may achieve nothing; and it is highly undesirable that a resolution of this kind shall become law in such form as to give the impression of insincerity; that is of pretending to do something which really is not done. But after much hesitation I concluded to sign the resolution because its defects can be remedied by legislation which I hereby ask for; and it must be understood that unless this subsequent legislation is granted the present resolution must be mainly, and may be entirely, inoperative.

Before specifying what this legislation is I wish to call attention to one or two preliminary facts. In the first place, a part of the investigation requested by the House of Representatives in the Resolution adopted February 15, 1905, relating to the Oil Industry, and a further part having to do with the Anthracite Coal Industry, has been for some time under investigation by the Department of Commerce and Labor. These investigations, I am informed, are approaching completion, and before Congress adjourns I shall submit to you the preliminary reports of these investigations. Until these reports are completed the Interstate Commerce Commission could not endeavor to carry out so much of the resolution of Congress as refers to the ground thus already covered without running the risk of seeing the two investigations conflict and therefore render each other more or less nugatory. In the second place, I call your attention to the fact that if an investigation of the nature proposed in this joint resolution is thoroughly and effectively conducted, it will result in giving immunity from criminal prosecution to all persons who are called, sworn and constrained by compulsory process of law to testify as witnesses; though of course such immunity from prosecution is not given to those from whom statements or information, merely, in contradistinction to sworn testimony, is obtained. This is not at all to say that such investigations should not be undertaken. Publicity can by itself often accomplish extraordinary results for good; and the court of public judgment may secure such results where the courts of law are powerless. There are many cases where an investigation securing complete publicity about abuses and giving Congress the material on which to proceed in the enactment of laws, is more useful than a criminal prosecution can possibly be. But it should not be provided for by law without a clear understanding that it may be an alternative instead of an additional remedy; that is, that to carry on the investigation may serve as a bar to the successful prosecution of the offenses disclosed. The official body directed by Congress to make the investigation must, of course, carry out its direction, and therefore the direction should not be given without full appreciation of what it means.

But the direction contained in the Joint Resolution which I have signed will remain almost inoperative unless money is provided to carry out the investigations in question, and unless the Commission in carrying them out is authorized to administer oaths and compel the attendance of witnesses. As the resolution now is, the Commission, which is very busy with its legitimate work and which has no extra money at its disposal, would be able to make the investigation only in the most partial and unsatisfactory manner; and moreover it is questionable whether it could, under this resolution, administer oaths at all or compel the attendance of witnesses. If this power were disputed by the parties investigated the investigation would be held up for a year or two until the courts passed upon it, in which case, during the period of waiting, the Commission could only investigate to the extent and in the manner already provided under its organic law; so that the passage of the resolution would have achieved no good result whatever.

I accordingly recommend to Congress the serious consideration of just what they wish the Commission to do, and how far they wish it to go, having in view the possible incompatibility of conducting an investigation like this and of also proceeding criminally in a court of law; and furthermore, that a sufficient sum, say fifty thousand dollars, be at once added to the current appropriation for the Commission so as to enable them to do the work indicated in a thorough and complete manner; while at the same time the power is explicitly conferred upon them to administer oaths and compel the attendance of witnesses in making the investigation in question, which covers work quite apart from their usual duties. It seems unwise to require an investigation by a commission and then not to furnish either the full legal power or the money, both of which are necessary to render the investigation effective.

THEODORE ROOSEVELT.

SPECIAL MESSAGE.

THE WHITE HOUSE, March 27, 1906.

To the Senate and House of Representatives:

I submit to you herewith the report of the American members of the International Waterways Commission regarding the preservation of Niagara Falls. I also submit to you certain letters from the Secretary of State and the Secretary of War, including memoranda showing what has been attempted by the Department of State in the effort to secure the preservation of the falls by treaty.

I earnestly recommend that Congress enact into law the suggestions of the American members of the International Waterways Commission for the preservation of Niagara Falls, without waiting for the negotiation of a treaty. The law can be put in such form that it will lapse, say in three years, provided that during that time no international agreement has been reached. But in any event I hope that this Nation will make it evident that it is doing all in its power to preserve the great scenic wonder, the existence of which, unharmed, should be a matter of pride to every dweller on this continent.

THEODORE ROOSEVELT

SPECIAL MESSAGE.

THE WHITE HOUSE, April 17, 1906.

To the Senate and House of Representatives:

I herewith transmit the report and recommendations, with accompanying papers, of the Insurance Convention which met in February last at Chicago. The convention was called because of the extraordinary disclosures of wrongful insurance methods recently made by the Armstrong legislative committee of the State of New York; the suggestion that it should be called coming to me originally from Governor John A. Johnson, of Minnesota, through Commissioner of Insurance Thomas D. O'Brien, of that State. The convention consisted of about one hundred governors, attorneys-general and commissioners of insurance of the States and Territories of the Union. The convention was seeking to accomplish uniformity of insurance legislation throughout the States and Territories, and as a prime step toward this purpose decided to endeavor to secure the enactment by the Congress of the United States of a proper insurance code for the District of Columbia, which might serve as a model for the several States. Before adjourning, the convention appointed a committee of three attorneys-general and twelve commissioners of insurance of the various States to prepare and have presented to the Congress a bill which should embody the features suggested by the convention. The committee recently met in Chicago, and in thorough and painstaking fashion sought to prepare a bill which should be at once protective of policy holders and fair and just to insurance companies, and which should prevent the graver evils and abuses of the business, and at the same time forestall any wild or drastic legislation which would be more harmful than beneficial. The proposed bill is discussed at length in the accompanying letter by Superintendent Thomas E. Drake, of the Department of Insurance, in the District of Columbia.

I very earnestly hope that the Congress at the earliest opportunity will enact this bill into law, with such changes as its wisdom may dictate. I have no expert familiarity with the business, but I have entire faith in the right judgment and single-minded purpose of the insurance convention which met at Chicago, and of the committee of that convention, which formulated the measure herein advocated. We are not to be pardoned it we fail to take every step in our power to prevent the possibility of the repetition of such scandals as those that have occurred in connection with the insurance business as disclosed by the Armstrong committee.

THEODORE ROOSEVELT.

SPECIAL MESSAGE.

THE WHITE HOUSE, April 18, 1906.

To the Senate and House of Representatives:

I submit herewith a letter of the Attorney-General, enclosing a statement of the proceedings by the United States against the individuals and corporations commonly known as the "Beef Packers," and commenting upon the decision of District Judge Humphrey. The result has been a miscarriage of justice. It clearly appears from the letter of the Attorney-General that no criticism whatever attaches to Commissioner Garfield, what he did was in strict accordance with the law and in pursuance of a duty imposed on him by Congress, which could not be avoided; and of course Congress in passing the Martin resolution could not possibly have foreseen the decision of Judge Humphrey.

But this interpretation by Judge Humphrey of the will of the Congress, as expressed in legislation, is such as to make that will absolutely abortive. Unfortunately there is grave doubt whether the Government has the right of appeal from this decision of the District Judge. The case well illustrates the desirability of conferring upon the Government the same right of appeal in criminal cases, on questions of law, which the defendant now has, in all cases where the defendant had not been put in jeopardy by a trial upon the merits of the charge made against him. The laws of many of the States, and the law of the District of Columbia, recently enacted by the Congress, give the Government the right of appeal. A general law of the character indicated should certainly be enacted.

Furthermore it is very desirable to enact a law declaring the true construction of the existing legislation so far as it affects immunity. I can hardly believe that the ruling of Judge Humphrey will be followed by other judges; but if it should be followed, the result would be either completely to nullify very much, and possibly the major part, of the good to be obtained from the interstate commerce law and from the law creating the Bureau of Corporations in the Department of Commerce and Labor; or else frequently to obstruct an appeal to the criminal laws by the Department of Justice. There seems to be no good reason why the Department of Justice, the Department of Commerce and Labor, and the Interstate Commerce Commission, each, should not, for the common good, proceed within its own powers without undue interference with the functions of the other. It is of course necessary, under the Constitution and the laws, that persons who give testimony or produce evidence, as witnesses, should receive immunity from prosecution. It has hitherto been supposed that the immunity conferred by existing laws was only upon persons who, being subpoenaed, had given testimony or produced evidence, as witnesses, relating to any offense with which they were, or might be, charged. But

Judge Humphrey's decision is, in effect, that, if either the Commissioner of Corporations does his duty, or the Interstate Commerce Commission does its, by making the investigations which they by law are required to make, though they issue no subpoena and receive no testimony or evidence, within the proper meaning of these words, the very fact of the investigation may, of itself, operate to prevent the prosecution of any offender for any offense which may have been developed in even the most indirect manner during the course of the investigation, or even for any offense which may have been detected by investigations conducted by the Department of Justice entirely independently of the labors of the Interstate Commerce Commission or of the Commissioner of Corporations,—the only condition of immunity being that the offender should have given, or directed to be given, information which related to the subject out of which the offense has grown.

In offenses of this kind it is at the best hard enough to execute justice upon offenders. Our system of criminal jurisprudence has descended to us from a period when the danger was lest the accused should not have his rights adequately preserved, and it is admirably framed to meet this danger. But at present the danger is just the reverse; that is, the danger nowadays is, not that the innocent man will be convicted of crime, but that the guilty man will go scot-free. This is especially the case where the crime is one of greed and cunning perpetrated by a man of wealth in the course of those business operations where the code of conduct is at variance, not merely with the code of humanity and morality, but with the code as established in the law of the land. It is much easier, but much less effective, to proceed against a corporation, than to proceed against the individuals in that corporation who are themselves responsible for the wrongdoing. Very naturally outside persons who have no knowledge of the facts, and no responsibility for the success of the proceedings, are apt to clamor for action against the individuals. The Department of Justice has, most wisely, invariably refused thus to proceed against individuals, unless it was convinced both that they were in fact guilty and that there was at least a reasonable chance of establishing this fact of their guilt. These beef packing cases offered one of the very few instances where there was not only the moral certainty that the accused men were guilty, but what seemed—and now seems—sufficient legal evidence of the fact.

But in obedience to the explicit order of the Congress the Commissioner of Corporations had investigated the Beef Packing business. The counsel for the beef packers explicitly admitted that there was no claim that any promise of immunity had been given by Mr. Garfield, as shown by the following colloquy during the argument of the Attorney-General:

"Mr. Moody. * * * * I dismiss almost with a word the claim

that Mr. Garfield promised immunity. Whether there is any evidence of such a promise or not, I do not know, and I do not care.

" Mr. Miller (the counsel for the beef packers). There is no claim of it.

" Mr. Moody. Then I was mistaken, and I will not even say that word."

But Judge Humphrey holds that if the Commissioner of Corporations (and therefore if the Interstate Commerce Commission) in the course of any investigations prescribed by Congress, asks any questions of a person, not called as a witness, or asks any questions of an officer of a corporation, not called as a witness, with regard to the action of the corporation on a subject out of which prosecutions may subsequently arise, then the fact of such questions having been asked operates as a bar to the prosecution of that person or of that officer of the corporation for his own misdeeds.

Such interpretation of the law comes measurably near making the law a farce; and I therefore recommend that the Congress pass a declaratory act stating its real intention.

THEODORE ROOSEVELT.

SPECIAL MESSAGE.

THE WHITE HOUSE, May 4, 1906

To the Senate and House of Representatives:

I transmit herewith a report by the Commissioner of the Bureau of Corporations in the Department of Commerce and Labor on the subject of transportation and freight rates in connection with the oil industry. The investigation, the results of part of which are summarized in this report, was undertaken in accordance with House Resolution 499, passed February 15, 1905, but for the reasons given in the report it has been more general and extensive than was called for in the resolution itself.

I call your especial attention to the letter of transmittal accompanying and summarizing the report; for the report is of capital importance in view of the effort now being made to secure such enlargement of the powers of the Interstate Commerce Commission as will confer upon the Commission power in some measure adequately to meet the clearly demonstrated needs of the situation. The facts set forth in this report are for the most part not disputed. It is only the inferences from them that are disputed, and even in this respect the dispute is practically limited to the question as to whether the transactions are or are not technically legal. The report shows that the Standard Oil Company has benefited enormously up almost to the present moment by secret rates, many of these secret rates being clearly unlawful. This benefit amounts to at least three-quarters of a million a year. This three-quarters of a million represents the profit that the Standard Oil Company obtains at the expense of the railroads; but of course the ultimate result is that it obtains a much larger profit at the expense of the public. A very striking result of the investigation has been that shortly after the discovery of these secret rates by the Commissioner of Corporations, the major portion of them were promptly corrected by the railroads, so that most of them have now been done away with. This immediate correction, partial or complete, of the evil of the secret rates is of course on the one hand an acknowledgment that they were wrong, and yet were persevered in until exposed; and on the other hand a proof of the efficiency of the work that has been done by the Bureau of Corporations. The Department of Justice will take up the question of instituting prosecutions in at least certain of the cases. But it is most desirable to enact into law the bill introduced by Senator Knox to correct the interpretation of the immunity provision rendered in Judge Humphrey's decision. The hands of the Government have been greatly strengthened in securing an effective remedy by the recent decision of the Supreme Court in the case instituted by the Government against the tobacco trust, which decision permits the Government to examine the books and records of any corporation engaged in interstate commerce; and by the recent conviction and punishment of the Chicago, Burlington and Quincy Railroad and certain of its officers.

But in addition to these secret rates the Standard Oil profits immensely by open rates, which are so arranged as to give it an overwhelming advantage over its independent competitors. The refusal of the railroads in certain cases to prorate produces analogous effects. Thus in New England the refusal of certain railway systems to prorate has resulted in keeping the Standard Oil in absolute monopolistic control of the field, enabling it to charge from three to four hundred thousand dollars a year more to the consumers of oil in New England than they would have had to pay had the price paid been that obtaining in the competitive fields. This is a characteristic example of the numerous evils which are inevitable under a system in which the big shipper and the railroad are left free to crush out all individual initiative and all power of independent action because of the absence of adequate and thorough-going governmental control. Exactly similar conditions obtain in a large part of the West and Southwest. This particular instance exemplifies the fact that the granting to the Government of the power to substitute a proper for an improper rate is in very many instances the only effective way in which to prevent improper discriminations in rates.

It is not possible to put into figures the exact amount by which the Standard profits through the gross favoritism shown it by the railroads in connection with the open rates. The profit of course comes not merely by the saving in the rate itself as compared with its competitors, but by the higher prices it is able to charge, and (even without reference to these higher prices) by the complete control of the market which it secures, thereby getting the profit on the whole consumption. Here again the only way by which the discriminations can be cured is by conferring upon the Interstate Commerce Commission the power to take quick and effective action in regulating the rates.

One feature of the report which is especially worthy of attention is the showing made as to the way in which the law is evaded by treating as State commerce what is in reality merely a part of interstate commerce. It is clearly shown, for instance, that this device is employed on the New York Central Railroad, as well as on many other railroads, in such fashion as to amount to thwarting the purpose of the law, although the forms of the law may be complied with.

It is unfortunately not true that the Standard Oil Company is the only great corporation which in the immediate past has benefited, and is at this moment benefiting, in wholly improper fashion by an elaborate series of rate discriminations, which permit it to profit both at the expense of its rivals and of the general public. The Attorney-General reports to me that the investigation now going on as to the shipments by the sugar trust over the trunk lines running out of New York City tends to show that the sugar trust rarely if ever pays the lawful rate for transportation, and is thus improperly, and probably unlawfully, favored at the expense of its competitors and of the general public.

The argument is sometimes advanced against conferring upon some governmental body the power of supervision and control over interstate commerce, that to do so tends to weaken individual initiative. Investigations such as this conclusively disprove any such allegation. On the contrary, the proper play for individual initiative can only be secured by such governmental supervision as will curb those monopolies which crush out all individual initiative. The railroad itself can not without such Government aid protect the interests of its own stockholders as against one of these great corporations loosely known as trusts.

In the effort to prevent the railroads from uniting for improper purposes we have very unwisely prohibited them from uniting for proper purposes; that is, for purposes of protection to themselves and to the general public as against the power of the great corporations. They should certainly be given power thus to unite on conditions laid down by Congress, such conditions to include the specific approval of the Interstate Commerce Commission of any agreement to which the railroads may come. In addition to this the Government must interfere through its agents to deprive the railroad of the ability to make to the big corporations the concessions which otherwise it is powerless to refuse.

The Government should have power by its agents to examine into the conduct of the railways—that is, the examiners under the direction of the Interstate Commerce Commission should be able to examine as thoroughly into the affairs of the railroad as bank examiners now examine into the affairs of banks.

It is impossible to work a material improvement in conditions such as above described merely through the instrumentality of a law suit. A law suit is often a necessary method; but by itself it is an utterly inadequate method. What is needed is the conferring upon the Commission of ample affirmative power, so conferred as to make its decisions take effect at once, subject only to such action by the court as is demanded by the Constitution. The courts have the power to, and will undoubtedly, interfere if the action of the Commission should become in effect confiscatory of the property of an individual or corporation, or if the Commission should undertake to do anything beyond the authority conferred upon it by the law under which it is acting. I am well aware that within the limits thus set the Commission may at times be guilty of injustice; but far grosser and far more frequent injustice, and injustice of a much more injurious kind, now results and must always result from the failure to give the Commission ample power to act promptly and effectively within these broad limits.

Though not bearing upon the question of railroad rates, there are two measures, consideration of which is imperatively suggested by the submission of this report. The Standard Oil Company has, largely by unfair or unlawful methods, crushed out home competition. It is highly desirable that an element of competition should be introduced by the passage of some such law as that which has already passed the House, putting alcohol used in the arts and manufactures upon the free list. Furthermore, the time has come when no oil or coal lands held by the Government, either upon the public domain proper or in territory owned by the Indian tribes, should be alienated. The fee to such lands should be kept in the United States Government whether or not the profits arising from it are to be given to any Indian tribe, and the lands should be leased only on such terms and for such periods as will enable the Government to keep entire control thereof.

                                    THEODORE ROOSEVELT.

SPECIAL MESSAGE.

THE WHITE HOUSE, June 4, 1906.

To the Senate and House of Representatives:

I transmit herewith the report of Mr. James Bronson Reynolds and Commissioner Charles P. Neill, the special committee whom I appointed to investigate into the conditions in the stock yards of Chicago and report thereon to me. This report is of a preliminary nature. I submit it to you now because it shows the urgent need of immediate action by the Congress in the direction of providing a drastic and thoroughgoing inspection by the Federal government of all stockyards and packing houses and of their products, so far as the latter enter into interstate or foreign commerce. The conditions shown by even this short inspection to exist in the Chicago stock yards are revolting. It is imperatively necessary in the interest of health and of decency that they should be radically changed. Under the existing law it is wholly impossible to secure satisfactory results.

When my attention was first directed to this matter an investigation was made under the Bureau of Animal Industry of the Department of Agriculture. When the preliminary statements of this investigation were brought to my attention they showed such defects in the law and such wholly unexpected conditions that I deemed it best to have a further immediate investigation by men not connected with the bureau, and accordingly appointed Messrs. Reynolds and Neill. It was impossible under existing law that satisfactory work should be done by the Bureau of Animal Industry. I am now, however, examining the way in which the work actually was done.

Before I had received the report of Messrs. Reynolds and Neill I had directed that labels placed upon any package of meat food products should state only that the carcass of the animal from which the meat was taken had been inspected at the time of slaughter. If inspection of meat food products at all stages of preparation is not secured by the passage of the legislation recommended I shall feel compelled to order that inspection labels and certificates on canned products shall not be used hereafter.

The report shows that the stock yards and packing houses are not kept even reasonably clean, and that the method of handling and preparing food products is uncleanly and dangerous to health. Under existing law the National Government has no power to enforce inspection of the many forms of prepared meat food products that are daily going from the packing houses into interstate commerce. Owing to an inadequate appropriation the Department of Agriculture is not even able to place inspectors in all establishments desiring them. The present law prohibits the shipment of uninspected meat to foreign countries, but there is no provision forbidding the shipment of uninspected meats in interstate commerce, and thus the avenues of interstate commerce are left open to traffic in diseased or spoiled meats.

If, as has been alleged on seemingly good authority, further evils exist, such as the improper use of chemicals and dyes, the Government lacks power to remedy them.

A law is needed which will enable the inspectors of the general Government to inspect and supervise from the hoof to the can the preparation of the meat food product. The evil seems to be much less in the sale of dressed carcases than in the sale of canned and other prepared products; and very much less as regards products sent abroad than as regards those used at home.

In my judgment the expense of the inspection should be paid by a fee levied on each animal slaughtered. If this is not done, the whole purpose of the law can at any time be defeated through an insufficient appropriation; and whenever there was no particular public interest in the subject it would be not only easy, but natural thus to make the appropriation insufficient. If it were not for this consideration I should favor the government paying for the inspection.

The alarm expressed in certain quarters concerning this feature should be allayed by a realization of the fact that in no case, under such a law, will the cost of inspection exceed 8 cents per head.

I call special attention to the fact that this report is preliminary, and that the investigation is still unfinished. It is not yet possible to report on the alleged abuses in the use of deleterious chemical compounds in connection with canning and preserving meat products, nor on the alleged doctoring in this fashion of tainted meat and of products returned to the packers as having grown unsalable or unusable from age or from other reasons. Grave allegations are made in reference to abuses of this nature.

Let me repeat that under the present law there is practically no method of stopping these abuses if they should be discovered to exist. Legislation is needed in order to prevent the possibility of all abuses in the future. If no legislation is passed, then the excellent results accomplished by the work of this special commtitee will endure only so long as the memory of the committee's work is fresh, and a recrudescence of the abuses is absolutely certain.

I urge the immediate enactment into law of provisions which will enable the Department of Agriculture adequately to inspect the meat and meat-food products entering into interstate commerce and to supervise the methods of preparing the same, and to prescribe the sanitary conditions under which the work shall be performed. I therefore commend to your favorable consideration, and urge the enactment of substantially the provisions known as Senate amendment No. 29 to the act making appropriations for the Department of Agriculture for the fiscal year ending June 30, 1907, as passed by the Senate, this amendment being commonly known as the "Beveridge amendment."

THEODORE ROOSEVELT.

SPECIAL MESSAGE.

THE WHITE HOUSE, December 11, 1906.

To the Senate and House of Representatives:

On November 21st I visited the island of Porto Rico, landing at Ponce, crossing by the old Spanish road by Cayey to San Juan, and returning next morning over the new American road from Arecibo to Ponce; the scenery was wonderfully beautiful, especially among the mountains of the interior, which constitute a veritable tropic Switzerland. I could not embark at San Juan because the harbor has not been dredged out and cannot receive an American battleship. I do not think this fact creditable to us as a nation, and I earnestly hope that immediate provision will be made for dredging San Juan harbor.

I doubt whether our people as a whole realize the beauty and fertility of Porto Rico, and the progress that has been made under its admirable government. We have just cause for pride in the character of our representatives who have administered the tropic islands which came under our flag as a result of the war with Spain; and of no one of them is this more true than of Porto Rico. It would be impossible to wish a more faithful, a more efficient and a more disinterested public service than that now being rendered in the island of Porto Rico by those in control of the insular government.

I stopped at a dozen towns, all told, and one of the notable features in every town was the gathering of the school children. The work that has been done in Porto Rico for education has been noteworthy. The main emphasis, as is eminently wise and proper, has been put upon primary education; but in addition to this there is a normal school, an agricultural school, three industrial and three high schools. Every effort is being made to secure not only the benefits of elementary education to all the Porto Ricans of the next generation, but also as far as means will permit to train them so that the industrial, agricultural, and commercial opportunities of the island can be utilized to the best possible advantage. It was evident at a glance that the teachers, both Americans and native Porto Ricans, were devoted to their work, took the greatest pride in it, and were endeavoring to train their pupils, not only in mind, but in what counts for far more than mind in citizenship, that is, in character.

I was very much struck by the excellent character both of the insular police and of the Porto Rican regiment. They are both of them bodies that reflect credit upon the American administration of the island. The insular police are under the local Porto Rican government. The Porto Rican regiment of troops must be appropriated for by the Congress. I earnestly hope that this body will be kept permanent. There should certainly be troops in the island, and it is wise that these troops should be themselves native Porto Ricans. It would be from every standpoint a mistake not to perpetuate this regiment.

In traversing the island even the most cursory survey leaves the beholder struck with the evident rapid growth in the culture both of the sugar cane and tobacco. The fruit industry is also growing. Last year was the most prosperous year that the island has ever known, before or since the American occupation. The total of exports and imports of the island was forty-five millions of dollars as against eighteen millions in 1901. This is the largest in the island's history. Prior to the American occupation the greatest trade for any one year was that of 1896, when it reached nearly $23,000,000. Last year, therefore, there was double the trade that there was in the most prosperous year under the Spanish regime. There were 210,273 tons of sugar exported last year, of the value of $14,186,319; $3,555,163 of tobacco and 28,290,322 pounds of coffee of the value of $3,481,102. Unfortunately, what used to be Porto Rico's prime cup—coffee—has not shared this prosperity. It has never recovered from the disaster of the hurricane, and moreover, the benefit of throwing open our market to it has not compensated for the loss inflicted by the closing of the markets to it abroad. I call your attention to the accompanying memorial on this subject of the board of trade of San Juan, and I earnestly hope that some measure will be taken for the benefit of the excellent and high-grade Porto Rican coffee.

In addition to delegations from the board of trade and chamber of commerce of San Juan, I also received delegations from the Porto Rican Federation of Labor and from the Coffee Growers' Association.

There is a matter to which I wish to call your special attention, and that is the desirability of conferring full American citizenship upon the people of Porto Rico. I most earnestly hope that this will be done. I cannot see how any harm can possibly result from it, and it seems to me a matter of right and justice to the people of Porto Rico. They are loyal, they are glad to be under our flag, they are making rapid progress along the path of orderly liberty. Surely we should show our appreciation of them, our pride in what they have done, and our pleasure in extending recognition for what has thus been done, by granting them full American citizenship.

Under the wise administration of the present governor and council marked progress has been made in the difficult matter of granting to the people of the island the largest measure of self-government that can with safety be given at the present time. It would have been a very serious mistake to have gone any faster than we have already gone in this direction. The Porto Ricans have complete and absolute autonomy in all their municipal governments, the only power over them possessed by the insular government being that of removing corrupt or incompetent municipal officials. This power has never been exer-

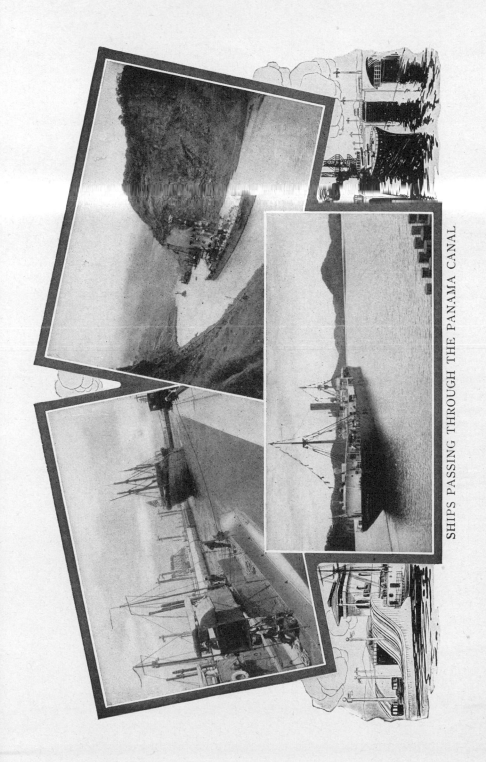

SHIPS PASSING THROUGH THE PANAMA CANAL

OPENING OF THE PANAMA CANAL.

On August 15, 1914, the Panama Canal was finally opened for passage of vessels drawing not more than 30 feet of water. It was not until some months later that the largest vessels were allowed to go through. The first vessel to make the journey through the Isthmus of Panama was the United States vessel *Ancon*. On board were the builder of the Canal, General George W. Goethals, and about two hundred guests of the Secretary of War of the United States, including the President of Panama and his cabinet. The *Ancon* made the trip in less than nine hours. On the following day, the first man-of-war to pass through the Canal, a Peruvian torpedo boat destroyer, made her voyage.

For a complete account of the Canal, see the Encyclopedic Index article, Panama Canal, and other illustrations listed therein.

cised save on the clearest proof of corruption or of incompetence—such as to jeopardize the interests of the people of the island, and under such circumstances it has been fearlessly used to the immense benefit of the people. It is not a power with which it would be safe, for the sake of the island itself, to dispense at present. The lower house is absolutely elective, while the upper house is appointive. This scheme is working well; no injustice of any kind results from it, and great benefit to the island, and it should certainly not be changed at this time. The machinery of the elections is administered entirely by the Porto Rican people themselves, the governor and council keeping only such super-vision as is necessary in order to insure an orderly election. Any pro-test as to electoral frauds is settled in the courts.

Here, again, it would not be safe to make any change in the present system. The elections this year were absolutely orderly, unaccompanied by any disturbance, and no protest has been made against the management of the elections, although three contests are threatened where the majorities were very small and error was claimed; the contests, of course, to be settled in the courts. In short, the governor and council are co-operating with all of the most enlightened and most patriotic of the people of Porto Rico in educating the citizens of the island in the principles of orderly liberty. They are providing a government based upon each citizen's self-respect and the mutual respect of all citizens—that is, based upon a rigid observance of the principles of justice and honesty. It has not been easy to instill into the minds of the people unaccustomed to the exercise of freedom the two basic principles of our American system—the principle that the majority must rule and the principle that the minority has rights which must not be disregarded or trampled upon. Yet real progress has been made in having these principles accepted as elementary, as the foundations of successful self-government.

I transmit herewith the report of the governor of Porto Rico, sent to the President through the Secretary of State.

All the insular governments should be placed in one bureau, either in the Department of War or the Department of State. It is a mistake not so to arrange our handling of these islands at Washington as to be able to take advantage of the experience gained in one when dealing with the problems that from time to time arise in another.

In conclusion let me express my admiration for the work done by the Congress when it enacted the law under which the island is now being administered. After seeing the island personally, and after five years' experience in connection with its administration, it is but fair to those who devised this law to say that it would be well-nigh impossible to have devised any other which in the actual working would have ac complished better results.

THEODORE ROOSEVELT.

SPECIAL MESSAGE.

THE WHITE HOUSE, December 17, 1906.

To the Senate and House of Representatives:

The developments of the past year emphasize with increasing force the need of vigorous and immediate action to recast the public land laws and adapt them to the actual situation. The timber and stone act has demonstrated conclusively that its effect is to turn over the public timber lands to great corporations. It has done enormous harm, it is no longer needed, and it should be repealed.

The desert land act results so frequently in fraud and so comparatively seldom in making homes on the land that it demands radical amendment. That provision which permits assignment before patent should be repealed, and the entryman should be required to live for not less than two years at home on the land before patent issues. Otherwise the desert land law will continue to assist speculators and other large holders to get control of land and water on the public domain by indefensible means. The commutation clause of the homestead act, in a majority of cases, defeats the purpose of the homestead act itself, which is to facilitate settlement and create homes. In theory the commutation clause should assist the honest settler and doubtless in some cases it does so. Far more often it supplies the means by which speculators and loan and mortgage companies secure possession of the land. Actual—not constructive—living at home on the land for three years should be required before commutation, unless it should appear wiser to repeal the commutation clause altogether. These matters are more fully discussed in the report of the public lands commission, to which I again call your attention.

I am gravely concerned at the extremely unsatisfactory condition of the public land laws and at the prevalence of fraud under their present provisions. For much of this fraud the present laws are chiefly responsible. There is but one way by which the fraudulent acquisition of these lands can be definitely stopped, and therefore I have directed the Secretary of the Interior to allow no patent to be issued to public land under any law until by an examination on the ground actual compliance with that law has been found to exist. For this purpose an increase of special agents in the general land office is urgently required. Unless it is given, bona fide would-be settlers will be put to grave inconvenience, or else the fraud will in large part go on. Further, the Secretary of the Interior should be enabled to employ enough mining experts to examine the validity of all mineral land claims, and to undertake the supervision and control of the use of the mineral fuels still belonging to the United States. The present coal law limiting the individual entry to 160 acres puts a premium on fraud by making it impossible to develop certain types of coal fields and yet comply with the law. It is a scandal to maintain laws which sound well, but which make fraud the key without which great natural resources must remain closed. The law should give individuals and corporations, under proper government regulation and control (the details of which I shall not at present discuss) the right to work bodies of coal land large enough for profitable development. My own belief is that there should be provision for leasing coal, oil and gas rights under proper restrictions. If the additional force of special agents and mining experts I recommend is provided and well used, the result will be not only to stop the land frauds, but to prevent delays in patenting valid land claims, and to conserve the indispensable fuel resources of the nation.

Many of the existing laws affecting rights of way and privileges on public lands and reservations are illogical and unfair. Some work injustice by granting valuable rights in perpetuity without return. Others fail to protect the grantee in his possession of permanent improvements made at large expense. In fairness to the government, to the holders of rights and privileges on the public lands, and to the people whom the latter serve, I urge the revision and re-enactment of these laws in one comprehensive act, providing that the regulations and the charge now in force in many cases may be extended to all, to the end that unregulated or monopolistic control of great natural resources may not be acquired or misused for private ends.

The boundaries of the national forest reserves unavoidably include certain valuable timber lands not owned by the government. Important among them are the land grants of various railroads. For more than two years negotiations with the land grant railroads have been in progress looking toward an arrangement by which the forest on railroad lands within national forest reserve may be preserved by the removal of the present crop of timber under rules prescribed by the forest service, and its perpetuation may be assured by the transfer of the land to the government without cost. The advantage of such an arrangement to the government lies in the acquisition of lands whose protection is necessary to the general welfare. The advantage to the railroads is found in the proposal to allow them to consolidate their holdings of timber within forest reserves by exchange after deeding their lands to the government, and thus to cut within a limited time solid bodies of timber instead of alternate sections, although the amount of timber in each case would be the same. It is possible that legislation will be required to authorize this or a similar arrangement with the railroads and other owners. If so, I recommend that it be enacted.

The money value of the national forests now reserved for the use and benefit of the people exceeds considerably the sum of one thousand millions of dollars. The stumpage value of the standing timber approaches seven hundred million dollars, and, together with the range and timber lands, the water for irrigation and power, and the subsidiary values, reaches an amount equal to that of the national property now under the immediate control of the army and navy together. But this vast domain is withheld from serving the nation as freely and fully as it might by the lack of capital to develop it. The yearly running expenses are sufficiently met by the annual appropriation and the proceeds of the forests. Under the care of the forest service the latter are increasing at the rate of more than half a million dollars a year; the estimate of appropriation for the present year is less than for last year, and it is confidently expected that by 1910 the forest service will be entirely self-supporting. In the meantime there is the most urgent need for trails, fences, cabins for the rangers, bridges, telephone lines and other items of equipment, without which the reserves cannot be handled to advantage, cannot be protected properly and cannot contribute as they should to the general welfare. Expenditures for such permanent improvements are properly chargeable to capital account. The lack of reasonable working equipment weakens the protection of the national forests and greatly limits their production. This want cannot be supplied from the appropriation for running expenses. The need is urgent. Accordingly, I recommend that the Secretary of the Treasury be authorized to advance to the forest service, upon the security of the standing timber, an amount, say $5,000,000, sufficient to provide a reasonable working capital for the national forests, to bear interest and to be repaid in annual installments beginning in ten years.

The national parks of the west are forested and they lie without exception within or adjacent to national forest reserves. Two years ago the latter were transferred to the care of the Secretary of Agriculture, with the most satisfactory results. The same reasons which led to this transfer make advisable a similar transfer of the national parks, now in charge of the Secretary of the Interior, and I recommend legislation to that end.

Within or adjoining national forests are considerable areas of Indian lands of more value under forest than for any other purpose. It would aid greatly in putting these lands to their best use if the power to create national forests by proclamation were extended to cover them. The Indians should be paid the full value of any land thus taken for public purposes from the proceeds of the lands themselves, but such land should revert to the Indians if it is excluded from national forest use before full payment has been made.

The control of grazing in the national forests is an assured success. The condition of the range is improving rapidly, water is being developed, much feed formerly wasted is now saved and used, range controversies are settled, opposition to the grazing fee is practically at an end, and the stockmen are earnestly supporting the forest service and co-operating with it effectively for the improvement of the range.

The situation on the open government range is strikingly different. Its carrying capacity has probably been reduced one-half by over grazing and is still falling. Range controversies in many places are active and bitter, and life and property are often in danger. The interests both of the live stock industry and of the government are needlessly impaired. The present situation is indefensible from any point of view and it should be ended.

I recommend that a bill be enacted which will provide for government control of the public range through the Department of Agriculture, which alone is equipped for that work. Such a bill should insure to each locality rules· for grazing specially adapted to its needs and should authorize the collection of a reasonable grazing fee. Above all, the rights of the settler and home-maker should be absolutely guaranteed.

Much of the public land can only be used to advantage for grazing when fenced. Much fencing has been done for that reason and also to prevent other stock owners from using land to which they have an equal right under the law. Reasonable fencing which promotes the use of the range and yet interferes neither with settlement nor with other range rights would be thoroughly desirable if it were legal. Yet the law forbids it, and the law must and will be enforced; I will see to it that the illegal fences are removed unless Congress at the present session takes steps to legalize proper fencing by government control of the range.

THEODORE ROOSEVELT.

SPECIAL MESSAGE.

THE WHITE HOUSE, December 17, 1906.

To the Senate and House of Representatives:

In the month of November I visited the Isthmus of Panama, going over the Canal Zone with considerable care; and also visited the cities of Panama and Colon, which are not in the Zone or under the United States flag, but as to which the United States Government, through its agents, exercises control for certain sanitary purposes.

The U. S. S. *Louisiana,* on which I was, anchored off Colon about half past two on Wednesday afternoon, November 14. I came aboard her, after my stay on shore, at about half past 9 on Saturday evening, November 17. On Wednesday afternoon and evening I received the President of Panama and his suite, and saw members of the Canal Commission, and various other gentlemen, perfecting the arrangement for my visit, so that every hour that I was ashore could be employed to advantage. I was three days ashore—not a sufficient length of time to allow of an exhaustive investigation of the minutiæ of the work of any single department, still less to pass judgment on the engineering problems, but enough to enable me to get a clear idea of the salient features of the great work and of the progress that has been made as regards the sanitation of the Zone, Colon, and Panama, the caring for and housing of the employees, and the actual digging of the canal. The Zone is a narrow strip of land, and it can be inspected much as one can inspect 50 or 60 miles of a great railroad, at the point where it runs through mountains or overcomes other national obstacles.

I chose the month of November for my visit partly because it is the rainiest month of the year, the month in which the work goes forward at the greatest disadvantage, and one of the two months which the medical department of the French Canal Company found most unhealthy.

Immediately after anchoring on the afternoon of Wednesday there was a violent storm of wind and rain. From that time we did not again see the sun until Saturday morning, the rain continuing almost steadily, but varying from a fine drizzle to a torrential downpour. During that time in fifteen minutes at Cristobal 1.05 inches of rain fell; from 1 to 3 A. M., November 16, 3.2 inches fell; for the twenty-four hours ending noon, November 16, 4.68 inches fell, and for the six days ending noon, November 16, 10.24 inches fell. The Chagres rose in flood to a greater height than it had attained during the last fifteen years, tearing out the track in one place. It would have been impossible to see the work going on under more unfavorable weather conditions. On Saturday, November 17, the sun shone now and then for a few minutes, although the day was generally overcast and there were heavy showers at intervals.

On Thursday morning we landed at about half past seven and went slowly over the line of the Panama Railway, ending with an expedition in a tug at the Pacific entrance of the canal out to the islands where the dredging for the canal will cease. We took our dinner at one of the eating houses furnished by the Commission for the use of the Government employees—no warning of our coming being given. I inspected the Ancon Hospital, going through various wards both for white patients and for colored patients. I inspected portions of the constabulary (Zone police), examining the men individually. I also examined certain of the schools and saw the school children, both white and colored, speaking with certain of the teachers. In the afternoon of this day I was formally received in Panama by President Amador, who, together with the Government and all the people of Panama, treated me with the most considerate courtesy, for which I hereby extend my most earnest thanks. I was driven through Panama and in a public square was formally received and welcomed by the

President and other members of the Government; and in the evening
I attended a dinner given by the President, and a reception, which was
also a Government function. I also drove through the streets of
Panama for the purpose of observing what had been done. We slept
at the Hotel Tivoli, at Ancon, which is on a hill directly outside of the
city of Panama, but in the Zone.

On Friday morning we left the hotel at 7 o'clock and spent the entire
day going through the Culebra cut—the spot in which most work will
have to be done in any event. We watched the different steam shovels
working; we saw the drilling and blasting; we saw many of the dirt
trains (of the two different types used), both carrying the earth away
from the steam shovels and depositing it on the dumps—some of
the dumps being run out in the jungle merely to get rid of the earth,
while in other cases they are being used for double-tracking the railway, and in preparing to build the great dams. I visited many of the
different villages, inspecting thoroughly many different buildings—the
local receiving hospitals, the houses in which the unmarried white
workmen live, those in which the unmarried colored workmen live;
also the quarters of the white married employees and of the married
colored employees; as well as the commissary stores, the bath houses,
the water-closets, the cook sheds for the colored laborers, and the Government canteens, or hotels, at which most of the white employees
take their meals. I went through the machine shops. During the day
I talked with scores of different men—superintendents and heads of
departments, divisions, and bureaus; steam-shovel men, machinists,
conductors, engineers, clerks, wives of the American employees, health
officers, colored laborers, colored attendants, and managers of the
commissary stores where food is sold to the colored laborers; wives of
the colored employees who are married. In the evening I had an interview with the British consul, Mr. Mallet, a gentleman who for
many years has well and honorably represented the British Government on the Isthmus of Panama and who has a peculiar relation to
our work because the bulk of the colored laborers come from the
British West Indies. I also saw the French consul, Mr. Gey, a gentleman of equally long service and honorable record. I saw the lieutenants, the chief executive and administrative officers, under the engineering and sanitary departments. I also saw and had long talks
with two deputations—one of machinists and one representing the
railway men of the dirt trains—listening to what they had to say as
to the rate of pay and various other matters and going over, as much
in detail as possible, all the different questions they brought up. As
to some matters I was able to meet their wishes; as to others, I felt
that what they requested could not be done consistently with my duty
to the United States Government as a whole; as to yet others I reserved judgment.

On Saturday morning we started at 8 o'clock from the hotel. We went through the Culebra cut, stopping off to see the marines, and also to investigate certain towns; one, of white employees, as to which in certain respects complaint had been made to me; and another town where I wanted to see certain houses of the colored employees. We went over the site of the proposed Gatun dam, having on the first day inspected the sites of the proposed La Boca and Sosa dams. We went out on a little toy railway to the reservoir, which had been built to supply the people of Colon with water for their houses. There we took lunch at the engineers' mess. We then went through the stores and shops of Cristobal, inspecting carefully the houses of both the white and colored employees, married and unmarried, together with the other buildings. We then went to Colon and saw the fire department at work; in four minutes from the signal the engines had come down to Front street, and twenty-one 2½-inch hose pipes were raising streams of water about 75 feet high. We rode about Colon, through the various streets, paved, unpaved, and in process of paving, looking at the ditches, sewers, curbing, and the lights. I then went over the Colon hospital in order to compare it with the temporary town or field receiving hospitals which I had already seen and inspected. I also inspected some of the dwellings of the employees. In the evening I attended a reception given by the American employees on the Isthmus, which took place on one of the docks in Colon, and from there went aboard the Louisiana.

Each day from twelve to eighteen hours were spent in going over and inspecting all there was to be seen, and in examining various employees. Throughout my trip I was accompanied by the Surgeon-General of the Navy, Dr. Rixey; by the Chairman of the Isthmian Canal Commission, Mr. Shonts; by Chief Engineer Stevens; by Dr. Gorgas, the chief sanitary officer of the Commission; by Mr. Bishop, the Secretary of the Commission; by Mr. Ripley, the Principal Assistant Engineer; by Mr. Jackson Smith, who has had practical charge of collecting and handling the laboring force; by Mr. Bierd, general manager of the railway, and by Mr. Rogers, the general counsel of the Commission; and many other officials joined us from time to time.

At the outset I wish to pay a tribute to the amount of work done by the French Canal Company under very difficult circumstances. Many of the buildings they put up were excellent and are still in use, though, naturally, the houses are now getting out of repair and are being used as dwellings only until other houses can be built, and much of the work they did in the Culebra cut, and some of the work they did in digging has been of direct and real benefit. This country has never made a better investment than the $40,000,000 which it paid to the French Company for work and betterments, including especially the Panama Railroad.

An inspection on the ground at the height of the rainy season served to convince me of the wisdom of Congress in refusing to adopt either a high-level or a sea-level canal. There seems to be a universal agreement among all people competent to judge that the Panama route, the one actually chosen, is much superior to both the Nicaragua and Darien routes.

The wisdom of the canal management has been shown in nothing more clearly than in the way in which the foundations of the work have been laid. To have yielded to the natural impatience of ill informed outsiders and begun all kinds of experiments in work prior to a thorough sanitation of the Isthmus, and to a fairly satisfactory working out of the problem of getting and keeping a sufficient labor supply, would have been disastrous. The various preliminary measures had to be taken first; and these could not be taken so as to allow us to begin the real work of construction prior to January 1 of the present year. It then became necessary to have the type of the canal decided, and the only delay has been the necessary delay until the 29th day of June, the date when the Congress definitely and wisely settled that we should have an 85-foot level canal. Immediately after that the work began in hard earnest and has been continued with increasing vigor ever since; and it will continue so to progress in the future. When the contracts are let the conditions will be such as to insure a constantly increasing amount of performance.

The first great problem to be solved, upon the solution of which the success of the rest of the work depended, was the problem of sanitation. This was from the outset under the direction of Dr. W. C. Gorgas, who is to be made a full member of the Commission. It must be remembered that his work was not mere sanitation as the term is understood in our ordinary municipal work. Throughout the Zone and in the two cities of Panama and Colon, in addition to the sanitation work proper, he has had to do all the work that the Marine-Hospital Service does as regards the Nation, that the health department officers do in the various States and cities, and that Colonel Waring did in New York when he cleaned its streets. The results have been astounding. The Isthmus had been a by-word for deadly unhealthfulness. Now, after two years of our occupation the conditions as regards sickness and the death rate compare favorably with reasonably healthy localities in the United States. Especial care has been devoted to minimizing the risk due to the presence of those species of mosquitoes which have been found to propagate malarial and yellow fevers. In all the settlements, the little temporary towns or cities composed of the white and black employees, which grow up here and there in the tropic jungle as the needs of the work dictate, the utmost care is exercised to keep the conditions healthy. Everywhere are to be seen the drainage ditches which in removing the water have removed the breeding places of the mosquitoes, while the whole jungle is cut away for a considerable space around the habitations, thus destroying the places in which the mosquitoes take shelter. These drainage ditches and clearings are in evidence in every settlement, and, together with the invariable presence of mosquito screens around the piazzas, and of mosquito doors to the houses, not to speak of the careful fumigation that has gone on in all infected houses, doubtless explain the extraordinary absence of mosquitoes. As a matter of fact, but a single mosquito, and this not of the dangerous species, was seen by any member of our party during my three days on the Isthmus. Equal care is taken by the inspectors of the health department to secure cleanliness in the houses and proper hygienic conditions of every kind. I inspected between twenty and thirty water-closets, both those used by the white employees and those used by the colored laborers. In almost every case I found the conditions perfect. In but one case did I find them really bad. In this case, affecting a settlement of unmarried white employees, I found them very bad indeed, but the buildings were all inherited from the French Company and were being used temporarily while other buildings were in the course of construction; and right near the defective water closet a new and excellent closet with a good sewer pipe was in process of construction and nearly finished. Nevertheless this did not excuse the fact that the bad condition had been allowed to prevail. Temporary accommodation, even if only such as soldiers use when camped in the field, should have been provided. Orders to this effect were issued. I append the report of Dr. Gorgas on the incident. I was struck, however, by the fact that in this instance, as in almost every other where a complaint was made which proved to have any justification whatever, it appeared that steps had already been taken to remedy the evil complained of, and that the trouble was mainly due to the extreme difficulty, and often impossibility, of providing in every place for the constant increase in the numbers of employees. Generally the provision is made in advance, but it is not possible that this should always be the case; when it is not there ensues a period of time during which the conditions are unsatisfactory, until a remedy can be provided; but I never found a case where the remedy was not being provided as speedily as possible.

I inspected the large hospitals at Ancon and Colon, which are excellent examples of what tropical hospitals should be. I also inspected the receiving hospitals in various settlements. I went through a number of the wards in which the colored men are treated, a number of those in which the white men are treated—Americans and Spaniards. Both white men and black men are treated exactly alike, and their treatment is as good as that which could be obtained in our first-class hospitals at home. All the patients that I saw, with one or two exceptions, were laborers or other employees on the canal works and railways, most of them being colored men of the ordinary laborer stamp. Not only are the men carefully cared for whenever they apply for care, but so far as practicable a watch is kept to see that if they need it they are sent to the hospitals, whether they desire to go or not. From no responsible source did any complaint come to me as to the management of the hospital service, although occasionally a very ignorant West India negro when he is first brought into the hospital becomes frightened by the ordinary hospital routine.

Just at present the health showing on the Isthmus is remarkably good—so much better than in most sections of the United States that I do not believe that it can possibly continue at quite its present average. Thus, early in the present year a band of several hundred Spaniards were brought to the Isthmus as laborers, and additions to their number have been made from time to time; yet since their arrival in February last but one of those Spaniards thus brought over to work on the canal has died of disease, and he of typhoid fever. Two others were killed, one in a railroad accident, and one by a dynamite explosion. There has been for the last six months a well-nigh steady decline in the death rate for the population of the Zone, this being largely due to the decrease in deaths from pneumonia, which has been the most fatal disease on the Isthmus. In October there were ninety-nine deaths of every kind among the employees of the Isthmus. There were then on the rolls 5,500 whites, seven-eighths of them being Americans. Of these whites but two died of disease, and as it happened neither man was an American. Of the 6,000 white Americans, including some 1,200 women and children, not a single death has occurred in the past three months, whereas in an average city in the United States the number of deaths for a similar number of people in that time would have been about thirty from disease. This very remarkable showing cannot of course permanently obtain, but it certainly goes to prove that if good care is taken the Isthmus is not a particularly unhealthy place. In October, of the 19,000 negroes on the roll 86 died from disease; pneumonia being the most destructive disease, and malarial fever coming second. The difficulty of exercising a thorough supervision over the colored laborers is of course greater than is the case among the whites, and they are also less competent to take care of themselves, which accounts for the fact that their death rate is so much higher than that of the whites, in spite of the fact that they have been used to similar climatic conditions. Even among the colored employees it will be seen that the death rate is not high.

In Panama and Colon the death rate has also been greatly reduced, this being directly due to the vigorous work of the special brigade of employees who have been inspecting houses where the stegomyia mosquito is to be found, and destroying its larvæ and breeding places, and doing similar work in exterminating the malarial mosquitoes— in short, in performing all kinds of hygienic labor. A little over a year ago all kinds of mosquitoes, including the two fatal species, were numerous about the Culebra cut. In this cut during last October every room of every house was carefully examined, and only two mosquitoes, neither of them of the two fatal species, were found. Unfaltering energy in inspection and in disinfecting and in the work of draining and of clearing brush are responsible for the change. I append Dr. Gorgas's report on the health conditions; also a letter from Surgeon-General Rixey to Dr. Gorgas. The Surgeon-General reported to me that the hygienic conditions on the Isthmus were about as good as, for instance, those in the Norfolk Navy-Yard.

Corozal, some four miles from La Boca, was formerly one of the most unsanitary places on the Isthmus, probably the most unsanitary. There was a marsh with a pond in the middle. Dr. Gorgas had both the marsh and pond drained and the brush cleared off, so that now, when I went over the ground, it appeared like a smooth meadow intersected by drainage ditches. The breeding places and sheltering spots of the dangerous mosquitoes had been completely destroyed. The result is that Corozal for the last six months (like La Boca, which formerly also had a very unsanitary record), shows one of the best sick rates in the Zone, having less than 1 per cent a week admitted to the hospital. At Corozal there is a big hotel filled with employees of the Isthmian Canal Commission, some of them with their wives and families. Yet this healthy and attractive spot was stigmatized as a " hog wallow " by one of the least scrupulous and most foolish of the professional scandal-mongers who from time to time have written about the Commission's work.

The sanitation work in the cities of Panama and Colon has been just as important as in the Zone itself, and in many respects much more difficult; because it was necessary to deal with the already existing population, which naturally had scant sympathy with revolutionary changes, the value of which they were for a long time not able to perceive. In Colon the population consists largely of colored laborers who, having come over from the West Indies to work on the canal, abandon the work and either take to the brush or lie idle in Colon itself; thus peopling Colon with the least desirable among the imported laborers, for the good and steady men of course continue at the work. Yet astonishing progress has been made in both cities. In Panama 90 per cent of the streets that are to be paved at all are already paved with an excellent brick pavement laid in heavy concrete, a few of the streets being still in process of paving. The sewer and water services in the city are of the most modern hygienic type, some of the service having just been completed.

In Colon the conditions are peculiar, and it is as regards Colon that most of the very bitter complaint. has been made. Colon is built on a low coral island, covered at more or less shallow depths with vegetable accumulations or mold, which affords sustenance and strength to many varieties of low-lying tropical plants. One-half of the surface of the island is covered with water at high tide, the average height of the land being 1½ feet above low tide. The slight undulations furnish shallow, natural reservoirs or fresh-water breeding places for every variety of mosquito, and the ground tends to be lowest in the middle. When the town was originally built no attempt was made to fill the low ground, either in the streets or on the building sites, so that the entire surface was practically a quagmire; when the quagmire became impassable certain of the streets were crudely improved by filling especially bad mud holes with soft rock or other material. In September, 1905, a systematic effort was begun to formulate a general plan for the proper sanitation of the city; in February last temporary relief measures were taken, while in July the prosecution of the work was begun in good earnest. The results are already visible in the sewering, draining, guttering and paving of the streets. Some four months will be required before the work of sewerage and street improvement will be completed, but the progress already made is very marked. Ditches have been dug through the town, connecting the salt water on both sides, and into these the ponds, which have served as breeding places for the mosquitoes, are drained. These ditches have answered their purpose, for they are probably the chief cause of the astonishing diminution in the number of mosquitoes. More ditches of the kind are being constructed.

It was not practicable, with the force at the Commission's disposal, and in view of the need that the force should be used in the larger town of Panama, to begin this work before early last winter. Water mains were then laid in the town and water was furnished to the people early in March from a temporary reservoir. This reservoir proved to be of insufficient capacity before the end of the dry season and the shortage was made up by hauling water over the Panama railroad, so that there was at all times an ample supply of the very best water. Since that time the new reservoir back of Mount Hope has been practically completed. I visited this reservoir. It is a lake over a mile long and half a mile broad. It now carries some 500,000,000 gallons of first-class water. I forward herewith a photograph of this lake, together with certain other photographs of what I saw while I was on the Isthmus. Nothing but a cataclysm will hereafter render it necessary in the dry season to haul water for the use of Colon and Cristobal.

One of the most amusing (as well as dishonest) attacks made upon the Commission was in connection with this reservoir. The writer in question usually confined himself to vague general mendacity; but in this case he specifically stated that there was no water in the vicinity fit for a reservoir (I drank it, and it was excellent), and that this particular reservoir would never hold water anyway. Accompanying this message, as I have said above, is a photograph of the reservoir as I myself saw it, and as it has been in existence ever since the article in question was published. With typical American humor, the engineering corps still at work at the reservoir have christened a large boat which is now used on the reservoir by the name of the individual who thus denied the possibility of the reservoir's existence.

I rode through the streets of Colon, seeing them at the height of the rainy season, after two days of almost unexampled downpour, when they were at their very worst. Taken as a whole they were undoubtedly very bad; as bad as Pennsylvania avenue in Washington before Grant's Administration. Front street is already in thoroughly satisfactory shape, however. Some of the side streets are also in good condition. In others the change in the streets is rapidly going on. Through three-fourths of the town it is now possible to walk, even during the period of tremendous rain, in low shoes without wetting one's feet, owing to the rapidity with which the surface water is carried away in the ditches. In the remaining one-fourth of the streets the mud is very deep—about as deep as in the ordinary street of a low-lying prairie river town of the same size in the United States during early spring. All men to whom I spoke were a unit in saying that the conditions of the Colon streets were 100 per cent better than a year ago. The most superficial examination of the town shows the progress that has been made and is being made in macadamizing the streets. Complaint was made to me by an entirely reputable man as to the character of some of the material used for repairing certain streets. On investigation the complaint proved well founded, but it also appeared that the use of the material in question had been abandoned, the Commission, after having tried it in one or two streets, finding it not appropriate.

The result of the investigation of this honest complaint was typical of what occurred when I investigated most of the other honest complaints made to me. That is, where the complaints were not made wantonly or maliciously, they almost always proved due to failure to appreciate the fact that time was necessary in the creation and completion of this Titanic work in a tropic wilderness. It is impossible to avoid some mistakes in building a giant canal through jungle-covered mountains and swamps, while at the same time sanitating tropic cities, and providing for the feeding and general care of from twenty to thirty thousand workers. The complaints brought to me, either of insufficient provision in caring for some of the laborers, or of failure to finish the pavements of Colon, or of failure to supply water, or of failure to build wooden sidewalks for the use of the laborers in the rainy season, on investigation proved, almost without exception, to be due merely to the utter inability of the Commission to do everything at once.

For instance, it was imperative that Panama, which had the highest death rate and where the chance of a yellow fever epidemic was strongest, should be cared for first; yet most of the complaints as to the delay in taking care of Colon were due to the inability or unwillingness to appreciate this simple fact. Again, as the thousands of laborers are brought over and housed, it is not always possible at the outset to supply wooden walks and bath houses, because other more vital necessities have to be met; and in consequence, while most of the settlements have good bath houses, and, to a large extent at least, wooden walks, there are plenty of settlements where wooden walks have not yet been laid down, and I visited one where the bath houses have not been provided. But in this very settlement the frames of the bath houses are already up, and in every case the utmost effort is being made to provide the wooden walks. Of course, in some of the newest camps tents are used pending the building of houses. Where possible, I think detached houses would be preferable to the semi-detached houses now in general use.

Care and forethought have been exercised by the Commission, and nothing has reflected more credit upon them than their refusal either to go ahead too fast or to be deterred by the fear of criticism from not going ahead fast enough. It is curious to note the fact that many of the most severe critics of the Commission criticize them for precisely opposite reasons, some complaining bitterly that the work is not in a more advanced condition, while the others complain that it has been rushed with such haste that there has been insufficient preparation for the hygiene and comfort of the employees. As a matter of fact neither criticism is just. It would have been impossible to go quicker than the Commission has gone, for such quickness would have meant insufficient preparation. On the other hand, to refuse to do anything until every possible future contingency had been met would have caused wholly unwarranted delay. The right course to follow was exactly the course which has been followed. Every reasonable preparation was made in advance, the hygienic conditions in especial being made as nearly perfect as possible; while on the other hand there has been no timid refusal to push forward the work because of inability to anticipate every possible emergency, for, of course, many defects can only be shown by the working of the system in actual practice.

In addition to attending to the health of the employees, it is, of course, necessary to provide for policing the Zone. This is done by a police force which at present numbers over 200 men, under Captain Shanton. About one-fifth of the men are white and the others black. In different places I questioned some twenty or thirty of these men, taking them at random. They were a fine set, physically and in discipline. With one exception all the white men I questioned had served in the American army, usually in the Philippines, and belonged to the best type of American soldier. Without exception the black policemen whom I questioned had served either in the British army or in the Jamaica or Barbados police. They were evidently contented, and were doing their work well. Where possible the policemen are used to control people of their own color, but in any emergency no hesitation is felt in using them indiscriminately.

Inasmuch as so many both of the white and colored employees have brought their families with them, schools have been established, the school service being under Mr. O'Connor. For the white pupils white American teachers are employed; for the colored pupils there are also some white American teachers, one Spanish teacher, and one colored American teacher, most of them being colored teachers from Jamaica, Barbados, and St. Lucia. The schoolrooms were good, and it was a pleasant thing to see the pride that the teachers were taking in their work and their pupils.

There seemed to me to be too many saloons in the Zone; but the new high-license law which goes into effect on January 1 next will probably close four-fifths of them. Resolute and successful efforts are being made to minimize and control the sale of liquor.

The cars on the passenger trains on the Isthmus are divided into first and second-class, the difference being marked in the price of tickets. As a rule second-class passengers are colored and first-class passengers white; but in every train which I saw there were a number of white second-class passengers, and on two of them there were colored first-class passengers.

Next in importance to the problem of sanitation, and indeed now of equal importance, is the problem of securing and caring for the mechanics, laborers, and other employees who actually do the work on the canal and the railroad. This great task has been under the control of Mr. Jackson Smith, and on the whole has been well done. At present there are some 6,000 white employees and some 19,000 colored employees on the Isthmus. I went over the different places where the different kinds of employees were working; I think I saw representatives of every type both at their work and in their homes; and I conversed with probably a couple of hundred of them all told, choosing them at random from every class and including those who came especially to present certain grievances. I found that those who did not come specifically to present grievances almost invariably expressed far greater content and satisfaction with the conditions than did those who called to make complaint.

Nearly 5,000 of the white employees had come from the United States. No man can see these young, vigorous men energetically doing their duty without a thrill of pride in them as Americans. They represent on the average a high class. Doubtless to Congress the wages paid them will seem high, but as a matter of fact the only general complaint which I found had any real basis among the complaints made to me upon the Isthmus was that, owing to the peculiar surroundings, the cost of living and the distance from home, the wages were really not as high as they should be. In fact, almost every man I spoke to felt that he ought to be receiving more money—a view, however, which the average man who stays at home in the United States probably likewise holds as regards himself. I append figures of the wages paid, so that the Congress can judge the matter for itself. Later I shall confer on the subject with certain representative labor men here in the United States, as well as going over with Mr. Stevens, the comparative wages paid on the Zone and at home; and I may then communicate my findings to the canal committees of the two Houses.

The white Americans are employed, some of them in office work, but the majority in handling the great steam shovels, as engineers and conductors on the dirt trains, as machinists in the great repair shops, as carpenters and time-keepers, superintendents, and foremen of divisions and of gangs, and so on and so on. Many of them have brought down their wives and families; and the children when not in school are running about and behaving precisely as the American small boy and small girl behave at home. The bachelors among the employees live, sometimes in small separate houses, sometimes in large houses; quarters being furnished free to all the men, married and unmarried. Usually the bachelors sleep two in a room, as they would do in this country. I found a few cases where three were in a room; and I was told of, although I did not see, large rooms in which four were sleeping; for it is not possible in what is really a vast system of construction camps always to provide in advance as ample house room as the Commission intend later to give. In one case, where the house was an old French house with a leak in the roof, I did not think the accommodations were good. But in every other case among the scores of houses I entered at random, the accommodations were good; every room was neat and clean, usually having books, magazines, and small ornaments; and in short just such a room as a self-respecting craftsman would be glad to live in at home. The quarters for the married people were even better. Doubtless there must be here and there a married couple who, with or without reason, are not contented with their house on the Isthmus; but I never happened to strike such a couple. The wives of the steam-shovel men, engineers, machinists, and carpenters into whose houses I went, all with one accord expressed their pleasure in their home life and surroundings. Indeed, I do not think they could have done otherwise. The houses themselves were excellent—bathroom, sitting room, piazza, and bedrooms being all that could be desired. In every house which I happened to enter the mistress of the home was evidently a good American housewife and helpmeet, who had given to the home life that touch of attractiveness which, of course, the bachelor quarters neither had nor could have.

The housewives purchase their supplies directly, or through their husbands, from the commissary stores of the Commission. All to whom I spoke agreed that the supplies were excellent, and all but two stated that there was no complaint to be made; these two complained that the prices were excessive as compared to the prices in the States. On investigation I did not feel that this complaint was well founded. The married men ate at home. The unmarried men sometimes ate at private boarding houses, or private messes, but more often, judging by the answers of those whom I questioned, at the government canteens or hotels where the meal costs 30 cents to each employee. This 30-cent meal struck me as being as good a meal as we get in the United States at the ordinary hotel in which a 50-cent meal is provided. Three-fourths of the men whom I questioned stated that the meals furnished at these government hotels were good, the remaining one-fourth that they were not good. I myself took dinner at the La Boca government hotel, no warning whatever having been given of my coming. There were two rooms, as generally in these hotels. In one the employees were allowed to dine without their coats, while in the other they had to put them on. The 30-cent meal included soup, native beef (which was good), mashed potatoes, peas, beets, chili con carne, plum pudding, tea, coffee—each man having as much of each dish as he desired. On the table there was a bottle of liquid quinine tonic, which two-thirds of the guests, as I was informed, used every day. There were neat tablecloths and napkins. The men, who were taking the meal at or about the same time, included railroad men, machinists, shipwrights, and members of the office force. The rooms were clean, comfortable, and airy, with mosquito screens around the outer piazza. I was informed by some of those present that this hotel, and also the other similar hotels, were every Saturday night turned into clubhouses where the American officials, the school-teachers, and various employees, appeared, bringing their wives, there being dancing and singing. There was a piano in the room, which I was informed was used for the music on these occasions. My meal was excellent, and two newspaper correspondents who had been on the Isthmus several days informed me that it was precisely like the meals they had been getting elsewhere at other Government hotels. One of the employees was a cousin of one of the Secret-Service men who was with me, and he stated that the meals had always been good, but that after a time he grew tired of them because they seemed so much alike.

I came to the conclusion that, speaking generally, there was no warrant for complaint about the food. Doubtless it grows monotonous after awhile. Any man accustomed to handling large masses of men knows that some of them, even though otherwise very good men, are sure to grumble about something, and usually about their food. Schoolboys, college boys, and boarders in boarding houses make similar complaints; so do soldiers and sailors. On this very trip, on one of the warships, a seaman came to complain to the second watch officer about the quality of the cocoa at the seaman's mess, saying that it was not sweet enough; it was pointed out to him that there was sugar on the table and he could always put it in, to which he responded that that was the cook's business and not his! I think that the complaint as to the food on the Isthmus has but little more foundation than that of the sailor in question. Moreover, I was given to understand that one real cause of complaint was that at the government hotels no liquor is served, and some of the drinking men, therefore, refused to go to them. The number of men using the government hotels is steadily increasing.

Of the nineteen or twenty thousand day laborers employed on the canal, a few hundred are Spaniards. These do excellent work. Their foreman told me that they did twice as well as the West India laborers. They keep healthy and no difficulty is experienced with them in any way. Some Italian laborers are also employed in connection with the drilling. As might be expected, with labor as high priced as at present in the United States, it has not so far proved practicable to get any ordinary laborers from the United States. The American wage-workers on the Isthmus are the highly-paid skilled mechanics of the types mentioned previously. A steady effort is being made to secure Italians, and especially to procure more Spaniards, because of the very satisfactory results that have come from their employment; and their numbers will be increased as far as possible. It has not proved possible, however, to get them in anything like the numbers needed for the work, and from present appearances we shall in the main have to rely, for the ordinary unskilled work, partly upon colored laborers from the West Indies, partly upon Chinese labor. It certainly ought to be unnecessary to point out that the American workingman in the United States has no concern whatever in the question as to whether the rough work on the Isthmus, which is performed by aliens in any event, is done by aliens from one country with a black skin or by aliens from another country with a yellow skin. Our business is to dig the canal as efficiently and as quickly as possible; provided always that nothing is done that is inhumane to any laborers, and nothing that interferes with the wages of or lowers the standard of living of our own workmen. Having in view this principle, I have arranged to try several thousand Chinese laborers. This is desirable both because we must try to find out what laborers are most efficient, and, furthermore, because we should not leave ourselves at the mercy of any one type of foreign labor. At present the great bulk of the unskilled labor on the Isthmus is done by West India negroes, chiefly from Jamaica, Barbados, and the other English possessions. One of the governors of the lands in question has shown an unfriendly disposition to our work, and has thrown obstacles in the way of our getting the labor needed; and it is highly undesirable to give any outsiders the impression, however ill-founded, that they are indispensable and can dictate terms to us.

The West India laborers are fairly, but only fairly, satisfactory. Some of the men do very well indeed; the better class, who are to be found as foremen, as skilled mechanics, as policemen, are good men; and many of the ordinary day laborers are also good. But thousands of those who are brought over under contract (at our expense) go off into the jungle to live, or loaf around Colon, or work so badly after the first three or four days as to cause a serious diminution of the amount of labor performed on Friday and Saturday of each week. I questioned many of these Jamaica laborers as to the conditions of their work and what, if any, changes they wished. I received many complaints from them, but as regards most of these complaints they themselves contradicted one another. In all cases where the complaint was as to their treatment by any individual it proved, on examination, that this individual was himself a West India man of color, either a policeman, a storekeeper, or an assistant storekeeper. Doubtless there must be many complaints against Americans; but those to whom I spoke did not happen to make any such complaint to me. There was no complaint of the housing; I saw but one set of quarters for colored laborers which I thought poor, and this was in an old French house. The barracks for unmarried men are roomy, well ventilated, and clean, with canvas bunks for each man, and a kind of false attic at the top, where the trunks and other belongings of the different men are kept. The clothes are hung on clotheslines, nothing being allowed to be kept on the floor. In each of these big rooms there were tables and lamps, and usually a few books or papers, and in almost every room there was a Bible; the books being the property of the laborers themselves. The cleanliness of the quarters is secured by daily inspection. The quarters for the married negro laborers were good. They were neatly kept, and in almost every case the men living in them, whose wives or daughters did the cooking for them, were far better satisfied and of a higher grade than the ordinary bachelor negroes. Not only were the quarters in which these negro laborers were living much superior to those in which I am informed they live at home, but they were much superior to the huts to be seen in the jungles of Panama itself, beside the railroad tracks, in which the lower class of native Panamans live, as well as the negro workmen when they leave the employ of the canal and go into the jungles. A single glance at the two sets of buildings is enough to show the great superiority in point of comfort, cleanliness, and healthfulness of the Government houses as compared with the native houses.

The negroes generally do their own cooking, the bachelors cooking in sheds provided by the Government and using their own pots. In the different camps there was a wide variation in the character of these cooking sheds. In some, where the camps were completed, the kitchen or cooking sheds, as well as the bathrooms and water-closets, were all in excellent trim, while there were board sidewalks leading from building to building. In other camps the kitchens or cook sheds had not been floored, and the sidewalks had not been put down, while in one camp the bath houses were not yet up. In each case, however, every effort was being made to hurry on the construction, and I do not believe that the delays had been greater than were inevitable in such work. The laborers are accustomed to do their own cooking; but there was much complaint, especially among the bachelors, as to the quantity, and some as to the quality, of the food they got from the commissary department, especially as regards yams. On the other hand, the married men and their wives, and the more advanced among the bachelors, almost invariably expressed themselves as entirely satisfied with their treatment at the commissary stores; except that they stated that they generally could not get yams there, and had to purchase them outside. The chief complaint was that the prices were too high. It is unavoidable that the prices should be higher than in their own homes; and after careful investigation I came to the conclusion that the chief trouble lay in the fact that the yams, plantains, and the like are rather perishable food, and are very bulky compared to the amount of nourishment they contain, so that it is costly to import them in large quantities and difficult to keep them. Nevertheless, I felt that an effort should be made to secure them a more ample supply of their favorite food, and so directed; and I believe that ultimately the Government must itself feed them. I am having this matter looked into.

The superintendent having immediate charge of one gang of men at the Colon reservoir stated that he endeavored to get them to substitute beans and other nourishing food for the stringy, watery yams, because the men keep their strength and health better on the more nourishing food. Inasmuch, however, as they are accustomed to yams it is difficult to get them to eat the more strengthening food, and some time elapses before they grow accustomed to it. At this reservoir there has been a curious experience. It is off in the jungle by itself at the end of a couple of miles of a little toy railroad. In order to get the laborers there, they were given free food (and of course free lodgings); and yet it proved difficult to keep them, because they wished to be where they could reach the dramshop and places of amusement.

I was struck by the superior comfort and respectability of the lives of the married men. It would, in my opinion, be a most admirable thing if a much larger number of the men had their wives, for with their advent all complaints about the food and cooking are almost sure to cease.

I had an interview with Mr. Mallet, the British consul, to find out if there was any just cause for complaint as to the treatment of the West India negroes. He informed me most emphatically that there was not, and authorized me to give his statement publicity. He said that not only was the condition of the laborers far better than had been the case under the old French Company, but that year by year the condition was improving under our own régime. He stated that complaints were continually brought to him, and that he always investigated them; and that for the last six months he had failed to find a single complaint of a serious nature that contained any justification whatever.

One of the greatest needs at present is to provide amusements both for the white men and the black. The Young Men's Christian Association is trying to do good work and should be in every way encouraged. But the Government should do the main work. I have specifically called the attention of the Commission to this matter, and something has been accomplished already. Anything done for the welfare of the men adds to their efficiency and money devoted to that purpose is, therefore, properly to be considered as spent in building the canal. It is imperatively necessary to provide ample recreation and amusement if the men are to be kept well and healthy. I call the special attention of Congress to this need.

This gathering, distributing, and caring for the great force of laborers is one of the giant features of the work. That friction will from time to time occur in connection therewith is inevitable. The astonishing thing is that the work has been performed so well and that the machinery runs so smoothly. From my own experience I am able to say that more care had been exercised in housing, feeding, and generally paying heed to the needs of the skilled mechanics and ordinary laborers in the work on this canal than is the case in the construction of new railroads or in any other similar private or public work in the United States proper; and it is the testimony of all people competent to speak that on no other similar work anywhere in the Tropics—indeed, as far as I know, anywhere else—has there been such forethought and such success achieved in providing for the needs of the men who do the work.

I have now dealt with the hygienic conditions which make it possible to employ a great force of laborers, and with the task of gathering, housing, and feeding these laborers. There remains to consider the actual work which has to be done; the work because of which these laborers are gathered together—the work of constructing the canal. This is under the direct control of the Chief Engineer, Mr. Stevens, who has already shown admirable results, and whom we can safely trust to achieve similar results in the future.

Our people found on the Isthmus a certain amount of old French material and equipment which could be used. Some of it, in addition, could be sold as scrap iron. Some could be used for furnishing the foundation for filling in. For much no possible use could be devised that would not cost more than it would bring in.

The work is now going on with a vigor and efficiency pleasant to witness. The three big problems of the canal are the La Boca dams, the Gatun dam, and the Culebra cut. The Culebra cut must be made, anyhow; but of course changes as to the dams, or at least as to the locks adjacent to the dams, may still occur. The La Boca dams offer no particular problem, the bottom material being so good that there is a practical certainty, not merely as to what can be achieved, but as to the time of achievement. The Gatun dam offers the most serious problem which we have to solve; and yet the ablest men on the Isthmus believe that this problem is certain of solution along the lines proposed; although, of course, it necessitates great toil, energy, and intelligence, and although equally, of course, there will be some little risk in connection with the work. The risk arises from the fact that some of the material near the bottom is not so good as could be desired. If the huge earth dam now contemplated is thrown across from one foothill to the other we will have what is practically a low, broad, mountain ridge behind which will rise the inland lake. This artificial mountain will probably show less seepage, that is, will have greater restraining capacity than the average natural mountain range. The exact locality of the locks at this dam—as at the other dams—is now being determined. In April next Secretary Taft, with three of the ablest engineers of the country—Messrs. Noble, Stearns, and Ripley —will visit the Isthmus, and the three engineers will make the final and conclusive examinations as to the exact site for each lock. Meanwhile the work is going ahead without a break.

The Culebra cut does not offer such great risks; that is, the damage liable to occur from occasional land slips will not represent what may be called major disasters. The work will merely call for intelligence, perseverance, and executive capacity. It is, however, the work upon which most labor will have to be spent. The dams will be composed of the earth taken out of the cut and very possibly the building of the locks and dams will taken even longer than the cutting in Culebra itself.

The main work is now being done in the Culebra cut. It was striking and impressive to see the huge steam shovels in full play, the dumping trains carrying away the rock and earth they dislodged. The implements of French excavating machinery, which often stand a little way from the line of work, though of excellent construction, look like the veriest toys when compared with these new steam shovels, just as the French dumping cars seem like toy cars when compared with the long trains of huge cars, dumped by steam plows, which are now in use. This represents the enormous advance that has been made in machinery during the past quarter of a century. No doubt a quarter of a century hence this new machinery, of which we are now so proud, will similarly seem out of date, but it is certainly serving its purpose well now. The old French cars had to be entirely discarded. We still have in use a few of the more modern, but not most modern, cars, which hold but twelve yards of earth. They can be employed on certain lines with sharp curves. But the recent cars hold from twenty-five to thirty yards apiece, and instead of the old clumsy methods of unloading them, a steam plow is drawn from end to end of the whole vestibuled train, thus immensely economizing labor. In the rainy season the steam shovels can do but little in dirt, but they work steadily in rock and in the harder ground. There were some twenty-five at work during the time I was on the Isthmus, and their tremendous power and efficiency were most impressive.

As soon as the type of canal was decided this work began in good earnest. The rainy season will shortly be over and then there will be an immense increase in the amount taken out; but even during the last three months, in the rainy season, steady progress is shown by the figures: In August, 242,000 cubic yards; in September, 291,000 cubic yards, and in October, 325,000 cubic yards. In October new records were established for the output of individual shovels as well as for the tonnage haul of individual locomotives. I hope to see the growth of a healthy spirit of emulation between the different shovel and locomotive crews, just such a spirit as has grown on our battle ships between the different gun crews in matters of marksmanship. Passing through the cut the amount of new work can be seen at a glance. In one place the entire side of a hill had been taken out recently by twenty-seven tons of dynamite, which were exploded at one blast. At another place I was given a Presidential salute of twenty-one charges of dynamite. On the top notch of the Culebra cut the prism is now as wide as it will be; all told, the canal bed at this point has now been sunk about two hundred feet below what it originally was. It

will have to be sunk about one hundred and thirty feet farther.
Throughout the cut the drilling, blasting, shoveling, and hauling are
going on with constantly increasing energy, the huge shovels being
pressed up, as if they were mountain howitzers, into the most un-
likely looking places, where they eat their way into the hillsides.

The most advanced methods, not only in construction, but in railroad
management, have been applied in the Zone, with corresponding econ-
omies in time and cost. This has been shown in the handling of the
tonnage from ships into cars, and from cars into ships on the Panama
Railroad, where, thanks largely to the efficiency of General Manager
Bierd, the saving in time and cost, has been noteworthy. My examination tended to show that some of the departments had (doubtless
necessarily) become overdeveloped, and could now be reduced or
subordinated without impairment of efficiency and with a saving of
cost. The Chairman of the Commission, Mr. Shonts, has all matters
of this kind constantly in view, and is now reorganizing the government of the Zone, so as to make the form of administration both more
flexible and less expensive, subordinating everything to direct efficiency
with a view to the work of the Canal Commission. From time to
time changes of this kind will undoubtedly have to be made, for it
must be remembered that in this giant work of construction, it is continually necessary to develop departments or bureaus, which are vital
for the time being, but which soon become useless; just as it will be
continually necessary to put up buildings, and even to erect towns,
which in ten years will once more give place to jungle, or will then be
at the bottom of the great lakes at the ends of the canal.

It is not only natural, but inevitable, that a work as gigantic as this
which has been undertaken on the Isthmus should arouse every species
of hostility and criticism. The conditions are so new and so trying,
and the work so vast, that it would be absolutely out of the question
that mistakes should not be made. Checks will occur. Unforeseen
difficulties will arise. From time to time seemingly well-settled plans
will have to be changed. At present twenty-five thousand men are engaged on the task. After a while the number will be doubled. In
such a multitude it is inevitable that there should be here and there a
scoundrel. Very many of the poorer class of laborers lack the mental
development to protect themselves against either the rascality of others
or their own folly, and it is not possible for human wisdom to devise
a plan by which they can invariably be protected. In a place which has
been for ages a by-word for unhealthfulness, and with so large a con-
gregation of strangers suddenly put down and set to hard work there
will now and then be outbreaks of disease. There will now and then
be shortcomings in administration; there will be unlooked-for accidents
to delay the excavation of the cut or the building of the dams and

locks. Each such incident will be entirely natural, and, even though serious, no one of them will mean more than a little extra delay or trouble. Yet each, when discovered by sensation-mongers and retailed to timid folk of little faith, will serve as an excuse for the belief that the whole work is being badly managed. Experiments will continually be tried in housing, in hygiene, in street repairing, in dredging, and in digging earth and rock. Now and then an experiment will be a failure; and among those who hear of it, a certain proportion of doubting Thomases will at once believe that the whole work is a failure. Doubtless here and there some minor rascality will be uncovered; but as to this, I have to say that after the most painstaking inquiry I have been unable to find a single reputable person who had so much as heard of any serious accusations affecting the honesty of the Commission or of any responsible officer under it. I append a letter dealing with the most serious charge, that of the ownership of lots in Colon; the charge was not advanced by a reputable man, and is utterly baseless. It is not too much to say that the whole atmosphere of the Commission breathes honesty as it breathes efficiency and energy. Above all, the work has been kept absolutely clear of politics. I have never heard even a suggestion of spoils politics in connection with it.

I have investigated every complaint brought to me for which there seemed to be any shadow of foundation. In two or three cases, all of which I have indicated in the course of this message, I came to the conclusion that there was foundation for the complaint, and that the methods of the Commission in the respect complained of could be bettered. In the other instances the complaints proved absolutely baseless, save in two or three instances where they referred to mistakes which the Commission had already itself found out and corrected.

So much for honest criticism. There remains an immense amount of as reckless slander as has ever been published. Where the slanderers are of foreign origin I have no concern with them. Where they are Americans, I feel for them the heartiest contempt and indignation; because, in a spirit of wanton dishonesty and malice, they are trying to interfere with, and hamper the execution of, the greatest work of the kind ever attempted, and are seeking to bring to naught the efforts of their countrymen to put to the credit of America one of the giant feats of the ages. The outrageous accusations of these slanderers constitute a gross libel upon a body of public servants who, for trained intelligence, expert ability, high character and devotion to duty, have never been excelled anywhere. There is not a man among those directing the work on the Isthmus who has obtained his position on any other basis than merit alone, and not one who has used his position in any way for his own personal or pecuniary advantage.

After most careful consideration we have decided to let out most of the work by contract, if we can come to satisfactory terms with the contractors. The whole work is of a kind suited to the peculiar genius of our people; and our people have developed the type of contractor best fitted to grapple with it. It is, of course, much better to do the work in large part by contract than to do it all by the Government, provided it is possible on the one hand to secure to the contractor a sufficient remuneration to make it worth while for responsible contractors of the best kind to undertake the work; and provided on the other hand it can be done on terms which will not give an excessive profit to the contractor at the expense of the Government. After much consideration the plan already promulgated by the Secretary of War was adopted. This plan in its essential features was drafted, after careful and thorough study and consideration, by the Chief Engineer, Mr. Stevens, who, while in the employment of Mr. Hill, the president of the Great Northern Railroad, had personal experience of this very type of contract. Mr. Stevens then submitted the plan to the Chairman of the Commission, Mr. Shonts, who went carefully over it with Mr. Rogers, the legal adviser of the Commission, to see that all legal difficulties were met. He then submitted copies of the plan to both Secretary Taft and myself. Secretary Taft submitted it to some of the best counsel at the New York bar, and afterwards I went over it very carefully with Mr. Taft and Mr. Shonts, and we laid the plan in its general features before Mr. Root. My conclusion is that it combines the maximum of advantage with the minimum of disadvantage. Under it a premium will be put upon the speedy and economical construction of the canal, and a penalty imposed on delay and waste. The plan as promulgated is tentative; doubtless it will have to be changed in some respects before we can come to a satisfactory agreement with responsible contractors—perhaps even after the bids have been received; and of course it is possible that we cannot come to an agreement, in which case the Government will do the work itself. Meanwhile the work on the Isthmus is progressing steadily and without any let-up.

A seven-headed commission is, of course, a clumsy executive instrument. We should have but one commissioner, with such heads of departments and other officers under him as we may find necessary. We should be expressly permitted to employ the best engineers in the country as consulting engineers.

I accompany this paper with a map showing substantially what the canal will be like when it is finished. When the Culebra cut has been made and the dams built (if they are built as at present proposed) there will then be at both the Pacific and Atlantic ends of the canal. two great fresh-water lakes, connected by a broad channel running at the bottom of a ravine, across the backbone of the Western Hemisphere. Those best informed believe that the work will be completed in about eight years; but it is never safe to prophesy about such a work as this, especially in the Tropics.

I am informed that representatives of the commercial clubs of four cities—Boston, Chicago, Cincinnati, and St. Louis—the membership of which includes most of the leading business men of those cities, expect to visit the Isthmus for the purpose of examining the work of construction of the canal. I am glad to hear it, and I shall direct that every facility be given them to see all that is to be seen in the work which the Government is doing. Such interest as a visit like this would indicate will have a good effect upon the men who are doing the work, on one hand, while on the other hand it will offer as witnesses of the exact conditions, men whose experience as business men and whose impartiality will make the result of their observations of value to the country as a whole.

Of the success of the enterprise I am as well convinced as one can be of any enterprise that is human. It is a stupendous work upon which our fellow-countrymen are engaged down there on the Isthmus, and while we should hold them to a strict accountability for the way in which they perform it, we should yet recognize, with frank generosity, the epic nature of the task on which they are engaged and its world-wide importance. They are doing something which will redound immeasurably to the credit of America, which will benefit all the world, and which will last for ages to come. Under Mr. Shonts and Mr. Stevens and Dr. Gorgas this work has started with every omen of good fortune. They and their worthy associates, from the highest to the lowest, are entitled to the same credit that we would give to the picked men of a victorious army; for this conquest of peace will, in its great and far-reaching effect, stand as among the very greatest conquests, whether of peace or of war, which have ever been won by any of the peoples of mankind. A badge is to be given to every American citizen who for a specified time has taken part in this work; for participation in it will hereafter be held to reflect honor upon the man participating just as it reflects honor upon a soldier to have belonged to a mighty army in a great war for righteousness. Our fellow-countrymen on the Isthmus are working for our interest and for the national renown in the same spirit and with the same efficiency that the men of the Army and Navy work in time of war. It behooves us in our turn to do all we can to hold up their hands and to aid them in every way to bring their great work to a triumphant conclusion.

THEODORE ROOSEVELT.

SPECIAL MESSAGE.

THE WHITE HOUSE, December 19, 1906.

To the Senate:

In response to Senate resolution of December 6 addressed to me, and to the two Senate resolutions addressed to him, the Secretary of War has, by my direction, submitted to me a report which I herewith send to the Senate, together with several documents, including a letter of General Nettleton and memoranda as to precedents for the summary discharge or mustering out of regiments or companies, some or all of the members of which had been guilty of misconduct.

I ordered the discharge of nearly all the members of Companies B, C, and D of the Twenty-fifth Infantry by name, in the exercise of my constitutional power and in pursuance of what, after full consideration, I found to be my constitutional duty as Commander in Chief of the United States Army. I am glad to avail myself of the opportunity afforded by these resolutions to lay before the Senate the following facts as to the murderous conduct of certain members of the companies in question and as to the conspiracy by which many of the other members of these companies saved the criminals from justice, to the disgrace of the United States uniform.

I call your attention to the accompanying reports of Maj. Augustus P. Blocksom, of Lieut. Col. Leonard A. Lovering, and of Brig. Gen. Ernest A. Garlington, the Inspector-General of the United States Army, of their investigation into the conduct of the troops in question. An effort has been made to discredit the fairness of the investigation into the conduct of these colored troops by pointing out that General Garlington is a Southerner. Precisely the same action would have been taken had the troops been white—indeed, the discharge would probably have been made in more summary fashion. General Garlington is a native of South Carolina; Lieutenant-Colonel Lovering is a native of New Hampshire; Major Blocksom is a native of Ohio. As it happens, the disclosure of the guilt of the troops was made in the report of the officer who comes from Ohio, and the efforts of the officer who comes from South Carolina were confined to the endeavor to shield the innocent men of the companies in question, if any such there were, by securing information which would enable us adequately to punish the guilty. But I wish it distinctly understood that the fact of the birthplace of either officer is one which I absolutely refuse to consider. The standard of professional honor and of loyalty to the flag and the service is the same for all officers and all enlisted men of the United States Army, and I resent with the keenest indignation any effort to draw any line among them based upon birthplace, creed, or any other consideration of the kind. I should put the same entire faith in these reports if it had happened that they were all made by men coming from some one State, whether in the South or the North, the East or the West, as I now do, when, as it happens, they were made by officers born in different States.

Major Blocksom's report is most careful, is based upon the testimony of scores of eye-witnesses—testimony which conflicted only in non-essentials and which established the essential facts beyond chance of successful contradiction. Not only has no successful effort been made to traverse his findings in any essential particular, but, as a matter of fact, every trustworthy report from outsiders amply corroborates them, by far the best of these outside reports being that of Gen. A. B. Nettleton, made in a letter to the Secretary of War, which I herewith append; General Nettleton being an ex-Union soldier, a consistent friend of the colored man throughout his life, a lifelong Republican, a citizen of Illinois, and Assistant Secretary of the Treasury under President Harrison.

It appears that in Brownsville, the city immediately beside which Fort Brown is situated, there had been considerable feeling between the citizens and the colored troops of the garrison companies. Difficulties had occurred, there being a conflict of evidence as to whether the citizens or the colored troops were to blame. My impression is that, as a matter of fact, in these difficulties there was blame attached to both sides; but this is a wholly unimportant matter for our present purpose, as nothing that occurred offered in any shape or way an excuse or justification for the atrocious conduct of the troops when, in lawless and murderous spirit, and under cover of the night, they made their attack upon the citizens.

The attack was made near midnight on August 13. The following facts as to this attack are made clear by Major Blocksom's investigation and have not been, and, in my judgment, can not be, successfully controverted. From 9 to 15 or 20 of the colored soldiers took part in the attack. They leaped over the walls from the barracks and hurried through the town. They shot at whomever they saw moving, and they shot into houses where they saw lights. In some of these houses there were women and children, as the would-be murderers must have known. In one house in which there were two women and five children some ten shots went through at a height of about 4½ feet above the floor, one putting out the lamp upon the table. The lieutenant of police of the town heard the firing and rode toward it. He met the raiders, who, as he stated, were about 15 colored soldiers. They instantly started firing upon him. He turned and rode off, and they continued firing upon him until they had killed his horse. They shot him in the right arm (it was afterwards amputated above the elbow). A number of shots were also fired at two other policemen. The raiders fired several times into a hotel, some of the shots being aimed at a guest sitting by a window. They shot into a saloon, killing the bartender and wounding another man. At the same time other raiders fired into another house in which women and children were sleeping, two of the shots going through the mosquito bar over the bed in which the mistress of the house and her two children were lying. Several other houses were struck by bullets. It was at night, and the streets of the town are poorly lighted, so that none of the individual raiders were recognized; but the evidence of many witnesses of all classes was conclusive to the effect that the raiders were negro soldiers. The shattered bullets, shells, and clips of the Government rifles, which were found on the ground, are merely corroborative. So are the bullet holes in the houses; some of which it appears must, from the direction, have been fired from the fort just at the moment when the soldiers left it. Not a bullet hole appears in any of the structures of the fort.

The townspeople were completely surprised by the unprovoked and murderous savagery of the attack. The soldiers were the aggressors from start to finish. They met with no substantial resistance, and one and all who took part in that raid stand as deliberate murderers, who did murder one man, who tried to murder others, and who tried to murder women and children. The act was one of horrible atrocity, and so far as I am aware, unparalleled for infamy in the annals of the United States Army.

The white officers of the companies were completely taken by surprise, and at first evidently believed that the firing meant that the townspeople were attacking the soldiers. It was not until 2 or 3 o'clock in the morning that any of them became aware of the truth. I have directed a careful investigation into the conduct of the officers, to see if any of them were blameworthy, and I have approved the recommendation of the War Department that two be brought before a court-martial.

As to the noncommissioned officers and enlisted men, there can be no doubt whatever that many were necessarily privy, after if not before the attack, to the conduct of those who took actual part in this murderous riot. I refer to Major Blocksom's report for proof of the fact that certainly some and probably all of the noncommissioned officers in charge of quarters who were responsible for the gun-racks and had keys thereto in their personal possession knew what men were engaged in the attack.

Major Penrose, in command of the post, in his letter (included in the Appendix) gives the reasons why he was reluctantly convinced that some of the men under him—as he thinks, from 7 to 10—got their rifles, slipped out of quarters to do the shooting, and returned to the barracks without being discovered, the shooting all occurring within two and a half short blocks of the barracks. It was possible for the raiders to go from the fort to the farthest point of firing and return in less than ten minutes, for the distance did not exceed 350 yards.

Such are the facts of this case. General Nettleton, in his letter herewith appended, states that next door to where he is writing in Brownsville is a small cottage where a children's party had just broken up before the house was riddled by United States bullets, fired by United States troops, from United States Springfield rifles, at close range, with the purpose of killing or maiming the inmates, including the parents and children who were still in the well-lighted house, and whose escape from death under such circumstances was astonishing. He states that on another street he daily looks upon fresh bullet scars where a volley from similar Government rifles was fired into the side and windows of a hotel occupied at the time by sleeping or frightened guests from abroad who could not possibly have given any offense to the assailants. He writes that the chief of the Brownsville police is again on duty from hospital, and carries an empty sleeve because he was shot by Federal soldiers from the adjacent garrison in the course of their murderous foray; and not far away is the fresh grave of an unoffending citizen of the place, a boy in years, who was wantonly shot down by these United States soldiers while unarmed and attempting to escape.

The effort to confute this testimony so far has consisted in the assertion or implication that the townspeople shot one another in order to discredit the soldiers—an absurdity too gross to need discussion, and unsupported by a shred of evidence. There is no question as to the murder and the attempted murders; there is no question that some of the soldiers were guilty thereof; there is no question that many of their comrades privy to the deed have combined to shelter the criminals from justice. These comrades of the murderers, by their own action, have rendered it necessary either to leave all the men, including the murderers, in the Army, or to turn them all out; and under such circumstances there was no alternative, for the usefulness of the Army would be at an end were we to permit such an outrage to be committed with impunity.

In short, the evidence proves conclusively that a number of the soldiers engaged in a deliberate and concerted attack, as cold blooded as it was cowardly; the purpose being to terrorize the community, and to kill or injure men, women, and children in their homes and beds or on the streets, and this at an hour of the night when concerted or effective resistance or defense was out of the question, and when detection by identification of the criminals in the United States uniform was wellnigh impossible. So much for the original crime. A blacker never stained the annals of our Army. It has been supplemented by another, only less black, in the shape of a successful conspiracy of silence for the purpose of shielding those who took part in the original conspiracy of murder. These soldiers were not school boys on a frolic. They were full-grown men, in the uniform of the United States Army, armed with deadly weapons, sworn to uphold the laws of the United States, and under every obligation of oath and honor not merely to refrain from criminality, but with the sturdiest rigor to hunt down criminality; and the crime they committed or connived at was murder. They perverted the power put into their hands to sustain the law into the most deadly violation of the law. The noncommissioned officers are primarily responsible for the discipline and good conduct of the men; they are appointed to their positions for the very purpose of preserving this discipline and good conduct, and of detecting and securing the punishment of every enlisted man who does what is wrong. They fill, with reference to the discipline, a part that the commissioned officers are of course unable to fill, although the ultimate responsibility for the discipline can never be shifted from the shoulders of the latter. Under any ordinary circumstances the first duty of the noncommissioned officers, as of the commissioned officers, is to train the private in the ranks so that he may be an efficient fighting man against a foreign foe. But there is an even higher duty, so obvious that it is not under ordinary circumstances necessary so much as to allude to it—the duty of training the soldier so that he shall be a protection and not a menace to his peaceful fellow-citizens, and above all to the women and children of the nation. Unless this duty is well performed, the Army becomes a mere dangerous mob; and if conduct such as that of the murderers in question is not, where possible, punished, and, where this is not possible, unless the chance of its repetition is guarded against in the most thoroughgoing fashion, it would be better that the entire Army should be disbanded. It is vital for the Army to be imbued with the spirit which will make every man in it, and above all, the officers and noncommissioned officers, feel it a matter of highest obligation to discover and punish, and not to shield, the criminal in uniform.

Yet some of the noncommissioned officers and many of the men of the three companies in question have banded together in a conspiracy to protect the assassins and would-be assassins who have disgraced their uniform by the conduct above related. Many of these non-commissioned officers and men must have known, and all of them may have known, circumstances which would have led to the conviction of those engaged in the murderous assault. They have stolidly and as one man broken their oaths of enlistment and refused to help discover the criminals.

By my direction every effort was made to persuade those innocent of murder among them to separate themselves from the guilty by helping bring the criminals to justice. They were warned that if they did not take advantage of the offer they would all be discharged from the service and forbidden again to enter the employ of the Government. They refused to profit by the warning. I accordingly had them discharged. If any organization of troops in the service, white or black, is guilty of similar conduct in the future I shall follow precisely the same course. Under no circumstances will I consent to keep in the service bodies of men whom the circumstances show to be a menace to the country. Incidentally I may add that the soldiers of longest service and highest position who suffered because of the order, so far from being those who deserve most sympathy, deserve least, for they are the very men upon whom we should be able especially to rely to prevent mutiny and murder.

People have spoken as if this discharge from the service was a punishment. I deny emphatically that such is the case, because as punishment it is utterly inadequate. The punishment meet for mutineers and murderers such as those guilty of the Brownsville assault is death; and a punishment only less severe ought to be meted out to those who have aided and abetted mutiny and murder and treason by refusing to help in their detection. I would that it were possible for me to have punished the guilty men. I regret most keenly that I have not been able to do so.

Be it remembered always that these men were all in the service of the United States under contracts of enlistment, which by their terms and by statute were terminable by my direction as Commander in Chief of the Army. It was my clear duty to terminate those contracts when the public interest demanded it; and it would have been a betrayal of the public interest on my part not to terminate the contracts which were keeping in the service of the United States a body of mutineers and murderers.

Any assertion that these men were dealt with harshly because they were colored men is utterly without foundation. Officers or enlisted men, white men or colored men, who were guilty of such conduct, would have been treated in precisely the same way; for there can be nothing more important than for the United States Army, in all its membership, to understand that its arms cannot be turned with impunity against the peace and order of the civil community.

There are plenty of precedents for the action taken. I call your attention to the memoranda herewith submitted from The Military Secretary's office of the War Department, and a memorandum from The Military Secretary enclosing a piece by ex-Corporal Hesse, now chief of division in The Military Secretary's office, together with a letter from District Attorney James Wilkinson, of New Orleans. The district attorney's letter recites several cases in which white United States soldiers, being arrested for crime, were tried, and every soldier and employee of the regiment, or in the fort at which the soldier was stationed, volunteered all they knew, both before and at the trial, so as to secure justice. In one case the soldier was acquitted. In another case the soldier was convicted of murder, the conviction resulting from the fact that every soldier, from the commanding officer to the humblest private, united in securing all the evidence in their power about the crime. In other cases, for less offense, soldiers were convicted purely because their comrades in arms, in a spirit of fine loyalty to the honor of the service, at once told the whole story of the troubles and declined to identify themselves with the criminals.

During the civil war numerous precedents for the action taken by me occurred in the shape of the summary discharge of regiments or companies because of misconduct on the part of some or all of their members. The Sixtieth Ohio was summarily discharged, on the ground that the regiment was disorganized, mutinous, and worthless. The Eleventh New York was discharged by reason of general demoralization and numerous desertions. Three companies of the Fifth Missouri Cavalry and one company of the Fourth Missouri Cavalry were mustered out of the service of the United States without trial by court-martial by reason of mutinous conduct and disaffection *of the majority of the members of these companies* (an almost exact parallel to my action). Another Missouri regiment was mustered out of service because it was in a state bordering closely on mutiny. Other examples, including New Jersey, Maryland, and other organizations, are given in the enclosed papers.

I call your particular attention to the special field order of Brig. Gen. U. S. Grant, issued from the headquarters of the Thirteenth Army Corps on November 16, 1862, in reference to the Twentieth Illinois. Members of this regiment had broken into a store and taken goods to the value of some $1,240, and the rest of the regiment, including especially two officers, failed, in the words of General Grant, to " exercise their authority to ferret out the men guilty of the offenses." General Grant accordingly mustered out of the service of the United States the two officers in question, and assessed the sum of $1,240 against the said regiment as a whole, officers and men to be assessed pro rata on their pay. In its essence this action is precisely similar to that I have taken; although the offense was of course trivial compared to the offense with which I had to deal.

Ex-Corporal Hesse recites what occurred in a United States regular regiment in the spring of 1860. (Corporal Hesse subsequently, when the regiment was surrendered to the Confederates by General Twiggs, saved the regimental colors by wrapping them about his body, under his clothing, and brought them north in safety, receiving a medal of honor for his action.) It appears that certain members of the regiment lynched a barkeeper who had killed one of the soldiers. Being unable to discover the culprits, Col. Robert E. Lee, then in command of the Department of Texas, ordered the company to be disbanded and the members transferred to other companies and discharged at the end of their enlistment, without honor. Owing to the outbreak of the Civil War, and the consequent loss of records and confusion, it is not possible to say what finally became of this case.

When General Lee was in command of the Army of Northern Virginia, as will appear from the inclosed clipping from the Charlotte Observer, he issued an order in October, 1864, disbanding a certain battalion for cowardly conduct, stating at the time his regret that there were some officers and men belonging to the organization who, although not deserving it, were obliged to share in the common disgrace because the good of the service demanded it.

In addition to the discharges of organizations, which are of course infrequent, there are continual cases of the discharge of individual enlisted men without honor and without trial by court-martial. The official record shows that during the fiscal year ending June 30, last, such discharges were issued by the War Department without trial by court-martial in the cases of 352 enlisted men of the Regular Army, 35 of them being on account of " having become disqualified for service through own misconduct." Moreover, in addition to the discharges without honor ordered by the War Department, there were a considerable number of discharges without honor issued by subordinate military authorities under paragraph 148 of the Army Regulations, " where the service has not been honest and faithful—that is, where the service does not warrant reënlistment."

So much for the military side of the case. But I wish to say something additional, from the standpoint of the race question. In my message at the opening of the Congress I discussed the matter of lynching. In it I gave utterance to the abhorrence which all decent citizens should feel for the deeds of the men (in almost all cases white men) who take part in lynchings. and at the same time I condemned, as all decent men of any color should condemn, the action of those colored men who actively or passively shield the colored criminal from the law. In the case of these companies we had to deal with men who in the first place were guilty of what is practically the worst possible form of lynching— for a lynching is in its essence lawless and murderous vengeance taken by an armed mob for real or fancied wrongs—and who in the second place covered up the crime of lynching by standing with a vicious solidarity to protect the criminals.

It is of the utmost importance to all our people that we shall deal with each man on his merits as a man, and not deal with him merely as a member of a given race; that we shall judge each man by his conduct and not his color. This is important for the white man, and it is far more important for the colored man. More evil and sinister counsel never was given to any people than that given to colored men by those advisers, whether black or white, who, by apology and condonation, encourage conduct such as that of the three companies in question. If the colored men elect to stand by criminals of their own race because they are of their own race, they assuredly lay up for themselves the most dreadful day of reckoning. Every farsighted friend of the colored race in its efforts to strive onward and upward, should teach first, as the most important lesson, alike to the white man and the black, the duty of treating the individual man strictly on his worth as he shows it. Any conduct by colored people which tends to substitute for this rule the rule of standing by and shielding an evil doer because he is a member of their race, means the inevitable degradation of the colored race. It may and probably does mean damage to the white race, but it means ruin to the black race.

Throughout my term of service in the Presidency I have acted on the principle thus advocated. In the North as in the South I have appointed colored men of high character to office, utterly disregarding the protests of those who would have kept them out of office because they were colored men. So far as was in my power, I have sought to secure for the colored people all their rights under the law. I have done all I could to secure them equal school training when young, equal opportunity to earn their livelihood, and achieve their happiness when old. I have striven to break up peonage; I have upheld the hands of those who, like Judge Jones and Judge Speer, have warred against this peonage, because I would hold myself unfit to be President if I did not feel the same revolt at wrong done a colored man as I feel at wrong done a white man. I have condemned in unstinted terms the crime of lynching perpetrated by white men, and I should take instant advantage of any opportunity whereby I could bring to justice a mob of lynchers. In precisely the same spirit I have now acted with reference to these colored men who have been guilty of a black and dastardly crime. In one policy, as in the other, I do not claim as a favor, but I challenge as a right, the support of every citizen of this country, whatever his color, provided only he has in him the spirit of genuine and farsighted patriotism.

THEODORE ROOSEVELT.

SPECIAL MESSAGE.

THE WHITE HOUSE, January 14, 1907.

To the Senate:

In my message to the Senate treating of the dismissal, without honor, of certain named members of the three companies of the Twenty-fifth Infantry, I gave the reports of the officers upon which the dismissal was based. These reports were made in accordance with the custom in such cases; for it would, of course, be impossible to preserve discipline in the Army save by pursuing precisely the course that in this case was pursued. Inasmuch, however, as in the Senate question was raised as to the sufficiency of the evidence, I deemed it wise to send Major Blocksom, and Assistant to the Attorney-General Purdy, to Brownsville to make a thorough investigation on the ground in reference to the matter. I herewith transmit Secretary Taft's report, and the testimony taken under oath of the various witnesses examined in the course of the investigation. I also submit various exhibits, including maps of Brownsville and Fort Brown, photographs of various buildings, a letter from Judge Parks to his wife, together with a bandoleer, 33 empty shells, 7 ball cartridges, and 4 clips picked up in the streets of Brownsville within a few hours after the shooting; 3 steel-jacketed bullets and some scraps of the casings of other bullets picked out of the houses into which they had been fired. A telegram from United States Commissioner R. B. Creager, at Brownsville, announces that 6 additional bullets—like the others, from Springfield rifles—taken from buildings in Brownsville, with supporting affidavits, have since been sent to the Secretary of War.

It appears from the testimony that on the night of the 13th of August, 1906, several crimes were committed by some person or persons in the city of Brownsville. Among these were the following:

(*a*) The murder of Frank Natus.

(*b*) The assault with intent to kill the lieutenant of police, Dominguez, whose horse was killed under him and whose arm was shot so severely that it had to be amputated.

(*c*) The assault with intent to kill Mr. and Mrs. Hale Odin, and their little boy, who were in the window of the Miller Hotel.

(*d*) The shooting into several private residences in the city of Brownsville, three of them containing women and children.

(*e*) The shooting at and slightly wounding of Preciado.

These crimes were certainly committed by somebody.

As to the motive for the commission of the crimes, it appears that trouble of a more or less serious kind had occurred between individual members of the companies and individual citizens of Brownsville, culminating in complaints which resulted in the soldiers being confined within the limits of the garrison on the evening of the day in question.

The evidence, as will be seen, shows beyond any possibility of honest question that some individuals among the colored troops whom I have dismissed committed the outrages mentioned; and that some or all of the other individuals whom I dismissed had knowledge of the deed and shielded from the law those who committed it.

The only motive suggested as possibly influencing anyone else was a desire to get rid of the colored troops, so strong that it impelled the citizens of Brownsville to shoot up their own houses, to kill one of their own number, to assault their own police, wounding the lieutenant, who had been an officer for twenty years—all with the purpose of discrediting the negro troops. The suggestion is on its face so ludicrously impossible that it is difficult to treat it as honestly made. This theory supposes that the assailants succeeded in obtaining the uniform of the negro soldiers; that before starting on their raid they got over the fence of the fort unchallenged, and without discovery by the negro troops opened fire on the town from within the fort; that they blacked their faces so that at least fourteen eye-witnesses mistook them for negroes; that they disguised their voices so that it least six witnesses who heard them speak mistook their voices as being those of negroes. They were not Mexicans, for they were heard by various witnesses to speak in English. The weapons they used were Springfield rifles; for the ammunition which they used was that of the Springfield rifle and no other, and could not have been used in any gun in Texas or any part of the Union or Mexico, or in any other part of the world, save only in the Springfield now used by the United States troops, including the negro troops in the garrison at Brownsville, and by no other persons save these troops—a weapon which had only been in use by the United States troops for some four or five months prior to the shooting in question, and which is not in the possession of private citizens.

The cartridge used will go into one other rifle used in the United States, when specially chambered—the Winchester of the '95 model— but it will rarely if ever go off when in it; and, moreover, the bullets picked out of the buildings show the markings of the four so-called " lands " which come from being fired through the Springfield, but not through the Winchester, the latter showing six. The bullets which I herewith submit, which were found in the houses, could not therefore have been fired from a Winchester or any other sporting rifle, although the cartridges might have been put into a Winchester model of '95. The bullets might have been fired from a Krag, but the cartridges would not have gone into a Krag. Taking the shells and the bullets together, the proof is conclusive that the new Springfield rifle was the weapon used by the midnight assassins, and could not by any possibility have been any other rifle of any kind in the world. This of itself establishes the fact that the assailants were United States soldiers, and would be conclusive on this point if not one soldier had been seen or heard by any residents in Brownsville on the night in question, and if nothing were known save the finding of the shells, clips, and bullets.

Fourteen eye-witnesses, namely, Charles R. Chase, Amado Martinez, Mrs. Kate Leahy, Palerno Preciado, Ygnacio Dominguez, Macedonio Ramirez, George W. Rendall, Jose Martinez, J. P. McDonald, F. H. A. Sanborn, Herbert Elkins, Hale Odin, Mrs. Hale Odin, and Judge Parks, testified that they saw the assailants or some of them at varying distances, and that they were negro troops, most of the witnesses giving their testimony in such shape that there is no possibility of their having been mistaken. Two other witnesses, Joseph Bodin and Genero Padron, saw some of the assailants and testified that they were soldiers (the only soldiers in the neighborhood being the colored troops). Four other witnesses, namely, S. C. Moore, Doctor Thorn, Charles S. Canada, and Charles A. Hammond, testified to hearing the shooting and hearing the voices of the men who were doing it, and that these voices were those of negroes, but did not actually see the men who were doing the shooting. About 25 other witnesses gave testimony corroborating to a greater or less degree the testimony of those who thus saw the shooters or heard them. The testimony of these eye and ear-witnesses would establish beyond all possibility of contradiction the fact that the shooting was committed by ten or fifteen or more of the negro troops from the garrison, and this testimony of theirs would be amply sufficient in itself if not a cartridge or bullet had been found; exactly as the bullets and cartridges that were found would have established the guilt of the troops even had not a single eye-witness seen them or other witness heard them.

The testimony of the witnesses and the position of the bullet holes show that fifteen or twenty of the negro troops gathered inside the fort, and that the first shots fired into the town were fired from within the fort; some of them at least from the upper galleries of the barracks.

The testimony further shows that the troops then came out over the walls, some of them perhaps going through the gate, and advanced a distance of 300 yards or thereabouts into the town. During their advance they shot into two hotels and some nine or ten other houses. Three of the private houses into which they fired contained women and children. They deliberately killed Frank Natus, the bartender, shooting him down from a distance of about 15 yards. They shot at a man and woman, Mr. and Mrs. Odin, and their little boy, as they stood in the window of the Miller Hotel, the bullet going less than 2 inches from the head of the woman. They shot down the lieutenant of police, who was on horseback, killing his horse and wounding him so that his arm had to be amputated. They attempted to kill the two policemen who were his companions, shooting one through the hat. They shot at least 8 bullets into the Cowen house, putting out a lighted lamp on the dining-room table. Mrs. Cowen and her five children were in the house; they at once threw themselves prone on the floor and were not hit. They fired into the Starck house, the bullets going through the mosquito bar of a bed from 18 to 20 inches above where little children were sleeping. There was a light in the children's room.

The shooting took place near midnight. The panic caused by the utterly unexpected attack was great. The darkness, of course, increased the confusion. There is conflict of testimony on some of the minor points, but every essential point is established beyond possibility of honest question. The careful examination of Mr. Purdy, Assistant to the Attorney-General, resulted merely in strengthening the reports already made by the regular army authorities. The shooting, it appears, occupied about ten minutes, although it may have been some minutes more or less. It is out of the question that the fifteen or twenty men engaged in the assault could have gathered behind the wall of the fort, begun firing, some of them on the porches of the barracks, gone out into the town, fired in the neighborhood of 200 shots in the town, and then returned—the total time occupied from the time of the first shot to the time of their return being somewhere in the neighborhood of ten minutes—without many of their comrades knowing what they had done. Indeed, the fuller details as established by the additional evidence taken since I last communicated with the Senate make it likely that there were very few, if any, of the soldiers dismissed who could have been ignorant of what occurred. It is well-nigh impossible that any of the noncommissioned officers who were at the barracks should not have known what occurred.

The additional evidence thus taken renders it in my opinion impossible to question the conclusions upon which my order was based. I have gone most carefully over every issue of law and fact that has been raised. I am now satisfied that the effect of my order dismissing these men without honor was not to bar them from all civil employment under the Government, and therefore that the part of the order which consisted of a declaration to this effect was lacking in validity, and I have directed that such portion be revoked. As to the rest of the order, dismissing the individuals in question without honor, and declaring the effect of such discharge under the law and regulations to be a bar to their future reenlistment either in the Army or the Navy, there is no doubt of my constitutional and legal power. The order was within my discretion, under the Constitution and the laws, and can not be reviewed or reversed save by another Executive order. The facts did not merely warrant the action I took—they rendered such action imperative unless I was to prove false to my sworn duty.

If any one of the men discharged hereafter shows to my satisfaction that he is clear of guilt, or of shielding the guilty, I will take what action is warranted; but the circumstances I have above detailed most certainly put upon any such man the burden of thus clearing himself.

THEODORE ROOSEVELT.

SPECIAL MESSAGE.

THE WHITE HOUSE, March 25, 1908.

To the Senate and House of Representatives:

I call your attention to certain measures as to which I think there should be action by the Congress before the close of the present session. There is ample time for their consideration. As regards most if not all of the matters, bills have been introduced into one or the other of the two Houses, and it is not too much to hope that action will be taken one way or the other on these bills at the present session. In my message at the opening of the present session, and, indeed, in various messages to previous Congresses, I have repeatedly suggested action on most of these measures.

Child labor should be prohibited throughout the Nation. At least a model child-labor bill should be passed for the District of Columbia. It is unfortunate that in the one place solely dependent upon Congress for its legislation there should be no law whatever to protect children by forbidding or regulating their labor.

I renew my recommendation for the immediate reënactment of an employers' liability law, drawn to conform to the recent decision of the Supreme Court. Within the limits indicated by the court, the law should be made thorough and comprehensive, and the protection it affords should embrace every class of employee to which the power of the Congress can extend.

In addition to a liability law protecting the employees of common carriers, the Government should show its good faith by enacting a further law giving compensation to its own employees for injury or death incurred in its service. It is a reproach to us as a Nation that in both Federal and State legislation we have afforded less protection to public and private employees than any other industrial country of the world.

I also urge that action be taken along the line of the recommendations I have already made concerning injunctions in labor disputes. No temporary restraining order should be issued by any court without notice; and the petition for a permanent injunction upon which such temporary restraining order has been issued should be heard by the court issuing the same within a reasonable time—say, not to exceed a week or thereabouts from the date when the order was issued. It is worth considering whether it would not give greater popular confidence in the impartiality of sentences for contempt if it was required that the issue should be decided by another judge than the one issuing the injunction, except where the contempt is committed in the presence of the court, or in other case of urgency.

I again call attention to the urgent need of amending the interstate-commerce law and especially the anti-trust law along the lines indicated in my last message. The interstate-commerce law should be amended so as to give railroads the right to make traffic agreements, subject to these agreements being approved by the Interstate Commerce Commission and published in all of their details. The Commission should also be given the power to make public and to pass upon the issuance of all securities hereafter issued by railroads doing an interstate-commerce business.

A law should be passed providing in effect that when a Federal court determines to place a common carrier or other public utility concern under the control of a receivership, the Attorney-General should have the right to nominate at least one of the receivers; or else in some other way the interests of the stockholders should be consulted, so that the management may not be wholly redelivered to the man or men the failure of whose policy may have necessitated the creation of the receivership. Receiverships should be used, not to operate roads, but as speedily as possible to pay their debts and return them to the proper owners.

In addition to the reasons I have already urged on your attention, it has now become important that there should be an amendment of the anti-trust law, because of the uncertainty as to how this law affects combinations among labor men and farmers, if the combination has any tendency to restrict interstate commerce. All of these combinations, if and while existing for and engaged in the promotion of innocent and proper purposes, should be recognized as legal. As I have repeatedly pointed out, this antitrust law was a most unwisely drawn statute. It was perhaps inevitable that in feeling after the right remedy the first attempts to provide such should be crude; and it was absolutely imperative that some legislation should be passed to control, in the interest of the public, the business use of the enormous aggregations of corporate wealth that are so marked a feature of the modern industrial world. But the present anti-trust law, in its construction and working, has exemplified only too well the kind of legislation which, under the guise of being thoroughgoing, is drawn up in such sweeping form as to become either ineffective or else mischievous.

In the modern industrial world combinations are absolutely necessary; they are necessary among business men, they are necessary among laboring men, they are becoming more and more necessary among farmers. Some of these combinations are among the most powerful of all instruments for wrongdoing. Others offer the only effective way of meeting actual business needs. It is mischievous and unwholesome to keep upon the statute books unmodified, a law, like the anti-trust law, which, while in practice only partially effective against vicious combinations, has nevertheless in theory been construed so as sweepingly to prohibit every combination for the transaction of modern business. Some real good has resulted from this law. But the time has come when it is imperative to modify it. Such modification is urgently needed for the sake of the business men of the country, for the sake of the wage-workers, and for the sake of the farmers. The Congress can not afford to leave it on the statute books in its present shape.

It has now become uncertain how far this law may involve all labor organizations and farmers' organizations, as well as all business organizations, in conflict with the law; or, if we secure literal compliance with the law, how far it may result in the destruction of the organizations necessary for the transaction of modern business, as well as of all labor organizations and farmers' organizations, completely check the wise movement for securing business cooperation among farmers, and put back half a century the progress of the movement for the betterment of labor. A bill has been presented in the Congress to remedy this situation. Some such measure as this bill is needed in the interest of all engaged in the industries which are essential to the country's well-being. I do not pretend to say the exact shape that the bill should take, and the suggestions I have to offer are tentative; and my views would apply equally to any other measure which would achieve the desired end. Bearing this in mind, I would suggest, merely tentatively, the following changes in the law:

The substantive part of the anti-trust law should remain as at present; that is, every contract in restraint of trade or commerce among the several States or with foreign nations should continue to be declared illegal; provided, however, that some proper governmental authority (such as the Commissioner of Corporations acting under the Secretary of Commerce and Labor) be allowed to pass on any such contracts. Probably the best method of providing for this would be to enact that any contract, subject to the prohibition contained in the antitrust law, into which it was desired to enter, might be filed with the Bureau of Corporations or other appropriate executive body. This would provide publicity. Within, say, sixty days of the filing—which period could be extended by order of the Department whenever for any reason it did not give the Department sufficient time for a thorough examination—the executive department having power might forbid the contract, which would then become subject to the provisions of the anti-trust law, if at all in restraint of trade.

If no such prohibition was issued, the contract would then only be liable to attack on the ground that it constituted an unreasonable restraint of trade. Whenever the period of filing had passed without any such prohibition, the contracts or combinations could be disapproved or forbidden only after notice and hearing with a reasonable provision for summary review on appeal by the courts. Labor organizations, farmers' organizations, and other organizations not organized for purposes of profit, should be allowed to register under the law by giving the location of the head office, the charter and by-laws, and the names and addresses of their principal officers. In the interest of all these organizations—business, labor, and farmers' organizations alike—the present provision permitting the recovery of threefold damages should be abolished, and as a substitute therefor the right of recovery allowed for should be only the damages sustained by the plaintiff and the cost of suit, including a reasonable attorney's fee.

The law should not affect pending suits; a short statute of limitations should be provided, so far as the past is concerned, not to exceed a year. Moreover, and even more in the interest of labor than of business combinations, all such suits brought for causes of action heretofore occurred should be brought only if the contract or combination complained of was unfair or unreasonable. It may be well to remember that all of the suits hitherto brought by the Government under the antitrust law have been in cases where the combination or contract was in fact unfair, unreasonable, and against the public interest.

It is important that we should encourage trade agreements between employer and employee where they are just and fair. A strike is a clumsy weapon for righting wrongs done to labor, and we should extend, so far as possible, the process of conciliation and arbitration as a substitute for strikes. Moreover, violence, disorder, and coercion, when committed in connection with strikes, should be as promptly and sternly repressed as when committed in any other connection. But strikes themselves are, and should be, recognized to **be** entirely legal. Combinations of workingmen have a peculiar reason for their existence. The very wealthy individual employer, and still more the very wealthy corporation, stand at an enormous advantage when compared to the individual workingman; and while there are many cases where it may not be necessary for laborers to form a union, in many other cases it is indispensable, for otherwise the thousands of small units, the thousands of individual workingmen, will be left helpless in their dealings with the one big unit, the big individual or corporate employer.

Twenty-two years ago, by the act of June 29, 1886, trades unions were recognized by law, and the right of laboring people to combine for all lawful purposes was formally recognized, this right including combination for mutual protection and benefits, the regulation of wages, hours and conditions of labor, and the protection of the individual rights of the workmen in the prosecution of their trade or trades; and in the act of June 1, 1898, strikes were recognized as legal in the same provision that forbade participation in or instigation of force or violence against persons or property, or the attempt to prevent others from working, by violence, threat, or intimidation. The business man must be protected in person and property, and so must the farmer and the wageworker; and as regards all alike, the right of peaceful combination for all lawful purposes should be explicitly recognized.

The right of employers to combine and contract with one another and with their employees should be explicitly recognized; and so should the right of the employees to combine and to contract with one another and with the employers, and to seek peaceably to persuade others to accept their views, and to strike for the purpose of peaceably obtaining from employers satisfactory terms for their labor. Nothing should be **done to legalize either a blacklist or a boycott that would be illegal at** common law; this being the type of boycott defined and condemned by the Anthracite Strike Commission.

The question of financial legislation is now receiving such attention in both Houses that we have a right to expect action before the close of the session. It is urgently necessary that there should be such action. Moreover, action should be taken to establish postal savings banks. These postal savings banks are imperatively needed for the benefit of the wageworkers and men of small means, and will be a valuable adjunct to our whole financial system.

The time has come when we should prepare for a revision of the tariff. This should be, and indeed must be, preceded by careful investigation. It is peculiarly the province of the Congress and not of the President, and indeed peculiarly the province of the House of Representatives, to originate a tariff bill and to determine upon its terms; and this I fully realize. Yet it seems to me that before the close of this session provision should be made for collecting full material which will enable the Congress elected next fall to act immediately after it comes into existence. This would necessitate some action by the Congress at its present session, perhaps in the shape of directing the proper committee to gather the necessary information, both through the committee itself and through Government agents who should report to the committee and should lay before it the facts which would permit it to act with prompt and intelligent fairness. These Government agents, if it is not deemed wise to appoint individuals from outside the public service, might with advantage be members of the Executive Departments, designated by the President, on his own motion or on the request of the committee, to act with it.

I am of the opinion, however, that one change in the tariff could with advantage be made forthwith. Our forests need every protection, and one method of protecting them would be to put upon the free list wood pulp, with a corresponding reduction upon paper made from wood pulp, when they come from any country that does not put an export duty upon them.

Ample provision should be made for a permanent Waterways Commission, with whatever power is required to make it effective. The reasonable expectation of the people will not be met unless the Congress provides at this session for the beginning and prosecution of the actual work or waterway improvement and control. The Congress should recognize in fullest fashion the fact that the subject of the conservation of our natural resources, with which this Commission deals, is literally vital for the future of the Nation.

Numerous bills granting water-power rights on navigable streams have been introduced. None of them gives the Government the right to make a reasonable charge for the valuable privileges so granted, in spite of the fact that these water-power privileges are equivalent to many thousands of acres of the best coal lands for their production of power. Nor is any definite time limit set, as should always be done in such cases. I shall be obliged hereafter, in accordance with the policy stated in a recent message, to veto any water-power bill which does not provide for a time limit and for the right of the President or of the Secretary concerned to fix and collect such a charge as he may find to be just and reasonable in each case.

THEODORE ROOSEVELT.

SPECIAL MESSAGE

THE WHITE HOUSE, December 14, 1908.

To the Senate:

I inclose herewith a letter from the Secretary of War transmitting a report of the investigation made by Mr. Herbert J. Browne, employed by the Department in conjunction with Capt. W. G. Baldwin to investigate as far as possible what happened at Brownsville on the 13th and 14th of August, 1906. The report and documents contain some information of great value and some statements that are obviously worthless, but I submit them in their entirety.

This report enables us to fix with tolerable definiteness at least some of the criminals who took the lead in the murderous shooting of private citizens at Brownsville. It establishes clearly the fact that the colored soldiers did the shooting; but upon this point further record was unnecessary, as the fact that the colored soldiers did the shooting has already been established beyond all possibility of doubt. The investigation has not gone far enough to enable us to determine all the facts, and we will proceed with it; but it has gone far enough to determine with sufficient accuracy certain facts of enough importance to make it advisable that I place the report before you. It appears that almost all the members of Company B must have been actively concerned in the shooting, either to the extent of being participants or to the extent of virtually encouraging those who were participants. As to Companies C and D, there can be no question that practically every man in them must have had knowledge that the shooting was done by some of the soldiers of B Troop, and possibly by one or two others in one of the other troops. This concealment was itself a grave offense, which was greatly aggravated by their testifying before the Senate committee that they were ignorant of what they must have known. Nevertheless, it is to be said in partial extenuation that they were probably cowed by threats, made by the more desperate of the men who had actually been engaged in the shooting, as to what would happen to any man who failed to protect the wrongdoers. Moreover, there are circumstances tending to show that these misguided men were encouraged by outsiders to persist in their course of concealment and denial. I feel, therefore, that the guilt of the men who, after the event, thus shielded the perpetrators of the wrong by refusing to tell the truth about them, though serious, was in part due to the unwise and improper attitude of others, and that some measure of allowance should be made for the misconduct. In other words, I believe we can afford to reinstate any of these men who now truthfully tell what has happened, give all the aid they can to fix the responsibility upon those who are really guilty, and show that they themselves had no guilty knowledge beforehand and were in no way implicated in the affair, save by having knowledge of it afterwards and failing and refusing to divulge it. Under the circumstances, and in view of the length of time they have been out of the service, and their loss of the benefit that would have accrued to them by continuous long-time service, we can afford to treat the men who meet the requirements given above as having been sufficiently punished by the consequences they brought upon themselves when they rendered necessary the exercise of the disciplinary power. I recommend that a law be passed allowing the Secretary of War, within a fixed period of time, say a year, to reinstate any of these soldiers whom he, after careful examination, finds to have been innocent and whom he finds to have done all in his power to help bring to justice the guilty.

Meanwhile, the investigation will be continued. The results have made it obvious that only by carrying on the investigation as the War Department has actually carried it on is there the slightest chance of bringing the offenders to justice or of separating not the innocent, for there were doubtless hardly any innocent, but the less guilty from those whose guilt was heinous.

THEODORE ROOSEVELT.

SPECIAL MESSAGE.

THE WHITE HOHSE, December 15, 1908.

To the Senate and House of Representatives:

In view of the constant reiteration of the assertion that there was some corrupt action by or on behalf of the United States Government in connection with the acquisition of the title of the French Company to the Panama Canal, and of the repetition of the story that a syndicate of American citizens owned either one or both of the Panama companies, I deem it wise to submit to the Congress all the information I have on the subject. These stories were first brought to my attention as published in a paper in Indianapolis, called " The News," edited by Mr. Delavan Smith. The stories were scurrilous and libelous in character and false in every essential particular. Mr. Smith shelters him-

self behind the excuse that he merely accepted the statements which
had appeared in a paper published in New York, " The World," owned
by Mr. Joseph Pulitzer. It is idle to say that the known character of
Mr. Pulitzer and his newspaper are such that the statements in that
paper will be believed by nobody; unfortunately, thousands of persons
are ill informed in this respect and believe the statements they see in
print, even though they appear in a newspaper published by Mr.
Pulitzer. A Member of Congress has actually introduced a resolution
in reference to these charges. I therefore lay all the facts before you.

The story repeated at various times by the World and by its fol-
lowers in the newspaper press is substantially as follows: That there
was corruption by or on behalf of the Government of the United States
in the transaction by which the Panama Canal property was acquired
from its French owners; that there were improper dealings of some
kind between agents of the Government and outside persons, representing or acting for an American syndicate, who had gotten possession of
the French Company; that among these persons, who it was alleged
made " huge profits," were Mr. Charles P. Taft, a brother of Mr.
William H. Taft, then candidate for the Presidency, and Mr. Douglas
Robinson, my brother-in-law; that Mr. Cromwell, the counsel for the
Panama Canal Company in the negotiations, was in some way implicated with the United States governmental authorities in these improper
transactions; that the Government has concealed the true facts, and
has destroyed, or procured or agreed to the destruction of, certain documents; that Mr. W. H. Taft was Secretary of War at the time that
by an agreement between the United States Government and the
beneficiaries of the deal all traces thereof were " wiped out " by trans-
ferring all the archives and " secrets " to the American Government,
just before holding the convention last June at which Mr. Taft was
nominated.

These statements sometimes appeared in the editorials, sometimes
in the news columns, sometimes in the shape of contributions from
individuals either unknown or known to be of bad character. They
are false in every particular from beginning to end. The wickedness
of the slanders is only surpassed by their fatuity. So utterly baseless
are the stories that apparently they represent in part merely material
collected for campaign purposes and in part stories originally concocted
with a view of possible blackmail. The inventor of the story about Mr.
Charles P. Taft, for instance, evidently supposed that at some period
of the Panama purchase Mr. W. H. Taft was Secretary of War,
whereas in reality Mr. W. H. Taft never became Secretary of War
until long after the whole transaction in question had been closed.
The inventor of the story about Mr. Douglas Robinson had not taken
the trouble to find out the fact that Mr. Robinson had not had the
slightest connection, directly or indirectly, of any kind or sort with

any phase of the Panama transaction from beginning to end. The men who attacked Mr. Root in the matter had not taken the trouble to read the public documents which would have informed them that Mr. Root had nothing to do with the purchase, which was entirely arranged through the Department of Justice under the then Attorney-General, Mr. Knox.

Now, these stories as a matter of fact need no investigation whatever. No shadow of proof has been, or can be, produced in behalf of any of them. They consist simply of a string of infamous libels. In form, they are in part libels upon individuals, upon Mr. Taft and Mr. Robinson, for instance. But they are in fact wholly, and in form partly, a libel upon the United States Government. I do not believe we should concern ourselves with the particular individuals who wrote the lying and libelous editorials, articles from correspondents, or articles in the news columns. The real offender is Mr. Joseph Pulitzer, editor and proprietor of the World. While the criminal offense of which Mr. Pulitzer has been guilty is in form a libel upon individuals, the great injury done is in blackening the good name of the American people. It should not be left to a private citizen to sue Mr. Pulitzer for libel. He should be prosecuted for libel by the governmental authorities. In point of encouragement of iniquity, in point of infamy, of wrongdoing, there is nothing to choose between a public servant who betrays his trust, a public servant who is guilty of blackmail, or theft, or financial dishonesty of any kind, and a man guilty as Mr. Joseph Pulitzer has been guilty in this instance. It is therefore a high national duty to bring to justice this vilifier of the American people, this man who wantonly and wickedly and without one shadow of justification seeks to blacken the character of reputable private citizens and to convict the Government of his own country in the eyes of the civilized world of wrongdoing of the basest and foulest kind, when he has not one shadow of justification of any sort or description for the charge he has made. The Attorney-General has under consideration the form in which the proceedings against Mr. Pulitzer shall be brought.

Meanwhile I submit to you all the accompanying papers, so that you may have before you complete information on the subject. I call your attention to my communications in my messages to the Congress of January 20, 1902, March 11, 1903, December 7, 1903, January 4, 1904, and December 17, 1906, in which I set forth at length the history of various phases of the whole transaction. I recall your attention to the report and opinion of the Attorney-General rendered to me, dated October 25, 1902, with the accompanying documents and exhibits. I call your attention to the correspondence of the officers and agents of the Panama Canal Company with the President and other officers of the United States printed in Senate Document No. 34, December 10, 1902; also to the copy of the official proceedings of the New Panama

Canal Company at Paris on the 30th of December, 1903, together with a report of the Council of Administration of that company, printed in Senate Document No. 133, January 28, 1904; and to the copy of the general conveyance by the New Panama Canal Company to the United States, also copies of certain telegrams from the president of the company making an offer of sale, and Attorney-General Knox's cablegram in response printed in Senate Document No. 285, March 23, 1906. I call your attention furthermore to the exhaustive testimony recorded in public document (Sen. Doc. No. 411, 59th Cong., 2nd sess.), which contains the searching investigation into the whole transaction made by the Congress for its information and fully considered by the Congress before it took action.

In the Act approved June 28, 1902, "To provide for the construction of a canal connecting the waters of the Atlantic and Pacific oceans," the Congress provided as follows:

" That the President of the United States is hereby authorized to acquire, for and on behalf of the United States, at a cost not exceeding forty millions of dollars, the rights, privileges, franchises, concessions, grants of land, right of way, unfinished work, plants, and other property, real, personal, and mixed, of every name and nature, owned by the New Panama Canal Company, of France, on the Isthmus of Panama, and all its maps, plans, drawings, records on the Isthmus of Panama, and in Paris, including all the capital stock, not less, however, than sixty-eight thousand eight hundred and sixty-three shares of the Panama Railroad Company, owned by or held for the use of said Canal Company, provided a satisfactory title to all of said property can be obtained."

It thereupon became the duty of the President, in execution of this statute, to purchase the property specified from the New Panama Canal Company, of France, provided he could obtain a satisfactory title. The Department of Justice was instructed to examine the title, and after such an examination Attorney-General Knox reported that a satisfactory title could be obtained. Payment of the purchase price was thereupon made to the New Panama Canal Company, in accordance with the act of Congress, and the property was conveyed by that company to the United States. It was no concern of the President, or of any officer of the Executive Department, to inquire as to what the New Panama Canal Company did with the money which it received. As a matter of fact, the New Panama Canal Company did distribute the money between its shareholders and the shareholders of the preceding Panama Canal Company in accordance with the decree of a French court, and the records of the French court show who were the shareholders who received the money; but that is no concern of ours.

I call your attention to the accompanying statement as to the attempt to form an American company in 1899 for the purpose of taking over the property of the French company. This attempt proved abortive. There was no concealment in its effort to put through this plan; its complete failure and abandonment being known to everyone.

The important points set forth in the accompanying papers, and in the papers to which I have referred you, are as follows:

The investigation of the history, physical condition, and existing value of the enterprise by the Congress, resulting in the enactment of the law of 1902 authorizing the President to acquire the property for the sum of $40,000,000 upon securing a satisfactory title and thereupon to undertake the work of construction; the failure of the Americanization of the enterprise in 1899; the transmission by me to the Congress from time to time of full information and advice as to the relations of this Government to transit across the Isthmus and under the treaties, as to the negotiations and final acquisition of the title, and later as to the progress and condition of the work of construction; the previous authorization of the sale to the United States by the stockholders of the new company and their subsequent ratification; the examination and approval of the title by Mr. Knox; the arrangements for payment through J. P. Morgan & Company as the fiscal agents of this Government, and the payment accordingly at the Bank of France upon proper official receipts to the liquidators acting under the decree of the French court, the French governmental body having jurisdiction in the matter; and, finally, the subsequent apportionment and distribution of the fund to the creditors and stockholders of the two companies under that decree.

The Panama Canal transaction was actually carried through not by either the then Secretary of State, Mr. John Hay, or the then Secretary of War, Mr. Elihu Root, both of whom, however, were cognizant of all the essential features; but by the then Attorney-General, Mr. P. C. Knox, at present Senator from Pennsylvania. I directed or approved every action, and am responsible for all that was done in carrying out the will of the Congress; and the provisions of the law, enacted by Congress after exhaustive examination and discussion, were scrupulously complied with by the Executive. While the transaction was pending I saw Mr. Cromwell but two or three times, and my communications with him were limited to the exchange of purely formal courtesies. Secretary Hay occasionally saw him, in the same manner; I doubt whether Mr. Root held any conversation with him. The Attorney-General saw him frequently, as he was counsel for the Panama Company; their communications were official, as representing the two sides. I enclose copies of my correspondence with Mr. William Dudley Foulke, who first brought these scandalous stories to my attention, and with Senator Knox and Mr. Cromwell, to whom I wrote in response to the request of a gentleman who wished to know about the stockholders in the Panama Canal Company.

The title to the Panama Canal properties was vested in the New

Panama Canal Company of France, which was the legal owner thereof, and the old or so-called De Lesseps Company had a large equity therein. The title was not in a New Jersey company nor in any other American company, nor did this Government have any dealings with any American company throughout the affair.

The exact legal status, to the most minute detail, appears in the exhaustive opinion of Attorney-General Knox approving the title to be given to the United States, which clearly establishes that the only party dealt with was the New Panama Canal Company of France (with the concurrence of the liquidator of the old company) and not any American corporation or syndicate.

The action of the United States Government was, of course, wholly uninfluenced by, and had nothing whatever to do with, any question as to who were, or who had been, the security-holders of either the new or the old company. Who such security-holders were was not our affair. If, as a matter of fact, the Canal companies, either or both, had been owned by American citizens or by citizens of any other nationality, it would not have altered in the slightest degree the action taken by this Government. Our concern was to get the canal property which was owned by the French Company, and to see that the title was clear. Our transactions were carried on openly, and were published in detail, and we dealt solely (so far as the interests of the old Panama Company were concerned) with the liquidator appointed by the proper French governmental body, the Civil Tribunal of the Seine, and in accordance with the decree of this same tribunal, with the New Panama Canal Company, which also went into liquidation upon the sale to the United States. All our transactions were carried on openly, and were published in detail.

The distribution of our payment of $40,000,000 follows the award of arbitrators chosen by the new company and the liquidator, authorized by the decree of this same Civil Tribunal of the Seine, and providing for a determination of the proportionate division between the new and old companies. We paid the money through the New York banking house of Messrs. J. P. Morgan & Company, acting as fiscal agents of this Government, into the Bank of France in Paris. The receipts and accounts of our Treasury Department show the payment of the money into the Bank of France and account for the money being paid over to the liquidator appointed by the Civil Tribunal of the Seine and to the New Panama Canal Company of France, the proportion of the forty million dollars being 128,600,000 francs to the liquidator of the old company and 77,400,000 francs to the New Panama Canal Company of France in liquidation. In these payments we followed to the letter the decree of the governmental tribunal of France which had the authority to make such a decree, the Civil Tribunal of the Seine. We had neither desire nor authority to go behind this decree of this proper governmental body, as all the conflicting rights of the security-holders of both companies had been settled by the decree of said court by ratification of the arbitration which resulted in that division.

I wish to make as clear as possible, and as emphatic as possible, the statement that we did not have anything to do with the distribution of a dollar of the $40,000,000 we paid as regards any stockholder or bond-holder of the French Companies, save that we followed out the award of the arbitrators appointed in accordance with the decree of the French court which had dealt with the subject in awarding a certain proportion to the old company and a certain proportion to the new company. Any question concerning the stockholders, bondholders, or other beneficiaries of the proceeds of sale was purely a question for the Civil Tribunal of the Seine, the French governmental body, with which this Nation had nothing whatever to do.

Under these circumstances there was not the slightest need for Mr. Cromwell to give any information on the subject of the companies for which he had been counsel. This Government has no concern with Mr. Cromwell's relation to these companies, or either of them, or with the amount of his professional compensation; it was not the affair of this Government to inquire who were the security-holders of the companies. Nevertheless, Mr. Cromwell, of his own accord, has submitted to me, together with a copy of his statement published on the 11th instant, and which I transmit herewith, a full list of the stockholders of the New Panama Canal Company of France on January 15, 1900 (numbering over 6,000), and a list of all stockholders who were present at a special meeting of the company held February 28, 1902, immediately after the cable offer of the company was made to the United States (January 9-11, 1902), to accept the appraisement of $40,000,000 made by the Isthmian Canal Commission, and to sell for said sum the Panama Canal, concessions, and other property, and the shares of the Panama Railroad Company. He has also furnished me a certified copy of the final report of the liquidator of the old company, which was filed on June 25th last and formally approved by the Civil Tribunal of the Seine, together with a summary account prepared and signed by said liquidator as late as the 24th ultimo. I also transmit a translation of the two resolutions, with the vote upon them, adopted at a meeting of the stockholders of the new company held on April 23, 1904, for the purpose of finally ratifying the sale.

All these documents I herewith transmit as a part of this message. It appears from them that the creditors of the old company number 226,296 parties who have received dividends out of the funds in the hands of the liquidator, who, in his letter, states that in this present month of December the second and last distribution to the creditors will be begun, and that the average dividend heretofore paid to each individual was 782 francs, or $156. No payment whatever was or will be made upon the stock of the old company, as it was worthless from the day De Lesseps failed, and this cuts out from consideration all misleading statements regarding a possible purchase by anybody of the stock of the old Panama Canal Company. It has not received, and will not receive, a penny. Even upon the bonded indebtedness the dividend, I am thus informed, will amount, in the aggregate, to only about ten per centum. It likewise plainly appears that this distribution by the liquidator of the old company has been openly conducted at his office in Paris, No. 50 Rue Etienne Marcel, where all the receipts, accounts, and records of his payments are on file.

The New Panama Canal Company of France is in liquidation. As the accompanying papers set forth, this liquidated company received as its proportion of the $40,000,000 the sum of 77,400,000 francs, and this amount was distributed by the liquidation in three payments through four leading banks of Paris, covering a period of the past four years, and to shareholders numbering about 6,000. Every step of the transaction was not only taken publicly, but was, contemporaneously therewith, advertised in the legal and financial papers of France, and the banks making the payments took proper receipts from all the parties to whom payments were made, as is customary in such cases.

The capital of the New Panama Canal Company of France was 65,000,000 francs, and the distribution thus made amounted to about 130 francs on each share of 100 francs. No dividends were paid during the ten years of the company's existence. It therefore resulted that the shareholders only recovered their original investment with annual interest of about three per cent.

The accounts and records of this liquidation which was concluded in June last, are on deposit with the Crédit Lyonnaise of Paris as a proper custodian of the same, appointed upon such liquidation. Recently a request was made by a private individual to inspect the records of these payments, but answer was made by the custodians that they saw no proper reason for granting such request by a stranger, and, inasmuch as there is not the slightest ground for suspicion of any bad faith in the transaction, it hardly seems worth while to make the request; but if the Congress desires, I have no doubt that on the request of our Ambassador in Paris, the lists of individuals will be shown him.

As a matter of fact, there is nothing whatever, in which this Government is interested, to investigate about this transaction. So far as this Government is concerned, every step of the slightest importance has been made public by its Executive, and every step taken in France has there been made public by the proper officials.

The Congress took the action it did take after the most minute and exhaustive examination and discussion, and the Executive carried out the direction of the Congress to the letter. Every act of this Government, every act for which this Government had the slightest responsibility, was in pursuance of the act of the Congress here, and following out the decree of the Civil Tribunal of the Seine in France.

Furthermore, through the entirely voluntary act of Mr. Cromwell, I am now able to present to you full information as to these actions in France with which this Government did not have any concern, and which are set forth in the accompanying papers.

It may be well to recall that the New Panama Canal Company of France did not itself propose or fix the figure $40,000,000 as the valuation of the canal and railroad properties. That sum was first fixed by our Isthmian Canal Commission in its reports to the Congress after two years of investigation and personal inspection of all the properties and work already done, whereby the properties and the work done were in detail appraised at that sum as their value to the United States. The French company steadily refused for over two years to make any offer whatever in answer to the many written requests of the Isthmian Canal Commission; and when its president did approach the question of price, it was on the basis of $109,000,000. Later, under conditions not necessary now to rehearse, the company, by cable, accepted the appraisement of $40,000,000 made by our Commission. This Government, therefore, acquired all the properties and concessions, both of canal and railroad, at its own valuation and price, the Congress approving the price, and authorizing the expenditure of the money, after the most exhaustive examination and discussion.

I transmit herewith lists of the documents in the possession of the Department of State, the Department of Justice, and the Department of War, so that, if the Congress sees fit, it may direct that they be printed. They are, and always have been, open to the examination of any Member of the Congress. There is no object in printing them, but there is also no objection to printing them, save that it is a useless expense.

I also transmit a list of the documents furnished by Mr. Cromwell.

THEODORE ROOSEVELT.

SPECIAL MESSAGE.

THE WHITE HOUSE, December 17, 1908.

To the Senate and House of Representatives:

The rapid increase of population in the national capital within recent years has greatly altered social conditions, necessitating changes in the machinery of its administration. Greater efficiency and a better provision for the protection of both the industrial and dependent classes are required.

Recognizing these needs, I have had a special report made to me on the affairs of the District of Columbia, which I transmit herewith. I cordially approve the recommendations in the report for the substitution of a single head or governor in place of three commissioners, the establishment of district or municipal departments in place of the existing bureaus, and the creation of a new department to be known as that of housing and labor. I ask your careful consideration of the entire report. Mr. Reynolds has rendered a great and disinterested service, for which our heartiest thanks are due him.

A single executive head would increase efficiency, determine responsibility, and eliminate delays and uncertainties inevitable under the present system. Municipal departments headed by commissioners to be appointed by the governor would yield the same advantage.

In the proposed scheme of reorganization the department of education should be coördinated with other city departments.

I especially urge that the proposed department of housing and labor be established. Poverty, disease, and crime are largely due to defects of social conditions and surroundings. The need of improved sanitary inspection of dwellings, rear alleys, and small shacks (such as, unhappily, still exist in Washington), and of stores, workshops, and factories should not be left to subordinate bureau chiefs, but should be brought under the direct control of a competent head of the above-named department.

An equally important public responsibility is the protection of the independent industrial class, which neither desires nor accepts charity, but whose members have often been led to misfortune, and even crime, through agencies licensed by the state, but defectively and inadequately supervised. Notable among these are pawnshops, loan and industrial insurance companies, and employment agencies. The supervision of these agencies is at present limited to the police. They should be under the direction of officials qualified to advance their efficiency and economic service to the public.

The above-named changes would vastly improve the efficiency of the District government, and would afford protection to its industrial and dependent classes which is imperatively needed.

I also transmit for the consideration of the Congress reports of the Committee on Building of Model Houses, which was appointed in accordance with the recommendation of Mr. Reynolds.

THEODORE ROOSEVELT.

SPECIAL MESSAGE.

THE WHITE HOUSE, February 15, 1909.

To the Senate and House of Representatives:

On January 25-26, 1909, there assembled in this city, on my invitation, a conference on the care of dependent children. To this conference there came from nearly every State in the Union men and women actively engaged in the care of dependent children, and they represented all the leading religious bodies.

The subject considered is one of high importance to the well-being of the nation. The Census Bureau reported in 1904 that there were in orphanages and children's homes about 93,000 dependent children. There are probably 50,000 more (the precise number never having been ascertained) in private homes, either on board or in adopted homes provided by the generosity of foster parents. In addition to these there were 25,000 children in institutions for juvenile delinquents.

Each of these children represents either a potential addition to the productive capacity and the enlightened citizenship of the nation, or, if allowed to suffer from neglect, a potential addition to the destructive forces of the community. The ranks of criminals and other enemies of society are recruited in an altogether undue proportion from children bereft of their natural homes and left without sufficient care.

The interests of the nation are involved in the welfare of this army of children no less than in our great material affairs.

Notwithstanding a wide diversity of views and methods represented in the conference, and notwithstanding the varying legislative enactments and policies of the States from which the members came, the conference, at the close of its sessions, unanimously adopted a series of declarations expressing the conclusions which they had reached. These constitute a wise, constructive, and progressive programme of child-caring work. If given full effect by the proper agencies, existing methods and practices in almost every community would be profoundly and advantageously modified.

More significant even than the contents of the declarations is the fact that they were adopted without dissenting vote and with every demonstration of hearty approval on the part of all present. They constitute a standard of accepted opinion by which each community should measure the adequacy of its existing methods and to which each community should seek to conform its legislation and its practice.

The keynote of the conference was expressed in these words:

Home life is the highest and finest product of civilization. Children should not be deprived of it except for urgent and compelling reasons.

Surely poverty alone should not disrupt the home. Parents of good character suffering from temporary misfortune, and above all deserving mothers fairly well able to work but deprived of the support of the normal breadwinner, should be given such aid as may be necessary to enable them to maintain suitable homes for the rearing of their children. The widowed or deserted mother, if a good woman, willing to work and to do her best, should ordinarily be helped in such fashion as will enable her to bring up her children herself in their natural home. Children from unfit homes, and children who have no homes, who must be cared for by charitable agencies, should, so far as practicable, be cared for in families.

I transmit herewith for your information a copy of the conclusions reached by the conference, of which the following is a brief summary:

1. *Home care.*—Children of worthy parents or deserving mothers should, as a rule, be kept with their parents at home.

2. *Preventive work.*—The effort should be made to eradicate causes of dependency, such as disease and accident, and to substitute compensation and insurance for relief.

3. *Home finding.*—Homeless and neglected children, if normal, should be cared for in families, when practicable.

4. *Cottage system.*—Institutions should be on the cottage plan with small units, as far as possible.

5. *Incorporation.*—Agencies caring for dependent children should be incorporated, on approval of a suitable state board.

6. *State inspection.*—The State should inspect the work of all agencies which care for dependent children.

7. *Inspection of educational work.*—Educational work of institutions and agencies caring for dependent children should be supervised by state educational authorities.

8. *Facts and records.*—Complete histories of dependent children and their parents, based upon personal investigation and supervision, should be recorded for guidance of child-caring agencies.

9. *Physical care.*—Every needy child should receive the best medical and surgical attention, and be instructed in health and hygiene.

10. *Coöperation.*—Local child-caring agencies should coöperate and establish joint bureaus of information.

11. *Undesirable legislation.*—Prohibitive legislation against transfer of dependent children between States should be repealed.

12. *Permanent organization.*—A permanent organization for work along the lines of these resolutions is desirable.

13. *Federal children's bureau.*—Establishment of a federal children's bureau is desirable, and enactment of pending bill is earnestly recommended.

14. Suggests special message to Congress favoring federal children's bureau and other legislation applying above principles to District of Columbia and other federal territory.

While it is recognized that these conclusions can be given their fullest effect only by the action of the several States or communities concerned, or of their charitable agencies, the conference requested

.ne, in section 14 of the conclusions, to send to you a message recommending federal action.

There are pending in both Houses of Congress bills for the establishment of a children's bureau, *i. e.,* Senate bill No. 8323 and House bill No. 24148. These provide for a children's bureau in the Department of the Interior, which

shall investigate and report upon all matters pertaining to the welfare of children and child life, and shall especially investigate the questions of infant mortality, the birth rate, physical degeneracy, orphanage, juvenile delinquency and juvenile courts, desertion and illegitimacy, dangerous occupations, accidents and diseases of children of the working classes, employment, legislation affecting children in the several States and Territories, and such other facts as have a bearing upon the health, efficiency, character, and training of children.

One of the needs felt most acutely by the conference was that of accurate information concerning these questions relating to childhood. The National Government not only has the unquestioned right of research in such vital matters, but is the only agency which can effectively conduct such general inquiries as are needed for the benefit of all our citizens. In accordance with the unanimous request of the conference, I therefore most heartily urge your favorable action on these measures.

It is not only discreditable to us as a people that there is now no recognized and authoritative source of information upon these subjects relating to child life, but in the absence of such information as should be supplied by the Federal Government many abuses have gone unchecked; for public sentiment, with its great corrective power, can only be aroused by full knowledge of the facts. In addition to such information as the Census Bureau and other existing agencies of the Federal Government already provide, there remains much to be ascertained through lines of research not now authorized by law; and there should be correlation and dissemination of the knowledge obtained without any duplication of effort or interference with what is already being done. There are few things more vital to the welfare of the nation than accurate and dependable knowledge of the best methods of dealing with children, especially with those who are in one way or another handicapped by misfortune; and in the absence of such knowledge each community is left to work out its own problem without being able to learn of and profit by the success or failure of other communities along the same lines of endeavor. The bills for the establishment of the children's bureau are advocated not only by this conference, but by a large number of national organizations that are disinterestedly working for the welfare of children, and also by philanthropic, educational, and religious bodies in all parts of the country.

I further urge that such legislation be enacted as may be necessary in order to bring the laws and practices in regard to the care of dependent children in all federal territory into harmony with the other conclusions reached by the conference.

LEGISLATION FOR THE DISTRICT OF COLUMBIA.

Congress took a step in the direction of the conclusions of this conference in 1893, when, on the recommendation of the late Amos G. Warner, then superintendent of charities for the District of Columbia, the Board of Children's Guardians was created, with authority, among other things, to place children in family homes. That board has made commendable progress, and its work should be strengthened and extended.

I recommend legislation for the District of Columbia in accordance with the fifth, sixth, seventh, and eighth sections of the conclusions of the conference, as follows:

1. That the approval of the Board of Charities be required for the incorporation of all child-caring agencies, as well as amendments of the charter of any benevolent corporation which includes child-caring work, and that other than duly incorporated agencies be forbidden to engage in the care of needy children. This legislation is needed in order to insure the fitness and responsibility of those who propose to undertake the care of helpless children. Such laws have long been in satisfactory operation in several of the larger States of the Union.

2. That the Board of Charities, through its duly authorized agents, shall inspect the work of all agencies which care for dependent children, whether by institutional or by home-finding methods, and whether supported by public or private funds. The State has always jealously guarded the interests of children whose parents have been able to leave them property by requiring the appointment of a guardian, under bond, accountable directly to the courts, even though there be a competent surviving parent. Surely the interests of the child who is not only an orphan but penniless ought to be no less sacred than those of the more fortunate orphan who inherits property. If the protection of the Government is necessary in the one case, it is even more necessary in the other. If we are to require that only incorporated institutions shall be allowed to engage in this responsible work, it is necessary to provide for public inspection, lest the State should become the unconscious partner of those who either from ignorance or inefficiency are unsuited to deal with the problem.

3. That the education of children in orphan asylums and other similar institutions in the District of Columbia be under the supervision of the board of education, in order that these children may enjoy educational advantages equal to those of the other children. Normal school life comes next to normal home life in the process of securing the fullest development of the child.

4. That all agencies engaged in child-caring work in the District of Columbia be required by law to adopt adequate methods of investigation and make permanent records relative to children under their care, and to exercise faithful personal supervision over their wards until legally adopted or otherwise clearly beyond the need of further supervision; the forms and methods of such investigation, records, and supervision to be prescribed and enforced by the Board of Charities.

I deem such legislation as is herein recommended not only important for the welfare of the children immediately concerned, but important as setting an example of a high standard of child protection by the National Government to the several States of the Union, which should be able to look to the nation for leadership in such matters.

I herewith transmit a copy of the full text of the proceedings.

THEODORE ROOSEVELT.

SPECIAL MESSAGE.

THE WHITE HOUSE, January 23, 1907.

To the Senate and House of Representatives:

I call your attention to the great desirability of enacting legislation to help American shipping and American trade by encouraging the building and running of lines of large and swift steamers to South America and the Orient.

The urgent need of our country's making an effort to do something like its share of its own carrying trade on the ocean has been called to our attention in striking fashion by the experiences of Secretary Root on his recent South American tour. The result of these experiences he has set forth in his address before the Trans-Mississippi Commercial Congress, at Kansas City, Mo., on November 20 last, an address so important that it deserves the careful study of all public men.

The facts set forth by Mr. Root are striking, and they can not but arrest the attention of our people. The great continent to the south of us, which should be knit to us by the closest commercial ties, is hardly in direct commercial communication with us at all, its commercial relations being almost exclusively with Europe. Between all the principal South American ports and Europe lines of swift and commodious steamers, subsidized by their home governments, ply regularly. There is no such line of steamers between these ports and the United States. In consequence, our shipping in South American ports is almost a negligible quantity; for instance, in the year ending June 30, 1905, there entered the port of Rio de Janeiro over 3,000 steamers and sailing vessels from Europe, but from the United States no steamers and only seven sailing vessels, two of which were in distress. One prime reason for this state of things is the fact that those who now do business on the sea do business in a world not of natural competition, but of subsidized competition. State aid to steamship lines is as much a part of the commercial system of to-day as State employment of consuls to promote business. Our commercial competitors in Europe pay in the aggregate some twenty-five millions a year to their steamship lines—Great Britain paying nearly seven millions. Japan pays between three and four millions. By the proposed legislation the United States will still pay relatively less than any one of our competitors pay. Three years ago the Trans-Mississippi Congress formally set forth as axiomatic the statement that every ship is a missionary of trade, that steamship lines work for their own countries just as railroad lines work for their terminal points, and that it is as absurd for the United States to depend upon foreign ships to distribute its products as it would be for a department store to depend upon wagons of a competing house to deliver its goods. This statement is the literal truth.

Moreover, it must be remembered that American ships do not have to contend merely against the subsidization of their foreign competitors. The higher wages and the greater cost of maintenance of American officers and crews make it almost impossible for our people who do business on the ocean to compete on equal terms with foreign ships unless they are protected somewhat as their fellow-countrymen who do business on land are protected. We can not as a country afford to have the wages and the manner of life of our seamen cut down; and the only alternative, if we are to have seamen at all, is to offset the expense by giving some advantage to the ship itself.

The proposed law which has been introduced in Congress is in no sense experimental. It is based on the best and most successful precedents, as, for instance, on the recent Cunard contract with the British Government. As far as South America is concerned, its aim is to provide from the Atlantic and Pacific coasts better American lines to the great ports of South America than the present European lines. The South American Republics now see only our warships. Under this bill our trade friendship will be made evident to them. The bill proposes to build large-sized steamers of 16-knot speed. There are nearly 200 such steamships already in the world's foreign trade, and over three-fourths of them now draw subsidies—postal or admiralty or both. The bill will encourage our shipyards, which are almost as necessary to the national defense as battleships, and the efficiency of which depends in large measure upon their steady employment in large construction. The proposed bill is of importance to our Navy, because it gives a considerable fleet of auxiliary steamships, such as is now almost wholly lacking, and also provides for an effective naval reserve.

The bill provides for 14 steamships, subsidized to the extent of over a million and a half, from the Atlantic coast, all to run to South American ports. It provides on the Pacific coast for 22 steamers subsidized to the extent of two millions and a quarter, some of these to run to South America, most of them to Manila, Australia, and Asia. Be it remembered that while the ships will be owned on the coasts, the cargoes will largely be supplied by the interior, and that the bill will benefit the Mississippi Valley as much as it benefits the seaboard.

I have laid stress upon the benefit to be expected from our trade with South America. The lines to the Orient are also of vital importance. The commercial possibilities of the Pacific are unlimited, and for national reasons it is imperative that we should have direct and adequate communication by American lines with Hawaii and the Philippines. The existence of our present steamship lines on the Pacific is seriously threatened by the foreign subsidized lines. Our communications with the markets of Asia and with our own possessions in the Philippines, no less than our communications with Australia, should depend not upon foreign, but upon our own steamships. The Southwest and the Northwest should alike be served by these lines, and if this is done they will also give to the Mississippi Valley throughout its entire length the advantage of all trans-continental railways running to the Pacific coast. To fail to establish adequate lines on the Pacific is equivalent to proclaiming to the world that we have neither the ability nor the disposition to contend for our rightful share of the commerce of the Orient; nor yet to protect our interests in the Philippines. It would surely be discreditable for us to surrender to our commercial rivals the great commerce of the Orient, the great commerce we should have with South America, and even our own communications with Hawaii and the Philippines.

I earnestly hope for the enactment of some law like the bill in question.

THEODORE ROOSEVELT.

SPECIAL MESSAGE.

THE WHITE HOUSE, December 18, 1906.

To the Senate and House of Representatives:

I inclose herewith for your information the final report made to me personally by Secretary Metcalf on the situation affecting the Japanese in San Francisco. The report deals with three matters of controversy —first, the exclusion of the Japanese children from the San Francisco schools; second, the boycotting of Japanese restaurants, and third, acts of violence committed against the Japanese.

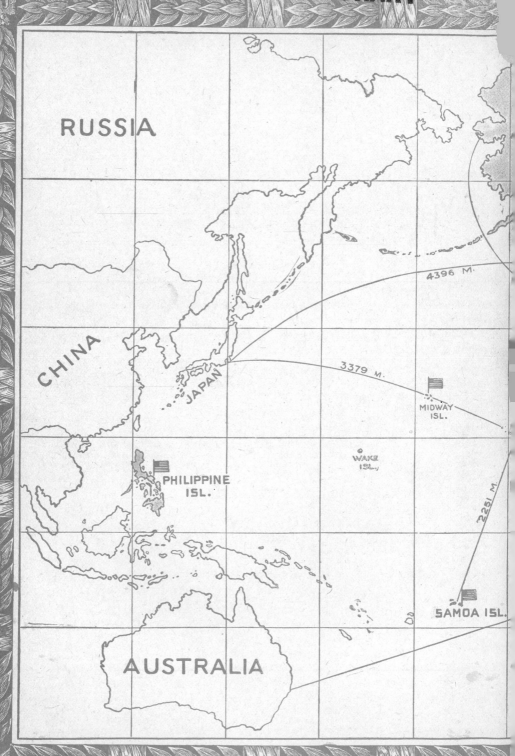